D1426690

COLD WAR
COMMAND

COLD WAR COMMAND

THE DRAMATIC STORY OF A NUCLEAR SUBMARINER

Richard Woodman & Dan Conley

Foreword by Admiral the Lord Boyce

Seaforth
PUBLISHING

For Linda

Copyright © Richard Woodman & Dan Conley 2014

First published in Great Britain in 2014 by
Seaforth Publishing,
Pen & Sword Books Ltd,
47 Church Street,
Barnsley S70 2AS

www.seaforthpublishing.com

British Library Cataloguing in Publication Data
A catalogue record for this book is available from the British Library

ISBN 978 1 84832 769 6

Typeset by MATS Typesetting, Leigh-on-Sea, Essex SS9 5EB
Printed and bound in Great Britain by CPI Group (UK) Ltd, Croydon, CR0 4YY

Contents

Foreword   vi

Prologue   ix

Introduction: The Sword of Damocles   xi

 1 The Twilight of Pax Britannica   1

 2 Dartmouth   8

 3 Midshipman   17

 4 Joining Submarines   40

 5 A Very Close Call   64

 6 Far East Interlude   68

 7 Submarine Activities in the Cold War   80

 8 First Nuclear Submarine   94

 9 Perisher   107

10 First Submarine Command   118

11 Torpedo Problems   135

12 From Barrow to Bear Island   146

13 Serving under the American Flag   163

14 To the South Atlantic   178

15 The Black Pig and the Red Banner Fleet   188

16 Arctic Bears and Torpedoes   215

17 A Kind of Victory   224

18 Back to the Shipyards   235

19 The Awesome World of Nuclear Weapons   252

Epilogue   266

Glossary   270

Index   275

FOREWORD

Admiral the Lord Boyce,
KG GCB OBE DL

As the Cold War unfolded after the end of the Second World War, the Soviet Union commenced building up a large submarine force which posed a serious potential threat to the vital sea lines of communication of the Western alliances. The nations of the West, and in particular those comprising the North Atlantic Treaty Organisation (NATO), aware of the devastating effects of submarine attacks upon shipping in both the Atlantic and Pacific during the Second World War, accordingly moved to counter this threat. As a part of this high-priority response, most of its member nations' submarines were modified or designed to fulfill a prime role in anti-submarine warfare (ASW), making them capable of seeking out and destroying Soviet submarines. The advent of the nuclear submarine in 1955, marked by the commissioning of the USS *Nautilus*, with its superior equipment and much greater endurance, range and mobility, enabled submarine operations against submarines to reach a new level of success. Meanwhile, covert intelligence gathering upon Soviet naval forces, which had been hitherto the province of diesel submarines, was to become an important peacetime task of nuclear attack submarines, colloquially known as 'hunter-killers'. Indeed, these vessels were routinely deployed to seek out and secretly follow Soviet submarines – particularly those capable of launching inter-continental ballistic missile attacks on Western cities – in order to be in a position pre-emptively to destroy them should hostilities break out. Such was the underwater confrontation of the Cold War.

In the decade after Britain's first nuclear submarine HMS *Dreadnought* was commissioned in 1963, the Royal Navy's Submarine Service changed from a force of conventional diesel submarines, many of which were of Second World War vintage and whose crews exuded a somewhat raffish buccaneering and independent spirit, to a highly professional – and arguably the most important – branch of the Royal Navy. It fully rose to the challenges of safely and effectively operating nuclear submarines, on the one hand delivering the nation's deterrent by means of the Polaris – and more latterly the Trident – intercontinental ballistic missile systems; and on the other providing a highly capable anti-submarine force of 'hunter-killer' submarines. The introduction into the Royal Navy of nuclear-powered submarines armed with Polaris was a remarkable achievement in itself, as the first British ballistic missile-armed submarine, HMS *Resolution,* went on patrol in 1968 only six years after the 1962 Nassau agreement – whereby the United States offered to provide Polaris technology and equipment to the United Kingdom in order to enable the Royal Navy to sustain a British independent nuclear deterrent.

At the same time, the Royal Navy underwent the painful contraction from a force deployed worldwide – at the core of which was a strike force of aircraft-carriers – to a much smaller navy, focused upon the 'Cold War threat'. Accordingly, in the three decades prior to the end of the Cold War, marked by the fall of the Berlin Wall in 1989, the United Kingdom invested a substantial proportion of defence expenditure in establishing and maintaining a potent flotilla of nuclear-powered submarines whose role was to maintain and support Britain's nuclear deterrent, and to counter the potential enemy's maritime threat directly by shadowing his units and covertly gathering intelligence.

During all these developments the Royal Navy benefited from its unique and close operational partnership with the United States Submarine Force. Whilst by no means on the same scale as the latter, by 1989 the Royal Navy Submarine Flotilla comprised twenty nuclear submarines complemented by twelve diesel boats, making a very substantial contribution to confronting and countering an ever expanding and increasingly capable Soviet nuclear submarine force. Indeed, the professionalism and the tactical adeptness of the Royal Navy's submariner, and the quality of his vessel, fully matched those of the major partner. This branch of the Royal Navy was truly in the 'premier league' of maritime fighting capability.

For very good reasons the part played by the submarines of the Royal Navy, United States Navy and those of other nations in the NATO Alliance during the tense years of the Cold War has been shrouded in secrecy. Even today many operations which occurred remain highly classified. In *Cold War Command,* Captains Dan Conley and Richard Woodman have succeeded in delivering a unique and evocative narrative which authentically captures the tensions and drama of this undersea confrontation which the West could not afford to lose. *Cold War Command* gives the reader thrilling insights into the physical and mental demands of operating a 'hunter-killer' in the Cold War era, and provides the reader with a hitherto undisclosed narrative of events based upon vivid and challenging experiences.

Cold War Command makes a significant contribution to charting the history of the Royal Navy Submarine Service in the latter half of the twentieth century when it underwent its greatest ever peacetime expansion. In particular, it describes the long and difficult gestation of reliable, effective anti-submarine weapons which it so sorely needed. And it is so important that individuals such as Captain Dan Conley who actually served throughout this era, witnessing many of its important events and milestones, record their experiences and observations. Having myself commanded a 'hunter-killer' and experienced first-hand similar encounters and events as are herein narrated, I can relate to much of its content – including the immense engineering and operational challenges which were so successfully met by the remarkable dedication and competence of the crews who manned the Submarine Flotilla during the uncertain years of the Cold War.

Admiral the Lord Boyce

Prologue

It was an evening in May 1985 and the sun was setting over the empty, heaving, grey wastes of the North Atlantic Ocean, where almost half a century earlier Great Britain had struggled to maintain her supply line in a world at war. On that day the world was at peace. The people on the western shore of the vast ocean were still about their business, those on the eastern side were on their way home from the toils of the day. Both were, for the best part, untroubled by thoughts of death and annihilation. The threat of the 'Mutually Assured Destruction' implicit in the stand-off between the countries of the NATO alliance and those of the Warsaw Pact kept that peace by the unrelenting maintenance of a crude but effective balance of power. For the NATO alliance, this strategic stalemate – the Cold War – depended largely upon the deployment of nuclear weapons in submarines deep in the North Atlantic Ocean.

On that May evening Britain's contribution to this delicate mechanism was the nuclear-powered, nuclear-armed submarine *Revenge*, patrolling somewhere in the North Atlantic. She was armed with Polaris intercontinental ballistic missiles, capable of striking at strategic targets deep inside Soviet Russia with their nuclear warheads, but she could be vulnerable to location and – if the international situation deteriorated due to some escalating circumstance – to potential destruction by Soviet submarines before she could launch her deadly weapons. That, at least, was the theory.

To protect her, and to ward off the inquisitive Russians, British submarines of a different type were also on patrol. These were smaller, highly manoeuvrable and also nuclear-powered, but conventionally armed, known in the naval jargon as 'hunter-killers', though all submariners, in acknowledgement of the unorthodoxies inherent in their branch of the naval service, continued to buck tradition and call their craft 'boats'. It was a grossly misleading simplification.

On that particular May evening, Commander Ian McVittie's *Revenge* had the distant support of Her Majesty's Submarines *Trafalgar* and *Valiant*, the latter of which was under Commander Dan Conley, a friend and neighbour of McVittie. The *Valiant* was then the Royal Navy's oldest nuclear-powered 'boat' which, thanks to the demands of maintaining her prototype propulsion plant and machinery, was known throughout the Submarine Flotilla as the 'Black Pig'.

Dan Conley was among those for whom the Cold War was a protracted test of professional skill, of pitting his wits against an opposition that was always an operation order away from becoming an enemy. For the first – and perhaps only time – this account reveals the true nature of the submarine brinkmanship that was played out off our shores.

The Sword of Damocles

To the generation of Britons born in the 1940s the shadow of the Second World War was long palpable, for the war's legacy lay all about them. Almost all had fathers who had been in the armed services or, if not, had worked in reserved occupations such as shipbuilding or the armaments industry. For the younger children dwelling in cities or large towns, but with no real recollection of the war itself, there was, nevertheless, a strong perception of its awfulness with the impact upon their landscape of bomb damage, and family members whose lives had been blighted.

Many British families were homeless, food was scarce, and rationing was retained as the realities of the post-war world called for further sacrifices. And so it remained for years as their government struggled with a shattered and worn-out industrial base, the heavy burden of a foreign debt, insurgencies in distant colonies and protectorates, while simultaneously attempting to rebuild an economy and provide a better life for its battered citizenry.

The destruction of the Japanese cities of Hiroshima and Nagasaki by atomic bombs had been intended to bring the war to a quick end. But the atomic bomb and other weapons developed during the conflict had awakened new possibilities. The German capacity to hit enemy cities and industrial plant with guided bombs and rockets had resulted in both the Americans and the Russians capturing and spiriting away German scientists and engineers who had worked on these fearsome weapons, in order to serve their own ends.

As a result of the appalling upheaval of the war, the world was a vastly different place in the months that followed the defeat of Germany in May 1945 compared with what it had been in September 1939. Stalin's seizure of the nations of eastern Europe as the Red Army rolled westwards in pursuit of the Germans turned into outright occupation of several countries and manipulation of elections in others, producing Communist regimes in them all. Thus was formed the Warsaw Pact, a vast buffer zone of satellite states, cutting Europe in two. 'From Stettin in the Baltic to Trieste in the Adriatic,' Britain's wartime Prime Minister, Winston Churchill, said during a speech made at Fulton, Missouri, in 1946, 'an Iron Curtain has descended upon the Continent.'

It had been clear by the time that the 'Big Three' victorious powers met at the Potsdam Conference in July 1945, following the disintegration of Germany under the hammer-blows of total war, that there was going to be no post-war accord between the Allies. The Soviet Union had suffered far more than either Great Britain or the United States of America, incurring immense damage to her infrastructure and losing some twenty million people; the consequent Russian obsession with the defence of her borders in depth is, therefore, unsurprising. After a war in which technology had played so profound a part, her natural xenophobia prompted her to seize those scientists and engineers who could serve the future ambitions of the Soviet Union, locating them away far beyond the reach of the West, where they were set to work further developing the use of rocketry to deliver devastation.

The United States, and less successfully the British, acted in a similar vein. The proximity of the British Isles to the western borders of the Soviet empire, combined with the awesome risk of a nuclear strike being launched by long-range ballistic missiles, transfixed the British, from the prime minister and the chiefs of staff to their intelligence chiefs and scientific advisers. There was the awful possibility of a pre-emptive strike by the Soviet Union, a 'nuclear Pearl Harbor', particularly pertinent after the Soviet Union detonated its first atomic weapon device in 1949. With the means in existence, and the ideological differences between the West and the Soviet Union providing ends seen by each side as legitimate, Russia was identified as the 'next enemy', a conclusion backed by deeper and more visceral convictions than mere conjecture, which had had taken root well before the end of hostilities in 1945.

Although a British admiral and his staff had attended the Japanese surrender aboard the USS *Missouri* on 2 September 1945, it had been obvious that Great Britain was emerging from the war as a weak partner to her greater ally, the United States of America. While British science had played its part in the technological triumphs of the war, Great Britain herself had borne a huge and disproportionate burden for her size.

Having dissipated one-third of her entire wealth, she was militarily overstretched and her industrial base was worn out by the demands of total war. Her people, tired of war and want, and feeling abandoned after President

Truman's abrupt and ungracious abolition of Lend-Lease in August 1945, confronted very daunting post-war problems at home and overseas. The country needed a rest, but was not able to seek such a luxury, for in her very weakness there remained the problem of her empire.

For the Labour government of Clement Attlee formed in 1945, priority lay with the reconstruction of a damaged country and the introduction of those social reforms the promise of which had so recently defeated Churchill. Notwithstanding these daunting challenges, it became clear that if Britain intended to retain her place in the world, she must exert herself yet further. While her chiefs of the imperial staff mooted the ambition of becoming a nuclear power, pleading it as a necessity, the strategic demands made by independence movements in her colonies, particularly India, demanded attention.

The British Empire had been carved out by its traders and their ships, its services and interconnectivity maintained by its merchant fleet and its order policed by the Royal Navy. As a maritime empire it therefore fell largely to the Navy to supervise the process of dismemberment. As a consequence of its worldwide deployment and the many tasks which it had undertaken during the late war, and despite the impoverishment of the British nation, the Royal Navy remained in the post-war decade a formidable enough force, at least on the face of it. Although its warships were ageing and qualitatively inferior to those of the United States Navy, and although it was sustained until the mid 1950s by conscription, the Royal Navy nevertheless possessed enough glamour to present itself as though little had changed. However, much of its upper-echelon thinking was antebellum in character and it had weaknesses that would occasionally be embarrassingly demonstrable. Nevertheless, to many boys of school age in the 1950s, when Navy Days were popular visitor attractions in the great naval ports of the kingdom, the Royal Navy's appeal remained potent.

In the early 1950s, Empire Day – 24 May – had not yet been abolished and although the term 'British Commonwealth' had long been in use, schoolchildren in Britain still waved the Union flag before being given a half-day holiday to celebrate their imperial legacy. But far away, on the other side of the world the French were fighting the Vietminh in Indochina and the Dutch were bogged down in an East Indies that was less and less 'Dutch'. When the outbreak of the Korean War involved United Nations forces against the Communist North Koreans and their Chinese allies, Britain was, of course, called upon to play her part. Once again the Royal Navy went to war and small boys watched with fascination, unaware of the horrors of that distant conflict. Although the long promised independence of India had been achieved by 1947, the pressures of domestic reconstruction had made this process precipitate and consequential. Elsewhere, would-be nationalists began to take up arms against the colonial power. With British troops fighting in Korea, a Communist insurgency in the Federated Malay States resulted in a euphemistically defined 'Emergency' that committed further resources to stabilising the future of the peninsula. Once this had been successfully suppressed, Malaysian independence followed; in the meanwhile, stirrings in Africa, the West Indies, Arabia and elsewhere required careful managing, all demanding the deployment of the British armed services.

With conflicts raging across the globe, the British and Americans continued to maintain forces in Germany to guarantee the security of the Bundesrepublik of West Germany. Opposite them, largely in East Germany and supported by the nations of the Warsaw Pact, units of the un-demobilised Soviet Red Army were stationed in overwhelming numbers.

Thus the two most heavily armed powers in the history of the world – ideological and socio-economic opposites – confronted each other in armed might. 'The West' was led by the United States of America in an alliance known as NATO, the North Atlantic Treaty Organisation, which had been formed in 1948 and had its strategic headquarters in Brussels. While this European confrontation led to military stalemate, for a period China, emerging from its civil war of 1949 as another Communist state, formed a loose alliance with the Soviet Union, very actively supporting the spread of Communism throughout Southeast Asia. It is indeed in retrospect very fortuitous that the several lesser conflicts, in which the West fought the wards of Russia and China in a policy of so called 'containment', did not escalate into yet another world war in which a nuclear exchange occurred.

The British Army on the Rhine was the most conspicuous British component of the front line in the stand-off between the West and the Soviet Union and the coerced allies of her eastern European satellites, which had become known as the 'Cold War'. There were other, perhaps less obvious aspects, particularly the nuclear deterrent maintained at this time by the Royal Air Force's V-bombers. Having played her part in the development of the atomic bomb, Britain argued her right to a share of American technology and, thanks to the exertions of Atlee's government and its desire not to allow the country to lose all of its international influence along with its empire, had acquired nuclear weapons.

This enabled the British, a junior partner to the Americans, to threaten any aggressive Russia intent on a 'first strike' with a retaliation amounting to 'Mutually Assured Destruction', a bleak policy whose acronym, MAD, seemed wholly appropriate. Owing to its proximity to the eastern borders of the Soviet Empire, Britain's early-warning system gave her population merely a 'four-minute warning', just sufficient time for its nuclear-armed V-bombers to take off to strike at targets within the Soviet Union.

These land and air defences were those most clearly in the consciousness of the British public. A strong peace movement emerged, along with a 'better red than dead' philosophy but, by and large, the popular reaction was that of stoic acceptance. Mutually Assured Destruction did at least offer the icy comfort of there being no winners. But there was besides these obvious realities another manifestation of the Cold War. Beneath the seas surrounding the British Isles, there was another confrontation taking place in which American, British and other NATO submarines – the 'Silent Services' – stealthily monitored and followed submarines and surface ships of the Soviet Navy. In operations cloaked in the highest secrecy, submarines of the West followed their Russian counterparts sometimes for weeks, if not months, totally undetected and where, upon occasion, they stole up to their opponents to within a dozen feet. At all times they were ready to fire their weapons and destroy their quarry should they receive that awesome signal indicating that hostilities had been initiated.

This book is about this underwater confrontation and focuses upon the career of one Royal Navy submarine officer, Dan Conley. How the vast and complex pressures of the Cold War affected the British Royal Navy in the years preceding the fall of the Soviet Union in 1989, and how it coped with the challenging task of providing the nation's nuclear deterrent are told through his experiences. Seldom has naval history had so close or revealing a witness to events.

1

The Twilight of Pax Britannica

IN 1956, AS BRITAIN disentangled itself from its imperial past, its complex Middle East embroilments threw up a new problem. Although India was no longer the jewel in the British imperial crown, the security of Britain's trade routes to the east and the Antipodes relied upon her part-ownership of the Suez Canal, which ran through a 'canal zone' leased from Egypt. The seizure of the Suez canal zone in July by the Egyptians led by Colonel Nasser so infuriated the British Prime Minister, Sir Anthony Eden, that he ordered its retaking. In a parlous co-operative venture with the Israelis, who were in a state of more or less constant war with the countries on their newly established borders, and Britain's canal co-owners, the French, Operation Musketeer was launched.

As Russian tanks rolled into the Hungarian capital of Budapest to suppress an uprising, in a demonstration of naked aggression by the Soviet Union, it appeared in Washington that the Anglo-French operation was just as unacceptable an example of neocolonialism. Despite Eden's protest that to capitulate to the Egyptians was appeasement such as had precipitated the Second World War, the American president, Dwight D Eisenhower, former commander of the Allied forces of America, Britain and Canada, vetoed the operation. Realising that the venture was doomed without American support in the United Nations Assembly, the British and French halted their successful landings and rapidly withdrew their troops. Even British schoolboys recognised this was a national humiliation, but there was one aspect of pride. Whatever the political misjudgements, one thing shone brightly: the amphibious operation had been all but flawless; the Royal Navy had accomplished its part to the letter. If they thought about it at all, the American reaction seemed like a betrayal and, coming from a much admired ally, a betrayal of the worst kind.

By the time those boys moved by these events came to sit their all-important eleven-plus examination, many considered a career in the Royal Navy a very desirable aspiration. A grammar school education, compared to that of a privileged public school, had its prejudiced detractors even in post-war Britain, but was nevertheless accepted as one possible route of entry as an officer-cadet. And so, with young heads stuffed full of a confusing mixture of paternal war stories, of politics gone wrong, of a vague but glorious past and, a few years earlier, of having been witness to a coronation of a young and glamorous Queen, many young lads of all backgrounds applied to join Britannia Royal Naval College in south Devon. This institution is perhaps better known by the name of the town above which its imposing structure stands – Dartmouth.

History aside, those among them in the early 1960s who had mugged up sufficiently to impress the fearsome Admiralty Selection Board would have been aware that the Royal Navy had recently acquired a new national status as the future guardian of the nation's nuclear deterrent. All would have comprehended the shadow of Mutually Assured Destruction, and most would have known that the nuclear deterrent was no longer exclusively in the hands of the USAF and the RAF, the responsibility for the ultimate deterrent having passed in America to the United States Navy, while in Britain it would in due course be handed over to the Royal Navy. Amongst the young men aspiring to become an officer in the Royal Navy of 1963 was a young Scotsman named Dan Conley.

Despite its supplanting by the United States Navy as the world's most powerful navy, the Royal Navy of the early 1960s remained a substantial force, with over two hundred and fifty warships and submarines, manned by more than 100,000 officers and ratings, supported by an equivalent number of civil servants and dockyard employees. In the twenty years following the end of the Second World War, Britain also possessed the world's biggest merchant fleet and a large deep-water fishing fleet. British shipbuilding continued to enjoy boom times, constructing a large proportion of the world's merchant shipping and directly employing a workforce of over 150,000. Everywhere there were symbols of Britain's maritime status: busy ports reached up rivers to penetrate centres of cities whose streets contained the offices of shipping companies, their windows filled with models of their latest vessels. Maritime influence was enshrined in such trivia as the nautical names of leading cigarette brands and the names of pubs; even the newfangled airlines adopted nautical terms and styles.

Naval recruiting posters, displayed at railway stations and on buses, portrayed a highly attractive life at sea in tropical climes. As if to cement this perception in the British psyche, the audience at the last night of the summer festival of promenade concerts at the Royal Albert Hall in London listened to a medley of orchestrated sea songs before participating in the culmination, a communal singing of *Rule Britannia*. Meanwhile, politicians murdered metaphors derived from seafaring, from 'the ship of state' to 'steady hands on the helm', a propensity that endured long after Britannia had ceased to rule very much, least of all the waves, a circumstance that was to overtake Conley and his fellow cadets within a decade of their obtaining their commissions.

In 1963 there was a very positive sense of opportunity, challenge and widening horizons in the Royal Navy. At its core was a force of five strike carriers armed with Buccaneer low-level bomber aircraft and Sea Vixen fighters which, together with radar-equipped airborne early warning Gannets, provided the Fleet with air cover. Plans were in place to build a new aircraft carrier of about 60,000 tons displacement, while to protect these heavy units and to provide trade protection to merchant ships in convoy in time of war, there was a force of ninety frigates and destroyers.

The submarine force of over forty 'boats' was being overhauled with the introduction of twenty one 'O'- and 'P'-class diesel submarines. Significantly, the navy's first nuclear-powered submarine, the prototype HMS *Dreadnought*, had been commissioned. Of even more importance, following the Nassau Agreement of 1962, the construction of five Polaris-armed nuclear-powered submarines had been started. These vessels, known to their crews as 'boats' but to NATO and the high command as 'SSBNs', would carry the British nuclear deterrent to sea undetected beneath the dark waters of the North Atlantic. Furthermore, to defend them by both acting as a distant support to their patrols and reconnoitring enemy countermeasure forces, a class of five nuclear-powered but torpedo-armed strike submarines was planned. Formally known as 'SSNs', the first two of these 'hunter-killer' submarines, HMS *Valiant* and HMS *Warspite*, were already under construction.

To maintain the security of inshore waters, the Royal Navy possessed about one hundred minesweepers, and an amphibious force capable of deploying a full brigade of Royal Marine commandos by means of helicopters was spearheaded by two commando carriers. To support these men-of-war at sea, over forty tankers, supply and ammunition ships were provided by the Royal Fleet Auxiliary. Ashore in Great Britain there were four Royal Dockyards: at Portsmouth, Plymouth, Chatham and Rosyth, with another at Gibraltar and a sixth at Sembawang, on the island of Singapore. Besides these shore establishments there were eight naval air stations and a number of naval bases scattered throughout the remnants of the empire including Bermuda, Malta, Hong Kong and Aden. For those officers and senior rates so inclined, these overseas locations offered the prospect of far-distant foreign postings. Well-appointed residences, generous allowances and, for the more senior, a retinue of domestic staff, added to their attraction.

It was not unusual for ships to undertake foreign service commissions of up to eighteen months' duration, operating from such exotic stations. Although officers could afford to fly out their families when their ships were alongside during extended maintenance periods, this was not the case for most of the crew, who would not see their kith and kin until their ship returned to the United Kingdom. The naval rating of the early 1960s required a robust outlook and a resignation to a disrupted, if not dysfunctional, family life. In such circumstances the character of a seaman's wife was of paramount importance in holding a family together during a husband's absence.

Such societal demands were increasingly old-fashioned as mainstream British society evolved during the permissive decade of 'the sixties'. If the situation of a seaman's wife was anachronistic, there were parallels in her husband's warship, where the inevitable entrenched perceptions of recent conflict reflected upon the overarching ethos within the naval service. Just as the 'Big Gun Club' of gunnery officers had predominated in the pre-war Royal Navy, aviators were pre-eminent in the Royal Navy in the early 1960s.

This naval aviation cadre had seen the post-war introduction of jet aircraft, often operating from carriers which were really too small and unsuited to this role. Coupled to aircraft with sometimes unreliable engines this was a highly dangerous occupation; even in peacetime 892 Squadron of Sea Vixen fighters embarked in HMS *Hermes* suffered a fatality rate of almost one in eight during a two-year commission. Although never actually used in aerial combat, of the 155 Sea Vixen aircraft entered into service, over sixty crashed and more than half of these accidents involved fatalities.

A particular hazard was a 'cold shot' when the steam catapult launching an aircraft from the bows of the carrier failed, tossing it into the sea ahead of the carrier. This then required its crew to exercise very great courage and incredible coolness, remaining in their sinking aircraft until the carrier's propellers had passed overhead and then ejecting safely to the surface to await rescue. Such stories were the stuff of legend and, remarkably, there was to be no shortage of volunteers for pilot training. However, the same could not be

4

said for the 'observers' who undertook the navigation and weapon-system control in the navy's two-man jet-propelled strike aircraft and fighters. Many of them were pressed men who had entered the service with no inclination to volunteer for flying. Naturally, being positioned in a cramped space underneath the cockpit of a Sea Vixen fighter known as the 'coal-hole' did not appeal to many of Conley's Dartmouth peers, since the fatality rate for Sea Vixen observers was even higher than that of the pilots.

In the early 1960s the Royal Navy's core strategy was geared to maintaining two strike carriers east of Suez. The tasks occupying the Royal Navy east of Suez smacked somewhat of the 'gunboat diplomacy' of the previous century, though it was usually in support of the civil power, rather than forcing British interests upon the citizenry of other countries. Among a number of influential interventions, in 1959 a British carrier-led task force successfully repelled the threat of Iraq invading the then British protectorate of Kuwait.

Despite the possibility of conflict in the Far East arising from the insidious spread of Communism fostered by the Chinese, the biggest maritime threat to the Western alliance of NATO at that time was that of over three hundred Soviet submarines. Considering that Hitler only possessed some forty operational U-boats at the outbreak of war in 1939, the Russians had profited from the German example, fully aware of the close-run nature of the outcome of the Battle of the Atlantic. The Soviet Union's submarine force, principally operating out of the Northern Fleet base at Polyanoe near Murmansk and increasing in numbers of nuclear boats, had the potential to seriously threaten the lines of communication across the world's oceans, but chiefly the North Atlantic. However, in the early 1960s the Royal Navy was principally focused upon Far and Middle East operations as opposed to putting the greatest proportion of its resources into Cold War containment, this task principally being that of the British Army on the Rhine (BAOR) and the Royal Air Force. In general, the Russians were not inclined to venture far from their own waters to any degree and arrayed against their submarines there was a large, if polyglot, NATO anti-submarine force which numbered in total hundreds of escorts, maritime patrol aircraft, submarines and helicopters.

Dan Conley joined the Royal Navy in 1963 through a cadet scholarship scheme. A Scottish grammar school boy from an Argyll fishing family, following the precedent of several generations of his forebears, he was set on a career at sea. An infant of the post-war baby boom, Conley had been born in Edinburgh in September 1946. His father finished his war serving in motor torpedo boats in the Far East, where hostilities did not end until

August 1945 and demobilisation was slow to follow. He then returned to his traditional job, that of a herring fisherman who hunted fish for a living. The family owned a herring trawler which operated from Campbeltown on the southeast tip of the Kintyre Peninsula, Argyllshire. The port boasted a local fishing fleet of about fifty boats which, together with its supporting infrastructure, formed the town's principal source of employment. Like all who live close to the sea, the young Conley was impressed by its awesome power in wild weather and the risks involved in making a living from fishing although, remarkably, serious accidents were few and far between in the Clyde herring fleet.

Clyde-based submarines frequently visited Campbeltown, allowing their off-duty men an evening's run ashore. Black, sleek and sinister, they inevitably attracted local attention, particularly on the part of curious boys who would rush down to the pier to watch as they came alongside. One stormy evening such a visiting submarine ran aground in the approaches to Campbeltown harbour, an event marked by a framed picture in a local hostelry of a postman in wellington boots, accompanied by his dog, standing underneath her bows delivering mail. Conley developed an early admiration for the crews, fascinated by their air of professional swagger that carried with it more than a hint of the buccaneer. Perhaps most influential was their demonstrable and characteristic cheerfulness. Later, these insights would prove influential in his decision to become a submariner.

Campbeltown was also often used as the forward base for the trials of the high test peroxide (HTP) propelled submarines, *Explorer* and *Excalibur*. Both had acquired a reputation, owing to the tendency of the volatile HTP to catch fire or explode. Nevertheless, hints that these submarines were capable of very high submerged speed added to the appeal of the Silent Service.

The appearance of submarines in the tranquil waters of the loch only emphasised the existence of a world beyond the horizon that remained inextricably linked with the upheavals and separations which occurred after the Second World War. During their schooldays Conley and his con-temporaries were well aware of the nuclear threat posed by the ideological hostility of the Soviet Union, not least through the activities of the civil defence organisation which included occasional radio or television informa-tion programmes and the distribution of leaflets describing in facile terms how to contend with a nuclear strike – hiding under the staircase or the dining-room table – and its fearsome aftermath of radiation risk. To a boy, however, such horrors seemed remote, and were easily forgotten.

In 1954 Conley's father became seriously ill. Although he recovered after a prolonged convalescence, he was no longer able to work at sea; his fishing career was over. The family boat was sold and in the summer of 1955 the family moved to Glasgow. Here Conley passed the eleven-plus examination and attended grammar school, where his education continued to be first-rate, but he conceived no fondness for the city and decided to join the Royal Navy as a seaman officer as soon as possible. Aged fifteen he applied for a scholarship to Dartmouth and was invited to attend the Royal Navy Reserve headquarters in Leith, where he was granted a preliminary interview by a captain and a rather benign Edinburgh headmaster. An aviator, the captain tested Conley's knowledge of naval aircraft, while the headmaster assessed the lad's potential. Conley progressed to the next stage, two days of interviews and tests at the Admiralty interview board in the shore establishment HMS *Sultan* at Gosport in Hampshire. Opposite Portsmouth itself, Gosport was also the home of another stone frigate, the submarine base HMS *Dolphin*. One evening the dozen young aspirants comprising Conley's selection group were taken aboard the new diesel submarine HMS *Finwhale*, which was lying alongside. Thirteen years later Conley, undergoing commanding officer's training, was to become better acquainted with the cramped control room of this particular submarine with its myriad of gauges and valves; at the time he was merely awed by its complexity. Subsequent to this unwitting peep into his future, Conley's full interview process was followed by an extensive medical examination in London, which included very stringent tests of colour vision. A failure in this courted instant rejection.

A few weeks later Conley's parents received a letter: their son's application had been successful. Subject to his achieving the required grades in his Scottish Higher examination, he was offered a scholarship. A year later Conley had cleared the final hurdle and, after a further trip to London for pre-entry medical tests and uniform measurements, in September 1963 the seventeen-year-old caught a train to join Britannia Royal Naval College, Dartmouth.

Unlike the other two armed services, or the indenture required of an apprentice in the Merchant Navy, where a formal process was undertaken, Cadet Conley was accepted for training as an executive (seaman) officer on the permanent career General List on the basis of a gentlemen's agreement.

2

Dartmouth

THE SUNNY AFTERNOON of 17 September 1963 witnessed the arrival of dozens of young men at Kingswear station, in the South Hams of Devon. They walked out of the station and boarded the ferry for the short crossing of the River Dart. Although possessed of a common purpose, all having been selected to train as potential officers for the Royal Navy, they remained individuals, staring about them and catching sight of the glitter of the sun on water, their nostrils filled with the scent of the sea. As soon as they disembarked at Dartmouth on the farther side of the river they began the process of conversion. Met by immaculately-dressed gunnery instructors, chief petty officers in naval uniform, they were ordered to put their luggage into parked lorries and then, with much shouting and direction from the instructors, they were formed into squads and began the march up the steep hill to Britannia Royal Naval College.

Seventeen-year-old Dan Conley marched among the loose ranks and files of the column. Like those marching with him, he was wondering what lay ahead. Of one thing he had little doubt: in going to sea as a naval officer he had chosen the right career. However, one of his new-entry colleagues was not so convinced about his forthcoming naval vocation and was observed two hours later boarding a taxi at the main college entrance, heading back to civilian life.

The imposing structure of Britannia Royal Naval College stands upon high ground overlooking and dominating the town of Dartmouth and the valley of the Dart. Completed in 1905 at the height of Britain's imperium, it replaced the old hulks of Her Majesty's ships *Britannia* and *Hindustan*, former ships of the line which had been used to accommodate and train several generations of officer cadets, despite the unhealthy conditions which prevailed aboard these ancient men-of-war. The college owed its existence to Admiral of the Fleet 'Jacky' Fisher, who wished to improve the professionalism of the Royal Navy's officer corps.

Despite Fisher's high-minded ideal, until 1948 the college had been little more than a public school, admitting fee-paying boys at the age of thirteen. The cadets passed out of the college at sixteen, going to sea in designated warships to complete their basic officer training. Although this had changed by 1963, the college retained a traditional British public school ethos, with all that this entailed by way of ritual and, of course, discipline. Up until the 1948 change to a sixteen-year-old entry, the latter included the administration of physical punishment for serious misdemeanours, the cane being applied in the college gymnasium under the supervision of a medical officer. Although the practice of matching a pair of new entrants in the boxing ring and encouraging them to beat the living daylights out of each other had been abolished, this was a comparatively recent reform. Indeed, the college retained many traditions and customs which were more in keeping with an imperial past, epitomised by the prominent inscription under the main building parapet which confidently declared – 'It is on the Navy under the good providence of God that our wealth, prosperity and peace depend'. It was soon, however, clear to Conley, among others, that much of the college training was unsuited to a modern navy, especially as that navy took on the challenges of the nuclear age where the age of officer entry would move from the late teens to the early twenties.

At the time, the majority of the college academic staff had not significantly developed their lecturing skills from those of teaching schoolchildren to delivering a graduate-level education. Therefore, whilst there were exceptions, the overall quality of tuition was at best unremarkable. This became particularly true when the young officer returned to the college for his sub lieutenant academic year. For the full career General List executive and supply branches this followed a first year as a cadet in college and a second at sea in the Fleet as a midshipman. The sub lieutenants specialising in engineering had after their midshipman's time, meanwhile, gone instead to Manadon College, Plymouth, to undertake their degree-level studies, a shift which acknowledged an inherent maturity not provided for their colleagues returning to Dartmouth.

For those returning to Dartmouth, the academic year consisted of indifferent teaching of English, physics, mechanics and mathematics to first-year university level. However, there was little encouragement of logical and challenging analysis, or focus on original thought. In particular, the opportunity was missed to inculcate contemporary naval strategy or the processes of decision-making in the Ministry of Defence. Significantly since it underpinned strategic thinking, curricular naval history was not only limited, but very badly taught, and there was no serious discussion or debate regarding force structures and the strengths and weaknesses of the Royal Navy, particularly in the Second World War. Unlike the United States Navy of the day, the Royal Navy did not take education sufficiently seriously and four decades were to elapse before the first Chief of Naval Staff (First Sea Lord) possessed a degree.

Perhaps more important, few junior officers leaving Dartmouth had an understanding of how the higher echelons of the country's defence management worked, let alone comprehended the interface between the other armed services, the civil servants and the politicians.

A product of the post-war baby boom, the seventeen-year-old Conley found himself among three hundred cadets. These included a number from Commonwealth and other countries, including Iran, Morocco and the Sudan. Later, on his return to Dartmouth as a sub lieutenant, among the foreign officers were half a dozen fiery individuals from Algeria who claimed they had most recently been Front de Libération Nationale (FLN) guerrillas, who had killed French citizens and should not, therefore, be messed around with. In later years, many of these overseas trainees were to die in civil wars in their respective countries, several of the Iranians being assassinated by their fellow countrymen.

On their first entry the cadets were organised into six junior divisions, each supervised by two divisional officers assisted by a sub lieutenant under training. A divisional chief, normally a retired chief petty officer, looked after their routine requirements and completed the management team of each division. On arrival, each cadet was allocated a bunk in the divisional dormitory, issued with a basic uniform and an all-important pay book which, amongst other detail, required the declaration of 'smoker' or 'non-smoker'. Smokers were entitled to coupons for the monthly purchase of 300 cigarettes especially produced for the Royal Navy and rumoured to consist of the floor sweepings of a well-known tobacco company. These were at a ludicrously low price, yet another hangover from a bygone era, and a benefit which could hardly be considered as conducive to good health. Almost the first lesson the cadets learned was to sign up as smokers in order to acquire the coupons, these being a negotiable currency.

Roughly half of the British cadets were from public-school backgrounds, most of the remainder coming from grammar schools. The General List entrants had been educated to university entrance qualification. There was also a sprinkling of so-called 'upper yardsmen', the quaint title for those individuals who, starting out as ratings, possessed outstanding qualities commending their promotion at an early stage in their careers from the lower deck into the General List. The former public schoolboys settled most easily into an existence with which they were already familiar. For many of the others, Conley included, induction was a more painful process as they struggled with the college routines and the very strict discipline which was enforced by all levels of the staff. Punishment for even relatively trivial offences, such as being late for lectures, involved extra drills, physical exertions or tedious changes of uniform. The practice of making recalcitrants run up and down the many steps leading to the River Dart had ended the previous year when an unfortunate youth under punishment had collapsed and died of heart failure.

Seemingly interminable time was spent undertaking training on the parade ground. Even with the Royal Marine Band attached to the college providing stirring martial music, there were those who found drill difficult, while taking charge of a squad and barking orders introduced Conley and many of his peers to a very novel and not entirely comfortable experience. Inculcating a parade-ground voice required in some cases the undertaking of 'backward shouting' classes, a public indication of a shortcoming somewhat hard to take. Moreover, much was made of defects in dress, such as wearing gaiters upside down, a mistake the consequences of which Conley afterwards recalled as 'the biggest humiliation in my entire Service career.'

The over-arching aim of the first two terms at Dartmouth was to instil basic naval knowledge and discipline, while developing character and leadership skills through adventure training or boat-work aboard one of the college's many boats. An apparent infinity of detail about the workings of the Royal Navy was instilled into the neophytes. However, a considerable amount of the instruction was of total irrelevance to their future careers such as, for example, a lecture upon the means of dealing with the anchor system on a long-scrapped battleship such as HMS *Nelson*. The cadets were also introduced to the more common weapon systems such as the anti-submarine mortar, all of which would be re-taught several times during the following years, just in case they had failed to hoist in the details on this first occasion.

Despite these intellectual shortcomings, as a quintessentially British institution the college offered a very wide range of sports, with recreational facilities second to none. Notably, the college possessed a very long-established beagle pack and fondly remembered hounds had their graves scattered throughout the college grounds. Other activities included flying in Tiger Moth biplanes from Roborough airfield, near Plymouth, horse riding and – besides boat-work in the college pulling boats and sailing dinghies – more extensive coastal cruises aboard one of the college's 36ft yachts. Before joining one of the warships attached to the Dartmouth Training Squadron, Conley spent a very enjoyable week aboard one of these, sailing round the south coast of Ireland. The yacht was skippered by Conley's divisional officer and his performance onboard the yacht was, he considered, a turning point from a rather poor start in his time at Dartmouth, as he felt that he had at last achieved the full confidence of this officer, Lieutenant Commander Chris Schofield. He was to be killed when the Avro Shackleton aircraft in which he was flying as an observer crashed into the English Channel.

Notwithstanding its deficiencies, or perhaps because of them, Britannia Royal Naval College successfully instilled the ethos, spirit and heritage of the Royal Navy, producing an elite, each of whom had an immense sense of pride in being part of a long-established armed service of the British Crown. The corridors of the college were arrayed with group photographs of previous cadet entries, and the knowledge that many of those faces staring out from the pictures had subsequently died serving their country endowed the impressionable young cadets with a profound sense of respect for what the college had achieved in the past. However, this pride was not to discourage Conley from being critical of the Royal Navy; on the contrary, his high regard for the institution was to create a desire to improve it, an aspiration formed within the hallowed precincts of the college.

The one fundamental issue Dartmouth failed to address, or even emphasise, was the requirement for reliable, effective weapon systems to enable British warships to be capable when in harm's way. Instead it bred an ethos of making-do, whatever the odds. After all, it seemed that, despite all its inadequacies, during the Second World War the Royal Navy had nevertheless emerged victorious. In this bland assumption, the often unnecessary loss of both warships and numerous merchant ships with their crews and cargoes was ignored. Such avoidable losses were in part a consequence of the failure to make historical discourse and operational analysis central to the development of the young and aspiring naval officer. Although Conley had yet to grasp fully the extent of all this, it was clear to him that the lacklustre college teaching left much to be desired.

In April 1964, along with fifty or so other cadets, Conley joined his first ship, HMS *Wizard*, an emergency-class destroyer completed in 1944, which had been converted ten years later to an anti-submarine frigate. The conversion had consisted of removing the ship's main armament and building up the superstructure with aluminium to keep the topweight down. The most up-to-date sonar had been fitted, supported by two triple-barrelled anti-submarine Squid mortars. The *Wizard*'s gunnery armament had been reduced to a high-angle twin 4in turret, facing aft, controlled by an obsolescent radar-driven gun director which would have been near useless in action. As a unit of the Dartmouth training squadron, *Wizard* had also been fitted with an additional open bridge above the enclosed one, abaft of which was a classroom which replaced a twin Bofors anti-aircraft gun mounting. Whilst her anti-submarine armament would have proved competent to deal with the conventional diesel-engined submarine of the day, like most former small warships of her era, *Wizard* lacked endurance and was incapable of crossing the North Atlantic without refuelling.

Conley and his classmates joined her in Devonport dockyard as she was completing a maintenance period. Here he first encountered the legendary 'dockyard matey', along with the many archaic and inefficient practices then commonplace in both private and state shipbuilding and ship repair facilities at the time. These very serious problems ensured that such places, run largely on assumptions of superiority which seamlessly begat complacency, were guaranteed a rapid demise as world competition exposed their actual chronic inferiority. Union demarcation was rife, leading to a bewildering number of different tradesmen assigned to simple tasks, resulting in great loss of working time and the high unit cost of each item on a ship's repair specification. Working hours were arcane, men clocking on at 0700, almost immediately breaking off for breakfast at 0800. Although this was only supposed to last half an hour, in effect little work was done before 0900 when the first dockyard mateys boarded a ship under repair. Management was in general very incompetent, individual managers rarely appearing on board the ships whose repair they were supervising, preferring to closet themselves in their warm and comfortable offices and allowing their foremen to run the show.

The average worker was relatively poorly paid and depended upon overtime to secure a reasonable income. This encouraged a management–worker relationship which, at best, could be described as abrasive, and at worst, hostile. However, perhaps the most shocking aspect of the dockyard matey was his attitude. Few felt any sense of loyalty to the Royal Navy, and many had little pride in their work. Too often too many arrived at their workplace intending to do the minimum possible during the course of the day, and it came as little surprise that under such conditions Devonport dockyard needed a workforce in the order of 16,000.

After the shock of this industrialised aspect of the Royal Navy's supporting infrastructure, *Wizard* herself proved to be an unhappy ship. Despite her recent winter training cruise having been to some delightful ports in the Caribbean, and in spite of imminent visits to Scandinavian ports, crew morale was depressed. Being new-entry cadets and therefore of low status on board, it did not take Conley and his colleagues long to smoke out the reason why the ratings were unhappy. They perceived themselves to be held in low esteem by their officers, while many of the senior leading hands and petty officers, no doubt similarly demotivated, failed to provide them with any leadership.

As for the officers, there was over-emphasis upon the cleanliness and appearance of the ship, which appeared to be the executive officer's only priority. One soon grasped that the life of many sailors revolved around very mundane and repetitive cleaning. Those recruiting posters depicting seamen manning guns or missile systems had clearly portrayed a very false picture of life at sea on a British man-of-war in the 1960s.

The cadets had first-hand experience of this, living and working as junior sailors, cleaning, storing and keeping watches accordingly. One of the most unpopular tasks was that of maintaining the unpainted aluminium upper deck, a job accomplished on one's knees and entailing the erasing of any marks with wire wool and soapy water. This was then finished by the application of Brasso and a vigorous polishing until the deck gleamed like silver. Apart from this being a damp, uncomfortable task, it was rather nugatory; at sea, a dollop of spray or deposit of funnel soot would quickly stain the bare metal.

HMS *Wizard* boasted two cadets' mess decks where the youngsters slept in hammocks. Conley never quite got used to this, either in or out of his berth. His usually badly stowed hammock which, when not in use, was supposed to be available to plug the hull in event of damage in action would rarely have been fit for purpose. Happily, however, being largely free from the curse of seasickness, he quickly settled into the cramped confines of living and working on a frigate, even one as miserable as HMS *Wizard*.

Under supervision, the cadets manned many of the watch-keeping and weapon system stations including the high-angled 4in anti-aircraft guns during live firing exercises. The most demanding position on the mounting was that of the loaders, who were required by hand to ram the 100lb combined shell and charge into the gun, keeping their fingers well clear as the breech block closed automatically once the cartridge was in place. This was followed by the piercing crack as the twin guns fired simultaneously, whereupon the gun recoiled, ejecting the brass cartridge casings which could catch an unwary cadet a nasty blow should he be in the way. The whole process was repeated at an interval of once every four seconds. Below the gun mounting, the aluminium bulkheads would audibly protest, bits of insulation fell from the deckhead, while loose gear flew around. It was all quite thrilling, despite the fact that the chance of hitting any of the aircraft targets was slender. Furthermore, the standard anti-aircraft shell fuse only exploded if the shell came close to the target. This differed from the earlier form of timed fuse which detonated a shell, thereby creating an intimidating barrage through which an attacking pilot must fly. Unless very close to the target, the proximity fuse produced nothing visible to put the attacker off his aim.

HMS *Wizard* was the oldest vessel of the Dartmouth training squadron and was accompanied by the more modern Type 12 anti-submarine frigates *Torquay* and *Tenby*, then both about eight years old. That summer the three warships visited Bergen in Norway and then Copenhagen, the capital of Denmark, before passing into the Baltic Sea. Here the squadron was met by a Soviet minesweeper which was soon joined by a Riga-class frigate, which were to be the squadron's constant escorts until it passed into Finnish territorial waters approaching the port of Turku.

This was Conley's first encounter with the Soviet Navy, the Royal Navy's principal Cold War opponent, and the actions of the Russians were but a foretaste of what he would come to know well as a game of intimidating cat and mouse as the two Soviet men-of-war came within a few hundred yards of the British warships. On leaving Turku, heading south, the three British frigates were again accompanied by Soviet warships units until they passed into Danish waters, a clear and demonstrable marker that the Soviet Navy regarded the Baltic as *mare nostrum* – 'our sea'.

After very enjoyable port visits to Gothenburg and Steinkjer in Norway, *Wizard* headed back home across the North Sea. It was noticeable on the homeward passage that three of the crew had been incarcerated in separate, temporary cells, and when not locked up could only move about under escort. This did not help an already fragile ship's company's morale and later the cadets found out that the three prisoners faced charges of serious assaults upon their shipmates. After being court-martialled, all three were given prison sentences.

The cadets' final week on *Wizard* was spent in the Firth of Clyde with her two other squadron consorts, acting as a targets for the strenuous command course undertaken by submarine officers. Known as the 'Perisher', owing to its relatively high failure rate, the unsuccessful suffered an instant termination to all hopes of a promising career in submarines. This was clearly an indication of standards of excellence as yet unseen by Conley and his fellows, an emphatic reflection of an elite, placing submarine commanders firmly and demonstrably in a class of their own. The lesson was not lost on Conley.

Each evening the three frigates anchored off Rothesay, where they were joined by the participating submarine, which emerged from the dark waters with an air of mystery. Along with other cadets whose interests were inclining them to consider specialising in submarines, Conley volunteered for a day at sea aboard her. The course submarine involved was HMS *Narwhal* and on the passage down to her diving position Conley found himself alongside the officer of the watch on her bridge. Wearing spectacles, very unusual for a seaman officer at that time, the officer of the watch (OOW) was a studious-looking Lieutenant Gavin Menzies, who in later years would not only command a submarine, but would go on to write the highly acclaimed but provocatively controversial bestseller *1421*, which rather convincingly set out the theory that in the fifteenth century the fleet of the Ming Emperor of China, commanded by the eunuch Zeng-He, had ventured as far as the North American continent and beyond.

Once *Narwhal* had dived, the 'Perisher' students, taking turns as commanding officer, were then put under the great pressure of having to contend with several warships proceeding at full speed towards their position with the instruction to ram the periscope if sighted. Of course there were copious safeguards to avoid this happening and the course instructor, known as 'Teacher', ensured the submarine went deep, well below the keel depth of the frigates, with plenty of margin to avoid collision. Spending some time in the control room, observing the students perform, gave Conley a vivid insight into the extreme intellectual pressures and emotional stresses he would place himself under if he made as far as the Perisher command course. As he returned that evening to the unhappy *Wizard*, Conley had a lot on his young mind.

3

Midshipman

THE CADETS DISEMBARKED from *Wizard* in late July 1964, the deployment ending the elderly frigate's service in the Dartmouth training squadron. Paid off the following year, she was sold for scrap three years later. For the cadets, however, their naval career was about to begin in earnest, for they were about to be promoted to midshipmen, Conley being destined for five weeks' training aboard the aircraft carrier *Eagle*. This was to be followed by appointment to the destroyer *Cambrian*, which was due to deploy to the Far East as part of the build-up of British forces assisting the Malaysian Federation in its 'Confrontation' with an aggressive Indonesia.

This would prove a long-lasting crisis which erupted in 1963 when President Achmed Sukarno of Indonesia threatened to withdraw his country from the United Nations (the first to do so since its establishment) and announced a policy of 'Confrontation' against the newly formed Malaysian Federation. This was little short of a declaration of war. Sukarno objected to the unification of the Federated States of Malaya, Singapore, Sarawak and Sabah (until recently British North Borneo), and claimed Sarawak and Sabah as Indonesian territories. To support the legitimate aspirations of the peoples of the new state, a significant proportion of the Royal Navy was deployed to the Far East, to be based in Singapore.

Although not a Communist himself but heading up strong nationalist armed forces, Sukarno's relationship with the well-organised Indonesian Communist Party had troubled Western intelligence services since the Second World War. During the late 1950s the latter had supported rebellions in the Indonesian territories of Sumatra and Sulawesi, the American CIA participating in some strength, including clandestine bombing. Sukarno's unfounded suspicions as to Western involvement in the establishment of the Malaysian Federation led him to declare 'Confrontation' with the new state. Incursions across the long, indistinct Borneo–Kalimantam border, combined with hit and run raids on isolated communities in Borneo and Sarawak, together with the threat of raids on international shipping in Singapore's Keppel Harbour and elsewhere in Peninsular Malaysia – where in the event parachutists were landed – led to major elements of the British armed forces being committed to support the Malaysians. Confrontation might have been a euphemism, but it became a war by any other name, forming part of the Western policy of 'containment' wherever Communism or its destabilising influences manifested itself. The Indonesian-Malaysian Confrontation ran concurrently with the first movements of American forces into Vietnam, which would in time lead to the United States' ultimately unsuccessful engagement in the long, bloody and very costly Vietnam War.

The commitment of the Western nations to a mutual containment policy encouraged the Royal Navy's high command, despite constraints on material resources, to nevertheless view hull numbers as an overriding factor. Set against the limitations in its warships' anti-aircraft defence systems this was a risky strategy, particularly since the major air threat to the Royal Navy in the 1960s was assessed to be the Soviet anti-ship cruise missiles launched from ships, submarines or aircraft. These missiles after launch would guide themselves to the target.

The first line of defence was the fighter or attack aircraft embarked on the five fleet carriers. However, although four of these ships had been completed after the Second World War, they were built to wartime design and were fitted with old-fashioned, inefficient steam propulsion machinery which was very expensive in fuel consumption and manpower-intensive to operate and maintain. Two, HMS *Hermes* and HMS *Centaur*, were not really big enough to operate efficiently and safely the 20-ton Sea Vixen and Buccaneer fighter and strike jets coming into service and whilst the others, *Victorious*, *Ark Royal* and *Eagle*, had the advantage of armour protection, particularly on the flight deck, this was at the cost of the number of aircraft embarked. Although the 45,000-ton *Ark Royal* and *Eagle* were the largest in the Fleet, they carried a maximum of fewer than fifty aircraft compared to the seventy or more carried by their American equivalents.

Ideally, the carriers would be operated in battle groups of two, which enabled comprehensive, continuous airborne protection to be maintained, together with the necessary capability to contend with multiple attacks. However, with a maximum of four operational carriers about to be reduced to three following the paying off of *Centaur* in 1965, it would have been impossible in practice to provide carrier air cover in more than two combat

18

scenarios. The incoming Labour government of 1964 was quick to realise how costly the carrier force was. However, their 1966 decision to phase out the fixed-wing carrier force ignored the considerations that it provided vital early airborne warning to the Fleet, and that the capability of its destroyers and frigates to protect themselves from air attack was very limited. These shortcomings were to make the Falklands War in 1982 a close-run thing, highlighting severe vulnerabilities in anti-aircraft defence of the Royal Navy.

In the early 1960s, besides the aircraft carriers, the Royal Navy possessed only four guided missile destroyers, the County class. These were armed with the rather cumbersome Sea Slug missile which was designed to destroy high-flying anti-ship missiles. As demonstrated in the Falklands War, this system was totally ineffective against attacking aircraft. The Fleet's medium-range gunnery systems depended upon the target remaining straight and steady so that the prediction systems could place the shells near the attacking aircraft: this type of co-operation could, of course, not be expected from an attacker. The Sea Cat missile was being introduced to provide short-range defence, but it was highly unreliable and was of low effectiveness. The remainder of the Fleet's short-range anti-aircraft capability depended on the 40mm Bofors gun, a weapon of Swedish design and Second World War vintage, which was also very limited in its effectiveness.

Indeed, it was not until the 1970s that the much more capable medium-range Sea Dart system was introduced into service. However, this was another missile much more effective at eliminating high-flying missiles, with their inherent predictability of trajectory, than successfully engaging a low-flying aircraft or missile, owing to its sluggish reactivity. This, then, was the state of play when Conley joined HMS *Eagle* at Plymouth, in company with a dozen or so fellow midshipmen.

The aircraft carrier had just emerged from an expensive five-year modernisation where she was fitted with a much better angled flight deck, a state-of-the-art and very capable detection and tracking radar, improved aircraft maintenance facilities and upgraded accommodation. HMS *Eagle* was, therefore, regarded as the premier ship in the Fleet, very smart in appearance as she emerged from the dockyard with spotless, comfortable accommodation which seemed to possess the ambience of a new ship. Against this was the depressing fact that she still had her original propulsion machinery fitted in 1946, including eight inefficient low-pressure open-furnace boilers.

On the arrival of the midshipmen, *Eagle* was undergoing a maintenance and leave period before completing a series of post-refit trials with no aircraft embarked. She was destined to take on onboard squadrons of twelve Buccaneer low-level strike aircraft and sixteen Sea Vixen fighters. Aerial reconnaissance and radar early warning would be provided by flights of Scimitar and Gannet aircraft, with a squadron of six anti-submarine Wessex helicopters topping out the complete air wing of over forty aircraft.

For the newcomers, familiarisation tours of the ship quickly revealed how complex she was internally. With a crew of over 1,500 required to navigate, operate her machinery and weapons systems and to meet the necessary logistical demands of stores, catering and personnel administration, she was a complex floating community. With the air wing embarked the complement would increase to 2,500. Armoured and subdivided into many watertight compartments to enable the ship to sustain substantial damage and yet remain afloat, Conley and the three of his colleagues who were also destined for small ships, and thus only onboard for a few weeks, were soon to get to know these compartments well.

Her fixed-wing aircraft would be launched over her bow by either of two steam-propelled catapults. On landing they would be arrested by hooking onto one of four wires which provided incremental hydraulic resistance. This was a crude but effective system which, although dating back to the early days of naval aviation, nevertheless proved adaptable to the jet age.

Conley and his three companions were initially allocated to train with the engineering department. However, on their first day with the department they soon realised there was a major problem which threatened the operation of this complex vessel. Inadvertently, seawater had been used to feed two of the ship's massive boilers. If the consequent salt deposits were not promptly removed, the intricate boiler tubes would suffer severe and disabling damage. Conley and his mates were soon into overalls, joining the boiler-room staff in the clean-up. This filthy task involved crawling into the pipework of the lower boiler, choking in the scale dust, and collecting small wire brushes which had been injected into the boiler tubes and propelled down them by compressed air. This abrasion would, it was hoped, remove the salt deposit. When all the brushes had been retrieved into a bag they were then carried up to the top of the boiler where a petty officer mechanic would again restart the process of firing them down though the mass of boiler tubes. Two days of continuous shift work completed the clean-up and gave the midshipmen experience of the many very unpleasant tasks they would expect their subordinates to undertake as a matter of course.

Having completed his fortnight's stint with the engineering department, Conley was sent to assist one of the officers in the air department. Without aircraft embarked there was little to do, and it soon became evident that in this situation many of the more than one hundred officers in the ship were seriously underemployed. This was due to an excessive specialisation; many of the roles could have been delegated to a senior rate such as boats officer or 'double bottoms' engineer, the specialist whose prime task was to look after these voids and tanks on the very bottom of the ship. During this participation in the daily work of the air department, Conley was given the unlikely task of hand-drawing graphs copied from a manual, in order to provide easy interpretation of the maximum landing weights of the newly introduced Buccaneer S2 variant against a range of relative wind speeds and angles of wind over the flight deck. He could not conceive then, or long afterwards, the Commander Air, situated in the 'Flyco' position on the wing of the bridge, clutching one of his scruffy drawings whilst asking the captain to alter the carrier's course to enable a safe landing.

Part of Conley's air training focused upon the stand-off attack techniques practised by the Blackburn Buccaneer strike bomber. These involved a very low and fast level approach at an altitude of less than 100ft. The Buccaneer would attack at around 600mph and then abruptly begin a steep climb, releasing its bomb at a range of about seven miles from its target, before immediately tightly turning onto a reciprocal course. The bomb's release velocity would then propel it until over the target. It was neither discussed nor admitted at the time, but this skilled and highly demanding form of attack was designed for use with a nuclear bomb and was an intrinsic element of the British aircraft carrier's Cold War capability of delivering tactical nuclear strikes against enemy targets at sea or ashore. The 25-kiloton atomic bombs which *Eagle* had on onboard were codenamed 'Red Beard' and required final assembly before being loaded onto the aircraft.

In their exploration of the bowels of the ship on one occasion, Conley and another midshipman, having ignored security signage, were chased out of a magazine wherein they had encountered specialists undergoing training in the bomb assembly procedures. At the time there was a strong rumour doing the rounds that a test version of one of these weapons (containing no fissile material) had been loaded onto a Sea Vixen at sea for transfer to a shore base. However, on taking off, the aircraft could not get its undercarriage up, and as a consequence had insufficient range to reach its destination. Since a Sea Vixen carrying this particular weapon could not land back safely on the carrier, there was no option but to jettison the device in deep water in the Southwest Approaches to the English Channel.

By this time *Eagle* had made her way into the English Channel, where she underwent machinery trials, working up to a speed of over 30 knots with all eight boilers on line and generating 150,000 shaft horsepower (shp). Vast quantities of boiler oil were consumed in the process. From time to time the ship would anchor and shore leave be granted to off-duty men. The *Eagle* spent one such weekend off Weymouth and Conley was assigned to act as coxswain of one of the large ship's boats. During his day of duty his boat had been used as a backup and all the trips to Weymouth harbour, over a mile away, had been for relatively few passengers. However, when it became apparent that there were still many of the ship's company ashore after the last scheduled trip had departed Weymouth – by which time it was assumed that the pubs would all have been shut – Conley and his crew were dispatched to do a final trip to collect the handful of men believed to be still ashore. The maximum number of passengers allowed in the 60ft launches was 100 but, as he approached the jetty, Conley realised that the assembled number far exceeded this. As he ran the boat alongside, it proved impossible to stop the sailors from boarding, most of them being the worse for drink.

As Conley headed the overladen boat seawards, he could feel her sluggish response to the sea as her bow dug into the waves and shipped spray. He was, therefore, greatly relieved to turn in under the lee of the carrier. However, his troubles were far from over and he could see, at the head of the gangway, an array of duty staff and regulators to deal with those among his human lading who were all but incapacitated. Failing to compensate for the additional weight of his excessive number of passengers, by reversing his engine too late the boat hit the landing platform with a loud noise of splintering timber and tortured steel guardrails. About 150 inebriated voices roared in appreciation of the hilarity of this miscalculation, leaving the duty officer high above to glower down in disapproving anger.

There remained one final task for the four short-term midshipmen to complete and that was to devise shutdown routes for crew members closing hatches, watertight doors and ventilation flaps in the different damage control configurations which might have to be ordered. It struck Conley as surprising that these routes had not been established long before the *Eagle* had begun her sea trials. It was even more of a surprise that the task, which was the responsibility of the senior shipwright officer, should be given to four trainee officers whose familiarity with the ship's complex internal compartmentalisation relied, up to this point, upon their own talent for exploration.

For over a week they gave it their best shot, each of them clambering round the many compartments of their respective quarter of the ship trying to develop fast, efficient routes which avoided those men assigned to the task of closing off and isolating compartments then being unable to return to their watch-keeping station. Later they learned that, when tried, their selected routes had led to 'utter chaos', but by that time they had left *Eagle*, on their way to their respective ships.

In September 1964 Conley arrived at Chatham Dockyard with two other midshipmen, one of whom had come with him from *Eagle*. Here they joined the destroyer *Cambrian* as she completed a refit. Like *Wizard* she was the result of the war emergency building programme, a destroyer of the CA class completed in 1944. Having spent fourteen years in reserve after the end of the Second World War, she was, with six of her sister ships, taken in hand for extensive modernisation and by January 1963 had been recommissioned. Fitted with a radar-controlled gunnery system to direct her three single, open 4.5in mountings, two forward and one aft, her superstructure had been modified to take the short-range Sea Cat system, though this was never installed and for close air defence *Cambrian* relied upon three vintage 40mm Bofors guns.

HMS *Cambrian* was of the classic destroyer profile, with an elegantly raked funnel and a raised forecastle approximately one-third of her length, and a low 'iron deck' that occupied the remaining two-thirds. The condition of her long, slender hull had been barely adequate after the long idle years in reserve had taken their toll. Corrosion had in several places proved so severe that whole plates had had to be replaced during her refit. A large amount of her internal space was taken up by the propulsion machinery required to generate the 30,000shp needed to drive her at over 30 knots. Her two boilers each consumed over 7 tons of furnace fuel oil per hour when steaming at maximum power (80 per cent of the energy generated going up the funnel) and her 500 tons of fuel gave her a maximum economical range of only just over 3,000 miles. Therefore she required frequent replenishments from oilers or larger warships which had spare fuel capacity. Entry into the machinery spaces was directly from the open after deck. The boiler rooms had an air-lock entry system which enabled powerful intake fans to keep these compartments pressurised, thereby improving boiler efficiency. But this crude arrangement risked a dangerous flame blow-back from the open furnace burners if the over pressure was inadvertently collapsed.

Besides the huge power plant, a large part of her hull was taken up by armament, ammunition handling gear, magazines, storerooms, fuel and freshwater tanks, so that the accommodation for her company of some two hundred ratings was extremely cramped and very uncomfortable. In harbour, with a minimum number of men on watch, many of the junior ratings slept in blankets and sheets on the tops of mess tables and benches. Most workshops were occupied by individual members of the crew berthing in camp beds to avoid their confined mess decks and the consequent smell of overcrowding. This became especially acute on the tropics. Whilst the ship had been fitted with localised air-conditioning units, these were unreliable, and in the tropics the heat generated from the additional electrical equipment fitted in the modernisation compounded an already torrid situation if the air conditioning failed.

The galley and food counters were situated in front of the funnel, requiring those in the after mess decks to carry their trays of food along the exposed iron deck. In rough weather *Cambrian* proved to be a very wet ship, the iron deck often out of bounds, awash in several feet of water. In these conditions the men accommodated aft messed in the fore part of the ship wherever they could find a space. In heavy weather the fetid mess-deck conditions were exacerbated by the clattering of loose gear rolling up and down the decks and the reek of vomit. In sum, the junior rates' accommodation could at best be described as squalid. Little wonder that the traditional 'tot', a generous slug of rum, was so welcome at lunchtime.

The officers fared much better, most occupying single-berth cabins, while the compact but comfortably appointed wardroom provided a pleasant area to relax in. The tradition of dressing for dinner even when at sea had endured, and most enjoyed a glass or two before sitting down to eat in the evening. The officers on the whole worked as a strong team and were a convivial bunch, which made a refreshing improvement from the anonymity of *Eagle*'s huge wardroom population, or *Wizard*'s dysfunctional leadership. Conley and one other midshipman shared a two-berth cabin situated in what was effectively a steel box on the upper deck, directly abaft the funnel and adjoining the radio transmitter room, which was packed full of hot equipment. When on one occasion in the Arabian Sea the cabin's air conditioner failed, the cabin temperature soared above 50°C.

Apart from these shortcomings, Conley was soon made aware of the ship's deficiencies in the way of armament. In the development of the modernisation specification for the CA-class gunnery system, one key element was missed out: that of aircraft target acquisition. A gunnery system relies upon the target being promptly detected by radar or visual means in order to direct the narrow radar-beamed gun director onto the target at adequate range for the prediction process to calculate precisely the offset required for the shells to be placed within detonation range of the target. The modern anti-aircraft shell transmits a high-frequency signal which within 100ft or so of the target causes detonation, with the intention of destroying or disabling the target. With a maximum effective anti-aircraft range of 7,000 yards, against an incoming aircraft flying at 600 knots, there were only 20 seconds available to defend the ship. Prompt target acquisition was therefore of vital importance but, in the case of the CA-class destroyers, radar target detection depended upon radar equipment from the Second World War, developed for defence against piston-engined aircraft of little more than 300 knots. Conley noted in his midshipman's journal that 'the Type 293 Radar did not perform satisfactorily as sometimes the test aircraft flew overhead still undetected'.

This poor performance, exacerbated by the proximity of land, was troubling. The alternative, visual target acquisition, relied upon a very rudimentary arrangement of a pair of standard binoculars being fixed to a crude device which transmitted target bearing and elevation to the gun director, and of course depended upon good visibility and sharp eyesight if the target was to be acquired in plenty of time to achieve successful engagement. There was much better and not over-expensive equipment available at the time of the *Cambrian*'s upgrading, but such additional expenditure was not considered an important enough matter to compromise the prime objective of maintaining an impressive number of hulls in the Fleet, for reasons already touched upon. In terms of anti-aircraft effectiveness, the resources expended upon the CA-class modernisations were squandered in the name of economy. What impact this would have had in the achievements of the class in a shooting war may be left to the reader's imagination.

Any anti-aircraft gunnery system depending upon the prediction of the aircraft's position is going to be seriously challenged by a low-flying aircraft adopting an evasive flight path – precisely what the Fleet Air Arm pilots flying the Buccaneers were trained to do to fox the enemy's radar tracking. In theory at least, the high-altitude Soviet cruise missile flying straight and steady should have been a much easier target. However, this proved a faulty premise when the Israeli destroyer *Eilat*, which was of very similar capability to the *Cambrian*, was sunk off Port Said in 1967 by cruise missiles fired from Soviet-built Komar-class missile boats of the Egyptian navy. This was exactly the type of opposition *Cambrian* was likely to be up against when deployed against the Indonesians in the Far East. That said, within the limitations of the gunnery system, the Commanding Officer, Commander Conrad Jenkin, himself a gunnery specialist, was determined that the ship would be as efficient as possible. Consequently, the ship's weapons maintenance team were to work very hard ensuring the system fully performed to its limited capability.

Notwithstanding the high-level reasons for doing so, reliance upon such local make-do and mend seemed to Conley extraordinary, the more so since it was a deficiency from which the Royal Navy had taken dreadful losses during the Second World War. Despite these hard lessons, for many decades afterwards the Royal Navy would continue with inadequate anti-aircraft weapon systems accompanied by a seeming lack of political or Service will to rectify this. The losses of ships to aircraft or missile attack in the Falklands War was to deliver a tardy and expensive wake-up call to the Ministry of Defence, but even then it was to take almost thirty years before the Royal Navy had a ship capable of effectively dealing with most types of air attack in the shape of the Type 45 *Daring*-class destroyer.

On the other hand, the *Cambrian*'s gunnery system would have been effective against surface ships and for use in shore bombardment. This had been dramatically demonstrated in her part in helping put down the East African mutinies that had occurred early in 1964 and which almost overthrew the government of Tanganyika which had gained independence in December 1961. The new nation's military forces consisted of only two battalions of the former King's African Rifles, reconstituted as the 1st and 2nd Tanganyikan Rifles, but still largely commanded by the same British officers who remained in the country. In January 1964 civil unrest occurred in the port city of Dar es Salaam and the 1st Tanganyikan Rifles mutinied, disarming their officers and packing them over the border into Kenya. The 2nd Regiment, stationed in Tabora, followed suit and with the British High Commissioner detained in his residence, the key points in the capital were occupied.

With his entire armed forces in revolt the Tanganyikan president, Julius Nyerere, appealed to London for help. The aircraft carrier *Centaur* was despatched from Aden with a portion of the garrison and an escort of destroyers including *Cambrian*. The *Centaur* and her consorts stood off Dar es Salaam until a request was received from Nyerere in writing, whereupon Royal Marines were landed on 25 January under the cover of a brief bombardment. As part of this intimidation, *Cambrian* fired at the mutineers' barracks, using anti-aircraft shells which, bursting in the air, did minimal damage. Casualties were light and little resistance was put up as the Royal Marines stormed ashore and attacked the barracks. Destroying the guardroom with an anti-tank missile, the cowed mutineers soon afterwards capitulated. Later that day the armoured cars of the Queen's Royal Lancers were landed and soon afterwards the remaining mutineers of the 1st Rifles threw in the towel. Hearing of the collapse of the rebellion in Dar es Salaam, the 2nd Rifles signalled their willingness to surrender, and a party of Royal Marines arrived at Tabora the following day to secure this. Within a week of the outbreak Nyerere's government was secured.

So much for *Cambrian*'s main armament, but what of her anti-submarine weaponry? This consisted of short-range sonars of Second World War vintage and six Squid mortars which, contrary to logic, were fitted aft. These had range of less than 400 yards and could only be effectively fired ahead. When discharged, the 300lb bombs soared in an apparently leisurely arc over the foremast to plunge into the sea a short distance ahead of the ship. In live firing trials they were invariably fired with the ship proceeding at slow speed and the bomb fuses set to explode quickly at a shallow depth to minimise the risk of damage to the warship. This system was no different from the final stages of anti-submarine weapons development during the Second World War and its effectiveness was limited to the conventional submarine of the day.

Programmed to sail for the Far East in January 1965, the inefficiency of Chatham Dockyard delayed her departure by prolonging her refit. Regarding the very sizeable workforce of 4,000 as they worked around the yard, Conley's sceptical opinion of the Royal Dockyards was confirmed. Frequent instances of work avoidance and poor efficiency, to which the upper management appeared indifferent, guaranteed that *Cambrian*'s departure date slipped further and further. Far from any sense of urgency to get the ship completed and ready to rejoin the Fleet, Conley sensed an almost palpable inclination in the opposite direction.

At last, in mid December, having completed post-refit trials, *Cambrian* finally left Chatham to the sound of a Royal Marine band on the jetty playing the tune of a popular song: 'Puff the Magic Dragon'. This hit by a group called Peter, Paul and Mary had been adopted by the crew, reflecting the ship's badge of the red Welsh dragon. Although HMS *Cambrian* was due to undergo several weeks of trials and work-up off Portland before deploying to Singapore, she was not at sea long, for Christmas was imminent. A few days later she entered Portsmouth, which was noticeably busy with more than sixty warships and submarines alongside, their crews enjoying leave over the festive period.

On New Year's Eve, all members of the wardroom went ashore to welcome the New Year in one of Portsmouth's pubs. Although this fell short of the spontaneity of a Scots Hogmanay, retreat to the home of one of the officers enabled conviviality to be maintained into the small hours of New Year's Day. However, 1 January was the day appointed for the port admiral's inspection which, despite the endemic hangovers, went well. The following day *Cambrian* sailed for Portland where her work-up would begin, her crew in a high state of morale, adopting the slogan '*Keepa sensa huma*' for the duration of the forthcoming period of intensive training.

By the time of *Cambrian*'s departure for Singapore, the Indonesian-Malaysian Confrontation had become a hot war in all but name. Strenuous diplomatic efforts to suppress any sense of escalation had proved successful, but in the dense rainforest of Borneo/Kalimantan, the probing patrols of both sides had engaged in fierce and deadly skirmishes, while it seemed that the old piratical days of the *Orang Laut* had been revived, with incursions from the sea on peaceful but isolated settlements along the littoral.

The importance of Singapore extended beyond the economy of the fragile new Federation of Malaysia, for it was an important port where cargoes were exchanged between oceangoing and smaller vessels and vice versa. Of global significance, Singapore was a great hub of world trade whose long curved sweep of Keppel Harbour was always fully occupied by vessels loading and discharging cargoes, with tankers servicing the offshore oil refinery and tank farm at Pulo Bukum, and two extensive anchorages, the Eastern and Western Roads, in which vessels of all descriptions either awaited berths, or transhipped cargoes from coasters or smaller craft. Protection of the port, and of the comings and goings of merchant shipping, was an important strategic concern and although the Royal Navy maintained a dockyard and naval base at Sembawang on the northern shore of Singapore, the island itself, situated at the southern extremity of the Malay Peninsula, was only a few miles from the northernmost islands of the vast archipelago that constituted the hostile state of Indonesia. Vulnerable to commando raids, or to the planting of limpet mines on ships at anchor or alongside, defence of the port and approaches to Singapore was the responsibility of the Royal Navy in its support of the Malaysian naval forces. Further offshore, the Malacca Strait lay between peninsular Malaysia and the large island of Sumatra. The strait was an international waterway of great importance, while Indonesian raids could be launched across it towards Port Swettenham.

There had been several exchanges of gunfire between British warships and

Indonesian gunboats, the *Leander*-class frigate *Ajax* having engaged several of the latter in the Malacca Strait. Meanwhile, the minesweeper *Fiskerton* had suffered several casualties, including a midshipman killed, when she had encountered an enemy craft off Singapore.

With battalion-strength raids by Indonesian forces across the disputed border between Borneo and Kalimantan increasing, British troop reinforcements had been flown out to increase the strength of the land forces opposing the Indonesians. In support of these operations small craft of the Royal and Malaysian Navies were involved in intelligence-gathering operations, a role in which several submarines were also utilised. Four British minesweepers and two inshore patrol craft had been taken out of reserve to bolster these inshore operations and these joined a force in excess of sixty allied warships in Malaysian waters. Besides the Royal and Malaysian Navies, these were drawn from Australia and New Zealand, and comprised men-of-war of all descriptions, from large warships to high-speed launches. Knowledge of this activity made the ship's company of the *Cambrian* eager to reach the scene of action.

The *Cambrian*'s work-up, undertaken in harsh winter conditions, more than put the ship and its crew through its full paces, comprehensively testing the stamina, competence and teamwork of the ship's company. There were numerous gunnery 'shoots' at various targets which did little to improve Conley's confidence in the ship's ability to contend with attacking aircraft, and many anti-submarine exercises. Considerable time was spent in dealing with the fast patrol-boat threat, in boarding suspicious vessels and in protecting *Cambrian* herself from saboteurs when at anchor or in harbour.

Replenishment at sea was frequently exercised with a Royal Fleet Auxiliary, combining re-storing with refuelling, while other 'evolutions' included rendering assistance to a stricken ship and taking a casualty in tow. Matters were even taken to an extreme, with a full nuclear fallout exercise when the *Cambrian* was shut down with 'pre-wetting' pipework used to cover her with a fine spray of seawater as, with her crew hunkered down in their citadel, she passed through a notional 'hot zone'. This evolution conveniently ignored the fact that it was impossible to shut down the boiler rooms and after a real nuclear attack, these would have become heavily contaminated, as would the open gun mountings.

Although risk of a nuclear encounter was minimal, in such an operationally variable theatre as the Far East it was necessary to consider all possibilities. Mindful of her last active engagement off Dar es Salaam and in common with all foreign deployments, *Cambrian*'s crew trained to 'aid the civil power'. In a war such as the Confrontation was, landing shore parties for a variety of purposes was highly likely. To these ends *Cambrian*'s ship's company were taught to assist in the suppression of riots and how to provide disaster relief. It was not all serious stuff; one evening, when alongside and at short notice, the crew were required to put on VIP entertainment, including a short son et lumière production which, using searchlights and piped Gilbert and Sullivan music, passed off surprisingly well, one positive result of training in the art of making-do. On another occasion, *Cambrian* entered harbour entrance in full ceremonial order, her ship's company manning the side in their Number One uniforms to carry out a 'Cheer ship' to a fictional state president. All in all it was a thoroughly testing few weeks during which *Cambrian*, despite her age and obsolescent equipment, did well, earning a commendation and passing her final inspection with flying colours. Notwithstanding the limitations of their ship, her company emerged as a strong, bonded team. This was, of course, the essential point of her work-up for, whatever the poverty of its pocket and the shortcomings of its weaponry, when it came to push of pike the Royal Navy retained the great asset of its tradition and the effect it could produce from its people.

For the minions aboard it had been a period of stimulation. It was fortunate for Conley that his commanding officer had been keen to delegate and he had been allowed to keep bridge watch on his own during daylight hours when things were reasonably quiet. The sense of satisfaction and responsibility that Conley experienced when Jenkin handed the ship over to him for the first time and disappeared down the bridge access ladder was memorable. To an eighteen-year-old, manoeuvring a powerful warship in close proximity to other vessels was exhilarating in the extreme, although mistakes risked the strong invective of the captain.

Their work-up completed, *Cambrian* returned to Portsmouth for a few weeks storing and maintenance, during which members of the crew were granted leave. Finally, however, their sailing orders arrived. It was now late March 1965. On the Friday before departure many of the ship's company brought their wives and families aboard and that evening a dance was held in a local sailors' club. This was one of the few opportunities the officers had to meet the wives and girlfriends of many of the crew. On the Monday the ship's company would be saying goodbye to their families for at least six months, able only to communicate by letter, but to a man they were looking forward to the deployment.

The morning of Monday, 26 March was overcast, dull and drizzling when *Cambrian* slipped from her berth, passed Fort Blockhouse and proceeded to sea. She was bound first to Aden by way of Gibraltar. The brief stay in Gibraltar proved enjoyable for the ship's company, but was marred by cases of drunkenness among the crew. There were several arrests, two junior ratings ending up in a Spanish jail in the border town of La Linea, charged with breach of the peace after a fight in the streets. Another was in hospital after being beaten up by a taxi driver. Excessive boozing, leading to trouble ashore and sometimes onboard, was an enduring feature of naval life, cheap alcohol and high-spirited young men being a fatal mixture, especially in foreign ports.

A few days after *Cambrian*'s departure from Gibraltar she arrived off Port Said. Entering the Suez Canal she led a southbound convoy of about thirty merchant ships of several nationalities. Passing a military airfield between the Great and Lesser Bitter Lakes, her officers noted some forty MiG-17 strike fighters, together with a score of obsolescent MiG-15s of the type which had so startled the Americans over Korea fifteen years earlier. To the observing British naval officers, the latter appeared in reserve but the increasing tension between Israel and her neighbours – which would culminate in the Six Day War of June 1967 – made the sight more interesting.

Clear of the canal *Cambrian* headed south down the Red Sea with temperatures onboard steadily increasing. Passing through the Strait of Bab-el-Mandeb, course was altered along the coast of Yemen until Aden was reached in early April.

At the time the Aden Protectorate was being rocked by civil unrest stirred up by armed and active groups backed by Yemen and Egypt, whose aim was to foment trouble compelling a British withdrawal. A number of deaths had been caused, large areas of Aden City were out of bounds to servicemen and their families and after midnight there was a curfew in place. This unrest was to touch *Cambrian* herself when, on the evening of their arrival, her captain, first lieutenant and two other officers were attending a formal dinner ashore. Despite being in a heavily guarded building, a grenade was thrown into the room. Fortunately, it failed to detonate properly and there were no serious injuries.

The *Cambrian* was further involved when the following day she was un-expectedly directed to proceed to sea to search for and intercept an Iraqi cargo vessel suspected of running arms to the rebels. For two days the ship slowly searched eastwards along the coastline, hoping to detect her quarry when she was within territorial waters but locating only a few dhows. In the prevailing light airs and high temperatures, life in the non–air-conditioned compartments became very difficult. For the ratings, toiling in the boiler and engine rooms in temperatures in excess of 40°C, frequent drinks and salt tablets were essential if they were to avoid heatstroke.

Returning to Aden for a few days' self-maintenance allowed an excursion or two. Conley joined a party of the ship's company on a trip to the Royal Engineers' camp in the Radfan Mountains. Bumping some fifty miles up the rough, unmetalled Dhala road in a convoy of army trucks led by a Scimitar light tank, they passed up into the arid highlands, an area which had been a hotbed of insurgent activity. Each member of the party was issued with an ancient .303 rifle and twenty rounds of ammunition, triggering a debate as to whether, if they got into a real firefight, twenty rounds would prove sufficient. Told to sit well forward, clear of the truck's rear axle, to minimise injuries if they detonated a landmine, they complied assiduously after passing the remains of several vehicles wrecked by mines. They were, however, blissfully unaware that there had been ferocious fighting on the Dhala road only a year earlier between British forces and insurgents.

The two-hour journey through the stark and barren mountain valley exposed them to the poverty and basic living conditions of the few villages through which they passed. Most male adults, they observed, carried a rifle of sorts, subsistence relying upon the sparse cultivation of a few vegetables and the tending of goats. It was an insight for Conley, the huge divide between the affluent West and the austere poverty of the Yemeni tribesmen they came across that day making a lasting impression upon him, in the light of which the emergence of al-Qaeda proved no real surprise.

They saw more Yemenis, men of the local militia who manned an ancient mud-walled fort which could have been straight out of the novel *Beau Geste*. This rag-tag band was of dubious reliability and loyalty. The Royal Engineers' tented camp was close by, and their hosts advised them that their neighbours frequently fired their guns in celebration and were not averse to occasionally shooting up the camp by way of amusement. Several of the soldiers' tents had bullet holes in consequence, and their more exposed facilities, such as the toilet blocks, were protected by armour plating.

The officers in the party enjoyed a very pleasant lunch in the officers' mess; even in this remote and forlorn spot the regimental silver was on the table. On the other hand, the naval officers detected a degree of scepticism regarding the building of a road which led to nowhere, the task which the engineers were engaged upon. After lunch they were given a tour of the camp and its outposts before heading back towards Aden. The return journey was memorable, the army drivers showing off by leaving the road and tearing over the rocky scrub to hoots of indignation from their passengers.

After nine days in Aden undertaking self-maintenance and exerting a naval presence, *Cambrian* sailed for the island of Abd al Kuri, which is situated about sixty miles west of Socotra off the Horn of Africa. The island was at that time part of the Aden Protectorate and a British possession, and the ship's mission was to conduct surveys of beaches on its northern coast. The purpose of this was to establish whether the beaches would be suitable for landing materials in order to construct a military airfield as part of the putative but, in the event, impracticable strategy of providing RAF air cover of the Indian Ocean. This policy was intended to compensate for the demise of the strike carriers by providing a circle of airfields around its periphery but, needless to say, it never got off the starting blocks.

The island of Abd al Kuri is about fifteen miles long and three miles wide; with mountains rising to about two thousand feet, falling away to a narrow and desolate coastal plain with few trees and little vegetation. Although the crew saw no sign of human habitation, fires were spotted at night on the eastern extremity, indicating that there were members of the local population about. The *Cambrian* first approached the more exposed southern coast where the British cargo ship *Ayrshire* lay beached. Two months earlier this eight-year-old ship had struck an uncharted rock to the south of the island and her master had deliberately driven her ashore in a sinking condition. The passengers had been lifted off, but her crew was still onboard and Dutch salvage tugs had arrived to patch her up and pull her off before the onset of the southwest monsoon.

The *Cambrian*'s captain and several of the crew visited the stricken vessel. Clearly, the warship's presence was welcomed, as some of the *Ayrshire*'s crew were becoming agitated about their prolonged isolation on such a remote island. The *Ayrshire*'s master offered Commander Jenkin any of the cargo which was transportable and of use. Two days later, *Cambrian* having anchored off the more sheltered northern shore of the island, a working party was landed and crossed the island to the *Ayrshire* to see what sort of loot they could acquire. On the way back, the party left a trail of discarded goods as the return traverse across the hot and rugged interior of the island proved too much for them. Nevertheless, a large Persian rug survived the land crossing, only to be lost into the sea on being hoisted aboard; after the strenuous efforts to get it thus far, it was observed that some of the raiding party were almost reduced to tears. The fate of the *Ayrshire* herself was no better for, sadly, the Dutch salvage attempt was not successful and she became a total loss.

While this diversion was in progress, surveying had begun on a beach on the northwest side of the island which was considered suitable for landing craft. The survey technique involved deploying the ship's whaler and taking hand lead-line soundings on the run into the shoreline, each sounding being fixed by observing the angles between three fixed and known points ashore. These angles were measured using a sextant horizontally and back onboard the destroyer were carefully and accurately transferred to a chart. However, the method suffered from being difficult to execute in a small whaler rocking in an ocean swell, and required both practice and time to accomplish successfully.

Conley learned something of its difficulties when on the third day of work he joined the survey team. After only two hours of surveying, the whaler worked too close inshore, where she was caught up and swamped by an incoming roller. With a saturated and defective engine the boat was beached, *Cambrian* was informed of the whaler's plight by radio, and her sodden crew awaited the ship's motor cutter to tow the whaler back to the ship. Offshore the odd shark could be seen, while the beach itself was littered with millions of dead blowfish forming a spiky obstruction at the high-water mark. With the waterlogged whaler baled out and towed back to the ship for repairs by the motor cutter, Conley and company were left ashore until finally assisted by some of the ship's temporary Royal Marines detachment (embarked to assist in the survey), who arrived in an inflatable to return them to the ship late that afternoon, most of them badly sunburned after being exposed on the beach for several hours.

This incident ended the survey. Enough data had been collected to verify the beach was indeed suitable for landing craft but that was the end of the matter. Abd al Kuri was in due course ceded to Yemen but in later years and in light of subsequent events, Conley often considered that had Britain retained the territory and built an airfield on it, how important it would have become in supporting both operations in the Persian Gulf and the protection of merchant shipping against piracy.

After leaving the island *Cambrian* made a rendezvous with HMS *Eagle* and her escorts, being assigned the duty of plane guard. The purpose of this was soon made crystal-clear, for very shortly after taking up her station on the carrier's quarter, one of *Eagle*'s Scimitar strike fighters experienced engine failure and the pilot ejected. He was quickly rescued by helicopter but

Cambrian's motor cutter, under Conley's charge, was lowered to recover one of the Scimitar's wings which was floating nearby. Unfortunately, the attempt proved futile, though they did pick up the pilot's helmet, a disconcerting experience since, at the time, they had no way of knowing whether the pilot was under it.

The following day Conley and his fellow midshipman who had served in *Eagle* were transferred by helicopter to the carrier to witness flying operations. The twenty-four hours the two young men spent aboard the carrier proved exciting, as from a grand vantage point they watched the Vixens and Buccaneers landing onboard in the dusk and darkness. Their pleasure was ruined after being spotted by the shipwright officer, who lambasted them for their incompetence in developing the damage control shutdown routes mentioned earlier. They also ran into a pilot instructor from their Dartmouth days who had impressed upon them the very high casualty rate incurred in flying Sea Vixens. Dressed in full flying gear and about to climb into his Vixen cockpit, he looked distinctly tensed up.

A few days later, having left the *Eagle* and her consorts, *Cambrian* headed for Singapore where she arrived in mid May. She was to conduct several patrols aimed at inhibiting Indonesian infiltration of Singapore or the Malaysian mainland. Prior to this and in the light of the experience of others, vertical steel plates were secured down either side of the iron deck. This was to provide some protection to any boarding party assembling where the freeboard was lowest, prior to scrambling onto an intercepted vessel. This was a vulnerable moment for those involved and several incidents of exploding booby traps had been encountered, the most recent aboard a minesweeper when a member of her crew had been killed by such an anti-personnel device on a boat ordered alongside for inspection. In addition to this extemporised armour, a Bren gun was set up above the bridge and this was complemented by two sharpshooters with high-velocity rifles.

During daylight hours the boarding and inspection procedures were exercised with any random small craft encountered at sea, but by night the ship was darkened, bereft of navigation lights, all noise suppressed as far as possible. A listening sonar watch was maintained in an attempt to detect any craft attempting a high-speed dash across the strait. In the event, there was an overwhelmingly high density of sonar contacts, and no suspicious craft were identified; nor were there any meaningful interdictions made during the course of the patrols.

In late May *Cambrian* returned to Singapore for storing and refuelling prior to proceeding to Hong Kong for an informal visit. The ship sailed with about fifty Chinese unofficially embarked on the upper deck for the passage, all of whom were reputedly 'cousins' of *Cambrian*'s Chinese laundrymen, and who brought with them an array of possessions: bicycles, sewing machines and laundry equipment.

As the *Cambrian* brought up to her anchor in Repulse Bay, prior to entry into Hong Kong, Conley received another shock at the world's poverty when he observed Chinese approaching in sampans to scoop up the garbage which had been dumped over the stern. In the main the Royal Navy maintained a benevolent attitude to those less privileged: in addition to the unofficial passage granted to the extended families of the *Cambrian*'s laundrymen, the official engagement of a local 'side party' was a long-standing tradition of the Service in Hong Kong. The side party invariably consisted of half a dozen women to which, on this occasion, a young girl was attached. They were supplied with paint, rollers and brushes, and undertook the painting of the *Cambrian*'s grey topsides in exchange for collecting unused galley food and some worn and redundant nylon mooring rope.

When the *Cambrian* put to sea a week later, the side party, dressed in their finery, accompanied the ship out of the harbour in their decorated sampan, detonating firecrackers of fulminate in appreciation of the ship's largesse; it was a strangely touching, even numinous moment, as they worked the long sculling oar or *yuloh* over the sampan's stern in an attempt to keep up with the lean grey shape of the destroyer. Eventually, they dropped astern and out of sight, an odd link between two vastly different cultures and part of the hail and farewell of seafaring.

On her return to Singapore, *Cambrian* undertook yet another maintenance period, berthed alongside the repair ship HMS *Triumph*. Owing to their own vessel being shut down, the ship's company were moved into temporary accommodation aboard the former aircraft carrier. On dumping his gear into the cabin allocated to him, Conley discovered in the wardrobe the uniforms of two midshipmen who had died in action during the Confrontation. Clearly, nobody had thought about the clothing's prompt return to the next of kin.

Life, Conley was quickly made aware of, went on and midshipman's examination boards were convened aboard the commando carrier *Bulwark*, with the practical engineering oral tests on board *Cambrian* herself. During the course of the predominantly oral examinations, in answering set questions Conley failed to cite correctly the formula used to determine the weight of an anchor cable link or to describe the 'Canterbury' test for the purity of the ship's boiler feed water. These examples were notable only for the futility of some of the detail a midshipman was supposed to absorb. Despite his failure on these two arcane points, Conley's board results were satisfactory, if unremarkable, marking his progress.

In early July, towards the end of her deployment to Singapore, HMS *Cambrian* joined the aircraft carrier *Ark Royal* and a number of other warships to carry out an exercise in the northern part of the Strait of Malacca. Despite her frequent stops for maintenance, *Cambrian* was showing her age, her smooth running interrupted by a series of defects culminating in a fire in pipe lagging in the engine room. It was minor and soon extinguished, but the threat of such occurrences only made the demanding duty of acting as plane guard even more stressful.

This role required the *Cambrian* to take up a station on *Ark Royal*'s port quarter at a range of half a mile. Keeping station at night at speeds of up to 30 knots, while frequent heavy tropical rain squalls markedly reduced visibility and caused severe sea clutter on the radar, was very challenging. The situation was exacerbated by *Ark Royal*'s occasional tardiness in communicating intended changes in her course and speed. On one occasion the carrier's stern loomed unexpectedly out of the darkness as *Cambrian* almost overshot her, not having received any signal indicating a drop in speed. Since this incident occurred shortly after the Australian carrier *Melbourne* had rammed and sunk her plane-guard consort, the destroyer HMAS *Voyager*, and eighty-two of the destroyer's crew had perished, it might have been assumed that procedures would have been tighter.

On completion of the exercise *Cambrian* headed for the island of Penang for a week's visit. One of the 'A'-class diesel submarines which had been engaged in operations off the Indonesian coast, HMS *Amphion*, was berthed alongside and her crew were very grateful to be offered showers and other facilities aboard *Cambrian*. Conley was struck by the high morale of the submariners, who had just enjoyed a very successful exercise as the opposition against *Ark Royal* and her escorts. At the end of a memorable run ashore, several of the ship's wardroom, including Conley himself, took part in a trishaw race in heavy rain. In this the trishaw owners were bundled into their own conveyances and relaxed under their hoods, pleased to earn a fare whilst the high-spirited naval johnnies did the pedalling.

Penang was the last port of call for *Cambrian* in the Far East and she soon afterwards left for Aden. After refuelling at Gan, the most southerly of the

Maldives, she escorted the commando carrier *Bulwark* across the Indian Ocean. In early August the two men-of-war entered Aden, where the security situation had deteriorated further. All ships in the harbour, both men-of-war and merchantmen, were on high alert for fear of attack by saboteurs.

Since Conley's year as a midshipman was coming to an end, he left the *Cambrian* on 6 August and transferred by boat to the British India Steam Navigation Company's *Waroonga*, which was bunkering in the harbour. He had arranged to complete his homeward passage aboard a merchant ship for the experience it offered. The *Waroonga* was a cargo liner, not quite the luxurious passenger liner he had hoped for, but a ship bound to a schedule, unlike a tramp ship. In the event, the several weeks he spent in her, visiting Djibouti (at the time a French Foreign Legion outpost), Genoa, Marseilles and Dunkirk, served to broaden his maritime knowledge. With a lascar crew, life in the *Waroonga* was comfortable and Conley was impressed by the professionalism of her officers, but for the young midshipman, with his sharp eye and quick perception, it seemed a life dictated by routine and commercial imperatives. With individual officers standing the same watches each day, this seemed a dull existence compared to the Royal Navy. Even the menu was governed by the day of the week, so that he began to expect curried chicken on a Sunday.

These comparisons forced on him during his passage home made him focus on his achievement so far. He had, he considered, learned a great deal during his midshipman's year about the workings of the Navy, how 'Jolly Jack' functioned, and what was expected of a junior officer undertaking basic seamanship and the more abstruse skills of bridge watch-keeping. He had been afforded and accepted responsibility, had had several adventurous experiences and served with a friendly wardroom alongside a resilient and committed ship's company in a happy ship. One of the most enduring benefits of his period as a midshipman in *Cambrian* was encountering and engaging with people from very different cultures and possessing values other than those of the West; like most seafarers, his eyes had been opened to a wider world.

On his return to the United Kingdom, Conley was promoted to acting sub lieutenant and returned to Dartmouth for his year of academic studies. When this socially very enjoyable but academically disappointing period was over, he spent a further twelve months in the Royal Navy's specialist schools – aviation, navigation, gunnery, etc – which existed at the time. When the year of courses ended, he and his fellows would be stuffed full of detailed information, a large proportion of which they would never refer to again, but from the social perspective, it was a very enjoyable time. Travelling round the country, staying in a number of stone-frigate wardrooms where a strong sense of camaraderie and first-class facilities existed, Conley was able to enjoy most of his evenings and weekends. Unsurprisingly, it was the serendipitous pleasures that left the most lasting impressions, and the highlight of these was a low-level flight over the north of Scotland from the Lossiemouth naval air station in a twin-seat Hawker Hunter jet trainer. It proved 'absolutely thrilling' to fly up a glen in brilliant sunshine at over 500mph, following the contours before cresting the summits of snow-covered mountains. However, kitted out in a tight fitting G-suit, the downside to the experience was a slight feeling of claustrophobia in the cockpit, a worrying paradox for Conley as he had already volunteered for submarines.

In 1967 the Labour government under the leadership of Harold Wilson had made the decision to withdraw British forces from east of Suez and, as mentioned earlier, started to pay off the aircraft carriers. On the other hand, they remained committed to the introduction of Polaris-armed nuclear submarines, despite many of them having been active in the Campaign for Nuclear Disarmament, better known as the CND. However, the number of submarines to be built to carry the missile would be reduced from the planned five to four. In addition Wilson's government also confirmed a commitment to build up a potent force of the nuclear attack submarines (SSNs) following the commissioning of HMS *Valiant*, the first all-British nuclear submarine.

Thus the Royal Navy with its limited resources was to shift focus from naval aviation to submarines, a clear indicator of Wilson's intention to abandon underwriting an increasingly outdated foreign policy and move towards shouldering more of the burden of Cold War confrontation. This appealed to Wilson both as an advocate of the 'white heat of technology' and as a means of signalling to Washington that in laying down her imperial burden, howsoever reduced her circumstances, she remained a key ally.

4

Joining Submarines

IN SEPTEMBER 1967, almost exactly four years after arriving at Dartmouth, Conley was appointed to the Submarine School at HMS *Dolphin* – the submarine base in Fort Blockhouse, Gosport. Here he would undertake the Royal Navy's twelve-week course intended to convert him into a submariner. The course concentrated on the operation of the Royal Navy's conventional submarines of the 'O'-class, the latest so-called 'diesel boats' in service. Conley and his colleagues would focus on learning in detail about the submarine systems and the skills necessary to monitor sensors, comprehend the control of the boat and undertake supervised control room watch-keeping when they joined their first operational submarine as a trainee officer.

There was a real buzz about Fort Blockhouse as the Submarine Service was rapidly expanding. The shift of Britain's nuclear deterrent from the Royal Air Force to the Royal Navy offered a change of gear in the Navy's fortunes and was the oxygen of liberation for ambitious young officers like Conley. Alongside the top-secret role of the nuclear-powered, Polaris-armed submarines, the first two of the five nuclear attack submarines of the *Valiant* class, popularly designated 'hunter-killers', but known to the navy as SSNs had been commissioned, and the first British nuclear submarine, HMS *Dreadnought*, had been in service for four years.

The decision by the Labour government of Harold Wilson to confirm stewardship of the nation's nuclear deterrent to the Royal Navy, while restoring to the Senior Service its traditional task of 'the nation's sure shield', also conferred benefits on the local economies on the banks of the Clyde, the Mersey and the northwest of England. British shipyards were a hive of activity, with six nuclear submarines under construction at Vickers Armstrong's yard at Barrow-in-Furness and the Birkenhead yard of Cammell Laird & Co. Besides these, three 'O'-class submarines were being built at HM Chatham Dockyard and Scotts of Greenock for the Canadian and

Australian navies, all of which provided a strong industrial base to underpin the Submarine Service's rapid expansion.

In the post-war years, many submariners had felt that the domination of naval aviation and the Royal Navy's commitments east of Suez had to an extent marginalised their arm of the Service. Although most of the submarines remaining in commission after 1945 – chiefly those of the 'T' and 'A' classes – had been modified, there had been no new construction. It was true that some of this modification, known as modernisation, which consisted of streamlining and in some cases enlarging battery capacity to increase submerged speed, extended the ageing boats' useful life, but it was into the 1950s before the Admiralty turned its attention to a new class of submarine. The result was the *Porpoise* class, the name vessel of which, HMS *Porpoise*, was commissioned in 1958. She was followed by seven other boats and to these were added thirteen of the similar 'O' or *Oberon* class. The latter differed chiefly from their predecessors in having a stronger hull construction and the outer casing and fin being made of glass fibre. Highly regarded, not least for their operational low noise level, these were capable of up to 17 knots when dived.

To the Submarine Service these new boats restored morale and offered something in the way of parity with the surface Fleet which in recent years had benefited from the introduction of several new classes of destroyer and frigate fitted with modern sensors and weapons. This question of morale was of considerable importance in view of Wilson's major shift in government policy. To undertake the stewardship of the nuclear deterrent required an elite force, not a run-down arm of a shrinking Navy which had found it difficult to adapt to its peacetime roles and was regarded with low esteem by some in the surface Navy.

The rundown from the high-stress pitch of the war to peacetime conditions had had a profound effect upon morale which reached a nadir when HM Submarine *Affray* was lost in the English Channel in April 1951. Although at the time this had been attributed to the failure of her snort gear, the cause of her loss, be it human error or material failure, has never been established. Bad enough as this was, the *Affray*'s loss was made far worse because she had on board an entire class of officers under training and these circumstances were held to be a contributing factor towards a culture of hard drinking within some elements of the corps of submarine officers.

Ten or more years later there remained a small but significant number of commanding officers who, having started their careers in this low period, drank excessively when in harbour. These men failed to exhibit those

41

professional standards expected of naval officers, let alone submarine captains, and were regarded askance by their subordinates. Thus when Conley's group of officers under training were dispersed from *Dolphin* and posted to their submarines, they were to discover that the best commanding officers had been selected for the new nuclear boats. In a number of cases, those who remained in diesel boats were in the last phases of their careers and although many of these men commanded a perverse respect on account of long service and experience, several were inadequate for the task, and had very limited tactical or war-fighting ability.

As for those commanding officers selected for the nuclear programme in command or at executive officer (second in command) level, many were to find their new charges very challenging. Contending with the much more complex task of being in command of a nuclear submarine required of them qualities which a fair proportion lacked; consequently, they found it difficult both to delegate responsibility and to exploit the full capabilities of their new, and much more capable, charges.

In 1967 the Flag Officer Submarines (FOSM) was Rear Admiral Ian McGeoch, who as a wartime submarine commander had lost one eye when HM Submarine *Splendid* was sunk in the Mediterranean. Many other senior officers had very accomplished war records, such as McGeoch's successor, Rear Admiral John Roxburgh, who had commanded his first submarine at the age of twenty-two. Such men exuded an undoubted aura of experience and professionalism, but there was a world of difference in offensive submarine operations in the Second World War, which was a young man's type of war where a touch of the bravado in the character was an essential for success, and the qualities necessary to command a nuclear submarine in the Cold War. The new Submarine Service was moving away from being a peripheral, semi-piratical organisation, regarded by the rest of the Fleet with a mixture of envy and affectionate scorn for its raffish disregard for the full panoply of naval protocols. The new, nuclear-powered Submarine Service was taking over the mantle of the nation's sure bulwark. Its ships' companies might cling to the anachronism of calling their submarines 'boats', but these were Great Britain's new capital ships.

Conley's training class consisted of twenty officers, including two Australians. Of the British officers on the course, four, including Conley, would eventually command submarines. Over time the others would leave the Submarine Service or the Navy either from choice, for reasons of health, such as degradation of eyesight, or unsuitability.

From the outset, these men were instructed in the detailed principles of how a submarine works by being able to vary its displacement. With her machinery, crew accommodation, power plant and weaponry contained in a central pressure hull, varying her displacement requires the filling and emptying of ballast tanks external to the pressure hull. On the surface its ballast tanks are kept full of air, providing positive buoyancy; to submerge, vents are opened, air escapes and is displaced by water. The vessel's displacement increases and she slips below the surface in what amounts to a controlled sinking. In addition to the main ballast tanks, there are also several variable seawater-filled compensation tanks inside the pressure hull which enable the submerged boat to be maintained precisely in a state of neutral buoyancy. In normal conditions this means she is trimmed horizontally fore and aft, providing a level platform for her crew. The content of these supplementary tanks is carefully adjusted prior to diving to ensure, as far as possible, that the submarine is neutrally buoyant: too little weight of water in these tanks will make it difficult for the submarine to submerge; and too much will result in loss of depth control when submerging. In the case of a conventionally powered submarine, prior to diving her diesel engines are shut down and her propulsion shifts to her battery-powered electric motor.

Once underwater, depth is changed by applying a bow up or down angle to the boat through the use of hydroplanes, one set fitted forward in the bows, the second set aft and close to the rudder. Older boats controlled both these hydroplanes and the rudder using separate handlebar levers, but modern submarines use a single or twin joystick. This arrangement is not dissimilar to an aircraft's controlling joystick. As a submarine goes deeper her hull compresses quite significantly, decreasing its displacement and making it vital that ballast water be pumped out in compensation for the increased negative buoyancy. To surface, high-pressure air retained in immensely strong compressed-air cylinders is blown into the ballast tanks where it expands, ejecting the ballast water, positive buoyancy being regained and the boat rising.

All combat submarines operate in a relatively shallow stratum below the surface of the sea, those of Western navies up to maximum safe depths of less than 1,500ft (455m) although some of their Soviet counterparts could operate significantly deeper down to greater than 3,000ft.

Some of the Royal Navy's older post-war boats were restricted to a safe depth of little more than 350ft, not much of a margin greater than the length of the hull. If a submarine goes below its safe depth through flooding, total loss of power or a high-speed uncontrolled dive, the boat risks crushing by the immense pressure of the sea with the loss of all on board. This point of no return is known as her 'crush depth' and is normally a factor of between one and a half to twice her safe depth. High speed can involve steep boat angles in excess of 30 degrees in both axes and, accordingly, nuclear submarine crews are taught ship control in three-dimensional trainers very much akin to those used for aircrews. Should a nuclear submarine be proceeding at depth and high speed when a catastrophic failure of her hydroplanes occurs, if these happen to be in the full-dive position, the crew must react very fast indeed to avoid the boat exceeding her crush depth.

For most of the Second World War, all submarines of all the belligerent powers had one thing in common: they were designed to operate on the surface the majority of the time. The low available speed underwater when under electric power deprived them of most of their tactical advantages beyond the obvious one of being out of sight. For this reason, German U-boat operations against Atlantic convoys commonly occurred in darkness and were often made by limiting the dived period during an approach to a convoy to ducking under the sonar search area of the leading escorts. Once inside the screen they could surface and attack several targets as the cumbersome merchantmen steamed past in their columns, before submerging under the tail of the convoy where the sea was churned by the passing wakes, further confusing the sonar operators of the rear escorts. To counter this, the escorts preferred to prosecute a U-boat well beyond the immediate vicinity of the convoy. In response, towards the end of the conflict the Germans came up with the expedient of operating at periscope depth under diesel power, drawing air into the U-boat using a raised intake, a pipe they called the 'schnorkel', anglicised to 'snorkel' or later, when adopted by the Royal Navy, 'snort'.

The fitting of these to the Type XXI U-boats operational in early 1945 introduced for the first time a submarine specifically intended to spend the majority of its sea-time submerged. Besides enabling a diesel-engined U-boat to remain continuously dived, by drawing air down the snort mast, the air quality within the boat was much improved, while her batteries could be kept charged. Engine exhaust gases are discharged through a separate mast, but 'snorting' carried risks beyond that of detection of the snort mast or her cloud of exhaust fumes. In heavy seas, the self-sealing head valve at the top of the snort mast functions less efficiently, allowing a considerable amount of water to come down the mast. While this is drained off into an internal tank, if this is not carefully monitored and regularly pumped out, it can result in a build-up of negative buoyancy which may only be evident when the boat slows down. Moreover, as the head valve shuts when the snort mast dips under waves, the running engines will suck air out of the pressure hull, thereby causing a vacuum in the submarine. This intermittent but cumulative situation, if prolonged, can cause serious loss of breathable oxygen unless the engines are promptly stopped. Alternatively, if the exhaust valves are shut with the engines still running, the boat can quickly fill with lethal carbon monoxide from the exhaust gases.

However, the biggest risk is failure of the snort system hull valve to shut when a submarine goes deep and shifts from diesel to electric power. If this occurs, severe flooding will follow. The loss of two French submarines, the *Minerve* in 1968 and the *Eurydice* in 1970, is thought to have been caused by this. Both sank in deep water in the Mediterranean and, as mentioned earlier, snort hull valve failure was considered a key factor in the foundering of HMS *Affray* in 1951. For these reasons drills and procedures associated with snorting were to feature as a very important part of the training class curriculum, a major feature of the prime element in the course: that of submarine safety. It was emphatically impressed upon the individual that error on the part of any member of the crew could very quickly imperil the boat.

Another key safety factor was that of battery ventilation. In the final stages of charging, hydrogen is emitted which, unless purged by the ventilation system, can quickly build up to dangerous explosive levels. Although modern British submarines have their batteries enclosed in separate compartments, unlike some other nations' boats, this did not prevent explosions occurring. Battery ventilation failures caused two explosions, one aboard HMS *Auriga* in 1970, the second the following year in *Alliance*, in which in several men were injured and one was killed. Among the losses of nuclear submarines, of which there have been several, the most plausible theory for the loss of the American hunter-killer, USS *Scorpion*, in 1968, was that a battery explosion killed or disabled the control-room team resulting in control of the boat being lost and it sinking to crush depth.

At the closing phases of Conley's own career in submarines, as the officer responsible for accepting new vessels from the shipbuilder, in 1992 he delayed the handover of HMS *Ursula*, the penultimate boat of the conventional *Upholder* class, until some damaged battery cells were replaced after a small explosion had occurred in her battery tank.

Should the worst occur, from whatever cause, it was essential that submarine crews should be able to escape from the confinement of their damaged boats. This could, of course, only occur if the submarine lay at a depth compatible with the ability of the human body to withstand the pressure, but if this was the case it was important that each individual had experience of such escape, for which nerve and a cool head were a prerequisite. The experiences of the late war combined with peacetime losses of submarines such as the *Affray* placed escape practice high on the trainees' agenda.

Although by the 1960s all British submarines were being fitted with separate escape chambers, prior to that the basic method of escape was to assemble all hands in a single compartment. Each man wore an escape suit and all were mustered for what was called a 'rush escape', which took place through a canvas trunking rigged under the compartment escape hatch. This would be opened when the compartment pressure had been equalised with that of the sea outside by flooding the compartment. This rudimentary method requires each man to breathe pure air through a mouthpiece which is discarded on entry into the escape trunk. The safe ascent then relies upon the disciplined blowing out of air through pursed lips all the way up to the surface if burst lungs or a very dangerous air embolism in the bloodstream are to be avoided.

The more sophisticated chamber escape method had the advantage of each individual being evacuated in sequence, continuing to breathe freely all the way up to the surface inside a totally enclosed escape suit. This type of escape was periodically tested down to a depth of 600ft from 'O'-class submarines sitting on the seabed, some of the crew volunteering to undertake the drill.

To familiarise trainees with the possibility of undertaking this hazardous procedure, training took place in the escape tank in Fort Blockhouse. This was 100ft deep and, in addition to having an escape chamber, had facilities at different depths which replicated the flooding of a whole compartment and the vertical escape to the surface following evacuation of the submarine. Such an evolution took place in benign conditions, in warm, well-lit water, with a number of instructors situated at various stages of the ascent to ensure the student was performing appropriately. Failure to blow out adequately in the training ascent was inevitably met by a firm prod in the stomach. All this would, of course, be a far cry from the darkness, the bitterly cold water and the fear prevalent in a real escape from a stricken submarine. Even so, it was not without inherent risk and in later years the value of pressurised escape training, with its occasional serious injuries or even fatalities, would be questioned. However, experience had indicated that it was highly likely that an untrained crew member would panic and fail to get out of the escape chamber, causing a fatal obstruction which prevented the remainder of the crew escaping.

Now aged twenty-one, Sub Lieutenant Conley completed the course in December 1967 and was appointed to the five-year-old 'O'-class submarine *Odin*. The *Odin* belonged to the Third Submarine Squadron based at Faslane, on the Gareloch, Scotland. The boat had been intended to be based in Singapore but the Wilson government, intent on withdrawing from the Far East, changed all that. Instead, her ship's company exchanged the intense tropical humidity which offsets the delights of Singapore, for the 65 inches of cold rain and the Scottish midge which assailed those who lived on the shores of the Gareloch. Despite being under training, he was *Odin*'s torpedo officer and was responsible for the casing – the external superstucture.

The 'O' class and their immediate predecessors, the 'P' class mentioned earlier, although of new post-war design, were built on traditional lines of a relatively long hull length, two propeller shafts and torpedo tubes in the bows and stern. Curiously, the earliest Royal Navy submarine, the *Holland I* of 1901, had a much more efficient underwater design than those that followed. This was because the short, rounded, single shaft hull design – known as an 'albacore' in shape and not dissimilar to the profile of a whale or porpoise – whilst highly manoeuvrable under water, tended to make for very wet, unstable operation on the surface. Since the traditional submarine was still essentially a submersible rather than a true sub-marine craft, until the adoption of the snort it was more important to design for surface efficiency.

This tradition was broken by the Americans one year after the lead vessel of the 'P' class, HMS *Porpoise*, entered service. In 1959 the United States Navy commissioned the conventional submarine *Barbel*, which was albacore in design. Submerged, she and her two sisters proved to be much faster and handier than the Royal Navy's 'P' and 'O' classes and they proved the superiority of the albacore hull form, sometimes called the teardrop, over the accepted style based upon the empirical development to that date. The true significance of this return to the form of the *Holland I* was that by this time the United States Navy possessed the means to drive a fully sub-marine warship: a nuclear power plant.

Nevertheless, the Os and Ps had many excellent features, chief of which was their absence of noise when running under electric motor propulsion. This was exemplified by one of these boats passing over an array of highly sensitive seabed hydrophones when the only noise detected was the patter of rain on the surface of the sea. They were also very seaworthy on the surface, possessed an excellent range of about 15,000 miles and were able to remain at sea for up to sixty days. With eight torpedo tubes, they carried an impressive outfit of up to twenty-six torpedoes and – for a limited duration of about forty minutes – could achieve a submerged maximum speed of 17 knots. Their accommodation was considered reasonable enough for long patrols, with separate mess areas, each fitted with bunks and tables, although some of engine-room staff lived between the after torpedo tubes.

Their disadvantages in handling lay in their slow turning rate, large turning circle and a relatively low speed of 7 knots at periscope depth, when the propellers would start making a significant noise owing to the onset of cavitation. Furthermore, unlike the submarines of some other navies, when running on the surface under diesel power, the engines did not have a separate air induction system. Instead, their air was sucked down the conning tower hatch and through the control room. Wet and salt-laden, this rapidly moving airstream did little good to the increasing amount of electronic gear being fitted in this location. In very rough weather, where lots of spray and the occasional lump of solid water could be expected down the conning tower, a plastic fabric trunking was mounted below the control room hatch. This in turn was lashed into a 3ft-high canvas receptacle with a hose connected to a pump set up to remove any overflowing seawater, an expedient known as the 'bird bath and elephant's trunk'.

In rough weather at night, with the control room in near-darkness, going on bridge watch, dressed in foul weather gear and safety harness, involved negotiating a wet, moving and slippery deck, climbing into the 'bird bath', avoiding falling into water it contained, before battling up the plastic trunking by way of the conning tower ladders through a very noisy and violent 100mph rush of indrawn air. Emerging onto the bridge, even the conditions of a force 8 gale would seem serene after the experience of the vertical climb against such odds. Fortunately, the later major modernisation of the 'O' class, which incorporated improved lock-out arrangements, where the submarine ran on the surface with all conning tower hatches shut and the snort system open, mercifully consigned the 'bird bath' to history.

Such things might be tolerated up to a point. Less easy to accept were the more important deficiencies in 'warfare capability'. Both the 'P' and 'O' classes were originally built with sensors and torpedo control equipment which had advanced little since 1945 and, indeed, this was still the case when Conley joined *Odin*. While these submarines had to be able to sink surface shipping, their primary combat role was to hunt and destroy other submarines, a task for which they required efficient sonar equipment and a capable anti-submarine (ASW) weapon. Their sonars, nearly always operated in the passive mode (not transmitting) to avoid counter-detection, had only a single narrow trainable beam and the long-range sonar, which had its hydrophones fitted in the ballast tanks, required the submarine to slowly circle to conduct an all-round search. The control room attack equipment relied upon a number of rudimentary paper or Perspex plots which, although foolproof, were manpower-intensive and required a considerable degree of skill to develop target parameters and solutions.

As to their offensive weapons, they could deploy the Mark 8 torpedo, which was of pre-Second World War vintage and, although reliable and capable of use against both surface ships and submarines at periscope depth, it was relatively short-ranged. For use against a hostile submarine the prime weapons were the Mark 23 and Mark 20 homing torpedoes, described by Conley as 'totally ineffective'. The former were wire-guided versions of the latter, but the wire arrangement was very unsatisfactory and, coupled with both poor homing performance and component reliability, made for a total system performance which was utterly inadequate. Although of course he could not know it, rectifying these deficiencies would occupy a significant part of Conley's naval career and would not be fixed until the eve of the end of the Cold War, a quarter of a century after the Royal Navy commissioned its first nuclear submarine, HMS *Dreadnought*, in 1963.

Throughout this period, when the Royal Navy replaced the Royal Air Force as 'the nation's sure shield' as steward of Great Britain's nuclear deterrent, the Submarine Service's senior officers on the whole reluctantly accepted these deficient weapons, somewhat failing in their duty to adequately thrust the issue under the noses of their civilian counterparts at the head of the Ministry of Defence, or those politicians responsible for the defence of the realm. In a period of such prolonged tension, with the threat of Mutually Assured Destruction ever present, the irony of this is inescapable.

Those responsible who regarded these serious deficiencies with such complacency focused upon the number of submarines, seemingly imbued with a touching confidence that, in event of hostilities, success would still be achieved even with inadequate weapons. Here the lessons of history were being thrown away with cavalier abandon. Clearly, these senior officers had failed to acknowledge the generally poor performance of torpedoes in the Second World War. They appeared ignorant of the wretched history of American and German torpedoes, the latter of which ameliorated Allied losses in the early stages of the Battle of the Atlantic – to the fury of Dönitz – whilst the former probably extended the Pacific War by at least six months.

Appreciation of all this lay in the future for Conley, who arrived at Faslane when *Odin* was still at sea. He checked into the brand new wardroom of the Clyde submarine base, HMS *Neptune*, which had been built specially to support the four new Polaris submarines which would become operational shortly. The base possessed new submarine jetties, workshops, shore accommodation and a floating dock, but was still under construction, with many other facilities in various stages of completion. To Conley it seemed that no expense was being spared in meeting the imperatives of the Polaris programme which was running to schedule and, despite the obvious outlay surrounding him, was on budget.

Officers' married quarters had been completed in the nearby village of Rhu and a large estate of ratings' quarters established behind the town of Helensburgh. This, however, was not very well built and in due course was to become very much a bleak, soulless place for families where the father could be away at sea, out of contact for several months. Although the officers' quarters had won an architectural prize, the exterior of most of the buildings looked like giant chicken coops and were ill-designed to cope with the winter weather of the west of Scotland.

In line with the United States' model, the base boasted very compre-hensive recreational facilities, including a petrol station and cinema which were to quickly prove commercially unviable. When off-duty the British submariner – unlike his US counterpart – spent as little time as possible in the base, preferring the very limited offerings of the Helensburgh nightlife or venturing further afield to Glasgow, some forty miles away.

On joining *Odin*, Conley experienced disappointment. The submarine was about to undergo annual inspection and all hands were focused upon bringing the boat up to the highest levels of cleanliness prior to proceeding to sea for two days of exercises when she would be put through her operational paces. Therefore, initially he felt himself to be a bit of a nuisance. Besides which, although *Odin*'s accommodation was considered adequate enough for sea-duty, it was the practice of all submarines in port to accommodate the crew ashore in barrack accommodation, leaving only a duty watch onboard overnight to deal with the routine running and security of the vessel, or to meet any arising emergencies. This tended to add further to Conley's sense of isolation and he experienced 'a fairly ragged time', being detailed to help the completion of painting and cleaning the torpedo com-partment, much to the embarrassment of the senior rating in charge. Also, greatly to his chagrin, he was instructed to remain ashore for the operational sea inspection and received the displeasure of his commanding officer when he was not there on the jetty to meet *Odin* when she returned to harbour unexpectedly early.

He had, meanwhile, been decanted from the shore wardroom accommodation to the 1938 vintage depot ship *Maidstone* that, prior to the base being established, had been the Third Submarine Squadron's shore support facility. Moored alongside, this venerable old ship had great character and there was a tremendous sense of camaraderie and spirit amongst the submarine crews billeted in her accommodation. Dinner in the wardroom was always a convivial occasion, a fair amount of drinking being buoyed by the ebullient presence of a number of Canadian and Australian officers on exchange appointments to British submarines whilst their boats were under construction. Also present were the officers of the Israeli submarine *Dakar*, until recently HMS *Totem*, who, conducting work-up prior to departure for Israel, added a friendly international dimension to the gatherings. Rather unusually, the commanding officer and first lieutenant of the Israeli submarine were brothers. Very sadly, a few weeks later *Dakar* was lost with all hands in the Mediterranean en route to her new home. The wreck, in deep water, was not located until 1999, but the cause of her sinking has never been established. Conley had got to know some of *Dakar*'s junior officers and this tragedy was a poignant reminder that submarining could be a dangerous profession, a cold douche to add to his nonchalant reception aboard *Odin*.

The depot ship's repair and maintenance staff were cheerfully helpful, a welcome contrast to the surly civilian dockyard mateys whose apathy and lack of urgency was legendary. Indeed, all departments of the *Maidstone* were committed, as was traditional, to deliver a level of support which the much larger shore staff of *Neptune* initially found difficult to replicate. Unfortunately, *Maidstone* left Faslane soon after Conley's arrival and, as the shore wardroom was now full, he moved into a cabin onboard the old landing ship *Lofoten*, which provided overflow officers' accommodation until the base facilities were complete.

By this time Conley was wondering if he and submarines were mutually suited. He was not to feel 'part of the team' until the *Odin* again put to sea after the Christmas leave period, whereupon responsibility was heaped on him. In company with other submarines, *Odin* left Faslane for exercises off the northwest of Ireland. Influenza swept through the ship's company and owing to shortages of fit watch-keeping officers, Conley soon found himself conducting watches on his own in the control room when the submarine was deep. His mentor and training officer was the *Odin*'s first lieutenant, the late Vice Admiral Sir Geoffrey Biggs, who quickly recognised Conley's abilities. On more than one occasion Lieutenant Biggs came on watch with Conley and discreetly disappeared, leaving the young sub lieutenant to it. Biggs was not only a good delegator, he was intelligent and capable and a great character; the two men were to serve together on a number of subsequent occasions.

Conley was soon to learn the hard way that diesel submarines spent a lot of time on the surface. Bridge watch-keeping in the winter off the British coast could be a very cold, wet experience. Watchkeepers slept in damp clothes to dry them off for their next duty period and, as the junior officer, Conley had been allocated the most uncomfortable of the seven wardroom bunks, in which it was almost impossible to sleep in rough weather. Here, jammed into the curve of the pressure hull and sharing the space with the brackets which supported the weight of the bunk above, he further pondered the wisdom of his career choice.

On completion of the exercises, *Odin* was programmed to make a courtesy call to Newcastle upon Tyne and headed for Cape Wrath. She had been scheduled to fire a torpedo at the small island of Garvie, situated off the Cape and used as a target by all three armed services. This 'proving warshot' with a live torpedo was, for some reason, cancelled and, as the weather deteriorated, *Odin* ploughed her way eastwards towards the Pentland Firth on the surface. This proved an exciting experience, with the rising westerly wind, now approaching storm force, blowing against the westerly setting tide of over 8 knots. The seas this generated were phenomenal for their steepness, and for a while little progress was made through the infamous very turbulent area – Merry Men of Mey – as one of the two main propulsion motors had failed, owing to a defective lubrication oil pump. A jury-rigged Black and Decker heavy-duty drill was ingeniously set up by the engineers to drive the pump, enabling the motor to be restarted, and ran continuously for the next thirty-six hours.

Clear of the Firth, *Odin* swung south into the North Sea on the night of the Glasgow 'hurricane' of January 1968, during which twenty Glaswegians were killed. On watch at 0230 as the storm was at its height, with the wind speed gusting at over 100mph, visibility was down to a few hundred yards. On *Odin*'s bridge the seas were breaking over Conley and his lookout. Radar performance was also poor thanks to the 'sea clutter', the echoes returned from the myriad surfaces of waves in their immediate vicinity. As a result, any other vessel would only have been detected at very short range, but fortunately there was little shipping around.

With access to the bridge through the conning tower airlock, and with air for the engines being supplied by the snort induction system, both Conley and the lookout were locked out of the submarine to prevent the control room flooding. When it came to his turn to be relieved at 0430, Conley experienced real trouble locking back into the submarine, as on climbing down to the airlock he found it flooded up by the breaking seas, which had filled the enclosed space in which the hatch was located. Attempts to pump it out proved fruitless, as every time he opened the upper hatch to climb in to the lock, the sea poured in after him. He therefore decided to stay in the chamber whilst it was pumped empty. Crouching at the top of the airlock ladder, his knees in water, suffused in the added surrealism of red lighting and with the pump drawing a vacuum, causing the seawater around him to start vaporising, he was very glad when the airlock was emptied and the control room crew swung the lower hatch open.

Having discovered that his bunk was untenable, he decided to sleep under the wardroom table where books, a typewriter and miscellaneous odds and sods fell on top of him when the *Odin* hit a particularly big wave.

Once alongside in Newcastle, and according to an unwritten tradition of the sea, as the junior officer Conley found himself on duty at the evening drinks reception. This was for local dignitaries and other guests, and towards the end of the gathering he was instructed to somehow manoeuvre a very drunken lady mayor out of the submarine by way of the access hatch and up a steep gangplank to her awaiting limousine. This was only achieved with a great degree of difficulty and the help of several members of the duty watch.

Solicitude for its submarine crews had persuaded the Ministry of Defence in the 1960s to grant them the privilege of living ashore when on courtesy visits to non-naval ports. On the day following his onerous duty of discharging the pickled recipients of *Odin*'s hospitality, Conley checked into the comfort of a central Newcastle hotel. However, owing to the cost of the hotel exceedingly the daily subsistence allowance, the first lieutenant decided the officers would move into the far cheaper local Mission to Seamen. This proved clean, friendly and hospitable, leaving sufficient of their allowance to be spent on enjoyment and *Odin*'s crew took advantage of the city's hospitality, so much so that, the appointed day for her departure being a Sunday, a large gathering of well-wishers watched from the quay. They were treated to the rather unedifying sight of the commanding officer and the first lieutenant rummaging through the dustbins placed on the quay for the boat's use, in search of a local telephone directory. This was required to determine why the ordered tugs had not arrived on time. This impasse resolved, the submarine slipped her moorings, made her farewells and began her passage downstream. On the way out of the Tyne, Conley received another reminder of the fragile mortality of submariners as *Odin* passed the spot where, a year earlier, one of his Dartmouth contemporaries had drowned after he was swept off his submarine's casing and his lifejacket had failed to inflate.

HMS *Odin*'s next task was to return by way of Cape Wrath to the exercise area off Malin Head where she was to take part in anti-submarine warfare (ASW) evolutions, in the role of the loyal opposition to a group of frigates and destroyers acting as convoy escorts, supported by maritime patrol aircraft (MPA). Notably, towards the end of the exercises the escort force encountered a Soviet Whiskey-class diesel submarine which, after several hours of prosecution by sonar, surfaced and requested a weather forecast. This incident was a reminder that the United Kingdom's naval forces and coast were subject to continuous surveillance by Soviet forces, surface and sub-surface. Indeed, for several decades a Soviet intelligence gathering ship was to be permanently stationed just outside territorial waters on SSBN patrol transit routes to the north of Ireland.

With the exercises completed, *Odin* headed for Lough Foyle and a visit to Londonderry, berthing alongside HMS *Stalker*. This was a large infantry landing ship which had been built in Canada for the D-Day landings and later converted to support submarines. The Joint Anti-Submarine Training School, which had run the exercise, was installed in HMS *Sea Eagle*, a shore establishment in the city. Inevitably, submarines arrived last into port and delivered their exercise records after the other participants. With inter-Service rivalry rampant, the trick for a submarine officer reporting in to the staff who had been monitoring the exercise was first to examine closely the large floor plot in *Sea Eagle*. Here the exercise had been followed and set out, so a subtle shift of one's own submarine's position away from the locations of reported submarine detections, especially those by aircraft, afforded an egregious satisfaction.

Many of the officers of the visiting warships congregated in the evenings in a local hostelry which usually reverberated to loud Irish Republican music, rousing in tempo and melody, if dubious in sentiment for officers of Her Majesty's Navy. 'The Troubles' were yet some months away and although fault lines fractured Ulster society, the lubricating effects of alcohol and Celtic music won the day. Nevertheless, late one evening, whilst Conley and his colleagues from *Odin*'s wardroom were enjoying this convivial and noisy hospitality after official closing time, the pub was raided by the police. The Royal Ulster Constabulary made rather futile attempts to take the names of the large number of customers present, which included a rather bemused group of officers from an American destroyer.

Another favourite haunt was the village hall dance in Muff just across the border in the Irish Republic, where Irish dance bands provided outstandingly good music and the local girls were willing to dance. The urbane intrusions of young British naval officers and ratings often provoked fights, which had the curious quality of proceeding at the pace of the music being played.

Conley and his shipmates were all struck by the friendly welcome they received from the people of Londonderry who, at that time, never bothered to lock their house doors. However, the city was evidently a poor place and the armed police patrolling the streets gave hints of the tensions which would tear apart a citizenry divided by two religious factions and plunge Northern Ireland into a dark and bloody era of widespread violence. Despite the disenfranchisement of the Roman Catholic population by the requirement of being a freeholder to vote in local elections, it was remarkable that Conley and his colleagues were struck by the genuine friendliness of the local population to the Royal Navy. However, it was little wonder that the Northern Ireland Civil Rights organisation was to be increasingly strident in its appeals for equality, while the repression of their demonstrations by the largely Protestant Ulster Constabulary was to act as a catalyst for the many years of 'the Troubles' then looming.

By this time Conley had settled into submarine life. Notwithstanding his early experiences, the *Odin* proved a happy and efficient submarine, well led and motivated by the strong team of her commanding officer Lieutenant Commander David Wardle and his second in command Lieutenant Biggs, her morale buttressed by the colourful tradition of the Submarine Service in allowing the wearing of exotic outfits at sea. This slackening of the strictures of naval discipline was a hangover from the Second World War, but added immensely to the bonding of a submarine's company, at the same time marking them as special – and to the individuals – an elite within the Royal Navy, part of that cocking a snook at the rest of the Fleet that went with their insistence that they served in 'boats'.

Aboard *Odin* at the time, the ratings manning the sonar system dressed as French onion sellers, engine room artificers wore Arab garb and the control room watchkeepers attired themselves as high Victorians. Conley stuck to a fisherman's sweater and slacks, which reminded him of his roots. This nonconforming and so–called 'pirate rig' would be prohibited in the early 1970s as, with its increasing number of nuclear submarines, the Royal Navy's Submarine Service underwent the major cultural shift discussed elsewhere. Moreover, the cleaner conditions aboard the nuclear submarines were more conducive to the wearing of formal uniform, whereas the old diesel-engined boats always smell strongly of diesel fuel, an acrid odour which permeates everything, including clothes, and pirate rig could be left on board when men went on leave, rather than risking the ire of their wives by bringing the very pungent stench into the home.

Shortly after visiting Londonderry, the commanding officer, extremely popular, was due to be relieved and prior to his departure, having finished a week of 'Perisher' work in the Clyde, the ship's company resolved to take him on a farewell run ashore into Campbeltown. Needless to say, it was an occasion of great revelry, which finished with a very noisy parade down the jetty with a chaired CO wearing a Viking helmet with replica Norse sword as baton, conducting a rendition of the submarine's song which had the repetitive chorus, 'Odin send the wind and waves to make it safe for snorting.'

The next day *Odin* proceeded to sea, dived and was then sat on the seabed for the morning, allowing her crew to recover from the excesses of the previous evening. Such was life in a typical diesel-engined submarines of the Royal Navy during the decade of the so-called swinging 1960s.

After her task in the Clyde, *Odin* was ordered to Chatham Dockyard where several weeks were spent undertaking repairs to her engines. This was necessary because the greater than normal high revolution running of her type of engines had proved detrimental.

Sub Lieutenant Conley's period as a trainee was coming to an end. Biggs had been impressed and Conley had grown into the niche the Navy had offered him; it was time to move on. The next hurdle was the successful passing of an examination, the submarine qualification. Given the importance the Royal Navy apparently attached to imbuing its young submarine officers with technical knowledge at the outset, this was a hurdle that in his case was not so much jumped, as kicked aside. Conley took the written part of the qualification in an office ashore in the dockyard, under the invigilation of a coxswain loaned from another submarine refitting alongside. Half way through Conley's papers, this helpful chief petty officer left the room and returned with two steaming cups of coffee. Sitting down beside the candidate he obligingly ran through the questions Conley could not answer, contacting his mates by telephone where he could not answer a specific question. As

Conley afterwards drily commented, 'At least I was spared the embarrass-ment of coming top of my training class in the examinations.' This collaboration proved successful and he duly received instructions to transfer to *Sealion* as navigating officer. Whilst this was a promotion and opened new prospects for him, it was not such good news and he would have preferred to remain in *Odin*.

Like his old boat, *Sealion* belonged to the Third Submarine Squadron. She had been completed at Cammell Laird's Birkenhead yard in 1961, the penultimate example of the 'P' class. However, she had a poor reputation; her commanding officer was a heavy, aggressive drinker in harbour and a bully at sea, a situation not helped by her first lieutenant being a very weak character, incapable of handling his superior.

Conley's worst fears were proved when he joined *Sealion* in what seemed like a forgotten floating dock in a remote corner of Portsmouth Dockyard, where she was undergoing repairs to both of her propeller shafts. She was filthy dirty, with crew morale palpably at rock bottom. The stench of her wing bilges, which contained remnants of packed food from past patrols mixed with oily water, was added to the usual pungent aroma of diesel oil. There was long-standing dirt and grime everywhere and much of the deck and bulkhead paintwork and finish had been damaged and not made good. She ought not to have been much different in her internal appearance from *Odin*, which was only a year younger, so the overall effect on her new navigator – or 'Pilot' as he would be called – was profoundly depressing.

There were, Conley discovered, some mitigating factors. *Sealion* was the last conventional British submarine to conduct intelligence-gathering patrols in the Barents Sea. During her first commission on one patrol she gathered data from Soviet nuclear bomb tests on Nova Zemlya and on another, whilst gathering information on missile firings, had been counter-detected. She was then harassed for many hours by a group of Soviet destroyers who, despite the interaction happening in international waters, during the prosecution dropped many warning charges on her in an attempt to force her to surface. *Sealion*, however, made it safely into Norwegian territorial waters. These northern patrols involved a long snort to and from the patrol areas with wear and tear upon both machinery and crew. She had finished these patrols about a year before but was mechanically worn out and many of her men were also in an exhausted frame of mind. In particular, those responsible for maintaining her weapon systems were a poor lot. If their equipment became defective, they often could not fix it: the best men were being drawn away and transferred to support the highly prioritised Polaris programme. Consequently, clapped-out boats like *Sealion* had to struggle with sub-standard technicians. This unhappy situation was worsened by a very defective character being in command.

As navigator, Conley inherited equipment which was adequate for coastal work, but was not up to the mark for operating in the deep ocean. The long range LORAN-C radio-navigation system was defective, taking months to get repaired, and the echo-sounder was incapable of taking the deep sea soundings for navigating using seabed contour charts. This left Conley with the periscope sextant. This was a very complex piece of equipment fitted with an artificial horizon which would enable him to take observations of the sun, but would prove totally unsuitable for star sights. 'In fact,' he recalled, 'I never came across anyone who successfully used this equipment to get an accurate star fix. The fallback position was to use dead reckoning with all its inaccuracies, owing to the unknowns of deep ocean currents or the boat undertaking an "action surface",' enabling him to take star sights at morning or evening twilight using a conventional sextant. 'This evolution strongly risked the ire of the commanding officer if my astronomical measurements did not result in an acceptably accurate navigational fix.'

In due course, with two new stern shafts fitted, *Sealion* proceeded down harbour and secured in Haslar Creek, alongside the Portsmouth submarine base at HMS *Dolphin*. Here she loaded torpedoes and stores prior to going to sea, and here Conley observed his new commander at close quarters. As duty officer on the final evening alongside, he had just finished dinner when the sentry on the casing reported that the commanding officer was coming aboard with some friends, one of whom had brought his dog. Conley then had to carry a very heavy Labrador into the submarine through the accommodation hatch and down a vertical ladder. At the end of an evening of excessive boozing, he had to reverse the process. Owing to the weight and nervousness of the Labrador, this proved more difficult than extricating the lady mayor in Newcastle.

Conley's ordeal was not yet over, for to his despair, having said goodbye to his chums, the captain returned onboard, sat in the wardroom where Conley was obliged to keep him company, and drank whisky until 0600. He then staggered ashore and off to bed in his shore quarters. As the off-duty crew came aboard at 0800 the duty officer welcomed them with bleary eyes. The commanding officer returned onboard just before noon and resumed drinking at a reception set up in the control room for the First Submarine

Squadron officers to thank them for their support and assistance during *Sealion*'s sojourn in Portsmouth. The guests departed at about 1400 and the ship's company went to harbour stations for leaving; *Sealion* slipped her berth at 1500. It was not to be expected that matters would go smoothly.

On reversing out of Haslar Creek, his judgement impaired by the vast quantity of alcohol he had consumed, *Sealion*'s commander successfully avoided a sand dredger by a violent alteration of heading. However, this caused the *Sealion* to be caught up in the strong ebb tide sweeping through the narrow entrance to Portsmouth Harbour on the western side of which lies the wardroom of HMS *Dolphin*, which has a large patio adjoining the sea wall. Here all the squadron officers were gathered to bid her farewell. They were treated to the sight of one of Her Majesty's submarines leaving for sea duty, beam on, athwart the line of the channel and with her bows pointing towards – and passing a few yards away from – them. With a modest shudder accompanied by a muddy disturbance and rising bubbles, *Sealion*'s bows grounded at the *Dolphin* saluting point, while her stern was swung by the fierce tide to point down channel towards Southsea Castle.

HMS *Sealion* was drawn off the bottom by the application of full astern power, thereafter continuing down the buoyed channel stern first until the commanding officer found a suitable position to turn her round. This was a very inauspicious start to Conley's time as navigator.

Having arrived in the Gareloch, *Sealion* undertook several weeks of work-up with the assistance of the squadron shore staff. Conley soon learned that when things went wrong the commanding officer was like a raging bull in the control room, yelling at everyone he conceived to have contributed to the cock-up. The first lieutenant was demonstrably ineffective and unwilling to support his fellow officers.

Part of the work-up involved passing at night through the stretch of water between Kintyre and the Isle of Arran in a submerged condition. This was very demanding, as there were very few navigational marks or lights from which to take bearings through the periscope, while the lack of a moon made it doubly difficult to identify significant features along the shoreline against the backdrop of the dark mountains. The evolution involved various scenarios which included exercising minelaying procedures, inshore photo-reconnaissance, the avoiding of ASW warships and penetrating a field of dummy mines which had been laid off the coast of Arran. As navigator in such close-quarters situations as these evolutions generated, Conley was on his mettle. Under an exemplary command team this would have taxed his abilities, even if he had been an experienced navigator; in his present circumstances this was to call from him extraordinary reserves. Properly, the first lieutenant should have reorganised the watch-keeping rota to avoid the navigator being kept at continuous fever-pitch for fourteen hours in the control room but, if the ordeal was to prove one of the most arduous Conley endured in the Submarine Service, it proved something else: he could run on little sleep for several nights running, and he could handle extremes. This was noticed by others, particularly *Sealion*'s captain who, despite his 'very aggressive behaviour' to Conley at sea, expressed every confidence in his new navigator, and gave up checking up on his work.

Whilst *Sealion* passed her work-up, just meeting the overall satisfaction of the squadron staff, her commander did not. Both he and the first lieutenant were soon to disappear, but not before *Sealion* undertook trials of a prototype Polaris submarine communication buoy. This involved fitting special rails to the after part of the casing to house and recover the buoy, which measured approximately 8ft by 6ft; it was attached to the submarine by about 1,000ft of wire. Fitting of the rails was taken in hand by Scotts Shipyard at Greenock, which had a distinguished history and where two 'O'-class submarines previously mentioned were being completed for the Australian Navy.

At the same time the opportunity was taken to replace many of *Sealion*'s very tired fabric and furnishings, all of this work being concealed in the cost of the rails. However, although the workforce evidently possessed a much better work ethic than their cousins in the Royal Dockyards, the senior directors were very uninspiring and the yard's infrastructure was very run-down and undercapitalised. The boat required dry-docking for a few days but the Scotts dock needed the continuous running of pumps to keep the wooden dock floor reasonably free of water. Other evidence of decrepitude was the use of ancient telegraph poles as side shores, to keep the submarine in position on the blocks. Unsurprisingly, like most other British shipyards which were living on an historical reputation for excellence, Scotts would go out of business a few years later.

The deficiencies of the yard were made manifest before the *Sealion* reached her trials areas. The buoy trials took place in the Mediterranean, in waters to the east of Gibraltar. Rough weather encountered crossing the Bay of Biscay on the surface tore the newly welded rails from the casing and a new set had to be manufactured and fitted by Gibraltar Dockyard. Once this had been accomplished, *Sealion* embarked on her trials which involved running eastwards daily from Gibraltar, testing different buoy types, configurations and towing wires at dived speeds up to 16 knots.

Besides having on board a number of technical staff – or 'trial scientists' – opportunity was taken to host a number of local guests at sea for the day, including army personnel, the medical staff from the naval hospital and local dignitaries. Accommodated in the wardroom, most commented on the bemusing array of cans strung out below the deckhead to catch water from a leaking cable gland. On one occasion *Sealion* departed from the dockyard with an army band playing on the forward casing, though some difficulty was experienced getting the drums below through the accommodation hatch once at sea.

The buoy trials proved successful in demonstrating the hydrodynamics at a range of speeds, but on the final day the trial scientists produced a tow wire covered in ostrich feathers, which had been fitted with the aim of avoiding wire 'strum'. This was a harmonic oscillation of the wire that occurred as it was drawn through the water and which, by being a 'potential acoustic counter-detection hazard', would possibly betray the position of any submarine deploying the equipment in an acute operational situation. An expedient relying upon ostrich feathers to reduce strum was predictably regarded with that scepticism 'Jolly Jack' has for the intellectually derived solutions of boffins. Jolly Jack won: on working up to full speed, the wire parted owing to the increased resistance of the feathers and the buoy was lost – never to be recovered.

The lax atmosphere that prevailed aboard *Sealion* guaranteed that a final departure time from Gibraltar two hours before midnight would result in a significant portion of the ship's company returning from shore leave one hour before sailing in less than sober state. This proved to be the case and shortly afterwards, true to form, the captain arrived by car a few minutes before departure and also staggered across the brow in a sorry state. Certain irregular preparations were made by members of the crew before leaving the berth while the commanding officer worked up his own departure plan. Ignoring all harbour speed restrictions, and determined to make his last departure a memorable one, *Sealion* was reversed from her berth at maximum speed and created a significant wash as she came abeam of the guard ship alongside, HMS *Zulu*.

The Tribal-class frigate had fitted to either side of her bridge large decorative Zulu shields which had been presented to her. These had somehow appeared secured to the *Sealion*'s fin and were unsubtly illuminated by lamps.

Their sighting by the frigate's watchkeepers caused a flurry of activity and a high-speed rigid raider was dispatched to recover the booty. By the time this reached *Sealion* she was already outside the harbour mole and her outgoing captain, in no mood to part company with the trophies his warriors had gleaned, took appropriate action. As the fast boat roared alongside, a Royal Marine officer, immaculately dressed in his mess kit, stood up in the stern to plead for the return of the shields, whereupon *Sealion*'s captain bombarded the boat with potatoes from a bag he had had sent up from the galley. The *Zulu* detachment repelled, the shields stowed securely away, he disappeared below to his cabin. Here he remained for most of the next three days as *Sealion* ran north, up the Portuguese coast and headed across the Bay of Biscay. Something of his psychological state of mind, not to say Conley's confidence, is revealed by the fact that he made no protest when Conley, guying his commander, kept the navigational charts under lock and key. Apparently indifferent to the *Sealion*'s progress until the diving area was reached in the Bay of Biscay, the wretched man departed without ceremony after speedily handing over to his relief when the boat berthed at Faslane.

With her 'booze-loving' commanding officer gone, the *Sealion* rapidly improved. Cleaner and more efficient, her crew, having undergone many changes, was more competent. The new captain, although initially lacking confidence, was nevertheless a big improvement. The same could not be said for the new first lieutenant, who was exceedingly eccentric, possessed an abrasive temperament and badly lacked management skills. In consequence, the other members of the wardroom, which had also undergone changes and which now included some very capable individuals, drew together like a 'band of brothers', supporting each other and developing into a very effective team. In this atmosphere lifetime friendships were formed.

Perhaps most enlivening was the arrival of a new wardroom steward who closely resembled the character of Baldrick, a servant played by Tony Robinson as a foil to the Blackadder of Rowan Atkinson in a the popular television series. Baldrick's common sense combined with his disreputable appearance producing risible solutions to his master's frequent plights made him extremely popular. The *Sealion*'s new wardroom steward displayed equally unsurpassable ingenuity in procuring extras for the wardroom. Many a supply officer of a warship berthed near *Sealion* must have wondered where their wardroom langoustines, fillet steaks or fresh strawberries had disappeared to, while the recipients of this cunning turned a Nelsonic blind eye.

For the remainder of the commission, *Sealion* undertook routine submarine work which more often than not involved acting again as the loyal opposition in exercises. Some of these were of large scale, including a NATO exercise in which a dozen merchant ships had been chartered to act as a transatlantic convoy.

The new captain proved somewhat accident-prone; early in his tenure of command *Sealion* struck the jetty when berthing in Portland harbour, causing it significant damage. He also had a minor collision with a fishing vessel whilst manoeuvring alongside in Funchal, Madeira, and temporarily grounded *Sealion* on the horseshoe bend in the River Avon on the way up to Bristol for a pre-Christmas visit in December 1968. She was quickly pulled off by the leading tug but in terms of seriousness none of these incidents were to match that of the following spring.

5

A Very Close Call

In March 1969 *Sealion* was snorting in deep water to the northwest of Ireland at 10 knots, her maximum snorting speed. She was acting as a sonar target for the first of Great Britain's Polaris-armed nuclear-powered submarines, the SSBN HMS *Resolution*, then undergoing her 'first-of-class' sonar trials. To avoid any possibility of a collision occurring, the two submarines were separated by depth zones, the *Resolution* running in the deeper of the two and in a position then unknown to *Sealion*. At about 0030 *Sealion*'s first lieutenant was about to hand over the watch to Conley and the weapons engineer. The control room was darkened, illuminated by a few dim red lights.

Suddenly, the after planesman reported that his hydroplanes had jammed to 'full rise'. He immediately transferred the control of the planes to a separate emergency system and applied 'full dive' angle to the hydroplanes which remained indicating 'full rise'. The submarine, however, adopted a severe down angle and increased depth.

The 'Stop snorting!' order was rapped out and the control systems watchkeeper urgently went though the tasks of shutting hull valves, lowering masts and – as part of his standard procedure – flooding the snort induction mast with seawater to avoid it being over-pressured. The forward planesman put full rise on his hydroplanes which limited the down angle to about 25 degrees, but he could not counter the effect of the larger and more effective after planes.

Part of the 'Stop snorting' drill on *Sealion* was to empty two small external compensating tanks using high-pressure air to counter the additional weight of water incurred in flooding the snort mast. Unfortunately, the control systems watchkeeper did this with the tank emptying valves shut and the effect of the high-pressure air caused the reliefs on both tanks to lift with a very loud and explosive report. The reliefs vented through the pressure hull into the control room wing bilges and the pulse of high-pressure air from the port relief forced an alarming jet of bilgewater into the control room. In the darkness and confusion of noise, at first it appeared that an explosion had occurred and the pressure hull had been breached. Spray hit the electrical starter of a pump, causing a second violent blast and a flash. This was followed by a major electrical short-circuit which caused the loss of most of the control room instrument illumination.

The runaway *Sealion*, with a significant bow-down angle, was going deep at speed. Preoccupied by their fight to regain control of the submarine, the two planesmen had failed to shut off their large shallow-water depth gauges. These registered a maximum of 140ft, which *Sealion* had long since passed, and now their gauge glasses fractured and more seawater sprayed into the control room.

As *Sealion* left her safe depth and she entered the depth zone of the *Resolution* beneath her, Conley manned the underwater telephone and broadcast the alarming report: 'Going deep! Going deep! Out of control!' Apart from warning the SSBN of their descent, he was determined that if *Resolution* was within reception range she would be aware that the *Sealion* was in trouble. There was, however, no response from *Resolution*; the *Sealion* headed for the depths out of control and apparently flooding. Unless the dive angle and speed were reduced *Sealion* would reach her crush depth within two minutes. Amid the terror induced by this prospect, Conley had the curious thought that it was unfair that this was happening before, and not after, impending visits to Copenhagen, Oslo and Stockholm.

Amid the shouting and confusion the *Sealion*'s captain had appeared in the control room and ordered the motors to 'Full astern'. The drag of the reversed propellers gradually slowed the submarine and slowly she levelled out. Much to everyone's relief, she adopted a bow–up angle and she was again put into ahead propulsion. Unfortunately, *Sealion* continued to make stern-way and increase her depth. This was because the motor room watchkeepers were having difficulty responding to the ahead order, owing to problems on the main motor control. By torch Conley noted from one of the small deep-depth gauges that at 600ft they were way below the safe depth of 500ft.

In response to the rapidly worsening situation, the commanding officer now ordered 'Stand by to surface!' Conley was alarmed to hear the first lieutenant instinctively ordering the manipulating of the main ballast tank vents as part of the normal surfacing procedure. The *Sealion* was far from being in a normal situation and Conley was fearful that, having opened the vents, they would be prevented from then promptly shutting them, which was vital to enable high-pressure air being put into these tanks to gain positive buoyancy and reach the surface. However, his heart beating and anxious about the state of the vents – were they open or shut? – Conley heard the air rushing into the main ballast tanks. Eventually, after what seemed like a long moment of suspended animation, *Sealion* began gaining headway as she headed for the surface.

As she approached the surface, the torpedo officer was assigned the duty of surfacing officer of the watch. Unfortunately, in the absence of the large-scale shallow-water depth gauges, it was difficult to judge when the boat had breached the surface. In consequence, the upper hatch was ordered opened while *Sealion* was still ascending. Fighting to open a hatch still under pressure, the torpedo officer was deluged by a torrent of water as, a moment or two later, *Sealion* surfaced and he got the hatch open with water still in the conning tower. A few moments later the officers of *Sealion* not immediately occupied assembled in the wardroom and, most unusually at sea, each had a glass of Scotch.

It was afterwards discovered that the incident had been caused by the failure of the after planes indication system, a defect compounded by the fact that there was only a single indicator in the control room. A further shortcoming was the limitation of *Sealion*'s deep-depth gauges which registered a maximum 750ft, well short of the 900ft-plus crush depth of the submarine's hull. Moreover, the small-scale calibration of these gauges made it difficult to determine quickly whether the submarine was increasing or decreasing depth, a situation exacerbated by the emergency. If, like the *Affray*, the *Sealion* had been lost, it would have been very difficult to establish the cause, giving rise to numerous improbable conspiracy theories, such as *Sealion* having collided with a Soviet submarine spying on *Resolution*.

In fact, *Resolution* had not been in close proximity and failed to hear Conley's underwater telephone transmissions. As for *Sealion*, she carried out repairs on the surface and after a few hours dived and continued with the trial. There was no subsequent inquiry.

Some time afterwards, Conley learned that on the night that *Sealion* made her uncontrolled dive, his grandmother had a premonition that he had drowned at sea. The following day she sent a telegram to this effect to an aunt of his who lived in South Africa. Although the incident shook up the *Sealion*'s crew, there had been no panic. At the time, as a twenty-two-year-old bachelor, Conley himself was not personally worried by what had happened, considering it 'all part of the deal'. On reflection, however, he considered it a sufficiently exceptional incident which had come close to losing the submarine. HMS *Sealion* could easily have been the fifth Western submarine to be lost between 1968 and 1970.

The Scandinavian visits, over which Conley had inconsequentially agonised in his extreme moment, were to be *Sealion*'s swansong before paying off into refit at Rosyth. As he had anticipated, they were thoroughly enjoyable, with the crew extremely well looked after by very hospitable locals. For Conley, calling at Stockholm marked a professional high-point in his career thus far, because the mandatory embarkation of a local pilot was frustrated by a strike. Conley therefore personally undertook the long and tortuous pilotage through the skerries of the outer archipelago, a passage in excess of forty miles.

Undertaken in calm conditions, in brilliant, early morning sunshine and passing close to the immaculate lawns of cottages where Swedes were enjoying their breakfasts, it was one of those wonderfully memorable occasions when a salary appeared to be an unnecessary bonus. On arriving alongside in Stockholm, the crew were saddened to hear that the Swedish host submarine had suffered a battery explosion involving fatalities and therefore would not be partaking in the social programme arranged for them.

When *Sealion* arrived at Rosyth for a long refit in July 1969 her ship's company was dispersed. Conley was part of this exodus. By the time he left *Sealion* he had served in submarines for just over eighteen months. His experiences in *Odin* and *Sealion* had been sufficiently varied to encourage a feeling of being a seasoned campaigner and to recognize that he had found his métier in life. It was not without some excitement that he learned that his next appointment was to the eight-year-old *Oberon*, then completing her extensive modernisation at HM Dockyard, Portsmouth. Destined to be a unit of the Seventh Submarine Division, *Oberon* was under orders to proceed to Singapore and he would, at last, be exchanging the inclement weather of the Western Approaches for the tropical climes of the South China Sea.

6

Far East Interlude

LIEUTENANT CONLEY JOINED the diesel submarine *Oberon* in refit at Portsmouth Dockyard in the summer of 1969. Commissioned in 1961, the boat was undergoing an extensive two-year modernisation. This included improved accommodation and, crucially, a much better air-induction system for the engines which, together with a significantly more capable air-conditioning system, would improve equipment reliability and make life much more comfortable for the crew. Despite the Labour government's declaration of withdrawal of British forces from the Far East at the end of 1971, when her refit and work-up were completed *Oberon* was to be deployed to this region.

As work in Her Majesty's Dockyards moved with its usual sluggishness, the refit was suffering delays and the ship's officers were constantly engaged in dialogue with the dockyard authorities in order to instil somehow a sense of urgency in getting the work completed. The more time in dockyard hands, the less time the boat would be based in Singapore and, as this would be an accompanied deployment, where the families would join married crew members at government expense, there would be less time for the dependents to live there and enjoy the many benefits and pleasures of this foreign posting. Besides generous overseas pay and allowances, Singapore naval base had its attractions of being very family-friendly and offered excellent recreational facilities. Already the completion date had slipped by several months, and departure was now no longer scheduled for early 1970. The Americans might have put men on the moon but Portsmouth Dockyard was incapable of delivering ships and submarines from refit to schedule.

Conley was designated as sonar officer and 'third hand', the most senior seaman officer after the captain and first lieutenant. However, on joining he was disappointed to discover that, despite the costly modernisation, there had been no updating of the sonar suite which remained essentially 1950s technology. Indeed, its long-range sonar was much less capable than that fitted in *Sealion*.

Shortly after he joined, the commanding officer addressed the entire ship's company and announced the introduction of the 'military salary', which put armed forces pay on a comparable basis of remuneration to broadly similar civilian occupations. It meant a substantial pay rise for most. However, for Conley and his bachelor peers the best part of the deal was that in the future they would be paid the same as married men, and the archaic practice of paying marriage allowance would be ended. A few months later what was called a 'delicate text' signal was received, announcing the end of the 'tot'– the daily rum ration. The Royal Navy was moving on. Today it is inconceivable to consider that Polaris missile technicians would carry on their work on nuclear-tipped missiles after having consumed a large slug of alcohol at lunchtime.

Recommissioned in February 1970, *Oberon* headed north to the Clyde for two months of trials and work-up. Unlike *Sealion* she was immaculate in cleanliness and appearance and with an experienced and competent sixty-five-strong crew, all bode well for her forthcoming deployment.

The trials and work-up mostly progressed in a highly satisfactory manner, although the two stern tubes, which could only discharge the useless Mark 20 anti-submarine torpedoes, never achieved a successful proving firing. These two tubes were subsequently only used for stowage of beer and the two embarked stern warshot torpedoes were carried out to the Far East and back again, effectively performing no role other than ballast. The quietness of the 'O' class was emphatically demonstrated during static noise trials in Loch Fyne with the boat suspended in a dived condition between four buoys above acoustic sensors on the seabed: the trials had to be put on hold on several occasions whilst noisy ducks feeding on weed on the buoy wires, causing more noise than the submarine, were chased away.

The commanding officer, Lieutenant Commander Terry Woods, was very keen to ensure that his officers were competent to navigate close inshore in a covert manner without the use of radar. Consequently, during the work-up he made certain that they all experienced the pressure of night watches submerged in shallow water close to navigational hazards. At night, keeping constant watch on the periscope whilst snorting among merchantmen and fishing vessels was good training for the congested waters off Singapore and Malaya.

During a break in the work-up *Oberon* berthed in Campbeltown for two days. Conley was surprised to see his brother on the pier as they secured alongside. The latter explained he had just attended their grandmother's funeral and burial. This was the grandmother who, on the night of *Sealion's* depth excursion and near-catastrophic accident, had had the premonition that her grandson had drowned at sea. By extraordinary coincidence the old lady was being laid to rest with the submarine as a backdrop a mere half a mile away as it passed Campbeltown cemetery.

Oberon sailed for the Far East in June 1970. To enable the passage to be conducted at a reasonable speed, and to avoid undue strain on the engines, the majority of the 12,000-mile route via South Africa was completed on the surface and, as most of the boat's tracks were well away from the shipping lanes, the bridge watchkeepers spent many a night under brilliant starlit skies without seeing another vessel, with the only sounds the subdued rumble of the diesel engines and the noise of the sea breaking on the bows. In starting to plan the passage the commanding officer had aired the option of conducting the entire passage to the Far East dived and thereby achieving a first for a diesel submarine and breaking several endurance records (the nuclear British hunter-killer *Valiant* had completed an entirely submerged transit from Singapore to the United Kingdom in 1967 in twenty-seven days). However, he was soon dissuaded from such a wild notion. As apart from morale factors and the crew forgoing a number of very attractive port visits, the sixty-plus days of snorting with its much increased seawater pressure on the engines would put a real stress on them and other equipment.

Having called at Gibraltar, Las Palmas in the Canary Islands, and the lonely and isolated outpost of St Helena, *Oberon* docked at Simonstown naval base near Cape Town in mid July during a sleet squall – not quite the South African weather the crew had envisaged. However, they were soon immersed in the remarkable hospitality offered by the local population which had a great affinity for the Royal Navy. This affection had been cemented during both world wars when Simonstown had served as an important Royal Navy base.

The apartheid regime of Prime Minister Verwoerd's National Party had for several years been subject to embargo, and the denial of British arms equipment made it difficult for the South African Navy to source spares for their predominantly British-built ships. Indeed, an unwillingness on the part of the British government in the 1960s to supply the South African Navy with 'O'-class submarines had led them to purchase three French *Daphné*-class boats in lieu. All named after Afrikaner nurses who worked in British Boer War concentration camps, the first of these, the newly commissioned *Maria Van Riebeeck*, was in Simonstown when *Oberon* arrived.

70

Conley and some of his fellow officers were invited to look round this first South African submarine and were immediately struck by how less robust in design it was in comparison to their own boat. Comparatively small, with a less-safe snort induction system and non-enclosed battery tanks, they sensed the *Maria Van Riebeeck* officers, most of who were not experienced in submarines, were uneasy about operating their boats in the notoriously large and violent seas off the exposed South African coast, which has few sheltered harbours or safe anchorages. No doubt the loss a few months earlier of a second French boat of this class, with its entire crew, was fresh in their minds.

After a few days' maintenance *Oberon* was off to sea for anti-submarine exercises with the South African Navy. The opposition consisted of their Clyde-built frigates *President Pretorius* and *President Kruger*. Towards the end of the exercises, Conley was transferred by helicopter for two days' experience onboard the *Pretorius*. He found many ways in which the ambience in the ship was like the Royal Navy two decades earlier. Even the wardroom china bore the obsolescent Admiralty crest. However, manned by white conscripts doing their national service, these ships did not spend much time at sea, and Conley noted that these men were demonstrably nowhere near as professional as their British counterparts. This observation proved prescient, as several years later the *Kruger* was to sink with heavy loss of life after collision with the replenishment tanker *Tafelberg*.

Leaving Simonstown, *Oberon* headed north towards Mombasa, meeting up with the frigate HMS *Lincoln*, on her forlorn and futile station off the port of Beira in Mozambique. The Beira Patrol was a blockade intended to choke off oil supplies to the white supremacist regime of Prime Minister Ian Smith in Rhodesia which had repudiated its colonial status by a unilateral declaration of independence. Sanctioned by the United Nations, the blockade lasted from 1966 to 1975 and involved a total of seventy-six Royal Navy ships, but it proved very ineffectual as fuel was trucked through South Africa and other contiguous countries. As a result of the combined effects of guerrilla warfare led by Robert Mugabe and Joshua Nkomo, and international pressure, the Smith regime conceded to the introduction of universal franchise in 1980 and subsequently Mugabe's long and often violent and repressive tenure as president of Zimbabwe began. The Beira Patrol and the many years Royal Navy ships spent on this thankless and lonely task have long since been forgotten.

Oberon arrived in Singapore in September and secured alongside the ageing depot ship HMS *Forth*, sister ship of the *Maidstone*. As in a few months the *Forth* would be returning to the UK, Conley elected whilst in harbour to live in the wardroom of the shore base, HMS *Terror*, a very comfortable, airy, colonial-style building, cooled by overhead fans as opposed to air conditioning. Living in a non-air-conditioned building had the benefits of rapid acclimatisation to the heat and humidity of Singapore where it rained most days, with a tropical downpour occurring generally in the afternoon.

The Singapore naval base of 1970 was very different in character from that which Conley had left in 1965. Confrontation had ended later that same year when President Sukarno's power base collapsed and the Indonesian threat faded. Fewer warships were now supported by the dockyard which had been taken over by a civilian entity, Sembawang Shipyard. This company had quickly turned it into a thriving commercial ship repair and maintenance facility. Everywhere else it was evident that the Royal Navy was winding its presence down and in the process of shipping equipment and stores back to the United Kingdom.

Being populated predominantly by immigrants from China, Singapore had withdrawn from the Malaysian Federation owing to its increasingly 'Malaysia for the Malaysians' policy which favoured those of Malay origin. The latter had sparked riots in several of Malaya's major cities in 1969 leaving hundreds dead, most from the minority Chinese communities. However, in late 1970 the region was enjoying peace and prosperity, despite the Vietnam War raging with increasing intensity a few hundred miles to the north.

Life in Singapore for the crew of *Oberon* was a far cry from that experienced at home. What was known as 'tropical' routine was worked in harbour, the crews arriving for work at 0700 in the morning and those not on duty securing at 1230. As there was a shortage of naval married quarters, accompanied ship's company members were found rented housing locally. For reasons of economy, most of the ratings' families were housed in the Malaysian district of Johor Bahru, across the causeway which linked Singapore Island to the mainland. Although living in very reasonable houses and sometimes electing to employ domestic help, many of the young ratings' wives found their existence in Johor when their husbands were at sea a very lonely and boring one, with no TV and a lack of family or friends. For this reason, although *Oberon* experienced few disciplinary incidents during her time in Singapore, a host of family welfare problems occurred, many exacerbated by the tropical climate and refuge being sought in alcohol to counter homesickness.

For Conley and his fellow officers, apart from the many attractions of the

72

very cosmopolitan city of Singapore only a few miles away, there was an excellent officers' club on the base with swimming pool, golf course and other sports facilities. He and the boat's other bachelor officers invested in a second-hand ski boat and many afternoons were spent waterskiing on the flat calm waters which separated Singapore from mainland Malaysia, taking picnics onto the smaller islands or many pristine beaches. During weekends there were often trips with his peers and their families into the Malaysian jungle to an idyllic, secluded spot with a river pool suitable for swimming, fed by a very picturesque waterfall. For both officers and ratings it was a very different existence from that of the Clyde submarine base, Faslane, with its cool, wet climate and much more onerous demands upon crews, with longer periods spent at sea and fewer port visits. However, it was somewhat surreal and was, in effect, the end of an era and it would be a real shock to their systems when they returned to Scotland.

As there was no naval threat in the region nor Soviet presence, the boats of the Seventh Submarine Division (*Oberon*, *Finwhale* and *Orpheus*) were primarily tasked to provide anti-submarine training for the still substantial number of Royal Navy warships in the area. *Oberon*, acting in the role of Soviet submarine, was to take part in several major exercises involving very large numbers of American and allied warships. There was also a fair number of port visits 'showing the flag', each involving a very crowded cocktail party in the crammed confines of the wardroom and control room where conversation with people having a limited grasp of English was difficult. On one occasion the commanding officer hosted a black-tie candlelit dinner party for a dozen dignitaries in the torpedo compartment, a table being set out between the weapon racks in close proximity to thousands of pounds of high explosive.

Whilst on long surface passages, in calm seas the opportunity was taken to hold barbecues on the casing or to stop and broadcast 'Hands to bathe', keeping a sharp lookout for sharks. At night in flat-calm conditions, the folded-in fore planes provided an excellent means of securing a cinema screen, enabling the watching of movies under the stars.

On one occasion, on surface passage in very poor weather conditions in the East China Sea off the southwest coast of Japan, as the submarine dived in readiness for exercise with Japanese warships, the bridge OOW brought below a racing pigeon which he had found resting in an exhausted condition just above the upper conning tower hatch. With the sea racing up towards the hatch, it had made no resistance to being picked up and stuffed down the

OOW's foul-weather jacket. The bird was taken forward to the torpedo compartment, and having been dried off and given some food and water, made a very rapid recovery from its ordeal. Within a few hours it had made itself completely at home using the top of one of the torpedoes as a roost. On the final day of the exercise the submarine surfaced briefly to embark a party of Japanese admirals. On reaching the torpedo compartment the visitors pointed excitedly to the bird and very clearly thought it was an emergency communications system. Their guides having used sign language to signify it was a racing bird, their excitement gradually subsided on grasping that the Royal Navy Submarine Service did not embark messenger pigeons.

A day later *Oberon* arrived in the port of Shimonoseki situated on the southwestern region of Japan and the pigeon was released, quickly heading off on its interrupted journey. No doubt a Japanese pigeon racer received his bird safely back, albeit the best part of a week late and, of course, with no idea that it had spent several days under the sea in a British submarine.

Both the civic dignitaries and the naval community of Shimonoseki were outstandingly hospitable to the crew of the British submarine and arranged a host of activities. Perhaps the most memorable of those was a large reception in the city hall, which included a performance of traditional Japanese singing and dancing. On its completion the convivial hosts, fired by copious quantities of sake, demanded that their British guests perform on the stage. A number of very enthusiastically delivered verses of 'Old MacDonald had a Farm' had the Japanese audience reeling in fits of laughter.

Sometimes the exercises *Oberon* took part in involved the clandestine night landing of special forces. One of the most common techniques of doing so was to embark four Royal Marines with two canoes. Surfacing well to seaward of the designated landing spot, the craft and their occupants would be placed on the casing and the submarine would be submerged underneath them. A raised periscope would then pick up a rope rigged between the two craft and the submarine would tow them towards the shore to a suitable release point where they were let go by simply lowering the periscope. The reverse was achieved at a predetermined rendezvous point in darkness by each of the canoes lowering a simple but distinctive acoustic device which the submarine would home onto using its sonar. Steering between the bearings of the two devices would enable the rope between the canoes to be snagged by the raised periscope and the tow out to sea effected. Communication between canoes and submarine was achieved by the means of a simple code passed both ways by red torchlight through the periscope lens.

Conley had but to admire the Marines as they headed towards tricky landing spots such as mango swamps which harboured a variety of unpleasant and venomous creatures. In later years, some of the 'O' class were fitted with diver lockout chambers in the fin which enabled Marines to be landed without the need for the submarine to surface. This could be a dangerous operation and one trial involving the *Orpheus* killed two Marines. The exercise, held in Loch Long, went wrong when the submarine, entering less dense water, suddenly lost her trim and went deep. Her commander increased speed to regain control and the two Marines, having left their chamber loaded with kit, were swept off the casing and were unable to reach the surface.

In November 1970 Lieutenant Conley was informed by his captain that he was to be elevated to the position of first lieutenant, second in command. There had been an evident personality clash between the commanding officer and his 'number one' and the latter was to be moved to a shore job in the base. With only three years' experience in submarines, the twenty-four-year-old Conley knew that he would not have been his captain's first choice, but presumed there was no alternative at short notice. Difficult months were to follow as Conley bedded into his new responsibilities and headed up a wardroom consisting now of close friends. However, learning from his *Sealion* experience, he was not to be afraid of privately challenging his superior, whose judgement on occasions could be eccentric.

All too soon the deployment was over, and in September 1971 *Oberon* left Singapore and headed home on surface passage to join the Third Submarine Squadron in Faslane. On 31 October 1971 the Far East Fleet sailed from Singapore for the last time, ending a ninety-year connection with Sembawang. Most of the remaining barracks and shore buildings were transferred to the Australian army under a five-power agreement (Australia, New Zealand, the United Kingdom, Singapore and Malaysia) but with no permanent Royal Navy units in the region.

Meanwhile, on 1 July that same year the 'A'-class submarine *Artemis* had sunk while lying alongside a jetty at HMS *Dolphin*. Fortunately, no one was killed in the incident and the three ratings trapped onboard overnight escaped successfully from the torpedo compartment. The sinking was not due to material failure, but incompetence and slack practices on the part of key personnel, who failed to monitor the trim of the submarine during fuelling, allowing flooding to occur through an open hatch near the waterline. Indeed, this incident, where there had been a litany of professional failures, was a severe jolt to the Submarine Service that prided itself in its professionalism.

Clearly, it needed to shake off the somewhat cavalier ethos embedded in a number of its officers and senior ratings. *Artemis* had been in refit at Portsmouth Dockyard at the same time as *Oberon* and therefore its officers were well-known to the *Oberon* wardroom who, on hearing about the event the following day, were very relieved to hear that no one had been killed.

Oberon's return passage was largely uneventful, again spending some time in South Africa visiting the ports of Durban and East London, in addition to a period alongside for maintenance in Simonstown. In early December the submarine arrived in the Clyde submarine base before departing a few days later for Barrow-in-Furness where she was to undergo a two-month routine docking and repair period in the hands of the Vickers shipyard rather than in the Clyde submarine base as originally planned. This was not welcome news for those married members of the ship's company, whose wives, having moved from Singapore to Faslane in August, now faced further separation from their husbands

The rather grim Cumbrian industrial town of Barrow was a stark contrast to the bright, vibrant, modern Singapore and although it had the redeeming feature of being very close to the stunning countryside of the Lake District, many of *Oberon*'s crew found it difficult to adjust to the much longer harbour working hours, the routines of submarine life in northern climes and the loss of their generous overseas allowances. Most of the longer serving officers and ratings, having done their standard two-year time onboard, were being posted elsewhere, but their replacements were not always up to the mark in terms of either attitude or competence in comparison to their predecessors. In particular, the new officers were rather an indifferent lot. For Conley's part, despite having been onboard well over the two-year mark, he was required to remain in post for another six months for continuity reasons.

Conley and Woods had made a good team, despite the significant gap in age and seniority between them, and the latter had delegated well. At sea he trained his second in command in how to conduct visual attacks against aggressive warships and proved a good mentor. He had also allowed Conley on his own to move the submarine between berths in the dockyard, a challenging experience on his first time, manoeuvring in a narrow basin crowded with warships. A year into the job, Conley had matured and gained much experience, developing into a capable second in command, and possessing a superb knowledge of the submarine's systems. They were both strict disciplinarians who ran a taut and efficient submarine, where the crew knew exactly what was expected of them in terms of standards of behaviour and performance. Therefore, Conley was sorry to say farewell to Woods, and he was never to build nearly the same level of confidence or rapport with his new captain.

With no barrack accommodation available in Barrow, it was a major challenge to get the crew's accommodation arrangements sorted out in the run-up to Christmas, most being set up in lodgings run by landladies of a very kindly and hospitable disposition. Conley arranged accommodation for himself in a remote Lake District cottage, where several officers standing by the build of the SSN *Swiftsure* were already ensconced.

In 1971 the Vickers shipyard and engineering works was a vast, sprawling complex which employed over 13,000 people. Barrow and Vickers were almost synonymous, most of the town's 80,000 population either working for the company or having a close relative involved in it. The shipyard was a hive of activity with two 'O'-class boats being built for the Brazilian Navy in addition to *Swiftsure* and two sister submarines in various stages of construction. Besides submarines, the first of the Type 42 destroyers, HMS *Sheffield*, was being fitted out, and a small liner was on the stocks. However, in marked contrast to Singapore's Sembawang, the yard was very inefficient: trade demarcation remained rife, the layout and geographic spread of its facilities were not in the least conducive to good working practices and planning/project management procedures were weak. That said, the management and workers exuded a great deal of pride in their work, and were scornful of many aspects of the standard of work which had been undertaken during the Portsmouth Dockyard refit.

The early 1970s were a dark chapter in British industrial history, with high levels of strikes and stoppages and very poor management–worker relations. In January 1972 there occurred the first of a series of strikes by the National Union of Mineworkers (NUM) which severely interrupted fuel supplies to power stations. An unprepared Conservative government led by Edward Heath declared a state of emergency on 9 February, which led to factories and offices being restricted to a three-day working week. This did not help *Oberon*'s passage through the repair period, which had already had been significantly extended by unforeseen defects and the shipbuilder's inclination to complete the work to a costly, gleaming, new-build standard.

During the national state of emergency, frequent planned power cuts occurred which made life challenging for Conley and his peers in their cottage. However, their local inn, demonstrating both resilience and initiative, lit by candles and oil lamps, remained warm and hospitable and somehow managed to provide hot food. Not that food was an issue as lunch was provided in one of three directors'/senior managers' dining rooms in the yard, the three known as the 'gold, silver and bronze troughs', where even the lunchtime repast was consumed strictly accordingly to seniority.

Oberon eventually left Barrow in April 1972 and started work-up and post-repair trials in the west of Scotland. This was a period of great difficulty for those members of the crew who had enjoyed a halcyon existence in the Far East. Whilst satisfactory results were achieved in the work-up, owing to a number of inveterate troublemakers amongst the crew, morale was very fragile and there had been several disciplinary cases, aggravated by what could be regarded as weak leadership on the part of some of the officers. In particular, in disciplinary matters Conley found it very difficult to work with his new superior, whom he felt had a rather laissez-faire attitude to standards of crew behaviour. The situation was made worse by the boat's new coxswain, the senior rate vested with the responsibility for crew discipline, who was both mercurial and perhaps not as loyal to the officers as he might have been. The three individuals were not in the least a team, with strong tensions between them, which in the confines of the submarine must have been evident to the crew. All this was exacerbated by several of the new officers proving to be short of competence and this contributed yet further to the atmosphere of poor spirits and motivation within the tight spaces of the boat. With four SSBNs in commission in 1972, each with two crews, and thirty other submarines needing to be manned, the Royal Navy was finding it difficult to find good people when it came to crewing *Oberon*.

Events reached a nadir whilst the submarine was secured to a buoy in Loch Fyne, off the picturesque town of Inveraray. Several of the off-duty junior ratings, when ashore and enthused by copious quantities of alcohol, decided to attempt to acquire the Duke of Argyll's flag flying from the top of the highest tower in his lochside castle. Breaking a window at ground level to gain illegal entry, one individual severely lacerated his leg on the broken glass and was abandoned unconscious in the Duchess of Argyll's dressing room whilst his compatriots, giving up on stealing the flag, instead removed four ancient muskets from the walls of the grand hall. Further damage was perpetrated on their leaving the castle, when they attempted to remove a cannon from the balustrade surrounding the building, and this ended up in a damaged state in a ditch.

The following day, when undertaking noise trials in the loch, an urgent signal was received from the captain of the Third Squadron requiring a full investigation into events in the Duke of Argyll's castle the previous evening. The duke was a personal friend of the First Sea Lord, Admiral Sir Michael Pollock, and consequently a great degree of disquiet was voiced at several levels of the command chain about the above happenings. This was further exacerbated after a search of the submarine revealed the four stolen muskets which had been brought onboard undetected, owing to the absence on the casing of the duty officer when the liberty boat arrived back from Inveraray. The local police handed the case over for the Royal Navy to deal with and disciplinary proceedings swiftly followed onboard against the miscreants, all of whom received suspended sentences of detention, but *Oberon*'s name had been very much sullied at a high level. All this confirmed Conley's view that it would have been best to change the entire ship's company when the submarine returned from the Far East.

Work-up was followed by several weeks during which *Oberon* was designated the training boat for a class of prospective NATO submarine commanding officers. This commitment gave Conley further insight into the severe stresses and demands of the Perisher course, which in the case of the NATO students was intensified by their unfamiliarity with the boat's equipment and the necessity of conducting their attacks issuing rapid orders in their second language, English.

This period at sea was to be Conley's last in *Oberon* and he was extremely pleased to be relieved and to hand his responsibilities over to someone else. Owing to a poor relationship with his captain and his feeling of isolation from several of the new officers, his last six months in the boat had not been a happy period. Furthermore, *Oberon* was no longer the elite, smart, efficient boat it had been in the Far East. After leave and professional courses, Conley was destined to join his first nuclear submarine, the brand new first-of-class *Swiftsure*, which he had enviously eyed some months previously when in Barrow.

7

Submarine Activities in the Cold War

IN OCTOBER 1973 Lieutenant Dan Conley joined his first nuclear submarine, HMS *Swiftsure*. This vessel and her sisters were being constructed in response to the relentless build-up of the Soviet fleet and the increasing level of confrontation under the sea which had its beginnings at the start of the Cold War in the late 1940s.

After the Second World War the Soviet Union embarked upon a construction programme geared towards establishing a very large submarine force, which culminated in the 1970s with more than 350 boats. Potentially, the Russian submarine fleet had the capability to choke off lines of communication in the Atlantic and Pacific and to win at sea without pursuing an all-out war on land.

Consequently, a technological race started between the Western powers and the Soviet Union, where each had the respective aim of gaining and retaining superiority in this highly charged undersea confrontation. This, for the nations of the Western alliance, was crucial: if the alliance lost superiority at sea it would have lost the Cold War.

This arms race, besides incurring great expenditure of national treasure, cost the lives of several hundred submariners on both sides, as technology was pushed to the very edge of operational safety. Each side constantly jockeyed for position, both in equipment design and capability, and in operational performance at sea. In the end by the late 1980s, losing the extremely expensive technological challenge, the costs of this arms race contributed directly to the Soviet Union's collapse. Staring into the abyss of financial bankruptcy, it was impotent to prevent both the break-up of its eastern European empire into constituent republics and the demise of what had been its all-powerful Communist Party.

In the post-war development of their conventional submarines, the Western naval powers, chiefly the United States, Britain and France, built up forces of submarines designed to destroy other submarines. These would be part of the vast armada of ships, aircraft and helicopters ranged against the Soviet submarine threat at a time when the memories of the experiences of the crucial war against the German U-boat were still fresh in the minds of military planners. Submarines have the advantage of stealth and with it the ability to approach and attack an enemy submarine undetected. Also much less vulnerable than ships and aircraft, they can deploy forward to choke points in the enemy's backyard where maximum damage can be achieved. The new prime role for the West's submarines was also reinforced by the consideration that in the first two decades after the war the Soviet surface navy was not seen as a major threat.

The anti-submarine role required streamlining of hulls and removal of guns and other external fittings both to reduce radiated noise, making the boats more difficult to counter-detect, and to improve sonar performance. A number of Second World War submarines were also enlarged to be able to take greater sized and more powerful main motors. This programme in the USN was known as the Greater Underwater Propulsion Programme (GUPPY), which gave the boats a maximum submerged speed of 15 knots instead of the 8 to 10 knots previously. This increase in speed further improved their anti-submarine capability. The Royal Navy converted eight boats of the wartime 'T' class to GUPPY-equivalent performance.

In their urgent quest for higher speeds and performance – as from 1943 onwards their U-boats were losing the sea battle – Germany developed experimental boats propelled by a fuel which made its own oxygen. Several boats of the Type XXII class were built, propelled by engines fuelled with concentrated hydrogen peroxide (high test peroxide – HTP) which does not require air to combust, but the war ended before they could be deployed. Exploiting this German technology, in the late 1950s the Royal Navy built two 800-ton prototype submarines which were HTP-propelled. However, although the two boats built, *Excalibur* and *Explorer*, reached speeds of 26 knots dived, the HTP proved to be highly volatile. Many fires and minor explosions occurred, so much so that *Explorer* earned the nickname '*Exploder*'. Fortunately, this hazardous technology was overtaken and made redundant by the advent of nuclear power at sea; this would revolutionise submarine propulsion. However, it did not entirely eclipse the modern diesel submarine, which is still a very potent weapon in littoral waters and, of course, is much less costly to build and maintain than the nuclear version. Several classes of the West's modern diesel boats are fitted with air-independent propulsion (AIP) using fuel cell technology. This can give them several days' duration at slow to moderate speeds without the need to surface or snort. If the potential threat nations acquire similar technology for their submarines, these boats, being extremely quiet and having extended endurance with AIP, would present a very difficult threat to counter.

In parallel to exploring the use of HTP for propulsion, the Royal Navy also tested this type of fuel in torpedoes, but this dangerous experiment came to an abrupt and violent halt in 1955 when a HTP-powered torpedo exploded in the submarine *Sidon*. At the time of the incident she was alongside in Portland Harbour, a fact that probably mitigated the death toll, but thirteen of her crew were killed and she sank at her berth. In 2000 a similar explosion aboard the Russian submarine *Kursk* occurred whilst she was at sea; the *Kursk* was totally destroyed with the loss of her entire crew of 118.

In 1955 the world's first nuclear submarine, the USS *Nautilus* became operational. Despite its public image, nuclear power was to prove a much safer submarine propulsion. The *Nautilus* introduced a revolutionary change in submarine technology and capability. Fast, manoeuvrable, virtually unlimited in range and with no need to surface or snort, paradoxically, the nuclear submarine was to become particularly potent in the anti-submarine role, and was to be accorded very high priority in the West's defence expenditure.

The first Soviet nuclear submarines were commissioned in 1959, but their nuclear plants were much less safe than their American counterparts. The crews of the first classes experienced many accidents and were exposed to high levels of background radiation. In expanding their submarine fleet, the Soviet Navy developed a number of differing types, each with a distinct purpose, all of which had to be met and outclassed by the navies of the Western alliance. In particular, they built both nuclear and diesel submarines (abbreviated SSGNs and SSGs respectively) which mounted anti-ship missiles which had the specific role of destroying the West's strike carrier forces. The earlier versions of these types had to surface to fire their missiles and, accordingly, were very vulnerable to attack when preparing for weapon launch.

As their nuclear fleet expanded, there were numerous classes and designs with little heed to achieving the benefits of commonality and standardisation. The Soviets pursued quantity rather than quality and their first-generation boats were very noisy and crude in design. Furthermore, their missiles used very hazardous liquid fuel propellant, essentially German V2 missile technology, always risky in a submarine environment. Additionally, their crews were mainly conscripts, often of varied ethnic and language backgrounds and on the whole were poorly trained. In summary, the Soviet submarine fleet was afflicted by a range of serious shortcomings which militated against safe operation and consequently a number of boat losses and major accidents were to occur.

In 1959 the United States Navy commissioned their first SSBN, the USS *George Washington*. She was armed with the solid fuel Polaris ballistic missile and was followed by forty similar submarines. These were built with an average construction time of less than two years in comparison to the seven or eight years it now takes to build this type of submarine. The Polaris programme was a tremendous technical and engineering achievement involving large numbers of highly skilled technicians and craftsmen and numerous American companies, both large and small, which collectively contributed successfully to the monumental effort involved. Because the Polaris missiles had a maximum range of only 2,500 miles, the boats were based in ports which were relatively close to their patrol areas, with facilities being established in the Holy Loch (Scotland), Rota (Spain) and Guam in the Pacific.

The establishment of American nuclear missile sites in Turkey was to the Soviet psyche a close pressing of its borders, a threat it found intolerable and which it countered by the establishment of launching sites for nuclear-armed missiles in Cuba. In turn, this produced a reaction in America, precipitating the Cuban Missile Crisis of 1962. This unequivocal nuclear threat to continental America produced an equally uncompromising response from Washington. President John F Kennedy imposed a naval blockade of the island of Cuba, aimed at preventing the Soviets shipping in the missiles and other arms. During the weeks of escalation of tension, the world stood at the brink of nuclear war. The manifestation of their worst fears in the holocaust of Mutually Assured Destruction appeared to people across the globe to be very possible. Eventually, however, Nikita Krushchev and his Politburo backed down and ordered their ships to put about and head back from whence they had come. The missile sites already built were dismantled and the world breathed again. As a quid pro quo, the USA disestablished their Turkish missile sites. However, it had been a dreadful warning, and called from the Americans leadership and coolness almost unparalleled in human history.

During the weeks of uncertainty and in response to the American blockade of Cuba, lacking substantial surface warships which were capable of operating at a long distance from the homeland, and realising that their nuclear submarines were not reliable enough to deploy at such long distance, Moscow sent four Foxtrot-class diesel submarines into Cuban waters. Each of these was armed with two nuclear torpedoes which they were authorised to use if attacked by American forces. All four boats were detected by US anti-submarine units and to coerce them to reveal themselves and surface, practice depth charges were dropped onto them. These charges had only a small amount of explosive, but on detonating under the water they made a loud report. In the dreadful conditions onboard the Russian submarines, which were entirely unsuited to operating in tropical waters with temperatures nudging into the 50s, oxygen levels low, and the propeller and sonar sounds of numerous anti-submarine warships above them, such explosions were very unnerving. One of the Foxtrot commanders seriously considered firing a nuclear torpedo at the harassing forces, but was persuaded by his political officer (at the time all Russian submarines carried an officer appointed by the Communist Party) not to do so. Had the submarine captain destroyed an American warship using a nuclear weapon, the inevitable American retaliation might have led to total war. This was the nearest the two Cold War super-powers came to a nuclear exchange.

To the Soviets the crisis highlighted the limitations of their existing naval power and under the stewardship of the head of their navy, Admiral Sergey Gorshkov, they thereafter built a navy capable of global power projection, spearheaded by a force of nuclear submarines, which culminated in numbers and capability in the late 1980s.

In 1963 the Royal Navy commissioned HMS *Dreadnought*, the first British SSN. Although built at Vickers Barrow, in order to hasten its entry into service the hull design and entire propulsion plant were of American origin. This very beneficial transfer of technology had been negotiated by Lord Louis Mountbatten, who was First Sea Lord during the period 1955–59 and who had excellent relations with his American opposite, Admiral Arleigh Burke. The first nuclear submarine of British design was HMS *Valiant*, which entered service in 1966. Although also constructed and fitted out by Vickers, her powerful reactor was of American design but built in Britain.

Great Britain was to build up to a force of twenty nuclear submarines in the 1980s but, contentiously, at a cost to the remainder of the Royal Navy. In particular, there were limited resources available to expend on air defence for the Fleet, including its anti-aircraft missile systems and carrier-embarked fighter aircraft. This vulnerability was to be emphatically demonstrated in the Falklands War, when the fragility of the Royal Navy's air defences resulted in the loss of important ships, which severely prejudiced the conduct of the operation and very much threatened its successful outcome.

During the late 1950s it was evident that Britain's V-bomber nuclear strike force with its freefall bombs was becoming increasingly susceptible to destruction before reaching its targets. Accordingly, a much less vulnerable stand-off capability to deliver the nuclear warheads was sought and, after desultory efforts to develop a home-grown version were abandoned, the RAF put its hopes upon the American *Skybolt* air-to-ground missile programme. This was cancelled in 1962 and, unless an alternative to the V-bomber was urgently developed, the United Kingdom faced the prospect of an ineffective nuclear deterrent.

At a meeting between President Kennedy and Prime Minister MacMillan in Nassau in the Bahamas in October 1962, the former agreed that the United States would provide Britain with Polaris missiles and technology. Six years later the first British SSBN, HMS *Resolution*, the lead vessel in a class of four, deployed on patrol on time and on budget. In 1969 the V-bomber force was stood down from providing quick reaction alert to counter the threat of nuclear attack. Since that date there has been at least one British SSBN on patrol at sea, ready to fire its missiles at short notice. From the mid 1990s Trident submarines assumed the role of providing the United Kingdom's independent deterrent.

Meanwhile, in the 1960s the SSN, the nuclear attack submarine, had established itself as the West's premier means of countering the Soviet submarine threat. Stealthy and fitted with first-rate listening sonars, they were to have marked acoustic superiority over their Soviet opponents. A further big advantage to the West was the very highly classified seabed sound surveillance system (SOSUS), listening and tracking acoustic arrays established on the seabed in the deep water of strategic areas of the oceans. SOSUS exploited an acoustic phenomenon known as the deep sound channel. It was capable of detecting the presence of a potentially hostile submarine over immense distances, sometimes exceeding thousands of miles on early classes of Soviet nuclear submarines. Nevertheless, it had its weaknesses: it was not feasible to set up in shallower or more confined seas, such as the Mediterranean, and could have been easily destroyed or debilitated in war. Furthermore, it lacked the ability to acquire an accurate bearing and therefore made the exact positioning of a submarine impossible.

In consequence, the location of a SOSUS contact by anti-submarine forces could take a long time, sometimes without success.

When in the 1970s the West's SSNs were fitted with passive listening sonars towed astern on long arrays, British and American boats gained the ability to make long-range acoustic detections of Soviet submarines. At this time the counter-detection capability of Russian submarines was very limited, enabling NATO submarines to follow or, in the jargon, trail, Soviet boats for prolonged periods undetected, sometimes for weeks or even months. Trailing of Russian SSBNs was a priority because it both gathered intelligence on their mode of operations and conferred on the pursuing submarine the ability to destroy its quarry before it was able to launch a nuclear strike in the event of hostilities. Thus successful and persistent trailing offered a further advantage in this risky but essentially defensive counter to any Soviet aggression. But the boot was occasionally on the other foot: Soviet counter-detections did occur and a Russian commander could become aggressive, turning directly towards the following submarine and making use of speed and active sonar to harass the hunter – now turned prey.

For their own part, the Soviets explored different avenues of submarine technology. In the 1970s they introduced the Alfa-class SSN. Highly automated, with a small number of crew (about forty instead of the 120 typical in British or American nuclear submarines), the Alfa was far faster than its Western counterparts. With its high-power liquid metal cooled reactor it could do over 40 knots, whilst its titanium hull enabled it to go to more than twice the operating depth of the West's deepest diving submarines. However, the liquid metal cooled reactor incurred severe technical problems and there were costs for its performance in terms of safety and quietness. Furthermore, the titanium hulls were immensely costly and consequently this class of boat was not successful.

Of course, the Soviets did not sit on their hands regarding the West's superiority and what they could not develop themselves they sought through espionage. In the 1950s they established a spy ring, the ringleaders – Lonsdale, Houghton and Gee – at Britain's Portland Underwater Research Establishment acquiring access to very valuable sonar technology. Perhaps most damaging was the Walker/Whitworth spy ring operating in the United States from 1968 to 1985. These individuals, being communications specialists, were able to select and pass ultra-secret signal traffic to the Soviets, in the process revealing the extent of the West's huge acoustic and anti-submarine superiority. In response, the Russians undertook a noise-quieting programme in their newest classes of submarines as a matter of the highest priority. Later Russian submarine classes have consequently been much quieter and the West's marked acoustic advantage was eroded from the mid 1980s onwards.

From the late 1940s the United States Navy deployed submarines on intelligence-gathering operations in the seas off the main Soviet Union naval bases in the Barents Sea and in the Western Pacific in the Sea of Okhotsk and off Vladivostok. Submarines operating covertly in the midst of Soviet naval forces provided hard intelligence which could not be gained by satellite surveillance. Furthermore, unaware of the intelligence-gathering submarine's presence, the Soviets undertook weapon tests which otherwise they would not have carried out in the overt presence of a NATO warship or aircraft. Besides gathering information on Soviet weapons and tactics, an objective of these operations was to provide early warning of a military build-up which could be a precursor to hostilities.

A submarine has several intelligence-gathering techniques at its disposal using visual, electronic and acoustic equipment. The underwater hull survey is a particularly challenging procedure, whereby a submarine takes station right underneath a 'target' warship as she makes way through the water, positioned below her keel at a depth where the raised periscopes are about 15ft below the warship's hull. Moving along the length of the hull, very close visual observation is gained of its features including sonars, propellers and other underwater fittings. This technique can also be employed on ships at anchor, but the anchor cable is an obstruction which clearly has to be avoided. If attempting this on a surfaced submarine there is also the risk of it diving unexpectedly on top of the observing submarine.

During intelligence-gathering missions, some occurring at close range, it was inevitable that collisions happened, particularly between two submarines. These may have amounted to no more than a glancing blow, but severe damage was sometimes inflicted. Despite these high risks, no submarine has been lost in this way, nor is it believed that any fatalities have been incurred. Nevertheless, an unexpected underwater collision is a very alarming experience to those involved.

The Royal Navy started to participate with the United States Navy in the Barents Sea operations in the 1950s and in due course extended their intelligence-gathering to Soviet naval forces in the Baltic and Mediterranean. For diesel boats the long snort passage to the Barents had its own challenges. In the winter months their crews incurred the stress of prolonged periods at periscope depth, conducting surveillance in conditions of near permanent darkness and in often violent seas. The control room watchkeepers worked in a very dark environment, the only illumination being their faintly red-lit systems and equipment dials. To allow their eyes to adjust quickly to varying levels of lighting, off-watch officers endured living in constant red lighting in their wardroom for weeks on end.

Events which occurred during these operations, routine or otherwise, were and still remain very highly classified, tightly controlled and not discussed even within the submarine community. However, inevitable leaks of information occurred from time to time within naval circles, for example the presence of HMS *Sealion* off Nova Zemlya in the early 1960s to gather information upon Soviet nuclear bomb tests.

In 1968 a Royal Navy SSN was for the first time committed to Barents Sea operations. Unlike their American colleagues, the Royal Navy designated a single specially-equipped submarine for the task, rather than affording a number of submarines the experience. Fitted with specialist listening and observation devices, this practice allowed the nominated British submarine crew to build up expertise in intelligence-gathering in these Arctic waters while minimising the additional costs incurred in the equipment fit.

The first British SSN dispatched on this task was HMS *Warspite*. In October 1968 she was involved in a collision with a Soviet Echo-class missile submarine. The Russians subsequently reported that their submarine was operating normally when it suddenly began listing to starboard, its hull shaking. The boat was consequently rapidly surfaced, whereupon her commanding officer spotted another submarine's silhouette through his periscope. With the conning tower hatch jammed, the crew used a sledge-hammer to open it, and it was several minutes before the commander could climb to the bridge, by which time the stranger had disappeared. Back at base, Soviet repair crews discovered a hole in the Echo's outer casing, described as so large that 'a truck could easily have driven through it'. On the basis of identifying navigation light remnants and some metal fragments stuck in the wreckage, the Soviets concluded that they had been hit by a foreign submarine. Meanwhile, *Warspite* limped back to Faslane with a badly damaged fin and the cover story that she had hit an iceberg.

In due course *Warspite* was replaced by *Courageous* as the designated and specially-fitted submarine for operations in the Barents Sea. During one patrol, whilst gathering data on an anti-ship missile firing, the latter's specialist Russian linguists, who were tuned into the radio frequency of an attendant destroyer which had VIPs embarked, reported extreme alarm onboard the destroyer when in error the missile hit it instead of the target barge. After *Courageous* there has been at least one *Swiftsure-* or subsequently *Trafalgar-* class boat designated for Barents Sea intelligence-gathering operations.

Among the nations of the NATO alliance, this elaborate game of cat and mouse was not solely the preserve of the British and Americans. Norway, Germany, the Netherlands and Australia have also conducted submarine intelligence-gathering patrols, demonstrating their own considerable achievements with remarkable resilience and skill.

Apart from the gathering of very valuable and exclusive intelligence, the experience of patrol operations provided NATO nations' submarine crews with invaluable training, manifesting the West's will and ability to confront successfully Russian naval forces in war. Indeed, it is remarkable to consider the West's submarines were the only element of its military forces which during the Cold War operated undetected as close as five yards from the opposition.

By the 1970s the Soviet Navy was much larger, more capable and had truly global reach. Besides maintaining a substantial permanent naval force in the Mediterranean, with normally a large number of naval warships anchored off Libya, the Russians periodically deployed significant numbers of submarines into the Atlantic, demonstrably projecting their own sea power and potentially seeking out NATO SSBNs. Moscow also established a network of intelligence-gathering auxiliaries, known as AGIs, stationed off naval bases of interest. These invariably shadowed Western naval forces when they were undertaking major exercises. Almost permanent residence was taken up off Malin Head, the most northern point of Ireland, by one such auxiliary, its purpose to monitor American submarines proceeding to or from their depot ship in the Holy Loch, and British boats on passage to or from Faslane and the Clyde.

The Russians also embarked upon a very comprehensive oceanographic research programme, gathering extensive hydrographic and ocean features information, constructing and operating a large number of oceanographic research vessels to achieve this. Besides enhancing the ability of their own submarines and ships to exploit the environment to the best strategic and tactical advantage, the programme potentially offered methods of detecting the West's submarines other than by acoustics, including wake detection or disturbance of the sea's micro-organic structure. However, achieving successful detections using such methods remained elusive.

With the advent in the 1980s of the massive 26,000-ton Soviet Typhoon-class SSBN with its missiles of much greater range, the Soviets started to withdraw their ballistic missile submarines from the Atlantic to home waters into so-called bastions – specifically protected areas – or under the Arctic ice pack. On the West's part, with the introduction of the much longer range Trident missile, America began to close its forward SSBN bases, in 1992 ending their presence in the Holy Loch.

These changes marked a new period of Cold War submarine operations. An expensive stalemate seemed to guarantee the peace of the world as the pioneering days passed into memory. Nevertheless, these had been remarkable. In 1958 the USS *Nautilus* made a passage under the Arctic pack ice from east to west, leaving the Pacific and heading through the Bering Straits between Alaska and Russia and leaving from the ice in the Greenland Sea. She was the first submarine to do so and the following year USS *Skate* surfaced at the North Pole. Since then there have been many British and American submarine operations under the ice, including torpedo test firings, the latter demonstrating the SSN's capability to engage and destroy the enemy successfully in this environment. Equally, Russian submarines became adept in operating under the ice, including surfacing through the ice to conduct ballistic missile firings.

Most of the Arctic ice pack is about 8ft thick with pressure ridges going down to around 50ft and the thickest ice an SSN can penetrate is about 6ft. Particularly in the summer, there will be areas of open water known as polynyas, and as the areas of sea ice contract owing to climate change, the frequency of these is increasing. In winter, polynyas, having refrozen, with their thinner ice features offer the SSN a surfacing location should they need to do so.

However, operating under the ice does have its risks, with sometimes a margin of only 25ft between the ice cover above the submarine and the seabed below it. During early American submerged passages of the shallow Bering Straits, one submarine encountered ice all the way down to the seabed and found itself in a canyon with ice closing in on all sides. Her commander had to stop and, using the boat's ability to hover, reversed course whilst stationary, during which the crew hoped and prayed that they could then get out the way they came in. Under the ice any accident or technical failure, such as loss of propulsion or navigation systems, can have very dangerous conse-quences. A serious fire on board a submarine in this environment is a particular hazard, forcing the submarine to surface through the ice or in open water to clear out the smoke. Such a fire occurred under the Arctic pack ice aboard the British SSN HMS *Tireless* and two of her crew lost their lives in consequence. If a submarine becomes stuck under the ice owing to catastrophic loss of propulsion, even if she is able to communicate her plight and position, a swift rescue would be impossible. The assembly of assistance in such circumstances must inevitably be a race against time insofar as the boat's crew are concerned.

Throughout this period, both sides were pushing the bounds of technology and losses were inevitably going to occur. Accidents and fatalities are an increased risk in submarines and only add to the normal hazards of seafaring. Shortly before the Second World War the submarine HMS *Thetis* flooded during post-build sea trials and most of those on board were lost, and in 1950 HMS *Truculent* was involved in a collision with a merchant ship in the Thames Estuary. Most of the crew were killed when it sank. As related in an earlier chapter, the submarine *Affray* disappeared in the English Channel in 1951 with the loss of its entire crew. The wreck was subsequently located off Alderney, but the cause of the tragedy has never been established.

In August 1949 the first of the American intelligence-gathering operations in the Barents Sea ended with loss of life when the diesel boat USS *Cochino*, in very heavy seas and in company with her sister vessel the USS *Tusk*, suffered a battery explosion. The *Cochino* subsequently sank and seven crewmen died during the rescue operation by the *Tusk*. The incident emphasised the very unforgiving environment of the stormy North Norwegian and Barents Seas.

The United States Navy lost two SSNs and their entire crews in the 1960s – *Thresher* in 1963 and *Scorpion* in 1968. The USS *Thresher* had emerged from refit to undertake trials in the western Atlantic when she suffered a major flood in the engine room. A seawater pipe joint had fractured and the effects of the flooding caused the nuclear reactor to shut itself down automatically. With the main propulsion lost, owing to the weight of the flooding water, the boat slowly slid backwards into the abyss. Her ballast blowing system was not fit for purpose and after a short period of use its valves froze up, rendering useless the submarine's only means of reaching the surface. As the *Thresher* sank deeper and deeper, her hull compressed and the rate of descent increased. It must have been a terrifying death for the crew, watching their gauges register an accelerating increase in depth and unable to do anything to reverse it. The submarine imploded into very small pieces at a depth of over 2,000ft, where the hull was under more than one million tons of pressure. Although the wreck of *Scorpion* has been located in 9,000ft in the mid Atlantic, the cause of her loss remains uncertain, although, as related in an earlier chapter, a battery explosion may have resulted in the boat plunging below its collapse depth.

As stated previously, the Soviet submarine force was large and had many different classes of submarine, most of which embarked weapons that had dangerous features. Moreover, its crews were often poorly trained and their boat manning levels inadequate. Quoting one Soviet submarine captain who took his Northern Fleet-based Victor-class submarine to the Mediterranean, lamenting the incompetence of members of his crew: 'During the deployment the crew did their best to kill themselves and three achieved it.' In November 1970 the Russians lost a November-class SSN in the Bay of Biscay. This was the first of several of their nuclear submarines to sink, adding to the post-war loss of six diesel submarines.

As well as outright losses of Russian submarines, sometimes involving the death of the entire crew, many serious accidents occurred. Amongst the worst examples of a hazardous boat was the *K19*, a Hotel-class ballistic missile submarine. This boat featured in the film *K19: The Widowmaker* starring Harrison Ford, the theme of which focused upon a very serious reactor accident which killed several of her crew. Incidentally, one of its crew members, a cook named Vladimir Romanov, having made a significant amount of money on leaving the Soviet Navy, in due course became the owner of Scottish Premier Division football club, Heart of Midlothian.

Perhaps one of the most dramatic losses was that of SSBN *K219*, some six hundred miles northeast of Bermuda in 1986. Looking very similar to the American *George Washington* class, this type of submarine had been given the NATO code name Yankee. The *K219* suffered a missile explosion when the weapons officer allowed fuel leaking from one of the missiles to come into contact with seawater. The missile effectively ignited in its tube, blowing the hatch open, spilling out its nuclear warheads, and killing several of its crew. The submarine subsequently surfaced, but it was so badly damaged by the explosion that it sank a few days later in deep water, taking its remaining fifteen missiles and warheads with it. Two years after the *K219*'s sinking, the Russians dispatched a survey ship to investigate the wreck using a deep-dive mini-submarine. The *K219* was discovered sitting upright on the seabed, but it is rumoured that its missile hatches were open and the missiles and warheads gone.

Despite their ingenuity, the Russians lost the technological race of the Cold War, particularly in respect of submarine operations, almost bankrupting themselves in the process. With the break-up of the Soviet Union, their submarine-building programme all but halted and although in recent years the Russian Federation has again started constructing submarines and warships, its navy is a shadow of its former self. The old Soviet submarine force is now a big environmental hazard, with nuclear-contaminated submarine hulks dumped in many places, including the Kara Sea. At the time of writing, its force level is now just over fifty submarines, down from the 350 or so at the height of the Cold War. Nevertheless, very capable and potent vessels are coming off the stocks and there is no room for complacency in the West.

The Royal Navy also now has a much smaller submarine force consisting of four SSBNs and seven SSNs, compared to the thirty boats it had in 1989. This small force is still highly capable and the Tomahawk cruise missile has given British SSNs a new role of land attack in post-Cold War conflagrations such as Iraq, Kosovo and Libya. Meanwhile, the British government is committed to replacing the four current Trident-armed SSBNs as they come to the end of their lives in the 2020s. However, for a variety of reasons, construction costs are increasing almost exponentially.

On the American side, many submarine bases have been closed or downsized, and from its peak level in the 1980s of forty SSBNs and ninety SSNs, the United States Navy has contracted for fourteen *Ohio*-class and about fifty SSNs, including four *Ohio*-class boats converted to launch Tomahawk missiles. As in Britain, submarine construction and equipment costs have risen significantly and issues of affordability cast doubt whether even this force level will be sustainable in the future. SOSUS has been stood down as an operational system and is on a care and maintenance basis.

For the foreseeable future, the West's nuclear deterrent will primarily be vested in SSBNs. Meanwhile, its submarine forces continue to conduct operational patrols, monitoring and intelligence-gathering among the naval forces of potential threats, such as Iran and China, in addition to maintaining a watch on Russian activities.

8

First Nuclear Submarine

LATE OCTOBER 1973 saw Lieutenant Dan Conley as officer of the watch (OOW) on the bridge of HMS *Swiftsure* in the English Channel, heading out to a diving area in the deep water of the Southwest Approaches. Making a comfortable 15 knots, he could sense the power of the hunter-killer, nuclear-powered submarine's propulsion, with well over 20,000shp available, compared to the maximum of 4,000 that *Oberon*'s diesels could generate. The only sound was the gentle breaking of the deep trough of water formed either side of the boat as its rounded bows parted the calm sea. The hiss of the curling water seemed to Conley, in a reflective moment, to exemplify the quietness and stealth of this new class of SSN. He had joined the boat in Plymouth on completion of its post-build work-up and had taken over as sonar officer, responsible for the operation of the submarine's suite of new, advanced types of acoustic sensor.

Designed to take on second-generation nuclear submarines which were emerging in large numbers from Russian shipyards, the Victor, Charlie and Yankee classes, the 4,500-ton *Swiftsure* class was a step improvement upon the *Valiant*s, being faster, deeper-diving, quieter and more manoeuvrable. The class had a safe operating depth of well over 1,000ft and their hulls could sustain the almost two million tons of pressure which would be exerted on them at 2,000ft deep. Although limited to about 16 knots on the surface, under the sea where their propellers were more efficient they could almost double this.

Subsequent to the lessons learnt from the loss of the *Thresher*, *Swiftsure* was the first British submarine to be fitted with a separate, high-pressure main ballast tank emergency blow system which would be effective at deep depths. The amount of internal piping required to sustain sea pressures had also been reduced, significantly decreasing the risk of flooding owing to a pipe fracturing or a joint failing. She was also fitted with the world's first submarine computerised contact data-handling system, although it only had a very limited memory of 64 kilobytes, negligible by today's standards but state of the art at the time. This system principally used bearings obtained from passive sonar and was revolutionary in that it could automatically calculate target parameters of course, speed and range provided the input was accurate. The first of a class of six boats, in overall performance she more than matched the contemporary United States Navy's *Los Angeles*-class SSN. However, there were inevitably going to be initial teething problems in such a complex machine and, of course, the designers and constructors wanted to test it to the boundaries of its capabilities. This sometimes made for challenging times for the crew.

HMS *Swiftsure*, like all previous British nuclear submarines, was fitted with a power plant based upon the American S5W pressurised water reactor (PWR) design. The PWR works by heating highly pressurised water in the reactor core, then pumping it into two boilers to produce steam from a separate water system which is not subject to radiation. This steam is then piped out of the reactor compartment and used to drive the main turbines and electrical turbo-generators which provide power to the myriad of systems and equipment. As the PWR is self-regulating in its fundamental physical characteristics, it is inherently a very safe design, and American and British submarine and warship PWRs have undergone tens of millions of operating hours without major incident.

Should the reactor need to be shut down at sea, a battery-backed diesel generator provided electric power and an emergency propulsion motor was capable of propelling the boat at a modest 4 knots. The battery provided power until the diesel was started but, of course, it could only support the emergency propulsion for a limited time.

During contractor's sea trials *Swiftsure* more than met expectations regarding her performance, but on surfaced passage it was evident there was a need to flood the after of four main ballast tanks, increasing the depth of the stern to provide acceptable steerage and better bite for the propeller. *Swiftsure* was fitted with a very large skew-bladed propeller, but most subsequent Royal Naval nuclear submarines would have pump jet propulsors (a shrouded rotor arrangement) which are quieter and more efficient than conventional propellers. The stern ballasting measure effectively removed 25 per cent of the surfaced reserve of buoyancy; and this contributed to making the bridge, which was much lower in height than the *Valiant*s, very wet in heavy weather. In the early days of the class there were a few instances of large quantities of seawater coming down the conning tower into the control room. Unlike previous types of British submarine, the fore planes were retractable into the hull, and the initial practice was to have them extended when on the surface, with rise applied to help to get the stern deeper. *Swiftsure*'s rudder was to prove excessively large for manoeuvring underwater at speed, and later boats were fitted with smaller versions.

Compared to diesel submarines *Swiftsure*, like all nuclear boats, offered much greater crew comfort, including separate messing and sleeping arrangements. Her atmosphere was closely controlled, air purification equipment removing carbon dioxide and other noxious gases whilst maintaining oxygen levels at an acceptable level. As her distilling plants were capable of making plenty of water, there were no restrictions on the sensible use of showers and a laundry service was available.

Her sonars and sensor equipment used cutting-edge technology, so her operators were required to develop operating procedures to ensure these systems were used in an optimum, efficient manner. However, on the downside, her torpedo armament consisted of the obsolescent Mark 8 anti-ship and the ineffective Mark 23 anti-submarine weapons.

Being part of the Royal Navy's 'new' Submarine Service, most aspects of operating *Swiftsure* were undertaken in a much more professional manner than hitherto. There was an end of the old buccaneering way of doing things and – symptomatic of this – the era of 'pirate' rig at sea had ended and the culture of heavy drinking when alongside was over.

Once more Conley was under the wing of his old *Odin* mentor, Geoffrey Biggs, now a lieutenant commander, who had taken over as executive officer and was therefore *Swiftsure*'s second in command.

The first major series of *Swiftsure*'s first-of-class trials took place in early 1974 in the tropical environment of the Atlantic Underwater Test and Evaluation Centre (AUTEC) which has its shore facilities in the Bahamian island of Andros. Completed in 1966, AUTEC provides excellent three-dimensional tracking facilities of ships, aircraft and submarines. Its main tracking range is about twenty miles long and fifteen miles wide and, with Andros to the west and unnavigable reefs and shoals to the east and south, AUTEC benefits from unique deep-water acoustic conditions. This, and the absence of interference from passing shipping, make it an ideal place to test sonar and underwater weapons.

During the deployment *Swiftsure* used the modern, well-equipped Port Canaveral as a base, and after enduring a Scottish winter the crew naturally very much appreciated the sunshine of Florida and the motels of nearby Cocoa Beach where they lived when off-duty and in harbour. With the ending of the Apollo Moon landings in December 1972, activity at Cape Canaveral had markedly reduced, and Cocoa Beach, developed in the 1950s, was already looking tired. Its motels, which had sprung up in the heyday of the space race, looked distinctly rundown. However, for the crew there was plenty of nightlife, and a particular favourite of the officers was a restaurant which had been frequented by astronauts and consequently displayed a very large and unique collection of their autographed photographs.

Another revelation at Port Canaveral was specific to *Swiftsure* herself. The AUTEC trials had been preceded by a docking in her base in Faslane. Included in the work undertaken was the gluing of one thousand noise reduction tiles to a section of the outer pressure hull. This was the first attempt to fit acoustic baffling to a British SSN, but as the tiles were applied in Scottish winter conditions of wind and driving rain, it is was no surprise that on arrival in Port Canaveral only about half a dozen had survived the submerged passage across the Atlantic. A more serious worry was the SOSUS detection during the crossing of a strong, discrete noise emission, which was established to be coming from the main engine cooling water inlets on the after stabilisers situated either side of the hull forward of the propeller. Eventually, this noise problem was to be solved, but not before the complete failure of trial stabiliser fairings which fell off whilst manoeuvring at sea temporarily increasing the noise problem by exposing the cooling water inlet pipes.

During the AUTEC trials period numerous senior visitors were embarked for a day at sea to witness the handling and capability of Britain's latest SSN. All were very impressed, including those from the United States Navy. To establish its handling and noise characteristics, the boat was put through very demanding manoeuvres, whilst scientists and engineers, both onboard and ashore, made acoustic measurements and collected data. One noise measurement trial involved the submarine in a dived condition being positioned stationary in tidal conditions at very close proximity to a large acoustic array suspended from a buoy attached to the seabed. Already one American SSBN had wrapped itself around the array with startling consequences, getting entangled in a mass of wires and hydrophones.

The tests to determine the dynamic manoeuvring characteristics of the submarine were often very dramatic, and with the trials scientists trying to push the boundaries of the boat's safe operating envelope, severe angles were experienced in both the horizontal and vertical planes. The *pièce de résistance* of the manoeuvring trials was a full-power run at depth, whereupon the boat's massive rudder was put hard over at 30 knots. With the crew closed up in maximum readiness at diving stations, on applying the rudder the boat listed alarmingly forty degrees to port causing engineering mayhem, as both of the vital turbo-generators tripped out on low lubricating oil pressure, the subsequent loss of electric power causing the reactor to shut down dramatically and start progressing into the very safe, but drastic, emergency-cooling mode. Main propulsion was lost and the crew had quickly to engage the very limited emergency propulsion whilst control of the submarine was regained. If emergency cooling had initiated, it would have required the boat to be surfaced and the engineering staff to undertake complex procedures to restore the reactor to its normal operating mode. Fortunately, this situation was narrowly averted by the quick reaction of the engineers, and within an hour the reactor was restarted and main propulsion restored. During the event, Conley recalled, 'never seeing and hearing so many different alarms simultaneously registering in the control room'. No damage was caused, and in due course the lubricating oil system was to be made more robust, but the experience frayed a number of nerves.

This incident chiefly demonstrated that events can get rapidly out of control in a nuclear submarine at high speed, with its potential to increase depth at over 1,500ft per minute making safe depths of around 1,000ft look modest. Several years later, the crew of the *Valiant*-class SSN, HMS *Churchill*, coincidentally also conducting manoeuvres at AUTEC, briefly lost control of their boat. Before control was regained, her bows reached a depth of over 1,200ft, close to her theoretical pressure hull collapse limit.

The AUTEC trials were followed by an eastward passage across the Atlantic to conduct torpedo discharge system proving trials in sea areas in the proximity of Gibraltar. A critical and fundamental evaluation of the boat's ability to destroy the enemy, should this become necessary, the location was chosen for the availability of deep water and the reasonably benign sea conditions which facilitated recovery of the discharged torpedoes. Weapons were launched down to 1,000ft, an unprecedented depth for a British submarine. Here, over a hundred tons of sea pressure is exerted on the few square inches of torpedo-tube rear-door retaining clips, all that stood in the way of the pressure hull and the Atlantic. Fortunately few, if any, of the crew would have undertaken this calculation; some information is best not considered.

For much of the duration of these tests, *Swiftsure* had the company of a smart and apparently businesslike Russian Kashin-class missile destroyer, stationed to gather what intelligence her operators could about this new British nuclear submarine. Both vessels exchanged the occasional friendly message by light using the International Code of Signals and on proceeding on the surface back to Gibraltar on a Friday evening for a two-day break, the destroyer requested *Swiftsure* to 'please stay at sea and keep me company'. This little cameo struck Conley as an example of the contrast in lifestyles between the West and the Soviet bloc. There was no run ashore awaiting the Russian sailors and, even if they had managed to land in Gibraltar, they would have had no money to spend in its shops or bars. Instead, they were confined onboard, with neither good food nor quality movies available to alleviate the monotony, while the enticing lights of Gibraltar and its fleshpots twinkled on the horizon.

The torpedo discharge tests involved launching inert trials Tigerfish torpedoes with their rear-mounted guidance wire dispensers. The dispenser was a cylindrical container which held a reel of 5,000 yards of guidance wire, intended to allow the firing submarine movement after launch. The torpedo itself held another 15,000 yards of wire for its controlled run to target which could take up to twenty minutes. After leaving the torpedo tube, the dispenser disengaged from the weapon, but remained connected to the submarine by armoured cable. When Tigerfish started coming into service in 1976 this crude arrangement proved very unreliable, and a considerable time later was replaced by a more robust system.

After the torpedo was fired, the deployed dispenser restricted the submarine to a maximum speed of 6 knots and, normally, at the end of the torpedo's run would be cut loose. However, the wire dispensers used in these trials had special recording gear fitted and consequently had to be recovered. Slowly returning to periscope depth, in one of the world's busiest shipping lanes with a bow cap open and dragging a guidance wire dispenser, was a manoeuvre fraught with risk and engendering tense nerves. Conley recalled that on one occasion whilst he was on watch, the submarine reached periscope depth almost underneath a passing merchant ship, and collision was only narrowly averted. Once the boat had surfaced, divers were used to bring the dispensers onboard.

On completion of the evaluations in the Caribbean and Gibraltar, it was back to Scotland for more noise trials. These included a unique first-of-class noise ranging in a 'dead ship' condition, all machinery being shut down in stages to a state where absolutely nothing was running. The measurements were conducted over a period of several nights, with the boat in a neutrally buoyant, static condition suspended at 150ft depth between four buoys, one on each quarter, at a noise range situated in Loch Goil in Argyllshire. The reactor had to be shut down for several days prior to the trials, to ensure the decay heat in its core had reduced sufficiently to enable its vital cooling pumps to be stopped for a period. Thus a miserably slow tow by tug from Faslane to the range was incurred, with the submarine's diesel engine providing power for its basic machinery load. As the navigator was on leave, during this evolution Conley undertook the pilotage on the bridge and for several hours he was immersed in a cloud of diesel fumes from the exhaust mast at the rear of the fin, augmented by a spray of the mast's cooling sea water. To this was added a dash of relentless Scottish drizzle: balmy bridge watches when on the surface on the AUTEC range seemed a long time ago.

On the final night of the trials, the plan was to switch all machinery off and consequently only a bare minimum crew remained onboard the boat, which was in conditions of near darkness with only emergency lighting providing dim illumination. In the eerie silence, with the ventilation shut down, scientists and technicians scuttled around the various compartments, excitedly taking readings whilst shore monitors measured the external radiated noise. The commanding officer, Commander Tim Hale, and Conley were in the control room as the final pieces of running machinery, the hydraulic pumps which supplied pressure to the submarine's hydraulically operated systems, were switched off. As hydraulic pressure was a vital element of operating the submarine's many valves and control components, this was the last plant to be shut down. A minimum level of pressure was sustained for a while by a number of pneumatic accumulators, filled with high-pressure air, incorporated into the hydraulic pipework.

After the hydraulic pumps were switched off, complete silence followed for a few minutes, but soon all onboard became aware of an ominous gurgling sound which grew progressively louder. Staring through the gloom at the hydraulic oil header tanks at the rear of the control room, Conley became aware of great quantities of heavy, brown oil vapours spilling out. These rapidly engulfed the control room personnel to waist level. Before catastrophe struck, either through the crew being disabled by breathing the thick vapours, or (being highly inflammable) they ignited, the trials were hastily terminated and *Swiftsure* was immediately surfaced using emergency hand control to work the compressed air valves. Once on the surface, machinery was restarted and the boat was quickly ventilated to get rid of these exceedingly dangerous hydraulic vapours. As surfacing OOW Conley opened the upper conning tower hatch and arrived on the bridge to witness the sun rising over the loch's mountains on a glorious still, summer morning with an accompaniment of cheerful birdsong, a very vivid contrast to the Stygian gloom beneath his feet. Subsequent investigations revealed that on the hydraulic pressure reducing, some of the internal fittings of the accumulators had ruptured. This caused high-pressure air to course round the system, ending up in the header tanks to generate the vapour cloud. After this escapade, the commanding officer and some members of the crew were evidently becoming increasingly stressed by the demands of the trials, with their very unpredictable outcomes.

The summer of 1974 saw *Swiftsure* being deployed for the first time on operational patrol, setting up a sonar search barrier between the Orkney and Shetland Islands. Her quarry was the Russian Whiskey-class diesel submarine which regularly patrolled the seas to the west of the United Kingdom. This submarine normally deployed from the Baltic, and was tasked with the training of prospective submarine commanding officers in potentially hostile waters, sometimes conducting submerged passage between the Mull of Kintyre and Rathlin Island to enter the Irish Sea. Besides training submarine commanders to operate in the potential enemy's backyard, these boats attempted to monitor NATO warship and submarine traffic in the Northwest Approaches. Despite being about twenty years old, when running dived on main motors, the Whiskey was very difficult to detect using passive sonar – listening as opposed to transmitting an acoustic pulse. It was *Swiftsure*'s task to covertly detect and track a deploying Whiskey and to establish exactly where it patrolled and what it got up to.

Despite *Swiftsure* being Britain's most capable SSN and having the support of maritime patrol aircraft, the patrol was not a success. The specific target submarine was lost by monitoring forces as it dived on leaving the Skagerrak, north of Denmark, to commence its passage to its patrol area. However, the British SSN did achieve an entirely serendipitous short period of passive sonar contact at close quarters on the elusive Russian in the Orkney–Shetland gap. Unfortunately, the command team was unskilled in dealing with the short-range situation and this contact was soon lost. A few mornings later, the Whiskey-class boat was again detected, this time at about fifteen miles' range, snorting to the west of the Outer Hebrides. However, the commanding officer, who as executive officer of *Warspite* had experienced the collision with a Russian nuclear submarine referred to earlier, was not keen to get close to him. Consequently, when the Russian stopped snorting shortly after sunrise, contact was again lost and not regained, despite a subsequent active sonar search, which would have given the game away to the Whiskey crew that a British submarine was looking for them.

The patrol highlighted to Conley that even when an SSN was equipped with the most modern of sonars, it was difficult to detect a diesel submarine when she was battery-powered. Also, once contact had been achieved, there was an evident need to develop tactics to deal with this threat.

Post-patrol, for crew relaxation *Swiftsure* headed for a few days' visit to the port of Barry, situated a few miles to the west of Cardiff. In the 1970s this former coal-exporting port was one of a large number of smaller British ports in terminal decline, owing to changes in trade and industrial patterns, restrictive labour practices and the advent of container ships which required larger, deeper water facilities than those offered by many of the existing older tidal harbours. As activities in these ports ramped down, pilotage and tug provision also declined consequently, making the entry of *Swiftsure*, with her deep displacement draught and sluggish surface handling, into Barry a difficult one.

The first impression of the harbour with its redundant coaling wharves was one of dereliction, with only one other ship alongside, the regular Fyffes-owned specialist refrigerated cargo vessel unloading her cargo of bananas from the West Indies. The perception by some of the locals that nuclear submarines were hazardous was reinforced by the local Royal Navy liaison officer distributing potassium iodide tablets to the port employers, with the advice that their staff swallow these radioactive material blockers if a nuclear accident should occur onboard the visiting submarine. This, of course, was a complete nonsense, as in the highly unlikely event of a serious nuclear incident onboard, the harbour environs would have been evacuated long before there was the remotest risk of contaminants getting into the atmosphere. That said, the crew were soon immersed in very generous local hospitality, which compensated for them being billeted in the somewhat shabby Butlins holiday camp. This, however, proved unexpectedly to have some tangible benefits in the friendliness of the female staff. Shortly after *Swiftsure*'s visit, Barry was deemed unsuitable for berthing nuclear submarines, and today it is no longer an active commercial harbour

The commissioning captain was replaced as a matter of due course in the autumn of 1974. Very unusually for a seaman officer, earlier in Tim Hale's career and prior to joining *Dreadnought* in construction at Barrow, he had received nuclear propulsion training in the American submarine force.

Accordingly, he had an excellent technical knowledge of *Swiftsure*'s machinery and systems that proved very advantageous during the trials programme, while his successor, Commander Keith Pitt, was to prove both tactically aware and capable of improving further the crew's fighting efficiency which had been somewhat patchy. Moreover, *Swiftsure* had been designated to start undertaking the Barents Sea intelligence-gathering operations the following year and he needed to raise significantly the operational sharpness of the command team to meet the unique demands of this task. As part of the preamble to these patrols, a number of exercises were undertaken with other Royal Navy SSNs, where the skills of covertly following another submarine were honed.

As the crew efficiency improved, Conley recognised that the ship's company of *Swiftsure* was much more professional and better disciplined than the crews of which he had been a part in diesel boats. Indeed, it was evident that several key individuals had been hand-picked to bring this world-leading nuclear submarine into operational service. Meanwhile, the boat had changed her operational base from Faslane to the Second Submarine Squadron in Devonport. During an extended docking period there in late 1974, there being no shore accommodation available in the base wardroom, Conley and several of his officer colleagues rented a farmhouse in the Devon village of Cornwood on the edge of Dartmoor. Life in the farmhouse and Devon countryside was very far removed from the stresses and strains of nuclear submarining and, over the three months of their tenancy, several lifetime friendships were cemented.

February 1975 again found Conley officer of the watch on the bridge at night, this time in extreme Storm Force 10 conditions. HMS *Swiftsure* was making a surface passage down the Minches between the Inner and Outer Hebrides towards a dived rendezvous with the SSN HMS *Conqueror* in the Northwest Approaches. Constrained to the surface until reaching sea areas where the submarine was cleared to dive, the commanding officer was concerned about making the rendezvous on time and was keen to press on, notwithstanding the heavy seas battering the boat and periodically covering the two bridge personnel, Conley and his lookout, in spray. Unlike ships, submarines tend to go through waves rather than ride over them, and on the bridge Conley and his assistant were frequently deluged by the occasional solid crest of a wave.

Having rounded Barra Head and left the lee of the Outer Hebrides to head southwest, the size of the waves increased. In the darkness and fury of the storm, Conley saw ahead an exceptionally large cresting wave and just had time to yell to the lookout to duck. There followed a heavy blow to the upper part of his body and several seemingly interminable seconds of darkness as the wave engulfed him. Undoubtedly, he and the lookout would have been swept overboard had it not been for their safety harnesses. As the effects of the wave passed, a gasping Lieutenant Conley and his lookout were left reeling and choking, with water up to their armpits. The bridge lifebuoy had been knocked over and its light activated under the receding water in the bridge well and in his now illuminated surroundings, cold and very wet, Conley mused upon the strange way he had chosen to make a living. The watchkeepers in the control room reported that their depth gauges had momentarily read 80ft as the wave passed over *Swiftsure* which, even allowing for the instruments' dial fluctuation and the 60ft between keel and bridge, meant that for a few moments there was at least a dozen or so feet of solid water above the heads of those on the bridge.

Reporting to the captain that either the submarine be drastically slowed down or the bridge watchkeepers risked being drowned, Conley and his lookout were brought below and the bridge was shut down. Having changed into dry clothes, Conley found maintaining watch below, with visual lookout on the powerful periscopes fitted with image intensification, was both much more comfortable and safer, a world away from the exposure of the bridge. However, it engendered a false sense of security, and soon the captain increased speed, although the boat was taking a real pounding.

Swiftsure had yet another surprise awaiting her crew. On diving a few hours later it soon became apparent that all was not well. All the signs were that the boat was massively heavy forward and it was proving very difficult to control her depth. After an hour of trying unsuccessfully to gain a reasonable buoyancy trim, concerned that *Swiftsure* was already late for her rendezvous with HMS *Conqueror*, the commanding officer ordered the boat deep and fast, directing the trimming officer to continue to sort out the apparent excess of ballast water which was being carried forward. A very significant quantity of forward ballast was removed, but a few hours later, on being slowed down to check the state of the trim, the boat rapidly headed out of control to the surface with a steep bow-up angle. Speed was applied just in time to avoid broaching the surface in the storm which was still raging. A hastily gathered investigation team soon reached the conclusion that whilst the fore planes' angle indicators were displaying 'normal' operating, the planes had been bent on their drive shaft by the exceptionally heavy seas to the full dive position.

An immediate return to harbour and docking confirmed this to be the case and thereafter the *Swiftsure* class kept their fore planes retracted whilst making passage on the surface in heavy weather.

In March 1975 Dan Conley married his long-time sweetheart Linda, a communications officer in the Women's Royal Naval Service (WRNS). For Linda, it was to mean giving up her successful career to be with her new husband, along with a future of frequent family moves which typify Service life. Their honeymoon was even put in jeopardy owing to the unplanned docking to fix the fore planes problem, but at the last minute it was agreed that a temporary relief would join, allowing their wedding arrangements to stand.

As the responsible officer for the sonar outfit, during the evaluations of these systems Conley started building up a substantial level of knowledge of the operation of sonars and of 'the acoustic environment'. However, at the age of twenty-eight he had been selected to undertake the submarine commanding officers' Perisher course, and consequently had to accept that he would not be present for *Swiftsure*'s first Barents Sea operation planned for later that year.

Conley's last period of sea-service in *Swiftsure* involved major sonar trials in deep water off the Canary Islands with a consort ship and submarine. Much to his dismay, once the trials had started, his departmental chief petty officer reported to him that, in error, inadequate stocks had been embarked of the photographic chemicals required to operate the main active sonar display. Normally, this would have not been an issue as active sonar was not often used, but on this occasion a key element of the trials was testing this mode of operation and display. Whilst pondering upon the best time to break the bad news to his captain, the Russian navy came to Conley's rescue. Intelligence reports indicated that a large Russian naval force had deployed into the eastern Atlantic and consequently being a far higher operational priority, the trials were terminated forthwith and *Swiftsure* was dispatched to shadow the Soviet force. The latter was successfully detected, but because of *Swiftsure*'s after stabiliser noise problem, which remained unsolved, Pitt was reluctant to get in close and very little intelligence-gathering or crew training were forthcoming. Having been spared the ire of his captain by the fortuitous Russian intervention, on return to harbour Conley handed over to his successor and bade farewell to the *Swiftsure* wardroom and his sonar team.

Conley had learnt a great deal during his twenty months onboard *Swiftsure*. He had developed an excellent knowledge of his first nuclear submarine's many complex systems. Moreover, the nerve-wracking engineering events and ship control problems he had experienced were to give him the ability later in his career to handle confidently and adeptly the nuclear submarines he would in due course command. For him it had been a very exciting appointment where he had enjoyed immense job satisfaction. However, the major career hurdle of passing the much apprehended 'Perisher' was now his immediate goal.

9

Perisher

In June 1975 twenty-eight-year-old Lieutenant Dan Conley reported to HMS *Dolphin* at Portsmouth to start the five-month submarine commanding officer's qualifying course, familiarly known as the 'Perisher'. He was only too well aware that if he 'perished', it was not only the end of his submarine career, but that his future elsewhere in the Royal Navy would be pretty bleak, with limited prospects of promotion. With no second chance or option of retake, it was make or break and he was determined to pass.

Originating in 1917, the Perisher course was a prerequisite for the command of one of Her Majesty's submarines. In Conley's time its training focused upon teaching its candidates to conduct a periscope attack upon surface ships, both men-of-war and merchantmen, and there had been only modest changes during the fifty-eight years of the course's existence. Indeed, the anti-ship, straight-running Mark 8 torpedoes available in 1975 had not changed much in the intervening period either. Conley joined eleven other prospective commanding officers, four of whom came from the allied NATO nations of Norway, the Netherlands and Denmark.

The course was split into two sections each allocated an instructor known as 'Teacher', and Conley's group of four British officers, a Dane and a Norwegian, was supervised by Commander Rob Forsyth, whom he had previously encountered seven years earlier during his trying times in *Sealion*. Forsyth combined great energy and dynamism with copious encouragement and consideration towards his charges.

Following several weeks of induction and training in an attack simulator, Conley's Perisher course was structured around two sea phases: five weeks of periscope training in the Clyde, followed by two weeks of operational exercises in both the deep ocean and inshore areas.

During the periscope training each of the students would take turns at being the duty commander for one target run, while his colleagues would fulfil the supporting roles of the command team. During this training phase the Teacher enjoyed the exclusive use of the after and more powerful binocular search periscope and combined the tasks of overall supervision of the submarine's movements and the all-important monitoring of his charges and submarine safety. The boat was, however, fully manned by her own captain and crew.

The trainees were confined to the smaller monocular attack periscope, the top few feet of which was barely three inches in diameter. The periscope training phase began with visual attacks being made on a single surface warship, usually a frigate, gradually working up in the final week to the penetration of a defensive screen of four escorting warships manoeuvring at maximum speed, in order to attack their charge, a fleet tanker.

In its simplest form a visual attack involves the submarine commander taking a set of periscope target range and aspect (angle on the bow) observations as he tracks his quarry. From this information he is expected to manoeuvre his submarine into a position from which to fire a torpedo. To achieve a successful attack using the then standard Mark 8 weapon, the submarine would ideally achieve the very close range of about 1,500 yards on the target's beam. Because the Mark 8 was a straight-running torpedo, it required an offset to be calculated which allowed for the target's movement during the torpedo's running time; this was known as the deflection angle. An instrument known as the torpedo calculator would produce this, and the command team would plot the target and work out its parameters of range, speed and course in support of the commanding officer's periscope estimations. To compensate for errors in the calculation of target parameters these torpedoes were normally fired in a spread of salvos of three or four weapons. In the era prior to the 1990s, when the Royal Navy introduced periscope television and digital imaging which allowed the control room team to view the surface picture, the commander would be the only individual who viewed the target through his periscope. The success or failure of such an attack was therefore the commander's sole responsibility – and if he failed and the target counter-attacked, the survival of his own submarine and her company were jeopardised.

In extremis, a competent commander could, without the aid of his team or instruments, undertake the mental calculations necessary to work out the target parameters, including the correct deflection angle, and then manoeuvre his boat into a firing position. Developing such mental agility was a core part of the Perisher training and demanded strong qualities of coolness and measured deliberation in situations of pressure.

In the vast majority of combat situations, the visual attack involves a number of factors which markedly increase its complexity and difficulty. The most obvious is in order to limit the chances of one's periscope being betrayed by a feather of wake, thereby inviting counter-attack, the exposure of the periscope must be limited to a few seconds for each viewing, keeping its elevation above the sea surface as low as possible. This, of course, risks even small waves blurring or obscuring the target image. Furthermore, to reduce the amount of wake the speed of the attacking submarine has to be kept low, ideally 4 or 5 knots. While the human eye has a field of horizontal view of over 180 degrees and a lookout may be alerted by that telltale periscope wake out of the corner of his vision, the horizontal view through a submarine periscope is very much smaller, normally less than 40 degrees. This constrained view requires the skill of rapid target location and, particularly where several hostile vessels are on the surface, of retaining a mental picture of where all enemy units are and what they are doing. Further difficulty and pressure are added if the target is protected by a screen of manoeuvring warships determined to hunt and destroy an attacking submarine before she can launch her torpedoes. Even in peacetime conditions, the unexpected close-range sighting of a destroyer's angry bows heading straight towards one at high speed drastically raises the adrenalin of the observer at the periscope.

With each student required to fire at least one salvo of four Mark 8 practice torpedoes, additional factors added to the trainee's woes because this element of the Perisher training took place in the Clyde Estuary. The necessity of ensuring a clear range before firing the weapons and then locating them when they had surfaced on completion of their 5,000 yards of run was complicated by the presence of merchant ships, leisure craft and the potential danger of fishing boats using trawls. Risk of collision with one of these was an ever-present hazard which had to be contended with.

A key part of the course was to train the prospective commanding officer to 'go deep', diving at the last possible moment to avoid collision with a counter-attacking escorting warship. This had to be done at a maximum range of 1,200 yards, or one minute of run at the combined speeds of a 30-knot warship and the submarine – and to add verisimilitude to actual warfare, the escorting warships were often instructed to try and ram any visible periscope. All this was intended to place the students under a degree of pressure as near as possible to the real thing.

Urgently going deep from periscope depth involved the submarine speeding up and applying a down angle by hydroplane, whilst filling a forward quick-flooding ballast tank – Q-tank – which held four tons of water. This enabled the boat within one minute to reach a depth of 90ft, allowing a margin of 25ft between the top of its fin and the escort's hull or propellers. If the student had got his calculations wrong, or had missed a threatening escort, the Teacher intervened and ordered the boat deep, earning the errant student a black mark. Conversely, if an over-cautious student went deep too early, this too would count against him. The trainees were taught to hold their nerve and, in reality, there was a small margin of safety because the submarine could reach 90ft in 50 seconds.

Determined as he was not to fail, Conley prepared himself for the task ahead, honing his developing skill at assessing the target aspect by using model ships mounted on a board. He also undertook a number of daily mental exercises to ensure that he was adept at calculating target parameters, periscope sighting intervals and torpedo settings. Early in the course, at the end of the initial shore-training phase, the students were granted their summer leave. During this break Conley and his wife enjoyed a week touring France by car. For an hour or so each day as he drove, Linda, equipped with a submarine attack calculation slide-rule, fired mental arithmetic calculations at him. As a convincing benchmark of his prowess Conley found himself confident that his mental agility was up to the mark after he had successfully answered a volley of questions at the same time as negotiating evening rush-hour traffic in the centre of Paris.

Thus mentally sharpened, Conley and his five course colleagues joined HMS *Finwhale* at Faslane in late August to start their periscope training. Meanwhile, the other half of the course had embarked in HMS *Narwhal*. The two boats operated on a daily running routine, returning in the evening to a buoy mooring in the Clyde port of Rothesay where the course staff and students would disembark to stay overnight in a small hotel.

Each day, when the submarines arrived in their respective diving areas to the east of the Isle of Arran, the surface warships would commence a series of north–south orientated runs in specific formations which were geared to train the students in different facets of the visual attack. Once the attack runs commenced, the Teacher would assume command of the submarine from the boat's commanding officer, although in theory the submarine remained the latter's ultimate responsibility. The last run completed for the day, the command would revert to the submarine's captain

One particular type of run involved each of the students going deep, ducking their 2,000-ton submarine under an approaching escort at the prescribed 1,200 yards 'go deep' range, then, once the warship had passed overhead, rapidly returning to periscope depth. Having checked the escort was still going away, the students concentrated on the prime target – most likely an escorted tanker – and re-established the overall tactical picture. This was a fraught exercise, completed in just over two minutes against the cacophony of sonar reports, propeller noises of both the passing warship and the submarine speeding up, periscopes being lowered and Q-tank being flooded and then blown empty. In the confines and noise of the cramped control room, the attack runs were highly stressful with the vibration and noise of fast-revolving propellers passing directly overhead reminding all on board of the very real risk of collision. The periodic practice torpedo firings added further complexity, with the student having to deal with internal weapon-readiness reports and tube launch preparations, and external pressure ensuring the range was clear and that no innocent vessel, such as the routine Ardrossan to Brodick ferry, became part of the action. Finally, there was the physical exertion of operating the periscope, crouching down to meet the eyepiece as it emerged from the deck, lowering the handles and then, once the top of the periscope broke the surface, rapidly swinging it onto the predicted bearing of the point of interest – the target. This was followed by determining the target's range and bearing and then snapping up the periscope handles and ordering it smartly lowered.

Mistakes made by the students were usually very evident to the boat's crew, who normally did their best to support the trainees. Nevertheless, there was an ongoing unofficial assessment by the more senior of them of the trainee's fortitude, character and leadership qualities. This boiled down to two essential questions: did his performance inspire confidence and if so, would they trust him sufficiently to have him as their captain? It would also become very apparent to Teacher if an individual was not getting the wholehearted support of the crew through bullying or abrasive behaviour.

The periscope course ran from Monday to Friday with weekends spent in Faslane. Here the students could relax and recharge their own personal batteries. During the week the daily routine would consist of leaving the hotel by bus at 0630, then a boat transfer out to the awaiting submarines, which had already slipped their moorings. The day's first duty student commander would then take the boat to sea and dive it under the supervision of the submarine's commanding officer.

Once underwater at around 0830, the attacks would start at intervals of approximately forty-five minutes. They would be relentless throughout the day, stressing not only the students – whether they were in the command role or the supporting team – but also the submarine's own commanding officer, and in particular his ship's company. The crew's responses to successive trainees, whose novice capabilities were all too obvious, demanded qualities of nerve beyond the normal. Needless to say, both their ship control and depth-keeping had to be exact within the tight margins of safety. Perhaps the most stressful job was that of the Teacher. To say that he monitored the students and intervened to prevent disaster when miscalculations occurred is an over-simplification, for within that process lay the crucial element of assessment. In order for the Teacher to carry out properly this essential element of the process on each individual student, a degree of leeway had to be allowed. The Teacher's intervention did not necessarily occur at the moment a student had made a mistake. Intervention had to be delayed until the precise moment when the student had demonstrated that he had missed the 'go deep' point, and the submarine had to be rapidly taken deep for safety reasons. All the time the Teacher was seeking evidence that a student – having made an error – could quickly recover the situation, which was invaluable in terms of assessing that individual's potential as a submarine captain.

Throughout, the Teacher, at the top of his game and continuously on his mettle, had to maintain the safety of the submarine, a particularly onerous task in the multi-ship high-speed target runs. He would be relieved for a short break at lunchtime by the boat's own captain, but otherwise his pace was extremely intensive until the last evolution was completed early in the evening. Once an attack was over the student commander would collect up his records and receive a debriefing in the semi-privacy of the captain's cabin. Conley's experience under Forsyth showed that he did not over-labour mistakes, such as the missed look on a threatening warship or mental arithmetic which had gone awry, most of which the student would be aware of anyway, but concentrated on advising how improvements could be made – a subtle and effective way of encouraging greater effort without undermining self-confidence.

In undergoing this protracted ordeal, Conley felt nervous and on edge before he assumed the command role, but once he had initiated the attack run, his apprehensions would melt away, replaced by a focus and aggression as he took control of the submarine and bent her to his will. 'It was all rather like an actor with stage-fright,' he reminisced self-deprecatingly. 'Once on stage one simply got on with the business in hand.'

For Conley and his peers, Perisher was the most intense and demanding chapter of their naval careers, requiring stamina and resilience, particularly when things went wrong. As he stood down from each exercise, no matter how it had gone, Conley's inner and unarticulated sense of feeling that he was fitted for this demanding task was profound.

The day's work over, the tension eased and the evening meal would be eaten in the submarine's tiny wardroom on her surface passage back to Rothesay. Finally, having returned to the hotel, both groups of students and the two Teachers would gather for a couple of hours in the bar, where they convivially mixed with the local regulars. Drinking was moderate and there was no implicit requirement for a student to join the gathering, but the Teacher would have thought it odd if a student had sought the solace of his own room.

Despite the intensity of the course there were periods of humour. A petty officer steward was assigned to each Teacher to assist with the course administration and help the boat's staff contend with the extra wardroom meals requirement. The two ratings were billeted in a separate hotel in Rothesay, and one morning they failed to make the bus as it left the officer's hotel. Just as the transfer boat was about to cast off and head out to the submarines, a council rubbish collection truck roared down the pier at high speed and as it screeched to a halt, the two petty officers leapt from its rear loading platform, shouting their thanks to the driver. The two Teachers appreciated the levity of the situation and there were no recriminations upon their assistants for oversleeping and missing the bus. For the watching students coping with their own apprehensions for the coming day's work, the episode was a welcome diversion.

As the course progressed, it revealed those who were struggling with their ability to handle a number of simultaneous periscope contacts, make the right calculations and the consequent decisions in manoeuvring the submarine. They began to lose confidence and became over-anxious, especially when next on to do an attack. Unless confidence was rebuilt by the Teacher through a series of specially structured runs, a descending spiral in self-belief and lack of awareness of what was going on around them in the control room could precipitate failure. Conley recalled his Teacher sorting out one student who was finding 'ducking under the escort' difficult. He set up four warships, 3,000 yards apart in line ahead, and coming straight towards the submarine at high speed. The student concerned was compelled to duck under each in succession, after which exhilarating make-or-break challenge, the evolution of 'ducking under and up' presented the individual concerned with little problem. While such a special, tailored exercise could steel a trainee and make him rise to the occasion, it was not always the case. A few students lost their nerve and it became evident that, no matter what tuition and encouragement they received, they would never make submarine commanding officers. But that was the purpose of the Perisher.

One of the rather bizarre traditions of the Perisher was the method of dealing with the student who failed. At the conclusion of yet another botched attack run, the Teacher – having over the duration of the course carefully assessed and concluded that the student concerned would never make the grade – would order the submarine to the surface. After a private, compassionate and very considered debrief, the failed student would be transferred to a fast launch and forthwith landed at Faslane. It was the Teacher's assisting petty officer steward who organised the logistics of this somewhat melodramatic event, including a stopping at Rothesay en route to collect the discharged student's belongings from the hotel. For the student, the abrupt and all too obvious rejection from the training submarine, over her casing and into a launch, the lone passage up the Clyde by way of Rothesay, and the lonely and conspicuous arrival at Faslane must have been a depressing experience, marking the end of the individual's ambition to command a British submarine. Although no one in Conley's group failed the periscope section of the course, twice on arrival at Rothesay, in the boat bringing them ashore it was noted that there was a missing face in the *Narwhal* section. These occasions rather dulled the evening's relaxation in the hotel bar.

During the weeks of periscope attacks Conley and his fellow students each conducted over forty attacks. As the course progressed, he inevitably assessed how well he was doing by comparing himself with his peers. Despite making the odd serious mistake, he knew he was up to the mark during the closing stages of these weeks when Forsyth started staging theatrics while he was acting in the command role and at his station on the periscope. These including a terrified rating running through the control room pursued by a ranting cook wielding a carving knife, histrionics that must have eased the tension for the ship's company, if not for the candidate under pressure. However, whilst feeling modestly confident and competent, Conley did not rate himself as a natural in handling visual attacks and tended to rely upon stopwatch timings, rather than trusting his innate instincts that it was time to look again at a given vessel.

On completion of the periscope attack training there followed several weeks ashore participating in a joint maritime warfare course at the Maritime

114

Warfare School in HMS *Dryad* near Portsmouth. There the students had the opportunity to meet and work with the prospective commanding officers of several frigates and destroyers, with the benefits of exchanging ideas and tactical initiatives. After this the Perisher candidates started the final two-week operational phase. Conley's section joined HM Submarine *Onslaught* at Devonport in early November. Travelling south by car, Conley's sense of well-being was disrupted by his Irish Setter defecating over the navigational charts in the rear of the car. These he had painstakingly prepared for various anticipated operational scenarios, such as exercising minelaying techniques and photo-reconnaissance of shorelines of interest, during which he would assume the role of duty commanding officer. He cleaned the charts off as best he could, and wryly annotated the resultant brown stains with an indication of their origin.

On her departure from Devonport, *Onslaught* headed for the Southwest Approaches to participate in a major joint exercise where the opposition was a multinational group of NATO ships supported by anti-submarine aircraft and helicopters. Conley found this phase to be a step-change from the highly structured weeks of periscope attacks and for the first time he had to conduct attack procedures at night in heavy seas. Nevertheless, this element of the course passed without any serious mishaps and was followed by the final inshore phase in the outer estuary of the Clyde. This was the Perisher's culmination, with each student taking it in turns to command the boat for a day in which to the challenge of close inshore navigation was added hostile opposition from patrol craft and anti-submarine helicopters. In these vital closing stages of the Perisher, Conley realised he was being over-cautious and risk-averse, but he was determined not to make a mistake and jeopardise his chances of success. With hindsight, he considered that he probably did not get the full benefit offered by this final fortnight at sea, but having upped his game and completed the course his achievement was considerable. To emphasise this, the course finally concluded with failure occurring right at the end. The Norwegian officer, who had been given every chance, conclusively demonstrated he could not handle the inshore situation in a safe manner.

As *Onslaught* headed for Faslane, Conley was called to the captain's cabin to hear of the outcome. There he found a smiling Forsyth, who informed him: 'Congratulations Dan, you are the new captain of *Otter*.' His elation and relief on being informed he had passed was somewhat tempered by the news that he was being appointed to the one Faslane submarine available, and not one of the six Portsmouth-based boats due for a change of commanding officer. His wife Linda had recently been appointed to HMS *Mercury*, the communications training school near Portsmouth, and they had set up house in the nearby town of Petersfield. He rightly anticipated that this would cause severe domestic upset and end his wife's successful career in the WRNS, but fate would have it that command of *Otter* would set him on course for a unique career path.

The Perisher course equipped Conley to be a competent, safe, confident submarine captain, able to handle the most demanding of inshore situations. He and his fellow students had been tested to the limit, demonstrating that they could handle extreme stress and that they would be able to knit their crews into efficient fighting units. However, ever an original thinker, he later recounted that he was dubious about 'devoting phenomenal time and effort doing Second World War style periscope attacks, with virtually no training on the underwater target scenario, which required an entirely different mindset. Here we were in 1975, with our main threat the submarines of Soviet Russia, spending little time addressing that potential foe and, specifically, how to successfully approach and attack a submerged target.'

Conley was only too aware that a submarine commander engaging an underwater opponent needed to be able to analyse information from all of his acoustic sensors, some of it imprecise or conflicting, to make rapid and expert assessments of the situation and, most importantly, keep his team appraised of his thoughts and intentions. It was, he was convinced, all about teamwork and trust between those in the sound room and the control room and all much less individualistic than the periscope attacks situation as practised in the Perisher. Indeed, it was a real art which not all successful Perishers would, or could, master. It required a significant degree of training to gain competence, and a further amount of hard work to raise that competence to the excellence Conley envisaged. In reviewing the Perisher privately, Conley quietly questioned the imbalance of resources in what was an extremely expensive course to run. The central problem was one of culture; at that time the Royal Navy's Perisher course had acquired a myth-like status and its format had been crafted by very accomplished Teachers such as Sandy Woodward, who as a rear admiral went on to command the Falklands campaign naval task group. It would have been very injudicious of Conley as a brand new lieutenant in command to challenge openly the Perisher content and conduct, still less its validity in the era of Cold War.

Across the Atlantic, the equivalent course run by the United States Navy, the submarine prospective commanding officers' course, committed a far greater proportion of operational training time on the anti-submarine scenario. This aligned with the American strategy in war of deploying their submarine force forward into the enemy's backyard, with the aim of destroying Russian submarines before they could break out into the Atlantic or Pacific, but the American submarine captain's prowess in periscope attacks could be less than refined, and as a rule he was not so skilled in handling the shallow water, coastal situation.

It was clear to an ambitious and very new submarine commander that, despite the reforms to the submarine service he had witnessed since joining the Royal Navy, there was still work to be done. Most important for Conley the private man, it was clear that he was increasingly able to be himself an agent of the change he so much desired.

10

First Submarine Command

ON A BLEAK winter's day in early December 1975, Lieutenant Dan Conley boarded the Third Submarine Squadron's *Oberon*-class diesel-electric submarine *Otter*, to take over as her commanding officer. The submarine was in dock in Faslane and, whilst his initial impressions were that she was in overall better shape than *Sealion* had been when he joined her, he soon realised that the machinery of the thirteen-year-old boat needed a refit and thorough overhaul. Altogether she was rather tired in condition and appearance.

As was traditional in the Submarine Service, the handover was brief and took less than two hours. Having met those officers who were not on leave, mustered a small quantity of highly classified commanding officer 'Eyes Only' material and codes, checked out the small holding of medicinal drugs, including a rather pathetic six ampoules of morphine, Conley declared he was happy to take over. The departing commanding officer was then 'piped over the side' for the last time and *Otter* was his.

HMS *Otter* was unique in the Royal Navy, being the only submarine acting as a target for torpedo tests and evaluations. To be able to withstand hits from practice weapons, the fibreglass superstructure standard in the *Oberon* class had been replaced by steel. She also had protective shielding fitted to those small areas of her pressure hull which were directly exposed to the sea and to the vents on top of the main ballast tanks, which were so vital to the boat's ability to dive and surface. These measures created additional top weight which reduced the boat's righting stability and Conley was to discover that in heavy weather she rolled much more than others of her class.

A quick walk-through revealed the submarine to be in a state of engineering upheaval, as the main work whilst in dock involved completing the final phases of a general programme throughout the Submarine Flotilla to replace a number of hull valve casings which were suspect. This was a messy job which incurred a considerable amount of restorative work after the base repair staff had finished.

In *Otter*, Conley inherited a boat containing much obsolescent equipment; even her outfit of ancient Mark 8 torpedoes were of a particular type which had been phased out elsewhere in the Flotilla. Her sonar was similarly antique, remaining essentially the same set as fitted on her completion in 1962. Of particular concern to the new commander was that the long-range wireless communication equipment relied solely upon hand-keyed Morse for both the reception and transmission of signal traffic. Conley was only too aware that the number of shore radio stations competent to handle this slow, out-of-date mode of transmitting messages was diminishing. Clearly, signal traffic handling was going to be at the top of his list of problems thus far.

On the other hand, for the first time in his career in submarines, Conley had his own cabin, a tiny cupboard-like space adjacent to the control room into which was squeezed a settee-bunk, a wardrobe and a fold-down washbasin. Apart from breakfast, as was the tradition in British submarines, he would eat in the wardroom very much on the understanding that this was the first lieutenant's fiefdom and he was a guest.

The *Otter*'s officers seemed a mixed bunch in terms of ability, very much less experienced than the *Swiftsure* team; the same could also be said of the ship's company, although in the event they were to prove a lively, high-spirited group of individuals, and they were sometimes a problem when on shore leave.

After the completion of repairs and with Christmas leave over, Conley took his first command to sea for the first time. *Otter*'s first major assignment in 1976 was to deploy to the Caribbean to the AUTEC range to act as a target submarine for a series of sonar and torpedo trials. First, however, was a short post-refit work-up, allowing him to get to grips with the boat, her equipment and her crew. On the second day at sea Conley conducted practice torpedo firings in the Clyde Estuary using the torpedo recovery vessel as a target, but the results were disappointing: the two Mark 23 weapons fired stubbornly refused to run, emphasising the uselessness of this weapon, and one of his salvo of four Mark 8s failed to surface for recovery at the end of its run.

Conley's next task was to take the boat into deep water in the Northwest Approaches where he would conduct a deep dive to test out the new hull valves and undertake other proving trials before heading across the Atlantic. During the deep dive the radar mast flooded, rendering this navigation and ship safety system inoperative, the first intimation that defective radar was to plague Conley's time in command of *Otter*.

Prior to final departure for the AUTEC range, *Otter* had to return to Faslane and experienced Storm Force 10 conditions on her return passage, made on the surface. During the night, a major electrical earth registered on the forward battery section and an inspection of the battery compartment revealed that the heavy rolling was causing acid to spill out and track across the tops of several defective battery cells, creating sparking and arcing. With a very real risk of a fire or an explosion, this was a potentially highly dangerous situation which required the boat to be rapidly put onto a course which reduced its movement, whilst electrical maintainers entered the very tight confines of the battery compartment to effect repairs and clean up the acid. Given the risks, this was a commendable though necessary process, revealing to Conley the spirit of some of his people.

Meanwhile, the remainder of the crew had been woken and ordered to their diving stations to ensure that they were in a high degree of readiness to contend with any eventuality. It was the first of many serious equipment problems Conley was to encounter in his three submarine commands, but since it was, after Perisher, the first real mishap he was called upon to deal with, the incident remained sharp in his memory.

On the return to Faslane to complete repairs to the defects which had arisen, and to undertake the final loading of stores and provisions before deploying, there was more excitement awaiting Conley. As he made his first night approach into a very tight berth, with the sterns of the SSN *Courageous* and the SSBN *Resolution* ahead and astern respectively, the rating in the control room operating the main motor telegraphs responded wrongly to orders from the bridge. Bringing *Otter* to a minimum speed in the final 200 yards of his approach, Conley ordered the propulsion astern; instead he got an ahead movement. As *Otter* lurched forward towards *Courageous*'s propeller, Conley ordered 'Full astern!' which had the opposite effect: *Otter* now began to make sternway towards *Resolution*. This was checked by a 'Full ahead!' order and eventually, after a series of further urgent telegraph movements, the ahead and astern oscillations diminished and Conley got his charge under control and somehow completed the berthing without causing damage to either of the two very important neighbouring submarines. Meanwhile, the squadron greeting staff gathered their breath having sprinted back and forwards up and down the jetty towards where they thought impact was about to occur.

A quick investigation revealed that the rating working the telegraphs was an inexperienced trainee who should have been supervised by an officer but the latter, about to be harbour duty officer, was in the wardroom changing his uniform. Later in the evening when his adrenalin had subsided, Conley made it very clear to the officer concerned that his absence from the control room at a critical time when berthing was an act of negligence, which could have resulted in millions of pounds of damage and the need to dock the other two vessels. But owing to the officer's inexperience, the matter ended there. In the privacy of his cabin, Conley mused self-critically on the last few days. They had been horribly eventful and did not amount to a very good start as a commanding officer. What, he wondered, lay ahead, on the far side of the Atlantic?

Otter left Faslane at the end of January 1976 for a transatlantic passage on the surface. Her first commitment was to act as target for sonar trials with the brand new SSN HMS *Sovereign* in an area to the northeast of Bermuda. Five days out, in mid Atlantic she encountered severe Gale Force 9 conditions and started suffering from a series of main engine problems and a recurrence of battery earths owing to her heavy rolling. As if this were not enough, one of the starboard engine's major hull valves had begun leaking and seawater was entering the submarine at a significant rate. With her obsolete wireless equipment, severe difficulties were also being experienced in both sending and receiving signal traffic concerning her engineering problems. As Conley sat in his cabin, his ears alert for the increasingly familiar sound of an engine stopping, the possible prospect of breaking down in the middle of the ocean with inadequate communications to call for assistance appalled him. For the first time he appreciated the meaning of that phrase 'the loneliness of command'. However, somehow his engineers managed to keep the engines running and when the gale eventually abated and the sea conditions moderated, the battery earth problems disappeared.

Having met up with *Sovereign*, a radio conversation with her commanding officer revealed that she too had had her own problems during the crossing. Her oxygen-making equipment had failed and it had been necessary periodically to ventilate the boat at periscope depth through the snort mast air-induction system. Whilst ventilating in the rough seas, she had incurred a small but serious explosion caused by seawater making its way down trunking to come into contact with the highly sensitive electrolysers which generated oxygen. This had been attributed to a defect arising from build – a stray piece of polystyrene left in the induction system seawater drain tank.

However, despite all this and after a slow start, the sonar trials were successfully completed. Owing to her leaking hull valve, *Otter* had been limited to periscope depth where the ingress of 20 tons of seawater an hour could just be coped with. Anything deeper was out of the question. The trials over, *Otter* headed for a port visit to Hamilton, Bermuda, where Conley was very glad there would be an opportunity to rectify at least some of his growing list of defects.

Whist strolling through the centre of the city on the second day of his visit to the Bermudan capital, Conley spotted a local newspaper with the front-page headline 'Sub Runs Aground'. On buying a paper to find out which unfortunate boat had had a mishap, he soon realised the headlines referred to *Otter*. As he had turned the boat round to make the final approach to the berth in the shallow, pristine, azure blue waters of Hamilton harbour, the propellers had stirred up a cloud of sand which an observing reporter assumed was caused by the submarine hitting the bottom. This was not to be the first time in his career that media misreporting would make life uncomfortable for him. A signal was sent to Flag Officer Submarines and the Squadron, refuting the newspaper article, but he knew that the promulgation of bad news, no matter how unfounded, tended to have an adverse effect.

Shortly after departing from Bermuda, Conley received a personal signal from the regional admiral expressing displeasure that the crew had caused some damage to the hotel they had been billeted in. With the engineering problems in the Atlantic passage, the reported grounding and crew misbehaviour ashore, he reflected that the deployment had got off to a somewhat dismal start.

Otter was now bound to the United States Navy base at Charleston, South Carolina. Here, during a ten-day stay, many much-needed repairs were undertaken by a very helpful submarine support team. The sprawling Charleston shore complex then based two large submarine squadrons, together with numerous destroyers and frigates. However, in 1996 as a cost savings measure at the end of the Cold War, it was completely shut down and no longer serves as a naval base.

As was a common experience in most American ports, *Otter*'s crew received immense hospitality from their hosts, despite the fact that they were beginning a year of commemoration of the 200th anniversary of the start of the American War of Independence. *Otter*'s host boat was the USN SSN *Grayling,* a unit of the Fourth Submarine Squadron, which had more operational nuclear submarines than the total in the Royal Navy. This fact alone emphasised to their British guests the scale of the American submarine fleet. The *Grayling* wardroom excelled themselves as hosts and for his part

Lieutenant Conley was feted by the area admiral and senior officers from the submarine squadrons, undertaking a number of official calls and attending several receptions and dinners. He got on very well with his American peers and was to make enduring friendships with two of the submarine commanders he met.

However, the serious business was about to start, and on departing Charleston, *Otter* headed for Port Canaveral, arriving there in late February for the fitting of range-tracking gear and special noise augmentation equipment. This was required for those trials where the Tigerfish torpedo would be tested. On 1 March Conley celebrated both his promotion to lieutenant commander and his first wedding anniversary, sharing a glass of champagne with his officers.

On the following day, *Otter* left Port Canaveral for six weeks on the AUTEC range. Here she would predominantly act in the target role in a dived state at varying depths for sonar and weapons trials. Her trial consorts were again the SSN *Sovereign* and the *Leander*-class frigate *Cleopatra*, the former firing Tigerfish heavyweight torpedoes at her and the latter launching the American-manufactured lightweight Mark 44 and Mark 46 weapons, either from her torpedo tubes or from her helicopter. *Otter*'s equipment problems continued, with the reliability of the diesel engines and their associated main electrical generators a constant source of worry. Conditions onboard when submerged, with sea temperatures of around 28°C, were extremely torrid. The air-conditioning system proved totally inadequate both in maintaining reasonable temperatures and reducing humidity, and consequently the deck-heads dripped with condensation.

During the weapon firings the boat's watertight compartment bulkheads were shut down as a precaution against the effects of damage from an inadvertent hit. This meant that ventilation had to be stopped, whereupon the air temperature soared into the 50s. On leaving Port Canaveral, several members of the crew had reported that they were suffering from symptoms of flu and this soon swept through the ship's company, its effects exacerbated by the very high humidity and the temperature differentials of up to 30° between the interior of the submarine and the bridge, when the submarine was running on the surface.

Conley succumbed, his symptoms becoming evident on the passage to AUTEC but with no one else available to take over command, there was no alternative other than for him to keep on going; it took over a week for him to recover to a near normal condition.

To give the crew a break and to enable them to get away from these very unpleasant conditions, two short port visits took place to nearby Nassau, the capital of the Bahamas. The first harbour entry, arranged at short notice and at night to allow proper medical care for the worse infected members of the crew, was very challenging for Conley. Full of influenza, with no operational radar, he discovered the buoys and beacon lights marking the approach were either extinguished or displayed totally different characteristics to those described on his charts. This fraught situation might have been eased by the early embarkation of the pilot, but this worthy boarded when just off the berth and was clearly in a very inebriated state. Once alongside, two of the crew who were showing signs of developing pneumonia had been landed into a local hospital where they were to make a good recovery. The following day, heading back to sea in daylight, viewing the harbour entrance and its various reefs and hazards, Conley counted his blessings that *Otter* had not come to grief.

A few days later *Otter* made a second, official, visit to Nassau. Conley's wife, enjoying her end of service leave from the WRNS, was able to join him here, but first he made his formal calls. These included the British High Commissioner, the Governor General and the Prime Minister of the Bahamas, Lynden Pindling, the first leader of this fledgling independent nation. The Bahamas had been granted independence in 1973 and Pindling was to serve as prime minister until 1992. Later in the visit, Pindling was clearly very pleased to be invited onboard *Otter* for a tour of the boat and arrived very informally dressed, accompanied by his two daughters. Conley found him to be a highly intelligent and personable man but was saddened to learn in later years of the allegations regarding the fortune he had made as payback for turning a blind eye to the use of many remote Bahamas islands, or cays, being used as a staging post for Colombian drug traffic into continental America.

A less welcome female guest had come onboard two days before the prime minister's family visit whilst the Conleys were dining with the High Commissioner. The young woman in question had obligingly removed her clothing, to the delight of several of the junior ratings. Seemingly harmless enough at the time, the ramifications of this incident were to bear heavily upon Conley and his officers when they came to light four months later.

Back at sea, engine and other mechanical problems persisted. Often only one of the twin diesel engines was in working order, parts of the defective engine being repaired ashore in the AUTEC workshops on Andros Island. The wireless mast was also defective owing to seawater ingress, making communications with the AUTEC staff or Squadron difficult. On one occasion, after surfacing in the evening at the end of a day's evasive manoeuvres against torpedoes, with the main battery absolutely exhausted, the one good engine available could not be started. With the submarine stationary, wallowing in a long swell, with very little power available other than for a few lights and essential equipment, internal temperatures climbed into the 50s from the heat exuding from the exhausted main battery. To a weary Conley, sitting perspiring in the near darkness of his cabin, the two hours it took to get the engine going seemed interminable. The roar of the diesel starting, and sucking relatively cool fresh air into the boat's interior, was one of best sounds he had ever heard.

Added to the myriad of electromechanical problems onboard was the external damage caused by several practice torpedo hits. Shortly after the trials had started, it became evident that the Tigerfish torpedoes were failing their specification. Although *Otter* had been fitted with special noise augmentation equipment upon which the weapons were supposed to home, in practice it was found that because of control deficiencies, the Tigerfish was finding it difficult to locate her, despite the boat's enhanced noise. These problems augured a long and difficult gestation for this well overdue anti-submarine weapon. There were many delays and aborted runs and Conley sensed a degree of frustration onboard the firing submarine, HMS *Sovereign*. Eventually, one good run was achieved with the weapon using its sonar in an active, transmit mode but perhaps overcome by exuberance, the *Sovereign* command team failed to heed the range control instructions to turn the weapon away from *Otter*. The high-pitched whine of the approaching 2-ton, 36-knot torpedo heard through the pressure hull was followed by a loud bang as the weapon struck forward in the area of the torpedo tube bow caps.

The boat was immediately surfaced and the range staff quickly flew out divers by helicopter to inspect and assess the damage. Braving a group of hammerhead sharks which were not too far away, the divers checked out the forward part of the submarine and on surfacing, clutching small fragments of torpedo, reported that a starboard torpedo tube bow cap was badly stove in, otherwise there was no other damage. A few days later a second inadvertent Tigerfish hit damaged the starboard battery cooling intake arrangement, followed by a tube-launched Mark 44 making an impact upon the starboard propeller shaft. *Otter* was taking a battering.

It had not been all hard work and no play during the boat's time in the Caribbean. In addition to the visits to Nassau, there had been calls at Fort

Lauderdale, Florida, and Freeport, Bahamas. Conley also ensured that, where possible when on the AUTEC range, some of the crew were landed ashore for relaxation in its facilities. Much to the pleasure of the sailors these included a pleasant beach bar. When there were breaks in the trials programme and the submarine was surfaced, the crew sometimes enjoyed a barbecue on the casing, or exercised their skills in attempting to catch game fish, albeit with very little success.

In early April, however, the trials were over and *Otter* headed back across the Atlantic on the surface to Faslane. Despite a series of mechanical problems, owing to Herculean efforts on the part of the engineering staff the boat had met all her commitments and was always at the right place at the correct time. Meanwhile, Conley had continued to drill the crew in emergency procedures, significantly improving their competence and efficiency, and in gaps between trials runs he took the opportunity to exercise his attack team against the other participating warships.

On returning to Faslane the boat was taken in hand for a docking and several weeks of repairs. It was cold comfort to Conley that on inspecting the main generators the shore maintenance staff expressed surprise that they had kept running and that the boat had made it back across the Atlantic at all. Meanwhile, two new officers had joined and were to prove highly competent. In particular, the new first lieutenant took a grip of crew discipline and set about improving the appearance of the boat. On the home front, Conley's wife Linda, having herself returned from her brief trip to the Bahamas, had set up home in temporary married quarters whilst the pair set about house-hunting in the local Helensburgh area.

The maintenance period over, Conley took *Otter* back to sea to participate in a number of major exercises. Gaining in self-confidence, he continued to improve the effectiveness and capability of the crew and the submarine began to gain a reputation for efficiency and tactical innovation. In July *Otter* took part in a large-scale Royal Navy exercise in the North Sea and achieved a host of successful simulated torpedo attacks against stiff escort and airborne opposition. During one part of the exercise Conley was required to surface and simulate a Russian Juliet-class submarine firing her missiles. These submarines were armed with Shaddock anti-ship cruise missiles with a range of 300 miles, but required the boat to be surfaced for launch. For exercise purposes two RAF Phantom fighters would replicate the missiles and their flight profiles once *Otter* had surfaced in a simulated launch mode. Conley assessed that it would be difficult to do this undetected since the area was under intense radar surveillance by maritime patrol aircraft radar. He therefore located a Spanish fishing boat lying stationary as she hauled her nets, knowing that if he approached close enough she would provide him with cover against radar detection.

Surfacing within 200 yards on the side of the fishing boat opposite to that over which she was hauling her nets, Conley recalled sighting through the periscope the great surprise on the swarthy fishermen's faces as the submarine unexpectedly arose abeam of them, to be followed within a minute by the roar of the two Phantoms streaking right over the top of their vessel at a very low height, before climbing near vertically as they assumed the character of missiles heading for their targets many miles away. *Otter* was back under the water within another minute, totally undetected by her hunters.

It proved a very successful exercise for HMS *Otter* and Conley was looking forward to the debriefing 'wash-up' in the Naval Base at Rosyth. However, on his arrival alongside he was met by the deputy squadron commander who was bearing bad news which was to utterly suppress his elation.

Once onboard in the confines of Conley's cramped cabin, the commander related that a well-known glamour model and pornographic actress named Mary Millington had approached the *London Evening Standard* and the *Sunday People*, selling the story that whilst *Otter* was in Nassau she had been invited onboard by the crew where photographs had been taken of her in the nude. In addition, a salacious article had been written in a pornographic magazine, which she owned and published, implicating the complicity of the boat's commanding officer in the invitation to her to board *Otter*. It was also alleged that she had then personally obliged several members of the crew. The deputy squadron commander's first question to Conley was whether he or his officers knew of any of this, to which the answer was a definite 'no'. It was, therefore, agreed that a full ship's investigation should be conducted forthwith and meanwhile Conley and his crew should be prepared for a barrage of unwelcome publicity. It was also decided that there was no point in Flag Officer Submarines' public relations officer attempting to refute Millington's claims, as this would risk putting the story into page three of the *Daily Telegraph*.

The investigation revealed that Millington had been staying in the same Nassau hotel as the crew. Meeting some of them, she had asked that she visit the submarine. On her arrival at the pier, the duty officer had granted permission for her to come onboard, where she was given a tour by some junior ratings of the duty watch. When aft in the engine room and motor room areas, she produced a camera and invited her escorts to take pictures of her in various sates of undress. Nothing else untoward happened onboard, although the investigation revealed that later on the same day she had intercourse in the hotel with one of the crew in the hotel at a cost to him of $50 and his wristwatch.

The story duly hit the front page of *The People* the following Sunday and included a rear shot of Millington in *Otter*'s motor room wearing only a sailor's cap. It also featured to a lesser extent in several other magazines and newspapers, and shortly afterwards a formal question about the incident was raised in the House of Commons and was responded to by Roy Mason, the Secretary of State for Defence. The sailors involved were subsequently disciplined by Conley, but awarded relatively light punishments in line with the official view that it was a caper which went badly out of control.

For Conley, the incident was an undoubted blemish upon his time in command of *Otter*. There was never an issue of complicity by his officers, while he himself had been lunching, with his wife, with the British High Commissioner. However, questions were asked about why, after the event, the officers were never informed by the senior ratings who had themselves known about it, but not reported it up the command chain. With an air of suspicion being sustained at Submarine Headquarters against *Otter*, the whole Fleet, of course, got to know about the story and on occasions at sea on encountering other warships Conley would be asked by signal if Mary Millington was onboard. Meanwhile, Millington had undertaken a similar jape appearing topless with the policeman standing outside No. 10, Downing Street and she was also rumoured to be having a relationship with a member of the Labour Cabinet.

Having relinquished command of *Otter* when she went into refit a year afterwards, Conley called upon Flag Officer Submarines, Rear Admiral John Fieldhouse (later Admiral of the Fleet followed by appointment as Chief of the Defence Staff). When the discussion got round to the Millington affair, the admiral declared that having survived the incident, the young commander could successfully meet all unexpected challenges. Privately, however, Conley was only too well aware that no matter what the circumstances, the behaviour of his ship's company and the good name of his boat were ultimately his responsibility. Later still, in 1979, he learned that Millington had committed suicide.

Across the Atlantic a few months previous to Millington's visit to *Otter*, as the US SSN *Finback* departed from Port Canaveral, a topless go-go dancer performed a routine on top of the boat's fin. It was very evident that the commanding officer had been complicit in this stunt and he was subsequently relieved of his command for being 'guilty of permitting an action, which could have distracted the attention of those responsible for the safe navigation of the nuclear-powered submarine maneuvering in restricted waters'.

As the publicity around the Millington affair gradually faded, *Otter* continued with a varied programme of tasks at sea. As the Royal Navy's target submarine, she participated in a number of torpedo trials at the British equivalent to AUTEC, the much smaller and more limited British Underwater Test and Evaluation Centre (BUTEC) situated in the Sound of Raasay to the east of the Isle of Skye. Compared to AUTEC, in addition to being much smaller in size and having less capable facilities, BUTEC was a very unprofessionally and inefficiently run set-up with which Conley, in due course, was to become intricately involved in after he left *Otter*.

A highlight of Conley's time in command was the conduct of two short operational patrols where he was directed to gather intelligence upon a large oceangoing Russian tug bristling with radio antennae, which had been stationed for some time just outside the then three-mile territorial limit to the west of the Shetland Islands, near the island of Foula. *Otter*'s task was to establish whether she was more than just a contingency tug, on station to provide assistance to Russian navy vessels in trouble in the northeast Atlantic. This would mean the submarine conducting an underwater survey of her hull to confirm there were neither sonar fittings, nor exit facilities for a submersible craft.

During the first patrol in October 1976, Conley spent two days covertly monitoring the Russian through the periscope, but she remained at anchor throughout the period, which made it almost impossible in the murky visibility conditions to obtain photographs of the underneath of her hull. To undertake an underwater look at a vessel at anchor required a final accurate, undetected visual set-up on the vessel on its quarter at a range of about 1,000 yards. Then, having gone deep to the observation depth (the top of the raised periscope about 15ft under the hull of the target), starting an approach at slow speed at an angle which offset effects of the tidal stream and current, ensuring at all costs that the other vessel's anchor cable be avoided. It was hoped there would be a few seconds glimpse of the under hull, sufficient to capture detail on the periscope-mounted cameras. However, in conditions of a strong tidal stream Conley found this extremely difficult to achieve without hazarding both vessels: if he had inadvertently got *Otter*'s forward hydroplanes entangled in the tug's anchor cable there was the risk that his 2,000-ton boat would drag the other craft under the sea.

On returning the following February to the Shetland Islands to continue the intelligence-gathering task, Conley had better luck. Shortly after starting to observe the Russian, the latter got underway at slow speed heading out to sea, enabling a successful underwater pass to be conducted without worrying about the anchor cable. Achieving a good station under the Russian for about half an hour, this surveillance produced high-quality photographic shots of the vessel's bottom and her underwater fittings, all of which revealed that the tug had neither unusual fittings nor sonar.

HMS *Otter* was also tasked to undertake two Perisher courses, embarking during the first his own Teacher, Commander Rob Forsyth, and on the second occasion a new Teacher, his mentor, Commander Geoffrey Biggs. Much to Conley's relief and satisfaction, both commended *Otter*'s crew for being thoroughly professional and well prepared. Clearly, the *Otter*'s reputation was gradually being restored after the Millington affair. Indeed, having quickly established confidence in Conley's periscope ability, Biggs significantly delegated to him, allowing him to take charge of a substantial proportion of the attack runs, barely a year after he himself had completed the Perisher course.

Between work at sea there were several port visits. A week in Gibraltar in the early summer of 1976 followed a Submarine Flotilla training period at sea involving a substantial number of submarines. After this *Otter* 'showed the flag' by visiting Rotterdam in the Netherlands. There were also two home-port visits to Blyth and Birkenhead. Apart from crew rest and recreation, the aim of the British visits was to afford the local community an opportunity to visit a submarine. In addition to the standard cocktail party in the control room for local dignitaries and officials, open to the public days were always very popular. Long queues formed of people very eager to gain an insight into life under the sea, and Conley's young crew rose to the occasion.

Blyth was another coal port in serious decline, but the crew enjoyed great hospitality from the locals, the older generation well remembering that the port was an operational submarine base during the Second World War. Indeed, Conley was invited to visit a local pub, the Astley Arms, which was a favourite of wartime submariners, where he was presented by a barmaid from the war era with a contemporary wartime bottle of Johnny Walker Scotch whisky which was an unclaimed raffle prize. The winner, a submarine petty officer, had failed to return from patrol to claim his prize, but the bar staff had kept the bottle in a safe place. The bottle, its contents now very dark in colour, is on display at the Royal Navy Submarine Museum, Gosport.

In early December faulty radar almost resulted in catastrophe during the final stages of the *Otter*'s passage into Birkenhead, the shipbuilding town situated across the Mersey from Liverpool. Arriving early in the morning at the pilot station, Conley gloomily noted a bank of fog sitting on top of the Mersey Channel. Soon after embarking the pilot and starting to make a cautious passage up the buoyed channel, visibility came down to only a few hundred yards and the boat had made no more than one mile into the channel when the radar failed completely. As it was soon evident that there would be no easy fix to the equipment, and having consulted with the pilot, Conley decided to turn *Otter* round in the narrow channel. Constrained by tidal bank training walls only about 400 yards wide, Conley had to stop the submarine to turn her short round, using her two propellers running in opposition, one ahead and one astern, to swing the long hull.

Notwithstanding a warning to all nearby shipping that a submarine was swinging short round in the channel, when halfway through the manoeuvre a small outward-bound Danish cargo ship appeared out of the fog heading straight towards *Otter*'s broadside. Conley ordered, 'Full astern!', sounded a siren warning to the other ship, ordered the crew to 'Emergency stations' and to brace for collision, shutting down bulkheads and closing hull valves. In the event, the cargo vessel passed less than 50 yards ahead, its officers in their enclosed bridge apparently oblivious of their near-miss with the submarine. Thoughts of *Truculent*'s sinking in the Thames after being rammed by a Swedish freighter flashed through Conley's mind for a few seconds, but his immediate imperative was to avoid the mudbank looming astern and to get the boat out of the narrow channel as soon as possible. The pilot's handling of the situation had been less than satisfactory, as Conley was unconvinced that he had clearly relayed to the harbour control authorities the intention to turn the submarine around in mid channel.

Having cleared the channel and left the fog bank, the radar fault was soon rectified, but although the visibility had improved considerably, the tidal window for entry into the Birkenhead dock system had been missed. Therefore, in late morning, having heard a forecast of reasonable visibility, Conley made the decision to head into the Mersey and to anchor off Cammell Laird's shipyard, Birkenhead, and await the evening tidal slot. This was achieved without difficulty and on this occasion the radar held up. However, having anchored, the visibility closed down again and the commanding officer's confidence in the pilot took a further knock when it became evident that having anchored in the position that he had advised, *Otter* was in poor holding ground and had dragged her anchor several hundreds of yards, right into the middle of the Liverpool–Birkenhead ferry crossing route: there was now a strong risk of being hit by one of these vessels.

With visibility down to 100ft, Conley moved the submarine to a more secure anchorage just out of the main Mersey shipping channel and then spent several very tense hours awaiting the rising tide. Unseen merchant ships passed only a few hundred yards away as Conley pondered how he was going to move into the locks when he could hardly see the *Otter*'s bows and forward anchor light from the bridge. Perhaps, he reflected, his decision to attempt an entry into the Mersey dock system had not been the right one and he had been over-keen to meet his programme. Now, confronting unpredicted and dismally poor visibility and with the possibility of the radar failing again, his only option was to somehow get into the safety of the Birkenhead docks.

At about 2000 the visibility improved a little, to about 200 yards, and after discussion by radio with the Birkenhead dock authorities it was agreed that they would place cars on either side of the dock entrance with their headlights full on to assist identifying the entrance through the murk. Having got underway once more, Conley found this improvisation to be a great help in identifying the entrance and safely got *Otter* into the harbour entry lock. Standing on the bridge awaiting the gate astern of him to close and the one ahead to open once the water level had matched that of the harbour, he was very relieved that he had not hit anything so far. However, again the visibility plunged to less than 100ft. Not trusting the pilot to direct competently the tug standing by to tow *Otter* to her berth, it was agreed that this vessel would lead the way while Conley stationed his second in command right forward in the bows in radio contact with the bridge to give guidance on the helm and motor orders.

Gingerly moving out of the lock and just able to see the powerful deck working lights of the tug which was only about 30 yards ahead, Conley negotiated a narrow swing-bridge gap, but in the final approach to his berth became totally reliant upon the first lieutenant forward giving the engine and rudder orders to get the boat alongside. The berth only appeared out of the pea-souper during the final swinging in of the submarine as she closed the dock wall. Once finally alongside, through the wet swirling fog Conley could see his wife and others of the welcoming party on the wharf and remembered that the boat's cocktail reception for local dignitaries and guests had been cancelled a few hours earlier. However, that had been the least of his worries in what had been a long and very tense day, during which he was relieved to have avoided collision or grounding. As he relaxed, the thirty-year-old lieutenant commander reflected that he had really earned his 30 pence command pay that day. Meanwhile the non-duty watches very cheerfully decanted ashore to their hotels, showing no semblance of appreciation of the risks encountered in the previous twelve hours.

In early March 1977, looking very smart and businesslike, *Otter* departed from Faslane with a large paying-off pennant streaming from her wireless mast to her stern. She was heading on surface passage for refit in HM Dockyard at Portsmouth, calling on the way for a visit to the port of Vjele, situated in southeast Denmark. After his Birkenhead experience, notwith-standing the impending refit, Conley insisted that the Faslane base support staff thoroughly overhaul the radar system – every component of it from the aerial downwards. This was fortuitous as, heading down the narrow channels of the Kattegat off the east coast of Denmark, thick fog was again encountered, but this time the radar performed well and the crew conducted a flawless night navigational passage to arrive off Vejle, where a pilot was embarked. In making the berthing, Conley was required to turn the boat in a very confined basin and then to undertake a difficult stern-first approach up the port's narrow harbour channel. This he skilfully achieved with no tug assistance and a minimum of manoeuvring: his first, very ragged, berthing in Faslane seemed a lifetime away.

Soon after arrival at Portsmouth for de-storing and final pre-refit preparations alongside at HMS *Dolphin*, Conley left *Otter*, admitting to a degree of relief that he had survived a number of near-misses. After leave, he was appointed to join the Submarine Tactics and Weapons Group (STWG) in Faslane, taking charge of the team responsible for the introduction into service of the contentious Tigerfish torpedo.

On looking back at his sixteen months in command it had certainly been a very eventful period in his life. Plagued by equipment and machinery failures and notwithstanding the Millington affair, which he considered his leaving interview with Rear Admiral Fieldhouse had at least mitigated, he felt that he had faced the challenges providence had strewn in his path. He had learned lessons, and the lonely experience of command had taught him that there would be more to learn; but the key to his sense of achievement was that he was able to meet and, as far as was humanly possible, overcome problems. As every commander must, he acknowledged that this had been due to the efforts of those supporting him and if there had been moments when he felt they had let him down, there were countervailing and important occasions when they had risen unequivocally to his support. Privately, he could do nothing other than welcome this as deeply satisfying. HM Submarine *Otter* was, he knew, in better shape at the end of his command time than she had been when he joined her. Her crew were a well-knit, happy, efficient team who had worked very hard to ensure *Otter* always met her commitments and tasks in a timely, well-prepared manner. Indeed, his final performance report from the captain of the Third Submarine Squadron lauded his strong leadership and 'priceless ability to raise his subordinates from a trough to a crest'. So much for his internal management and leadership, but what about the grand strategic picture that formed the great backdrop to *Otter*'s passing woes?

True, there had been little direct contact with the Russian opposition but in *Otter*'s target role Conley felt he that had made a significant contribution to improving the effectiveness of the Royal Navy's anti-submarine weapons and his new appointment offered an opportunity to carry that work forward, particularly in respect of the Tigerfish torpedo. In short, the whole experience of commanding *Otter* was, he felt, an excellent apprenticeship for whatever the future held in store.

11

Torpedo Problems

HAVING RELINQUISHED COMMAND of *Otter* in April 1977, Conley was appointed to the Submarine Tactics and Weapons Group (STWG) at Faslane, heading up the Tigerfish torpedo crew certification team. He was under no illusion that in comparison with his Perisher peers, this was not the most prestigious of post-command appointments. It was cold comfort to learn that the only one of his colleagues who seemed to have come off worse had done so after inadvertently hitting the seabed in his boat, HMS *Cachalot*. Nevertheless, there were aspects of the job which he considered vital, insofar as future Royal Navy submarine war-fighting capability was concerned. This ameliorated any disappointment he felt as he took charge of a small team of officers, chief petty officers and ratings, whose role was to train submarine crews in the competent handling and control of the new Tigerfish torpedo, a process known as 'weapon certification'.

Tigerfish was the long awaited anti-submarine weapon which Conley and other young officers of his mettle had been hankering after. Unfortunately, not only was the new torpedo many years overdue, it was rapidly acquiring a reputation for unreliability and poor performance, in consequence of which some of the disdain being heaped upon it by commanding officers was rubbing off onto the certification team.

Possessing a total strength of nine SSNs and four SSBNs, together with more than twenty diesel submarines, the Royal Navy's Submarine Flotilla was becoming a very potent force. Meanwhile, with an increasing amount of intelligence about Russian submarine movements and locations becoming available from sound surveillance system (SOSUS) chains in the North Atlantic, it had become vital to have central co-ordination for patrolling submarines and aircraft. This also ensured that British and American SSBNs were kept informed of any potentially threatening Russian vessels in their patrol areas. Accordingly, British submarines in the northeast Atlantic were now controlled from the Royal Navy and RAF Maritime Patrol Aircraft (MPA) operational headquarters in Northwood, London.

Thus in 1978 the Flag Officer Submarines and his staff decamped from their old-fashioned offices and facilities in Fort Blockhouse, Portsmouth, to Northwood, a sure sign of the abandonment of its past image of a buccaneering sideline in favour of being the Royal Navy's crack strike force. With the strategic increase in the activity of Soviet submarines of the Northern Fleet, this elevation of status was, of course, predicated upon having an adequate anti-submarine weapon and no longer relying upon a vintage, short-range anti-ship torpedo.

STWG was a recent response to this step-change and combined the existing Flotilla tactical analysis group with the new Tigerfish weapons team. This organisational concept was novel in the Royal Navy and was based upon the American model of a single organisation which developed tactics alongside the assessment of both the effectiveness of weapon systems and the competence of crews trained to use them. The logic of this is inescapable; a crew could not be called upon to execute a tactical task without the right weapon or training but, remarkably, comprehensive analysis of weapon system effectiveness was new to the Royal Navy. Its initial introduction at this level of rigour had been established with the adoption of the United States Navy's Polaris, where all facets of a SSBN's capability to launch and deliver its nuclear warhead on target were examined – thus underpinning the effectiveness of the terrifying concept of Mutually Assured Destruction – MAD.

The requirement to destroy, or at least inhibit, a potential enemy's ability to accomplish this had led, as we have seen, to the development of the hunter-killer submarine. Weapon system effectiveness in the submarine versus submarine scenario, therefore, analysed a number of factors from initial target detection by sonar, the approach to a firing position, followed by weapon launch and guidance onto the target. Only by thorough training and high degrees of weapon performance and reliability could this guarantee the destruction of the enemy; not only was a miss as good as a mile, it was likely to result in a possibly fatal counter-attack.

In its early days, some submariners regarded this concept with hostility or suspicion, not least because the resultant cumulative probability calculations often produced results of alarmingly low levels of success. This can be illustrated in the example where there is a 1 in 3 chance of a submarine detecting a given submarine target and achieving a successful firing position, to which similar odds, of one torpedo and its control equipment being reliable, have to be added. Thereafter, a 50:50 chance of the weapon's performance being adequate to destroy the target produces the startling outcome that a single attack opportunity yields a success rate of a mere 1 in 18. Of course, if two or more weapons were fired then the odds would shorten, but many in the Submarine Flotilla hierarchy did not want too much attention paid to such statistics, particularly when it was apparent that neither surface warships nor the Royal Air Force applied such rigorous analysis to their own weapon systems.

If any justification was needed for assessment of this nature in the submarine versus submarine scenario, it is important to note that, when applied to the effectiveness of Polaris, it produced a figure that was consistently in the high ninetieth percentile.

It was in this highly fervid atmosphere that Conley now found himself. As a douche of cold water, the apparent disinterest many senior submariners displayed in Tigerfish soon dismayed him: few demonstrated much enthusiasm in acquiring an understanding of its characteristics, let alone its nuances. This was very much the antithesis of the culture of the detailed knowledge of submarine systems which had been the basis of his early training. Most of the hierarchy were focused instead upon the Flotilla's concept of operations at the time, the orthodox buzz phrase for which was – 'By confronting the Soviet today, being prepared for tomorrow's war'. In other words, if it were demonstrated that the Royal Navy's submarines could gather intelligence upon and covertly follow Russian warships and submarines in peacetime, somehow all would be well in war. To Conley it was clear that many of his superiors were almost egregiously ignoring the lessons of history and, in particular, the severe impact that previously mentioned torpedo failures had upon the effectiveness of both the German U-boat campaign against Allied shipping in the Battle of the Atlantic and the American submarine campaign in the Pacific War.

Ironically, Conley fully appreciated that a commanding officer returning from a daring and very successful intelligence-gathering mission was bound to receive a much greater accolade and acclaim than one whose boat had excelled in the much more mundane certification process of handling and firing Tigerfish, the problems of which he now had to wrestle with.

The anti-submarine torpedo employs two principal homing techniques, the first of which uses its own sonar to seek out and guide itself towards the high-frequency noise being emitted from the targeted submarine. Its second homing method is to transmit high-frequency acoustic pulses to detect and intercept the target. Passive homing has the disadvantage that by emitting very little noise in the high-frequency spectrum a quiet submarine may elude pursuit by a torpedo. There is virtually no such emission in the case of a diesel submarine slowly propelling herself by electric motors, hence the necessity for a secondary method, that of active homing. However, the distinct pulses transmitted by the questing torpedo in this mode risks the targeted submarine being prematurely alerted, allowing it to use speed and/or decoys to successfully evade the attack.

The advent of the Russian nuclear submarine, with its much greater speed and agility, demanded a torpedo much more capable than the old Mark 23 wire-guided torpedo which was the Royal Navy's main heavyweight weapon from the early 1960s onwards. Severely limited in performance by its slow maximum speed of just 18 knots, a very limited depth capability and no active homing mode, it relied upon the targeted submarine making sufficient noise to attract its attention. Conley's experience indicated that this was not often the case and its modest speed made it highly unlikely to catch a nuclear submarine capable of 30 knots. It was considerations such as those fundamental deficiencies that sharpened the appetite of Conley and his ilk for a change of weapon, and much had been expected of the Tigerfish to answer this urgent need. The fact that it should have been in service in the late 1960s made its introduction all the more necessary, but a number of factors, including the reliability of its components – based to some extent on the failure of available technology to fulfil the designed specification – had delayed its entry into service by almost a decade.

The wire-guided Tigerfish was an electric torpedo which had a maximum speed of 36 knots and could home actively or passively. A number of different commands were transmitted from the attacking submarine down its wire, but its Achilles heel was the already described very unreliable arrangement for paying out the guidance wire. Apart from restricting the attacking submarine to a speed of about 6 knots, the outboard wire dispenser often 'tumbled' as it detached from the torpedo, causing the wire to break. Unlike the contemporaneous, much faster but noisier, active homing American Mark 48 torpedo, Tigerfish had to be 'command armed' after it had been launched, and a broken wire meant that even though it acquired its target and successfully homed upon it, detonation would not occur. The Mark 48, which armed automatically, was normally fired upon a target intercept course, with its appropriate offset, making it much less reliant upon wire guidance and thus was much more effective.

Tigerfish was, alas, introduced into service at a time when British manufacturing was at a nadir in terms of both quality of output and the industrial relations between management and the shop floor. This was most publicly made manifest by the poor quality of the products from the then leading British car manufacturer British Leyland, but it was common to other manufactories, a product of post-war malaise in management, a lack of investment and an air of entitlement among skilled workmen. It was also a period of parlous government finances, high levels of inflation and the infamous bailout of the United Kingdom by the International Monetary Fund in 1976.

It was against this background that the new Tigerfish torpedo was being manufactured by Marconi Underwater Systems Ltd. Thus poor component manufacture, exacerbated by a paucity of funding for the urgent rectification of its shortcomings, led to the serious delay in both the introduction of the Tigerfish and remedying its extremely poor performance. This situation was convincingly hidden by the Ministry of Defence behind the obvious imperatives accorded to the SSN building programme, though in fact there appeared to be a perverse lack of impetus to ensure that the primary strike force of the Royal Navy was adequately armed.

At Conley's end of this almost ludicrous situation there were other problems. The practice Tigerfish weapons, used for the crew assessments and certifications that he and his team were expected to carry out, used rechargeable propulsion batteries. These were different from the high performance single-use units fitted to the war-shot torpedoes. The former were prepared for firing by the MoD Armament Depot at Coulport, near Faslane, where the workforce were nicknamed the 'Coulport Bears' on account of their strident militancy inherited from their antecedents, who worked in the Clyde shipyards. Their preparation of the practice weapons was often less than thorough, further and significantly compromising an already low reliability.

Conley took over from a highly experienced lieutenant commander who had a brilliant intellect, but suffered from a very debilitating dependency upon alcohol. Most of the weapons firings took place at the British Underwater Test & Evaluation Centre (BUTEC) range, with its headquarters in the small Inverness village of Kyle of Lochalsh. The certification team would be landed overnight and as there was no Service accommodation available they would be billeted in local hotels or bed and breakfast accommodation. Conley soon realised that many of his staff enjoyed serious drinking in the local hostelries, displaying no sense of urgency to get the weapon firings completed as quickly and effectively as possible, let alone pass the records back to Faslane for in-depth analysis. This had become apparent to the submarine crews and was another factor which had done nothing to enhance the image of Tigerfish, or contribute to any sense of importance regarding its introduction.

Conley quickly applied change and made it clear to his subordinates that the days of going onboard a submarine in a lethargic state, suffering from a hangover, were over. From now on, only the highest standards of professionalism would be acceptable. This shake-up soon produced dividends.

The BUTEC tracking range, completed in 1973, was a very poor second in comparison to the American alternative, AUTEC. Only about five miles by three in size, its depth of water was relatively shallow and in its early days its tracking hydrophones on the bottom of the seabed were prone to be damaged by trawlers, until an exclusion area was rigorously enforced around its boundary. The range vessels and equipment required to support the torpedo firings were also not up to the mark, all of which further hampered the effectiveness of the firings conduction, and the testing of the submarine crews. The situation was worsened by the poor quality of the range staff, many of whom also had a penchant for excessive drinking, the curse of many communities in the west of Scotland.

During Conley's early days at the BUTEC the shore and jetty facilities were still under construction and its senior naval officer was temporarily ensconced in the Kyle of Lochalsh stationmaster's old office. The station platform was also used to transfer torpedoes on trolleys from the recovery vessels to the trucks which returned them to Coulport. This produced the public benefit of occasional family holiday snaps featuring children astride a Tigerfish, the Royal Navy's new secret answer to the massive Soviet submarine threat.

Conley quickly made himself unpopular with the range personnel by shaking up the whole BUTEC organisation. Well aware that submarine time was at a premium, he demanded extended range operating hours lasting until sunset, instead of the cosy practice of ending activities at 1600. He also insisted on the instigation of rigorous daily checks to ensure the range equipment was properly functioning at the start of the day's firings.

Prior to his arrival, the submarine crews undergoing certification only fired their weapons against unchallenging static noise targets which were a leftover from earlier development trials. He soon changed that by introducing mobile targets, both surface ships and submarines, which either by natural characteristics or by noise augmentation replicated closely the characteristics of Russian submarines. These were much more demanding for the crews to engage successfully and revealed a number of new problems, such as that of the noise made by a running torpedo masking that of the target on sonar, making accurate guidance difficult. In addition to testing the crews in conditions as realistic as possible within the constraints of the range, these early firings started the process of developing tactics to achieve optimum use of the weapons, notwithstanding the chronic reliability problems. Another initiative of Conley's was to start conducting firings away from BUTEC in suitable coastal areas in the west of Scotland which were much more conducive to the firing submarine being able to have more freedom to manoeuvre before weapon firing, thus adding further realism.

With the entire Submarine Flotilla being required to convert to Tigerfish within two years, the pace of certification was intense. Conley and his team took submarine crews through a comprehensive programme which included shore attack simulator training, instruction in the embarking and loading of Tigerfish, and testing and validation of the boat's weapon control equipment. During the sea phase, the team checked out that each submarine's crew were competent to use Tigerfish, usually firing up to eight individual weapons. This normally took two or three days to complete, as the torpedo recovery was ponderously undertaken by seamen in a rigid inflatable boat, or RIB, which deployed from a recovery vessel and who hooked the weapon and enabled it to be lifted out of the water. This evolution could only take place in daylight and was weather-constrained to a moderate sea state, unlike AUTEC, where helicopters could recover weapons up to gale-force conditions. There was also a host of other problems, both external and internal to the submarine, such as achieving clear range, which could delay weapon launch. It was hoped that out of the eight torpedoes embarked as standard, there would be at least three or four runners which would enable the certification process to be completed.

Perhaps unsurprisingly, the occasional crew failed and had to repeat the whole programme, but this was an exception, as much effort was put in by Conley and his team to ensure that the crews reached the required standards of expertise and capability first time round.

Over his sixteen months at STWG, Conley led the certification of over twenty submarine crews and experienced hundreds of Tigerfish firings. Inevitably, he built up a substantial expertise in the Tigerfish torpedo system, the reliability of which remained doggedly low at about 30 per cent for an individual weapon. In September 1977, a few months into the job, he was tasked to lead a team to Hardanger Fjord in Norway, to fire a randomly selected in-service torpedo in order to demonstrate the reliability of the warhead. The outcome was to prove a low point in Conley's experiences with Tigerfish.

A remote spot on the west side of the fjord had been used for some time to test straight-running torpedoes of both the Norwegian and British navies. With their limited range of a few thousand yards, these weapons were simply aimed at the steep sides of the fjord, exploding on impact with the sheer rock face. In the case of this first Tigerfish routine warhead proving shot, active homing was ruled out as with multiple echoes likely from the rock face, the weapon could possibly go awry – perhaps even posing a risk to the firing submarine, HMS *Ocelot*. Therefore, as passive homing was the only safe option, a noise source was suspended into the sea at a suitable point on the rock face. This was an essential prerequisite as the weapon needed to have strong target contact prior to detonation.

The firing did not go well. When the weapon was launched some 3,000 yards from the target, the wire dispenser failed to release. With the additional rear weight and drag caused by this imbalance, the Tigerfish careered on the surface across the fjord where Conley's shore observer spotted it close to the aim point 'disappearing behind a clump of trees'. Being unarmed, on impact with the shore the torpedo did not explode, but *Ocelot*'s sonar team reported breaking-up noises which reassuringly confirmed that it had not actually come up onto the shoreline.

After reporting the failure to the Northwood headquarters, Conley soon learned that the Norwegian naval authorities were extremely displeased. Apparently, they had not been informed by the MoD that the torpedo in question was an electric homing one with a maximum range of fifteen miles, as opposed to the two or three miles of the straight-running types. They took the view that it could have been a danger to numerous settlements or vessels further up the fjord. Conley was consequently summoned to the Royal Norwegian Navy headquarters at Bergen to provide an explanation. He travelled there by one of two Royal Navy Sea King helicopters which had been hastily arranged to collect a specialist diving team intended to recover the wreckage of the failed Tigerfish, and which had been urgently dispatched by commercial airline to Bergen airport. At a meeting with the local admiral and his staff, Conley explained that there were a number of safeguards on the weapon which prevented it exploding other than at deep depth, but the Norwegians insisted that the Royal Navy make every effort to locate the warhead.

The helicopter flight back from Bergen took them over the spectacular Folgefonna glacier before landing on the playing fields of the primary school (the only suitable site) in the village of Rosendal which, situated on the east side of the fjord, was the nearest suitable location to use as a base for the search. The school pupils, joyously pouring out from their classrooms, were thrilled at the noise and sight of the two unexpected aircraft which, having landed, decanted a burly team of divers and their equipment. Conley was more concerned about the bill for the evident damage the downdraught of the helicopters' blades had caused to the surface of their playing fields. For him, matters seemed rapidly to be going from bad to worse.

Meanwhile, a Royal Navy minehunter had been tasked to join in the search for the 300lb warhead and there was further assistance from a Norwegian Navy diving tender and its crew. Notwithstanding several days of search and the recovery of small fragments of the Tigerfish from a deep shelf on the side of the fjord, the warhead was never located. Accordingly, the search was terminated on the assumption that the warhead was lying in small pieces in several hundred feet of water.

On return home, Conley was required to conduct an investigation into the weapon's failure. The inquiry did not reveal much and it was duly concluded that the dispenser had been defective, just one of many potential failures in a thoroughly unreliable bag of tricks. The whole incident, of course, had done nothing for the reputation of Tigerfish and left Conley feeling very despondent about its many deficiencies. This was not what he had intended his working life to be when he had joined the Royal Navy's Submarine Service.

In the spring of 1978 Conley found himself back at AUTEC with his team. Their new task was to conduct a series of Tigerfish tactical evaluation firings from the SSN *Conqueror* using the diesel submarine *Porpoise* as the principal target. Conley and his deputy, a weapon engineer officer, had designed each of the firing runs, and his team were there to provide expert support to the *Conqueror*'s crew to ensure as far as possible perfect preparations for each of the shots. Ashore in the AUTEC headquarters building on Andros Island, a small cell of his staff analysed the firings, providing very rapid turnaround of the results, in order to highlight where improvements could be made on the weapon control.

Cape Canaveral was again used as a shore base and Conley's team was allocated offices in a building in the NASA Space Centre. This location offered several benefits, including the local NASA staff putting on a tour of several redundant missile-launch blockhouses. Conley later recalled how their visit to the Apollo launch control room had proved very moving; all the instruments and control stations remaining virtually untouched, gathering dust as the programme of manned missions to the Moon faded to become just a remarkable memory. Conley also received an invitation to attend the launch of an Atlas Centaur rocket with a payload of commercial satellites. The night firing under a canopy of stars appeared almost surreal as the ascending missile quickly disappeared into the single cloud created by its venting fuel before lift-off, turning the cloud bright red before emerging and accelerating upwards into space in what had been a flawless launch. Ruefully Conley reflected, 'If only Tigerfish could have similar reliability.'

There was a substantial cast of Tigerfish project civil servants and Coulport staff attending the weapon evaluations in a support role, many of whom had arrived in Cape Canaveral several weeks earlier and who were very much enjoying the benign spring climate in Florida. They were all under the charge of a senior submarine commander who was responsible for the conduct of the trials, although the purse strings for the whole operation were held by the Tigerfish project personnel. It soon became evident to Conley that, although the civilian staff of even the lowest status had been provided with rental cars for getting around Cape Canaveral and its environs, his own staff members were relegated to using a shuttle-bus service. A firm representation to the trials commander about the inequitable transport arrangements did not achieve any improvement. Conley was then subsequently loaned a car by an American space engineer with whom he had become friendly, but this generous act did not improve the frosty relationship which had developed between himself and the commander. However, it was a lesson to Conley about the power exercised by those in the Civil Service who controlled budgets. As the trials progressed, he also gained a dispiriting insight into a culture of ambivalence within the project team about the firing results, whether they were successful or otherwise. He reflected that it was no wonder that it had taken so long to get Tigerfish into service, and if this project was typical, the Navy's procurement organisation required a massive shake-up.

During these evaluation firings, an unusually good streak of Tigerfish reliability was experienced and Conley was pleasantly surprised by the efficacy of the weapon's active homing capability against *Porpoise*, even at a shallow depth where a lot of false surface returns could be expected. As achievement of the run objectives was exceeding expectations, Conley

(ABOVE) *Cambrian* arriving
Singapore Naval Base in May
1965. In the foreground left is
the Commander-in-Chief Far
East Fleet, Admiral Sir Frank
Twiss.

(ABOVE) Lieutenant Dan Conley, navigating officer, in the
control room of *Sealion*, March 1969.

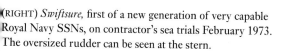

(RIGHT) *Swiftsure*, first of a new generation of very capable
Royal Navy SSNs, on contractor's sea trials February 1973.
The oversized rudder can be seen at the stern.

(ABOVE) *Otter,* Dan Conley's first submarine command, arrives at the US Naval Base Charleston, South Carolina, in February 1976. In the background is the submarine depot ship USS *Orion.*

(LEFT) The *Sunday People* headlines regarding the Mary Millington caper onboard *Otter.*

(BELOW) *Spartan*'s commissioning ceremony at Vickers Shipyard, Barrow, September 1979. The stand-facing starboard side has been freshly painted.

SAUCY SAGA HMS SEXY

By TONY PURNELL

RED-FACED Navy chiefs are investigating the saucy saga of the sexy model and the submarine.

Nude pictures on sub shock Navy chiefs

Minister fac quiz on nud 'Navy lark'

(ABOVE) *Courageous* departing Faslane, deploying on patrol.

(ABOVE) *Valiant* in April 1985 in lower Loch Long. On the right Dan Conley is conducting a short ceremony committing to the deep the ashes of wartime submarine hero Lieutenant Commander Alastair Mars, DSO, DSC*.

(LEFT) Commander Dan Conley is piped onboard *Valiant* for the first time, being greeted by Commander Chris Wreford-Brown on the right.

(ABOVE) The badly damaged Soviet Yankee-class submarine *K219* on the surface awaiting assistance. The damage was so extensive that she sank a few days later.

(ABOVE) The Soviet Alfa-class nuclear attack submarine. The fastest and deepest diving class of submarine ever built.

(ABOVE) A Soviet Whiskey-class diesel submarine. The class was built in very large numbers in the 1950s.

(LEFT) A Delta IV-class SSBN, the final version of this class of third-generation SSBNs which formed the backbone of the Soviet Union's seaborne deterrent from the 1970s.

(RIGHT) A Soviet Victor III class with its prominent pod on top of the rudder which housed a towed array sonar.

(LEFT) A Soviet Foxtrot-class diesel submarine. Built between 1958 and 1983, many of these were sold to other nations.

(ABOVE) During a quiet period at sea the officers of *Valiant* enjoy a mess dinner in the spring of 1985.

(BELOW) *Valiant* departs Faslane in June 1986 for a refit. She is flying an oversize pennant indicating imminent decommissioning.

(LEFT) A diver having attached a wire to it under the ice, a Tigerfish torpedo is pulled out from under the ice sheet by helicopter. The USN's Applied Physics Laboratory's Ice Station (APLIS), April 1988.

(BELOW) *Turbulent* surfaced in the Beaufort Sea during torpedo firings April 1988.

(ABOVE) The USN's Applied Physics Laboratory's Ice Station (APLIS) in the Beaufort Sea, spring 1988.

(BELOW) Captain Dan Conley, the last captain of HMS *Dolphin*, accompanied by his wife Linda, are cheered by the base officers as he leaves the establishment for the last time.

proposed to the trials commander that the weapon's active homing capability be explored further in more challenging scenarios. This would involve changing the authorised run plans, but his superior, possessing little knowledge of Tigerfish, refused such a request on grounds that approval would be needed from headquarters and that would take too long. A heated but nugatory debate followed, Conley submitting that a great opportunity was being squandered. This added to his increasing reputation of being a tartar who was not afraid to ruffle the feathers of his seniors.

On his return to the United Kingdom on completion of what had been a broadly successful series of firings, Conley started considering his next job. The duration of his STWG appointment was always going to be a brief one as there was a shortage of command-experienced executive officers (second in commands) needed to man the SSBN squadron and the ever increasing number of SSNs. Much to his concern, his appointer had indicated that he was most likely to be heading for an SSBN, an appointment he viewed with dismay, as he saw it holding limited challenges on very dull and monotonous deterrent patrols. Furthermore it did not make best use of his *Swiftsure* experience. To Conley's relief, however, a Campbeltown colleague who was destined to join the SSN *Spartan* at her builder's yard asked to be appointed to the SSBN for personal reasons of family stability. Accordingly, he immediately seized the opportunity arising of the *Spartan* job, to which his appointer agreed, and consequently prepared to go back to Barrow where the SSN was being completed.

Conley had worked very hard in his so-called 'shore' appointment, spending a considerable amount of time at sea and together with his team, working very long hours, particularly when at BUTEC. Alongside establishing high levels of crew competence in the use of their new torpedo, he had initiated the development of the optimum tactics to use it to the maximum effectiveness. He also took every opportunity to hammer home the message to his superiors that significant resources needed to be accorded to improving Tigerfish reliability if the Submarine Flotilla was to be effective in war. This was a lonely challenge but gradually by dint of effort he fostered the wholehearted support of some enlightened senior officers, including Commander Michael Boyce, the FOSM staff officer responsible for weapon system effectiveness: this officer was destined to head the Armed Forces as Chief of the Defence Staff at the time of the second Gulf War. Such highly capable individuals were able to make the case for getting an improvement programme underway – but this was to take many years and would be far from plain sailing.

12

From Barrow to Bear Island

DESPITE HIS ACHIEVEMENTS in training submarine crews, Lieutenant Commander Dan Conley was glad to receive a new posting and in September 1978 he returned to Vickers' shipyard at Barrow-in-Furness. His new appointment was to HMS *Spartan*, the fifth and penultimate SSN of the *Swiftsure* class, in which he would serve as executive officer, or second in command.

HM Submarine *Spartan* had been launched that April by Emily, Lady Lygo, a charming and lively Floridian, wife of Vice Chief of the Defence Staff Sir Raymond Lygo. As the traditional bottle of champagne broke against the hull, *Spartan* started a slow passage down the slipway, leaving behind as she slid into the murky waters of the Walney Channel the last of the class, HMS *Splendid*, still in the early stages of construction. She was then moved through the harbour lock system into a non-tidal berth for final fitting out and the testing of her machinery.

Conley observed sadly that the mode of working at the Vickers yard had changed little since his earlier spell there in 1972, despite its nationalisation. The slow decline of the British shipbuilding industry had provoked the Labour government to take the entire industry into public ownership and while these circumstances ought to have alarmed the management and workforce, the backing of the state had merely encouraged an endemic ennui. The shipyard, a sprawling complex of shabby, soot-stained Victorian buildings, sheds and workshops, was badly in need of modernisation to improve its production processes and to update much of its obsolescent plant, while its workforce continued its old ways, oblivious to the dangers of aggressive foreign competition. While shipyards building commercial shipping could go to the wall, a yard building the vessels so essential for maintaining and supporting Britain's nuclear deterrent, it was assumed by most at Barrow, was safe from such vicissitudes.

With a workforce of over 12,000, Vickers was heavily overmanned, but the management were hamstrung by very strong unions, which had an undue influence upon how the yard was organised and run. Whilst there was no significant industrial strife during *Spartan*'s building, this era marked the dog years of Jim Callaghan's Labour government and was a time of very weak management throughout British industry. Therefore, on occasions, Conley got the impression that the workforce dictated their own terms to the management and there were many practices of very evident inefficiency – for example the so-called night shift was a misnomer, as after midnight the shift workers took to sleeping in the most innovative of places. Nevertheless, he became aware that many of the senior management were legendary in terms of their ability to build and deliver nuclear submarines and they exuded a great degree of pride and confidence that they would produce a first-rate ship for the Royal Navy.

Apart from the two SSNs, *Spartan* and *Splendid*, the only other vessel under construction in the yard was the aircraft-carrier HMS *Invincible*. A year earlier a project to build three German-designed Type 204 coastal submarines for the state of Israel had been completed. Against a background of the loss of the *Dakar* and increasing difficulty in maintaining its ageing former British submarines built in the Second World War, the Israeli Navy badly needed new boats. Acquiring replacements from German shipyards would have been politically unacceptable, so a contract to build under licence was awarded to Vickers, a construction programme that was accomplished with a minimum of public notice.

Following a quick handover from the officer who had been appointed as executive officer on a temporary basis, Conley assumed the responsibility of second in command to an engineer commander, *Spartan*'s senior officer until relieved by the commanding officer when the boat was nearing completion. Conley found himself accommodated in a stark office in a draughty, prefabricated building, and got to grips with his task, the preparation of *Spartan* for her contractor's sea trials, only five months away. Well aware that in shipyard terms, five months was as the twinkling of an eye, there was much to be done. Pressing problems were exacerbated by the lack of any other seamen officers, due largely to external circumstances as the Royal Navy's Submarine Service went through a period of expansion. There were simply no qualified officers to fill several of the boat's key posts until the pressure of approaching sea trials compelled the necessary appointments. Indeed, even the captain, Commander Nigel Goodwin, did not arrive until after the trim dive in the yard basin had occurred in early December.

There was no such shortage of ratings and Conley had the challenge of keeping occupied an almost full complement of seamen, men who were well and truly engrossing themselves in the delights of Barrow. This was further complicated by the removal of one senior chief petty officer, the coxswain, who was under a charge in expectation of a court martial, owing to his dubious handling of the junior ratings' lodgings arrangements. Conley was not entirely sorry about this, as this was the same individual who had been his coxswain in *Otter* and whom, Conley was convinced, could have been much more forthcoming about the Mary Millington incident. However, although in the long term a blessing in disguise, this remained a setback, because the coxswain was not only responsible for discipline and the administration of the ship's company, but had the task of drawing up the watch and quarter bill, which set out the manning of the submarine when it was in different states of readiness, such as proceeding to sea or preparing to dive. Needless to say, there was also a shortage of submarine coxswains and a relief was not available until after the contactor's sea trials.

As was to be expected, the engineering department was provided with comprehensive formal documentation and operational procedures for the management of the nuclear propulsion plant. However, remarkably for such a complex vessel, there was no equivalent setting out the actions to be taken in the case of the failure of the general ship systems, or those specific to emergencies. For example, there were no properly documented procedures for what was to be done in the event of the after hydroplanes jamming. If this were to occur, vital and rapid steps needed to be taken and a drill by which the crew could swiftly and effectively deal with the problem should have been standard. The *Swiftsure* project in conjunction with FOSM's staff should have produced standard operating procedures, not least because system failures could imperil life and endanger the submarine, and were the moral responsibility of the design team.

However, such philosophical considerations would not solve the immediate problem and it was clear to Conley that it was up to him to produce *Spartan*'s own procedures. The task was made complicated by changes in the standard system of valve numbers adopted in earlier *Swiftsure*-class boats, so it was not just a matter of copying the documentation of *Spartan*'s predecessors. Without any seamen officers or a coxswain to share the load, Conley had his work cut out. On top of the daily demands on his time and attention, he was obliged to work late into many evenings, producing the myriad of operational and organisational documentation required before *Spartan* was ready to proceed to sea early in 1979.

Determined that the ship's company would be well prepared for the forthcoming sea trials and the work-up which would follow it, he started training the crew onboard in the early evening, before the night shift clocked on. This was an unpopular initiative, disrupting the ratings' routines, most of whom found their unpressurised existence in the yard highly congenial, and the pleasures of Barrow after work far more attractive than onboard training.

In spite of these multiple tribulations, Conley experienced immense job satisfaction. During his time in *Swiftsure* he had built up an excellent knowledge of this type of submarine's systems and characteristics which few, if any, of the crew could match. Pressed as he was, he felt himself very able to undertake the challenges with which the preparation of *Spartan* confronted him. To this there was also the compensation of some regular home life. Having packed up his work for the day, he would then head to the cottage he had rented near to the town of Broughton-on-Furness close to Coniston Water, a journey of twenty or so miles of winding roads edged with dry stone walls in stunning moorland countryside, providing a pleasant relief from the industrial grime of the shipyard.

Gradually, success bred success, and over time Conley experienced excellent co-operation between the shipyard managers and the submarine's staff who had, by now, accepted responsibility for the nuclear plant and watertight integrity of the submarine. Perhaps more important to future operational morale, the naval overseers appointed by the Ministry of Defence ensured that the crew's aspirations in terms of unauthorised improvements and embellishments were met, provided they were kept within reason. Conley took quiet pride in the number of unofficial changes which were achieved to meet the aim of ensuring that the submarine's habitability was to the best of standards.

Meanwhile, the final fitting out of the submarine progressed and the pace of individual machinery trials increased. Before the reactor was made to go 'critical' and start generating heat, a special barge secured alongside produced steam to test the main engines and the electrical generators. The first time of criticality of the reactor was an important milestone, when the control rods were gradually raised to allow a chain reaction to be initiated, thus generating the heat which would be turned into steam in the two boilers inside the reactor compartment. From a monitoring station – which had been set up on the dockside as a safety measure – Conley observed the elation of the engineering staff as the reactor went critical for the first time.

Another important event in the pre-trials process was the trim dive in the dock basin. HMS *Spartan* would carry both solid and seawater ballast to enable her to submerge without problems, having regard to a range of seawater densities and internal weight conditions. The easily removable liquid ballast allowed for the weight of additional equipment which would inevitably be fitted during the life of the vessel. The trim dive was a prerequisite to ensure that there was the right quantity of ballast and the boat was properly balanced fore and aft. This evolution took place in the yard's fitting-out basin which, whilst adequate for the trim calculations, was not deep enough to completely submerge the boat, the top of the fin remaining above the surface.

It was Conley's responsibility to ensure that when the submarine submerged in the basin it did so in a safe manner. Mindful that one of the previous *Swiftsure* class had ended up bow down, stuck in the shipyard mud, he ignored the official naval architect's diving ballast calculations because to him they appeared unsound. Instead, he rang around other vessels of the class and got hold of their trim data and calculations. On the assumption that the shipbuilder had built the submarine roughly the same size as the other *Swiftsure*s, it was not difficult to make an adjustment for stores and water density, and to work out a very acceptable and safe trim condition for the basin dive. The trim dive was successfully completed without incident, but the naval architect concerned stuck to theory in directing the shipbuilder to apply the final solid ballast corrections to the submarine.

In early 1979 the two key officers responsible for the navigation and sonar departments joined *Spartan*. Their unfamiliarity with the boat and her equipment required a great effort from them to get up to speed before the contractors' sea trials. The short space of time available necessitated Conley assisting, and their training was added to his daunting burden of tasks and responsibilities. The trials themselves would involve eight weeks of tests and evaluations, where the submarine was fully put through her paces in order to ensure all plant and equipment worked properly and that she had been built to the contract specification.

Late February 1979 saw *Spartan*, with tug assistance, move gingerly out of the dock complex into the open sea. The final culminating thrill of all his hard work in, as the phrase had it, 'getting underway in nuclear power', was tempered by the new captain, as he arrived on the bridge for departure, declaring that his children had contracted mumps and that he had feared he had caught the disease.

As *Spartan* moved past *Invincible*, the bow of which had been damaged earlier when she was being moved into the entrance lock, it was a reminder of the risks of locking back into the dock system, because it involved crossing a strong tidal stream. (Later, the entrance was significantly improved for the Trident submarines.) A shipyard joker had painted a large sign above *Invincible*'s damage, indicating that the remedial work was going to be undertaken by the local car body repair company. In the event both *Spartan*'s departure and re-entrance were achieved without incident.

Clear of the Walney Channel, *Spartan* moved out into deep water, having discharged her tugs, and headed north. On her maiden dive, undertaken in the sheltered waters of the Clyde Estuary, it proved difficult to submerge *Spartan* as she proved too lightly ballasted. Thus the submarine was obliged to spend a weekend in Faslane while a number of the Vickers shipyard workers attending the trials undertook the miserable task of securing tons of solid ballast under the casing in driving rain. With something of a sense of vindication, Conley saw the theoretical trim calculations disposed of to the 'classified waste'.

Proceeding back to sea for crew safety training, prior to embarking on full power trials, a serious problem soon emerged in that many members of the crew had become ill with violent stomach-ache and dizziness. Fortunately the symptoms, although very unpleasant, were short-lived, and the cause was determined as coming from contamination in a freshwater pipe. Meanwhile, the embarked shipyard personnel, who could be up to forty in number, had established themselves in the torpedo stowage compartment, nicknamed the 'casbah' owing to the amount of coloured material separating their temporary bunks. Fitted out with film projector and other comforts, this compartment was their sanctuary and was even out of bounds to the Faslane-based submarine work-up staff.

After several days of evolutions and emergency drills, the crew were cleared by the work-up staff as safe and competent enough to proceed with the trials. It was at this point that the captain's concerns on sailing proved accurate. The mumps laid him out and he was obliged to be landed, leaving Conley in command. This might have seemed like Conley's moment, a reward by providence for all his hard work, but prior to the acceptance of the new submarine into regular naval service – an important moment marked by the ceremonial hoisting of the white ensign – she was still technically the property of her builders, regarded as a merchant ship, and flew the red ensign. In recognition of his theoretical role of being their appointed shipmaster, Vickers paid Conley 5 pence per day, a sum deriving from the old Board of

Trade payment of one shilling per diem to a supernumerary aboard a British merchantman and reducing him – with something of an ironical twist of fate – to the status equivalent of a 'distressed British seaman'.

Having landed the captain, the first major element of the programme was to undertake machinery proving tests in the Irish Sea, working up to full power when dived. These were achieved travelling up and down the undersea valley known as Beaufort's Dyke, which bisects the Stranraer–Larne ferry route. This relatively deep trench of water is about thirty miles long but just over two miles wide. Working up to a maximum speed of 30 knots when only a few hundred feet above the seabed, and executing a sharp reversal of course at either end with a rather green crew, posed what today might have been an unacceptable degree of risk, not least because over two million tons of explosives had been dumped in the bottom of the Dyke after the Second World War.

For Conley this proved a nail-biting period. During all the high-speed runs he stationed himself in the control room, closely supervising the submarine ship control team, and ready to react immediately to any equipment failure. In particular, loss of control of the rudder or hydroplanes could have had catastrophic consequences. However, all went smoothly and on reaching 30 knots a 50-pence piece was successfully balanced on its edge on the wardroom table: there was virtually no vibration – an excellent example of British engineering at its best.

The remainder of the sea trials were completed very successfully and the first deep dive to a maximum safe depth of well over a thousand feet was undertaken without too many doors jamming or compartment partitions bulging from hull compression. To avoid this, the shipbuilder allowed adequate margins of clearance, and Vickers had achieved this very successfully. Meanwhile, the crew enjoyed the finest of cuisine because, although the catering staff ordered the food, the shipbuilder was paying for it. Surprisingly, the Faslane NAAFI food depot was not to be defeated by orders from *Spartan* at sea, which included such delicacies as frogs' legs, lobsters and Alaskan king crabl. It was all a bit of a game to see how far Vickers could be pushed, including charging them corkage on their own beer and wine, the proceeds of which went towards the ship's company commissioning dance, although, in reality, little of either was actually consumed.

Returning to the shipyard in April, *Spartan* embarked on a normal three-month 'post sea trials build completion phase'. In the event, however, this was extended by two months for her to be fitted with special protection to a number of her vulnerable external fittings. This would enable her to undertake the role of a target, the first Royal Naval nuclear submarine to be so modified and indicating to Conley that, like *Otter*, she was destined to spend significant periods of time at the AUTEC and BUTEC ranges. The prospect of having a variety of practice and test torpedoes fired against her, sometimes intended to actually strike her, added a zest to the future. The AUTEC trials were very welcome to the crew, who knew that they inevitably meant port visits to Florida.

On a fresh, sunny September morning, the commissioning ceremony took place in a shipyard berth back in Barrow, where a pavilion and stand had been set up. There was a substantial gathering of the families of the crew, Vickers's staff, local dignitaries and other guests, with the shipyard band providing a jaunty musical accompaniment. There was also a welcome contingent of 'old Spartans', veterans who had served in *Spartan*'s Second World War predecessor. Their Vickers-built *Bellona*-class light cruiser had been sunk off Anzio in January 1944 by a guided bomb. It was very much a humbling experience for the crew of the SSN to meet these stalwarts, several of whom had been severely wounded during the attack and, needless to say, they were delighted to be honoured guests and to be given a tour of a nuclear submarine. The crew were also extremely pleased that Lady Lygo was able to be present and, indeed, she was to maintain a strong interest in the submarine during its succeeding commissions.

The commissioning berth and everything around it had been spruced up and painted. This included the starboard side of *Spartan*, the side facing the bigwigs, making it at least five and a half coats of external paint applied since the initial coat. Indeed, the submarine had been completed to absolutely immaculate standards of finish and cleanliness, although Conley considered the employment of two women on their hands and knees using hacksaw blades to scrape off the piling from the wardroom carpet a bit over the top.

At the start of the commissioning proceedings the ship's company proudly marched on and formed ranks in front of the commissioning stand, their standard of marching and appearance absolutely outstanding for submariners. The commissioning ceremony was led by the Chaplain of the Fleet conducting a short service of dedication, which culminated in the captain reading out the commissioning warrant which authorised that HMS *Spartan* join the Fleet. On completion of the reading, the shrill of a bosun's whistle was the cue for the white ensign to be hoisted for the first time at the stern of the submarine and the Union Jack raised at the bows.

After the commissioning ceremony the VIP guests were conducted round the submarine and ended their visit with a glass of champagne in the wardroom. This plan encountered a hitch when the Mayor of Barrow's well-built wife proved a bottleneck, nervous of descending the vertical ladder of the main access hatch, despite much persuasion. The situation was resolved when the mayor himself threatened her with the deployment of the torpedo loading gear to get her below. All then proceeded well and was followed in the evening by a very successful ship's company dance in the town hall which concluded a happy and memorable day.

The seemingly interminable leaving parties now over and the final modifications and improvements extracted from the shipbuilder, HM Submarine *Spartan* prepared to leave her birthplace. After her work-up in Faslane she would join the Second Submarine Squadron, based in Devonport. However, the moment for *Spartan* to sever her connections with Barrow-in-Furness was not universally welcomed by the ship's company. A number of the crew had married Barrow girls and, characteristically, their young wives were not inclined to move out of the town and follow the drum. Their influence encouraged an aspiration in their husbands to return to another submarine under construction as soon as possible.

As he waited for the passing of the order to close up to stations for leaving harbour, Conley contemplated the moment of transition. He felt a strong attachment to *Spartan*, forged by the heavy but important workload that he had perforce been compelled to deal with on joining her. Moreover, he thought privately, those few days of command during the sick leave of Commander Goodwin had, in some odd way, confirmed this relationship. Sailors never quite love their ships, but they often have a regard for them and the part they play in their careers.

Her Britannic Majesty's submarine *Spartan* had cost about £200 million to build at 2013 values, much less than the cost of the *Astute*-class SSNs, which exceeded £1,000 million and were commissioned from 2010 onwards. She nevertheless had her limitations. Although fitted with the latest sonar and weapon-control equipment, against surface ships *Spartan* would have to resort to the over forty-year-old Mark 8 torpedo. However, she was equipped with the Tigerfish anti-submarine torpedo which, although a marked improvement on the Mark 23, as recounted in the previous chapter, suffered from serious defects.

Satisfaction with his new boat did not totally extend to the performance of her crew. To Conley's disappointment, and not for the want of enthusiasm and effort, the ship's company did not excel in the subsequent safety phase or the operational work-up. They were assessed to have achieved a satisfactory standard in both, but the breakdown in the personal relationship between the commanding officer and the captain heading the work-up staff undoubtedly proved an inhibiting factor in the outcome. Privately, Conley considered that the crew were capable of achieving a higher standard.

Once again, Conley observed that, exactly as in his Perisher course, the operational work-up programme was mainly geared towards fighting an 'enemy' who operated on identical lines to one's own or allied forces. To this was added training in intelligence-gathering techniques, but there remained a gaping lack of time devoted to dealing with the threat of hostile submarines. Apprehensive of the thrust of Soviet naval ambitions, Conley felt that they had received inadequate preparation for any forthcoming deployment against Russian submarines.

Although post-commissioning trials and work-up revealed few technical problems, an irksome fault was experienced with the anchor system, fitted under the bows outside the pressure hull. The anchor itself housed flush with the submarine's hull and behind it the cable lay in a cylindrical chain locker. Whilst serving in *Swiftsure*, Conley had witnessed a severe problem on weighing the anchor in a remote Scottish loch. As the final section of cable was hove in, it rode off the whelps of the windlass. The whelps grip each link, enabling the rotating windlass barrel to heave the cable in but once unshipped, the weight of the anchor would reverse the process. With a roar the whole of the cable ran out totally out of control, onto the bottom of the seabed. It was fortunate that the securing arrangements in the cable locker proved robust, or else all would have ended up at the bottom of the loch.

Employing manual seamanship techniques with which Nelson's sailors would have been familiar, the crew had had to haul in sufficient slack cable to work it back over the whelps on the windlass. This was a difficult and prolonged task, for the weight of the entire submarine had to be taken off the cable, while the weight of the cable itself as it dangled into the depths had to be lifted to recover a sufficient amount to accomplish its relocation. Once this was achieved the winding-in process could to be restarted. After many frustrations in trying to get the last part of cable into the locker, this proved so tight a fit that its accomplishment required the removal of one section of cable in order to house the remainder. This was a near-impossible task in the wet, cramped conditions of the *Swiftsure*'s windlass compartment. It was soon clear to all concerned that whilst the locker was adequate in capacity for initial use, as deposits built up on the cable, it became too small for the stowage of the full cable, causing the outer section to back up and jump off the windlass.

Based upon this experience, Conley had attempted without success to persuade the overseeing authorities to shorten the length of *Spartan*'s cable. It was therefore to his consternation that after anchoring off Rothesay one evening during the work-up, the crew endured a repeat performance of *Swiftsure*'s travails. Infuriated by the disconnect between the practical seamen and the naval architects which, in this case, had been made manifest by *Swiftsure*'s wretched experience, Conley had to be prevailed upon not to truck the surplus removed cable section to the submarine design department in Bath.

In April 1980, seven months after commissioning, *Spartan* was on operational patrol in the Norwegian Sea. For the first time she was fitted with a towed acoustic array – passive sonar – but the crew had no prior training in its use for target motion analysis (TMA) which was, in any case, rudimentary and underdeveloped. Submarine target motion analysis is derived from the changing bearing of a target yielding the data necessary to calculate its course, speed and range. That said, the resulting answers can often only be said to give a general indication of a target's location and movement.

The towed acoustic array consists of a long line of hydrophones – an acoustic array – streamed behind the submarine at a distance of several hundred yards. This ensures that the array is well clear of the submarine's own noise, while its features enable it to make long-range detection of discrete low-frequency emissions from the target's machinery. For example, a particular piece of plant, such as a generator, might emit noise at a very distinctive 270Hz. Such emissions, known as tonals, both aided the classification of a targeted submarine, but also provide information which assisted the TMA calculations. The disadvantage of the towed acoustic array is that it becomes destabilised for a period after any manoeuvre by the towing submarine. An alteration of course or depth results in a loss of contact for several minutes until the towed acoustic array is straight again. This breakdown in data acquisition inhibits the steady garnering of bearing change that resolves the course, speed and range of the contact. Other complications arise, compromising the accuracy of the acquired data, from sources such as the presence of anomalous sound propagation caused by contact noise reflecting off the bottom of the seabed, before being received by the array. Accordingly, TMA using towed acoustic array data is very complex and requires great skill and expertise to achieve the satisfactory results which, in themselves, tend to provide the 'ball park' referred to earlier.

Not long after *Spartan*'s patrol had begun, contact was made with a Charlie II-class cruise missile submarine (SSGN). Intelligence reports had indicated her to be participating in an exercise involving her trailing and marking the Russian helicopter carrier *Leningrad* and her surface escorts. This group was replicating an American aircraft-carrier strike force passing through the Norwegian Sea with the SSGN in the role of interdicting opposition. With the ability to launch its lethal SSN7 anti-ship missiles whilst submerged and at short range – thus affording very little warning – the Charlie II-class submarine at the time was the United States aircraft carrier's most dangerous foe.

Spartan patiently maintained her trail of the Soviet boat for two days at a range of about ten miles, but she never got close enough to generate an accurate 'fire control solution'. This would have marked the trail as a success but, in the event, only a rough 'range assessment' was held on her. Meanwhile, above the waves other intelligence sources recorded that the Russians had conducted simulated air attacks on the group, complete with gunnery exercises. Eventually, contact with the Russian force was lost among the noise made by coastal shipping and fishing vessels off the Norwegian coast as the Russians closed the final phase of their exercise. Despite the disappointment in failing to achieve that fire control solution, for the *Spartan*'s crew it was a good start; they had had practical experience in the field, trailing a potential 'hostile' using their towed acoustic array.

Spartan was next ordered north to intercept an Alfa-class SSN, reported to be the first which had deployed to seaward of local patrol zones off the north Russian coast. It was thought she too was partaking in a large Soviet maritime exercise. Soon *Spartan*'s operators were in contact with the Russian, which was detected at a range of over one hundred miles in an area to the north of Norway, but there was concern that she might be heading back to port for May Day celebrations and that a close-range intelligence-gathering approach might not be achieved. Accordingly, the captain was very keen to close on her as rapidly as possible. Unfortunately, Goodwin and Conley had not organised themselves into a proper command rota and over a period of several days with little sleep, their stamina was being stretched.

Heading east at high speed to intercept her quarry, but unable to hold the target on sonar whilst at speed, *Spartan* was slowed at periodic intervals to regain contact. About twelve hours after the initial sonar contact, Conley was summoned by Goodwin to the sound room. On entry he quickly observed that the towed array displays were indicating a very confused picture, almost saturated by noise from the Alfa, but curiously there was no contact on the hull sensors. Puzzled at first, he realised that the displays were indicating the close proximity of the Alfa, confirmed shortly afterwards by a contact of high rate of bearing change detected on the hull sonar on the port beam. This indicated the Russian was passing in the opposite direction and was evidently not too far away. Commander Goodwin now put his helm hard over and *Spartan* banked to port to maintain contact with and follow the Russian. It was soon evident, however, that the Alfa was herself altering course inside the British SSN's turning circle and had skilfully manoeuvred to a position astern of *Spartan*.

The Russian commander had clearly effected counter-detection and a situation had developed akin to an underwater dogfight, the two opposing submarines manoeuvring less than two miles apart and risking collision. Goodwin decided it was time to break away from the Russian and increase the distance between them. However, he had hardly done so when two very strong sonar transmissions were heard coming from directly astern. It was clear that the Russian commander was using his active sonar to classify *Spartan* as a submarine contact. Sonar transmissions now came from astern at regular intervals, a clear and unambiguous indication that 'the opposition' was well and truly in active contact and that, quite simply, *Spartan* was now the Russian's quarry.

It was evident that urgent evasion techniques had to be called upon and Goodwin put his boat through her paces, heading westwards at a speed approaching 30 knots. This proved insufficient, for with a top speed of 42 knots, the trailing Alfa remained on *Spartan*'s quarter, very close and clearly having no trouble in keeping up. There was little that could be done, other than hope the Russian would find it increasingly difficult to maintain sonar contact in the high-speed chase. Meanwhile, Conley observed that his captain, very much lacking sleep, looked absolutely drained and exhausted and was clearly upset about the loss of tactical control and the counter-detection.

Within an hour, the sonar transmissions had become faint and it was evident that *Spartan*'s evasive manoeuvres had confused the Alfa's sonar operators and contact had been broken. Having disengaged and continued to head west, no further Soviet contacts were gained during this patrol and *Spartan* returned to her base in Devonport.

There was no subsequent reproach for this incident, but there was a degree of concern expressed at headquarters that the Royal Navy's latest and quietest SSN had been detected by a relatively noisy Russian submarine. Close scrutiny of the results of a pre-patrol noise-ranging indicated a noise-short on a piece of machinery which could have given *Spartan*'s presence away. However, it was clear to Conley that tactical control had been lost and a very creditable detection at long range had developed into a less than satisfactory close-range encounter, in which the advantage had swiftly and decisively passed to the Russians as *Spartan* stumbled on top of her quarry. Conley concluded that a key lesson was the need to develop specific tactics when using data derived from a towed acoustic array. The question was – could better and more reliable bearing accuracy be obtained from the array itself? He privately felt that the designers and shipbuilder had been let down, and he became determined that *Spartan* would do a lot better in any subsequent patrol in which he participated.

By early February 1981, *Spartan* was back on operational patrol in the North Norwegian Sea, trailing a Victor SSN which was heading northeast towards her Northern Fleet base. In the intervening period the *Spartan*'s crew had had the benefit of two weeks' experience of operating with American submarines in a tactical evaluation exercise aimed at improving and refining the use of the towed acoustic array. They were therefore much better trained and prepared than they had been. This greatly encouraged Conley, who now found himself in a different situation. A new commanding officer had just joined: Commander Jim Taylor, who had had little previous experience in nuclear submarines or in encountering the Russian opposition. After discussing the matter with his executive officer, he had wisely delegated the tactical control of the submarine to Conley, who naturally relished the opportunity to make amends for the Alfa encounter.

The Russian Victor SSN had been detected to the northwest of the British Isles. However, owing to the difficult acoustic conditions of the Iceland–Faeroes Gap, caused by the noisy activities of fishing vessels and the confluence of ocean currents, the Gulf Stream meeting cold Arctic water, *Spartan* had broken off contact. Instead, she headed deep into the Norwegian Sea ahead of the Russian along his predicted track. This gambit paid off and, on cue, contact was regained and the trail continued.

When about a hundred miles southeast of Bear Island, hull sonar contact was achieved on the Victor, which had stopped moving forward and was randomly manoeuvring around a certain area. Using the much more accurate hull sonar bearings, *Spartan* closed range to about three miles to the east of the Victor's search locus and waited as events unfurled. Soon there was great excitement in the control room as a Delta-class Soviet SSBN was detected and classified, heading on a southwesterly track. Maintaining a prudent range, *Spartan*'s crew observed the Victor circling round the SSBN, conducting not very effective so-called 'delousing manoeuvres', aimed at detecting any trailing 'hostile' submarine. However, in this case, the inverse had occurred and the Victor had acted as a lure to a more valuable quarry. Using his experience from the Alfa encounter, Conley manoeuvred *Spartan* with great care to avoid any risk of counter-detection. At the same time he retained firm tactical control by carefully monitoring the movements and positions of the other submarines. He was well aware of the collision risks involved, with a trio of submarines operating within a three-mile radius of each other and remained alert for any unusual alterations in course or, a chilling thought, any hint of a fourth participant.

After several hours, having evidently completed his sanitising manoeuvres, the Victor headed southeast. Contact faded shortly thereafter, but now *Spartan* had established a trailing position on the port quarter of the Delta-class SSBN as she headed northwest. There was a great buzz throughout *Spartan* as word passed that they had collectively undertaken a unique piece of intelligence-gathering, of a Russian Victor SSN sanitising a deploying Delta SSBN. Moreover, they were now in chase of a strategically important contact; it was exactly what *Spartan* had been designed and built for, and for which they, as a ship's company, had trained.

Satisfied that all was under control, Conley left the control room for an early supper before relieving the captain for a stint as 'duty command'.

An hour or so later he returned to the control room and the boat was handed over to him. To his intense disappointment, contact with the Delta had been lost. Resolutely, Conley sought their elusive quarry. After two hours of searching to the northwest, Conley had the satisfaction of regaining contact and reported this to Taylor. Gratifying though this was, the evening was to have more surprises in store. Just before midnight it was clear that confusion existed in the sound room regarding the bearing of the Delta. The operators could not determine whether *Spartan* was on her port or starboard quarter, until it became clear that two distinctly separate sets of contact characteristics were being held on two different bearings. Conley quickly realised that *Spartan* was now behind not one but *two* 10,000-ton Delta–class SSBNs, which were about ten miles apart and heading deep into the Greenland Sea towards the ice edge. A second report went to the captain that they had additional company.

For the next day *Spartan* maintained her trail of the two Deltas as they headed towards the ice. On the second evening of the trail, as they approached the Greenland Sea oceanic front, a confluence of the remnants of the Gulf Stream and very cold Arctic water, a marked rise in sea noise ahead was detected: the characteristically noisy edge of the Arctic ice sheet. With no shipping contacts on sonar, Conley regarded this as rather eerie. Moreover, owing to the absence of an accurate navigational fix for some time, somewhat limited charts and a lack of knowledge of the exact location of the ice edge, he felt uneasy. To this sensation he had regard to the fact that neither of the Deltas had been held on SOSUS, so that naval headquarters at Northwood would have no idea where *Spartan* was operating in the very large patrol area designated to her. She was now approaching the limits of her sanctioned operational zone and, not being fitted with satellite communications and having no secure method of radioing for extra operating space, reluctantly her crew were obliged to abandon her wards and head south away from the ice. Despite the disappointment, however, both Taylor and Conley were satisfied that they had achieved a very successful and unique trail and that *Spartan*'s presence had not been detected.

A few days later, when back in the middle of the Norwegian Sea, contact was made with a homeward-bound Charlie II SSGN. The *Spartan* trailed her for a day or so before breaking off and returning to base. For Conley, who was about to leave the boat for a new appointment, it was a very satisfying end to his time in *Spartan* and their joint progress from fitting out to creditable operational patrol. The submarine returned to Devonport to accolades from the headquarters staff for what had been an outstandingly successful period at sea. *Spartan* was to go on to conduct several very accomplished operational patrols and took an active part in the Falklands War.

Although Conley would take no close part in the Falklands campaign, his experience in *Spartan* had brought him into contact with the potential enemy of the Cold War. They had crossed swords and been bested once, but he built upon this to achieve a *coup de main*. Commander Taylor's decision to delegate to him had given him a further opportunity to test himself and he consequently felt closer to his life's purpose and to his personal ambition, for his career had undergone a step-change. His performance and achievements in *Spartan* had erased the after-effects of his time in command of *Otter* and the ghost of Mary Millington had been laid to rest. Now selected for promotion to commander, his first appointment in his new rank would be on exchange duty with the United States Navy. He found himself a member of the staff of Commander Submarine Development Squadron Twelve, in Groton, Connecticut. Not only was this a prestigious posting, indicating some degree of official approbation of his conduct, but it would give him the opportunity to bring the extensive resources of the United States Navy to bear in his adopted crusade of developing towed acoustic array tactics. This was, he felt, a unique way of improving British SSN effectiveness in engaging the Russian submarine.

13

Serving under the American Flag

In July 1981 Conley and his wife arrived in Connecticut to move into a rented house in the pretty, historic town of Mystic, situated some twelve miles east of the US naval base at Groton. The prospect of living in a delightful corner of New England for two years seemed a fair swap for the rain and midges of the Gareloch, whither the American officer with whom he had exchanged places was destined.

Mystic had been a leading whaling port in the nineteenth century and its old seaport area had been transformed into a world-renowned maritime museum, which attracted a large number of visitors. The town's main street straddled the Mystic river and contained shops typical of small-town America, including an ice-cream parlour, barber and newsagent. Most of its houses and major buildings were of white, wooden clapboard construction and in many ways it epitomised the image of an affluent, well-ordered New England town. With the prospect of spending two years with Submarine Development Squadron Twelve, the Conleys soon immersed themselves in the local community and were made thoroughly welcome by several families who over the years had 'adopted' their exchange officer.

Submarine Development Squadron Twelve (CSDS12), known colloquially by the abbreviation of the 'Devron', was headquartered in America's largest submarine base, situated beside the sprawling town of Groton, on the River Thames opposite the city of New London.

The Devron had been formed in 1948 as an elite submarine squadron which had the specific role of developing war-fighting tactics as a result of the United States Navy's experiences fighting the Japanese in the Pacific. One of the conclusions drawn from the submarine campaign in the Pacific, which virtually destroyed all Japanese merchant shipping, was that 90 per cent of the sinkings were achieved by 10 per cent of the captains, a similar figure to the German successes against Allied shipping in the Battle of the Atlantic. Those individuals who employed the optimum attack tactics were both more likely to notch up kills and to survive enemy counter-attacks. This statistic assumed a greater relevance to possible operations conducted against the new enemy of the Cold War, where the tactical margins and their possible consequences held a new and thoroughly awesome threat for more than just those in the immediate vicinity. It was for these reasons that the United States Navy's high command placed an imperative priority upon tactical development, particularly as an increasing number of SSNs – known in the United States Navy as 'fast attack submarines' – came out of American shipyards.

When Conley joined the squadron it consisted of six SSNs and its naval shore staff were augmented by a number of contracted civilian specialists, several of whom were very highly qualified mathematicians. His first task was to lead a small team of civilian contractors in developing tactics for hunter-killer boats when they were required to provide cover for a strike force led by an aircraft carrier. This included the evaluation of an anti-ship version of the Tomahawk cruise missile which had a range of 300 miles. However, in this formidably intelligent mathematical company, he found himself addressing a more pressing problem. He was able to persuade his superiors that with the increasing threat of ever quieter and more capable Russian submarines, there was an urgent need to develop new methods of approaching these menacing craft using data from the towed acoustic array. Aware of the primary impor-tance of this stealthy method of acquiring target information, he was equally concerned that with all its vagaries and inaccuracies, at the time it was far from offering a real practical answer to the challenges faced by Western submarines confronted with the new generation of much quieter Russian boats.

With his recent experiences in mind he requested that he take a lead in this urgent problem and this was agreed. Conley also achieved an agreement to put greater effort into improving short-range submarine encounter procedures through the mechanism of a joint USN/RN-funded project which he would direct.

To a British naval officer, hitherto very much constrained in resources and trapped in entrenched orthodoxy, these opportunities were a godsend. Conley would be provided with the research facilities to develop computer simulations which comprehensively replicated the submarine versus submarine engagement. From expert analysis of the results of these, he and his team would then be able to develop tactics and procedures for testing at sea. During his tour of exchange duty, he and his consultants designed and ran six tactical evaluation exercises at sea, where the submarines acting in the Russian role were fitted with special noise augmentation equipment, in order that their characteristics would be as similar as possible to the opposition. A real benefit of the outcome would be that although there were equipment differences between the two navies, the Americans were very willing to make the results and the tactics developed available to the Royal Navy.

When Conley arrived in America, its submarine force was expanding at an unprecedented peacetime pace, aiming at a total number of ninety SSNs. Its workhorse of the 1970s, the thirty-seven '637' *Sturgeon*-class SSNs, were being joined by the bigger and faster '688' *Los Angeles*-class boats, of which there were twenty in commission and twelve under construction. (The numbers 637 and 688 were the hull numbers of the lead vessels of the respective classes.) There were also about twenty older-generation attack boats in commission, predominantly of the *Skipjack* and *Thresher* classes. At the same time the United States Navy's SSBN force totalled over thirty submarines armed with the Poseidon and Trident C4 missiles and the new 18,000-ton *Ohio*-class boats were about to start commissioning. In due course, these would carry the much more capable Trident D5 missile and would be built up to a total of eighteen submarines which would replace the older hulls.

In terms of numbers of vessels, the American all-nuclear submarine force was bigger than the entire Royal Navy, and the ongoing programme of expansion produced a very positive buzz within the Devron, with numerous ongoing projects addressing most aspects of submarine operations and warfare.

Outside the submarine base, a large and confidently presumptive sign proclaimed it as the 'Submarine Capital of the World', a declaration supported by the four operational squadrons of some forty submarines and a further dozen or so under construction at the General Dynamics Electric Boat shipyard on the east side of the Thames, a few miles downriver from the base.

Anyone who knew about shipbuilding, peering from the bridge linking New London with Groton into the Electric Boat yard, would be awed by the sight of several huge *Ohio*-class hulls protruding from the building sheds with a scattering of 6,500-ton '688'-class boats in the water at the fitting-out berths. However, the '688' build programme at the yard had encountered severe problems, owing to the detection of faulty internal welds in several hulls. These required significant restorative work which incurred serious delays, causing a backlog in the shipyard. On being given a tour of one of the delayed submarines after it had eventually been commissioned, Conley observed that its final finish was well short of the standards achieved in *Spartan*. In particular, the accommodation areas were notably austere and there were most certainly no carpets to hacksaw the piling from. However, he reflected that this was a warship, and rough edges and poor paintwork would not be detrimental to her fighting ability.

In 1981 the energetic, ambitious thirty-eight-year-old John Lehman was appointed by the incoming President Ronald Reagan as Secretary of the Navy. In due course, he went on to unveil an aggressive wartime maritime strategy of forward deployment of submarines and aircraft carrier battle groups into the Norwegian and Barents seas, the very backyard of the northern Soviet Union. It was also planned to deploy a large United States Marine force which could be landed rapidly in northern Norway to bolster NATO troops there, thus preventing the Russians from seizing the airfields that would be crucial to supporting the West's forward deployed maritime forces in case of a hot war.

Should it ever be necessary, the primary goal of this offensive would be rapidly to destroy all nuclear weapon-bearing Russian SSBNs on patrol in Arctic waters, and to prevent other enemy submarines from entering the Atlantic to attack shipping carrying crucial supplies and reinforcements to western Europe. Any surface units of the Soviet Navy at sea would also be destroyed, thus neutralising the enemy's submarine and surface fleets.

As part of this over-arching strategic plan, on the outbreak of hostilities both British and American SSNs would be deployed well forward into the Barents Sea and Arctic Ocean, whilst ASW aircraft and helicopters would provide protection for surface forces operating in the Norwegian Sea. A barrier of NATO diesel submarines would be set up in constrained areas, such as the seas between the Orkneys, Shetlands, Faeroes, Iceland and Greenland, colloquially known as the Greenland–Iceland–UK (GIUK) gaps. In these choke-points there would less need for mobility and speed to intercept and destroy successfully Russian submarines trying to get into the North Atlantic and, therefore, they were left for the diesel boats.

The United States Joint Chiefs of Staff and NATO High Command never formally approved the Lehman strategy, which drew its share of critics as many viewed it as suicidal to consider operating carrier groups in the North Norwegian Sea in the face of the massive Soviet air and sea power concentrated in the adjoining Barents Sea and northern Russia. However, the strategy underpinned the United States Navy's aspiration in the 1980s to

166

expand to a 'six hundred ship' force and governed many of the tactical development projects of the Devron.

Soon after taking up his post Conley was off to sea in local exercise areas on a familiarisation trip on the six-year-old USS *Richard B Russell*, the last submarine to be completed of the '637' class. She was armed with the Mark 48 anti-submarine torpedo, the Harpoon sixty-mile range anti-ship cruise missile and the thirty-mile range anti-submarine SUBROC missile with its nuclear depth-bomb warhead. Like British submarines, the torpedo compartment was also used to berth some of the crew or visitors in removable bunks close to the weapons and in the case of the USN, be they nuclear or conventionally warheaded. However, the British officer was spared the experience of sleeping alongside a nuclear warhead and was accommodated in one of the crew bunk spaces, where he enjoyed the comfort of sleeping between freshly laundered linen sheets. This was a new submarine experience, as Royal Navy submariners normally slept in nylon sleeping bags, which after a few weeks at sea developed a unique odour of their own.

The '637' class was capable of about 25 knots and had a maximum safe diving depth of 1,300ft, but had only four torpedo tubes compared to the six in the earlier *Skipjack* class and the British *Valiant* class. Nevertheless, they were very quiet boats, handling well at all speeds and were accordingly popular with their commanding officers.

Conley quickly settled into American submarine routines and procedures which were, in the main, similar to those in the Royal Navy. However, there were differences, in particular that of the majority of the officers being qualified nuclear engineers. Early in a junior American submarine officer's career, he would have to undertake the daunting double task of qualifying to watch-keep both in the control room, supervising ship control and conducting the navigation, and in the manoeuvring room, in charge of the reactor and propulsion plant. Although one of the more senior officers would have the responsibility of being the boat's engineer, the commanding officer ultimately made engineering decisions. Furthermore, the operation of the reactor was accorded the highest level of importance within a submarine's annual external inspection regime.

This was very different from the Royal Navy system of the executive branch filling the warfare roles of command, navigation and sonar, supported by officers of the marine and weapon engineering specialisations. Accordingly, the Royal Navy commanding officer relies heavily upon the advice of his engineers, and a key skill will be his ability to ask the right questions and to probe incisively but diplomatically the engineering advice proffered.

Conley concluded that both officer structure systems had their specific advantages and had evolved to suit the culture and background of their respective officer corps. However, he firmly believed that as Royal Navy submarine weapon engineer officers kept watches in the control room and many had developed excellent warfare and navigation skills, there should be no reason why exceptional individuals should not undertake the Perisher and, if successful, go on to command appointments. At the very least, such individuals would have a sea command experience base when they took up key jobs in the Ministry of Defence's procurement executive, which included managing the introduction and support of new weapon systems.

The voyage in the *Richard B Russell* might have turned out to be a long one as a Soviet Victor-class SSN intruder was reported to have been detected offshore. With the new SSBN *Ohio* on contractor's sea trials, the Victor's task would have been an intelligence-gathering mission, and to have measured the *Ohio*'s acoustic signature at that early stage would have been a real coup for the Russian. However, the *Richard B Russell* only intended to spend a few days carrying out independent exercises, did not have an acoustic towed array fitted, and consequently was out of luck in making detection in the difficult environment of high levels of shipping noise and fishing vessel activity.

Fourteen months later in October 1982, in the same sea areas, the small SSN, *Tullibee*, just out of refit, was also out of luck when after diving she became aware of a Victor SSN on her tail which commenced harassing her with close-range passes. She had probably been sighted by the Russian while on the surface preparing to go under the water and because she had a similar superstructure profile to an SSBN, although much smaller than an *Ohio*-class submarine, she could have been misidentified. The unfortunate *Tullibee*, owing to her small reactor size and limited power, was only capable of 16 knots and found it very difficult to shake off her pursuer. On hearing about this incident, Conley could only but envisage the highly alarming and unexpected situation the very green *Tullibee* crew found themselves in, especially operating in waters close to the American mainland, which would have been considered generally free of aggressive Russian submarine intrusion. Clearly, the Russian Bear was flexing its underwater muscles.

Back ashore, Conley's induction period included two weeks of instruction in the American Submarine School, joining the executive officers' course, learning about the state-of-the-art '688'-class sonar and torpedo fire-control systems. He was pleasantly surprised that the school hierarchy was very willing to disclose details of their latest submarine equipment to a foreigner, although paradoxically information about their reactor systems remained firmly out of bounds.

In October 1981 Conley was invited to attend the commissioning of the '688'-Class *La Jolla* at the submarine base. Afterwards, at a reception held in the base officers' club, he was introduced to the legendary Admiral Hyman G Rickover, cited as the 'father of nuclear power' in the United States Navy, who as Director Naval Nuclear Propulsion governed the commissioning and operation of naval reactor systems with a rod of iron. The octogenarian admiral, blunt, abrasive and confrontational in character, had become an increasingly controversial individual. His reputation had received a further dent whilst he was onboard *La Jolla* during sea trials: there had been reports that he overrode protocol and gave orders which resulted in a temporary loss of control of the brand new boat.

Never a friend of the Royal Navy, it was clear to Conley that Rickover was not interested in talking to him. This coolness was noted by a large bear of a man standing nearby who interjected, introducing himself as Takis Veliotis, managing director of the Electric Boat Company. Taking Conley aside, Veliotis, a Greek by nationality, told him in no uncertain terms of his derogatory views of the admiral; very evidently there were extremely strong tensions between the two of them, particularly regarding the debacle of the '688'-class faulty welds, the substantial costs of which eventually ended up being paid by the American taxpayer. At the time, Conley thought it decidedly odd that a Greek national should be managing America's prime submarine building yard which was delivering the highly classified *Ohio*-class submarines. The following year he was astonished to learn that Veliotis had fled America, wanted by the FBI on charges of taking kickbacks from subcontractors to the Electric Boat Company.

Two months after his encounter with Rickover and Veliotis, on Remembrance Day 1981 Conley and his wife attended the commissioning of the USS *Ohio*. A temporary stand to seat the four thousand guests had been set up on the berth, alongside of which was the truly awesome mass of the black painted SSBN, 560ft in length with her twenty-four missile tubes and the capability to launch up to almost 300 thermonuclear warheads. The cold, overcast weather added to the sombreness of the occasion. Shortly before the arrival of the guest of honour, Vice President George Bush, the diminutive and somewhat lonely figure of Rickover, wearing a civilian suit and raincoat, walked up the gangplank and took up his position on the superstructure. He looked passive and nonchalant about the proceedings, as if unimpressed that his achievement of delivering the world's first nuclear submarine – the USS *Nautilus* – in 1955 had eventually resulted in the building of this single, terrifying vessel, capable of destroying all of the Soviet Union's large cities.

Whilst the ensemble awaited the arrival of the vice president, Conley noted numerous secret service agents and police stationed in the surrounding buildings and vantage points. When Bush arrived in a limousine with escorting cars ahead and behind, the British officer was most impressed that when the entourage came to a halt, all the car doors opened in perfect unison and the bodyguards instantly took up precise station round their ward as he left his car. The Americans were taking no chances, even in a high security area such as the Electric Boat shipyard. It was also noticeable that if there had been any peace protests outside the shipyard, the protesters had been kept well away from public view.

In a short speech Vice President Bush declared that *Ohio* heralded a new dimension in national strategic security. In his own speech, Rickover summed up that *Ohio* had only one purpose which was 'to strike fear in the hearts of our enemies'.

In January the following year Conley was back at sea on the AUTEC range onboard the *Richard B Russell*, running an evaluation to try out new underwater dogfight tactics his team had developed. Another Devron '637'-class boat, the USS *Archerfish*, was acting as the target. It was planned to embark Navy Secretary John Lehman, who had a naval aviation background in the Reserves, and Conley was looking forward to the secretary's visit, not least as he would get first-hand insight into joint US/UK co-operation at the cutting edge of SSN tactics. He was, therefore, personally disappointed when he heard that at a few hours' notice Lehman's embarkation had been cancelled.

It was only after the exercise completed that Conley learned that the reason for the cancellation was that, on the day of the planned visit, Lehman had been instrumental in forcing the resignation of Admiral Rickover. On 31 January, at a very tense meeting in the Oval Office between President Ronald Reagan, the Navy Secretary and the admiral, it was made clear to Rickover that his services were no longer required. In his book *Command of the Seas* Lehman later recounted:

One of my first orders of business as Secretary of the Navy would be to solve the Rickover problem. Rickover's legendary achievements were in the past. His present vice-like grip on much of the Navy was doing it much harm. I had sought the job because I believed the Navy had deteriorated to the point where its weakness seriously threatened our future security. The Navy's grave afflictions included loss of a strategic vision; loss of self-confidence, and morale; a prolonged starvation of resources, leaving vast shortfalls in capability to do the job; and too few ships to cover a sea so great, all resulting in cynicism, exhaustion, and an undercurrent of defeatism. The cult created by Admiral Rickover was itself a major obstacle to recovery, entwining nearly all the issues of culture and policy within the Navy.

Lehman's criticism of Rickover coincided with the recovery of the United States, and in particular its armed forces, from the humiliations of the Vietnam War. The Rickover era of dominance in all United States Navy nuclear propulsion matters had thus ended, and Admiral Kinnaird McKee replaced him as the Director, Naval Nuclear Propulsion. However, Rickover's legacy of the highest possible standards of nuclear plant operation, and the primacy accorded within the United States Submarine Service to nuclear systems, was to be perpetuated. Lehman's intention was to build upon this, and to revitalise the United States Navy.

Oddly, however, it was not the United States Navy, with its commissioning of the mighty *Ohio* and her associated imagery of Armageddon, that was grabbing the headlines, but an apparently old-fashioned bushfire war in which the Royal Navy would play its part.

On 2 April 1982 Argentinian forces invaded the Falkland Islands and within weeks Great Britain had responded by dispatching a naval task force on a 6,000-mile passage to recapture the islands. As it became more evident that a diplomatic solution would not be forthcoming to solve the crisis, and war became more likely, Conley very felt uncomfortable about being in a foreign country when his peers and friends were going to war. Although the American national media were in general pro-British, there was an element which regarded the imminent conflict as yet another British colonial war, ignoring the uncomfortable fact that Argentina was ruled by a military junta which had an appalling human rights record. However, it was very evident to Conley that his colleagues in the United States Navy, together with his local civilian friends, were unquestionably on the British side and were very sympathetic to his isolated situation.

Conley felt that, at the very least, his expertise in the use of the Tigerfish torpedo and, in particular, the tactics needed to take on successfully a modern

Argentinian diesel submarine, would be called upon. Furthermore, had his advice been sought, he would have strongly advocated that each deployed submarine launch one of its Tigerfish as a drill exercise. This would both prove the weapon system and familiarise the crew in controlling a war-stock weapon which had a much longer endurance than the practice version; it would have been too late to discover latent problems when actually engaging the enemy. But to his disappointment there was no phone call or message seeking his advice and, indeed, later events proved that there was a serious, undiscovered defect in Tigerfish which could have been worked round if it had been identified as he had envisaged.

Meanwhile, harking back to his midshipman's time in the destroyer *Cambrian* with its low anti-aircraft effectiveness, he delved into the classified 'UK eyes only' documentation he held, which described the effectiveness and characteristics of the current Royal Navy shipborne anti-aircraft systems. These confirmed his fears that only the short-range Sea Wolf system, fitted to just a handful of frigates, would be effective in taking on aircraft near land, because the medium-range Sea Dart and Sea Slug systems were designed to engage the high-flying cruise missile in deep ocean scenarios. The Sea Slug in particular would be useless against low-flying enemy aircraft. He also knew that the short-range Sea Cat missile had a habit of diving into the sea post-launch and was generally regarded as very unreliable, while the gunnery systems available had not improved much from his time as a midshipman. Notably, no ships were fitted with anti-aircraft Gatling gun mountings. These were capable of spitting out a much more effective 4,000 rounds per minute than the twenty-five rounds per minute of which the latest Royal Navy 4.5in gun was capable. Therefore, there would be great reliance placed upon the Sea Harriers embarked in the small aircraft carriers, *Invincible* and *Hermes*, to engage enemy aircraft with any prospect of success.

In mid April Conley joined the '637'-class USS *Whale* for two weeks of evaluation of approach and attack tactics in the comparatively shallow waters of the Gulf of Maine. The USS *Whale* impressed him as being a very happy, efficient and well-led submarine, her captain, Commander Emmo Morrow, proving extremely co-operative and interested in the conduct of the evaluations. He furthermore did his best to read signal traffic which contained Falklands crisis information and pass the contents to the exchange officer. With the exercise successfully completed, *Whale* headed towards Halifax, Nova Scotia, for a port visit.

172

Meanwhile, Conley had learned about the sinking of the Argentinian cruiser *General Belgrano* by the British SSN HMS *Conqueror*. He speculated whether the submarine's captain, Dartmouth contemporary Commander Chris Wreford-Brown, had used Tigerfish torpedoes in the attack (the latest variant had an anti-ship capability), or whether he decided to fire a salvo of the much more reliable straight-running Mark 8 torpedo. In the event, Wreford-Brown had decided to use the latter on the grounds that its much bigger warhead would be required to severely damage or sink the former American Second World War vintage heavy cruiser. This decision was misconceived to the extent that the effect of a Tigerfish detonating underneath the target would be the equivalent of a direct hit by the Mark 8. Moreover, it would have been most likely that the Tigerfish would have homed onto the target's propeller noise, detonating under and breaking off the stern and almost certainly incurring fewer fatalities than the 321 crew killed by the two Mark 8s which struck the ship, one of which hit the hull amidships.

However, shortly after the Falklands War, a number of proving firings of Tigerfish revealed a serious reliability problem: the chances were that had Wreford-Brown chosen to use Tigerfish, the torpedoes would have probably proved absolute duds because of a propulsion battery actuation defect. If this had been known about it could have been worked round by manually priming the battery prior to firing, but at the time of the Falklands War the fault had been undiagnosed. Tigerfish problems thus continued, but this monumental deficiency at long last galvanised the application of adequate resources and effort to the solution of this weapon's chronic shortcomings.

The day after the *Whale*'s arrival Conley was met by his wife Linda, as it was planned that they would take several days' leave to drive back to Mystic, stopping off to stay in a small hotel in the very scenic environs of Mount Desert Island, Maine. Linda cheerfully disclosed that whilst he was at sea, because of small local pockets of pro-Argentinean support, the British embassy staff had suggested it might be a good idea to remove temporarily the large Union Jack which flew from a flagpole in the garden of their house. This she had done. However, on hearing of the good news of the recapture of South Georgia on 25 April, she had swiftly re-hoisted the flag.

While enjoying the solitude, stunning beauty and peace of the Acadia National Park, the Conleys heard the grim news on the car's radio that the destroyer HMS *Sheffield* had been hit by an Exocet missile. Both he and his wife knew *Sheffield*'s commanding officer, Captain Sam Salt, very well indeed, and there was no news about the number of casualties. Feeling utterly in the wrong place amid the green loveliness of the serene park, which was such a contrast to the bleak environment of the South Atlantic, Conley felt gut-wrenching sympathy for the crew of the destroyer.

A few months after the Falklands War had ended, one of his superiors gave him access to an American Defence Intelligence Agency (DIA) report of the analysis of the conflict, which was unique in being the only major maritime conflict to have occurred after the Second World War. Its analysis, therefore, had been awaited with interest. As was to be expected, the actual number of Argentine aircraft losses was substantially less than originally claimed by the British. Half of the kills in the air were attributable to the Sea Harrier and very few aircraft had been shot down by Sea Cat or guns (reportedly over eighty Sea Cats were fired for one confirmed kill). Along with the rest of the world, Conley also noted that after the sinking of the *General Belgrano* the Argentine Navy remained in harbour, with the exception of their modern German Type 209 submarine, *San Luis*. He later learned that the crew of this submarine had conducted two attacks upon Royal Navy warships, but their German-made SST-4 torpedoes malfunctioned owing to a fire-control system defect. Evidently, defective torpedo systems were not the exclusive preserve of the Royal Navy. Added to the fuse failures of many Argentine bombs, these factors significantly saved both British ships and British lives.

In June 1982 Conley was again at sea, this time in the USS *Dallas*, a very new '688'-class submarine, to undertake a new series of tactical evaluation exercises to the north of Bermuda. This class (the lead vessel *Los Angeles* commissioned in 1976) had been introduced to contend with the increasing number of high-speed Soviet submarines then coming into service, and the new role of providing anti-submarine support to carrier-led battle groups. It was assessed that both tasks required a dived speed well in excess of 30 knots, and a much more powerful propulsion plant than that fitted in the '637'-class. Rickover offered the S6G reactor and machinery system, which were based upon the design of the plant fitted in the nuclear-powered cruiser *Bainbridge*. It would be capable of delivering over 35,000shp and had several features which reduced radiated noise, but its installation required significantly greater space and the '688'-class boats, at over 6,000 tons displacement, were much larger and longer than previous SSNs.

Their long hull made them difficult to handle when manoeuvring under the water at high speed and their length of hull aft of the fin (known as the 'sail' in the USN) made them susceptible to broaching the surface when at periscope depth in rough weather. These deficiencies were improved upon in later vessels of the class by locating the forward hydroplanes in the bows, as opposed to the sail which had been standard in American nuclear submarines. Most of the class had propellers as opposed to the much quieter pump jet propulsors being fitted to all British nuclear boats. Such a change had been resisted by Rickover, perhaps on the grounds of the propulsor's lesser stern power, but all new American SSNs are now being incorporated with this form of drive.

The USS *Dallas* was the first American submarine to be fitted with totally computerised sonar and fire-control systems, and Conley, accompanied by a civilian expert in target motion analysis, was looking forward to evaluating the new equipment and continuing to refine approach and attack tactics using towed acoustic array data and nothing else. However, the *Dallas* was somewhat jinxed. The previous year she had run aground on the reefs at Andros near the AUTEC range, damaging her rudder and now, shortly after the evaluations had started, a very worried-looking commanding officer declared to Conley that the boat needed to be urgently surfaced and the reactor shut down forthwith. Crew error had caused all the freshwater onboard to be contaminated, including the vital feed water for the boilers in the reactor compartment. Continuing to use contaminated water in the boilers would have caused severe damage so the *Dallas* was bereft of effective propulsion. Conley recalled his own anxiety when *Otter* had been immobilised on the AUTEC range, but this situation was worse: *Dallas* was a nuclear submarine in a very vulnerable state, a long way from assistance in mid ocean to the north of the Bermuda Islands. The one ameliorating factor was the copious advice and guidance from headquarters on how to sort out and get the plant back on line.

To clean up the freshwater systems and to make new, pure water required almost three days of running the boat's one backup diesel generator providing all power whilst on the surface. Water was only available for drinking but, surprisingly, paper plates and tooth-cleaning plugs were produced from the boat's stores. With the *Dallas* stationary and wallowing on the surface of the tropical Atlantic and the Fairbanks-Morse diesel generator roaring away under the wardroom, life onboard was very uncomfortable. Nuclear submariners took for granted a plentiful supply of fresh water for daily showers and felt the lack of it acutely. However, the clean-up progressed successfully, the plant was recommissioned and the embarrassment of a tow to harbour avoided. Towards the end of the reactor restart, the commanding officer presented Conley with a large tinned-fruit can full of hot water from the engine room (which was off-limits to the British officer). Grateful for this forethought, Conley made his best ever use of a few pints of hot water to remove three days of grime and face stubble.

Despite the restitution of normality, it took Conley some effort to persuade a rather shaken commanding officer to continue the evaluations. However, these were successfully completed with very encouraging results from the new tactics being tested.

As the months past and his American superiors built up their trust in Conley, more responsibility was thrust upon him and rules of security access were relaxed. He undertook some of the short-range encounter work in the base attack training simulators, using the students of the prospective commanding officer (PCO) course – the United States Navy's equivalent of Perisher – as testers of the new trial tactics. It was noticeable to Conley that, when compared to the Perisher, the PCO course placed much more emphasis upon anti-submarine warfare training.

This short-range work also required him to set up an evaluation trial involving an American SSBN and SSN operating in the Marginal Ice Zone (MIZ) to the northeast of Greenland. This evaluation was undertaken as it was known that Russian SSBNs were making use of the high levels of ice noise in the MIZ to mask their presence, and the aim was to assess how difficult it was to trail another submarine in such conditions. This task broke new ground for Conley as it involved an American SSBN, and as an exchange officer by the rules he should not have been taking the lead in such sensitive areas: a Brit voice talking to Commander Submarine Atlantic operations staff about planning detail caused a bit of a ripple, and questions were asked about his access to No Foreign Dissemination (NOFORN) information, but to the best of Conley's knowledge there were no consequences upon his seniors.

Conley's superiors at the Devron, Commodore Dean Sackett, the squadron commander, and Captain Jim Patton his deputy, did much to support his work, contributing a great deal to the marshalling of innovative initiatives, together with providing submarine time at sea. They were also crucial to supporting the analytical effort that elucidated the invaluable lessons learned in these trials. Enduring and strong friendships were formed with both men, and Commodore Sackett very enthusiastically accepted the role of godfather to the Conleys' baby girl, named Faith, born in the base hospital in November 1982.

Unofficial honours were heaped upon Conley in the first six months of 1983, prior to his return home in the summer of that year. Conley ran two further evaluations in '688'-class boats, in the first of which, aboard the USS *Atlanta*, he was made an 'Honorary American Submariner' and presented with a submarine badge and a set of blue cotton coveralls (known as a 'poopy suit') which American submariners liked to wear at sea. In the USS *Philadelphia*, the commanding officer ignored the rules and invited him to witness drills in the engine room. The British officer was struck by how much simpler the layout and instrumentation were in comparison with Royal Navy submarine nuclear plants. In particular, the machinery configuration was much more conducive to access for maintenance and repairs. He was also impressed by the damage control and firefighting equipment available and, whilst he kept his illicit engine-room observations to himself, he did pass some of the damage control equipment details back to the Flag Officer Submarine's engineering staff. Some of these concepts were taken up by the Royal Navy and Conley was to personally benefit from the availability of American steam leak repair kits when he went onto command Britain's oldest SSN, HMS *Valiant*.

Meanwhile, it was becoming more evident from operational reports that, owing to improvements in the radiated noise of Soviet submarines, in part a result of intelligence being passed by the Walker-Whitworth spy ring, the West's marked submarine acoustic advantage was shrinking. It was becoming more difficult to detect and trail the latest Russian submarines and the number of counter-detections, whilst remaining small, was increasing. Accordingly, a highly classified cell was set up within the Devron to analyse so-called 'events'. The introduction of the new tactics and procedures, the development of which Conley had spearheaded, was very timely in respect of counterbalancing this decrease in technical advantage.

In July 1983 Conley and his family bade sad farewell to the many civilian and naval friends they had made in Connecticut. For the British officer it had been a most enjoyable two years, where solid advances had been achieved in sub-surface anti-submarine tactics. Conley was convinced that the war-fighting effectiveness of both navies had been raised thereby. On his return to the Royal Navy, Conley received a personal commendation from John Lehman, the citation recording that 'he [had] developed tactics that will result in prompt and immediate improvement in the tactical readiness of US and UK SSNs, significantly contributing to the national security of each nation'.

14

To the South Atlantic

BEFORE RETURNING TO the United Kingdom in the summer of 1983, Conley had lobbied hard to be appointed in command of a *Swiftsure*-class SSN. This was on two accounts: he saw a modern boat as his best opportunity to be deployed on operations where he would be up against Russian submarines and where he could try out for himself the tactics he had developed; second, he would be able to move his family from Scotland to the more benign climate of Devon where the *Swiftsures* were based. However, his appointer had other plans and informed him that he would be posted in November to the most modern of the *Valiant* class, HMS *Courageous*, and when she paid off into refit in the summer of 1984, he would then take over *Valiant* itself. Both of these boats were based in Faslane and, needing a bigger house, the Conleys bought an old manse requiring much work, situated beside the loch in the village of Garelochead, some two miles from the base.

Whilst Conley was in America, HMS *Trafalgar*, first of a new class of SSNs, was commissioned in May 1983. Very much based upon the *Swiftsure* design, *Trafalgar* was slightly larger in overall size and benefited from both an improved internal layout and better sensors, but essentially the hull and the machinery were unchanged. Meanwhile, in the previous year the British government had made the decision to replace the four ageing *Resolution*-class SSBNs with the same number of much bigger submarines, which would be capable of deploying the longer range and more accurate Trident D5 missile. Accordingly, the design of the new 14,000-ton boats was well underway, and the long overdue modernisation of the Vickers shipyard which would build them had started, funded by the MoD.

At the same time the Naval Staff was seeking government agreement for the procurement of a new class of diesel submarine to replace the *Oberons*, most of which were reaching the twenty-year-old mark. The requirement called for a low-cost submarine, which in war would be deployed to the

GIUK gaps, and in peacetime would fulfil an ASW training role. With increased use of automation, it was planned that the new class would have a significantly smaller complement than the *Oberons*, thus realising significant through-life cost savings. In the event the design chosen was the Vickers 2400 type (the number reflecting the size of its tonnage) and eventually four of these were built, named the *Upholder* class. Notably, Vickers had not in recent years undertaken the detailed design of a submarine, as that had been the exclusive province of the submarine designers at the MoD Bath.

The *Oberons*, meanwhile, were being updated with new sonars and fire-control equipment, replacing obsolescent fit much of which dated back to the 1950s. However, their hulls and machinery were becoming increasingly difficult to maintain.

The Trident-, *Upholder*- and *Trafalgar*-class build programmes were set to peak in the late 1980s and the Submarine Service continued to expand, with a total force level of thirty-four boats envisaged – four SSBNs, eighteen SSNs and twelve diesels. However, such a build-up was not without contention, with some senior officers within the Service arguing that a disproportionate amount of resources was being allocated to the Submarine Flotilla to the detriment of maintaining a balanced fleet.

The Trident programme required a significant extension of the Clyde submarine base to accommodate the much bigger submarines. New berthing, docking and training facilities, were built, altogether a challenging and expensive project in itself. Meanwhile, the shore infrastructure in HMS *Dolphin* would be modernised to take the *Upholder* class. Against a background of the continuing build-up and capability of the Russian Navy and its increasing number of vessels deployed overseas into such areas as the Mediterranean, the Submarine Service was most certainly the place to be for any ambitious officer or rating. However, all these programmes would push to the limit the specialist technical resources available within the United Kingdom to manage such wide-ranging equipment procurement and base modernisation projects.

Thanks to the intervention of the Falklands War, the surface fleet had survived the worst of the cuts planned in 1981 by the then Secretary of State for Defence, John Nott, and hulls which were destroyed in the war were being replaced. The operational success against Russian submarines of those *Leander*-class frigates fitted with towed acoustic arrays had spurred on the design and build of a new type of anti-submarine frigate, the Type 23 or Duke class, lead ship HMS *Norfolk*. These would have noise-reduction features which would make them ideal for ASW work using the acoustic towed array. It was envisaged that the class of sixteen vessels would be supported on station in the Norwegian Sea by specialist Royal Fleet Auxiliaries (RFA) supply ships, which would be fitted with their own Sea Wolf air defence systems.

Courageous had been completed at Vickers in 1971 and had been subsequently updated with the latest fire-control equipment and carried the sixty-five-mile range, very reliable, American-supplied Sub-Harpoon anti-ship missile. This was a step change from the fifty-year-old short-range Mark 8s, which at long last were being withdrawn from service. For both submarine and surface ship targets she also had the Tigerfish torpedo, which unfortunately still remained unreliable.

Capable of 26 knots dived and reasonably quiet, the *Valiant* class, however, suffered from very cramped engine room and machinery spaces, which were difficult to access and maintain. Furthermore, they had the vulnerability of a considerable amount of internal piping (even that providing toilet-flushing water) being subject to full external seawater pressure. In later, deeper-diving classes, for safety and cost reasons the amount of such piping was reduced to a minimum. The *Valiants*' maximum safe operating depth was 750ft with a theoretical crush depth of about 1,300ft, compared to the well over 2,000ft of sea pressure the *Swiftsures* could sustain. Within these margins, there would be less than a minute to take recovery action in event of a catastrophic plane jam at depth and speed and, furthermore, there was not the benefit of a separate deep, emergency ballast tank blowing system as fitted to the *Swiftsures*.

Prior to taking over *Courageous* from Commander Rupert Best, whom coincidentally he had relieved in New London, Conley undertook a two-week commanding officers' pre-joining course at sea, which was by chance onboard the same submarine. Joining her at Faslane, sailing was delayed by about twelve hours because of a steam leak in the engine room, the first of many he was to incur in his time in command of *Courageous* and *Valiant*. The training period centred upon a joint warfare exercise in the Southwest Approaches, during which he was informed that his father had died unexpectedly. However, like all seafarers, he had to contend with and contain such bad news, appreciating that there was no practical way of landing him other than in extreme emergency.

Rather than the usual two-hour handover, Conley used the period at sea to make sure he had a good appraisal of *Courageous* and her crew. First impressions were of a submarine in reasonably good mechanical condition, but a wardroom who were mentally very tired, having completed three South

Atlantic deployments in the previous eighteen months. Nobody was looking forward to a fourth patrol in the South Atlantic planned for the following March: the Falklands War was long over and such deployments, about three months in length, were characterised by tedium and boredom, at a time when the Falklands War was fading in the national conscience. It, however, remained MoD policy for several years after the war to deploy an SSN and several escorts to Falklands waters.

After Christmas leave and completion of a maintenance period, Conley took *Courageous* to sea for tests, trials and Tigerfish torpedo re-certification. The period at sea revealed that both of the boat's speed probes were defective and, therefore, the submarine was without an indication of speed through the water. An emergency docking was arranged to fix the defects, subject to *Courageous* immediately vacating the dock as soon as the repairs were complete. This proved to be a contentious issue, as the repairs were finished at 2200 on the evening of 28 February, and despite no pressing operational need to leave the dock overnight, the base organisation insisted the undocking proceed. Conley was not happy with this decision, as it meant bringing in additional crew overnight for the undocking evolution, with a twelve-week deployment only a few days away. Undocking at 0230, with the assistance of a tug for propulsion, he did a few circuits off the berths to check out the one probe under the waterline. This appeared to function correctly. Eventually getting alongside about 0400, allowing the non-duty crew to get home about 0500, Conley recalled that this was not a morale-building episode. However, such operational pressures, be they justified or otherwise, were considered the norm at the time.

Courageous sailed from Faslane on Monday, 4 March and started the 6,500-mile dived passage to the Falkland Islands to relieve the on-station *Warspite*. She was stored for twelve weeks, including over a hundred movies and hoards of Austrian smoked cheese and digestive biscuits, a favourite delicacy of the executive officer. Soon after diving both speed probes proved defective, but Conley pressed on, notwithstanding having no speed indication, having been persuaded by his weapons engineer officer that somehow repairs would be effected on reaching the Falklands.

Arriving off Port Stanley on 23 March after briefings from the Commander British Forces Falklands Islands (CBFFI) staff, *Courageous* undertook the first of three short patrols off the Argentine coastline, aimed at collecting general intelligence of air, maritime and military activity. This was achieved by cruising at periscope depth, just outside the twelve-mile territorial limit during daylight hours, which was the only time any military activity was detected. Two Spanish-speaking 'spooks' were embarked, who with their specialist equipment were able to tune into Argentine military radio circuits, particularly aircraft control frequencies. The first patrol's prime objective was to collect intelligence of aircraft activities at the air force base of Rio Gallegos, situated on the bleak, desolate coastline of southern Patagonia.

Although the seabed around the Falklands Islands had been reasonably well surveyed, when off the Argentine coast Conley frequently relied upon Admiralty charts, many of which were derived from surveys which had taken place in the 1920s using very basic hand-deployed, lead-line sounding techniques. Therefore, there was always the risk of grounding on a hitherto undetected shoal or pinnacle of rock. Already one submarine, the diesel boat *Onyx*, had badly damaged its bow when, after landing and recovering special forces during the hostilities, it had hit an uncharted pinnacle off the Falklands Islands. However, in the event, the charts used proved remarkably accurate, notwithstanding the dated surveys upon which they were based.

On patrol *Courageous*'s torpedo tubes were loaded with three Tigerfish Mod 1 torpedoes and three anti-ship Sub-Harpoon missiles. The extant rules of engagement directed that any submarine detected within a 150-mile radius of the Falklands, the exclusion zone still in force, be attacked and destroyed, but two years after the end of the war Conley doubted whether the British government would have welcomed news of such an engagement. In the event, Argentine military activity was at a very low ebb, and the only submarine detected was during the third patrol, when the radar transmissions were intercepted from a German-built '209'-class boat, firmly alongside in its base in the city of Mar del Plata.

There was very limited combat air activity at Gallegos air base and it was clear from communications intercepts that the Argentine air force was bent on enjoying a good, long Easter weekend. Conley, therefore, decided, for the want of doing anything else, to follow the route of Sir Francis Drake on his voyage of exploration to the Pacific, swinging into the Bay of San Julian where the great English seafarer had made landfall after crossing the Atlantic. The civil airfield at the port of San Julian, the closest runway to the Falklands Islands, had been used during the war for combat operations and thus it was also considered worth checking it out for military activity, admittedly an extremely remote possibility.

Arriving at the bay in stormy weather as darkness fell, Conley was dismayed to sight a considerable number of Argentine fishing boats emerge unexpectedly round a headland and effectively block his exit out of the bay. His Perisher training came to the fore, as he carefully manoeuvred the submarine at periscope depth between the fishing boats, avoiding getting caught up in their nets, and made his way out to the open sea. The difficulty of this was increased by heavy seas frequently washing over the periscope and the myriad of confusing lights the fishing boats were displaying. It occurred to him that this had been a foolish venture, and that if he had got caught up in the nets and consequently dragged a fishing boat under, this most certainly would not have been welcome news at headquarters. On the other hand, such ventures during a tedious patrol kept him and his crew on their mettle and ready for the unexpected. The fishermen, of course, remained blissfully unaware that there had been a British nuclear submarine in their midst.

During the tedium of these patrols, food was an important relief for the crew, and the cooks did an outstanding job in producing high quality, varied dishes. Each evening bread and rolls were baked, and a real treat was to enjoy a fresh hot roll and butter early in the morning. Periodic meet-ups with surface ships enabled a top-up of some provisions, including fresh bread and vegetables. For recreation, the crew watched films, read books and there was the occasional quiz night or whole ship entertainment such as a horse-racing evening. A return to harbour lottery was also run around estimation of the exact time of arrival back in the Faslane base, and one lucky young crew member was to win over £1,000 on the boat's return.

In between patrols anti-submarine exercises occurred with the on-station surface group consisting of four escorts and their RFA support ships. Most of the time the weather was inclement and on more than one occasion, at the end of a day's exercises, observing through the periscope the surface ships being severely battered by an Antarctic storm, Conley and his crew were very glad of the stable, secure environs of an SSN as *Courageous* slipped down to the placid calm of the depths.

Conley was determined to make the best use of *Courageous*'s time on deployment and, appreciating that for much of the time the surface ships had little to do, he and his officers developed a number of evaluations to test the long-range sonar and radar detection equipment's capability to track the ships and develop a fire-control solution which would support the successful targeting of the Harpoon anti-ship missiles.

Using accurate navigational data supplied by the ships, the reconstructed tracks were compared to the target solutions which had been developed on

Courageous fire-control equipment. The tests indeed proved that the boat's sensors could support the targeting of Harpoon out to fifty miles or more, but they fortuitously also identified a fire-control software defect which would have caused failure in specific missile targeting modes. The problem was signalled to headquarters and very quickly a software change was developed which rectified the defect and which was promptly issued flotilla-wide.

However, for Conley's part, despite such achievements, on patrol time often weighed rather heavily. Frequently, there were limited command decisions to be made or actions undertaken, and he found that reading for four or five hours a day was the maximum he could undertake in the cramped conditions of his small cabin. Besides a daily movie, he would sometimes pass the time away by playing chess on a simple computer. He also had a stock of tapes of the BBC *Archers* programme which he religiously listened to at 7pm each evening if nothing else was happening.

But it was not all monotony. On one memorable sunny evening, a large number of dolphins and pilot whales, including their young, gambolled round the submarine for well over an hour. Conley ordered the boat down to a depth where the periscopes were well below the surface. This enabled the crew to take turns to have a periscope view of their underwater activity, to an accompaniment of a sonar loudspeaker broadcasting the many chirps and squeaks emitting from the mammals, who appeared highly delighted to have encountered a submarine.

There was also an incident which could have terminated the deployment. Whilst operating off the Falklands, the opportunity was taken occasionally to embark some of the headquarters army personnel for a day's familiarisation at sea. Also when with the surface ships group, several personnel swaps took place. The mode of transfer was invariably by helicopter. Shortly after surfacing one morning in darkness to the south of the Falklands, in preparation for a helicopter personnel transfer to the frigate *Penelope*, with the submarine not yet in full buoyancy (achieved after surfacing by a blower passing low-pressure air into the ballast tanks), her bows dipped into an exceptionally big wave, causing a substantial flood of water to pour down the conning tower into the control room.

Having handed over command to the executive officer, Conley was in his cabin, getting ready for the transfer to spend a day in the frigate, when he was startled by a loud bang and vibration as the wave hit the conning tower. This was followed by the roar of several tons of water flooding into the submarine. On his dashing into the totally darkened control room, he sighted the officer in charge of the control room courageously saving the situation by climbing up through a torrent of icy water and pulling the lower conning tower hatch shut to stop the ingress. A lot of water was sloshing around the control room deck and flowing in the general direction of the wardroom. For a few exceedingly anxious and stomach-churning moments Conley could not establish contact with the surfacing OOW and lookout, and feared the worst – that they had been swept over the side where there would be absolutely no hope of recovery. It was thus a tremendous relief to hear the OOW testing his microphones when he had reached the bridge platform and completed the folding down of the steel flaps which faired in the top of the bridge when dived.

Fortunately, there was little damage to the submarine, other than a soaked wardroom carpet and a few officers' clothing drawers which had got topped up with water. A visiting officer from *Penelope* did sterling work in helping bail out the wardroom.

Conley reflected afterwards that he should have been paying more attention to the ongoing surfacing procedure, and that in rough weather the executive officer (fully command qualified, having passed Perisher) should have made sure that the boat had gained plenty of buoyancy before ordering the opening of the conning tower upper hatch. Command at sea sometimes depended upon a degree of luck, and instead of facing the situation of having a badly damaged boat wallowing on the surface in a very hostile sea environment, he had got away with a damp wardroom carpet and a few sodden shirts and socks.

Midway through the deployment, Conley and some of the crew were lifted off by Chinook helicopter to spend a day in Port Stanley. From his vantage position in the Chinook's cockpit, he was bemused on the final approach to Port Stanley airfield to see two Phantom fighters flying at speed overtake the helicopter from underneath. Air traffic control at the airfield was still rudimentary.

The town was still showing the ravages of the war, with the odd damaged building and lots of detritus everywhere. To Conley it reminded him of a very run-down Scottish village. However, the odd entrepreneur had moved in, and one venture was focused upon a 'lamburger' shop, which also supplied trail bikes for hire and, accordingly, was well supported by the local British forces who had little to do in their leisure time.

After receiving an operational briefing at the joint forces headquarters, he was taken to the governor's residence to call upon Sir Rex Hunt. He found him to be a very pleasant, avuncular individual, highly interested in *Courageous* and her crew, and very willing to recount his personal experiences during the war.

Official duties over, Conley and several of his officers headed to Port Stanley golf course, the most southern in the world. They found it to be a very demanding eighteen-hole challenge of rudimentary tees, extremely coarse fairways pitted with shell holes, and very rough and ready greens. There were two unique local course rules: owing to the presence of mines, areas of the rough were out of bounds and balls could be lifted out of shell holes without penalty.

Towards the end of her deployment, *Courageous* secured for two days at a buoy in San Carlos water. This gave some of the crew the option to go ashore to the local army base at Kelly's Garden, and the British supply tanker *Eagle* moored two miles away also provided very much welcomed hospitality. Conley and his officers took the opportunity to invite the San Carlos sheep station manager and other local civilians to lunch onboard. Sadly, they proved a somewhat uninspiring group, who showed little genuine appreciation for the lives which had been sacrificed to remove the Argentinians from their land.

Shortly after securing to the buoy, the sentry who was stationed on the after casing was joined by two penguins, which stolidly remained there for the next two days, enjoying titbits such as scones and jam from the crew. It was one of these penguins which featured in an iconic photograph, taking guard by the white ensign at sunset.

Courageous's return home was delayed for several days by the relief submarine, *Valiant*, being diverted to intercept and track a Soviet submarine which had been detected in the United Kingdom's Northwest Approaches. It was with some joy that the crew eventually received the information that she was on her way south and *Courageous* was released on 10 May to head north back to Faslane, gathering intelligence outside the Argentine naval base of Mar del Plata on the way. By this stage the very energetic and innovative weapon engineer officer, Lieutenant Commander (later Rear Admiral) Peter Davies, had achieved three working log speed probes, including a jury rig one mounted on the casing.

In early July, *Courageous* slipped from Faslane, paying-off pennant flying, base band playing and a large crowd of well-wishers gathered. She was heading on surface passage routed round the north of Scotland for a visit to the German port of Bremerhaven, prior to entering Devonport base for a long refit and nuclear core refuelling. Conley was again accursed by running into dense fog, which delayed the planned arrival off the Bremerhaven channel entrance into the River Weser. Having embarked the pilot, the latter advised he make maximum speed up the river to ensure the tidal window into the dock system was not missed. The fog had cleared, and making over 20 knots over the ground in a very busy, narrow shipping lane was both exhilarating and concerning to Conley. The German pilot, noting the commanding officer's worried brow, suggested that he relax and enjoy the scenery. He was curtly reminded that if a mess was made of the pilotage resulting in a grounding, both of their pictures would feature in the worldwide press the following day. The pilot took the point and concentrated very hard on the remaining part of the passage.

A successful and enjoyable visit completed, the submarine's departure was totally without incident, unlike the previous visit of *Courageous* to Bremerhaven, when she was involved in a minor collision with a tug on leaving the lock system. On this occasion the harbour authorities, with classic German efficiency, were taking no chances and an array of tugs awaited at the lock entrance, with a helicopter hovering overhead.

Arriving in Devonport, Conley reflected that *Courageous* had done him well in her last nine months of her second commission. There had been few serious problems with the plant or other equipment, and the crew had performed in a magnificent manner, displaying great professionalism and outstanding commitment. The South Atlantic deployment had not proved operationally challenging but there had been events and incidents which had added to his command experience and confidence. Well supported by his officers and crew, his short period in command had been much less demanding than his experience of *Otter.*

A few days after arrival in the dockyard Conley handed over to the executive officer, who gathered the entire ship's company on the casing to bid him farewell. It was the end of his first SSN command and he very much looked forward to the new ventures and many difficulties ahead when he took over *Valiant.*

The Black Pig and the Red Banner Fleet

In September 1984 Conley assumed command of HMS *Valiant*. The SSN, attached to the Third Submarine Squadron, was undergoing extensive maintenance in dry dock at Faslane following her recent three-month deployment to the South Atlantic. After an introduction to those officers not on leave, Conley completed a short handover from Commander Chris Wreford-Brown, who had been in *Valiant* since the end of 1982, following his critical period in command of HMS *Conqueror* during the Falklands War.

Commissioned in 1966, *Valiant* was the first nuclear submarine of all-British design, though her propulsion system owed much to the American model of two steam generators – or boilers – in the reactor compartment providing steam to two turbines, which were coupled through a gearbox onto one propeller shaft. However, unlike her American contemporaries, as previously stated, the machinery spaces were very congested and maintaining her equipment was very difficult. Worse, this was exacerbated by the inevitable first-of-class problems and the poor design of some of the auxiliary systems. Accordingly, *Valiant* was all too often affected by serious engineering defects which had earned her the nickname of the 'Black Pig'.

Since her commissioning, successive engineering teams had laboured in exceedingly hot and cramped conditions to repair yet another defect. The long hours of contorting repair work had often delayed her in harbour and the knock-on effect disrupted operational programmes, giving the boat a poor name and sometimes depressing the morale of her people. Despite individual instances of personal courage aimed at keeping *Valiant* operational, service in the Black Pig yielded few fond memories for her engineering staff.

During her first commission a fire was detected in the machinery spaces whilst the submarine was at sea. The propulsion plant was promptly shut down and the senior engineer officer immediately raced into the affected compartment dressed in his pyjamas with a hand–held extinguisher to tackle the flames. He thus prevented the fire becoming serious.

While shadowing a Soviet nuclear submarine in the Mediterranean on her second commission, a seawater pipe burst in the reactor compartment, activating a flood alarm. Rapidly brought to the surface, *Valiant*'s reactor was shut down and her diesel engines started. The noise of these evolutions alerted the Russian boat and it returned to periscope depth to find out what was going on. The bridge watchkeepers on *Valiant* spotted her periscope rapidly closing in what was assumed to be an aggressive approach, and a nearby American destroyer was called in to ward her off. It was only years later that it was established that the Russian captain had no hostile intent and, having seen smoke pouring from *Valiant*'s conning tower, thought she was in trouble and was closing to offer assistance. The smoke was in fact the exhaust from the diesel generators.

Nothing in this respect changed during Commander Conley's time in *Valiant*. For example, when deep in the Atlantic Ocean on 24 February 1986, his diary entry records the separate incidents of a serious flood caused by a fractured fully pressurised seawater pipe, a major steam leak in the engine room, and a temporary loss of propulsion. Against this catalogue of intermittent and demanding incidents, when HMS *Valiant* was at sea with her propulsion plant behaving itself, she notched up some notable operational achievements, of which her officers and ratings were justifiably proud.

In 1967, shortly after entering service, she became the first Royal Naval submarine to undertake a completely submerged passage from Singapore to home waters. In 1981 she had taken part in the Royal Navy's first tactical evaluation under the Arctic pack ice, which explored the problems unique to the approach and attack of a submarine in this environment. The following year she had played an active part in the Falklands War, stationed close to the Argentine coast, blockading the enemy's naval forces and providing the British Task Group with early warning of air raids. For his part, during 1985, Conley was to take the *Valiant* on two patrols in the eastern Atlantic, where she achieved success in hunting out submarines of that part of the Russian Navy based in the Arctic and known as the Red Banner Fleet.

However, Conley's first significant task after taking command was a diplomatic and social one, when in late November *Valiant* berthed in the Royal Norwegian Navy base at Haakonsvern, near Bergen, to participate in a series of events commemorating the seventy-fifth anniversary of the

189

Norwegian Submarine Service. The submarines of six other nations, including that of West Germany, were present and the culmination of the commemoration celebrations was a Sunday morning parade of the submarine crews and their inspection by Crown Prince Harald. Unfortunately, the West German contingent was conspicuous by its absence, the bus arranged to bring them from their boat to the parade ground having failed to materialise. Understandably, in that atmosphere of rapprochement, this failure was seen by the senior German officers present to be a snub, a reminder of Norway's sensitivity over German occupation during the Second World War.

With the parade over, *Valiant* then played host to the President of Norway, Per Hysing-Dahl, and his grandchildren who, needless to say, were enthralled at the invitation to explore the inside of a nuclear submarine. The visit was concluded by tea in the wardroom and members of the duty watch were much surprised by the informality of the occasion. There was no police escort and Hysing-Dahl emphatically insisted on absolutely no special arrangements being made for him or his kin.

On return from Norway, *Valiant* continued a varied programme of exercises and trials at sea, including a number of tactical evaluations run by the Royal Navy Devron equivalent – STWG. Conley noted that the structure and conduct of these evaluations was not on a professional par with those of the United States Navy. He considered that in order to reach an equivalent standard, much more effort would be required to hone tactical development and analysis within the Royal Navy. The *Valiant* also undertook a number of firings of the new heavyweight torpedo Spearfish, which was then undergoing development trials, prior to it being introduced into service to replace the unreliable and limited Tigerfish. Thus Conley was able to gain early and first-hand insight into the many problems which were to affect this new weapon system and significantly delay its operational introduction. Yet again, the Royal Navy was to face severe problems with a new torpedo.

It could not be supposed that service in the Black Pig would proceed smoothly. Perhaps the embarkation of the *Sunday Times* defence correspondent, James Adams, undertaking an 'off the record' familiarisation passage on the submarine, was too much of a temptation to the gods. In March 1985 *Valiant* was at sea, submerged in the Clyde Estuary, when she suffered a serious engineering problem. In the early evening, the senior engineer officer, Lieutenant Commander Andrew Miller, reported that a high-temperature alarm was registering in the reactor compartment. The port main turbine and the port turbo-generator, one of two vital steam-driven electrical generators, were already out of commission owing to suspected seawater contamination of their cooling systems. The reactor needed to be shut down quickly and its compartment entered to identify this second serious problem. This was rapidly accomplished and the engineers found a small, high-pressure leak on the starboard of the two boilers. Fortunately, it was on the non-radioactive part of the system, but it required that the affected boiler be shut down and isolated before the reactor was started up again.

All the intensive training of the nuclear engineering team came to the fore as they cross-connected the good port boiler to the available starboard turbo-generator and engine turbine. This provided sufficient limited power for the *Valiant* to surface and limp back to Faslane for repairs. For Conley this episode built up great confidence that his engineering team could contend with just about anything the Black Pig could throw at them. Whilst he could easily have published a story with sensational headlines along the lines of a British nuclear submarine having a hole in its reactor, Adams very honorably disclosed absolutely nothing about the incident.

After several weeks of repairs, *Valiant* was back at sea and on a mission which Conley relished – a three-week operational patrol aimed at detecting and trailing Russian submarines operating to the west of the United Kingdom. However, before proceeding out to the designated patrol areas, there was the task of committing to the deep the ashes of Lieutenant Commander Alastair Mars, DSO, DSC*. After a distinguished career as a submarine commander in the Second World War, Mars had had an unhappy time, incurring the displeasure of Their Lordships of the Admiralty. Finding it difficult to adapt to the peacetime navy and unable to live on his pay, Mars was for a while incarcerated in a naval hospital before being dismissed from the Service in 1952, having been found guilty of insubordination. At the time this was considered by many as a very contentious and undeserved sentence imposed upon a gallant officer – the future prime minister and former naval officer, James Callaghan, raised the matter in the House of Commons. Turning to writing, Mars had a number of novels and works of autobiography published, occasionally returning to sea as a watch-keeping officer in Ocean Weather Ships (OWS). He lived for some years near the Ocean Weather Ships' base in Greenock and died in March 1985.

A few days before *Valiant*'s departure, Mars's frail widow had brought his ashes onboard and handed them to Conley for safe keeping. Proceeding to Loch Long, the brief committal ceremony was conducted from the casing of the *Valiant* in very gusty conditions, a belated tribute recognising Mars's courage and very distinguished wartime record. The ceremony over, *Valiant* embarked her towed acoustic array from an auxiliary craft and then headed out to her patrol areas in the Shetland–Faeroes Gap.

Since joining *Valiant* Conley had spent a considerable amount of time training the control-room team in approach tactics using data from the towed acoustic array. To perfect his own methods, he had the array's tow cable length shortened and customised for *Valiant*, in order to achieve the correct balance between minimising array stabilising times after course alterations, set against ensuring the proximity of the boat's own noise did not reduce the detection capability of the array. Serendipitously, he benefited from a very experienced team of sonar operators, most of whom had been onboard when *Valiant* had encountered a Russian Victor-class SSN in the Northwest Approaches a year earlier. In sum, both crew and submarine were well-prepared for whatever was forthcoming.

Since the wartime role of HMS *Valiant* was to seek out and destroy enemy submarines, the key to her success would be her stealth. Stealth in submarine operations means quietness, maximising any opportunity of detecting an enemy submarine by listening using passive sonar. To accomplish this it was vital that no transmission or avoidable noise should be made by the hunting submarine – hence the term hunter-killer. Noise, in any form, could betray her presence, turning the hunter into the hunted in an instant. The imperative for quiet operation was the *sine qua non* of efficiency and had to be hard-wired into the psyche of every single crew member, as well as placing demands on design and operation of plant and equipment.

Like other SSNs, *Valiant* was fitted with a towed acoustic array capable of detecting the quietest of noises at a considerable distance. These in turn would be interpreted by the sonar operators, and the information thus gleaned provided the submarine's command team with the data for an attack. The approach of *Valiant* to her submarine quarry was comparable to the hunt of an aggressive wild predator in dense forest. Periodic bursts of noise enabled the unseen quarry's general direction and approximate position to be ascertained and stalked, but a noisy and revealing move on the hunter's part could either result in an aggressive charge by a thoroughly alarmed quarry, or an irrecoverable high-speed retreat out of danger.

It is clear, therefore, that approach of a hunting submarine requires patience, astute analysis of complex, fragmented and variable data, and skilful, careful manoeuvring to close the range to a position from which an attack can be made. Equally clear is the fact that a botched approach could develop into a very close-range situation, in which the enemy made a counter-detection and reacted accordingly.

The submarine close-range scenario has similarities to two opposing fighter planes manoeuvring around each other in poor visibility but, of course, is very different in terms of weight and speed. In reality, the situation of two nuclear-powered underwater 5,000-ton behemoths participating in a three-dimensional interaction, sometimes within ranges of a mile or less at closing speeds of over 25 knots, is very different. Although rare, underwater collisions have occurred and prove to be a very frightening experience for the respective crews. As far as is known, such encounters have not resulted in any breaching of the pressure hulls of the submarines involved, and no consequential serious flooding has thus far imperilled the survival of damaged vessels.

In war, it would be vital to maintain the fighting advantage by firing first and skilfully steering the torpedoes towards the enemy. Counter-fired torpedoes would require high-speed evasion away from the incoming weapons, the deployment of noise countermeasures to seduce their homing systems off the intended target, a rapid manoeuvre to turn the tables on the attacker and the successful firing of the torpedoes of the riposte. To achieve this, rapid reactions, a cool nerve and well-rehearsed manoeuvres by all concerned would be essential to survival in what would be likely to be a highly complex and confusing combat situation.

All of which emphasises the *absolute necessity* of stalking and striking first, and the *enabling imperative* of conducting operations in theatre in silence. Such an operational condition – which required teamwork of a very high order – was the nightly prayer of a submarine commander.

One of the key objectives of *Valiant*'s forthcoming patrol was to gather intelligence on what Soviet Russian submarines got up to when in the sea areas to the west of the United Kingdom. Most of these vessels would merely be in transit to and from the Mediterranean or heading out to the western Atlantic to take up strategic deterrent patrols off America's eastern seaboard, thus bringing their nuclear-armed missiles into range of the majority of United States cities. However, there were those bent on unknown purposes who disappeared into shallow water out of SOSUS coverage or used oceano-graphic features to mask their presence. These included diesel submarines which continued to operate in the United Kingdom littoral and which, when under electric propulsion, remained very difficult to detect.

Some of these Soviet submarines were assigned to detect and track the Royal Navy's single patrolling SSBN. With only one SSBN maintaining the

United Kingdom's independent nuclear deterrent, such a contact, if achieved and maintained, could have nullified British strategy at a stroke. To avoid an enemy hunter-killer being in a position to strike pre-emptively if the Cold War turned 'hot', it was imperative that the patrolling SSBN avoided detection.

Since this worked both ways, all patrols made by hunter-killer submarines were effectively war patrols. That is to say, the hunting and the clandestine stalking was always 'real' – only the launch of weapons was missing. For submariners, therefore, the Cold War was not a stand-off of chest-thumping and sabre-rattling, but a fully committed professional interaction, in which only the *coup de main* was not executed. To understand the encounters between submarines during the Cold War it is important to comprehend fully this state of affairs and the impact that it had upon the participants. It was in this atmosphere that Commander Conley and his ship's company took the ageing and awkward *Valiant* out to her patrol area north of the Shetland Islands.

Here Conley settled down to await news of an approaching submarine. Besides *Valiant*'s inherent defects, much else was at stake. Aware that he had accrued a reputation of being an astute tactician, Conley was very apprehensive that when a contact was made, he would conduct the approach and subsequent trail in an effective and successful manner. To carry this out and achieve a close-quarters position from which an accurate attack by Tigerfish torpedo might be made in war was a daunting task.

Fortunately, Conley did not have to live on his nerves for long, soon receiving intelligence of a southbound Victor SSN heading towards the Northwest Approaches. Thought to be fitted with special submarine-detection equipment, this vessel was of specific intelligence interest, particularly when it reached the United Kingdom littoral. This added an additional layer of importance to *Valiant*'s present patrol and the hunt was on.

After a few hours, a faint trace on one of the towed array displays indicated long-range detection of the Soviet submarine. Very much relieved, Conley commenced a careful approach from ahead, manoeuvring so as to allow the unsuspecting quarry to pass *Valiant*, before taking up a comfortable shadowing position at a range of ten miles on the quarter of the Russian, conducting periodic manoeuvres to refine the parameters of course, speed and range.

His next objective was to achieve the requisite accurate fire-control solution and conduct a simulated Tigerfish attack. This would subsequently be analysed ashore from the sonar and fire-control records to assess the

194

probability of its success. He would need to get within a few miles' range to achieve much more accurate hull sonar passive contact to ensure the required precision, but in doing so increased the risk of counter-detection through an unexpected manoeuvre on the part of the Victor.

To maximise the odds in his favour, Conley chose to make the final approach just after midnight, when he reckoned the Russian crew would be at their lowest state of alertness. As for the biorhythms of his own crew, the knowledge that they were running silent in pursuit of a Soviet Victor was sufficient to produce the required adrenalin.

Having gained firm hull sonar contact and having positioned *Valiant* astern of the Russian, confident that he had achieved an accurate target solution, Conley ordered 'Fire!' He then experienced the exhilaration of watching a simulated torpedo head out on the control display towards the real submarine target. The close approach had the particular satisfaction of converting a faint line on a sonar display into a firm aural contact, emitting a range of machinery whines and other noises. Besides the intelligence gained, being so close to the opposition gave *Valiant*'s crew a real buzz, proving that even in an old and often decrepit submarine, her people could cut the mustard.

After the simulated attack, Conley dropped *Valiant* back to a shadowing position and, twenty hours later, made a second close approach and engagement. Hunter and hunted were now to the west of the United Kingdom and it was very early morning. Matters were about to change, for the hour, though early in landsmen's terms, marked the start of an operational day. Suddenly the Victor's speed dropped; she had ended her passage and arrived at her patrol position, adopting a searching posture with frequent manoeuvres.

As this altered situation became apparent, Conley was called to the control room. During the preceding hours he had been catching some sleep and had handed the con over to the *Valiant*'s executive officer, with the instruction to open the range from the Russian, thereby minimising any risk of detection. On arriving in the control room Conley was not only aware that a close-quarters situation was developing, but was aghast to discern that one of his cardinal rules of frequently altering course to establish target range had been ignored.

Inadvertently, the range had not merely been closed but, even worse, *Valiant* was now *ahead* of the Russian. This was a potential disaster, at a stroke removing the satisfaction of the preceding day's success, and threatening the outcome of the patrol. Commander Conley immediately gave orders to open the range and began carrying out evasive manoeuvres. The anxious moments that followed stretched into an hour, the hour into two, as those in the control room strove to determine whether or not the Russians had made a counter-detection or that, if they had, they had been shaken off.

The Soviet commander had not conducted the typical counter-detection acts of blasting the detected 'shadow' with active sonar – a sort of crude submarine 'Boo!' – or, more sinister, the manoeuvre of charging straight towards the detected intruder at high speed, known to the NATO navies as a 'Crazy Ivan'. Unless he was a very subtle man, Conley hoped, if he had detected the presence of *Valiant*, he had not classified her as a submarine and decided that she was a passing whale or similar type of contact.

Much relieved and feeling, as one does at such moments, that one did not really deserve such luck, Conley was obliged to consider the culprit. This would prove to be only the first of several incidents in which Conley's confidence in his executive officer's ability to handle *Valiant* in operationally challenging situations was shaken. Well aware of the voids in the Perisher training of his second in command, Conley had compensated for these deficiencies by copious guidance on handling the underwater scenario. Despite such crafted mentoring, it was becoming evident that the executive officer was one of those individuals who found it difficult to assimilate a mental tactical picture exclusively from sonar bearings data. Although this aptitude is by no means common and despite the Perisher failing to determine whether or not an individual possessed it, such an ability had to be innate in a submarine commander if he was to be successful in war.

Although *Valiant* had successfully escaped counter-detection, Conley would have liked to hang onto his assignment, if only to dispel the feeling of irritation that what had been almost perfect simulated attacks had been all but nullified by a subsequent botch-up. Unaware of this personal sentiment, Northwood headquarters had other priorities and Conley was ordered to hand the shadowing of the Soviet Victor over to the *Leander*-class frigate HMS *Cleopatra*, commanded by Captain (later Vice Admiral) Roy Newman. Fitted with a towed sonar array, *Cleopatra* had been approaching from the Iceland–Faeroes Gap where she had been on patrol, and she was soon joined by Nimrod maritime patrol aircraft of the Royal Air Force. Clearly the Victor was a contact of high interest.

In conformity with instructions received from headquarters, Conley withdrew *Valiant* to a stand-off position where contact with the Victor had faded. However, it was soon apparent to Conley from signal messages that *Cleopatra* was experiencing problems maintaining contact and, to his quiet satisfaction, *Valiant* was directed by headquarters to close the last known position of the Russian and to relocate her. Less than eighteen hours after breaking off contact, *Valiant* had again taken up a position astern of the Victor, which had now resumed his transit to the southwest, presumably having completed his search task.

The situation had now grown a little more complicated, for *Valiant*'s operators had detected a second submarine tracking north. Conley accordingly reported holding a firm contact upon this, classifying it as in all likelihood a homeward-bound Soviet Yankee-class SSBN. Unfortunately, and worrying for Conley, a report had been received from headquarters informing him that one of the Nimrods had detected a serious noise emanating from *Valiant* herself. This was a considerable limitation; utmost care would now be needed in any close approach to another Russian submarine contact.

Despite extensive internal noise monitoring and a surfacing to check the casing and superstructure for loose fittings, locating the noise and its source would prove elusive.

Five days after making initial contact on the Victor, it was clear that this submarine was heading for the Mediterranean and no longer of significant intelligence interest or a threat to the on-patrol SSBN. HMS *Valiant*'s task in countering the potential neutraliser of the United Kingdom's nuclear deterrent had been accomplished successfully, despite the internal problems she had had.

Heading back towards the Shetlands–Faeroes Gap, *Valiant*'s next task was to intercept yet another southbound Victor SSN which had been detected on SOSUS. Meanwhile, *Cleopatra* had resumed her station in the Iceland–Faeroes Gap. Within two days this new Victor had been detected and a trailing station taken on her quarter, with occasional close-range fire-control solution and intelligence-gathering passes being accomplished. This submarine proved to be on a straightforward passage to the Mediterranean and of limited intelligence value. Accordingly, when it reached the west of Ireland, Conley made the decision to break off his pursuit.

However, shortly after contact faded, instructions were received to pass the Soviet submarine's position via a communications buoy message to a Nimrod en route from the Azores to its base at RAF Kinloss in Scotland. At the time, communication buoys, 4in in diameter and fired from a submarine signal-ejector, had a reputation for poor reliability. Furthermore, the positional data on the Russian was somewhat stale. However, the best estimates of its parameters were encoded and loaded into the small tape recorder contained within the buoy. As it was a Sunday, it was thought of adding a verse of the hymn, *He Who Would Valiant Be*, for the benefit of the Nimrod crew, but there were second thoughts about this extra possibly compromising operational security. A few hours later after ejecting the buoy, a signal was received from headquarters indicating that its transmissions had been detected by the Nimrod. But even better, immediate contact had been gained upon the Russian submarine when the aircraft deployed its first group of sonobuoys in barrier pattern across its predicted track

On the forenoon of the following day, as *Valiant* headed back towards the Rockall Trough area, an outward bound Echo II cruise missile submarine was encountered. Although one of the earliest, noisiest, primitive and most dangerous types of Russian nuclear submarine, this was something of a coup, because *Cleopatra* had been searching for her unsuccessfully. The Echo II was making about 11 knots in a southwesterly direction and appeared to be heading across the Atlantic. The contact stimulated some speculation aboard *Valiant* that, armed as she was with eight nuclear-tipped Sandbox cruise missiles, the Echo II may well have been trailing her coat in response to the forward deployment in Europe of nuclear-armed Pershing cruise missiles by the United States of America.

Conley and his team swung *Valiant* into position astern of the Soviet boat, making a very easy close approach after a short trailing phase. Under Conley's encouragement, and to give to those members of the crew whose duties were remote from the high-pitched atmosphere of pursuit some idea of the task to which they were all committed, a number of the crew took turns to listen to the noise emanating from the Echo II. From the *Valiant*'s sound room the loud whines and thumps of machinery in this ageing submarine of the Red Banner Fleet fascinated the ratings. They were not serving in the only old-aged submarine in the North Atlantic. As Conley and his officers broke off contact to enjoy a hearty lunch, they surmised that conditions onboard this very rudimentary nuclear submarine, with its high levels of radiation, would be pretty tough for its crew. Almost certainly they would not be relishing a roast beef lunch in a comfortable, well-furnished wardroom.

By this time *Valiant* had been on patrol for a fortnight. The encounters with Soviet submarines had quickly settled all hands into operational routines and established levels of competency and expectation, and all were very much working as a team. Moreover, a strong relationship of respect and confidence had developed between the commander and his crew, vital in a submarine if it was to maintain a high degree of operational effectiveness.

Off-watch life onboard was interspersed by plenty of movies, the weekly wait for football results on Saturday evenings, followed by short church services in the wardroom on Sundays. The temptations of a glass of sherry and nibbles afterwards had an effect upon the spiritual life of some of the crew, but for others the simplicity of the service and the reflective impact this had was a consolation.

Very content with his ship's company, Conley's preoccupation with the abilities of his executive officer continued to concern him. Unwillingness to break the tradition of sharing the command function with this officer meant that his sleep was light, one ear cocked to the stream of sonar reports emanating from the sound room adjacent to his cabin as *Valiant* carried out frequent ranging manoeuvres.

The final detection of the patrol was that of a Victor III SSN, homeward-bound from the Mediterranean. At the time, this type of SSN was the most capable of Russian submarines and with *Valiant's* own serious, unresolved noise problem Conley did not want to push his luck. This contact was, therefore, marked from a reasonable range. The Russian was moving at a speed of over 10 knots and keeping station on him exclusively using towed array data was very testing for *Valiant's* people as it involved high-speed sprints out of contact, interspersed by periods at slow speed to reacquire their quarry to re-establish his position.

During one of these sprints Conley was urgently called into the control room by the executive officer, who sensed all was not well. A quick scan of the sonar displays revealed to the commander that yet again an inadvertent close-range situation was rapidly developing: evidently the Russian had slowed down and *Valiant* had overhauled him up his port side. Conley had to quickly decide whether to turn towards the Victor III and gain a fire-control solution, or prudently to turn away and return to a trailing position on the Victor III's quarter. He decided upon the latter, regretfully forgoing the very rare prize of conducting a successful simulated attack upon this most modern of Soviet submarines.

After two days of trailing in deteriorating sonar conditions, contact was broken off with the Russian. With no more encounters likely, *Valiant* was directed to head back to her base in Faslane. In just over two weeks, the much-derided Black Pig had completed a successful patrol in the Western Approaches with an unprecedented five submarine detections to her credit. The later analysis of the significant number of simulated attack approaches which had been carried out revealed a very high success rate and, while this earned the crew of the Royal Navy's oldest nuclear submarine high praise, Conley had the difficult task of dealing with his executive officer's inability to contend with operational situations underwater.

Conley was quite clear in his own mind that the fault did not lie entirely with the individual officer and that some measure of the blame had to be attributed to the deficiencies inherent in the Perisher course. Conley was convinced that this was not fit for purpose in the context of training prospective commanding officers how to handle their boats when attacking submarine targets – whether real or simulated. The proof of this was the failure of the course trainers, the 'Teachers', to eliminate his unfortunate colleague, not because he was an inefficient naval officer, but simply that he did not possess one special quality necessary to the command of a hunter-killer submarine. After careful deliberation, it was amicably and mutually agreed between all parties, including the squadron commander, that the executive officer would best serve elsewhere. In vindication of Conley's assessment, he went on to successfully command a surface warship, while his replacement was a very experienced officer who had commanded a diesel submarine and had been executive officer of the SSN *Warspite*, Lieutenant Commander Huntly Gordon. He and Conley were to get on well, making a very strong team.

Two months later, in July 1985, *Valiant* was back at sea in the Northwest Approaches, taking part in a sonar trial when intelligence sources indicated that a significant Soviet submarine build-up to the west of the United Kingdom was ongoing. In view of the potential threat posed to the on-patrol UK SSBN – HMS *Revenge*, commanded by Conley's near neighbour in Garelochhead, Commander Ian McVittie – *Valiant* was directed to proceed at best speed to Faslane to pick up a towed array and then immediately return to sea to support the detection and location of the submarines of the Red Banner Fleet. Meanwhile, the SSN HMS *Churchill*, also operating in the Northwest Approaches, had made contact with and was trailing a Victor-class SSN.

However, on arriving in Faslane in the early evening, Conley was told that Northwood headquarters staff were concerned about *Valiant*'s noise defect, which had defeated all efforts to locate it. This would make her vulnerable to counter-detection and since this would prejudice the covert nature of the operation being conducted against the Russians, a quick noise ranging must be undertaken in the Clyde Estuary. Only then would a final decision be made as to whether or not to deploy her. Although Conley could see the sense in this, it was not good news. He felt the frustration of commanding a good team but being hampered by *Valiant*'s age and defects. Meanwhile, there was a hot situation developing; also at Faslane lay the brand new SSN HMS *Trafalgar*. She too was preparing to go after the Soviets.

Summoned ashore to speak to the duty submarine staff officer at Northwood through a highly secure voice link, Conley received a somewhat garbled briefing of the Soviet build-up, to the effect that there were numerous submarines operating to the west of the United Kingdom. As he strode back down the jetty to rejoin *Valiant*, he overheard two shore-based sailors discussing the fact there were an unusually high number of Soviet submarines at sea, and that *Valiant* and *Trafalgar* were being urgently scrambled. So much, he thought, for high-level security!

His elation at the prospect of again getting to grips with the Soviets was now tempered by *Valiant*'s excessive noise and the consequential possibility of having to act in a secondary supporting role to his contemporary in command of *Trafalgar*, Commander Toby Elliot. However, on arriving onboard he was greeted by his senior engineer, Andrew Miller, who declared enthusiastically that he had something to show him. The engineer was pretty confident that he had identified the noise defect as coming from a pipe valve under the casing. Following Miller along the casing, the two officers bent down at a spot on the after-casing and heard a distinct rattling noise. This was almost certainly the source of the problem; moreover, it could easily be fixed.

Getting underway at midnight with the towed array attached and having got the 'all clear' from the Clyde noise-range check, *Valiant* made a fast passage to the area where the Russian submarine activity appeared most intense. HMS *Churchill* had been withdrawn from the operation and the trail was rapidly going cold. Was all this to end in anticlimax? So it seemed until, a few hours after submerging, Conley's operators detected a Soviet submarine – *Valiant* had made contact with a Victor-class SSN, and he proceeded to close him to get within a comfortable trailing range. By coincidence the Russian turned out to be an old adversary, the specially fitted submarine they had trailed and 'attacked' on their previous patrol, and which was now returning from the Mediterranean. Once again the Victor was engaged in frequent manoeuvres in a patrolling and searching mode and proved a difficult contact to maintain, but one good intelligence-gathering close-approach and fire-control solution were achieved during the following day.

On the morning of the fifth day in company with the Victor, a second submarine of much quieter characteristics was detected and *Valiant* took up station behind them both. Although the second submarine was never properly classified, Conley suspected it was a Victor III. However, during the early evening, warning instrumentation indicated a potentially significant fault in the reactor compartment. Indications were that it was similar to that which presaged the previous episode in March. To Conley's despair, the shutting down of the nuclear plant and an investigative entry into the reactor compartment were going to be necessary to determine the problem. Meanwhile, HMS *Trafalgar* was searching to the eastwards but was not in contact with any of the Soviet submarines.

With the reactor shut down, the trail was continued in battery power, probably a first for a nuclear submarine, but speed was constrained to 5 knots and the battery endurance was very limited. As time passed the tension rose, all awaiting the emergence of the engineers from the reactor compartment with the result of their investigations. In due course, the reactor entry team emerged from aft, and the smiling face of Andrew Miller announced that the news was good: the instrumentation warning was a false alarm.

Having dropped back to a prudent range, the relatively noisy recommissioning of the nuclear plant took place and within an hour of the reactor being 'scrammed', *Valiant* was back in the trail with full power available.

Overnight both Soviet submarines were shadowed as they headed for the Shetland–Faeroes Gap but by lunchtime the following day strong Soviet surface ship sonar transmissions had been detected to the southwest, classified as emitting from an *Udaloy*-class destroyer. This was the most modern and capable of Russian anti-submarine ships and was fitted with a very powerful, long-range sonar. There were multiple ship noises coming from the same direction, although there was no intelligence to support the presence of a Russian surface squadron of any size.

As sunset approached, still in the company of the two Russian submarines, Conley decided that the Soviet surface force was close enough for him to take a look at. Rising to periscope depth, Conley found the sea state calm with good visibility. Almost immediately, he sighted the destroyer distant on the horizon, together with the masts of several other ships. The significance of this moment struck him forcibly. For all his experience and their recent close shaves with Russian submarines, this was the first time he had actually *seen* units of the Soviet Navy during the six operational patrols he had to his credit. Prior to this moment only the lines on a cathode ray trace or the noises on a sonar headset had told him where the 'opposition' was and what he was doing. It was the ability to distil detection information from such limited sensory inputs that made the acquisition of a mental tactical picture such a fundamental skill for a submarine commander. Without this the chances of success were negligible.

Conley and his team swiftly assessed that there were three or four Russian replenishment ships escorted by two or three destroyers. Moreover, since they were heading northeast, these vessels were probably simulating a NATO reinforcement convoy, allowing Soviet submarines to make dummy attacks for evaluation and exercise purposes.

However, as matters presently stood, *Valiant* lay in the grain of the approaching convoy where she was vulnerable to detection. Having no wish to add to the verisimilitude of the Soviet Navy's exercise by inviting an 'attack', Conley took *Valiant* deep and headed for the convoy's northern flank where the Victor was tracking, in the process keeping out of the way of the approaching *Udaloy*-class destroyer with its potentially very capable active sonar.

As the convoy passed, Conley headed *Valiant* to its southern flank to see what was going on there. On turning to run parallel to the most southerly ship, a submarine contact with a rapidly changing bearing was detected close to this vessel and Conley immediately suspected it to be the quiet second submarine. It was evident that the Russian submarines were carrying out exercise attacks on the convoy and the *Valiant*'s sonar and control-room teams had a real challenge in maintaining the overall tactical picture. Meanwhile, in the air the Soviets were carrying out simulated air attacks on the ships whilst anti-submarine aircraft played the role of their NATO counterparts.

Conley remarked later, 'This was real Cold War stuff – a Russian convoy playing the NATO part a few hundred miles to the west of the British Isles, being harried by Russian aircraft and submarines, whilst being followed by a Royal Navy SSN. Meanwhile, Russian maritime patrol aircraft were playing the NATO role.'

Conley shadowed the convoy during the night and on into the following day. This was a Sunday and *Valiant*'s crew settled down to a routine day and from the control room Conley continued to monitor the activities of 'the opposition' – the anodyne term for their potential enemy if things turned nasty. During the forenoon two Soviet auxiliaries and one escorting Kotlin-class destroyer were sighted and Sunday's roast lunch was interrupted by the Victor being detected going deep and at speed, crossing ahead of *Valiant* at close range as she shaped up for another dummy attack on the convoy. Quite clearly the presence of the *Valiant* remained undetected by either the Victor or the anti-submarine destroyers escorting the convoy. During the afternoon

Valiant's operators detected 'a probable' diesel submarine at close range astern of the convoy, and a good tracking solution was also achieved on him.

HMS *Valiant* continued her stealthy stalking of the Russian force, monitoring the comings and goings of various surface ships and submarines for a further two days. By this time the convoy was north of the Shetland Islands and it was becoming increasingly evident that the Soviet activity was dying down as the convoy had by now broken up and dispersed. Although contact with the two SSNs had been lost, two new Soviet nuclear submarines had been detected to the north at long range. As these were not accorded priority status, Conley headed *Valiant* back to the west of the British Isles to seek out any Soviet submarine which might still be lurking undetected off the Northwest Approaches. He was particularly focused on the possibility of locating any quiet diesel types, undetected by SOSUS.

Whilst making a sweep of the Rockall Trough, Conley received information that two Delta–class SSBNs, approximately twenty-four hours apart, were homeward-bound from their deep Atlantic patrol areas. Conley therefore laid off a course to intercept the first of these, and in due course *Valiant*'s passive sonar operators picked up the Soviet. Conley made a close approach and carried out a short trail then, having confirmed that the Delta was indeed heading for home, *Valiant* was hauled off and he decided to forgo making contact upon her consort and continued searching south for the more elusive diesel-type he had a hunch might well be lurking in the depths. The SSBNs were not priority contacts in terms of providing support for HMS *Revenge*. Nevertheless, later the same day the second SSBN was detected some distance away to the northwestwards. Conley recalled a discussion over dinner in the wardroom that evening in which it was considered what British public opinion would have thought if it was widely known that thirty-two nuclear missiles possessing immense destructive power had passed a mere two hundred miles off the British coast, borne by a pair of potentially hostile SSBNs.

The following Sunday, before Conley could complete his thorough investigation of the Rockall Trough, he received orders to intercept a reported outbound Victor II SSN which appeared to be heading for the Mediterranean. His task was to determine whether or not she had been ordered to search for any patrolling NATO SSBN, specifically Britain's single deterrent submarine. Accordingly, *Valiant* headed towards the likely transit route through waters off the northwest of Scotland. Whilst enjoying his lunch Conley was summoned to the control room; an unusual sonar contact had been detected at close range and the sound-room team found it problematical to classify. Such mysteries needed to be thoroughly investigated, so it fell to the commander to contribute his opinion. The sonar operators had detected a vessel emitting the noise of a diesel exhaust but – very unusually – with no accompanying propeller characteristics. This had raised their suspicions that it might well be a diesel submarine engaged in snorting at periscope depth.

This put Commander Conley in a quandary. His boat was by now in a particular area of the North Atlantic where *Valiant* was restrained by operational constraints to remain at a submerged depth greater than 400ft. This was because the shallower depth zone above this ceiling was allocated for use by friendly patrolling SSBNs. Such depth-zone separation removed the risk of collision between two very quiet submarines which were only likely to make sonar detection on each other at extremely close range. However, he needed to get to periscope depth to have a visual look at the contact to confirm it as a fishing vessel or, perhaps the snorting diesel submarine that his hunch suggested might be operating thereabouts. On the premise that, with a Russian Victor II SSN reported in the vicinity, it was highly unlikely that a British SSBN would be around, he bent the rules and ordered periscope depth.

As the steel periscope tube glided up from its well into the control room, Conley lowered its handles and stared through the powerful optics. As the periscope top broke the surface of the water he quickly spun it round, looking intensely for a fishing boat or similar vessel. There was nothing to see – it *must* be a submarine! He immediately ordered *Valiant* deep and the watch was stood to in order to commence tracking the new submarine contact.

Having taken *Valiant* well below 400ft, Conley ordered her levelled and almost immediately the sound-room team reported that the diesel-engine exhaust noise had ceased, and the contact being tracked was now emitting a classic nuclear submarine noise signature. However, as the minutes passed, all the pieces of the classification jigsaw were not fitting into place. Observing their displays intently, Conley and his team attempted to unravel the conundrum. From the characteristics of the noise signature, it slowly dawned upon them that this was no Soviet submarine and was most probably an American SSBN returning from her patrol area to her base alongside her depot ship in the Holy Loch, near Dunoon. The exhaust noise that had initially foxed *Valiant*'s sonar operators was probably attributable to the running of a diesel engine at periscope depth as an engineering drill.

This placed Conley in his second quandary of the day. What the Royal Navy was inclined to describe as 'an excess of zeal' had led him and his very efficient colleagues towards the possible compromising of an element of the Western alliance's nuclear deterrent. He was therefore obliged to make the transmission of a suitably contrite, 'exclusive-handling' signal to Northwood to the effect that he had probably harassed an allied SSBN. There was neither confirmation nor denial from headquarters of this assessment, nor was there any reproach over the incident beyond a gentle questioning over the breach of the depth-zone rules. Conley could only surmise that the staff at Northwood would be somewhat bemused that the Royal Navy's oldest SSN had 'bounced' an American SSBN. Whatever the truth behind the encounter, Conley's action had been initiated by the transmission of excessive noise by 'somebody'.

One more serious effect of this deviation was the escape of the targeted Soviet Victor II. It was most probable that she had slipped past *Valiant* by passing through the shallower and therefore sonically 'noisier' water conditions to the west of Scotland, a tactic used to mask a sonic 'signature'. The Victor II was eventually detected but, disappointingly for Conley and the *Valiant*, she was far to the south but had evidently not slowed down into a searching mode during her passage to locate any patrolling NATO SSBN.

Faced with this somewhat anticlimactic end to an otherwise eventful patrol, *Valiant*'s people were cheered up by a very long-range detection of another Russian submarine. This proved to be a homeward-bound Charlie II, upon which Conley closed and carried out a successful intelligence-gathering approach. The Charlie II was returning from the Mediterranean, where she would have been tasked to shadow the aircraft-carrier battle groups of the American Sixth Fleet, a strategic deployment intended to neutralise such a potent surface force with lethal anti-ship cruise missiles should hostilities occur.

With this intercept efficiently concluded, *Valiant* headed home, her ship's company in high spirits. Although they had been at sea only a little over three weeks, they had detected no less than nine Russian submarines.

The significance of this achievement was all the greater when *Valiant*'s run-down state was considered. With nine months remaining of her commission, some at Northwood were keen to deploy *Valiant* on further operations against the Red Banner Fleet, but she was increasingly showing her age and the need for a major refit. Her engineers had to work extremely hard to keep the boat going and on more than one occasion a minor fire had broken out onboard in harbour in Faslane, resulting in the arrival of the Dumbartonshire fire brigade. Fortunately, these incidents were not serious, but after a major fire aboard *Warspite* in 1976, when the nuclear submarine was visiting Liverpool, prompt fire brigade presence in such situations was considered a very wise precaution.

Aboard *Valiant* small problems had become endemic, and there was no knowing when any one of these might take a serious turn. A steam leak occurring on one of the many valves when 'flashing up' the plant in preparation for sea was a common occurrence and, as mentioned earlier, the necessary repair often compromised departure schedules. The deteriorating condition of the steam pipework in the engine room was of significant and possibly disastrous potential. The inexorable attrition of hot steam caused corrosion with a consequent weakening of the piping, lengths of which required urgent replacement. Accordingly, HMS *Valiant* was relegated to undertake less demanding tasks, including further Spearfish trials both as the firing vessel and, less gloriously, the targeted submarine.

At the end of February 1986 *Valiant* headed for the Mediterranean to partake in two major NATO submarine exercises. During these she called at Gibraltar and visited the Italian ports of La Spezia and Naples, home of the United States Navy's Sixth Fleet. In Gibraltar the stalwart senior engineer officer, Andrew Miller, was relieved, departing for a very well-deserved rest in a much less demanding shore appointment.

This whole period at sea was beset by more engineering problems than usual, the most serious of which, briefly referred to earlier, occurred at a time when *Valiant* was running both deep and at speed below the busy trade route for shipping along the Portuguese coast.

A serious flood occurred when the command team was closed up in the control room carrying out attack training drills in preparation for a forthcoming annual squadron inspection. A coupling on the wardroom heads flushing water failed, with a loud report followed by a roaring sound as highly pressurised water sprayed into the submarine. Immediately, Conley ordered an increase in speed and a twenty degrees bow-up angle to reduce depth and consequently the pressure of seawater forcing its way into the *Valiant*'s pressure hull. However, the steep cant of the submarine caused a bore of water to flood out from the wardroom passage, along the deck into the control room, where the nimble remained dry by leaping onto benches and stools. It then poured down the hatch to the compartments below, much to the alarm of the repair team trying to get up the ladder. However, the failed pipe was isolated very quickly and the ingress of water halted before any serious damage was done. The only casualties were sodden trousers and socks – the attack training drills continued with hardly a pause.

The second incident was a high-pressure steam leak which occurred towards midnight on the same day and was much more serious. Relaxing in his cabin with a book, Conley heard a shrill report from aft – 'Major steam leak in the engine room!' A violent, high-pressure leak of super-heated steam emitted into the cramped, Stygian confines of the engine room could fatally scald anyone in its vicinity; this was a life-and-death situation. The compartment was instantly evacuated, a repair party was assembled and the problem was tackled. Once again, the engineering staff rose to the occasion, quickly reaching the source of the steam and shutting it off. Despite the efficiency with which both incidents were neutralised, their occurrence and their causes shook up the new senior engineer officer and his team, giving Conley real concerns about the state of the boat's machinery. As if to emphasise *Valiant*'s increasing decrepitude, during the Mediterranean port visits, it was necessary to order a tanker carrying lubricating oil; like an old banger the Black Pig was consuming considerable quantities of lube oil.

Nevertheless, while involved in these exercises there was one final encounter with a Russian submarine. This occurred whilst participating in a NATO submarine versus submarine exercise in the Ionian Sea. Unimaginatively codenamed Dogfish by the NATO staff, it was inevitably renamed 'Dogshit' by the *Valiant*'s crew as they learned that *Valiant* – cast in the 'Blue' NATO role throughout – had in error received the exercise instructions setting out all the tracks and navigational way-points of the 'Red' submarines. It was thus all too easy locating and carrying out simulated attacks upon the opposing Red forces, which included the American SSN USS *Tullibee* and a number of NATO diesel submarines. From underwater telephone exchanges at the end of each attack phase, Conley noted a degree of despair on the part of the *Tullibee*'s crew as they grasped that they were being successfully engaged with unerring accuracy by *Valiant* in every section of the exercise.

However, for Conley and his team, these proceedings were a sideshow, as they were determined to detect a Victor II SSN, which was known to be in the Mediterranean and which had been trailed for a period by an American SSN with which Conley was thoroughly familiar – the USS *Dallas*, now commanded by Commander Frank Lacroix, who had been a near neighbour in Mystic, Connecticut. Contact had been lost with the Russian for several days, but Conley suspected that Dogfish would act as a lure to any inquisitive

Soviet submarine – the mirror image of his own stalking of the Russian convoy in the North Atlantic a few weeks earlier. Sure enough, with the exercise a few hours old, *Valiant* made contact with the Victor II. However, owing to her commitments to the exercise, Conley and his crew had to forbear investigating. The exercise was also evidently being monitored by a Russian 'research ship' bulging with sensor equipment; she was on more than one occasion sighted by *Valiant*. Not unnaturally, this prompted wild speculation among some of Conley's officers as to the impact upon any Soviet evaluation of the NATO staff cock-up in supplying a 'Blue' submarine with 'Red' information. Perhaps, the wags averred, this was a Bond-like double-bluff.

The days that followed assumed an air closely approaching farce, a bewildering mixture of *opéra bouffe* and the hardware of war. The blue waters of the Mediterranean were proving a very different place compared to the grey wastes of the North Atlantic.

During the final phase of the exercise, after conducting a successful approach against the 'Red' Italian submarine *Guglielmo Marconi*, *Valiant* was at periscope depth about two miles to the south of his victim. A USN Orion aircraft had been operating with *Valiant*, dropping active sonobuoys around the *Guglielmo Marconi* to emphasise the compromised status of the Italian boat. Suddenly *Valiant*'s sonar team reported a fast-moving submarine contact about four miles to the southward; it was tracking aft and emitting classic Russian SSN characteristics. As it was after sunset, Conley was constrained in taking rapid action, with the control room totally darkened and the need to pass locating details of the Soviet submarine to the aircraft using a cumbersome NATO numerical code difficult to use in poor lighting. The tactical situation was also confused by a high density of merchant shipping passing through the area and intense levels of biological noise from dolphins and other creatures in the vicinity.

When it appeared that the aircraft had got the message, Conley ordered *Valiant* deep to close with the Russian submarine but, on leaving periscope depth, the sonar contact was lost. However, soon afterwards a number of active sonar transmissions, characteristic of Soviet SSN equipment, were intercepted coming from the general direction of the Russian boat. These were followed by brief bursts of Soviet underwater telephone communications which made Conley think that the Soviet commander was liaising with either the so-called research ship or another submarine. What was certain was the increasing confusion of the underwater tactical picture. HMS *Valiant* was surrounded by a cacophony of noise: to the sound of passing shipping and cetacean wildlife there was now added the vocal Italian submarine captain of the *Guglielmo Marconi* chatting away on the underwater telephone, an Orion aircraft dropping numerous active sonobuoys and at least one Russian submarine which appeared to want to be part of the action. Looking back, Conley considered the whole incident a rather amusing finale to his operational engagements with Russian submarines.

The exercise over, *Valiant* headed first to Maddalena in Sardinia to leave her towed sonar array with the American submarine depot ship lying there. Here she embarked Captain Ken Cox, an American naval officer and long-standing friend of Commander Conley's, dating back to *Otter*'s visit to Charleston in February 1976. Whilst heading towards Naples for a port visit, Conley was able to give Cox a tour of *Valiant*. Afterwards, with a degree of perverse pride, Conley recalled Cox's astonishment at the amount of defect repair work which was ongoing in the machinery spaces. To Cox the exceedingly cramped confines of the submarine in general, but the machinery spaces in particular, were in extreme contrast to the well laid out, easily accessible compartments of most American nuclear submarines.

Once in Naples the majority of the ship's company, except the engineering department, could relax. Captain Cox was deputy to the American admiral commanding all NATO and United States submarine operations in the Mediterranean, and on the second day alongside, Cox invited his friend to attend the morning high-level briefings in the American naval headquarters. At the final and highest level of these briefings, Conley noted he was the only foreigner present, as the presentations focused upon the forthcoming deployment of an American carrier battle group across the so-called 'Line of Death' established by Colonel Gaddafi of Libya. This ran east–west across the Gulf of Sidra, along the parallel of 32° 30' N latitude. Quite unrecognised by international law, the sea to the south had been declared as Libyan territorial waters. Three days later, on Monday, 24 March 1986 the battle group, led by three aircraft carriers, the US ships *Saratoga*, *Coral Sea* and *America*, supported by destroyers and frigates, crossed the line. Libya responded with the use of anti-aircraft missiles and fighter aircraft, challenging the battle group's perfectly legitimate right of peaceful passage in international waters and airspace. In retaliation, American aircraft attacked several missile radar sites and destroyed or disabled several threatening Libyan naval vessels, including a Russian-built Nanuchka-class missile corvette and a French-built Combattante-class missile-armed patrol boat.

Having left Naples, a few days later *Valiant* berthed at La Spezia for an informal visit and a further break for the crew over the Easter holiday. Being billeted ashore in a small hotel, as there was no naval accommodation available, it came as a surprise to Conley and his officers that among the other residents was a small number of Libyan naval officers. They were standing by new patrol vessels under construction in the local Fincantieri shipyard. As one Italian admiral visiting *Valiant* cynically explained to Conley: 'We build vessels for the Libyan navy, the Americans sink them and then Gaddafi asks for more to be built. It is all very good for business.'

On leaving La Spezia in early April for a second submarine versus submarine exercise under the operational control of the Spanish Navy, the number of engineering defects occurring in *Valiant* continued to mount. To Conley, it was evident these were putting a severe strain upon the engineering department. In particular, a problem had occurred with one of the reactor's key instruments which meant that should the reactor be shut down for any reason, it might prove difficult to start it up again. Given the general state of *Valiant*, the inherent risk in such an event was exacerbated by a defect in the backup emergency propulsion motor which would render *Valiant* without any form of propulsion. Under the circumstances this worst-case scenario was not far-fetched and gave both Conley and his engineer officers plenty to contemplate, particularly as the exercise would be taking place in the Strait of Gibraltar. Crowded with international shipping, this was not an area where any vessel, submarine or surface ship would want to entirely lose the ability to manoeuvre. Two days into the exercise Conley reluctantly withdrew *Valiant* and headed for Faslane. This was a great disappointment to him as it was the only commitment which had not been met during his time in command.

After a week's repairs, *Valiant* was back at sea doing what her crew did best – covertly trailing another submarine for over twelve hours. True, this was an exercise and the quarry was a British SSBN, but the sweetness in the task was the impact on both the crew of HMS *Resolution* and the Naval Staff, for it raised issues regarding the vulnerability of Britain's ageing SSBN force. In something of a paradoxical conclusion, it was appreciated that *Resolution* was up against one of the Royal Navy's most capable and experienced SSN crews. Secretly pleased for his ship's company, Conley's disappointments over the Mediterranean deployment began to be forgotten as accolades followed from the squadron staff.

Whether or not this influenced the choice of *Valiant* to undertake an important task was not made clear, but Conley found his submarine selected to embark a contingent of the permanent representatives of the North Atlantic Council – the ambassadors appointed by each member state to NATO headquarters in Brussels. They would be taken to sea for a day to observe at first hand submarine operations in the Clyde Estuary. Such was the significance of the occasion that a full-blown rehearsal was staged on the preceding day. Happily, this included a trial of the splendid gourmet lunch prepared by the *Valiant*'s cooks, accompanied by some very fine wine. Aware that culinary triumph might add lustre of a more complimentary gloss to the Black Pig's reputation, Conley keenly anticipated the task. Despite *Valiant*'s age-related problems, he was justly proud of his ship's company and the virtues inherent in *Valiant*'s handling characteristics. Conley enjoyed putting the submarine through her paces and demonstrating her superb underwater manoeuvrability, all the more so as, on this important occasion, the propulsion plant and auxiliary machinery worked perfectly.

All the visitors appeared to have thoroughly enjoyed their day at sea and as they disembarked for a grand dinner in Culzean Castle in Ayrshire, the Spanish ambassador confided to Conley that he had thoroughly enjoyed the magnificent lunch and was very pleased that Spain had recently reaffirmed its membership of such a 'great organisation which allowed him to experience thoroughly pleasant events'.

Twenty-four hours later there followed an even more enjoyable event, when the families of *Valiant*'s crew were invited aboard for a day at sea. Ever resourceful, the cooks had sequestered sufficient of the NATO ambassadors' luncheon supplies to lay on a spectacular repast for wives and girlfriends.

In the closing weeks of *Valiant*'s third commission, she lay alongside at Faslane, preparing for an impending refit and nuclear refuelling at Rosyth Naval Dockyard. During this period the submarine was visited by a number of veterans, former midshipmen who had served aboard the battleship HMS *Valiant*. Commissioned in 1915, the previous *Valiant* had served until 1947 and the continuity of her name in the present SSN provided the Royal Navy with that important psychological thread of tradition. Conley's command, the fifth *Valiant* to serve, bore the battle honours of her predecessors on a splendid board outside her wardroom, including the battles of Copenhagen, Jutland and Cape Matapan.

The former inhabitants of the battleship's gunroom enjoyed both a tour of the submarine, a meeting with the present incumbents of the wardroom and a reunion, an event which could not fail to leave its mark upon all present. Conley remarked afterwards that they were a most pleasant and distinguished group of individuals, but the one notable absentee was HRH The Prince Philip, who had sent a telegram regretting very much that he could not join the gathering. He had served onboard *Valiant* as a midshipman during the period 1940–42 and had experienced some of the most intense fighting which took place in the eastern Mediterranean, including the Battle of Cape Matapan and the evacuation of the British Army from Crete, a very costly expedition in terms of loss and damage to Royal Navy ships.

Shortly after arriving at Rosyth on 19 May, Conley handed over command to his executive officer, Huntly Gordon. In his brief few days in the dockyard he was dismayed to see how quickly the internals of *Valiant* were being taken apart with scant regard for their reassembly. There had been intensive, detailed planning for the refit by *Valiant*'s officers and the senior dockyard managers, but there was a serious lack of communication and control between the planners and project leaders in their offices, and what was actually happening onboard the submarine. Inevitably, this dysfunction came at a price; the refit was to overrun, extending from two to three years with corresponding escalation in costs.

Unavoidably, there is a connection between a commander and his command; this has little to do with romance, but is a symbiotic function of the process itself. The latter becomes an extension of the former and the retrospective satisfaction – or otherwise – will embrace other components, chief of which will be crew efficiency, itself a measure of the commander's. Defects, such as had littered Conley's time in *Valiant*, though a serious nuisance, are also a challenge, and accepting and overcoming challenges in the circumstances peculiar to submarine operations provide the bedrock of job satisfaction. After nursing *Valiant* throughout her third commission, Conley regarded the achievements of his people as second to none and watching his boat carelessly torn apart by the dockyard seemed like a form of betrayal. He considered it all so unnecessary, but this costly inefficiency, carefully obscured from the taxpayers, had become standard in the refitting of nuclear submarines at this time.

Despite this disappointing terminal anticlimax, Conley's tenure of command of *Valiant* had been by far the most satisfying period of his naval career. He was sad to leave the 'Black Pig', but he considered himself extremely lucky to have avoided a serious, even a catastrophic, breakdown. HMS *Valiant* was in desperate need of a refit and during his final few months in command he had pushed her to the limit. He also acknowledged that he had owed much to the unsung heroes of his engineering department under Andrew Miller.

Their tremendous commitment and sheer hard work, often in awful conditions, had managed to keep the submarine going against the odds.

As for his operational successes, Conley had been blessed by an exceptionally competent and talented sound-room team which, combined with his own experience and tactical ability, had enabled *Valiant* – notwithstanding her age – to achieve notable success in hunting and tracking Russian submarines. Overall, he considered command of *Valiant* had given him the opportunity to capitalise on the knowledge and experience he had gained during his submarine career and with this came an acknowledgement of his good fortune and the privilege he had enjoyed. His achievements had not gone unnoticed. In the Queen's Birthday Honours List of 1986 he was made OBE and in the following New Year's Honours his stalwart senior engineer officer, Lieutenant Commander Andrew Miller, received an MBE.

Conley was now aged thirty-nine and *Valiant* was to have been his last seagoing appointment. However, his connection with submarines was to continue. In the near term his next posting was a year at the United States Navy's War College at Newport, Rhode Island. Here he would serve as the Royal Navy's representative on a prestigious international course. It was time for him and his wife Linda to pack up their possessions again and head back to New England.

16

Arctic Bears and Torpedoes

THE YEAR THAT Conley and his family spent at Newport, Rhode Island, was soon over. He had enjoyed a year's participation in the War College's international command course where his fellow students were commanders or captains from the navies of thirty-two other nations, some of whom would go on to head their respective services. Besides the valuable experience of working and socialising with such a diverse group, several weeks were spent touring America, enjoying unique insights into its institutions, history, industries and people. However, by September 1987 that was all behind him, along with the memories of the sunshine and beaches of Rhode Island. It was back to the grim realities of Faslane.

Here Conley took over responsibility for the Submarine Tactics and Weapons Group (STWG), then staffed by about forty people, mainly from the uniformed service, and was part of the Flag Officer Submarines (FOSM) organisation. Since he had left the STWG nine years earlier there had naturally been some changes to its work, notably the conduct of Sub-Harpoon anti-ship missile firings and the analysis of the 'approach to attack criteria' data from operational patrols. With the impending introduction into service of the new Spearfish torpedo and the need to improve the standard of tactical evaluation exercises at sea, plenty of challenges lay ahead.

Despite his and his fellow submarine commanders' demonstrably successful ability to stalk and close with Russian submarines, Conley knew that to achieve a real 'kill' in wartime relied upon a weapon system that was far from perfect. The old problem of recalcitrant torpedoes rose to confront him once again and he found himself immediately involved with a report on the analysed results of firings of Tigerfish torpedoes conducted in the early summer of 1987 in the open ocean by the SSNs *Warspite* and *Swiftsure*. These had been carried out in sea areas in the vicinity of St Kilda, the remote island

215

forty miles to the west of the Outer Hebrides. With each submarine alternating as target, these were the most realistic set of firings of Tigerfish to date but the success rate had been very low; unusually, this was predominantly due to crew error as opposed to the weapon's notorious unreliability. Conley's superior on FOSM's staff had been unwilling to release the results as they stood, because he feared that they would reflect badly upon the perceived effectiveness of the Submarine Flotilla. Very reluctantly, Conley set about creative manipulation of the report criteria, somehow producing a set of acceptable results which could be endorsed for promulgation to the wider Navy. Nevertheless, it disappointed and angered him that there still remained a culture at a high level within the Submarine Service by which weapon problems were either suppressed or ignored.

However, there was good news in the offing. After the Falklands War several Tigerfish warshot proving firings took place and the results of these had been awful. Accordingly, the MoD had put long overdue money and resources into finally fixing this weapon system. The result was the Tigerfish Mod 2 variant where the weapon's reliability had been much improved. Most notably, the guidance wire dispensing arrangement had been made robust by copying the American method of attaching the submarine end wire dispenser to the torpedo tube rear door, a great improvement on the previous system. The latter encompassed a 'bucket of wire' dangled by cable from the exterior end of the torpedo tube, a crude method which had constantly failed and compromised an expensive torpedo. There were now urgent imperatives for testing this modified weapon, not only in the so-called 'open ocean scenario', but in under-ice firings.

The difficulties experienced with the anti-submarine torpedoes carried by British hunter-killer submarines had, by this time, become acute because the Soviet Navy had introduced their huge Delta IV- and Typhoon-class SSBNs. These were, in effect the super-dreadnoughts of the Cold War, phenomenally expensive – the product of a truly centralised economy. Their advanced design enabled them to patrol under the Arctic ice from where their long-range ballistic missiles were within range of the majority of their American targets and there was increasing evidence that the Soviet Union was deploying these formidable submarines in precisely this environment. Since a SSBN of such potency, concealed close under the ice, stationary, with most of her machinery shut down and lurking in a quiet state would be exceedingly difficult to locate, American and British SSNs were tasked to demonstrate their capability to seek out – and potentially destroy – such a menace.

As the commander heading up STWG it was time to see what the Tigerfish Mod 2 could achieve in the Arctic. To further this, April 1988 found Conley clambering out of a twin turboprop Casa aircraft, gingerly stepping onto the ice of the frozen Beaufort Sea to the north of Alaska. The cutting blast of Arctic air reminded him that this was an odd place for a submariner; it was a lot more comfortable *under* the ice, cocooned in the warm pressure hull of a SSN.

He had arrived at the ice camp of the United States Navy's Applied Physics Laboratory Ice Station, or APLIS, to supervise a series of under-ice Tigerfish torpedo firings. Two British SSNs were involved, HMS *Turbulent*, Commander Ian Richards, and HMS *Superb*, Commander John Tuckett. They would be joined by the USS *Lapon* which was on her way from the Pacific Ocean, conducting a submerged passage below the ice by way of the shallow Bering Straits which separate the isolated American state of Alaska and the Soviet Union.

The Applied Physics Laboratory Ice Station had been set up on the first-year ice which had sealed off a former polyna – or ice-free channel. This meant that the ice was relatively thin and the fact that it was 'new' meant that it was also relatively flat: a sheet of ice, rather than the jumble of ragged projections formed by prolonged movement and collision to be found in 'old' ice. APLIS was situated 120 miles northeast of the oil town of Prudhoe. A landing strip had been established on the flattest area of the ice and a number of temporary prefabricated huts and framed tents provided accommodation and a command post. The base facilities included a three-dimensional range, which enabled the accurate tracking of both the submarines and the torpedoes they were to fire. This was a technical challenge, as the range equipment had to contend with both the complexities of ice drift, caused by the effects of the wind – up to six or seven miles a day – and the Coriolis effect, a phenomenon caused by the earth's rotation which creates a slow anticlockwise rotation of the ice sheet around the pole. The setting up and running of the APLIS organisation had been contracted to the University of Washington State, which would also remove all equipment and trials debris when the tests and trials were completed by the end of April. The station was under the command of the officer in charge of the Submarine Arctic Laboratory, based in sunny San Diego, Captain Merrill Dorman, USN.

In addition to observations, measurements and other data acquisition, there were the practical problems of recovering torpedoes at the end of their run. This was to be achieved by a combination of American civilian divers and helicopters. After recovery the weapons were then shipped by light aircraft to Prudhoe airfield where a team of civilian specialists from the armament depot at Coulport near Faslane would make them safe to be airlifted by RAF Hercules back to Anchorage airport for onward shipping. As these experimental firings were highly classified, the cover story for the Coulport team was that they were researchers from Nottingham University. For some reason they were dressed in Royal Marine camouflage fatigues, but as Arctic gear had been ordered but was not available, the team were to some extent hoist by their own petard in wearing jungle fatigues instead. It was also notable that, since they spoke with strong west of Scotland accents, few – Conley among them – were under any illusion as to the efficacy of this ruse.

The greatest danger to the people working on the ice was the presence of the Arctic's largest predator. Polar bears had been spotted near the ice station and all personnel were warned to be careful when leaving the immediate environs of the camp. In the station command hut there was an array of rifles and shotguns and it was normal routine to select a few weapons before any foray was made away from the station in case of having to deal with an aggressive bear.

A prerequisite for spending time at APLIS had been to undertake Arctic survival training in case the ice under the station unexpectedly broke up. This training largely consisted of surviving for several days in a snow hole in Maine, but as the decision that Conley would direct the initial phases of the firings was made late in the day, he had been unable to complete this prerequisite. In event, however, he found life at APLIS with its accommodation in heated framed tents very tolerable. During the time he was at the camp the temperature never dropped much below –25°C, but everyone had to be careful to protect themselves against the frostbite induced by the wind-chill factor in high winds and when subject to the downdraught from operating helicopters.

The danger of camping on first-year ice was demonstrated one night, when the ice separated and a large polyna formed, taking a chunk out of the landing strip. A further incident occurred the following morning when Conley and a party of three Americans took two snowmobiles to reconnoitre the extent of the polyna. One of his American companions incautiously approached the ice edge, which gave way, pitching him into the sea. Although the casualty was quickly pulled from the water, his snowmobile was lost to the Arctic Ocean. Fortuitously, a helicopter was readily available to fly the man back to the camp, where he quickly recovered in a sauna which had been put in place for such an emergency. As the senior officer present, Conley had to explain to the station commander how one of the party ended up in the sea with the loss of an expensive snowmobile. The whole incident was a reminder of the hostility of the Arctic environment, where Conley and 'the students from Nottingham University' now awaited the subjects of their study, the two British SSNs *Turbulent* and *Superb*.

The two submarines heading north for the under-ice firings each carried eight Tigerfish Mod 2 practice weapons, and their submerged passage of over 1,500 nautical miles under the ice from the Greenland Sea to APLIS was a new record for hunter-killer submarines of the Royal Navy. Conley had some appreciation of the anxieties of Commanders Richards and Tuckett; their only exit route to reach open water if anything went wrong was back the same way they had come. With their limited under-ice sonar capability, there was no prospect of them making a through passage to the nearer open water of the Pacific through the Bering Straits, with the possible presence of ice canyons stretching down to the seabed. Although the SSNs had high-definition sonars which mapped the ice either side of them, they were not fitted with ahead-looking ice detection equipment which would be needed to navigate around such features. A fully capable ice-detection sonar was still some time in the future for the British SSN.

As most of the Arctic ice pack was thicker than the two or three feet the two British SSNs could penetrate, any serious engineering problem or emergency occurring while under the ice pack would be compounded by their inability to surface without the delay in locating thin ice or a polyna. In the event of one of the submarines losing her propulsion, the contingency plan to dig the boat out from under the ice presumed both that it was able to send a distress signal successfully and that it could be located: neither was a certainty.

The Arctic ice sheet is characterised by a high density of pressure ridges which protrude above and below it. Above sea level these ridges rise to heights in excess of 30ft, but underwater they extend to depths – often called the 'keel depth' – of more than 100ft. Therefore, before attempting to surface through ice, a hunter-killer must use her sonar to map the ice thickness above her to both avoid pressure ridges, and to identify a surfacing location of flat thin ice or open water. Having got into the desired surfacing position and having stopped all horizontal momentum, the submarine then carefully de-ballasts to achieve an ideal ascent rate to use the fin (the 'sail' in American naval terminology) to punch through the ice.

The hazards inherent in this operation become even more complicated if it became necessary to surface quickly, say in the case of a serious flooding, when there was no time for a careful discovery of a suitable location. Such a scenario would call for rapid de-ballasting and any consequent contact with thick ice which frustrated the attempt to break through would result in an extremely precarious and dangerous situation. Highly positive in buoyancy, there would be a risk of a catastrophic roll of over sixty degrees, severely damaging equipment, putting the vessel into an irrecoverable situation and imperilling the crew.

In the preparation for the operation, Conley, in overall charge of its execution, had burned the midnight oil, carefully reviewing the plans and orders and all aspects of submarine safety. It had seriously concerned him that both *Superb* and *Turbulent* were fitted with a new type of inertial navigation system which had not been fully tested in very high latitudes. Considerably worried by the thought of a submarine under the ice losing its prime positional and heading reference, he accordingly had spent much time gaining assurance from its designers that this equipment would be totally reliable as the boats headed over the top of the world.

Once the operation was initiated, Conley could only head for APLIS and await the outcome and, as the estimated time of arrival of the two submarines approached, he could be found crouching next to the underwater telephone in the APLIS command hut in the Arctic twilight. It was thus a relief to hear faint and distant transmissions indicating the boats had made their passage successfully and would soon arrive.

On her arrival, Commander Richards of HMS *Turbulent* reported a serious problem with his oxygen-making electrolysers. Having had to fall back to burning special devices which generated oxygen – called 'oxygen candles' – she needed urgent replacements. Indeed, having penetrated the pack ice, *Turbulent*'s commanding officer had made the brave decision to press on to APLIS, past the point of no return in terms of having enough oxygen candles to return south, clear of the ice.

Conley swiftly made arrangements for a supply of oxygen candles, while Richards prepared to bring *Turbulent* to the surface in a polyna several miles distant from the ice station in order to ventilate the boat with fresh air. Meanwhile, Conley, having been landed by helicopter beside the polyna with a small group to await the surfacing, suddenly realised that the shotguns usually carried on such forays had been left in the helicopter. Preoccupied by carrying a portable underwater telephone and other equipment from the aircraft, the guns had been left behind. During the next few hours an apprehensive Conley kept a very sharp lookout for any polar bear stalking them behind the surrounding ice ridges. In due course, at a later surfacing, and in what may well have been the most unconventional 'replenishment at sea' ever, an adequate number of oxygen candles were supplied to *Turbulent*.

On reaching APLIS from the Pacific through the Bering Straits, the San Diego based USS *Lapon* conducted the first of a number of under-ice surfacing tests. Conley witnessed this evolution in the company of a number of scientists who were collecting data. A few minutes before the event, Captain Dorman arrived at speed on a snowmobile and declared that 'two bears were on the way', and would shortly reach the surfacing site. However, observing some people starting to check out their rifles, he quickly made it clear that the bears in question were actually Soviet Bear reconnaissance aircraft. Indeed, a few minutes after the *Lapon* surfaced, her sail having broken through the ice, she was overflown by the two Russian aircraft at very low altitude, closely pursued by two USAF F15 fighters.

Shortly after surfacing, the *Lapon*'s commanding officer, Commander J Mackin, climbed out of his submarine and joined the welcoming party on the ice. He was accompanied by his Arctic pilot, an experienced under-ice navigator who had provided guidance and advice to Mackin and his command team during the passage. After an exchange of pleasantries, Mackin revealed that he had concerns about a steam leak on his propulsion machinery. This potentially involved shutting his plant down to effect repairs; San Diego must have seemed a long way away.

Coincidentally, later that day, the ice station was overflown by one of the RAF Hercules freighters. Whilst at Prudhoe, one of the aircraft captains had indicated that he was keen to land his Hercules on the ice, as this had never before been achieved by the RAF. However, after a few passes, and no doubt having concerns about the landing strip's length, shortened by the fissure in the ice, the ambitious air crew wisely decided not to attempt a landing.

In the following few days both *Turbulent* and *Superb* fired their sixteen Tigerfish Mod 2 torpedoes in a near flawless series of evaluation firings, and all the weapons were successfully recovered. Most of the firings were conducted against each other, the submarines alternating as targets; however, some weapon runs were against static acoustic targets. These were configured to represent a stationary Typhoon or Delta IV SSBN hiding under the ice. The weapons performed extremely well in the quiet Arctic conditions, achieving long-range passive homing detections. Even in the active mode, where the torpedoes' homing systems had the problem of resolving the real target from contacts generated by returns from the ice features, the weapons homed remarkably reliably. Accordingly, the Americans observing the firings were impressed by both the weapon's very solid performance and their precision guidance, which enabled them to be parked under suitable flat, thin ice at the end of their run, ready for recovery.

At about 1,000ft or more the underwater visibility was remarkable, thus helping the job of weapon recovery. The routine for this consisted of creating two holes in the ice about 3ft in diameter, one for a diver, the other for the torpedo. Once the diver had attached a harness to the weapon, it was connected to, and drawn upwards by, a helicopter. Perhaps surprisingly, no weapon was significantly damaged, although at least one had to be recovered from underneath ice rubble about 20ft thick.

With the trials progressing successfully to Conley's satisfaction, his spell at the ice station was over. He soon found himself the sole passenger in the back of a Casa on the way back to Prudhoe, sharing a very noisy aircraft hold with two Tigerfish. About half an hour into the flight, he awoke from a doze to the noise of a distinct change of pitch on the aircraft's engines, simultaneously noting with great alarm that the pilot was wildly gesticulating downwards, pointing to the ice and circling the aircraft to lose altitude. The prospect of a crash landing on the ice, seated between two torpedoes, filled Conley with real foreboding, but then he spotted why the pilot was becoming so excited. There, on an ice floe a few hundred feet below, were polar bears – a magnificent mother and her two cubs.

The 1988 under-ice Tigerfish firings had firmly demonstrated the Royal Navy SSNs' capability to successfully engage submarines under the Arctic ice pack, putting its hunter-killer submarines' capability on a par with the US Navy in terms of under-ice warfare. Conley was extremely pleased with the efficient performance of both *Turbulent* and *Superb*, given the difficulties of navigating and operating under the deep ice pack. Both commanders and their respective ship's companies had demonstrated competence of a high order in conducting a series of torpedo firings unique to the Royal Navy. When FOSM Rear Admiral Frank Grenier subsequently briefed Prime Minister Margaret Thatcher about the operation, she was reported to have been 'absolutely spellbound', declaring great pride in what had been achieved. Despite having impressed the prime minister, there were no honours awarded to individual members of the submarines' crews which, given the constraints of security precluding any publicity in the media, struck Conley as a missed opportunity.

Conley was not to know it at the time, but the under-ice firings in which he had played such a central part, almost certainly marked the zenith of the Royal Navy SSN force's history. Extraordinary and unprecedented and unforeseen events in the following year, both at a grand-strategic and tactical level, were to produce dramatic effects upon the Submarine Flotilla. Unbeknownst to any of the participants, British, American and the reconnoitring Russian airmen, their activities in the high Arctic in those weeks of April 1988 marked the end of an era.

17

A Kind of Victory

THE MOST CURIOUS feature of the epochal events that were to transform the political map of the world and end the Cold War was their unpredicted arrival. In a divided world obsessed with suspicions, espionage and military intelligence appeared to lie at the heart of international interplay, overlaid by diplomacy. True, there were the easements of perestroika and glasnost, but the nature of the immense and accumulating forces underlying these tentative cracks in the bastion of Communist totalitarianism were quite obscure. For those whose business took them down to the great waters of the submarine front line in the Cold War, it was, in those last months of the 1980s, business as usual. Indeed, in contrast to what was to come, for the Cold War warriors there was much going on in the submarine tactical development arena, and copious resources were being put into addressing the many problems and deficiencies which existed.

For Commander Conley this meant a swift journey from the polar regions to the tropics where, at the AUTEC range in the Caribbean, another evaluation of the Tigerfish Mod 2 torpedo was underway. Handing over his Arctic clothing to an agent in Anchorage, he collected his tropical uniform and, after a succession of flights, he arrived at Andros Island to join the SSN HMS *Sceptre*. Together with the SSNs *Courageous* and *Churchill*, *Sceptre* was conducting tactical evaluation exercises run by STWG, to which was added the task of acting as target for test firings of the Royal Navy's Stingray lightweight torpedo, a weapon launched from aircraft, helicopters and surface warships.

Beyond these immediate trials and exercises there remained much work to do to improve the attack potential of British hunter-killer submarines, in particular honing the procedures for successful use of the now much more reliable Tigerfish, and evaluating the new Spearfish torpedo. Conley felt that the spirit of real improvement had both momentum and traction, and the fact that STWG was at the forefront of this demanding but vital task was enabling him to influence strongly the Royal Navy's Submarine Flotilla's war-fighting effectiveness.

This process had taken some years to get under way. In 1982, recognising the performance deficiencies of Tigerfish and, in particular, its limitations against the high-speed, deep-diving submarine, the Ministry of Defence had invited companies to tender for a replacement heavyweight torpedo ready to enter service in five years – 1987. In the event there were only two contenders: an advanced version of the United States Navy's Mark 48 torpedo known as the 'Adcap' and the British GEC-Marconi Spearfish torpedo. On paper, the latter was the better weapon, being considerably faster and more advanced in its homing system than the Adcap. Further-more, it would be a British weapon and its selection would ensure a heavyweight torpedo design and manufacturing capability would be maintained in the United Kingdom. It was, therefore, no surprise that the contract went to GEC-Marconi, notwithstanding it was the same company which had manufactured the troublesome Tigerfish, with its unenviable record of poor components and general unreliability.

To add to this augury, the five-year lead-time and the operational availability date of 1987 was unrealistic. This, it was later revealed, had been set in the competition process to meet the planned availability of the Mark 48-Adcap. In the event the latter entered service a year later, in 1988, but it would be another six years before Spearfish was sufficiently reliable to be adopted by the British Submarine Flotilla.

Spearfish was a very ambitious project, as the torpedo incorporated a new type of turbine engine which used a highly volatile mixture of two fuels. It also had a very sophisticated homing system, which was able to contend with a target submarine which laid a trail of powerful noise countermeasures aimed at deflecting an approaching torpedo. Furthermore, when used against a surface ship, its homing system was designed to place the weapon under a precisely specified part of the hull in order to achieve maximum damage. Combine all these novel features into one weapon, and significant develop-ment challenges were bound to arise.

Conley's team at STWG were responsible for the analysis of the Spearfish trials and he was therefore able to gain first-hand knowledge of the many problems the project encountered. This, on top of his experience gained in the several firings of the Spearfish from *Valiant*, engaged his professional interest as a submariner because, notwithstanding the successes of the torpedo as a highly destructive weapon in two world wars and sundry lesser campaigns, its history was littered with failure.

The holy grail of torpedo development prior to the Second World War was to achieve a reliable magnetic fuse which enabled a torpedo to explode under its target. This type of detonation creates a very powerful bubble of gases which lifts the targeted ship out of the sea and breaks its back, causing critical structural damage and sinking it. It is much more lethal than actually hitting the side of a ship where the effects of the explosion are – to a significant extent – dissipated by a ship's compartmented structure. To achieve this, both the German Kriegsmarine and the United States Navy adopted the magnetic fuse, only to discover that it proved unreliable. Premature detonation was very common, so too were the numbers of cases where a torpedo failed to explode under its target and only did so harmlessly at the termination of its run – thereby betraying the fact that it had been fired by a hostile submarine. Faced with this, both the German and American navies reverted for a period to sole use of the contact fuse in their torpedoes.

Initially, the United States Navy was extremely reluctant to adopt this expedient, carrying out extensive and prolonged investigations. The American Navy Bureau of Ordnance insisted that the weapon problems were caused by submarine commanding officers failing to fire their torpedoes with an adequately accurate target solution. This purblind infatuation with human error was not entirely confined to America; there were similar conclusions drawn elsewhere in other submarine forces.

The British also dabbled with the magnetic fuse during the Second World War, but suffered similar problems with its reliability. The Germans, meanwhile, developed the first acoustic homing torpedoes for use in their submarines, and these were specifically designed to lock on to the propeller noise of the convoy escorts as they located and attacked the U-boat.

The complex wrestling with the problems generated by the poor performance of the Tigerfish were but one chapter in this long history. The constant upping of expectations expressed in formal specifications seemed to constantly tempt design engineers to over-complicate mechanisms, resulting in expensive weapons being issued to highly-trained crews operating highly expensive submarines, but which would be of dubious effectiveness in war. Unsurprisingly, Conley was not alone in having being long very concerned that if he and his ship's company were ever pushed to the limit, their means of attack was, at best, of doubtful reliability. To discover that deficiencies were emerging in his team's assessment of several early Spearfish trials was not merely disappointing, but brought on a strong sense of déjà vu.

Specifically, Spearfish was displaying to Conley and his team a problem with its final approach and fusing arrangements against ship targets. The detonation of Tigerfish directly below its surface ship targets had been achieved by the relatively robust arrangement of the weapon actively generating its own magnetic field which, when broken by the target's magnetic field, initiated detonation. This had been taken to a much greater level of sophistication in Spearfish. However, Conley's efforts to persuade the Spearfish MoD project team there was anything wrong proved fruitless. His case was to an extent undermined by the contractor's flawed reporting of the results, which he despairingly observed on completion of several trial firings at AUTEC. Furthermore, the value of any fieldwork was impaired by the attitude of the project director in the Ministry, who proved far too optimistic about the progress of the weapon's development and failed to be inquisitive about potential problems.

Following a time-honoured tradition of ignoring the facts, the project's weapons specialists accorded the shortcomings in the final approach of the Spearfish to the artificial depth ceiling imposed upon the trials weapons. This ceiling was applied in order to prevent a torpedo actually hitting the target, success being measured by its dummy triggering at an offset distance. However, with his very extensive torpedo experience Conley was not convinced. Moreover, he was desperately disappointed that there were no plans or resources available to progressively update the homing software of the Spearfish to enable it to successfully contend with all types of target, such as the under-ice situation he had so recently perfected with Tigerfish at APLIS. Infuriatingly, these deficiencies were to affect the Spearfish programme for many years to come but, like his predecessors in the American and German navies, he was to learn that it was one thing to identify torpedo deficiencies, and quite another to persuade the hierarchy that they actually existed.

The passage of time also revealed that, in addition to its performance vagaries, Spearfish was unreliable. It gradually percolated to those responsible in the Ministry of Defence that they were grappling with another runaway project and that before acceptance for service a costly programme to rectify Spearfish had to be put in place. This would finally be done in the early 1990s, but not before the introduction of the new torpedo had slipped miles astern of its projected acceptance date, leaving Conley and his colleagues with the disturbing yet apparently ineluctable sensation of having been there before.

There was, however, one conventional submarine weapon system that was proving highly reliable for the Royal Navy – but it was not British, nor was it suitable for anti-submarine use. This was the American anti-ship Sub[marine]-Harpoon missile, the dependability of which was absolutely outstanding. Sub-Harpoon proved highly robust and reliable, homing convincingly onto its intended target. The missile was enclosed in a canister which, having been fired from a torpedo tube, rose to the surface of the sea. Here the missile's ignition system fired and it took off on its trajectory to its programmed target.

The introduction of Sub-Harpoon marked the culmination of a long search for such a weapon. Earlier initiatives to put conventional missiles into Royal Naval submarines included the submarine-launched airflight missile (SLAM) which *Oberon* had been fitted for – but not with – in 1972 after her return from the Far East. A Vickers initiative, SLAM featured a retractable mast in the submarine's fin, containing a pod of four Blowpipe missiles. These were intended to shoot down an anti-submarine helicopter hovering in the area dipping its sonar into the sea. However, the pod was conspicuous – particularly from the air – protruding above the sea, and the missiles required visual guidance onto the target through one of the periscopes. This was not a very practical proposition and, after a series of trials firings from the diesel submarine *Aeneas*, the project was dropped.

Another project which failed to get off the ground was Hawker Siddeley's Sub-Martel anti-ship missile. Fired from a torpedo tube, this would have been driven to the surface by a booster rocket whereupon a separate rocket motor took over. Conley had witnessed handling trials of a prototype Sub-Martel onboard *Swiftsure* in 1974 and was unimpressed. He and his peers within the Submarine Service were extremely pleased that the MoD cancelled the project in 1976, and went for the very much cheaper option of the proven, more powerful and longer-ranged American Sub-Harpoon. Almost certainly Sub-Martel, even if all its technical challenges had been overcome, would not have available in short order. By adopting Sub-Harpoon, the Royal Navy were able to deploy the missile for the first time onboard HMS *Courageous* in May 1982, at the end of the Falklands War.

STWG was responsible for the routine proving firings of Sub-Harpoon. Normally these were carried out on the Army-run Benbecula missile range situated to the west of the Outer Hebrides. Fired against remotely-controlled target vessels, the missiles were fitted with telemetry equipment which enabled range control to destroy them if they deviated from their intended flight path.

However, the periodic testing of a randomly selected Sub-Harpoon warshot was a very different matter. These were conducted well to the west of St Kilda using as target a warship hulk that had been towed into place by a tug, which then retreated to a safe distance. As there were no range-tracking facilities, a RAF Nimrod provided confirmation that there was no surface ship contact within an eighty-five-mile range of the firing submarine. A Buccaneer low-level strike aircraft would also be involved, ready to take up a station behind the missile as it emerged from the sea, following it and filming its flight until its impact on target. This in itself was a co-ordination challenge. Responsible for the safe conduct of these tests, it was always a worry to Conley – the son of a fisherman – that there might be a small, undetected vessel within the missile's 'search and acquisition envelope'. Furthermore, an errant missile could fly in any direction, with no method of destroying it in-flight until it ran out of fuel at the end of its sixty-five-mile range. However, at least during his own watch, the Sub-Harpoon missiles performed flawlessly.

During this period, as Conley and his people brought the Tigerfish to operational standards compatible with taking on the might of the Soviet Union's Typhoon and Delta IV SSBNs, the entire political and strategic fabric of the Cold War underwent tremendous upheaval. Such was the extent of this, that the year of 1989 effectively saw the Cold War end in a kind of victory for the West.

The struggle that had begun in the Far East in 1931, with the first Japanese incursions into China that would precipitate the Sino-Japanese War, had by September 1939 grown into a European war with the German invasion of Poland and the consequent declarations of war by Great Britain and France. With the German attack on the Soviet Union in the summer of 1941 and the Japanese attack on the United States of America that December, hostilities rapidly involved many countries, maturing into the Second World War. The events following the defeat of Nazi Germany and Imperial Japan in 1945 had in turn produced the impasse of the Cold War which, for forty-four years, had dominated the world. That this sudden transformation was about to take place was unforeseen, but among the several causes was the simple fact that the powerful imperatives which had driven both opposing sides in the confrontation to continually 'up the ante' in terms of military and naval posturing came at a massive cost. And this proved too high a burden for the

Soviet-led Warsaw Pact to sustain. In simple terms, the price of the sabres so necessary for a convincing rattle became excessive.

As far as the professional submariners were concerned, a sign that all was not well in the Red Banner Fleet came in April 1989 when a fire broke out onboard the modern Russian Mike-class SSN, *Komsomolets*, in the North Norwegian Sea. The *Komsomolets* was a prototype third-generation submarine which came into service in the early 1980s, and with its pressure hull built of titanium could dive about three times deeper than its Western equivalents. The fire spread, causing a catastrophic chain of events which would result in her sinking and the death of over half of her seventy-strong crew.

Captain Evgeny Vanin brought the *Komsomolets* to the surface using an emergency blow system and ordered her abandoned, but the sea conditions were rough. Although the majority of the crew escaped onto the casing, their plight was dire as the submarine was so badly damaged that she sank several hours later, the wretched survivors being swept off into the fatally cold water of the Norwegian Sea where many perished, long before any form of rescue could arrive.

Vanin and several of his crew, still being below as the *Komsomolets* began her final plunge, retreated to an escape capsule fitted under the super-structure. Wracked by extreme sea pressure and heading for the abyss carrying two nuclear-tipped torpedoes, the *Komsomolets* started to break up as Vanin and his colleagues released their capsule in which they succeeded in making it to the surface. Tragically, the inside of the capsule was at a very high atmospheric pressure so that, when its hatch was opened, it de-pressurised with catastrophic force, expelling and killing all but one of its occupants, whereupon it too sank.

This appalling death toll might have been much reduced if Norwegian search and rescue support had been sought promptly, but the Soviet Union still remained a very secretive state, reluctant to seek the help of others, even in such extreme conditions when, it might have been thought, considerations of humanity overrode all else.

The loss of the *Komsomolets* could, in part, be attributable to the Soviet Union pushing technical boundaries in their submarines beyond safe limits in their quest to outdo the Western alliance. Clearly, the technological challenges of the Cold War, particularly in the high-risk underwater confrontation played out largely in the North Atlantic and its adjacent seas had come at a tremendous cost. Having spent considerable quantities of national treasure trying to match the West's military capability, the Soviet

Union was teetering towards bankruptcy and the *Komsomolets* disaster was but one symbol of its failure. The fall of the Berlin Wall, the implosion of the Soviet Union, the loss of power of its Communist Party and the break-up of its empire in eastern Europe were only around the corner.

On a warm, sunny spring morning, a few weeks after Captain Vanin and his crew had been fighting for their lives, several hundred British submariners and their families gathered on the parade square of HMS *Dolphin* for the monarch's presentation of her colour to the Submarine Flotilla. This flag is periodically presented to branches and regiments of the armed forces and this occasion reflected the nation's recognition of the Submarine Service's achievements and its contribution to national security since the colour's previous presentation in 1959. It was also a rare opportunity for submariners – traditionally the more relaxed wing of the Royal Navy – to enjoy and participate in a gathering of some pomp and ceremony.

The Royal Navy's Submarine Service was reaching its zenith, with twenty nuclear and twelve diesel submarines in commission, including the brand new *Upholder*, first of a new class of twelve conventional submarines. Three of these were under construction at Cammell Laird's shipyard in Birkenhead and further up the coast at Vickers Shipbuilding & Engineering (VSEL), Barrow, HMS *Talent* and HMS *Triumph*, the final two SSNs of the *Trafalgar* class were being completed. Work was also progressing apace upon the build of the first two massive 14,000-ton Trident-class submarines, *Vanguard* and *Victorious*. Added to these projects the MoD was drawing up the specification for a new, highly capable third-generation SSN which would eventually replace the ageing *Valiant* class. The future of the Submarine Flotilla seemed very bright and this was reflected in the happy, family atmosphere of those gathered for the colour presentation, with a Marine band playing and a spectacularly smart guard of honour paraded to greet the sovereign.

Conley and a contingent from STWG were invited to attend the occasion with their wives. He proudly presented his team members to the Queen, relating to her their individual achievements and successes in trials and evaluations from the high Arctic to the tropics. His early days in STWG, struggling with Tigerfish submarine certification in the rain-swept mountains of northwest Scotland seemed a lifetime away.

Few who woke in the West on the morning of 9 November 1989 had much idea of the day's significance. Disturbances which had begun in the Polish shipyards of Gdansk and spread to other Warsaw Pact countries had precipitated an apparently expedient loosening of the constraints of

Communism under the leadership of Mikhail Gorbachev, but on that November evening, for the first time since the start of the Cold War, East Berliners were allowed unrestricted access to the western part of their city. As the 'Ossis' swarmed through the Berlin Wall, they were greeted by 'Wessis' waiting with flowers and champagne amid wild rejoicing. There followed a remarkable example of the domino effect: the withdrawal of Soviet forces from their satellite states in Eastern Europe, the break-up of the Warsaw Pact, the overthrow of Gorbachev and the disintegration of the Soviet Union. Almost at a stroke, the Cold War was effectively over.

In the years of chaos in Russia in the following decade of the 1990s, its submarine force, like most of its military arms, suffered serious neglect and upheaval. Added to the difficulties of running a large submarine arm with many different classes of boat, dangerous weapon systems, and conscript crews of varied ethnicity, was a chronic lack of money for pay, fuel, stores, maintenance and upkeep. 1987 had seen the last major surge of Russian submarines into the Atlantic and this was not to be repeated. Many hulls were laid up for disposal and the number of operationally available submarines decreased significantly. The Russian Navy withdrew its warships from the Mediterranean and other distant theatres and, in due course, with the rise of new nations within and outside the Russian Federation, the old Soviet Navy was split up. The most significant breakaway was the transfer of most of the Black Sea Fleet to the Ukraine. All of this resulted in the Russian Navy and its offshoots tending to stay in harbour and the tempo of its submarine operations declined remarkably.

Any sense of triumphalism in the Royal Navy was muted partly by a suspicious incredulity at what was happening, and the sensible precaution that a dying bear was capable of lashing out, but also because of sobering news from Devonport Dockyard. Here, that same November, the SSN *Warspite* was undergoing a routine refit when a technician, inspecting part of her reactor system, discovered alarming signs of cracks in critical welds within her two steam-generating boilers. This discovery was to have a crucial impact upon the Submarine Flotilla.

The defective welds joined two 14in diameter pipes – colloquially known as 'trouser legs' because that was what they looked like – through which the highly pressurised reactor cooling water flowed from the reactor core into the boiler heat-exchanger pipework which, in the non-nuclear secondary part of the plant, generated the steam necessary to drive *Warspite*'s turbines. The welds were about an inch thick and in *Warspite*'s case the cracks extended

232

across half their depth. This was extremely worrying, because if a weld failed an uncontrollable loss of reactor coolant would cause a major accident. Furthermore, it had to be assumed that potentially all the Royal Navy's nuclear submarines might well been in a similar condition.

In the prevailing situation of grave international uncertainty it was imperative both to limit submarine operations pending a thorough investigation, but very importantly to sustain one SSBN on deterrent patrol. As the problem was considered age-related, the older *Valiant*-class boats were immediately withdrawn from sea service whilst a testing and repair regime was developed, the newer *Swiftsure* and *Trafalgar* SSNs having priority for checking and repairing.

The ageing SSBN force was equally affected by the 'trouser-leg' problem but somehow continuous deterrence at sea was maintained by a thread. On occasion, deterrent patrol durations were significantly extended beyond the normal sixty-day mark, whilst the SSBNs in port had their steam generator welds examined and made good. Since access to the affected welds was through a very small hatch on the bottom of the generator, this required the innovative design and manufacture of robotic welding equipment. Such was the anxiety generated by this serious flaw that even the new Trident submarines under construction had their 'trouser-leg' welds strengthened. Sadly, all this appeared to fulfil Admiral Rickover's prediction – made in the 1950s when American nuclear reactor technology was passed to the British – that the Royal Navy would be incapable of the technical challenges of maintaining a nuclear submarine fleet.

As a consequence of the crisis, the MoD decided to decommission forthwith the SSNs *Warspite*, *Churchill* and *Conqueror*. The two remaining boats of the class in service, *Valiant* and *Courageous*, were in the early 1990s to fall victims to the British government's post-Cold War defence cuts – the so-called 'peace dividend'. Other savings in the defence budget were effected by decommissioning HMS *Swiftsure*, along with the remaining diesel-powered *Oberon* class, six of which had been modernised. Finally the decision was made to dispose of the four brand new *Upholder*-class boats and not to proceed with any new orders. The result was to geld the Royal Navy's Submarine Flotilla to a much reduced all-nuclear force of four SSBNs and twelve SSNs.

In this period of rapid retrenchment, Conley was selected for promotion to captain and in August 1990 he left STWG. In his last few months in Faslane he had observed with sadness the bored crews of the submarines tied up alongside whilst the 'trouser-leg' rectification progressed. For many it was up to eighteen months of inactivity, even extending to long-term uncertainty about their boat's future. For some junior officers this prolonged hiatus was to become a void in their career development, while the overall erosion of their core operational skills was an irreparable loss. The high standards achieved and maintained by Conley and his generation of highly competent submarine commanders inevitably waned, with only a single intelligence-gathering SSN being tasked to patrol the Barents Sea to watch the now largely supine Russians.

Even though the full impact of the 'trouser-leg' problem had still to be revealed and as yet unaware of the extent to which Soviet submarine activity was in decline, Conley left a depressed Faslane. On his appointment to STWG he had begun writing a manual encompassing tactical guidance on the approach and attack of Soviet submarines. Completing it just before he handed over to his relief, he was not to know that his publication would gradually gather dust on the bookshelves of his successors, but a hint of the future could be discerned from the parting remark of one frustrated submarine commander. 'You were very lucky to see the best days in submarines,' he was told. 'The good times are over'. The words rang in his ears long afterwards.

The threat of change breathed in the air of Faslane was obvious elsewhere. Despite his recent promotion, Conley sensed a likely curtailment of his aspirations as a naval officer. The looming prospect of a culling of senior officers resulting in redundancy called to mind the old adage, always useful at sea and equally sensible ashore, that one might hope for the best but should prepare for the worst. Before taking up his new job as the deputy of the Ship and Submarine Acceptance section, part of the Royal Navy's procurement organisation at Foxhill, near Bath, Conley found he had time on his hands. Not due to start at Foxhill until April 1991, he embarked upon a six-month sabbatical at Strathclyde University Business School, undertaking a Master's degree in business administration (MBA). Such a qualification would be an advantage if he had to leave the Service.

18

Back to the Shipyards

ON 2 AUGUST 1990 the Iraqi army invaded the kingdom of Kuwait. In response, an international coalition led by the United States of America began building up forces in the Middle East, prior to liberating the emirate from the Iraqi occupation. Conley, checking into Strathclyde University Business School in September, was aware that as a captain on sabbatical leave between appointments, he would probably be assigned to augment the Naval Staff in Whitehall. In the absence of any indication that the Iraqi leader, Saddam Hussein, would comply with the United Nations Security Council's resolution demanding the withdrawal of his forces, it thus came as no surprise when Conley receive a telephone call instructing him to join the Naval Staff for watch-keeping duties in January 1991. Having successfully completed his first term examinations, he withdrew from his MBA studies, which he completed in due course by distance learning.

In London, Conley joined a small group of naval officers, known as the Naval Advisory Group, whose task was to disseminate incoming campaign and logistics information and subsequently provide briefs to senior officers and ministers upon recommended actions or decisions to be made. An area of the MoD main building had been set up as an operations and intelligence centre from which the specific commitment of troops, ships and aircraft was determined in what was known as Operation Granby. The centre also managed logistical support and, when necessary, urgent equipment procurement. The main operational control of the British element of the coalition was undertaken at the RAF Headquarters, High Wycombe, just outside London. In the theatre of operations British ground and air forces came under the tactical control of the charismatic and ebullient American coalition commander, General Norman Schwarzkopf.

The MoD experience, both its organisation and its culture, was very new to Conley as, indeed, was the extensive intelligence and information network which supported the ultimate decision-makers. This included information gleaned from CNN and other television broadcasts. Indeed, in many cases television reporters at the scene of an action or event provided the most accurate and timely source of intelligence. Nevertheless, he was shocked by the amount of political micro-management that influenced the decisions under which the campaign was managed.

Early in his watch-keeping duties he received a request from the British air commander in theatre, asking that two additional Wessex commando helicopters be deployed to enable the eight of these aircraft already near the battlefront to be rotated out of the front line and fitted with additional protection devices. It astonished him that this very obviously pragmatic requirement, involving a modest expenditure, required the development of a written brief for the personal approval of the Secretary of State for Defence, Mr (later Lord) Tom King. Although this was rapidly effected, from his experience of dealing with this relatively minor issue Conley sensed that mistrust existed between the politicians and the military, the former being alert to the latter achieving inessential equipment improvements under the pretext of 'urgent operational requirements'. This would bypass the normal procurement process, characterised as it was – and is – by slow and prolonged scrutiny and cumbersome contracting procedures.

The air campaign of Operation Desert Storm began on 17 January. On 7 February, Conley's day of duty was spiced up when a series of loud explosions were heard coming from nearby. A rumour rapidly spread that the MoD main building was under attack by Iraqi special forces, but the alarm subsided when word was passed that the detonations were that of a mortar bomb fired by the Irish Republican Army from the back of a van in Whitehall. The mortar was aimed at No. 10 Downing Street where a War Cabinet meeting was in progress and although there had been some damage, no one had been seriously injured.

The coalition forces entered Kuwait on 24 February, rapidly rolling up the Iraqi army, which retreated across its own border in complete disarray. In four days the war was effectively over, though besides the withdrawal of coalition troops there remained the daunting tasks of clearing minefields and extinguishing blazing oil wells deliberately sabotaged by the retreating Iraqis. Despite these residual tasks, to minimise cost Britain rapidly withdrew its forces.

Observing the Royal Navy's part in the conflict from a distance, Conley had noticed that the warships operating in the north Persian Gulf near the

Iraqi littoral, where there was a threat from both Iraqi naval forces and mines, were either American or British. Vessels of other navies were generally deployed well to the south, out of harm's way. However, the first force to land in Kuwait from the sea was a French mine-clearance contingent and while the French tricolour was very evident, there was no sign of a British white ensign as Royal Navy mine clearance was being conducted well offshore; indeed, there was little visible presence of the British in Kuwait at all, the situation the British ambassador to Kuwait encountered soon after being reinstated.

The crisis organisation at the Ministry of Defence wound down during March, and the 31st, which happened to be Easter Sunday, was the final day of the Ministry's Granby organisation and Conley's last day of duty. Anticipating a quiet, anticlimactic day, his reading of the Sunday newspapers was interrupted by the receipt of an urgent telegram from the ambassador pleading that a battalion-sized British battle group of infantry be deployed to Kuwait forthwith. The diplomat was very concerned that with no 'boots on the ground', lucrative post-war reconstruction contracts were bound to go to America and France, both of which still had substantial ground forces in place. The ambassador also pointed out that since Prime Minister John Major was intending to make a statement in the House of Commons that there would be no new deployment of British forces to the Gulf, there was a real urgency in this situation.

With the help of his two assistant watchkeepers, a wing commander and a lieutenant colonel, Conley contacted the key members of the MoD hierarchy, most of whom had just enjoyed a substantial Easter Sunday lunch by the time he managed to speak to them. Armed with their verbal support, he succeeded in rapidly putting together a brief to the prime minister's office, strongly recommending the immediate deployment of a battle group to Kuwait. Two days later it was of some satisfaction to Conley that he heard on the radio the prime minister announcing that a battle group of infantry would immediately deploy to Kuwait. Never again would he experience such sensible, rapid and emphatic MoD decision-making.

During his brief spell of duty in the MoD, Conley had learned a little bit about the military/political interface and had observed how, in an emergency, major decisions could be made quickly. Nevertheless, he was about to join an organisation which was on the whole risk-averse and where the approval and decision-making process could be very ponderous.

Having moved his family to a new home in Wiltshire, in April 1991 Conley reported to the Commodore Naval Ship Acceptance (CNSA) organisation in

Foxhill, Bath. This small section, part of the Ministry's Procurement Executive (PE), consisted of about a dozen officers with their supporting staff. As its name suggested, it was headed by a commodore who was responsible for formally accepting ships and submarines from their builders on the completion of construction and successful sea trials. The section was also charged with advising when new weapon systems had met their MoD specification – defined as the 'agreed characteristics' – and that they were fully ready for operational service. This seemingly straightforward process was, to Conley's chagrin, full of pitfalls. These often arose from flaccid and imprecise specifications, the bane of any procurement programme, or worse, there could be a significant mismatch between the Ministry-endorsed detailed specification and the actual content of the contract placed by the PE. When this occurred there were inevitable disputes, and no available money to remedy voids or deficiencies.

Conley found the Foxhill site depressing. It consisted of a sprawling complex of single-storey brick buildings which had been built in 1944 as a temporary hospital to receive the anticipated high level of casualties from the D-Day landings. In the event, it was never used for this purpose and instead became home to the rump of the Royal Navy's division of the PE. This, in turn, came under the eye of the Controller of the Navy, an admiral who served on the Navy Board. With the Procurement Executive responsible for the design and procurement of ships and submarines, along with their weapon and command systems, a separate entity, known as Chief of Fleet Support, ran ship and submarine maintenance and stores support and it was also quartered in Bath.

Not only did Conley find the environment at Foxhill dejecting, but he found its culture weird and very difficult to assimilate. He was one of only a handful of seamen officers in a very large organisation dominated by the Civil Service and the Royal Corps of Naval Constructors, the MoD's naval architects and ship equipment designers. Despite a cadre of weapon and marine engineer officers in senior posts, and whilst there were several naval constructors with whom the new captain worked well, Conley perceived a strong vein of arrogance running through the establishment, manifested by a degree of disdain for the Royal Navy's seamen officers. If he thought that his extensive operational experience and knowledge of sonar – including state-of-the-art American systems – would be of value, Conley was to be disappointed. Instead, he discovered an organisation which was more focused upon processes as opposed to outcomes. Moreover, and significantly, in view of the challenges confronting the modern Royal Navy, many of his weapon engineer officer peers in the organisation lacked operational experience. Typically, they had undertaken only two sea appointments, yet they would be key in providing their particular projects with front-end user input. It was evident to Conley that the United States Navy's 'line officer' system, where the majority of mainstream officers had both warfare specialisation and engineering experience had real advantages within the procurement ambit, and that absence of any comparable system at Bath was damaging to the procurement process of the Royal Navy.

It was clear to Conley that within the overall procurement organisation there were groups of individuals pulling in different directions, be it politicians perversely directing contracts to underperforming firms in areas where they had historic political support or obligations, or civil servants charged with slowing down the whole process to meet annual budget targets. These problems were compounded by many important individuals, particularly Service personnel, normally being in post for only two or three years, an unacceptably short period of time when compared to the length of modern procurement cycles. With a lack of 'process ownership' and responsibility, this practice had a debilitating effect upon both continuity and accountability. To this woeful situation was added the MoD's inclination to demand unnecessary sophistication and/or capability in new projects that, within the set-price contract, was unattainable by British industry. Finally, in many areas the prevailing project management competence was very weak. In sum, it was little wonder to Conley that whilst it had had its highly commendable successes, the PE had an ongoing history of complex projects running into severe problems of overspend, underperformance and overrunning.

Conley had plenty to do when he joined CNSA. The Cold War might have been over, but the final submarine of the *Trafalgar* class, HMS *Triumph*, was nearing completion at VSEL Barrow, while the first of the huge Trident-class SSBNs, HMS *Vanguard*, was progressing well in the same shipyard. Meanwhile, on the Mersey, the final three diesel boats of the *Upholder* class were completing at Cammell Laird shipyard at Birkenhead.

On the downside, the highly capable third-generation SSN – the SSN 20 project – intended to replace the *Valiant* class, had been recently cancelled as unaffordable. In its place there were plans for a second batch of *Trafalgar*-class submarines, due to enter service in 2003, fitted with the PWR2 reactor, the larger and more powerful steam-raising plant of the Trident class.

Inevitably, this cancellation would induce a 'design and build gap' and it saddened Conley to see some very capable submarine designers and engineers leave Foxhill for early retirement. By the time the new SSN – designed by GEC-Marconi and known as the *Astute* class – was ordered, VSEL, the sole submarine builder, now owned by GEC-Marconi, had also lost a lot of its own internal expertise in submarine construction. The *Astute*s, which in the event had many of the planned improved features of the ill-fated SSN 20, had a long and difficult gestation. Almost 50 per cent bigger than the *Trafalgar*s, the first-of-class HMS *Astute* did not enter service until 2010, by which time she was years behind schedule and her hull cost had nearly doubled in real terms from the original £600m to £1,000m plus.

During the course of his appointment, Conley's responsibilities were extended to assisting his commodore in the acceptance of surface ships from the shipbuilders, most notably from the firms of Swan Hunter (Tyneside), Vosper Thornycroft (Southampton) and Yarrow (Glasgow). On the submarine weapons systems side of his remit, there were many projects long overdue for final acceptance, including the Spearfish torpedo, which a small section of his officers based in an outpost of the Procurement Executive at Portland were addressing.

The submarine acceptance procedure involved Conley and his team conducting a series of material inspections. The first of these confirmed that a submarine was safe to proceed to sea on contractor's sea trials, with the final inspection occurring when the building process was proved and the submarine was completed, just prior to commissioning. A key element of the procedures involved identifying and listing all extant defects and agreeing the rectification costs with the shipbuilder. Handover of the vessel and authorisation of the final staged contract payment occurred only after the successful completion of the post-commissioning sea trials.

As part of the peace dividend at the end of the Cold War, all four of the *Upholder* class were planned to be sold, but it was intended that the three boats still under construction be completed and demonstrated as being fully operational before being put up for purchase. Designed to replace the *Oberon* class, the *Upholder*s had the specific wartime role of conducting a six-week patrol in the Iceland–Faeroes gap. Designed by VSEL, they were the first British single-screw diesel submarines of streamlined, teardrop 'albacore' form. With a much smaller crew than the *Oberon* class, many of the systems fitted to the *Upholder* were highly automated and this was to cause a number of problems.

It soon became evident that the class had several serious technical deficiencies, the first of these manifesting itself in *Upholder* herself during her sea trials in 1989 when she suffered a complete loss of power and propulsion. This, it was discovered, had been caused by a design defect which was only fixed after several months. Other problems which soon became evident included a paltry range of about 4,000 miles, serious safety concerns with the torpedo tube operating system – described as being like a computer driven by hydraulics – and the snort exhaust system, which leaked badly after use.

Arriving at the Cammell Laird shipyard in Birkenhead for the first time, Conley was briefed by Gordon Howell, its managing director. Howell was an extremely experienced and astute ship and submarine constructor who had started his career as an apprentice with Vickers at Barrow. Returned to private ownership in 1986 and renamed Vickers Shipbuilding and Engineering Ltd (VSEL), the company had acquired the Cammell Laird yard as part of the deal. It was a sprawling 150-acre site on the west bank of the Mersey, a run-down complex of old buildings and sheds which, like many British shipyards at that time, was quite unsuitable for modern and efficient shipbuilding, though it did possess a covered construction hall. At the time Conley arrived, *Unseen* lay in the fitting-out basin with her sisters, *Ursula* and *Unicorn*, yet to emerge from the vast cavern of the hall.

Howell explained that, because there were no further orders in the offing, the workforce of about a thousand faced redundancy on completion of the present contract. Although he was trying his best to find a buyer for the yard, he was hamstrung because the yard did not qualify for either British or European Union intervention funding support for merchant shipbuilding. In the meantime, he was downsizing the estate, selling off pieces of land and other facilities where he could. He assured Conley that, notwithstanding this sad situation, he and his workforce were determined to complete the three boats to the very highest of standards. For his part Conley soon came to have the highest regard for Howell, with whom he got on well; together they formed a strong professional partnership.

Within a few weeks Conley and his team found themselves aboard *Unseen* in the early phases of her conducting contractor's sea trials in the Clyde Estuary. Climbing onto the bridge he noticed her slow speed as she headed on the surface to her diving areas; about 10.5 knots was her maximum on the surface, although she was capable of 18 knots dived. There was a following wind and the bridge was shrouded in the exhaust gases from the two diesels. Apart from its toxicity, the acrid fumes reduced the ability of the bridge team to keep an efficient lookout. For some reason the designers had not built in a bulkhead under the casing to prevent the exhaust causing this serious problem. Conley was very much bemused by this extraordinary deficiency – the bridge diesel-exhaust problem must have been learned years ago – but thought it would not be costly to remedy.

Having dived in the North Channel between Scotland and Ireland, the priority for Conley and his team was to witness the leaking snort exhaust hull-valve problem through a series of snorting runs of different durations and engine loads. It was evident that as the one-foot diameter hull valve heated up after a period of continuous use, it distorted in shape. Consequently, when the snorting evolution was ended and, as part of the routine, the engines crash-stopped, the valve did not seat properly for some time, thus allowing several tons of seawater to pour into the engine room as it cooled down. This, of course, had serious safety implications. However, Conley reluctantly acquiesced that there was to be no quick fix before acceptance of the boats, other than ensuring the crew had a drill and equipment in place to immediately pump out the engine room bilges on completing snorting. He could have done with the presence of the *Upholder* project director, a senior civil servant, during some of the sea trials, but the latter suffered from claustrophobia and never went to sea on any of his submarines – a ripe comment on the PE's placement policy and a reflection upon the little importance it placed upon its project directors actually getting to sea on their charges. Fortunately, the stalwart Gordon Howell was always present during the key sea trials phases and readily appreciated Conley's concerns.

This was but one serious design shortcoming amongst others, the most notable being a small but plausible risk of the torpedo tube flood valves opening to the sea when the tubes' rear doors were open. This type of problem was the cause of the catastrophic flooding resulting in the loss of the submarine *Thetis* in Liverpool Bay in 1939. Again, owing to the complexity of the torpedo tube control system, the only immediate solution was to introduce strict operating procedures to avoid serious flooding. Indeed, as the submarines were due to be disposed of and as the costs for the four boats had escalated to £1,350m at 2013 prices, there was no real impetus to fix the problems, other than the torpedo tube defect which had the most serious implications.

Despite these dispiriting observations, Conley observed that the *Upholder* class did have some commendable features. They handled well underwater, had a very quiet acoustic signature and they had an excellent fire control and sonar suite. Indeed, in the realms of war-fighting capability,

242

they were a real improvement upon the *Oberon*s. Unfortunately, these advances, which might be expected of evolving submarine design backed by the Royal Navy's experience of submarine operation, were offset by other constraints such as poor equipment accessibility and confined accommodation spaces which seemed to have put the clock back a generation. Moreover, with only two modestly powered diesels, they lacked power generation capability and Conley was driven to conclude the design as 'very disappointing', and that there was much evidence that the Procurement Executive had not adequately scrutinised the VSEL contract specification. Somewhat counter-intuitively, he pragmatically appreciated that the acceptance process would largely be confined to ensuring the shipbuilder had built the submarines to the contract criteria.

In April 1992 Conley was at the Cammell Laird yard for the launch of the last of *Upholder*s, HMS *Unicorn*. On a sunny spring morning, to the loud cheers of the remaining few hundred shipyard workers and their families, the submarine slid gracefully into the Mersey following a moment's anxious pause after the traditional bottle of champagne had struck the hull. The occasion marked the final launch of a vessel – any vessel – from the yard of Cammell Laird, ending a history stretching back 165 years. It was also probably the last dynamic launch down a slipway of a submarine from a British shipyard. Future submarine 'launches' would be achieved by gently lowering the vessel into the water using a huge lifting assembly known as a synchronised ship lift.

In the interim, *Unseen* and *Ursula* had been accepted into service after final trials in the Clyde. The acceptance formalities with the shipbuilder were completed onboard each of the boats in a very subdued atmosphere. Conley and his team were only too aware that many of the shipyard managers and workers aboard for the trials would be made redundant when they returned to Birkenhead.

In June 1993 *Unicorn* was commissioned in a very empty shipyard. It was Gordon Howell's swansong in shipbuilding, as he would not be returning to Barrow. At the commissioning lunch in the boardroom, surrounded by the paintings and the other memorabilia of what had been a great shipbuilding company, each of the guests was presented with a small crystal bowl. It was engraved with the words *Semper Commemoranda Unice Optima* – 'Always remember they were the best'.

The *Upholder*s were all paid off by 1994 and in due course were sold to the Royal Canadian Navy. They have since proved very expensive and difficult to maintain and operate, even making the headlines. When, in October 2004, the *Chicoutimi* (ex-*Upholder*) was crossing the North Atlantic, she took a considerable quantity of water down the conning tower whilst on the surface in rough weather. This caused a serious fire in which one man was killed. The cause of the fire was eventually discovered to be the fitting of the wrong type of watertight bulkhead electrical cable sealing arrangements: when saltwater came into contact with the seals they combusted.

Aside from the *Upholder*s, for Conley and his team there was much more important business to deal with. HMS *Vanguard*, the first of the new Trident submarines, was approaching commissioning and there were many problems to address. In the event, perhaps the biggest challenge he and his team would confront would be getting the Trident submarine project and the Ministry of Defence to accept there were any problems in the first place.

As a junior captain, he soon recognised that CNSA had limited leverage in getting the MoD to accept there were problems and to allocate resources to fix them. Perversely, his organisation was part of the Procurement Executive, yet was responsible for approval of the organisation's output in terms of delivering ships and submarines and their equipment to the standards and criteria set by the Naval Staff in the MoD. This was made more difficult by the frequent weakness of the MoD's vague or opaque detailing in their specified requirements. These could read like a wishlist, rather than hard and fast criteria, allowing fudging by either the PE or contractors.

Although throughout this appointment Conley was to be supported by an enthusiastic and very energetic boss, Commodore Stephen Taylor, he was not a submariner and in effect CNSA proved to have limited influence upon the Trident project. The latter was headed up by a senior naval constructor, who in turn reported to the Chief of the Strategic Systems Executive (CSSE), Rear Admiral Ian Pirnie. Admiral Pirnie had a daunting remit as he was responsible for all aspects of the Trident project, including the procurement of the missile systems and the construction of the requisite shore facilities.

Soon after taking up his post, Conley and his team visited VSEL and toured the Devonshire Dock Hall where there were three Trident SSBNs in various stages of construction, *Vanguard*, *Victorious* and *Vigilant*. Boarding *Vanguard*, Conley was immediately disappointed by her layout. Designed by the Ministry of Defence itself, the highly significant decision had been made to reduce the hull length by wrapping the forward and after ballast tanks around the pressure hull, reducing the hull diameters at either end. This was instead of adopting the precedent of the United States Navy's Trident SSBN in which uniform pressure-hull diameter was maintained throughout its length, with the ballast tanks attached at either end, thus creating much more internal space. There had been reasons for constraining overall hull length in context of the costs and the feasibility of the modifications required to the Barrow dock system to handle the Trident boats; there would also be an additional expenditure of building bigger shore facilities to accommodate longer hulls, but this appeared to be a case of cutting the head off the horse to fit it into the stable. The resulting non-uniform hull diameter, in addition to constraining layout design and adding complexities to the construction, ineluctably produced cramped propulsion spaces with very difficult machinery access. Indeed, Conley assessed the engine room as even more congested than *Valiant*'s, all of which, when combined with the complexities and space constraints of the other machinery spaces, would increase the cost of through-life upkeep and increase crew stress when maintaining and repairing engineering plant.

However, there was nothing Conley and his team could do about the SSBNs' layout other than press hard for improvements to the crew mess-deck areas, which had been completed as dining halls, as opposed to the submarine practice of doubling as recreational spaces. In fact, there was no provision of any recreational space where individual members of the ship's company could relax in peace and quiet away from their crowded mess decks, particularly when meals were in progress or movies were being shown. This facility had been called for in the Naval Staff requirement but had been missed in the design. The project management conceded this deficiency and agreed accordingly to adapt redundant space in the missile compartment; they also consented to the mess decks being improved. These were small triumphs for Conley and his team, but they would make a lot of difference to crew comfort during long patrols.

It was in the area of the sonar fit where Conley had most contention with the Trident project. It was evident to him that several key aspects of the submarine's sonar suite had been under-specified, resulting in a number of operational deficiencies which would either be costly or difficult to rectify. He firmly believed that the sonar system – which was unique to the Trident class – was not fit for purpose; in Conley's judgement, it would be unable to provide comprehensive protection against third-generation Russian submarines, the quiet and capable Victor IIIs and Akulas, which would be the SSBNs' main threat. Incomprehensibly – and almost egregiously, one might think – no expert operator input had been sought during the design stage of the sonar system. Furthermore, it was evident to Conley that weak and inexperienced project management was handling this vitally important part of the submarines' defences.

These views put Conley on a collision course with the hierarchy of the Trident project who saw him as awkward, unduly demanding and – from their perspective – of questionable judgement. However, none of them had knowledge or experience of operating submarine sonar in the contemporary threat environment. Conley afterwards recalled, 'It was like a Formula One racing driver trying to explain his car deficiencies to a bunch of people who have never been in a car in their life.' Perhaps seduced by the infallibility of the group, several members of the project team complained to Commodore Taylor that Conley was being unreasonable. With little or no support from either the Naval Staff or the specialists on the staff of Flag Office Submarines, Conley's voice was, for an inordinately long time, a lonely one.

In the autumn of 1992 Conley embarked on *Vanguard* for contractor's sea trials. He was immediately struck by the novelty of the submarine control room being situated two decks below the conning tower, as opposed to being directly below it. With the primary means of visual surveillance through remote periscope camera images which were then displayed on the submarine's state-of-the-art command system in the control room, this did not matter. Indeed, it was very conducive to an efficient and effective control-room layout. The 14,000-ton SSBN was much bigger than the SSNs to which Conley was accustomed, where most command positions, including the bridge, were a few feet away from each other. Accordingly, he assessed that operating on the surface would be more complex and difficult to manage. In short, he did not envy the challenges the commanding officers would confront when the boat was on the surface in dense shipping or poor visibility conditions.

A year later, during post-commissioning trials Conley authorised the acceptance of HM Submarine *Vanguard* into service on behalf of the project and the final stage payment of £80m to VSEL was endorsed (she had cost about £850m to build). Overall, the first-of-class trials were successful and in late 1994 *Vanguard* deployed on patrol for the first time. She had been delivered to time and cost, albeit the latter being helped by a favourable US dollar/sterling exchange rate. Conley had to concede that it was a remarkable achievement which – despite all his misgivings – reflected well upon the Ministry of Defence and British industry.

Predictably, however, soon after the submarine started sea trials, many of the sonar problems of which Conley had warned made themselves manifest. The Trident project senior management at last woke up to Conley's anxieties and began to investigate these emerging deficiencies, most of which would take both time and significant resources to fix. Although totally vindicated, Conley deeply regretted that, owing to lack of expert operator input at the outset of the design process and inept project management, the British taxpayer would be confronted with a substantial bill to fix the problems. But he was also aware that few in Foxhill were commercially minded, beyond meeting their own budget targets, and this too was part of the problem.

In 2011 the decision was made to extend the life of the four Trident boats from their designed twenty-five years to the thirty-year mark. As Conley had predicted, because of the poor equipment access and confined machinery spaces, the class has proved very expensive to operate. Furthermore, serious and underlying engineering problems, exacerbated by the accessibility constraints, have resulted in periods of very limited operational availability, putting the burden of extended patrol lengths on the sometimes single available SSBN in order to maintain continuous national deterrence. In 2007 the procurement and support organisations merged to form the Defence Equipment and Support Organisation (DESO), a major aim being to ensure that when warships and equipment are procured, there is equal consideration given to both initial production and through-life support costs. This reorganisation was, of course, very much overdue.

Conley's surface ship acceptance responsibilities proved much less challenging and contentious. His first ward was the 500-ton *Sandown*-class minehunter HMS *Bridport*, a real contrast to the complexity and scale of *Vanguard*. The class was being built in the small Vosper Thornycroft yard on the River Itchen in Southampton, an excellent, modern facility which specialised in constructing smaller warships. Highly manoeuvrable, fibreglass in construction and of a very low magnetic signature, *Bridport* and her sister vessels had the potential to be excellent minehunters but initially their variable depth mine-detection sonar had significant technical problems. These defects were preventing two of this class – completed by Vosper Thornycroft under the aegis of the BAE Systems Al Yamani contract – being accepted from the shipbuilder by Saudi Arabia. They had been alongside in the shipyard for a prolonged period, all ready to go except for the sonar deficiencies. Although in due course, when its technical glitches were sorted out, the minehunting sonar proved a world-beater, the acceptance delay did not augur well for further Saudi Arabian warship orders.

Vosper closed their Southampton shipyard in 2004, transferring their shipbuilding facilities to Portsmouth and, in the process, losing some of their highly skilled technicians. The site has since been developed into a housing and retail complex and, at the time of writing, the Portsmouth shipbuilding yard is scheduled for closure.

In addition to the *Bridport*, Conley was involved in the acceptance of two new, multi-role 30,000-ton Royal Fleet Auxiliaries (RFAs), *Fort Victoria* and *Fort George*. The former had been built at Harland & Wolff in Belfast but, owing to a number of factors, the yard had not had the manpower to complete it and this was initially undertaken by Cammell Laird before being passed on to Portsmouth Naval Dockyard. Meanwhile, Swan Hunter on the Tyne was struggling to complete *Fort George* and make a profit, owing to the contractual obligation for the yard to fund several significant structural modifications. Conley observed that the yard was under-capitalised. Furthermore, the amount of remedial work being undertaken in compartments of the ships under construction already deemed completed was at an unacceptably high level. This all compounded the shipyard's woes as, at the same time, the production costs of the three Type 23 frigates also under construction in the yard escalated, putting a further squeeze upon Swan Hunter's solvency. Indeed, sufficient anxiety was caused to move the MoD to make contingency plans; if necessary, the three frigates would be shifted elsewhere for completion if the yard went into receivership, which did indeed occur in 1993. In the event, these plans were not executed, but all was tragically symptomatic of British shipbuilding sliding into terminal decline.

The day of the final inspection of *Fort George* was a particularly poignant occasion for Conley and the CNSA team. The shipbuilders had done their best to present the ship, with its myriad of compartments, to the highest of standards, and even the directors and senior managers had rolled up their sleeves and helped with the final clean and finish. Overnight, a large team of cleaning ladies had worked hard to present every compartment, large or small, in a pristine condition. When the CNSA inspection team arrived early the following morning, these ladies were cheerfully checking off, clearly very proud of another fine Tyneside ship.

The inspection itself went very well and when it was complete in the early evening all who had partaken in it were invited to enjoy a can of beer in the ship's wardroom. Sitting there contentedly at the conclusion of the task, Conley could not but help noticing the insecure and concerned demeanour of many of the shipyard people, who were only too well aware of the contrast between his own secure future and their very precarious one.

Things were much brighter at Yarrow Shipbuilders on the Clyde. This shipyard, owned by GEC-Marconi, was in better shape under the redoubtable chairmanship of Clydeside shipbuilder, Sir Robert Easton. The latter's son, Murray, was his managing director, and the yard was doing well in its construction of a number of Type 23 frigates. It had much better undercover fabrication facilities than Swan Hunter and was also set to benefit from greater numbers of future frigate orders owing to the financial difficulties of the Tyneside company.

However, visiting the yard for the first time on a very wet and windy January day, Conley watched the struggles of a group of painters trying to apply a special non-slip coating to the flight deck of HMS *Monmouth* lying in the exposed fitting-out basin. Whilst the deck was protected to some extent by polythene screening, the conditions were quite unsuitable to apply any paint, let alone a specialist coating such as was required, and he doubted how durable it would be. Ideally, such external painting of the ship should have been carried out undercover, as it would have been in most yards in the world. Conley also noted the depressing fact that many fittings and prefabricated parts of the ship were being sourced from overseas: the anchor made in Spain, the upper deck guardrails in Sweden were but two examples. British shipbuilding had declined to such an extent that many of the British firms which had once made ancillary equipment had long since gone, and matters were now beyond redemption.

At sea on contractor's sea trials, Conley was highly impressed by the Type 23's handling and its very responsive combined gas turbine and diesel-electric power train. With a quiet acoustic signature and a low radar silhouette, these vessels, which would build up to a class of sixteen, had been designed specifically to conduct anti-submarine towed array operations in the Norwegian Sea. Six Fort-class RFAs, armed with Sea Wolf anti-aircraft missile systems, were planned to provide them with logistic support but, in the event, in the post-Cold War era only the two mentioned above were built, the *Fort George* and *Fort Victoria*. Although there were facilities for Sea Wolf in both ships, the missile system was never installed.

The main initial shortcoming of the Type 23 frigate class was that the early vessels were not fitted with a command system. This was needed to make the ship effective in combat. Furthermore, the Merlin helicopter they were planned to carry was experiencing technical delays. As for the sonar carried in the new frigates, Conley was convinced that there was an intrinsic signal-processing problem with their hull-mounted sonar set, as its submarine-detection capability compared unfavourably with other similar systems. He reported his concerns accordingly but, not for the first time, experienced a very lethargic response from the responsible project team.

It seemed incomprehensible to him, a submariner steeped in the cut and thrust of Cold War operations, that the surface element of the Royal Navy appeared to have lost all pride in its ships and people being leaders in anti-submarine warfare – the fundamental skill that had saved the country in the Battle of the Atlantic.

To this profound anxiety he could add a further defect: the frigate's single 4.5in Mark 8 fully automatic gun tended to jam after a few rounds had been fired. To his despair, it seemed to Conley that Royal Navy gunnery had hardly advanced since his *Cambrian* days.

Conley left the Procurement Executive in the summer of 1994. He was not sorry to depart. Although he had very much enjoyed working with the shipbuilders, there had been too many frustrations and a sense of personal impotence. His sparring with the Trident project had achieved successes, but in pressing the case for improving the SSBN's sonar system, he felt he had ploughed a very lonely furrow. What he could not comprehend was that many of his colleagues on the Procurement Executive's staff with whom he had engaged had had brilliant intellects, and were dedicated and committed to the Royal Navy. Why, therefore, was the organisation so dysfunctional?

To him, it could be all summed up by his experience soon after joining, when he made a courtesy call upon the senior civil servant at Foxhill, the Chief of the Underwater Systems Executive, who was responsible for the procurement of submarines and all underwater equipment and weapons. During the meeting Conley had raised the issue of the very poor results of a recent series of Spearfish trial firings. The mandarin had responded that he did not know about the Spearfish problems and furthermore he went on to express little, if any, interest in them.

Such a dismissive response should, he mused later, have sounded a warning call. What was clear to Conley after his experiences of the procurement process was that, despite periodic intensive reviews and reorganisations, it remained very inefficient and in many cases badly managed. It was thus both expensive to the taxpayer and in general unsuited to providing those going into harm's way with the best equipment affordable within the defence budget set by the government of the day. Conley afterwards reflected ruefully that during his time in the PE there was no one within the Royal Navy's hierarchy energetically and aggressively pursuing the necessary reforms, and all future significant change was to be driven by external initiatives.

19

The Awesome World of Nuclear Weapons

IN JULY 1994 Conley arrived on the seventh floor of the Ministry of Defence main building in Whitehall, colloquially known as the 'Madhouse', to join the directorate responsible for nuclear weapons policy and planning. He would be the Royal Naval captain who was specifically responsible for nuclear weapons target planning.

At this time, the Soviet Union was disintegrating under the turbulent leadership of Boris Yeltsin, and there existed the very real threat of nuclear proliferation in those former Soviet states which had nuclear weapon bases within their territory, although these were supposedly being dismantled. In the West, populations were seeking the so-called 'peace dividend' and within the United Kingdom the 1991 'Options for Change' defence reduction programme was just the start of two decades of protracted contraction in the size and strength of the country's armed forces. Meanwhile security agencies such as MI6 and the listening complex at GCHQ at Cheltenham were grappling with a rapid change of priorities from the confrontation of the Cold War in Europe to the troubled Middle East. It was into this not so brave new world that the Trident nuclear missile system was entering service as the replacement for Polaris, and already many within the defence establishment considered it was an upgrade that the United Kingdom could ill afford. This would manifest itself by pressure being applied to the assumption that the Royal Navy required four SSBNs to maintain the status quo of a minimum of one on operational patrol at any given time.

As Conley surveyed his office, the shabby furniture, the tarnished office walls streaked in coffee stains, a half–dead spider plant and an ancient electric kettle which gave him a belt when he first switched it on, he wondered what lay ahead of him in the very enigmatic environment of the Madhouse. To add to this very jaded ambience, his office window faced into an enclosed courtyard which was netted over to prevent birds nesting within the area, but which would frequently inadvertently entangle them. Consequently, the office occupant had an eye-level view of the rotting and half-devoured carcases of these unfortunate creatures scattered across the nets. It all seemed somehow more claustrophobic than the inside of any submarine. The office across the passageway was occupied by an immaculately dressed Irish Guards colonel who every night, at the stroke of five, packed up his papers and left his desktop in perfect order with his coffee mug and utensils placed in a touchingly careful, strict layout on a tea towel. Further down the passageway, a Scots infantry officer had his desk covered in tartan and played a few bars of the bagpipes every morning when he arrived in his office. Such minor habits were metaphorical comfort blankets, forming a link to the individual's past and seemingly distant existence of being an officer in the comparative sanity of front-line service.

The Nuclear Policy Directorate, staffed by a score of people from both the armed and civil services, was part of the policy department of the Ministry of Defence and was headed by a civil servant ranking as a deputy permanent secretary. Conley became aware that whilst possessing a brilliant intellect, the latter's leadership and management skills left a lot to be desired, exemplified by the fact that during the captain's two years in the organisation, his ultimate superior never walked round his department to meet and encourage the hundred or so people who worked for him. Nor did he make any attempt to manage the resources at his disposal to best effect and efficiency. However, he was clearly very impressive in his support and briefings to Sir Malcolm Rifkind, the then Secretary of State for Defence; undoubtedly he knew his priorities in terms of career progression.

Conley soon concluded that the Ministry's main building and its organisation were often totally dysfunctional. Two weeks after he had taken up his new post, one of the department's office administration staff who dealt with paperwork and publications up to the Secret level was arrested in her office and removed by Ministry of Defence and Home Office police officers. It was revealed that she was an illegal immigrant of Nigerian nationality and had been apprehended prior to deportation. Astonishingly, a foreign national who had no status in the United Kingdom had managed to get through the Ministry's security vetting process and for a period had unfettered access to classified information regarding the nation's nuclear weapons programme. Conley observed that: 'Even worse, she could have been removing documents by the bag load and no one would have been the wiser: there were no security checks at the building's exit doors.'

One reason that contributed to the MoD's nickname of the Madhouse was the inter-Service rivalry which was absolutely rife in the building and was quickly apparent to Conley. It was particularly virulent between the staff of the Royal Navy and the Royal Air Force, the former remembering the very creative but unrealistic case the latter had made in the 1960s for providing air cover to the Navy in the Indian Ocean. This issue was considered to be a significant factor in the demise of the Royal Navy's fixed-wing carrier force in the 1970s, which had an extremely deleterious impact upon the size and shape of the contemporary Fleet.

Conley had already experienced this rivalry when, as a newly promoted captain in the first three months of 1991 during the first Gulf War, he had been a Naval Staff watchkeeper in the Ministry of Defence. He recalled the naval hierarchy's extreme enthusiasm to get the light carrier HMS *Ark Royal* into the Gulf, despite absence of a genuine military need, on the grounds that it was thought that such a move would bolster the 'naval case'. A personal letter had gone from the First Sea Lord, Admiral Sir Julian Oswald, to the head of the United States Navy, Admiral Frank Kelso, asking that he make a request to the British Secretary of State for Defence, Tom King, that *Ark Royal* join the Alliance naval forces deployed in the Gulf. The American response was strongly supportive but it was despatched by sea mail and did not arrive until the war was over.

Also apparent to Conley was a cultural chasm and mutual suspicion between the senior civil servants and the higher level armed services officers. The former were the better educated, and in general they were very intellectually gifted. Unfortunately, however, they were given to engagement in esoteric debate for its own sake, irrespective of the effort and resources devoted to such a luxury. In consequence, many of them made very poor managers. On the other hand the so-called armed service 'warrior' working in the Ministry could be prone to over-zealously presenting the case for the procurement of equipment for his or her own Service, providing unrealistic financial costs, timescales and other criteria. On occasions this mutual lack of co-operation resulted in the suppression of bad news by both parties. One such extreme example Conley stumbled across in his most classified files had occurred in the 1980s. A serious problem concerning the reliability of the Polaris warheads had arisen, but had not been communicated to any of the senior civil servants in the Ministry of Defence, not least head of the Ministry, the Permanent Secretary. When, after the problem had been rectified, the latter found out that for a period the deterrent had been in a parlous state, there was inevitable rancour and recrimination which contributed to sustaining the continuing lack of mutual trust between the senior military officers and their civilian equivalents.

Besides the divisions between the Navy, Army and Royal Air Force, Conley observed that there was also a clear disparity in working practices, with army and air-force officers working largely normal office hours, but the naval staff often putting in very protracted hours in developing papers which supported their case, whether it was dealing with strategy or procurement, often without any successful outcome.

One of Conley's major responsibilities was the development of the target plans for Trident. He recalled that, on reviewing the plans for the first time alongside the existing Polaris targeting options, the hairs on the back of his head rose as he contemplated the almost unthinkable consequences of these devastating weapons being used. However, he fully appreciated that nuclear weapons would not constitute an effective deterrent unless they were complemented by plans for their actual use, no matter how horrific this eventuality would be. The British Trident system is committed to NATO and, therefore, his remit required developing plans that would meet both national and alliance requirements.

In all situations, the ultimate decision to use the United Kingdom's nuclear weapons lies with the prime minister or, in his absence, a designated member of his government. It is within this context that the prime minister, on taking up office, is invited to write his personal instructions in a sealed envelope provided to the commanding officer of each SSBN. This is provided in the event of all communications and command and control being totally lost through a devastating nuclear attack upon Great Britain. An early task of Conley's was to liaise with the Cabinet Office to produce the outline of options for the then Prime Minister, John Major, in order that he could set out the requisite sets of instructions for the new Trident SSBNs then coming into service. This remit was completed with much greater ease than was the case with Jim Callaghan's instructions for the use of Polaris when he assumed office in 1976. Callaghan had prevaricated from making a decision on his chosen option for several months so that – at least in theory – for a period the commanders of the SSBNs on patrol were devoid of instructions for the ultimate use or otherwise of their Polaris missiles in event of a nuclear strike against the United Kingdom.

The targeting of nuclear weapons in Great Britain is subject to an extremely rigorous process which involves the input of several agencies, including national intelligence. Not surprisingly, accuracy and quality control are absolutely paramount and an independent organisation scrutinises both the effectiveness of the completed plans, together with the capability and availability of the patrolling SSBN. For his part, Conley managed a small cell of nuclear targeting experts who worked within the concrete complex deep beneath the Ministry's main building. Very professional and committed, this unsung and unknown group of naval officers worked very hard in doing their part to deliver the targeting plans which ensured that the national deterrent remained totally credible.

Conley's first tour of the underground bunker revealed a Cabinet room with an identical table to that in Downing Street. Moreover, the prime minister had his own compact bedroom upon the walls of which were watercolours of scenes of the British countryside. He wondered who had thought of this level of detail.

As part of his wider induction, his responsibilities took him to the Atomic Weapons Establishments (AWE) at Aldermaston and Burghfield, where the nuclear warheads are manufactured and assembled. These two sites, whilst modern, did not initially meet his vision of immaculate, high-tech facilities populated by persons of grave and serious mien. Instead, he encountered a relatively small-scale establishment, retaining an enduring recollection of:

> a very large man on the warhead assembly line who bore a very strong resemblance to 'Jaws' of James Bond fame and of a middle-aged woman who opened the storage vaults to show me a number of the RAF's nuclear bombs. She had a visage and demeanour which would not have been out of place in Macbeth's witches. I was later advised that people who work in the very tense environment of handling explosives all day long are no ordinary types.

Conley's main contact at AWE was a scientist who, in support of the targeting process, had been contracted to investigate the effectiveness of nuclear blast upon different land topographies. One of the scientist's key experiments involved purchase of a large number of Christmas trees which, planted in the ground at Shoeburyness firing range near Southend in Essex, were subjected to the effect of 20 tons of TNT, and then assessed for the scaled-up damage of a nuclear blast upon a wooded area. In sum, AWE was not the high-powered, technologically advanced organisation the captain had envisaged, though it appeared that it worked well, with safety absolutely paramount.

In 1994, as a savings measure, the decision had been taken to phase out the Royal Air Force's free-fall tactical nuclear bomb, the WE177, with a version of the Trident missile which would be configured with a much lighter warhead payload. Known as Sub-Strategic Trident, this would allow politicians the flexibility to use nuclear weapons in a limited strike, of particular importance in circumstances of escalation to a nuclear exchange without recourse to a massive attack. This flexibility reinforced the credibility of nuclear deterrence, although it could be argued that it might be more likely to induce the decision to 'go nuclear'. Conley observed that some of the higher strategists of the RAF attempted to reverse their loss of capability and the exit of their Service from the 'nuclear club' of which they had been a member for over forty years. These officers pointed out the very strong deterrent advantage of highly overtly deploying nuclear-armed Tornado bombers to forward air bases as part of a NATO strike force, as opposed to a SSBN deployed unseen and unheard in the depths of the oceans.

In a cash-constrained ministry, where the cost of nuclear weapons had to be reduced, the no-cost Sub-Strategic Trident argument won the day. However, it bemused Conley that one entrepreneurial wing commander had attempted to secrete some WE177 bomb casings in an airbase store, just in case this capability needed to be restored in a hurry.

Owing to the ending of NATO nuclear weapons war-gaming exercises, where communications networks and command and control procedures were tried out, once a year the Nuclear Policy Directorate organised a tabletop nuclear war game in the command and control room of the MoD bunker, where politicians, senior civil servants and the heads of the three Services were presented with conflict scenarios which were geared towards them debating and considering the use of nuclear weapons. Conley had already come to the conclusion that most senior military officers within the ministry demonstrated a distinct disinterest in nuclear deterrence, seeing nuclear weapons as essentially a political capability of limited military utility. In view of this, his departmental heads considered the three-hour annual war game to be very important, as key participants included the most senior decision-makers, including the chief of the defence staff and the single Service heads. During the course of the war game these officers would be compelled to consider the many complex political and military factors which would govern their recommendation to the prime minister as to whether to deliver a nuclear strike. It was the norm for the Secretary of State for Defence to chair such exercises.

For a number of the reasons the first of these war games that Conley attended did not go well. Ever the Scottish lawyer, Secretary of State Malcolm Rifkind was most unenthusiastic at being presented with information during the course of the exercise with little time to grasp its detail. Clearly angry, he challenged the efficacy of the structure of the exercise, after which the whole process went downhill.

The following year the directorate head, licking his wounds, instructed Conley to organise and direct the war game. Having learnt lessons, he ensured that there would be no surprises of the type which, at short notice, challenged the intellect or knowledge of the participants. To this end, Conley's written and verbal briefing packages were very comprehensive. The BBC were in the process of making a documentary about the United Kingdom's defence organisation, including one episode devoted to Trident. It was, therefore, agreed that the production team would film the opening few minutes of the war game, set at an unclassified level and taking advantage of this unique ensemble. The military staff working in the main building do not normally wear uniform, but as this did not align with the public's perception of 'top brass', the Service participants were invited to be dressed in military attire. Beneficially in the dim lighting of the command room, the uniforms engendered a much more realistic ambience as the exercise got underway.

Michael Portillo had succeeded Rifkind as Secretary of State for Defence and on the morning of the exercise Conley met him at his office and escorted him down to the bunker. As they descended, exchanging general conversation, Portillo remarked how daunting it was going to be for him to both face the television cameras and chair a war game with the heads of the Services, addressing a difficult subject which a few weeks previous he had known little if anything about. Conley concluded that in an increasingly complex world there were very high expectations upon those politicians holding ministerial post. On his arrival in the command room and taking his place at the head of the gathering, the minister spotted a large brass key on a plinth in the middle of the conference table. Before the cameras rolled he enquired whether this was the nuclear release key. He was assured that it had been presented by the contractor who had built the bunker as a memento and had no military significance whatsoever. However, this little cameo did illustrate to those gathered the everyday challenges of being a high-level politician in the public eye.

Despite a number of the participants unduly striving to impress the Secretary of State, this second war game, set in highly plausible scenarios which were very professionally briefed, went well and led to the very difficult and daunting decision by the participants to use Trident in a sub-strategic mode. As Conley emerged afterwards into the fresh air of a pleasant sunny spring afternoon with people enjoying their lunch in nearby gardens, the proceedings of the previous three hours seemed chillingly possible, but very surreal.

Meanwhile, Conley had become involved in the arrangements for phasing out Polaris. The latter had been updated in the 1980s under the secretive 'Chevaline' programme, where the warhead package incorporated a range of decoys to enable penetration of the Moscow anti-ballistic missile defences. This was an ingenious system which involved a team of talented people who had unique knowledge and expertise in the physics and engineering of ballistic flight. Because of Trident's much greater capability, there was no future requirement for the decoy package and the team was being disbanded. In the process of attending meetings to wrap up the programme, Conley came across some members of this very dedicated and committed group of mathematicians and engineers. 'Most were destined for early retirement, looking forward to golf or tending their roses – such a sad waste of talent and skill.'

In June 1996, in the absence of apparent interest from anyone else in the MoD, Conley sent a message to the prime minister's office, informing him that as the last Polaris patrol had been completed, and as two Trident submarines were fully operational, the scrapping of the Polaris weapon system would commence. It seemed to him that times had markedly changed from the heady days of 1967 when he arrived at the Clyde Submarine Base in its final phases of construction to be able to support and base HMS *Resolution*, in an era when the nuclear deterrent was very much at the forefront of the nation's attention and interest.

Since the 1950s the United Kingdom has enjoyed very close links with the United States in all aspect of nuclear weapons technology. As part of this relationship, the British Nuclear Policy Directorate and its Pentagon equivalent met twice yearly to discuss a wide range of issues, the venue alternating in each country. These talks were always frank and forthcoming with few, if any, security classification constraints. However, Conley got the impression that the Americans did not always put their best and most talented people into the field of nuclear policy, despite the fact that the United States' team was led by a very impressive senior civil servant named Frank Miller, who clearly had a wealth of experience, coupled with an excellent intellect and the ability to think laterally. Moreover, he was a great friend of the British and a supporter of its nuclear weapons programme. The United States continued to possess a 'triad' of nuclear weaponry, submarine-launched missiles, land-based intercontinental ballistic missiles (ICBMs) and bombs delivered by aircraft. However, the START I nuclear weapons treaty limitations, which constrained the number of warheads and delivery platforms on each side, were beginning to bite. Although the United States Navy's SSBNs were considered to be the ultimate deterrent, under the provisions of the treaty their numbers were being reduced by four to fourteen. For the ambitious and talented American naval officer, the nuclear programme, in long-term contraction, was not seen as a desirable posting.

These talks, normally spread over two or three days, included visits to each country's nuclear weapons facilities or bases and involved a social gathering aimed at providing a unique cultural experience to the visiting delegation: a visit to Wimbledon greyhound racing and a junior league baseball match featured as events during Conley's time with the directorate. Whilst the British range of facilities of interest was very limited, in America there was plenty to see in their bases or nuclear weapons laboratories.

One of the series of talks Conley took part in incorporated tours of the Los Alamos and the Sandia laboratories, both facilities in New Mexico, the first of which had seen the development of the first atomic bombs. The Comprehensive Nuclear Test Ban Treaty (finally adopted by the United Nations in 1996), which prohibited the detonation of nuclear weapons either in the atmosphere or underground, was engendering the twin challenges of ensuring that existing stocks of warheads remained reliable, and that the capability of developing new warhead designs was retained. Accordingly, the Americans had started putting resources into these areas. At Los Alamos the British delegation were shown round a very ambitious and costly facility which enabled the sequence of the conventional trigger explosion in a nuclear device to be recorded to very fine degrees of accuracy. This was complemented by a presentation by a physicist explaining the concept of the National Ignition Facility which, by using high energy lasers, would enable experiments to be achieved examining the complexity of nuclear fusion – turning an atomic detonation into a much more powerful nuclear explosion. This controversial facility in terms of value was to become operational in 2009 at a cost of several billion dollars, but it would ensure the maintenance of a baseline of expertise in nuclear weapon design. Such facilities put into context the relatively small scale of the British nuclear weapons maintenance programme.

260

The lecturing physicist also presented a large number of viewgraphs, the content of which was mostly incomprehensible to the British visitors. This contrasted with the clarity of a talk the following day about nuclear warhead design delivered by a Chinese-American scientist, Wen Ho Lee. Remarkably, a few years later he was arrested by the FBI on allegations of providing nuclear weapons design information to China; in the event these charges were never proven and he was released.

On completion of their visit to Los Alamos, the British party travelled by road through the New Mexico desert to Sandia Laboratory, which was of specific interest in that it provided support to testing and ensuring the reliability of the Trident warhead fusing and detonation components supplied to the Royal Navy. However, perhaps of most interest at Sandia was an insight into the ongoing American programme aimed at improving the safety and security of former Soviet nuclear weapons and materials, thus reducing the risk of unguarded proliferation. This programme included helping former Soviet republics destroy their nuclear weapons delivery vehicles. In a related effort, the United States and Russia had agreed to co-operate in converting highly enriched uranium from former Soviet weapons into reactor fuel for possible sale to the United States. It was a surprise for the visitors to learn that the United Kingdom had provided financial support to the security element of the programme, but even more remarkable for them was viewing real-time images of nuclear warheads in a Russian storage facility, where the Americans had set up surveillance cameras as part of the nuclear weapons security enhancement initiative.

All this was a very different scenario to the confrontation and abrasive relationships of the Cold War. Indeed, in an illustration of changed times, whilst being given a tour of the facilities in the Trident Base, in Kings Bay, Georgia, Conley observed his hosts to be concerned over something. Once the tour was over, it was explained by an American officer that a Russian START inspection delegation was about thirty minutes ahead on a similar tour route, and there was concern that the two sets of visitors would get mixed up. Asked about any problems with the Russian delegations, the response was that they tended to quickly empty the minibars in their US paid-for hotels and accordingly because of the horrendous hotel bills incurred, use of this facility had been banned.

Since the British nuclear deterrent is primarily committed to NATO, joint target planning was conducted at the headquarters of Strategic Command (STRATCOM), at Offutt Airforce Base, Omaha, Nebraska – right in the centre of continental USA. The Royal Navy provided a captain and lieutenant commander as liaison officers. These were lonely postings, as the representatives of other NATO nations that had a tactical nuclear capability had been gradually withdrawn; the two British officers fulfilled a role more symbolic than substantive, in almost complete isolation in a well-appointed suite of empty offices within the base's large underground complex. That said, during Conley's periodic visits to STRATCOM, he noted that the host-nation staff were very hospitable and welcoming. He particularly recalled the large screen presentation in the command centre of a simulated all-out nuclear strike, ICBMs being made ready, SSBNs being sent on patrol, and the dramatic scrambling of B-52 bombers – all to very upbeat music with no suggestion that Armageddon was just round the corner. Memorably, the visiting officer accommodation was to the highest standard he had ever encountered. General Curtis Le May, the controversial head of the US Strategic Air Command in the 1950s, had ensured his aviators were very well looked after when not flying.

Conley happened to serve in the Ministry of Defence at a time which coincided with rekindled interest on the part of the French in taking forward nuclear weapons co-operation with the United Kingdom. France had developed an entirely independent nuclear deterrent and retained a triad of SSBN, land and air based missiles – the *Force de Frappe* – although the land-based missiles were being phased out in the mid 1990s. As France was not a member of the NATO military structure, there was no joint targeting or exchange of information upon each other's systems, and co-operation had historically been confined to low-level talks of little substance. Needless to say, as Britain was completely dependent upon the United States for its missile system, great care had been exercised to ensure there was no compromise of the unique bilateral relationship.

However, perhaps owing to the advent of Trident, it was evident that the French were keen to explore all viable avenues of enhanced co-operation and had sent delegations to the MoD to oil the wheels, prior to a formal visit by the directorate's staff early in 1996 to the French naval air station at Istres, near Marseilles. This was the base for a squadron of nuclear-capable Super Étendard attack aircraft.

The delegation, which included Conley and was led by an air vice-marshal, flew to Istres on an Andover aircraft of the Queen's Flight. In Istres they were feted for two days by their French hosts, embarking upon a culinary adventure at each meal and being enthusiastically shown the base facilities and the actual nuclear missiles. After lunch on the final day, having been softened up with excellent food and the finest of wine, the rear admiral heading the French side put the case forcibly for significantly escalating the level of nuclear weapons co-operation between the two countries. Although the British team had an interpreter, the French, as is their practice, conducted their part of the talks in their national language and, being highly technical, most of the content of their presentations floated above the heads of Conley's colleagues. Nevertheless, the British visitors got the general thrust and took away the remit for looking at ways and means of taking forward the joint initiatives which the French clearly sought.

Conley was directed to take forward options and accordingly devised a number of very innocuous proposals, including each country's SSBN participation in submarine rescue exercises and an exchange of port visits. Also, it was to be agreed that an improved 'hotline' be set up between the MoD and the French military headquarters in Paris. Subsequently, the general principles of enhanced nuclear weapons co-operation were agreed between Prime Minister Major and President Chirac at the May 1996 Anglo-French talks in London. It was evident, however, that the French wanted the British to go much further towards developing a European nuclear deterrent and tabled much more ambitious options such as the possibility of sharing communications systems and exchanging information concerning SSBN patrol areas to ensure no chance of inadvertent encounter between submarines on patrol. For a number of very sound reasons, some of which arose from the British relationship with the United States, and perhaps an underlying historical distrust of the French, such proposals were resisted. The wisdom of this conclusion is understandable but, as an incontrovertible footnote, in 2009 HMS *Vanguard* and the French SSBN *Triomphant* collided when on patrol in the same area in the eastern Atlantic, neither vessel realising the close proximity of the other before impact. Fortunately, the damage incurred was not serious. On the other hand, it was agreed by treaty in 2010 that the United Kingdom and France will share in developing nuclear warhead reliability-proving facilities in Valduc, France and at AWE Berkshire.

There was one final twist to Conley's time in the Ministry of Defence. The complex customised software which supported the targeting process had been supported by a private contractor. For a number of years this company had done an excellent job in terms of its competence and responsiveness to problems but, as the contract term was due to expire, there was the necessity under MoD rules to place the contract re-renewal under a competitive tendering process. In ministry terms it was a very modest deal of about £10m in value at 2013 prices spread over five years. The contracted company put in a very acceptable proposal but a second firm also submitted a tender which happened to be below the price of the former. Despite the fact that this second company was known to Conley's staff as not having the competence or expertise under the existing competition rules, it was they to whom the contract was to be awarded.

Conley accordingly raised his serious concerns with the department responsible for placing and awarding the contract. In due course he was summoned by the head of naval equipment procurement, the Controller of the Navy, to explain his concerns. In a somewhat confrontational set-up, the controller – an admiral – flanked across a table by a number of senior civil servants and a second admiral, the head of the strategic systems executive, he was asked to explain why the cheaper company should not be awarded the contract. Conley outlined the ramifications of the Trident targeting software failing and his serious reservations about this company's ability to deliver against the contract specification when set against a very satisfactory and proven track record of the existing contractor.

Having heard out Conley's misgivings, the controller sought advice from his head of contracting who was emphatic that as the undercutting company's proposal was entirely compliant with the contract criteria, and as its price was below that of the incumbent, by law it must be awarded the contract. The controller agreed and stated that there was no alternative. For his part, Conley was completely astounded by the total absence of common sense, and in the contracting process by the lack of incisive deliberation regarding the ability of the new firm to fulfil the specification.

This divorce from reality in the contracting process was but one minor occurrence in a culture of incompetent defence procurement by the Ministry of Defence, which was to result in the effective bankrupting of the United Kingdom's defence organisation a decade later.

Conley left the Ministry of Defence shortly afterwards to take up appointment as captain of HMS *Dolphin*. He learned a few months later that, as he had anticipated, the new contractor had failed to fulfil the requirements of the contract, which had accordingly been terminated and awarded back to the original contractor. He recalled that:

In the interim, lack of competent software support had caused a great deal of extra effort and frustration on the part of the targeting team and, of course, did nothing for their confidence in the MoD organisation. Neither of these two factors, of course, was measured or reported, and no one was held accountable for the very poor contracting decision. The whole set-up was truly that of a Madhouse.

Epilogue

THE SUMMER OF 1996 found Conley back at HMS *Dolphin* in Fort Blockhouse as captain of the shore base, his appointment at the Ministry of Defence thankfully behind him. However, it was a very different *Dolphin* from the one he had joined twenty-nine years earlier as a trainee sub lieutenant, and now was an empty place echoing with past glories. The submarines had gone, the berths were empty and the workshops lay silent; his posting would be a short one, preparing the establishment for handover to the Royal Defence Medical College and other tri-Service medical training organisations.

For the time being, however, his staff was accommodated within the old submarine headquarters and he was ensconced in what once had been Flag Officer Submarine's office. The last link the establishment had with submarines, the Submarine School, also lay within his bailiwick, but plans were already well advanced to relocate it to the training establishment HMS *Raleigh* in Torpoint across the River Tamar from HM Dockyard Devonport.

Conley was also responsible for heading up the Fleet Warfare Development Group (FWDG) which was a recent amalgam of the surface fleet, air and submarine tactical development organisations. The Submarine Tactics and Weapons Group (STWG) had been divided, the weapons element remaining in Faslane. This distressed Conley, as he viewed one of STWG's great strengths to have been the co-location of the separate disciplines of tactical and weapons' development. He found the FWDG to be an organisation which lacked a sense of direction and focus, with many of its staff neither possessing the requisite analytical competences nor being adequately motivated in what they did. It too was also on the move, to be co-located with the Maritime Warfare Centre in the training establishment HMS *Dryad* situated just outside Portsmouth. Time was therefore against him achieving any significant changes to the quality of either its output or effectiveness.

In early September 1997 Captain Dan Conley, the last captain of HMS

266

Dolphin, and his wife were given a very convivial farewell lunch by the wardroom officers. On leaving the building they both took up positions astride a large model of a nuclear submarine on a trailer roped to a contingent of officers. To a loud cheer from the assembled gathering, they were pulled out of the parade square; it was not quite a going into retirement, but to Conley the occasion effectively and poignantly marked the end of his career in submarines.

Despite the decline he found all around him, he had taken part in the Submarine Flotilla's greatest ever peacetime expansion and had witnessed a period of unprecedented technical change and challenge. He had served in the highly successful *Swiftsure*-class SSN and had been at the cutting edge of the Royal Navy's undersea confrontation with the Russian submarine force. He had also been involved in the introduction into service of the less successful *Upholder* and *Vanguard* classes amid the shrinking of Britain's industrial and shipbuilding capacity, factors adversely affecting the country's ability to maintain a home-built nuclear submarine force.

There had been the very rapid downsizing of the Flotilla in the 1990s, spurred on by the end of the Cold War and the marked diminishment of the Russian submarine threat. Accordingly, he concluded that he had enjoyed almost certainly the best and most professionally satisfying of times for a peacetime submariner. Furthermore, he had immensely enjoyed working with highly professional and committed officers and ratings.

Conley had one more job in the Royal Navy, as a director of the United Kingdom Hydrographic Office (UKHO) in Taunton, a quasi-commercial agency which remains the world's leading producer of nautical charts. The United Kingdom's maritime triad of the Royal Navy, Merchant Navy and the fishing fleet might all have drastically diminished in size and capability, but the UKHO still provides the charts of many other countries' navigational waters, and is renowned for the quality and accuracy of its Admiralty chart series and other supporting products.

However, like all organisations, the UKHO faced change, and in particular the conversion of thousands of paper charts to a digital format. Included in his responsibilities, Conley was in charge of the electronic navigational chart (ENC) development and production project. Early on he had to take the unpopular and unprecedented initiative of outsourcing elements of the paper chart conversion to an Indian company. This was for reasons of both cost and skilled manpower availability, demonstrating that even the very successful UKHO could not escape financial and efficiency pressures.

At the same time, he and his team had robustly pressed the Ministry of Defence to make a modest outlay for the provision of digital charting systems to all ships in the Fleet. A basic system cost as little as £10,000 and with highly accurate navigational positional input from the American global positioning system (GPS) and the availability of an automatic alarm facility providing warning should a hazard be approached, digital charts significantly enhance navigational safety. But this was not agreed by a key civil servant in the Ministry decision-making chain, who rejected such a proposition with a counter assertion that: 'There is no evidence to support the case that digital charts enhance navigational safety'. Consequently, the few million pounds of expenditure required to fit all ships of the Fleet with this equipment was turned down on both the occasions that Conley made a submission to the Ministry, notwithstanding that the First Sea Lord at the time, Admiral Sir Nigel Essenhigh – himself a former Hydrographer of the Navy – was an ardent advocate of digital charts.

Captain Dan Conley left the Hydrographic Office and the Royal Navy in October 2000. Less than two years later, the destroyer HMS *Nottingham* grounded on rocks off Lord Howe Island to the east of Australia. The ship was only saved by exceptional damage control efforts and the cost of the repairs was over £40m. The cause of the grounding was sloppy navigation, but it would not have occurred if a digital charting system had been available. Eight years later, in 2010, the brand new £1bn submarine HMS *Astute* went aground off the Isle of Skye during contractor's sea trials and incurred over £2m of damage. The cause of this extremely embarrassing accident, where the submarine was televised well and truly stranded, was a poor navigational and pilotage organisation. Incredibly, *Astute* did not have an electronic chart facility, which again would highly likely have prevented the grounding. To Conley, by then deep into retirement, both incidents reflected just one more procurement debacle, evidence of a system which was well and truly broken.

He had not quite hung up his seaboots, as on leaving the Royal Navy he was back to his fishing roots, joining the Royal National Mission to Deep Sea Fishermen as its chief executive. Fishing remained the nation's most dangerous industry, its 13,000 seafarers suffering on average sixty fatalities or serious injuries each year during Conley's eleven years with the charity from 2001 to 2012. Moreover, vessel losses in the 6,000-strong fleet averaged two a month, largely due to flooding or groundings; there was, therefore, much work for the society to do in supporting the bereaved and injured, while proactively contributing to a range of safety measures.

In the early 1950s, the British fishing industry employed over 50,000 fishermen, but for a number of reasons, including loss of the right to fish Icelandic waters and more effective catching systems, it had declined significantly in size, like the Royal and Merchant Navies. Most of the great fishing harbours of the past, such as Grimsby, Hull and Fleetwood, had in effect ceased being fishing ports.

During his time Conley was to witness further downsizing, as the catch quota system imposed by the European Common Fisheries Policy bit harder each year, driving boat owners out of business and perversely causing tens of thousands of tons of perfectly good fish to be dumped at sea each year. Another colossal enigma involved the decommissioning of fishing boats in some countries, including the United Kingdom, while the European Union subsidised the building of new vessels in other countries, most notably the Republic of Ireland and Spain. The fishing villages of the northwest of Scotland were particularly badly affected, such remote communities as Mallaig, Lochinver and Kinlochbervie losing not only jobs but a centuries-old way of life. Towards the end of his time in the Fishermen's Mission, on return to his childhood town of Campbeltown, Conley observed that its fleet of boats had also virtually gone. It was a truly depressing sight.

The coalition government's Strategic Defence and Security Review of 2010 heralded more draconian reductions in the armed forces with entire areas of capability, such as the maritime patrol aircraft squadrons, being disestablished. The Royal Navy was reduced to a mere nineteen frigates and destroyers, its aircraft carriers either mothballed or disposed of, and its manpower decreased to about 30,000 personnel compared to the 100,000 when Conley joined in 1963. The Submarine Flotilla was spared the worst of the cuts and a force level of four Trident SSBNs and seven *Astute*-class SSNs is envisaged.

Reviewing his career, Dan Conley reflected that he had been very fortunate in being an officer in a navy which had had a worldwide outreach. He also considered himself privileged to serve in the Royal Navy's Submarine Flotilla during the height of the Cold War, at a time of continuous tension when there was a clear and evident threat, and when maritime matters were much more prominent in the national conscience. However, he is certain that today's submariners face similar challenges to those he had confronted, that there is probably still a 'Black Pig' somewhere within the Flotilla, and somewhere close by are young men capable of mastering her.

Glossary

Submarine Classes

Soviet submarines – NATO designations

Whiskey – diesel-powered, 1,100 tons surface displacement, torpedo-armed patrol submarines built in large numbers between 1951 and 1957. Total in the class: 236. Later some hulls were converted to carry cruise missiles. Went out of service in the late 1980s.

Foxtrot – diesel-powered, torpedo-armed patrol submarines which succeeded the Whiskey class. Total of fifty-eight were built between 1958 and 1983. Went out of service in 2000.

November – first type of Soviet nuclear attack submarine (SSN). Torpedo-armed, a total of fourteen were completed between 1958 and 1963. Went out of service in 1991.

Hotel – a first-generation, nuclear-powered, ballistic missile submarine – SSBN. A total of eight were completed between 1960 and 1962. Was armed with three medium-range ballistic missiles but initially needed to be surfaced to launch them. This was rectified in later modernisations of the class. Went out of service in 1991.

Echo – nuclear, anti-ship cruise-missile armed submarines (SSGNs), the prime role of which was to attack NATO strike carrier forces. There were two variants Echo I and Echo II and a total of thirty-four were built between 1960 and 1967. Fitted with eight missile launchers but required to be surfaced to launch missiles. Went out of service in early 1990s.

Juliett – a large diesel submarine of 3,200 tons surface displacement, armed with four anti-ship cruise missiles (SSG). Required to be surfaced to launch missiles. A total of sixteen were built between 1963 and 1968. Went out of service in early 1990s.

Yankee – a second-generation SSBN of 7,500 tons surface displacement which carried a total of sixteen intercontinental ballistic missiles (ICBMs). Built in response to the American Polaris submarine threat. Thirty-four were completed between 1967 and 1974. Went out of service in the early 1990s.

Victor – second-generation SSN. Three types – Victor I, Victor II and Victor III. A total of forty-eight were built between 1967 and 1991. The Victor III was much quieter than its predecessors and was capable of launching anti-ship cruise missiles. Four Victor IIIs remain in service (2014).

Charlie – second-generation SSGNs which could launch their cruise missiles whilst dived. Two variants, Charlie I and II – a total of seventeen were built between 1968 and 1980. Went out of service in the 1990s.

Delta – third-generation SSBN of four variants – Delta I to Delta IV – which could carry between twelve and sixteen ICBMs. A total of forty-three vessels were commissioned between 1972 and 1990. As of 2014, approximately ten remain in service.

Alfa – torpedo-armed nuclear attack submarines. Very fast – 42 knots – deep-diving, and highly automated, a total of seven built between 1977 and 1981. Very difficult to maintain, went out of service in 1996.

Typhoon – a third-generation class of SSBNs. At 26,000 tons displacement, by far the world's largest submarines; six were built between 1981 and 1989. They carried a total of twenty intercontinental ballistic missiles. The last of this class went out of service in 2012.

Mike – prototype SSN completed in 1983 – the *Komsomolets* – which sank in 1989.

Akula – third-generation class of SSN capable of firing anti-ship missiles. Very quiet acoustic signature on a par with USN *Los Angeles* class. Fifteen completed between 1984 and 2009. Eight still in service (2014).

BRITISH SUBMARINE CLASSES

Conventional diesel-powered submarines (SSKs)

'S' class – a class of sixty-three submarines of 750 tons surface displacement built in the late 1930s and during the Second World War. Had a maximum underwater speed of 10 knots. Post-war a few were streamlined for the ASW role and fitted with snort (snorkel) masts. All were paid off by the early 1960s.

'T' class – a class of fifty-three submarines constructed in the late 1930s and during the Second World War. Post-war many were streamlined and converted to the ASW role and fitted with snort masts. Eight had their hulls extended in length and greater battery capacity fitted, giving them burst speeds of 15 knots dived. All were paid off by the late 1960s.

'A' class – a class of sixteen submarines built for the Pacific campaign, but all were completed post-war, a total of sixteen being built. Most were streamlined for the ASW role, but with a maximum dived speed of 8 knots they had limited capability and often were used as training targets. All were paid off by the early 1970s.

'P' and 'O' classes – virtually identical classes, these very quiet submarines were designed specifically for the ASW role and were completed in the late 1950s and early 1960s, twenty-one being built for the Royal Navy. Had a top underwater burst speed of 17 knots. Torpedo-armed for both for anti-ship and ASW tasks, could be fitted with the anti-ship cruise missile Sub-Harpoon. All were paid off by the early 1990s.

Upholder **class** – first Royal Navy diesel submarines to be completed of the 'albacore' teardrop hull shape. Of 2,400 tons surface displacement and designed for the ASW role, they could also embark Sub-Harpoon anti-ship missiles. Four were built and the class had a top underwater speed of 18 knots. Soon after completion of the first, HMS *Upholder* in 1988, as a cost-savings measure the decision was made to dispose of all the hulls once they were completed. All were sold to the Royal Canadian Navy in the late 1990s.

Experimental submarines

Explorer **and** *Excalibur* – two 800 tons surface displacement experimental unarmed submarines completed in the late 1950s and propelled by steam turbines fuelled by High Test Peroxide (HTP). Reached 26 knots dived but HTP proved very volatile and this type of propulsion was eclipsed by the advent of nuclear power at sea in submarines. Both were disposed of in the early 1960s.

Nuclear attack submarine (SSNs)

HMS *Dreadnought* – prototype completed in 1963 of 3,500 tons surface displacement and capable of 30 knots dived. Design based upon the USN *Skipjack* class and was powered by a Westinghouse reactor and machinery. Noisy and not a very capable ASW platform, it was withdrawn from service in 1980.

Valiant **class** – all-British design but nuclear reactor was based upon the US S5W plant. Had significant noise reduction features and prime role was ASW with secondary role of anti-ship. Maximum speed 26 knots dived. Class of five built between 1966 and 1971. Latterly armed with the Sub-Harpoon missile and Tigerfish dual role torpedo. All withdrawn from service by 1992.

Swiftsure **class** – second-generation attack submarines; quieter, faster and deeper diving than *Valiant* class. Prime role was ASW but Tigerfish/Spearfish dual-role torpedoes and Sub-Harpoon missiles gave them a good anti-ship capability. Six were built between 1973 and 1981 and all withdrawn from service by 2010.

Trafalgar **class** – improved *Swiftsure* class with slightly bigger hull and similar performance. Fitted with improved sonar systems. Seven were completed between 1982 and 1991. Armed with Spearfish torpedoes and Sub-Harpoon anti-ship missiles; in the late 1990s the latter were replaced with Tomahawk missiles which provide a thousand-mile-plus range land-attack capability

Astute **class** – class of seven planned to replace the *Trafalgar* class, first HMS *Astute* commissioned in 2010. At 7,500 tons surface displacement, this class of SSN is significantly larger than previous classes and has much greater weapon capacity, carrying the Spearfish torpedo and Tomahawk missile.

Nuclear ballistic missile submarines (SSBNs)

Resolution **class** – armed with sixteen Polaris intercontinental ballistic missiles, four of this class were completed between 1967 and 1970 and constituted the UK's independent nuclear deterrent between 1969 and the mid 1990s.

Vanguard **class** – armed with up to sixteen Trident D5 intercontinental ballistic missiles, the four vessels of this class were completed between 1993 and 2001. Of 14,500 tons surface displacement, the first deployed on patrol in 1994.

UNITED STATES SUBMARINE CLASSES

Conventional diesel-powered submarines (SSKs)

Fleet boats – large numbers built in the Second World War (300-plus hulls), many of which were streamlined and converted to the ASW role post-war. Considerable numbers were modernised under the Greater Underwater Propulsion Programme (GUPPY) which gave them much greater underwater endurance and burst speeds of 15 knots dived. Many were sold to overseas navies, but this class had been disposed of in the USN by the early 1970s.

Barbel **class** – the last diesel submarines built for the USN, a class of three completed in 1959/60. Of 'teardrop' hull construction, these submarines had a dived burst speed exceeding 20 knots .

Nuclear attack submarine (SSNs)

Nautilus – the world's first nuclear-powered submarine, commissioned in 1955. Of 3,500 tons surface displacement, had a maximum dived speed of 25 knots. Both ASW and anti-ship capable. Decommissioned from active service in 1980.

Skipjack **class** – completed between 1959 and 1960, six of a class. First nuclear submarines of 'albacore' hull form and single propeller. Fitted with the S5W reactor. Capable of 30 knots dived. Last of class paid off in 1986. Primarily had an ASW role and were armed with Mark 37 and Mark 48 torpedoes.

Thresher **class** – fourteen submarines completed between 1960 and 1967, of 3,700 tons surface displacement. Prime role was ASW and in addition to being armed with Mark 37 and Mark 48 torpedoes, embarked the Sub-Roc stand-off missile fitted with a nuclear depth-bomb.

Tullibee – one of a type, small ASW SSN of 2,200 tons surface displacement but limited to a maximum dived speed of 16 knots.

Sturgeon **class** ('637' class) – the workhorse of the US Submarine Fleet in the 1970s and 1980s, thirty-seven of this class were completed between 1967 and 1975. They had a prime role of ASW. Similar in size, performance and armament to the *Thresher* class; for the anti-ship role, in addition to the Mark 48 torpedo they embarked either Sub-Harpoon or Tomahawk ship-attack missiles. Possessed an excellent under-ice capability.

Los Angeles **class** ('688' class) – designed to achieve a speed well in excess of 30 knots dived, these are large – 6,500-ton surface displacement – SSNs fitted with the powerful S6G reactor. Sixty-two of these vessels were completed between 1976 and 1996. Prime role is ASW but later versions were armed with vertical launch tubes for Tomahawk land-attack missiles. Armed with the dual-role Mark 48 Adcap torpedo. Earlier vessels of the class started decommissioning in the 1990s.

Nuclear ballistic missile submarines (SSBNs)

George Washington **class** – five of this class were completed between 1959 and 1961 using the basic *Skipjack*-class hull configuration and S5W power plant. Of 6,000 tons surface displacement. Fitted with sixteen intercontinental ballistic missile tubes and the Polaris missile system. Class phased out in the 1980s.

Ethan Allen **and** *Lafayette* **class** – thirty-six of this all-SSBN designed class were built between 1961 and 1967. Similar to *George Washington* class, were fitted with sixteen missile tubes and in the 1980s were outfitted with the Trident C4 weapon system which replaced Polaris. Were all decommissioned by the 1990s.

Ohio **class** – eighteen of these 18,500-ton submarines were completed between 1981 and 1997. Armed with up to twenty-four Trident D5 missiles, four of these vessels have been decommissioned as SSBNs and converted to undertake a land-attack missile (Tomahawk) role.

Index

'637'-class US SSN 165, 167, 170, 172, 174

'688'-class US SSN 165, 168, 169, 174, 177

Abd-al-Kuri 33, 34

Adcap (torpedo) 225

Aden Protectorate 4, 26, 31–3, 37, 38

Aeneas, HMS 228

Affray, HMS 41, 45, 46, 66, 91

Ajax, HMS 29

Akula-class Soviet submarines 245

Alfa-class Soviet submarines 86, 157–60

Alliance, HMS 45

Amphion, HMS 37

Applied Physics Laboratory Ice Station (APLIS) 217–21, 227

Ark Royal (1955), HMS (fleet aircraft carrier) 18, 37

Ark Royal (1985), HMS (light aircraft carrier) 254

Artemis, HMS 75–6

Astute, HMS 268

Astute-class submarines 154, 240

Atlanta, USS 177

Atlantic Underwater Test & Evaluation Centre (AUTEC) 96–8, 100, 119, 120, 123, 124, 126, 129, 140, 141, 143, 153, 170, 175, 224, 227

Atomic Weapons Establishment (AWE), Aldermaston 256, 263

Auriga, HMS 45

Ayrshire, SS 33, 34

Barbel, USS 47

Barents Sea 57, 87–9, 91, 103, 105, 166, 234

Barrow-in-Furness 40, 75, 76, 79, 84, 102, 145–9, 153, 154, 231, 239, 241, 243, 245

Beaufort Sea 217

Beira Patrol 71

Belgrano (Argentinian warship) 173–4

Best, Commander Rupert 180

Biggs, Vice Admiral Sir Geoffrey 52, 55, 56, 96, 130

Birkenhead 40, 57, 130–3, 231, 239, 241, 243

Borneo 17, 18, 28, 29

Boyce, Admiral Lord (Michael) 145

Bridport, HMS 247, 248

Britannia Royal Naval College, Dartmouth 2, 7, 8–12

British Underwater Test & Evaluation Centre (BUTEC) 129, 139, 140–1, 145, 153

Buccaneer (strike aircraft) 3, 18, 20–1, 25, 35, 229

Bulwark, HMS 36, 38

Burke, Admiral Arleigh, USN 84

Cachalot, HMS 135

Cambrian, HMS 17, 23–38, 172, 250

Cammell Laird shipbuilding yard 40, 57, 131, 231, 239, 241, 243

Campbeltown 6, 56, 69, 70, 145, 269, 248

Centaur, HMS 18, 26

Charlie–class Soviet submarines 94, 157, 161, 206

Chatham Royal Naval Dockyard 3, 23, 27, 40, 56

Churchill, HMS 98, 200–1, 224, 233

Cleopatra, HMS 123, 196–8

Cochino, USS 91

Commodore Naval Ship Acceptance (CNSA) 237, 239, 244, 248

Comprehensive Test Ban Treaty 260

Comsubdevron Twelve (Devron) 163–70, 176–7

Conley, Linda 105, 110, 116, 126, 173, 214, 267

Conqueror, HMS 103–4, 143, 173, 188, 233

Courageous, HMS 88–9, 120, 178, 180–7, 224, 228, 233

Cox, Captain Ken, USN 210

Cuban Missile Crisis 83–4

Dakar (Israeli Navy submarine) 51, 147

Dallas, USS 174–6, 208

Daphné-class French submarines 70

Dartmouth (town) 2, 8

Davies, Rear Admiral Peter 186

Delta-class Soviet submarines 159–61, 204, 216, 221, 229

Devonport Royal Naval Dockyard 13–14, 103, 115, 154, 158, 161, 186–7, 232, 266

Dolphin, HMS 7, 40, 42, 58–9, 75, 107, 133, 179, 231, 264, 266–7

Dorman, Captain Merrill, USN 217, 221

Dreadnought, HMS 3, 40, 49, 84, 102

Dryad, HMS 115, 226

Eagle, HMS 17–24, 34–5

East African mutinies 26–7

Echo–class Soviet submarines 88, 198

Eilat (Israeli Navy destroyer) 25

Elliot, Commodore Toby 201

Eurydice (French Navy submarine) 45

Excalibur, HMS 6, 81

Explorer, HMS 6, 81

Falklands War 19, 26, 85, 116, 161, 171–4, 179, 181–5, 188–9, 216, 228

Fieldhouse, Admiral Lord (John) 128, 133

Finback, USS 128–9

Finwhale, HMS 17, 73, 110

Fisher, Admiral of the Fleet Lord (John) 8

Fiskerton, HMS 29

Forsyth, Commander Rob 107, 112, 114–15, 130

Fort George, RFA 248–9

Fort Victoria, RFA 248–9
Forth, HMS 71–2
Foxhill, Bath 234, 238, 240, 247, 250
Foxtrot-class Soviet submarines 84

Gannet (aircraft) 3, 20
George Washington, USS 83
Gibraltar 60, 61, 98–9, 211
Gibraltar naval base 3, 31, 60–1, 70, 99, 130, 207, 211
Goodwin, Captain Nigel 147, 154, 157–8
Gordon, Commander Huntly 200, 213
Gorshkov, Admiral, Soviet Navy 84
Granby (Operation) 235, 237
Grayling, USS 122
Grenier, Rear Admiral Frank 222
Guglielmo Marconi (Italian Navy submarine) 209
GUPPY-class US submarines 81

Hale, Commander Tim 100, 102
Hermes, HMS 4, 18, 172
Holland One 47
Hong Kong 4, 36
Hotel-class Soviet submarines 92
Howell, Gordon 241–3

Indonesian Confrontation 17–18, 28, 30, 36
Invincible, HMS 147, 150–1, 172
Istres, France 262

Jenkin, Rear Admiral Conrad 26, 30, 33

K19 (Soviet submarine) 92
K219 (Soviet submarine) 92
Kelso, Admiral Frank, USN 254

Kashin-class Soviet warships 99
King, Lord (Tom) 254
Komar-class missile boats 25
Komsomolets (Soviet submarine) 230–1
Kotlin-class Soviet warships 203
Kursk (Soviet submarine) 82
Kuwait 5, 235–7

La Jolla, USS 169
Lacroix, Rear Admiral Frank, USN 208
Lapon, USS 217–18, 221
Lehman, John 166, 170–1, 177
Leningrad (Soviet warship) 157
Lincoln, HMS 71
Lofoten, HMS 51
Londonderry 54–6
Los Alamos 260–1
Lygo, Admiral Sir Raymond 146

McGeoch, Vice Admiral Sir Ian 42
McKee, Admiral Kinnaird, USN 171
Mackin, Commander John, USN 221
Maidstone, HMS 51, 71
Malaysian Federation 9, 17, 72
Maria Van Riebeeck (South African submarine) 70–1
Mars, Lieutenant Commander Alastair 191
Menzies, Lieutenant Commander Gavin 16
Mercury, HMS 116
Miller, Lieutenant Commander Andrew, 190, 201–2, 207, 213–14
Miller, Frank 259
Millington, Mary 127–30, 133, 148, 161
Minerve (French Navy submarine) 45
Morrow, Captain Emo, USN 172

Mountbatten, Admiral of the Fleet
Lord (Louis) 84
Murmansk 5

Narwhal, HMS 16, 110, 114
Nassau Agreement 3
Nautilus, USS 82, 90, 170
Neptune, HMS 50–1
Newman, Vice Admiral Sir Roy 196
Norfolk, HMS 179
Nottingham, HMS 268
November-class Soviet submarines 92

Oberon, HMS 67, 68–79, 94, 228
Oberon class 41, 118, 178, 179, 233,
240, 243
Ocelot, HMS 142
Odin, HMS 47, 50–7, 67
Ohio, USS 168–71
Ohio-class US SSBNs 93, 165, 168–9
Onslaught, HMS 115
Orpheus, HMS 73, 75
Oswald, Admiral Sir Julian 254
Otter, HMS 115–16, 118–34

Patton, Captain Jim, USN 176
Perisher 16, 56, 79, 105–6, 107–16,
130, 155, 168, 176, 183, 196, 200
Philadelphia, USS 177
Pirnie, Rear Admiral Ian 244
Pitt, Commander Keith 103, 105
Polaris missile system 3, 39, 40, 50, 58,
60, 64, 69, 83, 85, 136–7, 252,
254–5, 259
Port Canaveral 96–7, 123, 128
Portillo, Michael 258
Portland naval base 27–8, 63, 82, 86,
240

President Kruger (South African
warship) 71
President Pretorius (South African
warship) 71
Procurement Executive (PE) 168, 238,
240, 243–4, 250

Radfan Mountains 32
Red Beard (atomic bomb) 21
Resolution, HMS 64–6, 85, 120, 211, 259
Resolution class 178
Revenge, HMS 200, 204
Richard B Russell, USS 167–8, 170
Richards, Commander Ian 217
Rickover, Admiral Hyman, USN
169–71, 174–5, 233
Rifkind, Sir Malcolm 253
Riga-class Soviet warships 15
Rosyth Royal Naval Dockyard 3, 67,
127, 212–13
Roxburgh, Vice Admiral Sir John 42
Royal Marines 26–7, 34, 74

SLAM (missile) 228
SOSUS 85–6, 93, 97, 135, 161, 193,
197, 204
STRATCOM, Omaha 261–2
SUNROC 167
Sackett, Rear Admiral Dean, USN 176
San Luis (Argentinian submarine) 174
Sceptre, HMS 224
Schofield, Lieutenant Commander
Chris 12
Scimitar (strike aircraft) 20, 32, 34–5
Scotts shipbuilding yard 40, 60
Sea Cat (missile) 19, 23, 172, 174
Sea Dart (missile) 172
Sea Eagle, HMS 54

Sea Slug (missile) 19, 172

Sea Vixen (fighter) 3, 5, 20–1, 35

Sea Wolf (missile) 172, 249

Sealion, HMS 57–70, 75, 88, 107, 118

Second Submarine Squadron 103,
154

Sembawang Naval Dockyard 4, 28, 72,
75, 77

Seventh Submarine Division 67, 73

Sheffield, HMS 77, 173

Sidon, HMS 82

Simonstown Naval Base 70–1, 76

Singapore 4, 17–18, 27–9, 35–7, 47,
67–77, 189

Skate, USS 90

Skipjack class 165

Sovereign, HMS 121, 123, 125

Spartan, HMS 145–61, 166

Spearfish (torpedo) 190, 207, 215,
224–5, 227, 240, 250

Stalker, HMS 54

Stingray (torpedo) 224

Sturgeon class 165

Submarine Tactics and Weapons
Group (STWG) 133, 135–6, 141,
145, 190, 215–16, 224–5, 228, 231,
233–4, 266

Sub-Martel (missile) 228

Suez 5, 31, 39, 41

Suez crisis 1

Sukarno, Achmed 17, 72

Sultan, HMS 7

Superb, HMS 217, 219–22

Swan Hunter (shipbuilders) 240, 248–9

Swiftsure, HMS 77, 79, 80, 94–105, 119,
145, 149, 155–6, 215, 228, 233

Swiftsure class 89, 105, 146, 148, 150,
156, 178, 180, 233, 267

Tafelberg (South African warship) 71

Talent, HMS 231

Taylor, Commodore Jim 159–61

Taylor, Commodore Steve 244, 246

Tenby, HMS 15

Terror, HMS 72

Thetis, HMS 91, 242

Third Submarine Squadron 47, 51, 57,
75, 118, 134, 188

Thresher, USS 91, 94

Thresher class 165

Tigerfish (torpedo) 99, 123, 125,
133–4, 135–45, 154, 171–3, 180–2,
190, 194, 215–22, 224–7, 229, 231

Tireless, HMS 91

Tomahawk (missile) 93, 164

torpedo, Mark 8: 49, 96, 107–9, 119,
154, 173, 180; Mark 20: 49, 69;
Mark 23: 49, 96, 119, 138, 154;
Mark 44: 123, 125; Mark 46: 123;
Mark 48: 138, 167, 225

Torquay, HMS 15

Totem, HMS 51

Trafalgar, HMS 178, 201–2

Trafalgar class 89, 179, 231, 233

Trident missile system 90, 165, 178–9,
244, 246–7, 250, 252, 255, 257–62,
264

Trident-class SSBN 85, 93, 151, 231,
233, 239, 244–5, 247, 255, 259, 269

Triomphant (French Navy) SSBN 263

Triumph, HMS (repair ship) 36

Triumph, HMS (submarine) 231, 239

Truculent, HMS 91, 131

Tuckett, Commander John 217, 219

Turbulent, HMS 217, 219–22

Tusk, USS 91

Type 23 frigate 179, 248–9

Type 45 destroyer 26
Typhoon-class Soviet submarines 90, 216, 221, 229

Udaloy-class Soviet warships 202–3
Unicorn, HMS 241, 243
United Kingdom Hydrographic Office (UKHO) 267–8
Unseen, HMS 241, 243
Upholder, HMS 231, 241, 244
Upholder class 45, 179, 233, 239–40, 242–4, 267
Ursula, HMS 45, 241, 243

Valiant, HMS 3, 39, 70, 84, 177–8, 186–7, 188–214, 225, 233, 245
Valiant class 40, 94, 95, 98, 167, 178, 180, 231, 233, 239
Vanguard, HMS 231, 239, 244, 246–7, 263
Veliotis, Takis 169
Vickers shipbuilding yard 40, 76, 77, 84, 146–53, 178–80, 228, 231, 241
Victor-class Soviet submarines 92, 94, 159–60, 168, 192, 194–7, 199–206, 208–9, 245
Victorious, HMS (aircraft carrier) 18
Victorious, HMS (SSBN) 231, 244

Vietnam War 18, 72, 171
Vigilant, HMS 244
Vosper Thornycroft (shipbuilders) 240, 247–8
Voyager, HMAS 37

Walker/Whitworth spy ring 177
Wardle, Commander David 55
Waroonga, SS 38
Warspite, HMS 3, 88, 101, 181, 200, 207, 215, 232–3
WE177 (nuclear bomb) 257
Wessex (helicopter) 20, 236
Whale, USS 172–3
Whiskey-class Soviet submarines 54, 101–2
Wizard, HMS 12–17, 23–4
Woods, Commander Terry 69, 76–7
Woodward, Admiral Sir Sandy 116
Wreford-Brown, Captain Chris 173, 188

Yankee-class Soviet submarines 92, 94, 197
Yarrow (shipbuilders) 240, 249
Yemen 31–2, 34

Zulu, HMS 61–2

DATE DUE			

Fighting for Mental Health

Norman Sartorius is one of the most prominent and influential psychiatrists of his generation. As Director of the Division of Mental Health at the World Health Organization, and subsequently President of the World Psychiatric Association, he has, over many years, been in a position to survey the state of psychiatry worldwide, to campaign for greater equity and honesty in the clinical and research agenda, and to point out some deficiencies and anomalies.

The essays collected in this stimulating book represent the author's latest thinking as well as a few chapters he selected from among his innumerable speeches and previously published articles. They range from trenchant critiques of mental health service delivery and prevention to more light-hearted, anecdotal pieces on the use of language and how to get things done. All point to the core concerns for mental health programmes today: definition of needs; the role of psychiatry, both in general health care and in the developing countries; and the challenges that our times present for mental health. In every essay the author's well-known wit, candour and scientific authority are well illustrated.

This is a book that every psychiatrist will wish to own, both as a survey of current debates in their discipline, and a reflection of one of the sharpest minds brought to bear upon them.

Norman Sartorius has held professorial appointments at the Universities of Geneva, Prague, New York and Zagreb. He is a member of the Council of the World Psychiatric Association and of the Expert Advisory Panel of the World Health Organization. He has honorary doctorates in science and in medicine at the Universities of Umea, Prague and Bath and is an Honorary Fellow of numerous professional organizations, including the World Psychiatric Association, the Royal Colleges of Psychiatry (in the UK and in Australia and New Zealand) and the American Psychiatric Association. He has written over 300 scientific papers and co-authored or edited over 40 books. Among his many positions he has been Director of the Mental Health Division at the World Health Organization, President of the World Psychiatric Association and President of the Association of European Psychiatrists.

Fighting for
Mental Health

A personal view

Norman Sartorius

Department of Psychiatry
University of Geneva, Switzerland

CAMBRIDGE
UNIVERSITY PRESS

PUBLISHED BY THE PRESS SYNDICATE OF THE UNIVERSITY OF CAMBRIDGE
The Pitt Building, Trumpington Street, Cambridge, United Kingdom

CAMBRIDGE UNIVERSITY PRESS
The Edinburgh Building, Cambridge CB2 2RU, UK
40 West 20th Street, New York, NY 10011–4211, USA
477 Williamstown Road, Port Melbourne, VIC 3207, Australia
Ruiz de Alarcón 13, 28014 Madrid, Spain
Dock House, The Waterfront, Cape Town 8001, South Africa

http://www.cambridge.org

First published 2002

Printed in the United Kingdom at the University Press, Cambridge

Typeface Swift Regular 10/14pt.   *System* QuarkXPress® [SE]

A catalogue record for this book is available from the British Library

Library of Congress cataloguing in Publication data

Sartorius, N.
Fighting for mental health: a personal view/Norman Sartorius.
        p.   cm.
Includes bibliographical references and index.
ISBN 0 521 58243 1 (hbk.)
1. Psychiatry – Anecdotes.   2. Mental Health Services.   I. Title.
RA 790.5 .S275 2002
362.2 – dc21   2002019250

ISBN 0 521 58243 1 hardback

To Vera, my spouse and beloved companion in dreams and realities, with thanks for being a source of inspiration, strength and sunshine, at all times.

Contents

Acknowledgements   ix

Introduction   1

Part I
The context of health and mental health programmes

1 Updating 1789   13

2 Doubts about three of the many dogmas of development   21

3 Overlaps and confusions   33

4 Nearly forgotten: mental health needs of an urbanized planet   43

5 The Mozart effect and the Keshan disease   57

6 The paradoxes about psychiatry   71

7 On advice and consultation   81

Part II
Mental health and medicine

8 Psychiatry in the framework of primary health care: a threat or
   boost for psychiatry?   91

9 The limits of mental health care in general medical services   107

10 The mental health adventure of the World Health Organization   123

11 Mental health care for the elderly? Another 30 years to wait   141

12 On words I like to hate   157

Part III
Psychiatry and mental health programmes

13 Assessing needs for psychiatric services   171

14 Why are mental and neurological disorders not being prevented?   179

15 The seven vices of psychiatry   187

16 Brueghel's Everyman: a cover page for a book on research in
psychiatry   201

17 And then there were five . . .   209

18 Enabling   219

19 Psychiatry in developing countries   231

Index   253

Acknowledgements

It is a pleasant duty to acknowledge, with many thanks, the help that I received during the production of this volume from several people. Dr Richard Barling encouraged me to write the book and had the patience and magnanimity to wait for the manuscript that was delayed for quite a while, for a variety of reasons. Sir David Goldberg read many of the essays and made valuable comments about the book as a whole and about most of its chapters. Gavin Andrews gave me very useful comments and contributed a number of suggestions for further reading. Vera Sartorius read the text, told me what she found interesting and gave me invaluable help in the selection of the illustrations for the book. In the latter task I also had fine suggestions from Danielle Sartorius. I wish to thank Lydia Kurkcuoglu for her excellent help in the technical preparation of the manuscript. Finally, Pauline Graham had editorial responsibility for the book and helped competently and cordially in the different stages of its production.

Introduction

My friends tease me because I often use threefold arguments and classify matters into three groups. This habit seems to be the sin of many. Even philosophers and religions seem to be attached to it. Pythagoras felt that three is a perfect number expressing the beginning, the middle and the end – thus being the symbol of Deity. Classical mythology had three Graces, three Fates, three Furies, three main Gods, Jupiter (heavens), Neptune (sea) and Pluto (hell). Humans were considered threefold, with body, mind and spirit. Outside Europe too, Egyptian and Hindu gods are grouped in threes. The great and ancient Mayan god, Huracan, was the Triple Heart of the Universe. Three-legged stools are more stable than chairs with more legs. And so on.

It is thus not surprising that this book is divided in three parts – the first dealing with the context of health and medicine, the second dealing with the relationship between medicine and mental health and the third with psychiatry and mental health. This division, however, is not the consequence of my habit of dividing things in three groups. It corresponds to the three phases of my comprehension of psychiatry and of my tasks in relation to it.

Many years ago I decided to become a physician. This seemed to be a logical choice. For several generations of my family, at least one of the children selected medicine as their field of action. Sometimes, there were more than one, never none. Medicine seemed to offer a good chance of leading a useful and, overall, agreeable life. Also, the political and other circumstances prevailing at the end of my adolescence made me (and those whom I asked for advice about my career) feel that it would be wise to have a profession that would make it possible to find work in any country. I also had some uncertainty about that choice. One of the reasons for hesitation was that I wanted to become a pediatrician: my mother, however, was a successful and well-known pediatrician and founder of social pediatrics in the country in which I grew up, and I knew that it would be very difficult to avoid continual comparisons with her and the attribute of being the son of a well-known person rather than an individual making one's own way. Accounts by friends and books like Sinclair's *Martin Arrowsmith* and Paul Kruif's *Microbe Chasers* seemed to indicate that there were many other parts of medicine that could be attractive and so I took the entrance examinations, passed, studied and graduated.

When I got my diploma, there were few openings in the fields of medicine that I considered to be particularly interesting. Psychiatry was one of them. At the time, it was possible to start postgraduate studies while working in the department of psychiatry, provided that the candidates agreed to carry out clinical duties without being paid for it. I did so and complemented the support that I received from my family by working as a tourist guide. The latter proved to be immensely useful later in life, when I often had to make people who had no particular interest in what I was showing them become awake, emotionally engaged and ready to listen or help.

Half-way through my postgraduate studies in psychiatry (and neurology) I became aware of the fact that I was not learning enough about normal psychology (nor about research methods). I took on studies in psychology and got my doctorate on the basis of a study of changes in the thinking processes in schizophrenia. I learned a great deal about various technical matters in the process: the most important lesson was, however, that psychiatry – or for that matter any other branch of medicine – does not contain all the knowledge and insights that are necessary to practise it well. I continued searching these in epidemiology and later on in public health in general. The latter turned out to be inextricably linked with issues of overall socioeconomic development and change.

Although I have written the essays contained in this book in the past few years, they belong to the three stages of my understanding of psychiatry and its role in society. At first, I thought of psychiatry as a self-sufficient discipline dealing with fascinating oddities of mind, making sense out of confusions, bringing solace to people tortured by inner emotional turmoils and distress. Gradually, it dawned on me that psychiatry is part of medicine and, psychiatrists one of the many helping professions. I began to understand that psychiatry has to do with diseases as well as with distress, and that the bizarre ideas are often symptoms of dysfunctions that perturb the patients and make them unable to perform in their personal and social roles. Later still, I understood that psychiatry and medicine cannot stand alone either, that they should be studied and practised with constant awareness of the social and physical context that surrounds the persons who suffer from diseases and the physicians who are trying to help them. Medicine, as part of the armamentarium that societies use to make the life of their members better, implies the necessity to pursue its goals using political as well as scientific means. Psychiatry, as an academic discipline examining puzzles of nature and dwelling on convolutions of thought, is therefore neither the only nor the most desirable of its definitions.

Psychiatry, as any other medical discipline, has thus three sets of roles that have to be performed synchronously if psychiatry is to be as useful as it can be. It must be a discipline that is solidly based on evidence and experience about mental disorders, about their recognition at different levels of care, and about their treatment and prevention. It must be part of medicine and develop mutually supportive relationships with it. It must also grow in conjunction with overall socioeconomic development, helping to make it optimal from a humane point of view and drawing strength from being harmonious with it. My own contributions and tasks in professional life, I understood, must therefore also be in keeping with those three sets of roles of psychiatry. In order to make the best use of my working life, I applied myself to strengthen psychiatry, ethically and scientifically as a profession; I sought ways of bringing psychiatry closer to medicine for the benefit of both; and I tried to see ways in which political tools can be used to improve education, research and training in the field of mental health and in developing mental health programmes.

It is obvious that many psychiatrists will concentrate on the recognition and treatment of mental disorders. They will want to have an independent discipline unencumbered by the need to deal with diseases other than those that have been labelled psychiatric. They will be driven by the twin engines of wanting to help their patients and of hoping to live a life of quality. Their interest in public health will be negligible and they will make no sustained effort to understand the intricate relationships between psychiatry and overall development nor draw guidelines for their own behaviour on the basis of such an analysis. They will be the vast majority of the world's 150 000 psychiatrists. Their contribution to the welfare of their patients is important and they feel that making that contribution justifies the existence of the profession.

Some of the psychiatrists are constantly, and sometimes painfully, aware of the fact that they can only deal with a minute proportion of people with mental illnesses. Even the most conservative estimates indicate that the total numbers of people with mental disorders who never see a psychiatrist are enormous. Most of them come to seek help from general practitioners or other non-psychiatric medical practitioners. Their disease is sometimes recognized and sometimes not. Even in highly developed countries, about half of the people who come to doctors because of their mental disorders receive a diagnosis of some other disorder or no diagnosis at all. Of those who are recognized, some are given treatment, often in inappropriate doses and too late. This second group of psychiatrists will therefore argue that general health services should therefore somehow be changed. The non-psychiatrists, if given some additional training, can provide adequate treatment to most of the patients who come to see them. Operational and functioning links between general medicine and psychiatry are an important ingredient in this respect. These links gain further importance from the fact that a large proportion of people with mental disorders also suffer from some physical disorder that should be treated simultaneously with the mental disorder for better outcome of both.

But, even if the links between psychiatry and general medicine were to function very well, and if all the patients with psychiatric problems who come to general health services were to receive their treatment, much would remain to be done. In developing countries most of the population is not covered by psychiatric or by general health care services. In many of the developed countries a significant proportion of the population lives in poverty or does not receive the benefits of appropriate medical care for other reasons. In a vast majority of settings in almost all countries, people who had a mental illness and were treated for it do not receive good-quality aftercare. The rehabilitation of people who have a mental impairment – as a result of a mental illness or for other reasons (e.g. brain trauma) is deficient in most parts of the world. The stigma of mental illness, and the consequent negative discrimination of people who have it, represent a powerful obstacle to success of any intervention undertaken to help the patients and their families during the illness or after it.

It is thus clear that a significant improvement of the fate of the majority of the 500 million people with mental illness (and of their families) depends on the existence of mental health programmes that involve not only mental health and general health care services, but also other sectors of governments and many members of the community. Mental health programmes should have components that deal with the prevention of mental illness, with the organization of treatment and rehabilitation services and with activities that will make it possible to use knowledge about psychosocial issues in overall socio-economic development. They should be carried out by people working in different social sectors and must be based on knowledge and skills from many disciplines, including psychiatry. No single profession or sector of government can design, carry out or evaluate mental health programmes alone: they must be like mosaics composed of many pieces that, together, can make a coherent picture and be useful to all.

In this book the first seven essays deal with the context of mental health programmes. The elements of that context include some of the basic principles of society important for mental health programmes – equity, solidarity among people and the recognition of duties and rights of members of the society, including those who have a mental illness. These principles are of direct relevance to psychiatry: but they are also of determining significance for overall socio-economic development that is at present, in many countries, misguided by dogmas and logical fallacies. In addition, for mental health programmes, the situations is made even more difficult because of the overlaps of the semantic spheres of words that are used to discuss the subjects of mental health programmes, their role and their value. Two essays discuss the reasons for being pessimistic about the potential that currently funded (or otherwise supported) research could have in speeding up progress and about the hope that countries in the process of development will learn from the examples of others or accept advice that is based on other people's experience. The impact of urbanization on mental health, and the low priority of mental health programmes, are the subjects of the remaining two essays in this part of the book.

The second group of essays deals with issues at the border between medicine and mental health. They discuss the ethical basis and dilemmas of the incorporation of mental health elements into primary health care and define the limits of interpenetration of mental health and general health care services. Two case studies are included in this part of the volume. One uses the example of the mental health programme of the World Health Organization as an illustration of the difficulty of including mental health into the public health arena from which it has been, traditionally, absent. The other presents the probable difficulties of developing new health programmes on the basis of an analysis of obstacles to the growth of mental health programmes for the elderly. A brief essay deals with some of the words that we use frequently in medicine and in psychiatry to illustrate that we are often unaware of their premises, although they are influencing our behaviour.

The third part of the book focuses on psychiatry. It starts with a discussion of ways in which mental health needs should be assessed if we are to build services that respond to them. The next essay deals with the reasons that might explain why there are so few programmes of primary prevention of mental and neurological disorders and argues that this is because many of the measures of primary prevention of mental disorders are the responsibility of sectors other than health and, if of health, of disciplines other than psychiatry. The reasons for the poor position of psychiatry among other medical disciplines, and the poor utilization of the potential that psychiatry might have for the improvement of health in general, are discussed in the next two essays, which are followed by proposals for a different organization of mental health programmes and a different orientation of programmes of rehabilitation of people with mental illness. A chapter on psychiatry in the developing countries closes that part of the book.

What will happen with psychiatry in the years to come? Is it worth pursuing the directions that were selected after so much debate and argument a few decades ago? Should we still make efforts to heighten the priority of psychiatry and mental health services on the governments' agendas? Preach the integration of mental health into general health care services? Diminish or eliminate the large mental hospital and promote community care for people with mental illness? Build mental health programmes in collaboration with various sectors of the government and the representatives of other actors in the field of mental health, for example, the organizations of families of people with mental illness? Try to introduce psychosocial concerns into overall development programmes? Or, should we drop these goals and concentrate on making psychiatry a respected discipline of medicine leaving the other concerns now included in mental health programmes to others to do? After all, there are no national programmes of surgery, and yet surgeons and surgical departments are doing fine. We could argue that many of the efforts that were made in the past are not necessary. Once we are as successful as other disciplines of medicine in making diagnoses and treating diseases in our field – and psychiatry is certainly almost there – things will fall into their places. Public health authorities will then be including action in the field of psychiatry into their plans just as they do today with dermatology, orthopedics, internal medicine, and so many others.

The answer, in my opinion, is that we do not have that choice. We cannot abandon the previous lines of action of mental health programmes – for ethical and for immediate practical reasons. First, there are hundreds of millions of people who suffer from mental disorders for which we now have effective treatment. Most of the people with mental disorders could be provided with that treatment in general health services. For some, it would be necessary to provide specialized treatment facilities. In areas in which health service coverage is poor, it would be possible to educate village elders and other persons, including in particular members of families of people with mental illness to provide care to those who need it.

The cost of that treatment – including the necessary in-service training, establishment of referral lines, regular supplies of medications, development of rehabilitation services, changes in the curricula of psychiatry in schools of health personnel, and related expenditures – is considered high because mental health has a very low priority on the agenda of governments and of communities. That situation argues for a change of emphasis for mental health programmes: their first objective and main focus should now be – more than ever before – the elevation of position of mental health on the scale of values of individuals, communities and governments. Previously, promotion of mental health – the increase of value that people give to it – was of lesser importance: psychiatry had few effective interventions at its disposal and having more money or support would have had less impact on the care for people with mental illness than it would have today.

Second, there are very many people with chronic mental illnesses, who are surviving in the terrible conditions that prevail in many of the dilapidated institutions that should be stripped of the name of hospital that they now have. People with chronic mental illness and impairment are sometimes better off living as vagrants, although they might be ridiculed, abused and sometimes exposed in wild places. Either condition – being in hospitals without proper care or being outside of them and receiving no treatment or other help – should be recognized as unacceptable. Mental health programmes and mental health professionals worldwide should be among the first and most vocal to denounce that situation which is, at present, often hidden or forgotten.

Third, the treatment of other, so-called somatic illnesses, co-morbid with mental disorders, is usually less efficient and therefore more expensive when the latter are not recognized and treated. Similarly, the neglect of the humane and psychosocial factors in general health services renders them less effective and makes the population which they are supposed to serve less satisfied with them. The neglect of psychosocial components of health care will also increase the probability of emotional burn-out, an expensive side-effect of current trends of seeking managerial efficiency and economic rentability of health care and services while forgetting that medicine should be a noble vocation.

Fourth, overall socio-economic development that disregards psychosocial elements will convert dreams of a better world into a richer nightmare for all concerned, and fail to contribute to the growth of civic societies which should be the ultimate goal of such development.

Even if science were to discover a completely effective treatment for all mental disorders tomorrow, much of the above agenda would remain relevant and urgent. The debts of societies to people with mental illness and their families are of vast magnitude and have to be paid. And, consequently, even though it might be much easier to remain a clinical psychiatrist helping one's patients, psychiatrists must also fight the social and political battles that are necessary to improve the fate of people struck by mental illness, and make psychiatry and related disciplines and sciences useful to society and responsive to its ethical duties.

Part I

The context of health and mental health programmes

Eugene Delacroix (1798–1863): *La Liberté guidant le peuple* ('Liberty Guiding the People 28 July 1830'), 1830. (Courtesy of Peter Willi, the Louvre, Paris, and Bridgeman Art Library, London.)

1

Updating 1789

The mottos of the French Revolution 'Fraternity, Liberty and Equality' may have seemed in themselves sufficient goals when they were chosen. Today it is clear that, at least in relation to mental health problems, equality before the law should be complemented by equity in resource distribution, fraternity needs to be understood as solidarity with people who need help, and liberty should be interpreted in the light of duties and responsibilities that all of us should accept as members of societies that strive to be civic.

Marxists believe that great leaders are no more than midwives who help the birth of progressive ideas that have matured in the body of history. The mottos of the French revolution – Equality, Fraternity, Liberty – would thus have been ripe to be born and spread across Europe by the rivers of blood of the Napoleonic wars.

Today's psychiatry was born at about the same time. The Age of Enlightenment brought with it the marvellous notion that human beings can, through conscious action, improve their society, their environment and their lives. In tune with this and with similar ideas that became popular in the late eighteenth century, institutions that served to protect mad people from crowds (and families and communities from the nuisances that the mentally ill could produce) began to be seen as places in which madness, given appropriate treatment, could subside. In his treatise on madness in 1758 Battie (the owner of two mental asylums in England and, for a while, the President of the College of Physicians) argued that mental asylums can help to improve the mental health of its inmates – a new idea that was accompanied, some 30 years later, by instructions on how to go about this in the volumes *On insanity* by Chiarugi. Chiarugi took off the chains that were on people in the San Bonifacio hospital; and Joly in Switzerland and Pinel a few years later followed suit, freeing people in asylums from their chains and preaching that mental hospitals were hospitals in which people should be given treatment.

The mottos of the French Revolution, as well as the Declaration of Human Rights that Louis XVI, the King of France, signed at the time, were important for the formulation of European moral and legal provisions in the years that followed. Like most ideals, the goals of the French revolution were sufficiently big to be visible from afar – which was useful because it soon became clear that reaching them will take time and that the road towards them will be long and arduous.

But, while there is no doubt about the historical significance of the mottos, it now seems that concentrating only on the achievement of these goals might carry dangers for people with mental illness and for some other population groups. Equality, for example, presupposes that people will obtain, say, the same compensation for the same amount of work. If they do not receive it, they would probably have the right to ask for it: but people vary greatly in their capacity to ask for what is theirs. Legal provisions concerning health care border on the perfect in many countries but the health care received by the majority of the population is often substandard only a minute proportion of people, however, will have the energy and know-how necessary to obtain what the law proscribes for them[1]. In addition to differences in the capacity to demand and obtain what is rightfully theirs, people also differ in their needs: the application of the equality principle might be interpreted as an invitation to disregard differences among people in terms of age, gender, wealth and health states, culture, previous experience and expectations.

In addition, the interpretation of rights differs: the right to work, for example, was interpreted in the 1970s as the obligation of the government to provide work for all citizens (in the socialist block countries of Europe), while Canada and some other countries interpreted it as the right to get work if there are openings commensurate with the person's ability and qualifications. The interpretation of rights is well regulated in some instances and very poorly or not at all in others. Moral and legal rights differ considerably from country to country, and from one time period to the next.

Thus, it seems that asking for equality is not sufficient and that the quest for social justice and equity must accompany the first of the three mottos of the Revolution. Equity takes differences between people and their needs into account. Its application still does not protect people against abuses, but it makes it more easy to identify and fight them. Application of the principles of equity and social justice might, in the end, make people more equal whilst respecting their differences.

Applied to the field of mental health, advocating equity means arguing for parity of care in the sense of providing services and support in response to needs[2]. People with mental disorders, for example, may have to receive support in order to be able to realize their rights to treat-

---

[1] This, of course, applies only in the few countries in which there are established legal procedures for complaining and suing services or parts of government administration.

[2] In many countries services for people with mental disorders do not receive the same amount of resources as do those dealing with people suffering from other diseases (e.g. in terms of compensation for days spent in hospital).

ment or disability pensions. Fighting stigma and discrimination because of mental illness must be an essential part of mental health programmes and most receive appropriate additional resources. The families of people with some forms of mental illness need more (and different) support than families dealing with other long-lasting diseases.

Fraternity does no better in terms of usefulness to people with mental illness than did equality. It implies that people united by some formal link – for example, that of being members of the same family – will accept the obligation of sharing their time, energy and other assets with other members of the same cluster. Brothers do not select, by free and informed consent, to become brothers: they are brothers because they were born to the same parents. They share a proportion of their genes and sometimes have physical similarities. They do not necessarily like each other nor are they always willing to demonstrate their fraternal love. They also fight against one another and sometimes become bitter enemies.

It is therefore necessary to conceive society as being dependent on solidarity rather than to expect that societies will survive by relying only on groups and networks that have been linked by some externally imposed rule. Societies can live and flourish if they augment their social capital as well as their human and economic capitals[3]. Social capital has been defined as the public good that results from the totality of the mutually supportive relationships that exist in a society. While useful in simplifying the description of elements that are important in describing a society, the notion of social capital carries with it the danger that the value of relationships between people will be assessed in the same way as the value of other goods on the market – coffee, computers, sugar, copper ore or chemical fertilizers. Should this happen, it would be logical to discard some types of relationships as being too expensive and to introduce others which are less costly. To an extent this danger is diminished by defining the social capital as the public good, i.e. a good that belongs to all members of the society and not to any one member. It is, however, also necessary to be constantly

---

[3] The economic capital refers to the totality of material goods of a society and the human capital to the numbers of economically productive members of a society.

aware that social relationships have components that cannot be converted into monetary value.

Social capital is reflected in the participation of the members of a population in civic activities, in the acceptance of norms of reciprocity of useful actions and in the amount of trust in other members of the group. Social capital has its structure – networks governed by certain rules and procedures leading to mutually beneficial relationships – and its cognitive content – the value system that is shared by members of a society. Relationships among people are often divided into horizontal (e.g. among friends) and vertical (e.g. among generations) links: horizontal links are further examined to establish whether they are restricted to members of the society or whether they stretch to reach others outside of a defined group in society. When links with those outside of the immediate social group are weak, the dangers of confrontation between groups grow and the disadvantages of those who live on the territory of a group without links with others on it are numerous.

The amount of the social capital depends on its use – the more intense the use of the relationships, the more likely is the increase of the society's social capital – and the less the social capital is used, the more likely it is that it will be depleted. Importantly also, the increase of social capital will usually lead to an increase of the human capital, and through this to an increase in the economic capital of societies: the opposite is not necessarily going to happen.

Solidarity as implied in the framework of social capital can produce significant benefits in the economic and political domains and improve the quality of life of citizens of a society. Civic association, adherence to the rules of reciprocity and mutual trust can help in efforts to provide feebler members of a community, e.g. children, the disabled and the elderly, with essential care and protection. Well-structured societies have lesser crime rates. Bonding ties (e.g. within family) coexistent with positive bridging links (e.g. to other societies) can help in the avoidance of conflict and violence while preserving the cultural heritage of a society. Strong social networks have been shown to have a positive influence on the outcome of disease and on its course. In terms of social capital, every member of society has value. Even persons who are totally dependent on others for their survival have value because caring for them represents moral earnings and demonstrates the values that the society has accepted.

Civic societies are characterized by abundant social capital. This, in addition to the fact that such societies are likely to accept the supremacy of ethical rules over moral norms, makes it possible for the members of a community to take care of those of its members who are weak (such as those impaired as a result of a disease or other reason) or a passing through a crisis without collapsing or experiencing burn-out and consequent problems. Indeed, the level of civilization – the closeness to civic society – can be measured by the amount of attention and care that a society gives to its weakest and most voiceless members.

There are obvious relationships between the growth of social capital and well-designed mental health programmes. The care for people with mental illness depends to a significant degree on the social relationships in the society in which they live. Negative attitudes concerning people with mental illness will decrease access to treatment. If the members of a society have no respect for people in distress, they will not respect those with a mental illness. This will be particularly painful and detrimental to the people who suffer from such illnesses. People with mental illness have to be able to find their place in a supportive network that is willing to accept that in certain characteristics they are different from others. This will only happen if the society's social capital is sufficiently developed to maintain such supportive networks.

Mental health programmes can also contribute to the growth of social capital. They can help by providing care to individuals who have mental disorders likely to be accompanied by disruptive behaviour so as to make it easier for them to control it. They can promote mutually supportive relationships involving family members, patients and health care workers. They can reduce the indirect cost of mental illness by providing timely and appropriate support to carers. If well structured, mental health programmes can produce methods for the prevention of burn-out and social malaise.

Many of the measures that help to improve mental health programmes will also contribute to the growth of social capital. Legal measures that support social cohesion and family health can help mental health care and increase social capital. School and other early-age programmes directed to the enhancement of tolerance for difference and abnormality make for better human relationships and facilitate mental health care. The recognition of merit of those who provide care for people with a chronic mental illness (e.g. people with dementia) will help carers in their tasks and life: at the same time such recognition will promote other forms of civic contributions to society. Emphasis on maintaining norms of mutually useful reciprocity, and on the creation of civic associations, is helping to make societies function better in every respect, including their reaction when faced with disability, violence and other psychosocial problems.

The insistence on the development of horizontal links among the members of the community does not negate usefulness of closed links established among traditional social groups such as families: it complements them. Nor does it stand in the way of the establishment of vertical links between related and unrelated members of the community. It is therefore sensible to propose that the motto of Fraternity of the Revolution should be complemented by the motto of Solidarity among members of the broader community, particularly when the society is faced with the need to help people in distress.

The third part of the French Revolution's slogan – Liberty – will also have to be complemented in civic societies. The liberty of action of any member of the society has its limits in the responsibility towards other members of the community. Responding to needs of the less fortunate – for example, impaired – members of a society increases the liberty of all its members. In societies striving to become civilized, responsibilities are never limited to those related to the members of the narrow social group – for example, the family or the clan: they refer to all the members of a society and indeed of humanity.

Balancing liberties and responsibilities prevents the acceptance of boundless liberty, a state that does not always improve the quality of life. Dealing with liberty and matching duties requires training and experience. Without it the imposition of liberty can be experienced as a burden. In the countries of Eastern Europe, for example, political changes led to changes in the lives of large numbers of people who, for several generations, saw their duties and activities defined for them by others. Whether the activities and way of life were good or bad is of less importance than the fact that the decisions about them were not in the hands of the people themselves. Suddenly these rules, tasks (and merit for performing them) vanished. People were supposed to decide for themselves – and their families – how to proceed, how to live their lives. They were given the freedom to do as they pleased but had not been trained or prepared for so much liberty of action. Combined with economic insecurity, with the bankruptcy of many of the ideals that were considered sacred and with the shattering of beliefs into matters such as military might – the liberty to do as they please (in conditions of unexpected scarcities) was experienced as a burden. People who spend years in mental hospitals may have a similar experience. The weakening of restrictive and paternalistic cultures and traditions occurring in developing countries, hailed as a new freedom by some, has been experienced by many as a stressful time; in addition, it has affected the capacity of communities to contain disabled members and the elderly. Learning how to live with liberty may take time and support in order to learn how to enjoy it and how to accept the social and personal responsibilities that go with it.

The Declaration of Human Rights that the unfortunate king of France has signed (and which never got him much credit) also needs an update in the year 2002. Human rights – like Liberty – depend on the fulfilment of duties of those who claim the rights and of others who surround them. The right to have free time is linked to the duty to contribute to society and its other members – through work or other means, for example, kindness and understanding. The right to be respected is linked to the duty to respect others. The right to be protected against abuse in illness or old age is part of the system of rights and duties that require tolerance of difference, engagement in civic associations and participation in the functioning of societies.

Thus, with the wisdom of hindsight it would seem sensible to complement the quest for equality with that for equity; that for fraternity with that for solidarity; the striving for liberty with the insistence on the acceptance of responsibilities by all concerned; and the emphasis on the realization of human rights with that on the fulfilment of civic and other duties.

2

Doubts about three of the many dogmas of development

Increasing resources given to health and education, arresting population growth and conducting health service research (so as to rationally develop health care) are among the dogmas of development. On closer examination, however, these dogmas look less convincing and it is obvious that there are a number of conditions that have to be fulfilled if they are to retain any value.

Ivan Lackovic Croata (b. 1932): 'The Village on an Altar' (1969). (Courtesy of Ivan Lackovic Croata.)

There are statements that have been repeated so often and by so many that they have the ring of truth and seem to be self-evident. Most of them are half-truths and one of the halves is usually expressing something that we would really like to believe. Three dogmas concerning the improvement of health that seem to be particularly widely held will be discussed below, to exemplify some of the many fallacies of thinking about socio-economic development.

In developing countries a relatively modest financial support to health and education will have significant results

It is perfectly true that in many developing countries the health situation is poor and the educational needs are great. Communicable diseases still rage and non-communicable diseases are growing in numbers and rates. More recently some of the communicable diseases that were considered to be under control reassumed importance and reappeared as public health problems. Malaria and tuberculosis are among the best examples of this trend. New communicable diseases have made their appearance: Lyme disease, hanta virus pulmonary syndrome, Legionnaires' disease, toxic shock syndrome, AIDS and erlichiosis (Harvard Working Group, 1995).

A large proportion of the population is illiterate. Many educational institutions are dilapidated and the educational methods used in primary and secondary schools and at university level are outdated. There are no training materials. Emotional burn-out is frequently seen in teachers. There is corruption, degree buying and political abuse of schools.

It seems logical therefore that more resources should be invested in health and educational programmes, but perhaps this is not the case. In many countries increases of the health budget will not change the situation in the sense that we would like to see it changed. Increases in the amounts given to health care are very likely to be spent in capital cities to develop top-class facilities equipped with every possible modern diagnostic and therapeutic apparatus. It might also be that the number of young and promising scientists that will be sent abroad for training will be increased. The purchase of some of the modern and more efficacious medicaments might also be on the list of items competing for parts of the augmented budget. In some instances particularly important people of great merit or their friends might be more regularly sent abroad when in need of examination and treatment.

None of these ways of spending the additional money is wrong. It is natural and important that developing countries also develop facilities of excellent quality so that they can use the most modern treatment techniques or develop new ones. People who were sent for training abroad often have to have exceptional facilities to use what they have learned because they would otherwise not return to their country after training abroad. Excellent facilities might also be used for the training of young graduates so that they do not have to go abroad to be trained in modern medicine. Medicine is developing very rapidly and it will be very important that a developing country follows the improvement of technology. There is nothing wrong either in sending bright young doctors abroad so as to enable them to bring home new technology.

And, as for people who have done a great deal for their country and for humanity: what could be wrong with flying them to the best centres in the world so that they can receive the best possible treatment for their ailment[1].

So the additional money may well be spent on these worthy purposes (or on others similar to them) without improving the overall health situation in the country very much. The fact that modern and excellent new medicaments have been introduced in the country and can be provided at government's expense to a certain proportion of patients does little to improve the treatment of the same disease in the country as a whole. The increased probability that well-trained young graduates will return from their training abroad and work at home will do very little to prevent the burn-out of the health care workers on the periphery toiling for many years with a miserable salary, without incentives or rewards for the often excellent work they have done. Sending people with merit for treatment abroad will once more confirm the belief of

---

[1] It is questionable whether this privilege should also be extended to their friends, although some of them may have merit in their own right.

the indigenous population that their hospitals are not particularly good.

The situation is somewhat similar in the field of education. Additional investments are often used to increase the number of graduate and postgraduate training facilities. Some of the training institutions are provided with special educational equipment. The numbers of students are increased and so is the number of graduates. Graduate and sometimes even secondary education is provided in a foreign language so as to facilitate postgraduate training and communication with other scientists or educational specialists. Occasionally, the whole system is thoroughly evaluated in preparation for an educational reform.

But, here again, these laudable changes have their dark side. In some developing countries vast investments have been made to increase opportunities for graduate education. In Colombia, for example, several years ago some 28 medical schools were in operation producing medical graduates in large numbers. In other countries too, the number of graduate institutions has grown much faster than the country's capacity to provide appropriate employment to the graduates. The resulting difficulties were sometimes entrusted to another sector, the Ministry of Labour for example, who conducted retraining courses. Occasionally, brain drain resolved part of the problem and reduced pressure to create jobs, at a huge loss of the investment into training people who will be working in other countries. Sometimes it was possible for a government to export young graduates as part of a political commitment to help another country: numerous Cuban doctors, at one point of time, could be found in the most remote of African countries. Sometimes the graduates took on other jobs which had nothing to do with their original training.

Training given in a foreign language usually resulted in a higher likelihood of emigration of the graduates to other countries. Most of the total revamps of the educational systems resulted in failure after a very short time. Personnel of an educational institution, faced with a bold reform, rarely accepted relearning of their trade, and continued teaching as before giving their instruction a new name. Sometimes reforms followed each other quite rapidly, sometimes they touched some parts of the system but not others, leading to differences in qualifications of people carrying the same title.

In addition, all these changes and innovations resulting from additional investments usually leave peripheral schools with their problems and do little to correct the functional literacy of the population at large. The epidemic of burn-out among teachers in primary schools and the continuous deterioration of the quality of their teaching continues unabated. The physical condition of schools and other training institutions deteriorate further.

What is the answer then? The other side of the half-truth that health and education in developing countries need more support is that they need a very, very great deal of support. It is unlikely that reasonable increases will make a real difference. There will be wastage. Some of the money will disappear because of mismanagement, corruption and errors. Some of the irrational investments – the translation of some textbooks into Esperanto, perhaps – will still occur. But, by the mechanism of overflow, if there is enough money to build an outstandingly advanced hospital and still much more is left over, it becomes probable that the peripheral health services will also receive some attention and that the distribution of medicaments to rural areas will begin to become regular. Once there is sufficient money to fund a large number of fellowships, it will become possible to invite some of the peripherally located doctors or nurses to apply with a chance of being selected. Once the quality of the hospitals in the country obtains the reputation of being excellent, it is possible that people of special merit will accept being treated there rather than seeking treatment abroad.

Such a manna, however, is not very probable. Sometimes a major political upheaval results in a huge influx of resources into the field of health or education, but such events are rare, and political promises of investments and foreign help often remain words without follow-up. For many years to come, it will be necessary to accept that additional investments into health and education will be meagre and rare. They may be received from abroad on a single occasion or for a (unpredictably) short time. There might even be occasions when support to the strategically most important activities is received: whether it will be well used and for long and whether it will continue to come, however, remains open.

It is therefore reasonable and necessary to foresee how best to survive with the meagre resources that exist, rather than to expect continuing significant input from elsewhere. That stance calls for considerable patience and tolerance of constraints for years and years. It also calls for an acceptance of the fact that health and education sectors will improve in parallel with improvements in other sectors, e.g. the judiciary, which, if strong, could help in the implementation of laws and agreements about the use of resources, regular or special that the country will receive. The probability that a single sector of governmental activity, e.g. health, can develop more quickly, if given additional support for a while, is on the whole low.

Population growth has to be controlled because it is a major reason for delayed development

Another half-truth, fervently held and proclaimed by numerous inter-governmental and non-governmental agencies engaged in activities supporting socio-economic development is that population growth is dangerous. It is stated that population growth decreases the amount of resources for the health care per child and that this in turn reduces the probability that they will grow well. Other pundits predict that the Earth as a whole, and most developing countries in particular, cannot sustain the necessary increase of food production, and that every effort to do so will harm the ecological balance of the country and the world. Health agencies and organizations concerned with the welfare of women put forward the fact that too many children will exhaust the women giving birth to them, and prevent them from taking full part in their country's development. Nationalist-minded politicians in some countries attract their voters by painting a spectre of vast numbers of immigrants from countries characterized by rapid population growth. Health economists show that it is less expensive to reduce population growth than to provide better conditions for the growth of children or for family development. Educational specialists argue that the large numbers of children in classes, that in their opinion are the inevitable consequence of the larger number of children, does not permit appropriate instruction.

Although there is no firm evidence for some of the above statements – it is, for example, uncertain whether the increase of numbers of children will increase emigration, and it is not certain at what number of children per class the quality of instruction significantly decreases – it is possible to accept that all the above statements are true. And yet, the conclusion that rapid population growth is the main obstacle to development is unacceptable unless it is postulated that several conditions relevant to this assessment are stable and unalterable.

There is no reason to believe, for example, that it is impossible to increase the capacity of health services to a level at which they will be capable of looking after the health of more children than they do now. Recent debates seem to indicate that the increase of productivity of investments into industry is so large that it is well possible to give a larger part of the gross national product to health and other social services without harming the investments into other sectors of concern to the governments and industries. The often cited proposal to decrease expenditures for arms and wars and use the savings for the improvement and expansion of health care is not intrinsically impossible and might happen once politicians' wisdom comes closer to ethical and social maturity.

The argument that the increase of population will exhaust the resources of the Earth was advanced many years ago. Since then it has been put to rest many times. Undoubtedly, the resources of the world are finite and the general strategy of sustainable development has much merit. This, however, does not mean that the resources of the developing countries will be exhausted primarily because of population growth. Corruption, dishonesty, mismanagement, ignorance and unrealistic plans, are much better targets to go for than population growth if the resources of the world are to be preserved. Population density in the developed countries is incomparably higher than that in the majority of developing countries. The surface of sub-Saharan Africa is enormous and much of the land is arable. In Latin America the expanses of uninhabited land are huge and there is no need to annihilate the tropical forests to get agricultural land. Some of the developing countries in Asia still have unused land and possibilities for expanding it. In all instances it is not the land that is at issue but the political realities of the world today. A flow of resources from developed into developing countries could increase the latter's agricultural productivity many times. A more equitable approach to the Earth's resources would make population growth a minor issue for a very long time to come. Undoubtedly, population growth will have to be reduced, in time: it has reduced itself in the developed countries, not before the economic development, but in parallel with it.

Women can be exhausted if they give birth to too many children. This is, however, so provided that all other circumstances negatively affecting the woman's position in the world remain equal. But these can be changed and should be changed before, or simultaneously with, the insistence on the control of childbearing. Women could be given an equitable position in relation to health care in general so that they can obtain advice and help when they need it and without delay, on all matters including childbearing. Women could be given better and easier access to education and learn a great deal more about the way in which life could be organized and children raised. Society could begin to recognize the tremendous contribution that a woman makes by giving birth and bringing up a child – not by empty phrases but by providing a salary to a mother for the supreme task of producing valuable citizens of today's world. A reduction of child morbidity and mortality would also reduce the risk of losing several children before a sickly one remains alive; this would have a powerful influence on decisions about childbearing. Governments could become more generous in their support to the family and more flexible in their decisions concerning child rearing, allowing, for example, a sufficiently long time off work for the mother or the father to take care of the child. None of these requirements is in the way of the recommendation that women should space their children in a manner that will be best for the family, for themselves, for their children and their societies. They are listed here because they are at least equivalent to the quick fix of tubectomy, vasectomy or prolonged hormonal or other contraception with all their possible side effects. Some of the international and national agencies in this field have gradually changed from promoting contraception and family planning to the promotion of appropriate child and family care including contraception: the acceptance of this more general approach is often more in words than in deeds because a more comprehensive approach requires more effort, more money and greater investment into the change of attitudes, none of which is welcome to the authorities.

The argument of reducing immigration to a country by the expedient of supporting efforts to control population growth in its poor neighbouring countries borders on the ridiculous and is certainly unethical. There are many reasons for immigration and many obstacles to it that have little to do with the size of the population. Even if the connection existed, it would be unethical to promote a reduction of the population size because some of its members might wish to live elsewhere.

The economists' argument is also easy to refute. It might be true that it is less expensive to slow down population growth than to improve conditions for children's and families growth and welfare. This might be true in the immediate future: the gains from an increase of the population able to produce and contribute to society while consuming less health care because of better conditions of life might easily outweigh the initial savings obtained by opting for a reduction of population growth.

Population growth is an important factor in development and there are many measures that are necessary to optimize it. The control of its rate may also be advisable in certain circumstances. The presentation of these two arguments, however, must be made remembering the complex tissue of social and economic factors that have to be taken into account before making the reduction of population growth the main target of developmental efforts.

Health services research will help the development of health services in developing countries

Some time ago, research into the functioning of health services and other forms of operations research was hailed as a major potential contributor to the development of health services.

It was argued that good health services research could indicate where resources are spent sub-optimally; that results of such research can guide health policy makers in their arduous tasks; that participation in such research can help to acquire the habit of rational thinking about health problems; that advice, that can be formulated on the basis of monitoring and observation done in a scientifically impeccable manner, will be vastly superior to any other advice. In many countries – in the developing and developed world – governments invested in health research. In some cases institutes or governmental departments were created to carry out investigations of the functioning of health services, and to formulate advice about further investment into health care. The production of books and other materials, facilitating the understanding of how health services research should be done and how to use its findings, soared. International networks of individuals and institutions working in the area came into existence. Planners of health services grabbed the mantle of health services research and declared that their predictions and recommendations concerning the development of health services were scientifically grounded and therefore should be protected from change or modifications. Health service research was declared useful for health service development, although there was no evidence that the results of health service research significantly influenced the development of health programmes or that its findings modified health policies and consequent action.

There are several reasons that can be invoked to explain why findings of health services research failed to have any significant impact on their development. First, the rhythms of research and that of service change rarely showed synchrony. Governments make changes when the political situation requires that this be done, not when the results of research are ready. Sometimes, they fund health service research so as to be able to postpone an unpopular decision pretending to await results of studies. Sometimes, however, a government official would use the results of research in decisions: only too often relevant studies take too much time (or have to be complemented by additional studies) so that the results are ready long after the date when the decision has to be made.

But there are also real difficulties in making results of research on social sector services (such as health care) useful and used. One of them is the uncertainty about the homogeneity of groups that are studied. Researchers often have to take shortcuts or deliberately omit the consideration of the complexity of a variable, assuming that this will not affect the results too much. Groupings such as urban, of foreign descent, or aged 20–50, hide a universe of differences that can seriously affect the interpretation of findings. Sometimes, the canons of social research help to avoid errors of this type, but there is often not enough evidence about the impact that a grouping of variables might have, so that the investigators 'for the time being' use composite variables as if they were suitable for the description of groups. Numerous other methodological difficulties besetting the field of services research have had no real or easy answer until now and, for some of them, it is unlikely that there will ever be one.

It is therefore probable that the statement that health service research is useful for service development has to be accompanied by an enumeration of the conditions that will make it useful. These might include (i) that health service research should not be undertaken unless there is a high probability that the government or other service providers will use the results once they are produced; (ii) that it must be possible to terminate the study in the time defined by the decision makers; if that is not possible the investigations should not be undertaken; (iii) that health service research should concentrate on well-specified aspects of service functioning rather than attempt to examine the health system as a whole. The interpretation of results of such focused, short-term studies, however, should be made taking the broader picture and the variety of factors known to be of importance in these matters into account; (iv) that health service research findings should never be taken as the main input to the formulation of recommendations for action: such recommendations should be made taking into account the results of research and all other factors that are of relevance; (v) and that service research should involve the eventual users in the conduct of research.

The doubts about these three dogmas of development are no more than examples of ways in which widely held beliefs do not stand up to even superficial scrutiny. The reduction of complexity of a problem summarized in the form of a dogma is useful in searching for money and in mobilizing people. It is less useful, and sometimes harmful, when allowed to govern programme planning and implementation. Perhaps the time has come to critically examine the many dogmas of development in order to understand why so many development programmes have failed. This would perhaps result in a new paradigm of development – a change that I believe would save effort and resources and make development possible and useful for the welfare of people that should at all times be at its centre.

REFERENCE

Harvard Working Group (1995). New and resurgent diseases. *The Ecologist*, **25**, 21–26.

3

Overlaps and confusions

A major obstacle to the development of psychiatry and of mental health programmes is the vagueness of their fundamental concepts. There is confusion about the ethical, moral and legal prescriptions for behaviour in society and about their hierarchy. Definitions of mental health abound and range from being in bliss and happiness to the absence of psychosis: under these circumstances, it is difficult to rally forces and take united and firm action, which is necessary for any successful programme.

Four sets of terms overlap and produce harmful confusion in the mental health field. They concern mental malady, the adjectives to describe it, the frames in which it is handled and the needs that arise because of it. Each of the terms concerned describes a specific notion and can be well defined. Yet, their semantic spheres overlap and they are often used wrongly. The resulting confusions are each a major obstacle to the development of mental health programmes.

Mad, bad and mentally ill

Some of the acts that are transgressing against the basic ethical principles or deeply ingrained moral rules – such as killing others or robbing people – are committed under circumstances that exculpate those who commit them. Soldiers are expected to kill when defending their country and sometimes in other circumstances. Revolutionaries do not necessarily respect private property and take things without permission of the owner.

When such circumstances do not prevail, acts of this kind are labelled criminal. People who commit them usually show no overt signs of mental disorder. Their cognitive functions are in good order. They do not behave as the ethical, moral or legal rules prescribed, but seem to be otherwise no different from the rest of their peers. People who suffer from mental illness also commit such unacceptable acts. They might kill, steal, or disturb others in serious ways.

And then there are some who do things quite out of the ordinary or engage in other sports that are so dangerous that they might die in the

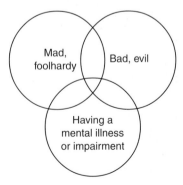

effort and leave their families without any source of support, or end up disabled for life.

In some instances people who do not respect moral or ethical requirements – who are bad – also get a mental illness. Sometimes, foolhardy people are also criminal. Sometimes, mentally ill people are very brave and will also put their life at risk during their mental illness. But, the associations are relatively rare and there are no causal connections between these three types of reasons for unusual, dangerous or unacceptable acts. It would be immensely useful if unusual behaviour were to be examined to establish to which of these three groups of reasons it can be ascribed.

The control of unusual behaviour should also follow the logic of its causes. The measures for the prevention of evil acts committed by people who do not show signs of derangement of mental functions should be in the hands of authorities that societies have established to protect themselves against dangers stemming from asocial acts committed by individuals. What will be considered mad will vary from society to society and it will be up to the mores of the society in which such individuals live to decide who may engage in what kind of dangerous activity. Society might wish to prohibit the climbing of some mountains, declare some streams forbidden for swimming or boating, or request that boxers wear helmets and very large gloves. And, people who have a mental disorder should be offered help and treatment that will diminish or remove the impairment of their mental functioning.

Clarifying at every relevant level – in the course of formal and informal education, through the media, in laws and in social sectors services – that socially undesirable or dangerous acts have different explanations might diminish the stigma from which people with mental illness suffer. It might also improve the chances of success for activities undertaken to prevent behaviours that are socially unacceptable. The current confusion about reasons for abnormality leads to confused and harmful interventions. People with mental illness are put into prisons. Bad people avoid punishment by acting or being declared mentally ill. Evil acts are sometimes also forgiven because they are seen as being an expression of foolhardiness and vice versa.

Moral, legal and ethical

Ethics is the study of good and bad and the search for features that distinguish them. *Morals* describe standards of rectitude prevailing in a particular society at a given point in time. *Ethical* denotes accordance of an action with general or ideal standards of good and bad, of right or wrong. *Moral* (as an adjective) is used to describe the accordance of an action with the standards prevailing in a particular society at a given point in time[1]. Finally *legal* describes the accordance of an action with the laws in a given society.

A central issue in ethical study is to know what is good and what is bad. There are at least four ways in which good and bad have been defined. The first is by the intervention of a divine being who has from time immemorial defined the good and the bad and ordered humankind to maintain the original distinction or be punished. The second is by reference to the evolutionary advantages that the acceptance of certain rules has for the species. The third is by historical analysis showing the immutability and repeated appearance of the same rules in different cultures and in different religious systems. The fourth is by consensus of the just and wise, by the so wise that they can, despite their own anchors in time, see or sense the eternal truth.

Ethical rules are, for all intents and purposes, fairly immutable.

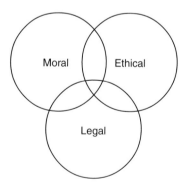

---

[1] For a more extensive discussion of this difference, please see also Ethics and societies of the world in Okasha, A.J., Arboleda Florez, J. and N. Sartorius (2000): *Ethics, Culture and Society*, American Psychiatric Press, Washington and London, pp. 3–13.

Their change is probably possible but happens rarely, and when it does happen occurs in a manner similar to that described in the writings about the change of paradigms of science.

In most societies and at most times, there is an overlap between ethical and moral requirements and standards. Moral rules, however, change more quickly. They are created by a particular group of people at a given time. Sometimes, moral rules are imposed by the majority on the minority and sometimes the reverse is true. On occasion, a mighty country will force a less powerful country to accept its moral rules. They are often imposed under the false pretence, declared to be ethical.

Legal rules are usually in harmony with the moral rules prevailing in a society. Sometimes they become obsolete, or refer to the rules of a previous time in the same society. In the preambular paragraphs, laws also sometimes make oblique or direct references to the ethical requirements. In most societies, legal rules are imposed with threats of punishment for their non-observance. When they are harmonious with moral norms, the society – and particularly its middle class – will also help to ensure their observance by imposing social sanctions on those who do not behave in accordance with legal standards.

Unfortunately for psychiatry, the overlap and the significant difference between these three concepts are rarely recognized. Moral rules are mistaken for ethical prescriptions. Laws are made to try to approach moral principles rather than to reflect ethical standards. The adjective ethical is used to justify actions that are inspired by society at the time of consideration and that might even be in direct contradiction to the ethical rules. The behaviour of the health system and of psychiatrists is inspired by morals: the abuse of psychiatry might therefore at one point be morally and legally acceptable (although ethically unacceptable) and at some other point in time considered abhorrent. The current morals say that scientific evidence should be used in decisions about therapy, involuntary detention in psychiatric institutions and similar matters. Science is supposed to tell us the truth and should therefore guide: but scientific evidence is incomplete and actions of psychiatrists continue to be guided by other considerations that have little to do with science.

Legal prescriptions concerning the mentally ill are obsolete in many countries. In others there are no laws that deal with people suffering from a mental illness. Most of the laws become obsolete soon after (and sometimes before) they are enacted. They should be changed whenever necessary to reflect the state of knowledge and our comprehension of what is good and bad. Their relationship with morals should be a subject of debate and evaluation. They should be harmonized with ethical tenets and morals recognizing that ethical rules and moral rules have set hierarchies within them. Laws have to be written with reference to the actual situation in the country in which they are to be used. So, for example, requesting two signatures by qualified medical practitioners to certify that an involuntary admission is necessary is supposed to protect the rights of the mentally ill. This is an ethical requirement. The law should reflect this requirement except if it is to be enacted in a country where there are so few qualified medical practitioners that it would take a long time to obtain the two signatures, which would make it impossible to protect the patient from harm by admitting him to an institution. In this instance, the need to protect the life of the patient and others surrounding him or her has a higher (ethical) priority than the protection of the right to self-determination.

Disease, illness and sickness

The English language has the luxury of having at least three different words for the concept of malady: illness referring to the experience of the individual patient; disease referring to the medical decision that there is a pathological process that can be diagnosed and often be stopped or slowed down by specific medical interventions; and sickness referring to the society's recognition that an individual's state of health has to be recognized by society as a state of lesser functional capacity, for example, leading to the payment of sickness benefits.

With the exception of severe forms of physical disease, the conceptual areas covered by the three terms are significantly different. People often feel very ill, although doctors cannot discover any changes in body tissues, nor any significant abnormality in body functions. Illness is usually the main reason for consulting the doctor or another person thought to be able to help. Most cultures and languages have specific words to describe illnesses: such words are, by and large, not available for the labelling of diseases. The medical language containing the labels used by doctors to describe diseases has, in recent years, invaded the language spoken by the people. Ordinary people now use medical terms such as 'depression' to describe their illness. When they do, doctors sometimes believe that patients are referring to the same state that makes doctors use a particular disease label: this, however, is rarely so.

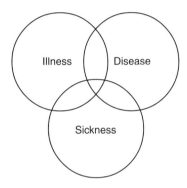

Terms that describe illnesses are not particularly welcome in health services. The instructions regulating the health care practice prescribe treatments for diseases not for illnesses. The past century has been characterized by hope, nay, conviction that all morbid states will reach the nosological status of a disease. To call a condition a disease, we must know its causes, its pathogenesis, the symptoms and syndromes that the pathological process produces and the way in which the condition will progress, with and without treatment. Unfortunately, the expectation that that much will be known about all morbid states has proven to be far too optimistic: in recent years we have had to admit that our knowledge about most of the non-communicable conditions does not allow us to call them diseases. Discarding the terms by which people described illnesses has obviously been premature: perhaps it would be valuable to return to the notes of anthropologists and to read records of doctors who lived and wrote about the things patients told them in the past centuries.

The term 'sickness' is another reminder of the fact that medicine must remain conscious of its role as an art of helping people in distress. Societies decide what they will admit as a state of sufficient impairment to provide help, give a pension, offer or impose treatment. The abuse of psychiatry for political purposes has been, and remains, a sad example of what can happen when medical terms and the health professions are taken as a convenient excuse to remove people who are disturbing by being different (or are asking unpleasant questions) from the public arena. The abuse of medicine for political purposes is not limited to psychiatry: the definition of blindness in the USA, for example, has been heavily influenced by the estimation of the monies that would have had to be paid out, if almost complete blindness had been accepted as the limit of blindness. Doctors have accepted the dubious privilege of being given the authority of declaring that a morbid state is sufficiently incapacitating to deserve the label of sickness that will lead to a permission to stay off work. The severity of illness that accompanies disease states is only rarely given sufficient weight in this process. And yet, it is usually the severity of illness which determines the behaviour of the patient. It determines whether the patient will seek help, take the prescribed treatment and follow advice about his or her lifestyle.

Needs of individuals, families and communities

The previously used ways of estimating needs for psychiatric services have been shown to be of little use. Counting those who have a particular type of illness and then estimating what services are needed to treat these individuals is neither easy nor useful.

There are several reasons for this. First, the needs of the patients, of the community and of the family are not identical although they overlap. Governments, for example, are interested in diminishing costs of treatment and will therefore insist on the use of the cheapest possible treatment among those that are similar in their efficacy. Patients will insist that their treatment should not only diminish their suffering but also that there should be no side effects that impact on their quality of life. The families might also be keen to ensure that the treatment is given by the most qualified specialists and reject care offered by primary care workers. A question that arises for those planning health services will therefore be: whose needs are most important? Sometimes, doctors will be forced to accept limitations and constraints imposed by the government, although they know that their patients will not be very happy with the treatment or with other services that the government decided they should receive.

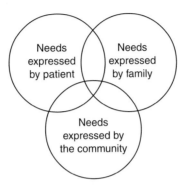

Another question, close to the first, also arises: should health services cater for diseases, for illnesses or for sickness? Psychiatrists, as members of the medical profession, should in their treatment plans be primarily influenced by the disease of their patients. Patients, on the other hand, are particularly keen to get treatment that will deal with their illness. Psychiatrists also have to accept their role as agents of society and decide on the level of sickness of the individuals they treat. The overlap between the three aspects of malady – the disease, the sickness and the illness – is not always very large, and the treatment interventions might differ depending on what is taken as the primary target for action.

The overlap of needs also influences the evaluation of effectiveness of treatment. The decision about which needs have to be addressed first might upset the routine of doctors. Physicians may wish to eliminate or suppress all symptoms of a disease, even if that can be done only at the cost of producing unpleasant side effects. Patients, on the other hand, might wish to be free of side effects even if that means that some of their symptoms will not be controlled by the treatment.

The four areas of overlap described above are of direct relevance to the development of mental health programmes, to their evaluation and to their acceptance by society, by the patient and by the health professionals. A consistent use of definition of these terms would be a blessing for all concerned. The confusion that now reigns harms everyone.

4

Nearly forgotten: mental health needs of an urbanized planet

By 2020 most of the world's population – an estimated 80% of it – will live in cities. Health care in most of the world's cities is deficient in coverage and quality. The political and social consensus about the development of primary health care was useful but focused mainly on the provision of care in rural settings. There is, as yet, no consensus nor international political backing for a strategy that would ensure health and mental health care in cities. Reaching agreement on strategies for urban health care has become urgent.

Pedal rickshaws and motor vehicles clog the streets of Dhaka, Bangladesh. (Photograph by Rafiqur Rahman, courtesy of Reuters and Popperfoto.)

It is an amazing fact that governments of the world, faced with rampant urbanization, have not developed a strategy for the provision of health care in cities. In less than 30 years' time four-fifths of the world population – in developed and developing countries – will be living in urban areas. This represents a steady growth for industrialized countries and a revolutionary change for most of the others. It is easy to predict that this change will bring new health problems or magnify those currently facing health care in an unprecedented manner: it is also probable that a well-formulated plan of action to counter these problems might make it easier to deal with them.

These predictions have to be considered against the background of three arrays of facts. The first concerns the size of future cities: it is very unlikely that cities will cease to grow when they reach the size of today's largest towns; judging from tendencies already visible in some developing countries the cities of the future will grow to unprecedented sizes – to agglomerations of dwellings of 20 or 30 million people. Megalopolises are not only cities grown big: they are likely to be different creatures – in the same vein as adults are not big children, although they continue to belong to the same biological species when they are children and when they grow up. This change – a revolution in Hegelian sense – means that most of the knowledge and administrative skills developed to manage cities will be only partially applicable to deal with life of a megalopolis; that health care organization as well as other social services will have to examine the applicability of their current strategies and ways of functioning systematically if they are to be useful. This change of size also means that cities will no longer have a decorative town hall and a ceremonial mayor: a future megalopolis the size of a country, or even a group of countries, will have the political processes and powers of a country the size of Romania, or of all the Nordic European countries put together.

The second array of facts concerns the locus of fastest growth. Urban growth is already much faster in the developing than in the industrialized countries. Life in Third world towns, with all its dangers and shortcomings, is still better than life in rural areas. Towns act as an irresistible magnet for the populations in the rural areas. Villagers in many countries become exhausted by their battle against corrupt administration, failing crops, the harsh environment and consequences of disasters rendered ever more costly in human life because of growing population density. Their vital forces get sapped up feeding guerrilla wars, by economic difficulties reflecting speculations at faraway stock exchanges, by expenses of pharaonic buildings, and by the continuing presence of (often preventable) communicable diseases. The apparent easy availability of all things in cities also exerts its influence, as do stories of successes and easy lives that some of the first migrants to cities have been able to lead.

Villagers no longer migrate to towns in small numbers and slowly: their move to cities is massive. They bring with them their culture and their habits, their manner of life often incompatible with functioning of large aggregations of humans sharing a restricted area. They are, at first, amazed by all that can be obtained, then despondent because all this wealth cannot be theirs; their search for a better life then takes different paths, from work for minimal wages (and without protection) to crime, violence and prostitution. Health care for newcomers to towns is neither that appropriate for the villages from which they came nor that of towns in which they now live.

Third world cities are not only growing faster than their counterparts in industrialized countries: they also differ from them in many other ways. The population density in Cairo in 1995 was 375 inhabitants per hectare and in Calcutta 220: in comparison, London had 40, and New York 44, inhabitants per hectare. The number of children and adolescents in the developing country cities is much higher than in the developed countries, reflecting the difference in demographic structure between those two types of countries in general. There are other differences, often neglected, that matter a great deal in organizing health care; the number of abandoned children and adolescents without family, for example, in some developing countries (e.g. in Latin America) is much higher than in the developed countries and continues to grow at a fast rate.

The third set of facts concerns the dramatic changes of the demographic composition and function of rural areas, the main donors of population to cities in many countries. Young and able-bodied people are often the first to leave home, with the resulting increase in proportion of the disabled, elderly and those too young to leave the rural areas. In some instances those who fail to succeed in towns or become disabled because of working conditions return to villages, further decreasing the capacity of the rural areas to function independently.

Villages near towns become dependent on them and on demands that towns make. Modern agricultural production reduces employment opportunities in rural areas, greatly increasing the numbers of the rural proletariat and of seasonal migrant agricultural populations now reaching vast numbers, for example, in the Americas. The change of production style in rural areas further contributes to the reasons for leaving villages and migrating to towns, without any hope or wish to return to the rural area.

Mental disorders in towns

The prevalence of mental disorders in cities differs from that in rural areas. In China, for example, schizophrenia seems to be more prevalent in cities and learning disability in villages (Cooper & Sartorius, 1996); in the UK, a 1995 survey showed that depressive disorders, generalized anxiety and phobias are higher in urban areas than in rural areas (Meltzer et al., 1995). There are more lonely chronic mentally ill people in cities than in villages. The homeless mentally ill in urban areas of industrialized countries are comparable to vagrant psychotics described in developing countries. It is uncertain, however, whether the mortality of these two groups is similar. It is also probable that mental disorders linked to early brain damage should be more prevalent in areas – urban slums or remote villages – in which access to health care and appropriate nutrition is difficult: unfortunately, these are also areas in which statistics (or results of studies) about morbidity from mental illness and mental impairment are less reliable, if available at all.

Drug and alcohol dependence have been described as urban mental health problems: there are, however, many areas in the Third world in which rural areas are just as strongly hit by drug dependence problems as the populations of towns (e.g. Pakistan, Thailand), and there is little doubt about the ravages that alcohol abuse and dependence create in rural areas in many countries.

Studies of schizophrenia showed differences in course and outcome of mental disorders between developing and developed countries. Systematic comparisons of course and outcome of schizophrenia and other mental disorders in urban and rural areas of developing and developed countries are, however, lacking and it is unlikely that such data will become available in the immediate future. What is true for major mental disorders such as schizophrenia may also be true for other mental disorders and for neurological disorders. Differences in the prevalence of mental disorders in urban and rural areas have also been described: there is, however, little agreement about the reasons for these differences, which may well, at least in part, be the result of variations in course and outcome of diseases.

While there is some information about differences in the prevalence of mental disorders in urban and rural areas, data about the differences in the severity of the psychosocial problems of cities are, by and large, lacking. Loneliness, anomia, stress-related disorders (e.g. hypertension) as well as various forms of antisocial behaviour (e.g. violence) are seen as being typical of cities: it is difficult to know whether the situations that have been described in cities of industrialized countries also exist in developing countries and to what extent they are qualitatively differ-ent from them. Violence has been epidemically and then endemically present in certain countries, in both rural and urban areas (e.g. Mexico, Colombia), and it is difficult to declare violence in those countries as a typically urban problem.

It may be that, in the future, the differences in prevalence rates of mental and physical disorders in towns and villages will diminish. In developing countries today, for example, people suffering from a chronic disease will move to towns where help for their condition is available and then stay there, thus increasing the prevalence of certain chronic diseases. The increased density of families that contained a person suffering from a mental disorder around hospitals has been demonstrated in the past in the USA: similar phenomena are even more visible in the newly created settlements at the doorsteps of mental hos-pitals, for example, in front of the Aro Mental Hospital in Abeokuta,

Nigeria. With the development of communications, i.e. roads and cheaper transport between towns and surrounding areas, this type of migration of selected groups of population might decrease, thus diminishing differences between towns and rural areas.

A recent report (Harvard Working Group on New and Resurgent Diseases, 1995) provides a gloomy forecast of diseases of the future by pointing out that infectious diseases remain the leading cause of death in the world, and that numerous diseases that were considered to be under control have made their way back to the top of the killing charts. Diphtheria has emerged as a major killer of adults in the countries of the Community of Independent States (in Russia alone the number of cases doubled between 1985 and 1992). Malaria and tuberculosis are creating major problems in many countries. Plague has made its way back in India and cholera has emerged in Latin America. Dengue fever, hemorrhagic fever and yellow fever as well as some diseases about which little was known (e.g. Lyme disease, hanta virus syndrome, toxic shock syndrome, AIDS and ehrlichiosis) have appeared on the lists of priorities for public health authorities. Changes of ecosystems, water management, major development programmes, pollution and over-harvesting of certain species (e.g. fish) as well as other excesses of socio-economic development combined with an increasing vulnerability of the human organism seem to make it certain that communicable diseases will continue to grow and create public health problems – the major difference probably being that they will no longer be restricted only to rural or only to urban areas but will hit both areas, and in them particularly the poor, with similar power.

Opportunities for health care interventions in cities

At present, urban areas offer opportunities for health care interventions that would be difficult to find in villages. The population is easier to reach in health campaigns. Health care personnel are concentrated in towns and are likely to stay there. Slum dwellers, particularly in the developing countries, are resourceful and can be motivated to participate in health care activities. Funding for health care is easier to find. In-service training for personnel of health and other social services is easier to organize. Quality assurance of health care facilities is less complex. Supplies of health care materials are easier to organize. Laboratories can function more efficiently. Politicians and other individuals of high public visibility can be shown health services in difficulty and be involved in improving them. Gaps between academia and practice can be diminished, and training of different categories of health care personnel can be carried out in health facilities serving the majority of the population.

Many of these opportunities for improving or providing health care in towns are not utilized; it is, however, important to remember them in defining health strategies for cities and in calculating investments that might be necessary to put urban health care into operation.

Possible areas of action

A prerequisite for the formation of a useful and usable strategy is agreement on the meaning of terms and concepts used in its formulation. In the instance of a strategy for health care in cities, the meaning of many of the concepts that have to be used changed in the past few years. There is no commonly accepted definition of a city, or of a village, township or town. Villages previously inhabited by farmers toiling the land nearby have become inhabited by middle class and richer people from towns who establish secondary residences in those villages now being described as romantic, charming, quaint and culturally traditional. Townships have forever lost their previous meaning and now remain synonymous with the aggregations of prefabricated and concentration camp-like structures established during apartheid in Zimbabwe and South Africa. Cities in the developing world have grown rapidly and often have the appearance of a huge camp of migrants or refugees situated around a dilapidated nucleus of a previously established small or medium-sized town housing the administrative centre of a province or a country, built over the past 100 years or so. The periphery of the settlement may contain the newest migrants to town; but there are vast differences in the manner in which these towns have grown and in which the population groups that make up the town have distributed the space occupied by the city. In some instances the original tribes or villages re-establish themselves in the new settlement; in other instances the social class structure prevails and the rich live with the rich, the poor with the poor. Developed country towns have also become different from what has been described by writers, sociologists and demographers in the past six or eight decades, during which much of the writing on the subject was done. Inner-city slums have been turned into expensive property and house the chic and rich; and the huge buildings or groups of buildings housing several thousand people have not infrequently turned into citadels, better depicted by artists in films or novels than by scientists who seem to write little about the structure and functioning of such conglomerates. Currently growing gaps between scientific disciplines do not help to learn more about these matters: geographers who produced excellent descriptions of new urban arrangements rarely write in a manner that is attractive to doctors; and even if they did, it is unlikely that public health decision makers or psychiatrists would be following this literature.

Even the concepts of a street or a park have different meanings from one setting to another. The streets in which house numbers go up to 10 000 or more represent different concepts from the street in most European towns, which never had more than a couple of hundred house numbers and in which it was highly probable that everybody knew everybody else. Towns that came into existence at different points of time bear characteristics of that time that distinguish them architecturally and functionally from one another, to a degree that makes it necessary that they organize the lives of their citizens and their health care in radically different ways. While basic medical skills required to work in towns may be similar, demographic features of a town, e.g. the preponderance of elderly persons, or of children, and various other characteristics of the city will require special or more skills in one area than in another.

Terms used to describe towns are not the only ones that have changed their meaning: the same is true for other frequently used notions and concepts, for example, that of the community. A community was defined earlier as a population subgroup occupying a defined geographic area and having links of mutual support: nowadays, the criterion of living in the same area is only rarely useful. Links of mutual support are still important but do not, any longer, exist primarily among neighbours. People inhabiting the same geographical area in modern towns often do not know each other and have little in common with the exception of their address: links of support are defined differently, by family ties, by the enterprise employing the bread-winner, by minority or language grouping. Administrative authorities still do not recognize this change of definition of community, and establish community health centres, for example, that are wasteful because they serve only a small subgroup of the population.

Nor is there agreement on the way in which the functioning of a town or the success of a health care intervention will be assessed. Indicators of change differ from one setting to another and their definition is often slightly, but significantly, different so that comparisons across services, across towns or across time are flawed.

It would be too ambitious at present to seek agreement on indicators of progress, on the definition of criteria, on methods of definition of areas of intervention (e.g. of 'communities'), or on criteria for the assessment of levels of priority, although this would be highly desirable. An immediate objective at present should be to work on the definition of terms in a manner that will allow their clear comprehension and a rational interpretation of the results of studies or of monitoring service interventions.

Next, it will be necessary to admit that towns have their personalities and that there is no such thing as a strict doctrine that will be applied in each case. The best that can be expected is agreement on certain principles that can serve as the frame for health care activities. These principles will have to be formulated, proclaimed and then used in developing plans, in educating the general public and in creating new generations of health workers. The essence of most of these principles can already be stated: the challenge is to formulate them sufficiently clearly for all to understand and use.

One such principle is that health care in cities cannot and should not be planned or executed by the health care sector alone. This principle of multisectoral involvement has also been put forward in the Alma Ata Declaration: over time, it has been implemented in a number of settings, often with reluctance and usually with reservations. Successful services developed already, in some countries show how health and social services can collaborate; how the voluntary sector can be included in mental health services; and how users themselves can contribute to the overall service. The political backing for multisectoral collaboration should not be sought as an afterthought: rather it will be of importance to assert that no significant improvement of health in cities can be expected until, and unless, the political authorities and leaders make that their own priority and force the administrative authorities to find structures and manners of function characterized by collaboration and resulting in better quality of life for citizens. Those who can demonstrate that their efforts can make a significant contribution to that goal can then be given an opportunity to do so.

It is also clear that long-term planning in conditions of rapid social change and amid economic upheavals cannot be realistic. While general principles of health care – such as equity in distributing benefits of health care and parity in service provision for mental and physical disorders – must be stated and used as a framework for short-term specific plans, 'rolling horizon' planning and programming are imperative: in order to make them possible and realistic, resources of health care services will have to be structured in a manner that will allow changes in the direction of care or a major reorientation of activity at short notice.

Parallel to the principle of flexibility must be the principle of accountability and transparency of expenditure and investment. If the population is to be a willing partner to health care authorities, it must be given respect and opportunities to see what is going on and what its own contribution to health care might be. In the first instance this will involve a major investment in a different type of health education – education on how to plan, execute and evaluate health care programmes. Health education of the type that was promoted previously, for example, on the reproductive cycle of disease vectors, will have to continue, but should not be seen as sufficient for health care purposes.

The acceptance of the population as an equal partner in the planning and execution of health care requires a significant change of the definition of the health professions and their life course: this is, however, the price to pay if a new paradigm of health care is to be introduced. A corollary of these principles is that investments have also to be made in activities that will promote health and mental health on the scale of values of individuals and communities. Once the population values health highly, it will be willing to participate in efforts to prevent diseases or make arrangements for their treatment (Sartorius, 1998).

Another principle that might be useful for the improvement of mental health care in cities is that progress should be achieved by learning from others – in the same country or elsewhere – and by sharing one's experience with them. This commonality in progress will involve the creation of networks of information exchange and the development of an attitude of humility about one's own achievements or country.

Coda and invitation

Thirty years ago, the World Health Assembly that brings together Ministers of Health or their envoys from the member countries of the World Health Organization expressed appreciation and unanimously adopted the various measures that were necessary to put the Alma Ata Declaration on primary health care into operation. The Declaration, and the documents that accompanied it, defined a new strategy of health care for the world. It introduced principles and guidelines that directed health systems into a new manner of operation. It underlined the need for delegation of most health care tasks to relatively simply trained personnel, the imperative necessity to rationalize health care expenditures, the unavoidable assignation of priorities to health problems, the need for new alliances between health and other social sectors in all health care action and the usefulness of monitoring progress and achievements. Primary health care was a strategy (see Chapter 8) expressing the manner in which health care should reflect ethical principles governing societies at the end of the twentieth century. It harnessed energy, knowledge and goodwill of many into a common framework of health care for the next three decades.

Useful as it might have been at the time of its formulation, the Primary Health Care strategy was deficient in that its prescription was primarily applicable to developing countries and, in them, to care in rural areas. It did not anticipate changes in the trends of urban development, nor foresee a viable mechanism for its own evaluation and revision in time. It was clearly overawed by the magnitude of health problems of the 1970s and was captured in the political tensions that prevailed at the time of its formation.

The consequences of these shortcomings are emerging in a variety of ways. Primary health care as a single strategy, and as the only locus of investment in the health care system, has lost its appeal in many countries and for most of the public health and other decision makers. Faced with urban health problems and changes in the rural areas, ministries of health and social welfare employ a variety of strategies that are often in part, or in their totality, contradictory to one another, although concocted in the same country or even in the same city at two points of time. Health plans are based on obsolete public health notions and lack foresight. Investments in health care are spasmodic and often governed by the need to deal with yet another crisis. Data on which public health action should be based are not collected regularly, or are losing credibility for a variety of (usually political and managerial) reasons. Economic imperatives are invoked to justify decisions whose ethical features are often at the very limit of acceptability. Complex mental health systems, involving many agencies and bringing together expertise from different sources that need to be developed go well beyond a simple reliance on primary care services as the remedy for all problems.

Mental health problems of cities of today and even more of tomorrow are many and severe. They complement and aggravate other health problems that endanger existence and quality of life of citizens of urban and rural areas. They must be faced and overcome if the majority of mankind is to have a future worth living.

The formulation of a strategy to overcome mental and other health problems of the cities of the future will have to proceed in an inductive manner, basing its formulation on examples of successes often achieved under conditions of tremendous scarcity and deprivation of resources of all types. It will have to draw its strength from the motivation and creative power that was demonstrated in towns that have developed mental health and other services. It will have to use the experience gained in developing health care and in many other areas of humanitarian effort.

Developing strategies and services that can provide appropriate health care for the cities of tomorrow is a venture of survival in an unknown territory replete with problems, but also with promises of progress in a material and moral sense. In this game success will depend more than ever before on the collaboration of many, on the creation of a productive alliance between the population at large, patients and users of health services, scientists, health professionals, decision makers in the fields of health, mental health and other industry, nationally and internationally. The creation of a strategy formulated jointly by all concerned and then used by them, is an essential task for all of us at the point of entry into a new millennium in which people should not only end up by being in cities but should share a determination of making cities a liveable place, in which they can grow together and continue to improve the quality of life for themselves and for all those who will follow them in time.

REFERENCES

Cooper, J.E. & Sartorius, N. (eds.) (1996). *Mental Disorders in China. Results of the National Epidemiological Survey in 12 Areas*. London: Gaskell.

Harvard Working Group on New and Resurgent Diseases (1995). New and resurgent diseases: The failure of attempted eradication. *The Ecologist*, **25**, 21–26.

Meltzer, H., Gill, B., Petticrew, M. & Hinds, K. (1995). *The Prevalence of Psychiatric Morbidity Among Adults Living in Private Households*. London: HMSO.

Sartorius, N. (1998). Universal strategies for the prevention of mental illness and the promotion of mental health. In *Preventing Mental Illness – Mental Health Promotion in Primary Care*, ed. R. Jenkins & T.B. Üstün. Chichester, UK: John Wiley.

Evaristo Baschenis (1607–77): *A guitar, cello, lutes, musical score, books and an armillary globe.* (Courtesy of Bridgeman Art Library, London.)

5

The Mozart effect and the Keshan disease

The Mozart effect, a serendipitous finding that listening to a particular piece of music can enhance mental capacity for a while and can reduce the number of otherwise uncontrollable epileptic fits, failed to attract research that might have resulted in useful results and could have opened new avenues of research. The Keshan disease is a syndrome that is due to a lack of selenium in the diet. It was discovered, explained and shown to be preventable and curable in less than two decades; yet there is little information about the scientists who made this discovery. Information about the severity of mental health problems and their public health significance has also been available for a number of years, but in most parts of the world this did not stimulate the vigorous action that would be necessary to deal with them.

In these and other instances the information that could have stimulated research, given greater credibility to research conducted by Scientists in developing countries, or given rise to public health interventions led to little action (or fame). The reasons for this are different and contain important lessons for the development of mental health programmes in the world today.

Listening to the Mozart sonata for two pianos (K448) can reduce the frequency of epileptic fits in a person suffering from a severe and otherwise therapy-resistant epileptic illness. It also enhances spatial reasoning skills (Jenkins, 2001). It might have other effects on the mental capacity, but the evidence about this is less firm.

The Keshan disease is a cardiac disease characterized by multifocal necrotic lesions of the myocardium. In severe cases it leads to death. In less severe cases cardiomegalia can be the only symptom.

The Mozart effect may be an important finding. The study of the effects of this particular opus, or of music in general, could be an avenue for the study of brain function. Perhaps it could tell us how to specifically improve cognitive performance. Perhaps the Mozart effect might also lead to revolutionary changes in the treatment and care for epilepsy and possibly for other paroxysmal disorders. At present at least 40 million people with epilepsy receive no treatment. The main reasons are that (i) they have not been seen by a health worker who could prescribe treatment; (ii) they cannot find (or pay for) medicaments that could help; (iii) they do not take the medication regularly or cease taking it altogether because the fits have become less frequent; (iv) they forget to take it, (v) nobody has explained to them that they must continue taking drugs even if they feel well; or (vi) the side effects are so unpleasant that they prefer to have occasional fits.

If it were proven that listening to a particular type of music can control epilepsy, it would be possible to consider using this in treatment programmes – particularly in developing countries in which the frequency of epilepsy is up to ten times higher than the frequency of epilepsy in the industrialized countries. And in the same developing countries, of all the inventions of the industrialized world, music from these countries is the most popular import. Listening to music is certainly likely to have fewer side effects than the long-term ingestion of antiepileptic drugs and could be a much cheaper treatment than anything else invented so far.

Also, if music exerts an effect on certain types of brain functions, it might also be helpful in the treatment of some types of mental illness. Some years ago it was shown that mentally retarded people have different preferences for music from those suffering from schizophrenia. Are these findings related to the same brain structures as the Mozart effect? What other diseases are responsive to music? What other music has the same effects on the brain? Or on the functioning of other body systems?

But the demonstration of the Mozart effect and its possible benefits failed to excite neuroscientists, psychiatrists and epileptologists alike.

In a different but related manner the discovery of the causes of Keshan disease did not make much noise in scientific literature. And yet, here is a curious disease that has been discovered only 65 years ago in people living in the foothills of the Keshan mountain. Since then it has been found in almost all other provinces of China – Jilin, Liaoing Shansi, Kansu, Shandong and half a dozen others. It damages the heart of people in hilly rural areas and does not strike those living in cities or coastal areas. Its incidence shows seasonal variation: in North China it is higher in severe winter seasons while in the Southwest it becomes frequent in hot summers. Its incidence also varies from year to year. In the North it most frequently strikes women in the child-bearing age, while in the Southwest it is more often seen in children aged 2 to 7 years (Rotschild, 1981). During endemics, several members of the family might be affected. When it was discovered and described, there was no cure for it. Relatively soon, however, the pathogenesis of the disease was clarified and the lack of selenium identified as the cause of the disease. Provision of selenium will cure the disease or prevent it.

There are other diseases that appear in only one or two areas of the world. It is rare, however, to see a disease that is not due to an infectious agent and yet has the rather extraordinary associations with, seasons, weather and residence. It is also rare to see a disease, which has no apparent genetic basis, appear in only one ethnic group. What is even rarer is to see that the pathogenesis of such a disease is successfully unravelled and a cure as well the prevention of the disease found and put at the disposal of medicine and public health.

The Mozart effect and the Keshan disease have one thing in common. The discovery of the special effects that a particular music had on the brain did not awaken much interest in the medical community[1]. The discoveries linked to the Keshan disease – one of the few non-communicable non-hereditary diseases whose pathogenesis, cure and prevention have been firmly established in the past few decades – remained unknown and unheralded by all. The discoverers themselves did not boast with their achievement, although they have very good reasons to do so. Their government does not seem to have rewarded them. Cardiological or other societies have not awarded them any prize, to my knowledge.

Epidemiological information about the frequency and severity of mental disorders in different parts of the world presents the same puzzle. Why did the estimations, made some 30 years ago, that there are at least 400 million people in the world suffering from mental or neurological disorder not cause a vast influx of funds into mental health programmes or into research into their causes and treatment? Treatment for many of those disorders was available and not expensive and some of them could have been avoided by the application of measures of primary prevention.

The three examples of the lack of impact of information can be explained in a number of ways. Keshan disease strikes a population far away from the USA and European countries in which most of the research on cardiovascular disorders has taken place. The descriptions of the disease have appeared in scientific journals that are not widely read. They are mainly in Chinese. The description of the largest series of cases, for example, appeared in a publication of the Heilongjiang Endemic Disease Research Institute. The report is not signed. Another report, a description of the disease in children, this time signed by a Z. Lu, appeared in a local journal in Guangzhou. Some other relevant articles appeared in European journals but most of them deal with selenium and some of its effects, not specifically with the Keshan disease. Harrison's textbook of internal medicine – undoubtedly one of the most important books in the field – gives a very brief description of the

---

[1] It did affect the producers of compact discs and cassettes – who produced a variety of Mozart's works with the announcement that listening to these is good for your brain and intelligence.

disease, but lists no reference to any article about the disease. Some of the major medical dictionaries do not list the illness at all.

But such is the case also for most other publications and discoveries made in the developing world. In a recent article Patel and Sumathipala (2001) report that, of the nearly 3000 articles published in six leading English language journals (three published in the USA and three published in Europe), only 6% were from countries other than USA and Europe. Patel and Sumathipala put forward several possible reasons for this imbalance. The investigators might have had difficulties with the English language. The papers might have been of low quality. It might be that there is a bias against the papers from the rest of the world (in fact, the rejection rate of papers submitted to some of the journals that kept relevant statistics is higher for papers submitted by authors from the Third world countries). The number of papers submitted for publication is low. The editors might feel that information about, or from, developing countries would be of less interest for their readership, mainly located in the developed countries of Europe and North America.

The most worrisome of Patel and Sumathipala hypotheses – and the most likely to be confirmed – is that the number of submissions is low because little research is done in the developing countries. The scarcity of resources for research is only part of the explanation for this depressing fact. The lack of research expertise may also be contributory, but does not explain it either. The overload with clinical work because the salaries are low is often put forward as a reason: but working long hours in a clinic and then doing research in one's free time was (and still is) the way of doing research in many developed countries. An explanation that is not mentioned in the Patel and Sumathipala article (nor in discussions about this matter) is that the motivation for becoming engaged in research in the developing countries – but also possibly worldwide – is diminishing.

The reasons that were driving clinicians to do research included academic recognition and advancement, the increased respect of their peers and supervisors, and the possibility of entering into a world different from the clinical world – in one's own country and internationally. The curiosity and the wish to understand the functioning of the human body, the universe or other matters were important motives for some, but not for the majority of, people who engaged in research. All of these reasons for the popularity of research seem to have weakened. In many countries the respect for scholarship and scientific achievement are on the wane. They are not the only ones to go. Over the centuries, people could use various ways to self-assertion and fame. Those who were not born aristocrats could become priests, military officers, scholars, and politicians, and become rich. In modern times, many of these sources of recognition have lost their attraction, leaving their place to affluence. Making a lot of money seems to have become more desirable than becoming recognized as a scholar.

In addition, the number of medical schools, university institutes and other institutions of academic orientation has grown so much that it is increasingly difficult to command the field in one's country. In some of these institutions – otherwise indistinguishable from the rest – the acquisition of a professorial degree depends on a variety of factors in addition to (or instead of) the number of publications and scientific achievements. The opportunity to establish international contacts through research has also lost some of its attractiveness in parallel with the increasing array of other possibilities to do so that are available to clinicians of a good reputation and/or reasonably well-supplied bank accounts in their own country or abroad.

The sophistication of research technology has also increased. A clinician who wanted to become engaged in biological research in previous decades could do so after completing his postgraduate training or residency; today, such a late entrant in the field would have to face competition with neuroscientists who started their research career 10 or more years earlier and since then have done little else but research. The increasing sophistication of methods of epidemiological and social science research make it difficult to start such research without considerable effort and funds. Clinical research is thus the most likely area in which clinicians can become engaged: this type of research, however, does not lend itself to publications as easily as laboratory or population investigations. In many of the poorer countries the main form of research is participation in studies of new medications. Research protocols for such studies are fully developed by the sponsors of the investigations and there are sufficient funds to do the research, to improve the state of one's department and to make some money. There is also the added advantage that such investigations often include provisions for travel to meetings of investigators or to congresses or both. And – what might be particularly attractive for many – the conduct of this type of research does not require fighting one's way through national or international bureaucracies that could be a source of money for research. The dangers of being exploited or otherwise damaged in some of these studies, as well as in some of the investigations sponsored by individuals or institutions in the highly developed countries, are by now well recognized and seem therefore to be declining (Sartorius, 1988).

But, as the case of the Keshan disease illustrates, even when there is a significant medical achievement in a developing country, the chances are that it will remain unknown to scientists and clinicians in the countries outside the country of discovery. The exception might be discoveries that have a direct impact on the diseases of the developed world. The situation is similar with research and discoveries in the Eastern European countries, which are in any case viewed with suspicion, perhaps in part justified by the history of some of the 'discoveries' in Stalin's era. The flow of scientific information is, by and large, unidirectional: from the northwestern European countries and the USA to the developing countries of the world and to the countries of Eastern Europe, and, more and more, from the USA to Western Europe.

What of the Mozart effect? Why did the information about this discovery fail to excite epileptologists and neuroscientists in general? All the work on the Mozart effect has been done in the developed countries. Intractable epilepsy is a problem for both developed and developing countries – perhaps more visibly so for the former group (because people with forms of epilepsy that respond to treatment usually get treatment and are therefore not a problem for health services). Neuropsychology and cognitive investigations are *en vogue* at present. There are numerous excellent institutions in the USA and Europe that have the potential to explore the effect and assess its scientific and practical interest.

I see two possible explanations for this lack of interest: first, the exploration of the effects of music on the brain is somehow in no man's land. It is not the primary field of investigation for epileptologists. The neuropsychologists have turned their interest to other areas – the investigation of cognition, the localization of brain structures involved in specific cognitive functions and neuroplasticity. Psychiatrists have stopped at the findings that certain types of illness seem to make people like one type of music more than another. Medical Research Councils and other organizations funding research prefer to remain in the area of established research rather than venture into high risk (and therefore potentially high gain) territory, lest they be accused to be insufficiently serious in their selection of topics worthy of support. They have often adopted the 'back the winner' strategy – deciding what to fund on the record of previous achievements rather on the listing of potential benefits of a particular line of work in the future.

The second possible explanation of the little interest in the Mozart effect is that potential investigators came to believe that the controversial results that surrounded the discovery indicate that the chances are high that the Mozart effect is a curious artefact and nothing more. To spend years in high-risk research might be a significant drawback for the researchers and their institutions. In the current atmosphere of having to produce publications and results in order to receive an extension of a grant or further funding from a Foundation, any painstaking, long-lasting high-risk investigation has a poor chance of being tolerated, let alone funded, regardless of the potential gain from a discovery.

These two explanations hang together. Lesser chances of funding will make scientists turn elsewhere. If there is no research and no further advances of understanding of the matter under study, the attractiveness of such research for other scientists and funding agencies will, in turn, decrease. The current trend of changes in the manner of funding research may also be responsible for the neglect of high-risk/high-yield investigations. In earlier times, high-risk research would (and often was) undertaken without any difficulty (provided that the head of the department said yes). More recently, research funding has to be applied for in elaborate ways. The applications are read by committees that are often anything but adventurous in their thinking. The chances that a high-risk research will be undertaken are therefore lessened – and so may be the gains for science. It is a pity that, at present, the former way of funding research is becoming less and less popular; having a mixture of both might have been a more promising recipe for further progress of science.

The lack of impact of epidemiological information on the policies of most governments in the field of mental health is another riddle, more grave in its immediate consequences than the two preceding examples. There are at least four possible explanations for this anomaly. First, the data about the seriousness of mental illness was offered in a manner that made it incomprehensible. Second, the data was well presented but the presentation was ill timed. Third, the data was presented well and comprehensibly, on time and to the right people but the decision makers did not want to act upon it because of their prejudices, because of the need to observe already established priorities, or because of other reasons. Fourth, the data was presented well, to the right people but will have an impact with a considerable delay, somewhat in a manner of a slow virus acting after a long incubation.

Incomprehensible data presented to decision makers can have two forms: either the data is presented in a messy, inconsistent, or even illegible form; or the data is presented in a manner that makes a lot of sense to the epidemiologist but none to the decision makers. The latter are often not experts in psychiatric matters and have little interest in them. Epidemiologists often expect that the decision makers will be like themselves; in fact, they usually are not. Barbara Wooton wrote in 1980 about the differences between the 'registers' of the criminals and their judges.

Judges and magistrates seem to think that offenders' mental processes are much as they imagine their own would be in similar circumstances and they envisage both the man in the dock and themselves as, potentially at least, liable to similar temptations. In looking into his heart, they appear in fact only to see what lurks in their own. Legislators, likewise, in drafting the criminal law seem equally disposed to draw upon introspective evidence: as when advocates of capital punishment project images of how they would refrain from carrying guns on a robbery if to do so would put their own life at risk.

Up to a point, of course, this works . . . But the point at which the courts' traditionalist psychology really breaks down is in relation to what are often called 'motiveless crimes', that is to say crimes which we cannot imagine ourselves committing or even being tempted to commit . . .

The public health worker who comes to the government officials to present his data often appears to them as the motiveless criminal did to Wooton's magistrate. Why, for example, should the government official listen to the presentation of figures about the numbers of mildly mentally retarded persons? Nobody seems to have asked for specific action about them. Their relatives do not complain too much, the disability is not lethal, and anyway the world has to be made up of all kinds of people. What should the official do with the data even if he took the time to listen to the presentation? The epidemiologist's belief that full mental life and capacity are among the most highly desirable goals of health efforts is not necessarily shared by the ministry officials. The data will not have any impact in this situation.

In order to convince decision makers about the need to act, epidemiological data probably has to be presented differently. First, it should be accompanied by information that is relevant to the frame of reference of the government. Second, it should be given in a way that will show how it can be used, by the decision maker, say, the minister. Ministers worry about being re-elected and about saving the government and themselves from all kinds of embarrassment. They have to deal with pressure groups in the area of their responsibility, and prevent dissatisfaction and strikes of health care personnel. They have to protect their area of responsibility and budget from the voracious appetite of other Ministries. And, being human, they usually have a variety of problems in their own life. Hearing that a disease has an incidence of 14/100 000 population per year is not likely to propel them into frantic action.

It follows that epidemiologists who would like to see their findings become the basis for government action have to study the frame of priorities of the government and present their figures, showing their relevance to the personal and official set of priorities of decision makers. Perhaps it would have been better to speak of the total number of people now suffering from the disease than to give the incidence figure. The presenter could have linked that data with some other fact, e.g. with possible savings if interventions were to be undertaken and the public health (and electoral) impact that the establishment of treatment facilities of good quality would have had.

Unfortunately, postgraduate training in epidemiology rarely includes specific training on how to do this. A course on the preparation of scientific reports would be considerably more useful if it were accompanied by another course on presenting data (in a manner that will show their importance) to politicians with little time, little money, under stress and without any in-built love for matters psychological.

The second explanation of the perceived neglect of data by authorities has to do with its timeliness. For a variety of reasons inherent in research and in policy making, it is only rarely possible to produce data that are relevant to the policy options available to decision makers just at the time of data production. Sometimes, epidemiologists keen to present the best information will take extra time to update their data or complete the study before presenting any of its results. Both strategies might mean that none of the (now perfect) data will be used. The political process does not work with perfect certainties; it uses best estimates and produces decisions amid ambiguity and guesses as to what will work.

The choice of people to whom the data should be presented is a considerably more difficult problem. There are few decision makers with appropriate training in psychiatry or in mental health. In most developing countries they were perhaps exposed to psychiatry by a 5-day visit to the local 'lunatic asylum'. There, they were amused by the curious behaviour of the inmates and made to admire the courage of the personnel who dared to work in a place with so many dangerous people. Even those who had better training in psychiatry are often unaware of the effectiveness of treatments developed in the past few decades. The stigma attached to mental illness and all that touches it – treatment institutions, psychiatric personnel, psychiatric treatments, patients' families – is also at work: politicians will score better by building sophisticated cardiac surgery departments than by helping develop humane and open mental health services.

The sheer size of the estimates that are presented to the decision makers is also a deterrent. The size of investments that would be necessary to deal adequately with mental health problems is vast. The fact that a significant proportion of people contacting general health services has mental health problems means that it would be necessary to organize training of all general health practitioners and change the medical curricula in schools of medicine and other schools of health personnel. The dismal state of institutions in which people with mental illness live requires considerable investment into the buildings, into re-education of staff, into better supplies of food and into medication. Decision makers usually do not have the possibility to divert such sums to psychiatry. Since public pressure nevertheless requires action, they will act – even in very poor countries – and, not infrequently make paradoxical investments into building one, or a few, well-equipped expensive clinics to deal with an infrequent problem.

But even the well-informed decision makers may not be inclined to act when presented with figures about the frequency of mental disorders. As a rule, decision makers are forced to spring into action when there is a change, an emergency, imminent catastrophes and political embarrassment. By its nature, mental disorders are not spreading epidemically: in one form or another they have been around for a long time and for just as long there was little that could be done and that could have a dramatic effect on the disease or on its prevalence. The officials therefore receive epidemiological estimates with quiet resignation and no impatience to act.

The distance from the problem plays an important role as well. Predictions that the mortality due to a particular problem, e.g. the environmental pollution, will increase in 20 years are characteristically unheeded or are countered by one of the numerous excuses that governments usually have in stock. A promise of results in a short time – in time for the next elections – often works wonders.

Finally, it cannot be excluded that the data presented to the decision makers and politicians operate like slow viruses. Once entered into the political system, epidemiological information makes its way slowly, eroding obstacles on its way. Occasionally, there are signs that the process is under way, but not always. The information that sounded so unbelievable when first presented over time becomes well known and is finally accepted as the basis for action. Repeated presentations of the same information to the same people and repeated reports from different sources may shorten the incubation. The absence of contradictory reports can also help to speed up the process, and so does the dramatic presentation of the data about groups of people with whom the decision makers can identify emotionally, like data about drug use by their adolescent children, for example.

Smoking is a good example of the incubation hypothesis. Data about the harmful effects of smoking were presented to the Executive Board of the World Health Organization in the late 1960s. The ashtrays were removed from the room in which the Board was meeting some 20 years later. It took a few more years to create a post that allowed the recruitment of an expert[2]. Ten further years later the fight against smoking became a priority of the Organization. The incubation of data about the harmful effects of smoking – one of the main causes of health problems in the world – was nearly 40 years.

Incubation of data about the frequency and severity of mental health problems and about possible measures to deal with them is, for the moment, of similar duration. The welcome signs that the World Health Organization has made the fight against mental illness and its consequences one of its priorities now, some 40 years after the data about the magnitude and severity of mental health problems were first presented, seem to confirm the hypothesis as well.

REFERENCES

Jenkins, J.S. (2001). The Mozart effect. *Journal of the Royal Society of Medicine*, **94**, 170–172.

Patel, V. & Sumathipala, A. (2001). International representation in psychiatric literature. *British Journal of Psychiatry*, **178**, 406–409.

Rotschild, H. (ed.) (1981). *Biocultural Aspects of Disease*, pp. 347–348. New York: Academic Press.

Sartorius, N. (1988). Crosscultural and international collaboration in mental health research and action. Experience from the mental health programme of the World Health Organization. *Acta Psychiatrica Scandinavica*, 78 Suppl. **344**, 71–74.

---

[2] It is amusing to recall that the first incumbent of that post was a lawyer from Cuba, which at the time still depended on the production and exportation of tobacco for a good part of its national budget.

René Magritte (1898–1967): *La Clairvoyance* (1936). (Courtesy of Galerie Christine et Isy Brachot, Brussels, DACS, London, and ADAGP, Paris 2002.)

6

The paradoxes about psychiatry

Practitioners of the mental health sciences have knowledge and techniques that could help in overall socio-economic development, yet they are only rarely invited to participate in the planning or execution of development projects. There are numerous declarations and publications about principles of modern mental health care, yet relevant legislation and procedures that would facilitate their application are changing very slowly or not at all. There is much to be gained from collaboration between psychiatry and the rest of medicine, yet the gap between the two still exists and in some settings increases. The reasons for these paradoxical situations are not fully known, but it is possible to make reasonably good guesses about them.

Three paradoxes mark the role of psychiatry outside of its main field of action. They concern the role of psychiatry in socio-economic and health development programmes, the legislation concerning psychiatric care, and the relationship of psychiatry with general medicine. All three are somewhat more evident in developing countries than in the industrialized world where their presence is less starkly visible for a variety of reasons. Health decision makers and public health authorities seem to accept these paradoxes calmly. Psychiatrists are not much more excited either: they concentrate on their clinical work, on their research or on their teaching and only rarely generate public debate to dissolve one or more of these paradoxes. The tacit acceptance of the three paradoxical situations described below makes psychiatry less useful to the population and less attractive as a discipline to those who practise it and to those who consider doing so.

The paradox of socio-economic development

Governments claim that their purpose is to increase the quality of life of its citizens. Industrial development and economic solvency are seen as important ingredients of the effort to achieve this goal. The final goal – better quality of life – is somewhat vaguely defined but usually refers to the feeling of satisfaction that individuals have when they reach – or sense that they will soon reach – goals that they have set for themselves in terms of social status, security, health, spiritual fulfilment and freedom. It is evident that relationships between people and their motivation to participate in the society's effort to improve everyone's quality of life play a determinant role in such progress. It is also evident that well-developed cognitive faculties and emotional balance can facilitate the participation of citizens in these efforts and might enhance the value of their contributions.

What is more, it is beyond doubt that industrial development and rapid changes of the socio-cultural networks in a country represent a source of stress to which many of the traditional sources of strength of a society have no answer.

And yet, indicators of mental health are rarely used in planning or monitoring the developmental process. Governments rarely see investment into mental health programmes as a potential source of support for their developmental programmes[1] (Gonzales, 1990).

They do not call on mental health programmes to propose action that would use knowledge and techniques produced in order to facilitate adjustment to social change or to strengthen participation in community activities.

I see three reasons for this paradoxical situation. First, the mental health sciences have failed to clearly describe what they have at their disposal and what effects their techniques might have; second, the motivation of mental health workers to work on matters related to socio-economic developments is, by and large, low; and third, much of the knowledge that mental health sciences have produced is still not translated into techniques that are easy to use by non-specialists.

So, for example, if mental health workers were to be asked what knowledge they have about the upbringing of children, it is as likely as not that they would refer to the fact that a child's emotional and intellectual development is likely to be better when the child lives in a family in which the parents have a harmonious relationship and the basic material needs of the family are covered. This knowledge is (correctly) seen by the government officials as banal and useless for immediate action. If asked to try again, mental health specialists might admit that the central element of knowledge about upbringing is that children do better if they can establish a trusting and lasting relationship with at least one responsible adult who looks after them. From there, they will still have to be pressed further until they produce the suggestion that, in hospital and day-care facilities, it would be useful if the children were to be entrusted to the care of the same nurse or educator rather than to many, changing frequently. And yet, it is this type

[1] There was a notable exception to this habit. In the early 1980s, the President of Venezuela decided to invest into the development of intelligence of the citizens of his country. In his opinion, informed participation in the democratic process required well-developed intelligence and comprehension of issues at stake: citizens had to be able to understand what they voted for and what the consequences of their voting might be. He saw the active participation of citizens in the development programmes as the essential determinant of development and felt that participation and the commitment of the intellectual, emotional and social resources of each individual to the joint cause depended on the health and intelligence of the citizens. The programme had numerous useful outcomes, but failed to survive and continue for a long time because of political changes.

of suggestion that will be seen as useful by the government, not the recommendations to provide each child with a well-functioning harmonious family.

The paradox of legislation about psychiatric care

The United Nations Resolution 119, adopted in 1991, declared that the protection against abuse and access to appropriate treatment for mental illness are human rights. Ministers and other plenipotentiary representatives of the World Health Organization's Member States adopted a number of resolutions over the years covering most of the aspects of care for people with mental illness. The need to develop community mental health care and to introduce mental health elements into primary health care, the importance of paying attention to psychosocial aspects of health and overall development, the usefulness of reducing the size and numbers of outdated mental hospitals, the principles of training for mental health care and numerous other subjects, have all been covered in these documents. National and international non-governmental and governmental conferences contributed further guidelines and recommendations about the way in which services for the mentally ill should be organized and run.

Yet, a recent survey of legislation concerning mental illness and people suffering from it conducted in 45 countries showed that the laws governing lives of the mentally ill and the management of services supposed to help them are often out of date, and sometimes more of an obstacle than a help to the provision of care. In nearly two-thirds of the 45 countries surveyed there had been no changes of legislation in the past 25 years, despite the vast changes in the principles of mental health care and the enhancement of its potential that have occurred in those years. Most of the countries in which there was no change are in the developing world – where change is probably even more necessary since so many of these countries either have no laws or have inappropriate laws copied from their past colonial masters. Only four countries among those surveyed reflected the need for the decentralization of mental health care in their laws. More than half of the countries surveyed have only broad principles governing non-voluntary hospital-ization and nearly a third of them do not specify a limit to the duration of involuntary hospitalization. A third of the countries do not specify any overseer or review bodies (Poitras & Bertolote, 2001).

The situation is similar concerning procedures governing the admin-istration of mental health services. It is as if the past decades have brought nothing of sufficient importance to warrant changes of laws and procedures concerning mental health care. The introduction of quality assurance procedures into mental health services – a very welcome development – has also been slow. Many countries have not yet introduced any mechanism to control the quality of services regu-larly, and even countries in which it has been introduced do not neces-sarily apply it in all of the services.

The fact that governments frequently subscribe to the need for changes of mental health programmes, yet do little to change the prac-tice of psychiatry by changes in legislation, might have several explana-tions. Perhaps mental health laws and procedures are thought to mean so little that it is not worth anyone's trouble to go through the arduous procedure of getting the legislators to re-examine mental health laws and change them. This would be a pity. Although unevenly observed, well-formulated laws have been shown to be helpful in providing care and in protecting the rights of patients. They also, if well constructed, diminish the stigma of mental illness and subsequent discrimination against people who have it.

Another explanation might be in the scarcity of champions of the cause. Psychiatrists, particularly in less-developed countries are busy people, and few among them will be willing to spend a great amount of their time learning about the intricacies of the new international and national documents and convincing their own legislature to intro-duce changes. Some of them seem to be willing to do so, but often have difficulties in getting hold of instructions and guidelines to help in the reformulation of laws and procedures.

Also, particularly in the developing countries the pressure to gain a livelihood (and a little more) is so great that it is difficult to identify someone who will find the free hours, days and months needed to change the legislation and supervise the changes of procedures in mental hospitals and elsewhere. Organizations of patients and their families are feeble, non-existent or forbidden. Where they exist, they usually suffer because their resources are scarce and are received irregularly and their personnel consists of volunteers with little preparation for the many tasks that are before them. Other non-governmental organizations – for example, the psychiatric associations – have no permanent personnel or money to take on tasks other than organizing meetings and possibly sending out a newsletter. Government offices dealing with mental health would be logical candidates to undertake this work: but in most countries their administrative power and resources are derisory.

A third possible explanation is that things will change but that that takes several decades – somewhat in the manner of maturation – regardless of the urgency of change or of the amount of advocacy. Unfortunately, preparations for the moment when change becomes possible are important but often insufficient or neglected.

The paradox of relationship between psychiatry and medicine in general

Medicine in general and psychiatry would both gain if they were closer together. Most people with mental health problems seek help in general health services where their disease is often not recognized and where the treatment for it – even when the disease is recognized – is not always appropriate. The mental health problems present in people suffering from a physical illness are usually not treated simultaneously with the physical illness. Conversely, physical illness in people with mental illness is often not properly handled in the psychiatric services. Psychiatrists' knowledge of general medicine is often obsolete, and their awareness of new methods of treatment less than optimal.

Burn-out in personnel working in general health services is becoming epidemic in many settings. The population's satisfaction with medical care is declining. Neglect of the need to develop interpersonal skills of medical personnel is, to a large extent, responsible for the increasing numbers of complaints about the dehumanization of medicine.

It is therefore likely that general medical care and psychiatric services would gain in quality if psychiatrists and other medical specialists were to be closer and if new knowledge in general medicine and in psychiatry and behavioural sciences were to be shared and used in both types of services. This is happening in a few places – but, on the whole, the gap between psychiatry and general medicine is not diminishing and in some settings it has even increased.

Much of the distance between the two can probably be traced back to the past. The physical separation of the usual place of work, the difference in diagnostic and treatment techniques, the differences in the relation to legal procedures and numerous other reasons can be listed as being the culprits for the separation. But why does the gap persist?

Perhaps it is because the image of psychiatric services as being custodial, and of psychiatrists as being uninterested in physical medicine, persists despite the creation of a significant scientific basis for psychiatry. The popularity of psychoanalysis and the inclination of psychiatrists to use it (to excess) to explain social, political (and almost all other) phenomena has undoubtedly contributed to the opinion that psychiatry is not likely to be useful in dealing with real illness. Biologically oriented psychiatrists and their skills in psychopharmacotherapy have probably helped to slightly change the idea that psychiatry is a talk-shop based on little science. Yet since they are often not seen as being true representatives of the psychiatric tribe but as useful renegades from psychiatry to 'true medicine' – much of the old image of psychiatry persists.

Perhaps the gap persists because psychiatrists have fallen so far back in their knowledge of modern medicine that they prefer a distant relationship with it. General physicians are also often behind today's psychiatry and have no particular wish to upgrade their knowledge, since they do not think that there is much to psychiatry anyway even if it is advanced. They deal with mental symptoms in a manner similar to that which they use for physical symptoms – by prescribing pharmacological treatment. If this does not work, they have the option of referral and consultation. Neither of the two contributes much to learning about psychiatry nor to developing practical skills. Referrals from general medicine to psychiatry is often more influenced by the amount of nuisance that a patient creates on the general medical ward than by a desire to obtain guidance about psychiatric diagnosis and treatment. The stigma of psychiatric illness carries with it the notion that all mental patients are dangerous and that they should be sent somewhere else. General health care staff are not immune to such prejudice.

These reasons, however, do not fully explain the separation that is harmful for both parties. The creation of new disciplines – such as liaison psychiatry and psychosomatic medicine – are helping to overcome the gap in some countries. In others, those practising psychological medicine are seeking their own disciplinary identity and define, as their exclusive area of concern, all those disorders that would otherwise be the natural domain for collaboration between psychiatry and medicine. Where this has happened, psychiatry thus becomes reduced to being a discipline that deals with the most severe cases – chronic alcohol dependence, chronic forms of schizophrenia, the dementias and multiple handicaps.

The paradoxes of today's psychiatry are most likely related to the same central cause: the stigma that is attached to mental illness and to all that is in contact with it. Psychiatry (and behavioural sciences) are not perceived as a useful ally socio-economic development projects. The changing of laws that would make it possible for psychiatry to function well and to be useful to overall development programmes is not seen as worthwhile. Psychiatry – because of its image – is still not accepted as a real part of medicine except in a few countries. It is more or less clear what needs to be done to resolve these paradoxes: the challenge before psychiatry is to do it.

REFERENCES

Gonzales, R. (1990). Ministering Intelligence: a Venezuelan experience in the promotion of cognitive abilities. *International Journal of Mental Health*, **18**, 5–19.

Poitras, S. & Bertolote, J.M. (2001). Mental Health Legislation: International trends. In *Contemporary Psychiatry*, ed. F. Henn, et al. **2**, pp. 269. Heidelberg: Springer.

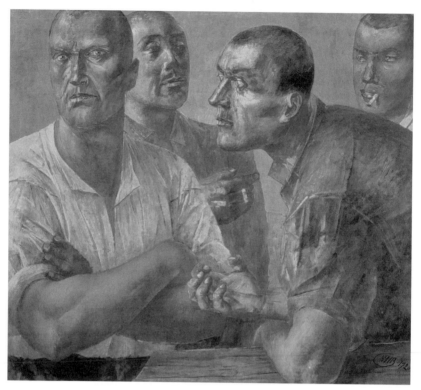

Kuzma Sergeevich Petrov-Vodkin (1878–1939): *Labourers* (1926). (Courtesy of the State Russian Museum, St Petersburg, and Bridgeman Art Library, London.)

7

On advice and consultation

Progress in health – or other development programmes – could be speeded up if the knowledge and experience gained already could be made available to those responsible for development programmes. Consultants and advisers could be vehicles for this transfer of information. But advice which they offer is only rarely used. Some of the reasons for this are known and could be avoided, others are not. The hope that advice and consultation will be a significant part of development strategies is not likely to be fulfilled.

Most of the very successful people in international health work – including some of the top advisors to governments or major health agencies – whom I have had the pleasure to meet, rarely if ever give advice to anyone.

I believe that this is because they have learned that advice is only rarely requested with the intention of it being followed. Sometimes, it is requested in order to flatter the advisor. Sometimes, it is requested because it is hoped that the advice given will tell a great deal about the advisor. Sometimes, the request is an excuse for spending time with the advisor, because his or her room is nicer than other places or because the advisor is an interesting person, a good listener. It happens that advice is requested on the order of someone else whose command must be obeyed. Occasionally, the request for advice is an introductory sentence, a polite preface to a lengthy statement of the requester's opinion. Asking for advice can also be a way of apologizing for numerous occasions when advice or orders have not been followed in the past.

On occasion, a decision maker does want a neutral and well-balanced opinion before proceeding further, say with an administrative reform or other change. He might wish to consult a foreign adviser uninvolved in local politics. Finding the best adviser inevitably takes time and it is rarely possible to get the right person before the window of opportunity has vanished. Highly placed persons, interested and powerful enough to make the change, also change positions quite often. The successor in the position who has 'inherited' the consultant when he finally arrives does not really want to see too much of him or her and rarely welcomes their suggestions.

Such advice, requested by the predecessor in one's post will be handled like any other unsolicited suggestions. Advice, which we did not request, is almost always experienced as a nuisance. It is not welcome even when it would be logical to accept it. When invited to come to a country and examine the health situations or to assess the effectiveness of health services, it is tempting to conclude that the findings of the visit should be formulated in the form of recommendations about future action. Most frequently this is not the case. The invitation to visit a country is often the result of complex negotiations within the

Ministry of Health that has issued the invitation. It might have been, for example, that a particular department wanted to use the presence of the foreign consultant as a reason for introducing a change in the health service or for frightening a particular person into action. It might also be that the Ministry felt that it would be useful to gain time by inviting a foreign consultant to come and assess the situation. Even in well-functioning bureaucracies (and those are hard to find), the process of finding a person, and getting a consultant of sufficient seniority to come, might take several months, a decent period to let spirits cool down or to postpone action to the next budgetary period. Advice and recommendations from a consultant in such a situation are irrelevant since there was never an intention to follow them, no matter what they were. The added nuisance for the government is that something might have to be done because the consultant has drawn attention to a conveniently forgotten problem. Consultants also sometimes copy their reports to others in the Ministry or elsewhere: some of these others might use the fact that the suggestions of an important visitor were ignored as ammunition to attack the agency that has invited the advisor if the advice was not followed.

When aware of such situations, advisors sometimes produce recommendations (requested in their terms of reference) at such a level of generality that no action is either forbidden or supported by the recommendations. Sometimes, the main recommendation in such instances will be that another consultation is needed later; or that another agency should be involved in an in-depth analysis. Both of these types of recommendations – the sweeping and the delaying ones – are usually well received, considered with much solemnity. They are also recompensed by statements of gratitude and by (held) promises of future invitations to give advice.

It does happen that the urge to give advice, even when not asked to do so, is irresistible. Such is the case when something is obviously wrong or wasteful, and when a minor change would suffice to put everything right. When this happens, it is likely that the chances that advice will be followed increase if the advice is couched in terms which will hide its nature. Using an opportunity to tell a story of a success of a course of action in a similar situation in another country might be a way to do it, particularly if the story can be accompanied by a true or imaginary account of another health official who failed to understand the advice or recommendation. It is even better if the story can be placed in an admired friendly competing country (or in a totally unknown country) rather than in a country that is either far richer or well known for its failures in various undertakings. The key element in this strategy will be the timing of the disguised advice. The timing errors are usually in giving advice too early: the recipient must be ripe to accept the suggestion. If the advice cannot be given at the optimal time, it is better to give it late than early. The almost too late advice ('you could have told me this earlier, but I hope we can still do something') is on the whole better received because decision makers can imagine problems much better when they are approaching them. The example of the social workers who mounted the night train from Madrid to Paris in order to advise immigrant workers about their rights and the dangers that will await them next morning is an excellent example of well-timed advice given at a point of doubt and anxiety about the future and about the validity of previously used coping strategies. The same advice given earlier, e.g. in school or in talks given to people who might become immigrants at some other point in time, would have been, in all likelihood, less well listened to or remembered.

Another disguise for advice is to dress it up in the form of a question or a request for guidance. Decision makers – and other people – find such an invitation to present their views welcome and can occasionally be steered to solutions that they would have rejected if they had been presented to them as recommendations or options for action. A sub-form of this way of proceeding – requiring considerable skill if done on purpose – is the formulation of a recommendation in such vague and confused terms that the recipient takes the matter in his or her own hands and becomes engaged in efforts to understand what is going on and how it could be logically presented.

Regardless of the guise that advice will assume, the person who cannot control the urge to advise has to face three major challenges: first, to understand the frame of reference of the recipient; second, to use formulations that are harmonious with the characteristics of the culture in which the advice is offered; and third, to package advice in amounts that are digestible.

Understanding the frame of reference of the person advised requires its study. Once understood, its description will have to be rehearsed with the recipient of advice and from then on serve as a constant part of the introduction to any discussion, debate or joint effort to find solutions to problems. Comprehending the frame of reference of a decision maker is a fascinating task because its exploration is also a study of culture and of human relationships in a given situation. At the end of the process, the advisor will know as many facts as the decision maker but – since the responsibility is with the decision maker – these facts will not have the same emotional loading for the advisor as it does to the decision maker. The degree to which the advice is likely to help in resolving the decision makers' emotional unease in a situation is proportionate to the probability that advice will be followed: an equation difficult to express numerically or in other measurable terms. In thinking about it, it is important to remember that the advisors do not have to accept the frame of reference of the persons whom they advise: but they must be conscious of them and seek solutions that will be acceptable, despite possible differences in the value systems between them.

Understanding the characteristics of the culture in which the decision makers or other advised people live requires more than the awareness of wedding ceremonies, fasts and other rituals. It must include an awareness of the cultural construction of concepts such as time, of visible and invisible hierarchies prevailing in the society, of systems of rewards and punishment, and of the manner of distribution of information in the community and in selected social groups.

When saying this, it is also important to remember that cultural differences have often been exaggerated. People who have the same profession and have been dealing with similar problems, who read the same books and spent periods of their training with the same teachers, will have a common ground for a good understanding even when they seem to belong to very different cultures. The relatively simple rules of behaviour – to treat others and their opinions with respect, for example – are transculturally remarkably robust. There are specific traps that one can quickly learn to avoid – for example, to presume that all people share the same conception of time[1] or that all people use the same logic: forgetting these cognitive determinants makes one's advice just as useless in one's own culture as it does when working with people from other cultures.

The third challenge is to break down one's recommendations and suggestions into pieces that can be understood and applied. A proposal for a major change will almost always be rejected: the only persons who can propose revolutionary reforms that will do good things to all people are – or so it seems – the politicians seeking election to a public office. The corollary to this rule of providing advice in small doses, is that the pride of the advisor must lie in the fact that the advice leads to the course of action that the advisor suggested and not to the public recognition of the origin of the idea. The recognition of the origin of ideas is, at all times, a bonus not a normal event.

Even if all these precautions are taken, it is highly unlikely that advice, particularly if it provides a new idea, will be immediately understood. Sometimes, the recipients do not listen very carefully; sometimes, they take the advice as part of the preamble for some spectacular advice and do not pay much attention to it; sometimes, the presentation of the advice employed jargon, or was otherwise unclear and arcane. Advice should therefore be presented several times, in different forms and presentations, perhaps with an allegorical reference, with reference to other lands, told as a story or several stories, sometimes by reference to some topic that is particularly precious to the recipient. Once it appears that the advice has been understood, it should not be repeated again: every repetition after it has sunk in will weaken the attractiveness of the course of action proposed and give the advisor the reputation of being repetitive, slow and, worst of all, boring. The accep-

---

[1] The chronological concept of time by which time is perceived and used as an axis defined by the chronology of events that follow one another is not very widespread. The ordering of events on that axis by importance, for example, as well as other ways of structuring time seems to be more widely used. Among these other ways, the 'punctual ordering' of events, by which a new event covers all those that have preceded it (and therefore the past has no depth) is fairly widespread and may necessitate a special effort of explaining arguments – based on some specific sequence of events in the past. The World Atlas of cultures has divided all cultures into the 'now' and the 'before and after' cultures by the amount attention they give to the present as opposed to the longitudinal vision of time – clearly demonstrating how important the time concept is for the definition of a culture.

tance of this way of going about things also means that an advisor should not work on more than one piece of advice at a time.

Giving advice is never free of a certain amount of involvement of the advisor in the course of action that the recipient will undertake subsequently. The advisor must be able to live with the results of his action and should therefore never give recommendations that are contrary to his inner convictions, scales of values and the ethical and moral principles by which he lives.

I cannot resist the temptation to close this chapter by (unsolicited) advice to the reader: avoid advising but if you have to do it remember that most often advice will not be followed, that you will not usually be better liked for giving it and that you will often discover that your advice was not all that great. Remember, however, also that the chance to help good things happen should never be missed and that, occasionally your advice will be the keystone, making the arch possible.

Part II

Mental health and medicine

A Mole in a Hole by Hatao. (Courtesy of Hatao Masuda.)

8

Psychiatry in the framework of primary health care: a threat or boost for psychiatry ?

Psychiatrists are apprehensive about the provision of care to people with mental illness by health workers in primary health care services. They say that they are uneasy because primary care personnel may not be capable of providing good care to those with mental disorders. In private practice they are also uneasy about the potential decrease in the numbers of patients who may no longer consult them if they can get care in a general health care facility.

To a large extent, these feelings can be related to the fact that the term 'primary health care' refers to two largely independent matters: to a philosophy of health care and to services provided at the point of first contact between patients and health care agents. The primary health care philosophy is embedded in the Alma Ata Declaration and in subsequent documents that provide the ethical framework for prevention of illness, the provision of care and other interventions aiming to improve the health of a given population. The acceptance of this framework would provide a boost to psychiatry while sharing the provision of care with health personnel other than psychiatrists.

In order to be able to discuss the place of psychiatry in the framework of primary health care, it is necessary to first define primary health care and psychiatry.

Definitions

'Primary health care' is a term describing a strategy of provision of health care. The term was formally adopted by the World Health Organization (WHO) in 1978 during a huge international conference held in Alma Ata, then the capital of Kazakhstan. Ministers or their envoys from most of the world's countries debated the concept for days and finally agreed to adopt the strategy of primary health care as the preferred way of organizing health care in all of their countries. The (WHO, 1978) conference said what primary health care was; it did not, however, discourage the use of the same term to describe other health care concepts. To an extent, this was dictated by the determination to reach consensus on a set of principles for the provision of health care that will be applicable in all countries of the world. It was felt at the time that this objective was most important and that, for the sake of consensus, it was allowable for some countries or health system organizations to use the term in a somewhat different sense. (It should be remembered that 'consensus' does not necessarily mean unanimity; the *American Heritage Dictionary of the English Language* in its third edition, for example, defines consensus as an 'opinion or position reached by a group as a whole or by majority will'.

As it is a strategy, primary health care was defined in terms of principles that should govern action in the field of health rather than in terms of activities. It listed areas of action rather than specific tasks and proposed ways to decide about priorities rather than priorities themselves. It was described as 'essential health care based on practical, scientifically sound, and socially acceptable methods and technology, made universally accessible to individuals and families in the community through their full participation and at a cost that the community and country can afford to maintain at every stage of their development, in a spirit of self-reliance and self-determination'. From this definition it is clear that the descriptors of primary health care are ethical and epistemological and that improving first-contact care might, but will not necessarily, be among the chief features of the health system accepting primary health care principles.

The definition says that primary health care must concern itself only with essential health care: the word 'essential' is used in relation to society's survival. Hence, criteria for the choice of diseases to be considered among priority targets are their frequency, the damage or concern they cause society, and their constraining impact on socioeconomic development.

'Essential' does not define the nature of the interventions: under this criterion it is irrelevant whether the measures are simple, such as vaccination, or complex, such as neurosurgery after traffic accidents.

The second descriptor states that primary health care must use methods that are scientifically sound; that is, they must have been examined by the best of science and shown to be efficacious. Since the proof of efficacy is to be obtained through scientific inquiry, the health care system must include means of continually monitoring the effectiveness of health care methods, of evaluating them, and of comparing them with effects of new methods so as to ensure the use of the best method known. The Primary Health Care strategy thus imposes on the health system the obligation to collect data, to monitor experience, and to establish research units in the framework of the health system itself if sufficient data cannot be obtained from other sources (e.g. university research departments).

The requirement that governments must ensure a scientific evolution of treatment methods (even if that means that they must establish research units) is certainly a novelty for many of the poor countries. What was even more novel and not traditional was the requirement that treatment must be socially acceptable. This implies complex negotiations with sectors other than health; it means that, in one way or another, the people concerned must be given an opportunity to accept or reject health care methods that the health sector proposes.

The next requirement of primary health care, that it be universally accessible, that everyone – male or female, in any part of the world, regardless of race, religion, sex, age, or nationality – must have access to care, is possibly even more difficult to accomplish. This principle is easier to accept than some of its corollaries: it is easier to agree that all should be given care than to make those who will undoubtedly have to relinquish certain privileges (if an equitable distribution of care is indeed to be achieved) give these up.

All of this, however, is not simply to be given to the population: health care, according to the fifth descriptor of primary health care, requires active participation of individuals and their families in the process of care. There are few precedents for this requirement in the history of medicine. In sum, this descriptor means, for example, that the health care system has no right to decide on what will be done without the agreement of individuals suffering from a disease and their families. It implies a redistribution of authority and responsibility, a profound change of the health system, for any country.

Finally, the sixth descriptor of primary health care is that the cost of care must be congruent with the place health holds in the scale of values of a society. No society can afford to have everything; the decisions on what to do and how much to spend on it depend on the value attached to the goal by all those concerned – the individuals, the government, the press, society at large. Self-reliance and self-determination have been written into the definition as having a higher value than health, but no other contender for the society's budget has been listed. The word 'afford' in the definition clearly refers to the amount of resources corresponding to a specific value assigned to health at a given point in time; an increase in the value accorded to health directly influences the amount of resources reserved for health care. Those resources will, of course, have to be increased at the expense of other items whose priority in the scale of societal values has to drop when that of health is increased.

The definition of psychiatry is somewhat easier. Psychiatry is a medical discipline that is concerned with the recognition and treatment of mental disorders. It is important to recall that there is a distinction between psychiatry and mental health programmes. Mental health programmes are broader than psychiatry and somewhat different in their nature. They are aggregates of activities designed to (i) promote mental health, (ii) prevent mental illness, (iii) ensure the treatment of the mentally ill, (iv) rehabilitate those who are disabled by mental disorders, and (v) provide technical support to efforts aiming to diminish psychosocial problems such as violence of the erosion of families in conditions of rapid social change (WHO, 1992). Psychiatrists are sometimes leaders of mental health programmes; however, this is not always the case, nor is it necessary. While knowledge residing in psychiatry is a necessary part of the fund of knowledge on which mental health programmes are built, having it is not a sufficient qualification for a programme leader. The multitude of activities that must be included in comprehensive mental health programmes is such that skills and knowledge of many experts – ranging from anthropologists and economists to practitioners of biological sciences and philosophy – will be involved in the planning and implementation of these programmes.

Criteria for the inclusion of care for the mentally ill into primary health care

Having definitions of psychiatry, mental health programmes, and primary health care, it is possible to examine their relationship.

Public health importance

With regard to the first descriptor of primary health care – requiring that priority be given to problems that are of public health importance (i.e. problems that are frequent, grave in their consequences, and exert an impact on socio-economic development) – it is obvious that psychiatric disorders must be among those considered as a priority. Psychiatric disorders are frequent in all societies. They strike people at all ages and in all cultures. They cause suffering and can result in disability. They stigmatize people who have them, their families, and all that surrounds them, including medicaments for their treatment and institutions in which treatment is provided. The estimates of the total numbers of mentally ill people in the world are staggering; even by conservative estimates, at least 400 million people suffer from mental disorders of a severity sufficient to disable them. Recent estimates by WHO and the World Bank indicate that nearly 10% of all years lost because of disability are being lost because of mental disease. These estimates do not include mental retardation, which represents a serious impairment for at least 30 million people and less serious impairment for at least 100 million people in the world. Several forms of neurotic disorders as well as the psychiatric consequences of brain trauma, of epilepsy, and of stroke are also left out of the World Bank's calculations and have to be added to obtain correct estimates of the total burden that mental disorders present for society. Alcohol- and drug-related problems should also be added to the score; this is often not done because of the notorious methodological (and political) difficulties in the estimation of their magnitude.

In addition to mental disorders defined in accordance with standard psychiatric nosography, there are also psychosocial problems that are usually of major concern to governments and the population. These reach from intrafamilial violence to the interruption of the transition of culture in societies undergoing rapid social change. Estimations of their impact on socioeconomic development are difficult, but there is little doubt that it is enormous. Furthermore, psychosocial factors play a role in the origin of many diseases – for example, those determined by health behaviour – and influence the course and outcome of all of them. Psychiatry cannot deal with these problems nor control psychosocial factors. It can, however, provide substantial help in the recognition of psychosocial problems and factors and in the design of measures that can control them.

Problems for which there are no solutions cease to be problems and become givens of life; problems for which there are solutions are challenges to which we should respond with action. Until recently, it was believed that mental disorders are not amenable to preventive or curative intervention. This belief was perhaps at the origin of the low priority that mental health programmes and psychiatry receive in too many countries of the world. Today it is certain, though not universally known nor accepted, that primary prevention can be used in mental health programmes and that it can have substantial results (Sartorius, 1989; Sartorius & Henderson, 1992). It has also been demonstrated that many mental disorders are amenable to treatments and that such treatments not only reduce the time spent in illness but also reduce the probability that mental disorders will result in lasting impairments.

The two requirements for the declaration that mental disorders are a major public health problem – that the problem is severe (in terms of frequency, disability, and suffering that it produces) and that effective interventions are available – are therefore fulfilled.

It is thus possible to say that, using the first criterion of primary health care, the resolution or control of mental health problems must be given priority in national health programmes and that psychiatry must be among disciplines that will be called upon when these national programmes are drafted and implemented.

Scientific soundness of treatment and prevention methods

The second descriptor of primary health care requires, however, that national programmes designed to improve health use only methods that are scientifically sound. Here, traditions of psychiatry present a problem. For a long time and in many countries, psychiatrists have used methods of treatment that seemed useful, often without definitive proof of their effectiveness. Other branches of medicine were doing the same: gradually, however, evidence about the effectiveness of treatment has been accumulating in most medical disciplines. Psychiatry lagged behind, even after the introduction of a number of pharmacological remedies. Their effectiveness has since been extensively examined. Similarly, other biological treatments have been tested, and some had to be rejected because it was impossible to prove their effectiveness (e.g. insulin coma treatment), while for others (e.g. electroconvulsive treatment) the indications were sharpened. The value of other treatments in psychiatry has yet to undergo the rigorous testing that is required for admitting them as methods 'scientifically proven to be sound'. Among these are most psychotherapeutic techniques, as well as techniques used by traditional medical systems, and procedures such as meditation and various dietary regimens. Providing clear evidence that the treatments that are recommended for mental illness are effective is a major challenge for psychiatry in the framework of primary health care. Failing to demonstrate that psychiatry has at its disposal appropriate therapies would effectively eliminate psychiatry from health programmes if the strategy of primary health care were to be strictly applied.

Social acceptability of interventions proposed

The third descriptor of primary health care also represents a challenge for psychiatry. Not only does psychiatry have to prove that its methods are effective, it has also to ensure that its treatments are socially acceptable. Social acceptability is a complex criterion: treatments that are socially acceptable are not always acceptable to the patient and vice versa. An additional complication springs from the fact that the role of the family of the mentally ill is different from the role of the family of people who suffer from illnesses that do not diminish the capacity of the individual to make decisions about his or her treatment. In some cultures it is the head of the family who will decide whether the patient should be admitted to hospital; and even if he or she is against the treatment, it is the word of the head of the family that counts, so that the patient is counted as a voluntary admission. The words 'social acceptability' also have deeper undertones – for example, that of social interest and society's survival, both of which have been used to justify the intervention of psychiatry for political purposes.

The criterion of social acceptability is also complicated by the fact that education and other means can be used to change people's attitudes and that it is not clear whether, and how many, resources should be invested in making a particular treatment or intervention socially acceptable. Furthermore, social acceptability may change with time, and it could be argued that social acceptability must be examined at regular intervals even if this is expensive and difficult. Social acceptability also depends on the effectiveness of the measures proposed and on the changes in ideology and mores of communities. The criterion is thus clearly difficult to use, and there are many confounding factors that have to be kept in mind. The treatment of psychiatric illness has traditionally been considered as a rather vague set of procedures, possibly useful and certainly dangerous. The necessity to change the image of psychiatric treatment and provide clear, well-documented evidence about psychiatric interventions, which will allow patients and communities to make informed decisions about acceptability, remains therefore a major challenge before the psychiatric profession and leaders of mental health programmes.

Universal accessibility of care

At the present time the criterion of universal accessibility can only be met if a considerable proportion of tasks relevant to the prevention and treatment of mental illness is delegated to other health professions and in particular to those working at the level of primary-contact care. The number of psychiatrists in most countries of the world is small and will for a long time grow only slowly. In most developing countries, in which the frequency of mental and neurological disorders is the same or higher than the frequency of these disorders in developed industrialized countries, there are very few psychiatrists. In some developing countries there is no more than one psychiatrist for several million people. But even in the far better endowed developing countries – for example, India – there is still only one psychiatrist for every 300 000 people. It is probably impossible to provide an 'ideal' figure and say what the density of psychiatrists in a country should be. In Switzerland, for example, there are areas in which there is one psychiatrist for every 1000 inhabitants, and yet patients have to wait for weeks to see a psychiatrist while the health service is considering the need to increase the number of psychiatrists.

The story does not end there, however. Even in highly developed countries, most of the mentally ill will first seek help from general practitioners or physicians other than psychiatrists. The general health workers who deal with the large majority of the mentally ill are often poorly trained in psychiatry and do not recognize mental disorders when they see them. The treatment provided to those who are recognized is also often not adequate, leading to outcomes that discredit psychiatry and its therapeutic armamentarium.

Universal accessibility also means that, in the countries in which there are sufficient numbers of specialists (as well as in those in which there are few), everyone should have equal access to care, a requirement that at present does not seem to be satisfied even in the richest countries with most resources. Members of minority groups, the poor, the elderly and many others do not have as easy access to care as their more fortunate brethren who are better educated, richer, more vocal or more politically important.

Involvement of the population

The fifth criterion of primary health care – that the population must be involved, take an active part in the processes of treatment and the prevention of mental disorders – is a particularly difficult challenge for psychiatric services. The stigma still attached to mental illness and to those who suffer from it makes it difficult to mobilize anyone's help and participation, possibly with the exception of the close family of the patient. Involvement and active participation also seem to dwindle as the illness takes a chronic course, so that help becomes less and less available as the need for it grows. In many developing countries the first few months of illness will witness much support to the patient, from family members and from the community, in money and in kind. As the illness progresses, the family finds itself facing the impossible dilemma of continuing to spend its resources for the treatment of one of its members or looking after the needs of all the others. In such cases, as elsewhere in poor families who have no access to social insurance, chronic patients will not infrequently lose their place in the community of origin and become ostracized 'vagrant psychotics' overexposed to health hazards and hardships of all kinds.

Prospects are fortunately less bleak for less severe forms of mental disorder, and it is probable that the gradual introduction of different forms of social services for the general population will help in providing mentally ill people with the support they need even if they happen to be poor or otherwise disadvantaged. It is also probable that the increased effectiveness of treatment methods will help in reducing the time spent in illness and the cost of treatment – both important factors in any campaign seeking social support for a service or other action. Social involvement, compassion, and support to those who are impaired or otherwise in difficulty is a cardinal goal for civilized societies, with or without well-functioning social services. The challenge is its extension to cover stigmatized and severely disadvantaged groups.

Affordability

Finally, the last criterion of primary health care strategies refers to the services that a community or a country can afford. This is a rather vague statement allowing governments to set the expenditures for health at a level that is decided by other competing priorities. It would have been better if the Alma Ata Conference had stated the percentage of national budgets that should be at the disposal of health services, and then adopted recommendations for ensuring that the sum is spent in a just and scientifically justifiable manner. Clearly, it was difficult to expect that the member states of WHO could decide on such a matter without an intensive and extensive set of discussions within member countries, ensuring that there is consensus about the way in which the national priorities are set. It is probably utopian to hope that there will be international agreement on such a percentage calculated on the basis of the real health needs of the population. The word 'afford', however, does permit debate about the amount that should be given for health care and represents a beginning in the process of ensuring that people's health needs are fairly considered at all levels of government.

There then remains the difficult question of distributing the funds within the health sector. No country seems to have found a way to do this to the satisfaction of all the disciplines, institutions, and patients concerned. Mental health programmes have been particularly vocal in requesting more resources for the large numbers of patients suffering from mental illness and their many neglected needs. The most recent chapter of this everlasting battle concerns parity of insurance coverage for patients regardless of the diseases from which they suffer. In some countries this battle has been won; in many others it has not even begun. The difficulty that psychiatry and mental health programmes have to face at present also concerns the conversion of resources. Large buildings housing mental hospitals, for example, represent a huge financial value that cannot be used in the manner modern mental health care would require.

Experiences in the application of the primary health care strategy relevant to mental health care

It is thus obvious that programmes designed to deal with mental disorders would receive high priority if the primary health care strategy were to be applied. Unfortunately, primary health care is often interpreted in a manner that those who defined it would have never accepted. The reasons for this are many. The development of health care relying on principles of equity and scientific evidence would require a fundamental change in the current approaches to the provision of health services and to their evaluation, a change that would impose a redistribution of resources and authority in society as a whole. The estimation of the prevalence of a group of disorders and the consideration of the cost that their existence produces for society is an explicitly public health approach to decision making; few of the current leaders of the medical profession reach their decisions by using such approaches. Many sectors of society have vested interests in the maintenance of the presently existing system of health care. The notion that health care could change its objectives, its actors, and the sites of its performance is therefore likely to meet with resistance not only from those responsible for health care but also from many others.

The translations of the principles of primary health care into recommendations and guidelines for national health programmes are many. The difference between them is not in the overall descriptions of necessary action; rather, it is in the emphasis that has been given to components of the primary health care strategy. In some countries, for example, the emphasis has been put on ensuring that the health care system has a representative, e.g. a health station, near the people who will use the system. This enterprise, intended to implement the principle of accessibility of care, is costly and in many instances has failed to be beneficial for anyone. The peripheral health stations have often been established without ensuring a proper referral system. The health workers in the peripheral stations, in the beginning, did their best for a minimal salary, excited by the perspectives of a better future for all. The health authorities gave praise to the staff of these units in general terms; the individual recognition for work done, however, was often neglected. As time went on, working in peripheral stations lost all attraction. In some instances the health workers took on other – not always legitimate – tasks, for example, the sale of medications. In other settings the development of communications with cities and larger health institutions made it possible for a substantial proportion of patients to travel elsewhere for health care, so that the peripheral stations dealt only with the poorest people, who could not afford to go elsewhere and those residing nearby who had scratches and bruises or other banal problems.

The effort to ensure widespread coverage by rural primary care units also lost significance when the rate of migration to towns increased. Villages changed their demographic structures, often having a disproportionately large number of elderly and disabled people who could not migrate to towns, presenting problems for which the health workers had no solutions and no training. On the other hand, the rules and equipment foreseen for peripheral health units in villages proved to be at the limit of uselessness when the units were established in the huge peripheral region of towns. In more highly developed countries, the units also had to compete with a multitude of other institutions and systems providing care. Health workers in such units found little satisfaction in their work and began to suffer in increasing numbers from emotional burn-out syndromes.

In other settings the national health programme concentrated on developing another component of the primary care strategy – that of intersectoral cooperation. The efforts to ensure coordination between persons working in the sectors of health care, education, social welfare, labour, and so on often progressed well on the central government level. Problems arose, however, when the intention of coordinated work was proposed to the periphery, where there were considerable differences in the level of development and strength of the local representatives of the different systems, unable therefore – and often unwilling – to work together.

Another set of translations of the principles of primary care into practice emphasized the need to develop first-contact specialist care. Patients, it was said, should not have to be referred to a specialist; they should have the possibility of reaching the specialist directly, without delays. While it would probably be attractive for some patients to reach the best specialist for their disease as soon as possible, there were also many disadvantages to a system structured in this way. First, the system would require many specialists, often expensive to produce and often unwilling and unable to work far away from their specialized equipment. Second, the system presupposes that patients will know enough medicine to be able to decide which specialist to consult. They would have to know that numbness in their feet may be a consequence of a defect in sugar metabolism and that they should therefore consult a diabetologist (as well as other specialists), who may have the right solution for their problem. It is unlikely that the majority of patients will reach such knowledge about diseases in the near future and that all specialists will be able to deal with diseases outside their (narrow) speciality. Third, it is also possible that such an approach would further contribute to the fragmentation of medicine and to its dehumanization. Placing emphasis on disorders of specific organ systems may reduce the understanding of the total predicament of the patient and of his or her suffering.

Other examples of problems that the implementation of primary health care strategy encountered could be listed. It is probable, however, that the few examples given are sufficient to show that the main shortcoming of all attempts to introduce the concept was the uneven emphasis placed on the components of the strategy, which could work if all of its principles and elements are handled in a balanced manner and with similar zeal.

The tentative conclusions that one could draw from these arguments are the following. (i) Psychiatry stood to gain a great deal if the primary health care strategy had been introduced in all countries in the sense that its originators had intended. (ii) The primary health care strategy has to be reviewed because of changes in the health situation and socio-political and demographic changes worldwide. (iii) The argument about the best person or persons to provide treatment for mental illness is a relatively minor issue in the conundrum of decisions about the way in which the knowledge of psychiatry can be brought to bear on new primary health care strategy and consequently on the development of medicine and national health programmes. (iv) It is of the utmost importance that psychiatry and psychiatrists find a way of actively participating in the formulation of strategies for health care.

REFERENCES

Sartorius, N. (1989). The World Health Organization views on the prevention of mental disorders in developed and developing countries. In *Epidemiology and the Prevention of Mental Disorders*. ed. B. Cooper & T. Helgason pp. 321–326. New York: Routledge.

Sartorius, N. & Henderson, A. (1992). The neglect of prevention in psychiatry. *Australia and New Zealand Journal of Psychiatry*, **16**, 550–553.

World Health Organization (1978). Primary Health Care: Report of the International Conference on Primary Health Care, Alma Ata, 6–12 September 1978. Geneva: WHO.

World Health Organization (1992). *Mental Health Programmes. Concepts and Principles*. Geneva: WHO.

Reproduced with kind permission of the American Psychiatric Association.

His Head is Always in the Clouds by Hatao. (Courtesy of Hatao Masuda.)

9

The limits of mental health care in general medical services

In the second half of the twentieth century research showed that a large proportion of people with mental health problems do not seek help from health services and, of those who do, a great majority will contact general health services rather than psychiatrists even in countries in which the number of psychiatrists is high.

A consequence of these findings was that a number of countries began to provide additional training to general health care staff. It was soon demonstrated that these staff, with relatively simple training, can provide competent care to a significant number of patients who come to general health care facilities. Governments have also started proclaiming that mental health care should be provided in the general medical framework and, in some instances, reduced support to mental health services. In time, however, it became obvious that there are limits to this strategy and that the inclusion of mental health components into general health care must be accompanied by the development of mental health services of good quality and by the establishment of other services providing support for people with mental illness.

Texts concerning health care organization over the past several decades are unanimous in at least one recommendation: that primary and general health care services should take on the responsibility for the treatment (and prevention) of a number of illnesses that have been handled by specialist services (or by nobody) until now. Mental health planners have been particularly vocal in this respect. This is easy to understand. The prevalence of mental disorders in the general population and in general health care services is high and there are effective relatively easy-to-use methods of treatment. Skills and knowledge necessary for the application of these methods can be conveyed in a reasonably short time and the cost of treatment can be kept low. Preventive interventions are also possible – and most of them have to be implemented by general health care services or social sectors other than health. Examples of primary prevention measures range from the iodination of salt to prevent cretinism and appropriate perinatal care to avoid early brain damage, to the avoidance of hospitalization of the elderly to prevent cognitive and sensory overload: most of them can be suggested by psychiatrists but have to be implemented by others, outside of the mental health system.

The recommendations of the Alma Ata Conference on Primary Health Care (World Health Organization, 1978) included mental health care as one of the essential elements of primary health care and a number of countries have taken specific steps to provide care to those with a mental illness at the level of primary care. An important factor in accepting this recommendation was the results of studies done in Northern and Western Europe showing that a significant proportion of people with mental illness seek and receive help from general health care services and in particular from general practitioners. Meanwhile, such studies have been carried out in other countries producing similar results (Sartorius et al., 1990). Two decades ago, an international study of the frequency of mental disorders in primary health care services in developing countries combined with an operational study, demonstrated that it is possible to train general and primary health care staff in methods of treatment of several mental disorders and that staff so trained can provide useful and effective service to people contacting the services (Sartorius & Harding, 1983). Other studies since then confirmed these findings and showed that mental disorders are frequently seen in general health care services and that many of those seeking help do not receive it because their illness does not get recognized; and even when it is recognized appropriate treatment is only provided to a proportion of those ill (Üstün & Sartorius, 1995).

In some developing countries it has been possible to do all that is necessary to introduce mental health care into primary care. National mental health programmes have been drafted and accepted by the government, resources for the training of general health care have been made available and the medicaments for the treatment of some of the most severe mental disorders have been provided on a regular basis. In other countries some of the steps have been taken, but a broad-scale application of mental health measures at primary health care level still remains only an objective, although all concerned believe that its achievement is of the highest priority. In other countries still, governments and the professionals have not yet fully accepted the notion that mental health care should be provided in the primary health care services and mainly by primary or general health care staff. In many of these situations it is easy to obtain declarative support from the authorities and the professional associations but programmes do not go further than that.

In situations in which there was an extension of mental health care to the periphery there was invariably an individual or group of individuals who were determined to introduce the change and who often succeeded – although on occasion the new strategy is applied only on a limited territory and also often loses sharpness and power in parallel to the departure, ageing or promotion of the individuals who were the leaders of the original programme. This is not to say that progress is not being made: gradually, attitudes change, services are organized differently, training in medical schools is adjusted to the situation in the field and budgetary provisions are beginning to support peripheral mental health care in general health care services.

The above considerations do not only apply to developing countries: many highly industrialized countries are still committed to a model of provision of care in which most of the serious or longer lasting mental disorders are treated by the psychiatric service system and the remaining mental health problems are dealt with by psychiatrists in private practice, by psychologists and by a proportion of general practitioners who seem to have a special interest in mental health matters. Traditional health practitioners[1] see a significant number of people with mental health problems and play an important role in their treatment in both developing and developed countries: their activity however, is often not taken into account in official documents reporting on mental health care nor in planning for services.

It is therefore legitimate to ask why it is so difficult to fully implement a strategy of extension of mental health care to the periphery using primary and general health care services. At first glance, everybody stands to gain from the acceptance of this way of proceeding. The patients would receive help from clinics which are located close to their domicile. The health services would save money because it would be possible to treat patients under supervision of primary health care workers at their home and the side-effects of institutional treatment would not come into play. The cultural background and the home situation of the patient and their family would be well known to the service providers, which would help to avoid some of the difficulties that usually arise when patients are treated far away from home by individuals who are often not familiar with the culture and the situation in which the patients live. Doctors would feel better because they would know that their field of action has been expanded. The psychiatrists and other mental health specialists could give their attention to therapy-resistant cases, spend some time teaching and doing research. And yet, progress towards the introduction of mental health components into general health care remains slow or has been arrested.

Factors that limit the introduction of mental health components into general health care

An analysis of the reasons for the slow introduction of mental health care into general health services shows that limiting factors

---

[1] 'Traditional health practitioner' refers to an individual who has not completed formal training in a recognized health care school and is usually not officially permitted to treat people with mental illness.

belong to the personal, technical, social, administrative and professional domains.

Limiting factors: the personal domain

Factors belonging to this group are undoubtedly the most important and most difficult to manage. They refer to the attitudes and other personal characteristics of the main actors in the process of providing care – the patients, his or her family, the service provider and the decision makers in the field of health.

People suffering from mental illness (as well as their families) are aware of the nefarious consequences of being recognized as a 'mental case'. They will therefore – if they suspect that mental illness might be the reason for their suffering – seek help from people who are not part of their immediate social surroundings. Sometimes they will go for treatment to another town or village, sometimes they will see a privately practising psychiatrist, even if they have to pay for this treatment themselves. In many countries patients and their families do not believe that the information about a person's illness will stay in the records of the general practitioner: they feel that it is very likely that in one way or another an indiscretion by the nurse, home visitor or even the doctor, will give away the diagnosis or indicate the nature of ailment from which the patient suffers.

Sometimes, patients and their families will go to traditional healers who, by and large, never make the distinction between mental and physical illness but operate using a different system of grouping illnesses. The classification of problems used by traditional healers is usually more comprehensible for the patient and the treatment that is being prescribed is harmonious with cultural beliefs and previous experience of the patient and of the family. Primary health care is closer to most patients than the large and often dehumanized hospitals, but it is still in many cultures a foreign import, far less their own than traditional health practices and practitioners.

The fear of stigma and possible discrimination because of mental illness and the wish to be treated by an acceptable practice are not the only reasons for the selection of someone other than the primary health care provider: to these reasons is added the uncertainty about the knowledge and treatment skills that the general practitioner has and might use to deal with mental illness. This lack of confidence is not without justification: for a very long time general medical practitioners had little training in psychiatry (particularly concerning the treatment of 'banal' mental illnesses such as anxiety states) and were reluctant to treat people suffering from mental illness. The population often sees the general practitioner as a person who can help with emergencies and can treat minor physical illness: when it comes to more complex problems, it is felt the general practitioner will act in accordance with a specialist's advice.

The personal reasons that make physicians at primary care level reluctant to handle mental health problems are more complex. In some instances the lack of knowledge and absence of treatment skills drives the general practitioner to refer the patient elsewhere. The medical school training in most countries of the world and in most medical schools still lacks emphasis on psychiatric treatment skills for the general practitioner; even such an elementary skill as the mental state examination is not taught in practical exercises. The total number of hours that medical undergraduates spend in direct contact with people who are suffering from mental illness is still appallingly low in most medical schools of the world: the total number of hours of instruction about psychiatry is often restricted to 50 hours, most of which are given to lectures.

Stigma and the image of a mental patient also play a role in the reluctance of the general physician to take on the care of the mentally ill: among the elements of the stigmatized image of the mentally ill, the myth of incurability of those who suffer from diseases of the mind may also make the treatment of mental illness less attractive. When a mental disorder and a physical disorder are both present, both the doctor and the patient may prefer to pay attention to the physical illness, thus avoiding talking about mental illness or seeking treatment for it ('tacit collusion').

The working conditions of the majority of general health care personnel are also of importance. In many countries long hours of work, relatively low income, absence of career prospects, excessive administrative demands and other factors, reduce the motivation of the primary health care personnel to do their work. The 'burn-out' syndrome appears to have become common in peripheral health care workers (and some other professionals, e.g. teachers in peripheral schools) and health decision makers in various countries complain that it is becoming exceedingly difficult to introduce any measure requiring additional work or learning into primary health care services. The proposal that general practitioners and other primary health care personnel should participate in service training or refresher courses is usually found acceptable by the administrative heads of the service: the attendance at training courses and the enthusiasm to learn new things, however, remains low and incentives other than increase of knowledge have to be provided in most instances.

Similar factors might also be at work in creating the reluctance of health decision makers to promote the introduction of mental health care into general health services. The health decision makers of today have often received inadequate training in psychiatry and may have left their medical school believing that all mental disorders are like those that they have seen during their brief visit to the mental hospital. They know that such patients are rare in general health care services and are therefore not convinced that much would be gained if an intensive effort were to be made to train general practitioners or to reorganise the services. Even when they have a broader comprehension of mental health problems and have accepted data about the prevalence of mental disorders in general health care facilities, they do not believe that today's psychiatry has the means to help those patients given the constraints of primary health care activity. They therefore do not do much to help the introduction of psychiatry into primary care. This can be changed: in the All India Institute of Neurosciences and Mental Health in Bangalore (India) for example, health decision makers have been invited for information sessions about mental health and illness, which greatly facilitated the introduction of changes into the health service system.

Limiting factors: the technological domain

Technological constraints (using the word technology in its original sense of the application of scientific knowledge) are also of considerable importance in the provision of mental health care in primary care settings. Once research produces methods that can reduce particularly disturbing symptoms of mental illness (e.g. extreme agitation) even more rapidly than is possible using today's techniques, it will be reasonable to expect that general health care services retain patients who show such symptoms. For the time being, the settings in which primary health care is usually practised do not permit the management of acutely disturbed, severely psychotic or aggressive patients *in loco*: referral to a facility that is equipped to deal with this type of behavioural disturbance will be necessary while these symptoms last. The discovery of modern pharmacological means to deal with various types of symptoms of mental disorder has already significantly changed the organization of services for the mentally ill. Further advances of science and of treatment tools will make the treatment of mental illness in the framework of primary health care much easier and more similar to other interventions in emergency situations often used in primary care settings.

Other technological problems also limit the possibility of transferring responsibility for mental health problems into primary health care. The irregularity of supply of medicaments to the peripheral health services and pharmacies, for example, is a persistent problem in many developing countries and more recently also in countries of Eastern Europe. Transport to a referral centre takes a long time and has to be prepared well in advance: under such conditions it will often be considered safer to send the patient to an inpatient facility even if that is far away, to avoid complications and legal problems.

Limiting factors: the social domain

Stigma of mental illness is not limited to the disease or the person who suffers from it. It extends itself to the family of the patient, the medicaments used to treat the disease, to the institutions where people receive treatment for mental illness and to mental health workers. It is pervasive and frightening in its consequences. The idea that a nice primary health care facility could be used to treat mentally ill people is not acceptable for many who receive treatment in the primary care centre (for other types of ailments), to the authorities that run the facility, the population living in the area and, last but not least, also to many of the health staff working in the centre. It is certainly possible to overcome these resistances, but not in all situations and not without a major effort often involving legal measures, long-lasting disputations and difficulties with colleagues, friends and politicians. The line of lesser resistance is therefore often chosen and even when the architectural and other plans have foreseen that mental health care would be provided in a department of psychiatry located in a general health care facility, things somehow soon change and the treatment of the mentally ill is done elsewhere. The reasons given for this move are remarkably inventive and usually sound very rational, referring to more pleasant surroundings, better access, more space for parking and various other apparent advantages. It is encouraging to watch how the departments of psychiatry in general hospitals previously often located in the basement floor or in a separate building at the far end of the hospital grounds gradually move closer to 'real' medicine departments; unfortunately, however, in order to be acceptable to other colleagues in the hospital or the medical school the psychiatrists select the best behaved patients for admission in the general hospital, sending other patients – who often need particularly careful attention – to other facilities in which the patient/staff ratio and other conditions are considerably worse than in the general hospital wards. This two-tier psychiatry, which has made its appearance in recent years, is a real danger to the discipline as a whole: in often elegant settings there are numerous psychiatrists and other mental health personnel – psychologists, social workers, case managers all dealing with 'attractive' patients – while somewhere else, understaffed and otherwise poorly resourced facilities break down under the load of patients who have diseases that are difficult to manage and are poor, often homeless, and with many social problems. The previous battle to enter into the general hospital and general health care facilities will probably now have to be replaced by a battle to open the upper quality mental health facilities to all or most of the patients and to ensure that mental health resources are equitably distributed within psychiatric services, not only between psychiatric and other health services.

Limiting factors: the administrative domain

Resources that are spent on mental health services are in many settings, considerable. Mental hospitals – although often catering only for a small proportion of those with mental illness in the population (among whom many are resident in the hospital for years) – cost a lot of money. Staff in mental hospitals may be low-paid, the food and other facilities for patients may be miserable and the buildings and parks surrounding them may be in need of repair: the annual budget for the institution as a whole (and for its 'sisters' or 'brothers' carrying the name of 'mental health institute' or some other, e.g. 'rehabilitation centre') is nevertheless high and represents a significant proportion, sometimes almost the whole, of the allocation for mental health care in the country. Reformers have, for a long time, pointed to the resources reserved for the maintenance of mental hospitals stating that the mental health budgets do not necessarily have to be increased to provide better service to a much larger number of patients. All that would have to be done would be to reallocate resources to outpatient services, to the training of general health staff in psychiatry, to the development of half-way institutions, to the strengthening of social services. All in vain: over the years and through many a bitter experience it became clear that (i) it is relatively easy to discharge some of the patients with chronic illness and impairments but that it is difficult to discharge all of them, (ii) that staff in mental hospitals, although not well paid and often lacking prospects of scientific or other careers prefer stability and when given a choice of working outside the hospital or in it, select the latter, (iii) that the economy of the villages surrounding the hospital depends on its existence and that their inhabitants can create a lot of opposition to its closure, (iv) that there are often considerable difficulties in converting an empty mental hospital with its grounds into readily available cash to be used exclusively for the development of mental health care, (v) that there are patients who need inpatient care for a variety of reasons and that, unless or until another mental hospital or inpatient facility has been built, such patients will come back to the mental hospital and that (vi) when there are no mental hospital beds, acute wards have to use part of their resources to house chronically disabled patients, which in turn changes the nature of the acute community service in a major way. Operational research has shown that it is necessary to nearly double the investments in mental health services during the period of emptying the mental hospital so as to build alternative facilities and establish appropriate mental health care in the community (Trieman *et al.*, 1998). As a consequence of such experience and findings, administrative authorities have become reluctant to begin the process of deinstitutionalization, and the introduction of mental health care in general health services has become dependent on an enlargement of the budget for mental health (naturally at the cost of diminution of some other budget line whose proponents always seem to fight back with vigour). In current times of financial stringency and administrative conservatism it is therefore becoming even more difficult to introduce such changes, and detailed and well-reasoned programmes to do so lie idly in many places, waiting for better times.

Limiting factors: professional domain

Most of the knowledge about mental health problems and of the techniques for their treatment is produced by the psychiatric profession. Psychiatrists are engaged in research on mental illness and serve as a bridge to other disciplines carrying out related research. Psychiatrists teach medical students, study the epidemiology of mental disorders and its changes under the impact of new service arrangements, provide forensic psychiatric service and represent – well or not so well – the interests of psychiatric patients and of the discipline of psychiatry before the administrative and academic authorities.

When it is proposed that mental health care should be carried out by general health care services, that biological research into the causes and pathogenesis of mental disorders should be left to fundamental scientists and that rehabilitation of the impaired should be taken on by the rehabilitation services, psychiatrists begin to feel uneasy: those in private practice feel that the patients whom they normally treat will be taken away by the general practitioner and that their income will therefore diminish; those in teaching positions foresee that teachers of other subjects, for example, internal medicine, will begin teaching about the recognition and treatment of, say, depression; and those engaged in research see their field of inquiry drastically diminished. Psychiatrists are therefore, in most instances, not very ardent supporters of the delegation of mental health tasks to the general health care workers.

The fears that there will not be enough patients to treat and that teaching will be taken over by others are not supported by evidence. The introduction of treatment of the mentally ill in general health services usually increases the number of those requesting help, and there is little movement from the specialist to the generalist. The teachers of other disciplines are rarely keen to begin teaching psychiatry. There is, however, a danger that one of the consequences of a broad-scale reform will be a significant reduction of the resources that are put at the disposal of psychiatry, which might reduce its productivity in terms of new knowledge and in terms of its capacity to provide adequate teaching to medical students and others in the health care system. The reformers should keep this in mind and argue for a strengthening of mental health components of general health care, while maintaining the function of psychiatry that has to support the providers of care at the point of primary contact and has to continue to lead in the development of new knowledge and skills that can be used by others in the health sector.

Overcoming obstacles to the introduction of mental health care into general health care

While it is obvious that some of the factors limiting the introduction of mental health components into general health care are expressions of true dilemmas, others are not. The latter should be removed: at the present state of our knowledge there is no other way but the introduction of mental health care into general health care to increase the probability that those suffering from a mental illness will receive adequate help. In many countries of the world there are few psychiatrists. The prevalence of mental disorders in developing and developed countries is high and the total burden of mental disease worldwide is second highest in terms of the years lost due to disability produced by disease. No less than one person out of every five who contact general health care services has psychological disorder as a primary reason for consultation and most of those disorders are amenable to treatment.

Table 1 summarizes the factors limiting the introduction of mental

Table 1. *Introducing mental health care: limitations and interventions*

Domain	Limiting factor	Intervention
Personal	Reluctance of patients to present problems to general health care worker	Health education
	Reluctance of health workers to deal with mental health problems	Training of health workers to increase their technical competence and change attitudes
Technological	Imperfection of treatment tools	Research to produce better treatment interventions, with particular emphasis on the possibility of their use in primary health care
	Irregularity of supply of medicaments	Reorganisation of supporting services
Social	Stigma on mental illness and on mental health services	Anti-stigma actions within the health care system and in the general population (e.g. in school health programmes)
		Examination of legal provisions concerning discrimination
Administrative	Transfer of allocations of funds to general health care, earmarked for psychiatry often difficult	Lobbying for an increase of funding for the mental health programmes Development of long-term gradual programme of diminution of inpatient services and their replacement by outpatient services
Professional	Reluctance of psychiatrists to participate in programmes of introduction of mental health care into general care	Involvement of psychiatric society as well as general practitioners in planning for change and provision of incentives for training of general health care staff

health care into general health care and proposes interventions that could remove or lessen some of the limitations. In examining this table it is important to remember that there is usually more than one limiting factor at work and that the measures listed are examples of a variety that have been used in different settings to reduce some of them.

Conclusion

As in many other instances, programmes and strategies are important for any change. At the same time however, it is useful to recall that people change faster in response to emotional and social pressures than they do in response to logic and public health imperatives. Change to new ways of doing things should therefore, wherever possible be proposed by leaders who have the confidence of the profession and of the population because of their knowledge, previous achievements, personality and political skills. Transfer of responsibility for care is also a transfer of power – an operation that will involve readjustments and often sacrifice. A vast majority of those involved in changes are reasonable people, of reasonably good will. Proceeding with respect for concerns and wishes of all involved, and carefully choosing the pace and manner of achieving change, is therefore an indication of good sense and a guarantee that changes will survive and last after the reformers have left the field.

REFERENCES

Sartorius, N. & Harding, T.W. (1983). The WHO collaborative study on strategies for extending mental health care I. Genesis of the study. *American Journal of Psychiatry*, **140**, 1470.

Sartorius, N., Goldberg, D., de Girolamo, G., Costa e Silva, J.A., Lecrubier, Y. & Witchen, H.U. (eds.) (1990). *Psychological Disorders in General Health Care*. Bern, Toronto, Lewiston (NY): Hogrefe and Huber.

Trieman, N., Hughes, J. & Leff, J. (1998). The TAPs Project 42: the last to leave hospital – a profile of residual long-stay populations and plans for their resettlement. *Acta Psychiatrica Scandinavica*, **98**, 354–359.

Üstün, T.B. & Sartorius, N. (eds.) (1995). *Mental Illness in General Health Care.* Chichester, UK: John Wiley.

World Health Organization (1978). *Primary Health Care: Report of the International Conference on Primary Health Care,* Alma Ata, 6–12 September 1978, Geneva: WHO.

Reproduced with permission.

Martin Schouman (1770–1848): *Shipping in a Swell*. (Courtesy of Bonhams, London, and Bridgeman Art Library, London.)

10

The mental health adventure of the World Health Organization

Fifty years ago it was not customary for public health agencies to have a department of mental health. The inclusion of such a programme in the World Health Organization is a testimony to the wisdom of the founders of the Organization. Yet, over the years the mental health unit had numerous ups and downs reflecting the fact that the promotion of mental health and the control of psychiatric disorders have not been fully accepted as part of WHO's public health mission. In the most recent past, however, the WHO administration has given the mental health programme considerable attention and support.

The history of the programme seems to confirm that it takes several decades before an idea can gain acceptance and a change can be introduced in the public health machinery.

World Health Day for the year 2001 was devoted to Mental Health. The Annual Report of the World Health Organization for the year 2001 was devoted to mental health. The Mental Health Department of the WHO has been significantly strengthened by staff and funds. Additional resources were made available to the Department by voluntary donations from a number of countries. These are good news for the field of mental health and particularly for mental health programmes in the many countries in which they have very low priority. The history of the mental health programme of the WHO illustrates the perils and the sinuous way of making mental health everybody's concern and ensuring that people with mental disorders and their families get the care they need.

The Constitution of the World Health Organization was written in 1948, shortly after one of the most terrible wars in human history. The citizens of the world – or at least the majority of those who lived in its parts that the war had ravaged, met peace with hopes and expectations of a better future for all. Many of the villains had been punished. There seemed to be no obstacles to the vast improvement of the world. The sense of togetherness born in the struggle against the common enemy made it easy to find volunteers. Everyone seemed to be ready to continue making sacrifices in order to build a better future. Associations of people of goodwill[1] sprang up and it was easy to establish intergovernmental organizations such as the World Health Organization. The basic documents of the organizations and associations that came into existence at that time make beautiful reading. They are inspired by the devotion of their writers to humanitarian causes and by their visions of a prosperous future in which equity and solidarity will continue to reign.

The Constitution of the World Health Organization also reflects these feelings (WHO, 1996). It defines health as being a state of physical, mental and social well-being rather than as a 'mere absence of disease'. It proclaims that the achievement of the 'highest attainable' standard of health is one of the fundamental rights of every human being. It holds governments responsible for the health of their people.

---

[1] For example, the World Federation for Mental Health.

It proclaims that the extension of 'medical, psychological and related knowledge' is essential to the attainment of health. The Constitution's Article 2, enumerates the activities that are necessary to fulfil WHO's role as 'a co-ordinating and directing authority' in the field of international health – such as the development of standards, conventions, information systems, and diagnostic procedures and the provision of advice to member states. It lists three general functions – the promotion of research, the improvement of teaching in schools of health and related personnel and the study and reporting on techniques that can be useful in the prevention and treatment of diseases. Finally, it gives four specific areas of action – the prevention of injuries, the promotion of environmental health, the promotion of maternal and child health and the fostering of '... activities in the field of mental health especially those affecting the harmony of human relations'.

When the time came to create the infrastructure of the World Health Organization, various units were created and given the task to fulfil the constitutional functions of the Organization. Not all of the functions of WHO were reflected in its units: but mental health, surprisingly for many, was. The reasons for this are not clear. Perhaps this was due to the fact that the Director-General of the new agency was a military psychiatrist, Dr Brock Chisholm. The fact that the army of the Allies had introduced screening for psychological problems and had managed to diminish casualties among their pilots and other military personnel – information well known to Dr Chisholm – might have played a role in his decision. Maybe he decided to do so, feeling that all constitutional mandates of the Organization must have a specific focal point, but ran out of staff necessary to create units for all of WHO's constitutional mandates. Maybe he truly saw the promotion of mental health as one of the primary tasks of the Organization. We shall never know.

A mental health unit in a public health organization was an oddity: schools of public health only rarely had such a department. D. Chisholm must have had difficulties in creating the mental health unit: its size was small (a chief and a secretary) and its budget was modest. But it began working and, with this, started the adventure of a mental health programme in an organization, that like other public health agencies, had no particular interest in mental health matters. WHO in its early days concentrated on matters such as fighting communicable diseases, the eradication of malaria, the provision of training fellowships to doctors from disadvantaged areas, on the collection and publication of information about health matters[2] and on convening Expert Committee meetings that were producing outstandingly good reviews of knowledge and recommendations for the development and management of health services and other matters related to health. In its structure the Organization had similarities with an army created to fight the war with disease. Terms used in WHO reflected this. The Head of the Organization was the Director *General* who resided at the *Headquarters* of the WHO that carried out its work through the action of a number of *Divisions* dealing with the major parts of the programme. Smaller programmes were undertaken by *Units*. An overall *strategy* governed the orderly execution of activities including WHO's *campaigns* against diseases or other health damaging factors. The rules of operation – some written and some transmitted by word of mouth – were strict covering even minute details, for example, the colour of ink used by officers at different levels of the Organization: the Director General used mauve/purple ink, his Deputy green, the Assistant Directors General red, the Chief of Budget turquoise and the Divisional directors black ink. Other staff were not supposed to use ink of these colours, and so wrote in pencil and royal (or other shades of) blue.

The constitutional mandates of the WHO were similar to those of a school of public health. The Divisions of the WHO had tasks that were similar to the departments of the same name in public health schools. The promotion of mental health and the control of mental and neurological disorders did not belong to the usual array of tasks of schools of public health, and it was not quite clear to anyone why mental health should be among WHO's units, nor what it should be doing. In addition, many of the staff of the Organization in those years, who had served in colonial health services before or during the Second World

---

[2] For example, the *Weekly Epidemiological Report* and the annual statistical reports on health services.

War, had little to do with mental health services in their previous career and, with rare exceptions, did not think that it was worth doing anything about mental illness. The widely prevailing opinion was that mental health problems are not as frequent in the developing world as they are in industrialized countries, that the families can cope well with the few cases that exist and that there is, anyway, little that can be done to help those struck by mental illness.

The odds that the mental health unit would survive for long in such an environment were low. The Unit concentrated its attention on two subjects: the organization of Expert Committee meetings, each resulting in an excellent report and a series of assessments of country needs mainly done by consultants who wrote reports and visited government offices.

The former activity covered a lot of ground: Table 1 gives the topics that the Expert Committees and Scientific Groups convened by the Unit tackled over the first 25 WHO years (1949–1974).

Each of the meetings involved 10 to 12 experts, members of the Mental Health Expert Panel. The members of the Panel received no remuneration for their being on the panel or for their participation in the meetings. Their travel and accommodation expenses were covered, and it was customary to offer the expert a cocktail reception lasting approximately 1 hour. The Chiefs of the Unit that convened the meeting usually invited the experts for a meal at their home or in a restaurant, without receiving an allowance for such entertainment.

The meetings were regulated by strict rules: the most important of these, for practical purposes, was that the experts had to produce a report by the end of the week of their meeting. The reports usually went through three drafts and the result was a publication of some 60 to 80 pages. The reports were submitted to the Executive Board of the Organization and discussed by the Board in considerable detail. The discussions in the Board were detailed and useful in the implementation of the recommendations. The members of the Executive Board at that time had usually been highly placed and experienced public health experts.

The visits of consultants to countries resulted in reports of the actual

Table 1[3]

Habit-Forming Drugs, 1949
Mental health, TRS No. 9, 1950
Mental Hygiene, PAHO, Scientific Publication No. 1, 1953
Community mental hospital, TRS No. 73, 1953
Mental Hygiene in the Nursery School, 1953
Mental health aspects of adoption, TRS No. 70, 1953
Alcohol, TRS No. 84, 1954
Drugs liable to produce addiction, TRS No. 76, 1954
Mentally subnormal child, TRS No. 75, 1954
Children in Hospitals, 1954
Mental Health through Public Health Practice, 1955
Legislation affecting psychiatric treatment, TRS No. 98, 1955
Human relations and mental health in industrial units, 1956
Psychiatric nursing, TRS No. 105, 1956
Juvenile epilepsy, TRS No. 130, 1957
Psychiatric hospital as a centre for preventive work in mental health, TRS No. 134, 1957
Treatment and care of drug addicts, TRS No. 131. 1957
Ataractic and hallucinogenic drugs, TRS No. 152, 1958
Medical Rehabilitation, TRS No. 158, 1958
Mental health aspects of the peaceful uses of atomic energy, TRS No. 151, 1958
Public Health Aspects of the ageing of the population, 1959
Mental health problems of ageing and the aged, TRS No. 171, 1959
Mental health problems of automation, TRS No. 183, 1959
Social psychiatry and community attitudes, TRS No. 177, 1959
Epidemiology of mental disorders, TRS No. 185, 1960
Programme development in the mental health field, TRS No. 223, 1961
Undergraduate teaching of psychiatry and mental health programmes, TRS No. 208, 1961
Role of public health officers and general practitioners in mental health care, TRS No. 235, 1962
Training of psychiatrists, TRS No. 252, 1963

---

[3] This table only contains topics addressed in Expert Committees and Scientific or Study Groups. These were usually published as Technical Report Series (TRS). Numerous less formal meetings addressed other topics.

Table 1 (*cont.*)

Psychosomatic disorders, TRS No. 275, 1964
Mental Health Research, 1964
Research on genetics in psychiatry, TRS No. 346, 1966
Research in psychopharmacology, TRS No. 371, 1967
Services for the prevention and treatment of dependence on alcohol and
    other drugs, TRS No. 363, 1967
Neurophysiological and behavioural research in psychiatry, TRS No. 381, 1968
Organization of services for the mentally retarded, TRS No. 392, 1968
Biochemistry of mental disorders, TRS No. 427, 1969
Biological research in schizophrenia, TRS No. 450, 1970
Clinical pharmacology, TRS No. 446, 1970
Psychogeriatrics, 1970
The Use of Cannabis, TRS No. 478, 1971
Detection of dependence-producing drugs in body fluids, TRS No. 556, 1974

situation. Their main purpose, however, had been to demonstrate WHO's interest in the field of mental health, to establish contacts with public health authorities and to identify mental health workers able and interested in participating in WHO programmes.

The first 10 years of the programme were mainly spent in this way. The budget of the programme remained low but steady[4]. Other WHO programmes went from strength to strength and WHO grew considerably. Regional offices of the Organization were established in five regions (Southwest Asian, Eastern Mediterranean, European, African and Western Pacific). In the Americas, WHO found an arrangement by which the Panamerican Sanitary Bureau also began to function as the WHO Office for the American region. The regional offices grew rapidly. Their main task was to provide direct services to countries. Strategic recommendations remained Headquarters' responsibility. In two of the offices a mental health unit came into existence – in the Americas and

---

[4] In the early years of the WHO programme, the Heads of the mental health unit were Drs G. Hargreaves, E. Krapf, P. Baan, B. Lebedev and F. Hassler.

in Europe. These units reported to the Regional Directors but maintained technical liaison with the Headquarters mental health staff.

At the end of the 1950s and early 1960s it was proposed to add a post of a psychiatric epidemiologist to the mental health unit, which has meanwhile grown by the addition of a psychiatrist transferred from an organization that dealt with refugee problems and an editor. The post was meant to employ an expert from Taiwan, then the country representing China as a whole. Taiwan was also a loyal ally of the USA. There were politically tainted comments about the recruitment, discussions and bargaining ending in the creation of two posts, one for the expert from Taiwan and the other to balance matters for a Russian psychiatrist who had specialized in biological psychiatry and psychopharmacology. The latter field was of growing importance and of considerable scientific as well as economic interest. Everyone seemed to have gained by this process of balancing – the mental health programme had grown, Taiwan could be proud that its citizen could come and initiate the programme of epidemiological psychiatry and the Russian Government had gained a post in the Headquarters of the Organization. I joined the Organization shortly after this development: its echoes were still audible and highly interesting for a newcomer.

It turned out that the employment of the expert in psychiatric epidemiology brought with it a new opening for the programme: personal contacts and relationships with leading experts in the field as well as the fact that the National Institute of Mental Health[5], at the time had much interest in psychiatric epidemiology made it possible to apply for a grant and get it thus nearly doubling the budget of the mental health programme. A four-stage programme was put into operation: Part 1 was to deal with psychiatric diagnosis and classification; Part 2 was to facilitate pilot studies of major psychiatric disorders and develop transculturally applicable psychiatric assessment instruments; Part 3 was to support the expansion of this work and allow the conduct of epidemiological studies of mental disorders in geographically defined populations; and Part 4 was to develop training in psychiatric epidemiology so

---

[5] The National Institute of Mental Health has subsequently been divided into three National institutes, one dealing with mental health, one with alcohol problems and one with drug abuse and dependence.

as to enable countries to train their own staff and carry out studies in preparation of rational programme development (Cooper, 1999).

The effects of this injection of funds from outside of the Organization were varied. Most of them were positive. The funds have made it possible to hire staff to work on the project thus increasing the technical strength of the unit. The work in the field resulted in the establishment of groups of investigators who were advocates of the WHO in scientific circles. These groups were located in the developing and developed countries: the fact that good research could be carried out in countries that were poor and had no long-standing tradition of research came as a surprise to many and facilitated influx of funds from other sources into these countries. The publications that resulted from the programme made the mental health programme of the WHO known as a place where international research was being done.

The studies carried out by the WHO in those years resulted in several 'firsts' in science – the first-ever confirmation that people in very different countries suffer from the same form of schizophrenia and some other mental illnesses, the first-ever array of assessment methods that could be reliably applied in different cultural settings (and many languages) (Sartorius & Janca, 1996), the first-ever methods of achieving reliability in psychiatric assessment in different parts of the world, and the first major confirmation of a few indicative previous findings that schizophrenia has a better outcome in the developing than in the developed world.

The WHO administration did not consider these developments as being of particular importance. The administration of the WHO argued that the influx of funds from elsewhere frees it from adding to the budget of the programme in the following years. There were doubts about the legitimacy of this undertaking: after all, WHO was a public health agency and not an institution that should be engaged in research, particularly in a field that is not a priority concern of the organization. There were occasionally some political comments as well: on one occasion the ambassador of France – a country always concerned with the preservation of the French language and traditions – sent one of his attachés to enquire why there were so few references to French publications in the book reporting on findings in the international pilot study of schizophrenia[6]. This visit was of considerable interest – it showed that WHO publications were, regrettably, more regularly scrutinized, on the whole, by political than by scientific bodies. Political changes did not affect the programme very much, but occasionally they did. Thus, for example, when the representation of China to the United Nations (and in the WHO) changed from Taipeh to Beijing the collaboration with the field research centre in Taiwan had to stop[7]. WHO's stated policy of non-interference with national health care systems was among the reasons why for many years, WHO, did not get directly involved in the movement against the abuse of psychiatry in the USSR (and elsewhere). In the 1980s this policy changed and lead to WHO's action against health discrimination in the apartheid regime of South Africa and to its involvement in improving health care for displaced populations. Sometimes, there were pressures to give priority to this or to the other candidate in the selection for posts. That politics did not interfere in the work of the programme might have been one of the few positive consequences of the small size of the programme and of the fact that it was not being considered a priority for the organization.

Although no grants and few additional resources were received for work in biological psychiatry, collaboration with centres engaged in biological research progressed as well leading to the establishment of a network of collaborating centres and publications. The collaborating centres of different orientation participated in a fairly large number of collaborative studies under the aegis of the WHO (Sartorius, 1989) and developed into a worldwide network including centres of excellence in psychiatry and neurology in more than 40 countries.

Other programmes were also launched with minimal funds – for example, dealing with mental retardation, with the prevention of suicide and with alcohol-related problems. Occasional meetings of expert committees and study groups continued to happen, gradually becoming less clear in their recommendations.

The support to the mental health programme in WHO remained

---

[6] None directly relevant to the report were published.
[7] The data from the Taipeh centre were later published in an American journal.

steadily low, hovering around 1% of the Organization's total regular budget. Although professionals and a number of countries recognized the need for mental health programmes and urged the WHO management to increase the regular budget for the programme, nothing much happened. The recognition of the importance of the mental health programme within the organization came from a different source.

In the early 1970s there was a change of the Director General and his Deputy: Dr M. Candau, the second Director General of WHO under whose directorship the Organization grew enormously, left the Organization and Dr H. Mahler, a Danish tuberculosis expert was elected as his successor. Dr Mahler had a different set of priorities and ideas about the direction of the Organization. With the change of WHO leaders and in tune with socio-economic changes in countries, characteristic of the mid-1970s, the strategic aims of the Organization changed. The ambition of the early years of WHO to be the ultimate technical authority in public health was abandoned. WHO was to become the coordinator of national efforts in the field of health. A whole range of changes followed this shift. The Advisory Committee for Medical Research, for example, containing a small group of the world's best scientists changed its name to become the Advisory Committee on Health Research (ACHR), and its membership was increased by adding public health decision makers. The meetings of the Advisory Committee became less regular, its discussions swerved away from scientific, epidemiological and laboratory research to issues of health care provision. The recommendations of the ACHR Committee became broader, dealing, for example, with the involvement of ministries of health in research.

The deputy of Dr Candau the Director General, Dr Dorolle was French and had in the years before joining the WHO for a while been responsible for the management of a mental hospital in Vietnam. His opinion of the mental health programme and its function was probably inspired by this experience. His successor in this position was Dr T.A. Lambo, a psychiatrist from Nigeria. Prior to joining the WHO, Dr Lambo gained fame because of his efforts to reduce and complement mental hospital treatment by the placement of people with mental illness into homes of families that agreed to look after them. He had also collaborated in a landmark epidemiological study carried out in Nigeria, together with Canadian scientists. He was successful in building up his medical school, and his university. Tall, of imposing presence, he was important for the programme in two ways: first, by being a psychiatrist in the almost highest position in the Organization, and second by being inclined to help the programme of the discipline to which he belonged. As could be expected, over time, the feeling of professionally belonging to the discipline of psychiatry dwindled and many other interests and priorities invaded his agenda: in the early days of his presence, however, he helped to introduce a number of administrative changes that were immensely useful to the programme. These included the merging of the unit of drug dependence originally embedded in the Division of Pharmacology into the Mental Health Unit, an increase of the numbers of staff of the mental health programme by transfers from other units and the elevation of the status of the Mental Health Programme first to an independent office that reported directly to him and then to the level of a Division[8].

Though administratively elevated, the programme still retained its low budget and was in a precarious position. Not many in the Organization supported the idea that the mental health programme should be raised to the level of other major programmes. Although the personal relationships of the mental health programme staff with the rest of the organization's staff were pleasant and cooperative, the usual prejudices against psychiatry did not abate. It was necessary to find ways of defending the programmes. I felt that a way to do this was to strengthen the relationship with the Regional Directors in order to convince those who did not yet have a mental advisor about the usefulness of establishing a mental health post or unit at the regional level. This effort was, to an extent, influenced by my early experience in WHO. Soon after joining the Organization, I was transferred to India to work there as a member of an interregional team on the epidemiology of mental disorders. This was an unforgettable experience in many ways. Among the lasting impressions of that time was the realization of the vast possibilities of achieving much, even with little resources – for

---

[8] The Directors of the Mental Health Division were myself (1977–1993), Dr J.A. Costa e Silva (1994–1998) and Dr B. Saraceno (1999–present).

example, by being around and making people in the field of mental health become more aware of their value and potential. I also learned that WHO staff at the regional office, or at country level, were hardly aware of mental health needs. As long as this was so, the changes to get more visibility for the programme and more support for it were feeble. The effort to bring mental health to the regional level was successful and, by the early 1980s, all the Regional Offices of the WHO had a mental health advisor and a regional mental health programme. The links between the headquarters of the programme and the officers in the regions were very good, probably better than those of any other programme of the WHO. Regular meetings with regional office staff, exchange of information, and a considerable investment into the creation of good personal relationships and occasions to build friendships, made it possible to maintain a certain degree of harmony between the regional and headquarters programme, unusual for WHO at the time. The staff at the Division of Mental Health were young, able and willing to expand the programme; and by good fortune and considerable effort it was possible to also find and employ regional advisors who were highly motivated and competent.

On the programmatic level another important component was added to the Mental Health Programme by the Member States' representatives. In a passionate speech the Minister of Health of Belgium said to the World Health Assembly that progress towards health is not possible unless the psychosocial aspects of health and development programmes are given appropriate attention. Representatives of the Netherlands and Norway, as well as influential leaders of public health, supported the notion. The Assembly gave in and adopted a resolution putting a programme on psychosocial factors and health into place. Some funds were made available by Belgium, the Netherlands and Norway and later by other enlightened governments, and an impressive array of proposals for country level activities were defined. The Advisory Committee on Medical Research recommended to WHO starting a large-scale research (and research training) programme on biobehavioural sciences and health. WHO was to provide funds for this work from its regular budget but, as before, relied on voluntary contributions instead of increasing the programme's budget. Once voluntary contributions were used up, the psychosocial programme had to be cut down, in keeping with the meagre resources that the Mental Health Division had at its disposal.

One of the aims of the psychosocial programme was to raise the awareness of decision makers – in the WHO and elsewhere – of the importance that behaviour plays in health care and in promoting health. To achieve this, we made a variety of presentations, talked to staff of other divisions, published the World Health Assembly discussions. The World Health Assembly discussed the matter and adopted resolutions: yet the reluctance to take behaviour seriously continued in most programmes. Authorities and decision makers outside WHO were urging the Organization to do more for this psychosocial programme. WHO finally decided to discuss how to strengthen programmes dealing with human behaviour in relation to health care. The Headquarters Management Committee – the top administrators of the WHO in Geneva – initiated a series of discussions about the best way to deal with behavioural issues in their committee.

These discussions were a welcome test of the attitudes of the management to the further development of the mental health programme and to its psychosocial component. The discussions were held behind closed doors, the mental health programme specialists were not allowed to participate in the discussions nor to contribute background documents for the committee discussions. The leader of the team that was to guide these discussions was the head of the tropical disease programme. The discussions led to nothing new and the Committee dropped the subject having, however, also decided not to increase funding for activities designed to help the introduction of behavioural and psychosocial components into national health programmes.

Another event also illustrated that the stigma attached to psychiatry did not vanish from WHO and that the feeling that mental health has no place in the world of public health was still strong. In 1978 the World Health Assembly examined the overall strategy of the organization. It decided that too many of the Organization's resources were concentrated in Geneva and requested that a redistribution of the Organization's resources be made within a year. The Assembly's resolution was specific: it requested that at least 60% of all WHO's regular budget resources[9] have to be located in the Regional offices and in country programmes. A cut of budget was applied to all programmes at Headquarters, regardless of their size, to ensure that within each of the programmes the distribution of resources was in keeping with the Assembly's resolution. The Mental Health Division was to absorb a cut of nearly 30% of its posts and budget – a cut among the highest in the Organization. Despite remonstrations this was effected although the mental health programme was close to the 60/40 distribution when the resolution of the Assembly was adopted and before any cuts were done.

Demands for an increase of the mental health programme's budget were made on a number of occasions by the Member States and by the Executive Board, to no avail. The usual answer was that the size of budget does not reflect the importance that the management gives to programmes. The requests to increase the moral support to the programme – for instance, by devoting one of its annual World Health Days to mental health went unheard[10] for 30 years. The programme had to continue its existence relying on extrabudgetary contributions, on its network of collaborating centres and on the remarkable and continuing support of experts and service leaders the world over.

Late in the 1980s Drs Mahler and Lambo left the Organization and the Assembly elected a new Director General, this time a Japanese psychiatrist, Dr H. Nakajima. Early in his time, Dr Nakajima decided to separate the parts of the programme dealing with drug and alcohol dependence from the mental health programme, perhaps hoping that more extrabudgetary resources might become available if the activities concerning drug dependence were to be made more visible. This weakened the programme and reduced its staff and funds. The budget for mental health was also reduced. Paradoxically – as on previous occasions – the lack of interest in the programme seemed to continue to protect it against other major reforms or cuts.

---

[9] WHO's regular budget refers to the budget that is composed of the regular contributions of the WHO Member states. 'Extrabudgetary' resources refers to contributions that the organization received from other sources, usually with a specification of the programme area in which they should be spent.

[10] The Organization has devoted the Day to mental health on two occasions – in the years 1959 and 2001.

At the point of my departure from the Organization the – possibly justified – rumour spread that the Mental Health Division will be abolished. Various non-governmental organizations raised their voice asking the Director General to continue the programme that has been so useful to them and to country programmes. The programme was not disestablished, and it will never be certain whether the rumour had reflected intentions or whether it represented an unjustified conjecture. The programme thus continued, depending heavily on dwindling extra-budgetary support. Some of the regional office activities have been stopped, and staff dealing with mental health who left the regional office posts were not replaced. No new research was initiated and the studies that were started earlier gradually ceased. The publications produced by the programme became rarer. The network of collaborating centres continued to function but gradually became much less active and only a small number of centres remained in operation.

Dr Nakajima left the Organization at the end of his second term of office and the Assembly elected Dr G.H. Brundtland as Director General. She soon appointed a new Director of the Mental Health Department, Dr B. Saraceno. In the second year of her mandate Dr Brundtland declared that mental disorders are a public health problem of such dimensions that the Organization will place it high on its list of priorities. In support of this statement she quoted the figures of a report that compared the amount of disability that different diseases were producing[11] (Murray & Lopez, 1996). Dr Brundtland did not stop at making this statement. In 2001 World Health Day was devoted to mental health, and the Annual Report of the Director General for the same year was devoted to mental health (WHO, 2001). The Division of mental health has been brought back to strength in terms of staff and obtained both an increase of regular budget and extra-budgetary resources. The alcohol and drug dependence programme was returned to the mental health programme amidst a variety of other reforms. It is very probable that the programme will continue doing well and will gain the position of importance that the seriousness of mental health problems requires.

---

[11] The report was published several years earlier and had been generally neglected by the WHO administration in so far as mental health was concerned.

It thus appears that it has taken some 50 years to introduce mental health fully into public health programmes. Individuals played their roles in making this possible, but the story of this programme seems to confirm that little can be done to speed up changes of administrative structures that govern health care. It is terrible that this takes so long: it is marvellous that it is possible to achieve it even when it looks highly improbable at the onset.

REFERENCES

Cooper, J.E. (1999). Towards a common language for mental health workers. In De Girolamo, G., Eisenberg, L., Goldberg, D.P. & Cooper, J.E.: *Promoting Mental Health Internationally*. London: Gaskell.

Murray, C. & Lopez, A. (1996). *The Global Burden of Disease*. Boston: Harvard School of Public Health.

Sartorius, N. & Janca A. (1996). Psychiatric assessment instruments developed by the WHO. *Social Psychiatry and Psychiatric Epidemiology*, **31**, 55–69.

Sartorius, N. (1989). Recent research activities in the WHO's mental health programme. *Psychological Medicine*, **19**, 233–44.

WHO (1996). *Basic Documents*, pp 1–18 Geneva: World Health Organization.

WHO (2001). *The Report of the Director General on the Year 2000*. Geneva: World Health Organization.

Marinus van Roejmerswaelen (*c.*1493–1567): *St Jerome in his Study*. (Courtesy of La Musée de la Chartreuse, Douai, France, and Bridgeman Art Library, London.)

11

Mental health care for the elderly?
Another 30 years to wait

Although the ageing of the world's population began to receive increasing attention, and although studies show that mental health and physical problems need considerable attention, governments, with few exceptions, continue to invest little into this area of health care. Although at first glance this may seem surprising, an examination of the arguments for a significant strengthening of programmes dealing with mental health of the elderly show that these are not as strong as they might seem. Regrettably, therefore, it seems that in many countries of the world a few more decades will have to go by before mental health in the elderly receives the attention it deserves.

The proportions of the elderly in the populations of the world are rapidly increasing. The increases in the numbers of the elderly are likely to increase their political importance, particularly in countries with a democratic government. Epidemiological research has produced good estimates of health needs for the elderly. Science and experience have created knowledge necessary to define and provide treatment for many of the mental disorders of the elderly. General improvements of health care have given people more years of old age which they can enjoy. Science has also provided knowledge that allows an optimization of conditions of life of the elderly and an improvement of their quality of life. The increases in numbers of the elderly will lead to the development of better services for them and increase the tolerance and acceptance of the elderly by the rest of the population.

All the above statements can be found in scientific literature and in newspapers. They are usually parts of the framework used for formulation of scenarios for the future. They help gerontologists (and others interested in the improvement of quality of life of the elderly) to find courage and endurance in their efforts. They are supported by findings of research. They are clear and appear just.

Why, then is the mental health care of the elderly not improving much faster than it does and why is it that in many countries it is not given any priority? Why do surveys and anecdotal reports show that mental health care for the elderly is improving very slowly and only in some countries? Whence the recent reports of the high prevalence of the abuses of the elderly, in institutions and in the communities, the world over? Perhaps the reasons for optimism listed above are not as solid as they seem to be: perhaps they are not the truth but only part of the truth. Perhaps some of them are fallacies born out of frustration and constitute no more than wishful thoughts of noble people who want to help the elderly and cannot wait patiently any longer. The comments that follow examine the planks composing the platform on which we have erected the optimistic scenarios for the development of mental health care for the elderly. Before doing so it is necessary, however, to define 'health care for the elderly' and the word 'elderly'.

Definition of mental health care for the elderly

There is little agreement about the contents of mental health care programmes for the elderly. In some instances care is defined as the provision of treatment for conditions for which an effective treatment methods exists (e.g. for depressive disorders). In other definitions mental health care is conceived as a much more ambitious undertaking including all that is necessary to improve the quality of life of the elderly and make them live longer, better, and in good health. For the purposes of this discussion, mental health care is defined in a broad sense. It is seen as including the prevention and treatment of mental illness as well as measures that can improve the autonomy and independence of the elderly. It also includes measures that will foster interdependence between the elderly and those who surround them as well as support to the family or other carers involved in the provision of services to the elderly. Further, it also encompasses health education about old age offered to the general population and to the members of the professions concerned with the elderly – for example, health workers.

Definition of the elderly

Old age can be defined in different ways. Chronological age refers to years since birth and is easy to establish in countries where birth registers or other ways of systematically recording data about the population are in existence. In many countries of the world such registers and records are not in existence or function poorly in terms of coverage and correctness. Estimating the age structure of the population in such settings is therefore a game of approximations and guesses. Individuals sometimes link their age or year of birth to some event of major significance for the place in which they lived at the time, a big flood or a landslide for example. This serves quite well for a variety of purposes: it is, however, not very suitable for accurate demographic investigations. Landslides or floods have different dimensions in the eyes of those who are involved in them and those who are not: linkage between such events and the age of the respondent is therefore neither sensible nor should be made. Even in countries in which records are well kept, there are often gaps in good reporting due to wars or other events of that nature: also, most countries of the world have introduced good statistics and recording systems relatively recently – the people living in the next century will, in many countries, have much better records of their birth than those of their age living today.

Physiological age

Physiological age, estimated by the function of body and mind, varies among individuals and populations. It is not easy to measure reliably, and even when it is, serves better in the care of an individual than in epidemiological or demographic estimations. There is also some evidence that people age with different velocity in different cultures. Whether this is due to genetic factors, food, average levels of stress or other reasons, is uncertain. Recent years have brought up information showing that people are getting old after more years after their birth than before. Sports injuries, for example, have come up as an important reason for medical interventions in people over 65 years of age. This probably reflects that they are more energetic and physically able at that age than those of 65 a few decades ago. For the moment this is no more than good news for all of us: soon these findings will help governments to define administrative old age differently, make the age of retirement (or the age at which the government provides additional help to individuals) higher. Once this happens, the proportion of elderly people in the population will have to be corrected downward. The downward correction will, however, have to be done differently in different countries (or for different population groups, the poor and the rich for example) – a complication which makes statements about the proportion of the elderly in a population difficult.

The validity of reasons for optimistic predictions about mental health care for the elderly

The proportion of the elderly in the populations of the world are rapidly increasing

Demographic reports from many countries indicate an increase of the numbers of people in the age groups of 65 years and over. These reports are used to argue for more services and more investment into the health care of the elderly. The argument, however, often falls on deaf ears. Perhaps because it is flawed: although the absolute numbers of the elderly grow and although in relative terms too, i.e. in terms of proportions there is a clear increase – the elderly are still in most parts of the world a small minority of the population as a whole. This is true when the traditional limit for old age, e.g. 65 years, is taken as the basis for calculations. It is even more true when the higher chronological age is taken as the limit for being elderly. There is thus some justification for ignoring the reports about the increases of the numbers: twice a very small number is still a very small number.

The increased numbers of the elderly are likely to increase their political power
The announcements that the 'grey tigers' will be able to influence political decisions was received with much satisfaction by the elderly and by those who are promoting their welfare. It was argued that political leaders will no longer be able to ignore the elderly since they make up a significant proportion of the electorate. Political power, it was hoped, will then be used to improve services for the elderly and their quality of life; this in turn will make the elderly more eager to use their power for the purpose and will, in the long run, increase the numbers of the elderly people surviving and thus add to the size of their group.

But this was only partly true and only in a small number of countries. The reasons for this are obvious. In addition to the fact that, even in countries in which the population of the elderly are highest, they still remain a minority, there are two other factors of importance. First, the elderly are not a homogeneous groups, speaking with one voice. Their needs vary from one social class to another and from one cultural group or sub-group to another. Those who survive often belong to the upper social classes, who are not likely to ask for more services because they already have access to them. Second, the elderly are not well organized and rarely have the energy and skills to harness all of their power to exert pressure in a particular direction. Becoming a political party defined by age is difficult: too many of the elderly who are politically active already have loyalties to parties defined by other goals and features. A person who has voted for a political party all his or her life will continue to do so, regardless of the fact that another party (that has

defined itself having members over a certain age) has come into existence. Also, major political parties usually build a plank of helping the
old and infirm into their political platform, which makes it easier to
stay with that party than to join a grey tiger party. It is likely that the
establishment of a unified political stance will become easier once
being old again becomes a sign of distinction rather than an indication
of decrepitude and of a high risk of becoming dependent on someone
else.

Epidemiological research has produced good evidence about the needs of the elderly

Numerous fine studies about mental illness in the elderly have been
conducted in recent years. They have produced credible estimates of
the frequency of diseases such as dementia and depressive disorders[1].

Now that we know, the argument goes, how many of the elderly
suffer from mental disorders and that we have data about the type and
severity of disorders, we are in a good position to state what kind, type
and quantity of mental health care we should provide. Data from
cohort studies of healthy and diseased elderly are also becoming available and further strengthen our position in this respect.

Unfortunately, however, this argument is not as strong as we would
like it to be. First, most of the credible studies of mental disorders of old
age have been conducted in a very small number of countries. It is possible to say that the situation in other countries is probably the same:
the justification for such a statement is, however, weak. Differences
between findings of epidemiological studies carried out in the same
country illustrate the need to be prudent in generalizations for areas
that seem to be similar to one another. Lack of prudence, however,

---

[1] They have also produced evidence about the importance of comprehensive assessment
and reporting of findings of such studies. The finding, for example, that depressive disorders (defined in accordance with the ICD-10 classification of mental disorders or the
DSM-IV classification) are less frequent in the elderly than in the rest of the population
is counter-intuitive and does not tally with reports from clinicians who emphasize the
importance and high prevalence of depressive disorders in the higher ages. Full reporting has shown, however, that depressive symptoms in the elderly populations are frequently found and often lead to much suffering and disability. This underlines the
need to re-examine the criteria that have been taken by these classifications to define
the depressive disorders of old age rather than accept low prevalence rates as the basis
for planning services.

turns into obvious scientific error, when generalizations are made from studies on one continent to another and to populations that differ in ways of life, experience of disease, speed of ageing, cultural traditions and many other factors that are of importance in the occurrence of diseases in their course and their outcome. Outcome of schizophrenia in developing countries is different from its outcome in industrialized countries: why should the outcome of depressive disorders in Africa be the same as the outcome of depression in Finland?

This, however, is not all. Even if we had valid studies carried out on representative samples of different populations of the world, we would still be in a relatively weak position when it comes to predicting or estimating needs for mental health care for the elderly. The concept of needs for care has been significantly revised in recent years. The relation between needs for care and the prevalence or incidence of mental disorder is far from being simple or straightforward. Needs for care are defined by numerous factors including the frequency of the disorder in a population: that datum, however is becoming recognized as being of relatively little importance. In order to be realistic in our estimation of needs, we must know what the patients want; what their families wish and hope to receive from health or other social services; who the patients are, to what social class and cultural group they belong; what other resources are at their disposal or could be mobilized; what technological means for the treatment of the disease in question are available to the health service; how acceptable these means of treatment are to the population in general, to the patient and to their families; and finally whether the disease can be given priority by the government because it is a public health problem[2].

In all, despite the accumulation of knowledge about mental disorders of the elderly in some countries, we are still not in a position to determine the needs for mental health care of the elderly adequately

---

[2] Criteria for deciding whether a disorder is of public health importance and therefore deserves priority in the allocation of resources by public health authorities includes the frequency of the disorder; its severity in terms of suffering it produces of the patient and the family; the disability or other consequences that the disease might produce; the availability of acceptable treatments or care methods; and the trends in the development of the disease in the individual and the population with and without intervention.

and scientifically for a vast majority of the world's population. This, of course, does not mean that we should not ask for care that appears to be most urgent and necessary; in making our requests, however, we should be aware that these are *ad hoc* requests rather than parts of a master plan based on strong and complete evidence.

Science and experience created enough knowledge to define effective treatment for many mental disorders of the elderly

Psychiatry, as well as other medical disciplines, until very recently seemed to live in a dream world in which patients suffered from only one disease at the time and in which each of the sufferers had clearly expressed symptoms appearing in a well-ordered time sequence. Chapters about mental disorders in most textbooks often end by suggesting that a particular method of treatment, e.g. a particular drug should be applied: there is rarely a specific suggestion how a particular mental disorder should be treated in the presence of other (sometimes many) mental or physical disorders. Just as badly, the difference between treatment in hospital settings and in community care is given little attention forgetting that most treatments will differ – in dosage and manner of application depending on the setting in which the therapy is given. The indicators of progress in treatment are vague, and criteria for switching from one method of treatment to another because the first one does not work sufficiently well are not defined.

Well-conducted research in a growing number of countries clearly demonstrates that a vast majority of people with mental illness consult general practitioners and specialists in disciplines other than psychiatry. They relatively rarely refer patients to a psychiatrist. This will happen only if the patient shows signs of a major mental disorder, for example, those of an episode of schizophrenia, or when they have tried various types of treatment in a particular patient and nothing seems to work. General practitioners and other specialists often do not recognize mental disorders in patients who consult them. This is true in most settings: a recent study in 14 different countries (Üstün & Sartorius, 1996) showed that some 50% of general health care patients in whom an independent and reliable assessment confirmed the presence of a mental disorder did not receive a diagnosis of mental disorder from the general practitioner. The general practitioners, however, gave the diagnosis of a mental disorder to a number of patients who did not satisfy criteria for any mental disorder listed in the tenth revision of the International Classification of Mental Disorders, basing this on a variety of criteria in addition to (or instead of) those listed in the diagnostic guidelines accompanying the Classification. The practitioners then undertook to treat approximately half of those whom they recognized as having a mental disorder. It is uncertain how many of those whom general practitioners recognized were either sent or went to specialist psychiatrists; in all probability they will be few. The two worlds do not seem to mix much. Psychiatrists have created most of the descriptions of mental disorders basing them on their experience, and their observation of patients who came to them by referral or directly. The development of descriptions of mental illness have rarely taken into account the form that mental illness takes in people who never reach a medical doctor or a psychiatrist.

The general practitioner sees other types of patients – often suffering from a variety of illnesses, with symptoms of mental disorders that are not always similar to those that were described by psychiatrists. Knowledge about these patients is not yet well systematized even in countries in which there are many mental health specialists and a tradition of precise description of patients. Data about the differences between countries in the form that mental illnesses takes, in the manner in which they are treated and in the outcome of the disorder after treatment are, by and large, not available. Cross-cultural research has concentrated on mental illness that was seen in patients in contact with mental health services. There is some information about patients who were found in other places in which people with mental illness are brought for treatment, e.g. those in the care of traditional healers. Studies that systematically examine the multitude of forms of mental illness seen in general health care, often in the presence of physical illness, are still lacking. There is even less information about special patient groups across cultures, e.g. about the elderly mentally ill and their mental health problems. Treatments tested in a small number of countries in the developed world are applied in countries and to populations that are different in all relevant aspects. Reports of the effects of those interventions are difficult to obtain and usually are no more than anecdotes and personal observations of doctors or other members of the health professions. Worse still, knowledge that has been gathered many years ago about the form and course of mental illness is still taken as the basis for education and recommendations concerning management. The fact that ways of life have changed, that illnesses have assumed different forms, and that people have changed their attitudes to work, food, their appearance and other features, are not taken into account in those writings.

The knowledge on which we base our plans and teach future doctors is not sufficient. It has to be enlarged, described in terms that people in different countries can understand. There should be more exchange of clinical experience and research evidence between countries. For the time being we must operate with little knowledge – and we should not cease health care activities because we do not know enough: but we should act in full cognisance of the imperfection of our estimates and recommendations and systematically gather experience and knowledge so as to be able to use it.

The demographic changes, higher life expectancy, better health care and higher incomes result in an increase of years in the post-retirement period and it is now necessary to plan for the leisure years gained

It is true that the expectancy of life at the point of retirement has increased in the past few decades, in a number of countries. The increase of disability-free years, however, has been much slower and, in many instances, has not happened at all. People live longer but their diseases not only have not disappeared but have got increasingly more difficult to manage because of the synergy between problems of ageing and problems of chronic disease. The limping progress in adjusting the retirement pensions to price increases and inflation add a further difficulty for the retired person, who loses purchasing power and cannot afford to buy tools for life provided by technology. In the developing countries only a small proportion of people have retirement benefits. They are expected to work for as long as they can, after which the family looks after them. The decreasing size of the family and the increasing number of elderly surviving into higher age with diseases to treat, strains the resources of the family to a point at which it cannot continue to provide care, food and shelter for the elderly.

There is thus, for the time being at least, no urgency to plan for leisure years; what is urgent is to plan and think how best to make the life of the elderly liveable and how to provide families support so that they can sustain the elderly for more years than was expected. The double burden of the developing countries which have to deal with problems of communicable diseases and other diseases (producing, for example, high child mortality), while the number of the elderly and the need for heir care grows, also needs to be addressed now. Help for these countries in the fight against communicable disease, against malnutrition and improvement of sanitary conditions, will help the old and the young. Furthermore, if appropriate legal measures are taken now, it is possible that resources now used for the control of illnesses of yesterday will be – after these diseases and problems are vanquished – invested in the care of the elderly. Both of these strategies are, however, on shaky grounds: it is no way certain that quick success in the battle against the communicable disease will be forthcoming: nor is it certain that resources liberated in one area of health care will be used for the care of elderly.

The increasing numbers of the elderly will increase the tolerance of the population for them

This argument is used interchangeably with the opposite one that states that increased numbers of the elderly will decrease the population's tolerance for them and lead to a massive rejection of the elderly. Both statement are, in part, true and, in part, false. Behaviour of the majority to minorities follows a fairly predictable course. While the number of individuals belonging to a particular group is very small, the tolerance is usually good: in a way they are treated as curiosities, as mascots. In the past the rare persons reaching advanced age have been respected and many societies in which the elderly were rare have proudly spoken about the excellent care that their communities gave to the elderly and about the prestige that they enjoyed.

As the number of members of a minority grows, the attitude of the population towards them usually changes. The massive influx of immigrants to a country raises frank opposition by some, thoughts about the best and most humane way to reduce their numbers by others, and an uneasiness in most of the remainder of the community. The growth of the numbers of elderly people is likely to have a similar effect on their popularity. The population, for example, is likely to become less inclined to vote for parties that propose significant amounts of money to make the elderly's participation in traffic easier and safer. Later, the situation changes again. When the number of individuals belonging to a minority increases further, and when it becomes obvious that they are and will remain numerous, the tolerance and the willingness to do something for them might increase.

The increased numbers of the elderly will force the development of better services for them

The socio-economic and health service change, which has led to an increase of the numbers of the elderly, has not affected only the elderly. In societies in which life expectancy is increasing, the trend is not restricted to the elderly; the expectation of life for population groups of other ages is also growing. This has several consequences for the development of health services. First, the competition for funds in such situations will remain as sharp as before, health services for the adult population and its various sub-groups being requested with just as much vigour as the services for the elderly. Second, the numbers of people with diseases typical for other age groups will also increase. The fact that child mortality is lowered and that more people enter into the age of 18–25 increases the number of individuals who fall ill with schizophrenia. The swelling of the population group 35–45 increases the numbers of individuals at risk for the development of unipolar depressive disorders. Increase in the numbers of the population entering into the reproductive age will increase the need to combat the spread of venereal disease. The advocates for more resources for the elderly will thus have to fight with just as many opponents as before, with a possible added difficulty stemming from the fact that increasing need for maintaining population groups that can produce major economic returns to the government by being employed will result in larger investments into work, medicine and protection of the economically active population.

Sociological and other studies have produced knowledge that will allow the rational development of health and other social services for the elderly and this increases their quality of life

In the past two decades a significant proportion of the elderly have chosen lifestyles that are new and could not have been studied in the past. The numbers of elderly persons who have selected to spend several years in travel from place to place, in trailers or in other ways, grow in many developed countries. The organization of health care for that group of people represents challenges that are similar to those that have to be faced when health care for nomadic populations is being built up. The increase in life expectancy is not only happening to the healthy: it is even faster for people with disability and chronic impairments or diseases. Health services have now to face the challenge of providing care to persons who have suffered from schizophrenia and now are likely to outlive their parents who were their main carers, or see these become very old. Those persons will now be entering into old age with the burden of impairments that remained after their schizophrenic illness and with the responsibility to look after very old parents. The numbers of people in such a predicament are growing with the progress of medicine and the improvement of our capacity to postpone death from disease or other reasons. We have no clear strategy of care for these 'new elderly', nor data about the effectiveness of measures that are taken in different settings to provide services for them.

The barriers to the provision of care to the elderly are mainly of financial nature

Obstacles to the provision of care stem from various sources: the lack of financial resources is an important, but certainly not the main barrier to the development of mental health programmes for the elderly. Some of these stem from the elderly themselves. Their attitudes and expectations may be inimical to the development of mental health programmes. An elderly who believes that symptoms of diseases he or she experiences are signs of old age, is not likely to seek help from health services, which have to spend considerable amounts of money and time to educate the elderly and find those who need health care. Health staff often lack knowledge that would allow them to identify and treat mental disorders in the elderly. The changes of social arrangements – for example the increasing numbers of women who become employed and are therefore unable or unwilling to provide care for the sick and elderly at home – present challenges that cannot be corrected by financial investments alone. The urbanization prevalent in all countries changes the way in which health care has to be organized, particularly for the elderly; at present, there is no clear plan that could be recommended nor evidence that would allow to develop it in different socio-cultural settings. Major upheavals that have become so frequent – wars, mass accidents, migration and flight from political or other persecution – are pernicious for the elderly and can be insurmountable obstacles to the provision of care. The rapid development of technology makes the skills of the elderly obsolete and increases the probability that they will become dependent on others for their survival. Thus, it is necessary to do much more than only (!) increase the funding of services for the elderly – but there are few coordinated efforts to address the variety of obstacles of which some are listed above.

What to do meanwhile?

The above trends and facts indicate that the development of mental health programmes for the elderly will not be easy nor rapid. This, however, is not a reason for despair. Most new services take time to develop and become truly useful. Science is making giant steps forward and it might bring solutions that we cannot even foresee today. Meanwhile, however, it might be useful if we admitted our ignorance about the true needs of the elderly in many societies and about the most effective and efficient ways of responding to them. It might also be useful to direct a significant part of our research to the solution of practical, day-to-day problems, arising, for example, in the provision of services in urban settings of the developing countries, in dealing with negative attitudes of health care personnel, in providing treatment for a mental illness in a person with many other illnesses and impairments, in changing the expectations of the elderly. We should also accept that, for a time, progress will have to be directed by opportunities rather than by an all-out acceptance and support to the programmes of the elderly.

REFERENCE

Üstün, T.B. & Sartorius N. (1996). *Mental Illness in General Health Care – An International Study*. Chichester/New York/Brisbane/Toronto/Singapore: John Wiley & Sons.

Bob Lescaux (b. 1928): *Sower of the Words.* (Courtesy of Bridgeman Art Library, London.)

12

On words I like to hate

There are words that are introduced to describe a new concept, but then get overused both to describe the original idea and other notions. Sometimes this surpasses uneasiness about the repetitive style, and their use becomes harmful because it obscures differences between concepts, diminishes the clarity of messages and leads to confusion. For me, some such words are 'Western', 'compliance', 'Third world' and 'consumer'.

There are words denoting concepts that are manifestly wrong. Despite objections, by many, they continue to be used giving false credence to notions which should be abandoned. Some of them were introduced with a particular, for example, political purpose. In some instances those who introduced them were aware of the distortion that they were proposing. Among those the best known are words that had been used by the propaganda offices of warring states. Sometimes, the authors genuinely believe that the use of a word is correct and have no bad intentions. Later, although it became obvious that the notions were never valid (or that they ceased to be valid), the authors and others continue to use the word. Sometimes, such words are euphemisms. Sometimes they are just translations of a common word into Latin or into a scientific language to reify a banality.

I will list a few of them, hoping against reason that readers and others will add to the list and that one day all journals will have a column arraying words whose continued use is misleading, unnecessary or harmful – a little like the stamp at the bottom of a tin saying that the tinned product should not be used after the date indicated because it could be dangerous or have a bad taste.

Western

The word 'Western' is often used to refer to the mythical notion that all European countries, the United States of America, Canada (and Australia!) have one culture and therefore can be contrasted with Eastern cultures (as if there were only one Eastern culture) and with countries of lesser industrialized development. The word was probably made popular by the writings of North American anthropologists and may well have its roots in the notion of the Western (Roman) Empire, which was called that way to distinguish it from the Eastern (Roman) Empire[1]. The grouping under Western disregards the fact that European countries have different histories, that Europeans speak different languages and confess religions that are, in many of their rituals

---

[1] The fact that in English 'to go West' may also mean being lost, is in curious contrast with the notion that the 'Western' countries are supposed to be predominantly populated by calculating, heartless and efficient individuals.

and prescriptions, different from one another. It also neglects the facts that the many groups of inhabitants of Europe organize their family and other social life in different ways, that they eat very different food, live in different climates.

Even geographically the term 'Western' makes no sense. The only European countries that are to the West of the Greenwich meridian are Ireland, a part of Portugal and Iceland: all other countries in Europe are geographically Eastern. Morocco is more to the West than are most countries on the European continent and Australia is more to the East than Japan.

The Third world, developing countries

The term 'Third world' is a translation of the French term *tiers monde* mentioned for the first time in an article by Alfred Sauvy in 1952 (Lacoste, 1993) to refer to countries that were neither of explicitly communist nor of capitalist orientation. A convinced republican, Sauvy could not but introduce an allusion to the third layer, *le tiers état* (after the nobles and the clergy) – the townspeople and the peasantry – fighting for their rights in the last two decades of the eighteenth century and thus coined the term *tiers monde*. In the atmosphere of the Korean war and its undertones, Sauvy vaguely indicated that these countries might be searching for a different way to progress. The term was translated into English and used by few and without consistency, until it was officially adopted during the Tri-continental conference in Havana in 1966 by a variety of anti-imperialist movements. It was used in that sense – of being neither communist nor capitalist – until the mid-1970s when the Chinese theorists reinterpreted the term to mean a different scheme: the First world consisted of the two imperialist powers – the USA and the USSR. The Second world were the industrialized countries at present without imperialist ambitions such as the European countries. The Third world were all other countries (provided, of course, that they were not too closely related to either the USA or the USSR). China was supposed to be the leader of these countries: a notion, accepted by few apart from China and Maoist movements in some other countries. Since then, and for a few years, the term was used with the idea that, after all, the non-industrialized countries have many things in common. In the late 1970s – after the Vietnam war (in which some of the communist and socialist countries aligned themselves with a developing country in the fight against the USA) and Vietnam's invasion of Kampuchea, it became clear that the 'Third world' countries were sharply different from one another and cannot be put into the same group so easily. A further change of content gradually took place and the term 'Third world' began to be used to describe the non-industrialized countries characterized by poverty and state indebtedness, by insufficient health services and other dire features.

'Developing countries' was a term that competed with the 'Third world' and gained more general acceptance in the early 1980s. It is not much better than the term 'Third world' but it sounds more optimistic and does not have the ideological background of the 'Third world'. Ideally, one should avoid the use of such a label because it obscures differences and over-simplifies.

After all, each country has its own cultural, economic, intellectual and emotional traditions and characteristics that make it, to a significant degree, unique. Also, most of the countries of the world are mosaics of developed and developing regions of modern and traditional parts, of noble and ignoble components. Just how much of each of these is present will vary with time and from one part of the world to another. Grouping countries should therefore be done only very rarely bearing the consequences of such reductionism in mind.

Affordable

'Affordable' is undoubtedly among the words that I like to hate very much. It crops up everywhere, in health policies, in national health programmes, in guidelines, in declarations. It is a terrible word because it usually annihilates the preceding recommendation or policy statement. The definition of primary health care in the Alma Ata Conference refers to the essential components of primary care – components that governments should provide to all people and accompanies this requirement with the word affordable – thus primary health care should be provided if there is nothing else that the government considers more important. Because, if there is a thing that the authorities consider as more important, they will spend the money to get it and then declare that primary health care was not affordable. They have thus lived by the solemn obligation that they have accepted when adopting the Declaration: it just so happens that there is not enough money for the work that they agreed was essential for the health of their population.

Mental health programmes in most parts of the world – and other health programmes as well – often fall into the affordability trap. The scenario is simple. The Authorities provide the persons responsible for the mental health programme with a certain amount of resources. He or she develops a programme using the resources obtained. Next year the Authorities provide fewer resources. The reasons given for such a reduction vary and often surprise by their improbability. The mental health programme leader proceeds to readjust the service to a lower sum. The same may happen also in the year that follows. The service will deteriorate and occasionally there will be scandals because people hospitalized because of mental illness died of hunger or of an infectious disease that could have been successfully treated, had it been possible to buy antibiotics or food. Low salaries and poor conditions of work make most good staff go away. Emotional burn-out weakens the health team. People with doubtful motivations stay and often make the life of the patient even more difficult than the disease and its consequences already made it.

Finally, the blame has to be placed on someone – why not on the leader of the health programme and his colleagues who provide such a miserable service? After punishment has been meted out and the image of psychiatry further damaged, the routine can be established again. At no point has the leader of the programme been asked or allowed to define what his team would need to provide decent service. Brave leaders sometimes say what would be necessary: the authorities in such instances usually take the cover of non-affordability. After all, they had stated in advance that they would provide as much as they could afford. The 'affordability trap' could be avoided if an international and national consensus about minimal needs for mental health care were to exist; in that case the authorities would have to explain to the electorate that they are not providing minimal care for whatever reason they might wish to choose. At present, their position is much more comfortable. They can tell the electorate that they have given enough resources (or 'as much as they can afford') to the service and that the reason that care is not of good quality lies in poor management, too high salaries of, say, doctors, unreasonable ambitions of the service providers, unbelievably immodest requirements of the families of patients, pilfering or any other cause that they fancy at that moment.

In the 1970s the World Health Organization tried to promote programme budgeting (i.e. developing programmes first and then deciding on the budget necessary to implement them) which was to replace budget programming in health care administration. Programme-budgeting would require service providers to state what they wanted to do and why. The authorities would then, it was proposed, examine the demands and provide the resources for the execution of the programme. Although logical and reasonable, the proposal was, by and large, ignored by all. The service providers were usually not trained in matters such as the assessment of needs, the management and evaluation techniques and the preparation of specific proposals and medium-term plans. They therefore said that the task was impossible and that it was in any case condemned to fail because things were never done this way (they were not far from being right when saying this). Even those who were willing to try and who succeeded in overcoming the barriers of management language often gave up when faced with the state of the treatment doctrines in psychiatry. Treatment guidelines for most diseases do not exist, or if they do, they do not command general agreement. There are few exceptions to this rule. There is also disagreement between professional peers about the minimal care that patients suffering from specific disorders should receive. The authorities (rightly) felt that this way of proceeding would reduce their freedom of action and force them to become much more familiar with programmes than they wanted. In some instances, parts of the government infrastructure were interested in applying the programme budgeting method of administration of services, but other parts of the service were not and usually succeeded in blocking the change.

Consumers

The wave of anti-psychiatry that rolled over some of the countries in the industrialized world in the 1960s and 1970s had a number of effects, some positive and some negative. Among them was the increased reluctance of the governments to invest into the development maintenance or improvement of mental health services; the drop in the attractiveness of psychiatry as a career choice for the best medical graduates; and the worsening of the image of psychiatry as a medical discipline among other health professionals. The image of psychiatry in the general public was already bad and became worse.

On the positive side there were also important developments. Mental health services in some of the countries were improved in structure and function. In some countries – for example, Germany – the governments initiated a thorough examination of their mental health services and acted to improve them. Politically also, there were significant gains. The need to protect the human rights of people with mental illness was officially recognized in a number of settings. Formal resolutions were passed addressing the issue of rights of those with mental illness. Among them, the most important was the resolution UN 119 adopted by the General Assembly of the United Nations in 1991. The most remarkable feature of that resolution is that it not only recognizes the need to protect the human rights of people with mental illness but also urges UN member states to ensure that people suffering from these illnesses have access to appropriate medical and social services because this also is a human right[2]. Simultaneously – and perhaps facilitated by the developments during the anti-psychiatry era – patient and family organizations came into existence in a number of countries.

The need to find a term that will describe people who had experienced mental illness and were now politically active resulted in a number of proposed names. Some among them were 'loaded' (e.g. 'survivors of psychiatry'), did not find general acceptance and gradually ceased to be used. Among those that stayed around is the term 'consumer' that I

---

[2] The resolution is accompanied by guidelines that give specific recommendations in this respect.

truly dislike. There are two main reasons for this. First, the term 'consumers' implies that persons who have a mental disorder (and their families) are using up resources, consuming them. The term indicates that they are not contributing to society. It tells others that these people are taking, not giving. It accuses them of not usefully participating in their society which, after all can only survive if it has developed and protects mutually supportive relationships among its members.

I dislike the word consumer because this is not so. People who have mental illness can, and should, contribute to society within the limits of their capacity, in the same way as society – other people – should support people with mental illness to the limit of their capacity. Even in instances in which disease has made a person unable to be economically productive or socially active, those who take care of them will have moral earnings which should be recognized in the same solemn way as that in which governments recognize other services performed to maintain and protect society. Years of looking after a severely ill person deserves just as much (if not more) praise as being wounded on a battlefield protecting one's country. Living with disease and nevertheless making a contribution to society is an achievement that often requires enormous effort and personal investment. It should be recognized and praised, not obscured by calling it health service consumption.

Second, the fact that there are consumers of health services indicates that health is a commodity that can be purchased and sold like other commodities – sugar, salt or cotton. Medicine, in that logic, is a trade. More money allows you to purchase more health: less money means that you will not be able to make use of all that medicine of today can offer. Perhaps, the times are such that medicine is no more than a financial transaction in which doctors and other health workers dish out health and receive payment for it. Perhaps, times are such that compassion and the spiritual components of the relationship between a person in distress and another who has the knowledge and tools to help him or her are no more part of medicine. If that is so, medicine is in a bad state. Use of the term 'consumers' is a tacit acceptance of this degradation of medicine and it is therefore wrong.

The schizophrenics

There are diseases that last a long time and are of great importance for the daily life of the individuals concerned and for those who live with them. Sometimes people who suffer from a disease will be described as carriers of their disease, not as individuals. A package of attributes, usually derogatory, travels with them. Diabetics are obese, do not want to eat like other people, inject themselves with insulin, and are often irritable. Schizophrenics are dangerous, hear voices, and think that they are Napoleon. Depressives cry all the time, shy away from work. Lepers are deformed and highly contagious. Stigma is often attached to the label, and negative discrimination is frequent.

I hate these terms because they are an impediment to treatment of the disease (and to the process of rehabilitation) and because they are harmful in other ways. The stigma attached to the label will make people reluctant to come forward and seek treatment. It will also prevent them from maintaining or regaining respect for themselves in their own eyes.

These consequences are aggravated by the discrimination related to stigma that makes it difficult to provide appropriate services and support to those who need them most. Labelling people as if they were carriers of the disease rather than individuals is also harmful to the treatment process. People who have a disease are different even when the disease is the same. And, furthermore, the disease is also express-ing itself differently in different people. To be adequate, medical treat-ment must be individualized, tailored to the form of the disease and adjusted to the needs of the individual who is suffering from it. Calling people who have a disease by the name of their disease is negating these differences and thus leads to poorer treatment and lesser chances for the social rehabilitation of individuals who have suffered from the disease.

These terms are also unjust. Most of us suffer from one disease or another and bear it less or more well. Yet, most of these diseases, even when serious, do not make us lose our individuality, our membership in the community of our peers. There would be an uproar if people suffering from pneumonia were to be called pneumonics and then prevented from obtaining driving licences because they might begin to cough and lose control of their vehicle.

Having a disease is usually bad enough for the individuals who have them and for those who care for them. To rob them of their identity is adding insult to injury, aggravating the disease and transgressing against one of the most basic human rights – the right to be a member of one's community, to be expected to help others and to be helped in distress.

Compliance

Compliance – the act of complying with a wish, a request or a command – has been used in medicine to describe the willingness to follow a prescribed course of treatment. It seems that it is a term that was introduced in medicine (or gained popularity) recently – colleagues of earlier vintages do not seem to remember that the word was used or discussed in their medical studies. It is now a constant refrain of reports about treatment, giving prominence to a banality – that a treatment that was not applied will have less effect than a treatment that was applied. There is surely no dispute about the fact that assessments of the value of treatments must include evidence that the medication was taken and that the actions considered to be effective have been implemented.

Why is self-evident truth then gaining no such prominence? Why are practising doctors and scientists now talking about compliance? Was it that earlier they did not care whether the medication was taken or not? The word doctor comes from the Latin *docere* – to teach: doctors might have seen themselves as teachers, telling patients what would be the best treatment and then, having done their educational task leave it to the patients to decide whether they would like to proceed along the lines taught, go and see another doctor, forget about the treatment altogether or modify it according to their desire. Or perhaps, was it that the patients in earlier times always followed doctors orders so that compliance was not a problem? Or is the insistence on compliance an expression of surprise that the treatments do not work and an attempt to ascribe the fault to the patients' behaviour? Or is it that pharmaceutical companies have helped to bring about the awareness that doctors should see to it that their patients take the medications that were prescribed for them?

Be that as it may, the word compliance expresses an unacceptable premise of the doctor–patient relationship. Doctors and their patients should be partners in the process of treatment. Partners discuss the course of action; they do not expect that their requests will be followed without an appropriate explanation, without a discussion about the consequences of a proposed course of action and without an agreement about the best route to take. Sometimes, the effects of the disease make it difficult to have such discussion and it is normal that in those circumstances action proceeds in accordance with rules that have been formulated to create a framework for treatment and other medical intervention. In most instances however it is possible to reach an agreement about the treatment and about the compliance of both doctor and of patient to the plan of treatment developed together not a doctor's command.

The *American Heritage Dictionary of the English Language* contains several definitions of the word compliance. One of them is 'unworthy acquiescence'. An essential requisite for good medical treatment is that following a course of treatment should never become compliant with that meaning.

REFERENCE

Lacoste, F. (1993). *Dictionnaire de Geopolitique*. Flammarion.

Part III

Psychiatry and mental health programmes

Edvard Munch (1863–1944): *The Scream*. (Courtesy of the Nasjonalgalleriet, Oslo, Norway.)

13

Assessing needs for psychiatric services

One of the doctrines of public health is that health care should be planned and rationally structured. A first step in the process of making relevant plans is the assessment of need. In the past this was done by interpreting epidemiological data. Nowadays, it is becoming clear that estimates of prevalence and incidence have much scientific value (e.g. in the search for risk factors for diseases) but cannot be used in planning health care if they are not accompanied by several other sets of data. These include information about the demands for health care by people with the disease and their families; information about the cost and effectiveness of interventions that might have to be employed to diminish the problem; and an appraisal of the speed and nature of socio-economic and other changes in the area for which health care is being planned.

Life is becoming more complicated by the day. In times past, when asked how much should be invested in providing services for a particular mental or physical illness, we could provide an estimate of the number of people who had such an illness. Then we could state how many personnel, drugs and beds are necessary for appropriate care and how they should be used. It is still possible to do this today but, in many settings, it will no longer be correct.

There are several reasons for this. First, the needs of the patients, the needs of the community and the needs of the government only partially overlap. For example, governments are particularly interested in avoiding high costs for disease control, while the community places a high premium on diminishing or preventing disturbance to the normal ways of societal functioning. Patients and their families are more insistent that quality of life, before and during treatment, is an important criterion of treatment acceptability. Consultation between these three groups, therefore, emerges as a necessary part of the estimation of needs.

Second, it has gradually become accepted that the notion of calculating needs, outcomes or costs by using averages, is misleading. Average (demographic) citizens, average reactions to treatment, and average outcomes are often not applicable in individual cases.

People are different whether well or ill. They belong to different cultures, have different personalities, physical constitutions and personal histories, all of which makes them perceive their diseases in a specific manner. They cope with the consequences of diseases in individual ways, and thus require different types of help. Some of them do not want anyone to help them; others want more help than could sensibly be expected given the impairment or suffering that their disease produces. Some of them do not want help from a health service; if convinced that their disease is a consequence of someone's magical influence they may prefer to seek the help of traditional healers, exorcists or others that deal with black magic.

Third, the needs of the health professions play a particularly important, yet neglected, role in planning health services and assessing and providing care for a sick population. Health workers, for example, will not take jobs in places where their children might not get acceptable schooling. In some countries, this keeps the density of health care agents in rural areas low and, in turn, affects the expression of demands for, and availability of, care in a rural population.

Fourth, it has become clear that plans made to cover long periods must be vague, addressing only overall objectives and goals. The notion that a 5-year plan should be precise and include operational details, as was promoted in countries of Eastern Europe, lost much of its attraction when it became clear that services in those countries did not develop in accordance with the plans, and that the making and announcing of those plans had served mainly political purposes. These reasons and others – unforeseen political changes, methodological problems in the planning and evaluation process, incompetence of planners because of insufficient training – have led to an increasing recognition that the previous standardized ways of planning are not very useful. In many countries during the late 1970s and early 1980s this type of planning has resulted in the gradual disappearance of planning institutes, planning departments in the ministries of health, and planning courses in public health training programmes.

More recently, planning and evaluation services have regained momentum under the pressure of economic factors (expressed mainly as the wish of governments and/or insurance companies to reduce the costs of care) and through the population's insistence that they receive more care of better quality.

This new wave of planning is, however, different from previous versions in that it has begun to define the three key elements of planning in a new way.

(i) Investment is measured in terms of total expenditure – not only the money spent to build services and pay health personnel, but also implicit expenses such as the time that relatives spend looking after sick members of their family.

(ii) The main indicator of health care productivity is now assessment of outcome in terms of improved health, whereas it used to be assessment of improvement in the process of providing health care.

(iii) The definition of needs for health services are changing. There are now four elements in the process of defining the needs for health care services: (a) the need for health care should consider the expressed demands of the community; (b) the needs of the health professionals' quality of life should be assessed and addressed; (c) the need for health care must consider the availability of effective and ethically acceptable solutions; and (d) the health sector's involvement must depend on how much the solution lies within the health sector's competence and responsibility.

The consideration of these four elements raises several unresolved issues.

Whose need is the most relevant?

The demands expressed by people affected by a disease are not necessarily the same as those of their families. As previously mentioned, planning for health services has become less popular because of disparities between the expressed needs of those who are sick, their families, and the community. It is imperative to consult all those concerned when defining needs. In theory, this sounds reasonable; the difficulty lies in applying the process, which requires all concerned to learn new ways of behaving.

Are demands linked to disease, illness or sickness?

The English language has the luxury of having three terms that can be used for the three aspects of a morbid condition: disease corresponds to a specific pathological substrate and a specific course and outcome of the condition; illness corresponds to the subjective experience of the morbid condition; and sickness corresponds to the societal recognition that the disease prevents an individual from contributing to society. Psychiatrists – and other health workers – have to deal with diseases and illnesses in their clinical practice and with sicknesses when they are acting as agents of society. Illnesses, diseases, and sicknesses cover different grounds (see also Chapter 3). People sometimes feel more ill than their disease warrants in terms of average values; sometimes people have diseases that do not make them feel ill; and sometimes the term sickness is used to describe individuals who do not feel ill and have no demonstrable pathological substrate for their condition. What then is a 'true' intervention? – the one that responds to a disease? Or to an illness? Or to a sickness? Or only to the area of overlap of all three?

What is an effective intervention?

A problem becomes a need when there is an effective and ethically acceptable intervention that can be performed by the health services. It is therefore necessary to define an effective intervention. There is a growing consensus that the value of interventions should be assessed on the basis of the results of scientific investigations. This does not resolve everything. Sometimes, interventions deal with the disease or its consequences in totality; sometimes, they can only deal with part of the problem caused by a disease. Different interventions may be effective for different parts of the disease problem. The question that arises is whether the gains of using the different interventions (each dealing with a different part of the disease problem) are equivalent – and from whose point of view? The population? The population in general, or the population affected by the disease? Alternatively, should experts, for example experts on the social impact of disease, be invited to advise? For a long time, psychiatrists have valued interventions by how well they relieve symptoms. Their patients might have preferred a treatment with fewer side effects, even if that meant a less complete relief of symptoms. The population might have been particularly keen to see the application of treatments or other interventions that reduce disability, diminish dependence on others, or eliminate public disturbance.

There is also confusion about who is responsible for the implementation of some interventions. When the intervention requires knowledge and skills unique to health service staff, the issue is easy to resolve; unfortunately, for many diseases the situation is not that clearcut. For example, as science has not yet provided an answer to dementia, should health staff decline to be involved with the problems faced by people with this disorder? Yet families need help in dealing with, say, the symptom of fecal incontinence, which is a consequence of the dementia. Should health care staff become involved in the provision of incontinence pads and the education of carers as to how to persuade the demented person to wear them? At one level this can be seen as preventing decubitus ulcers, a proper concern of medicine, but at another level the supply of incontinence pads and education about their use could well be the responsibility of general services for the elderly. Similarly, if a person with a chronic psychosis refuses to take medication until he or she is given appropriate housing, is it the responsibility of the health service to provide and pay for suitable accommodation? The boundaries between health and education, health and child-care services, between health and housing or health and the criminal justice services are often unclear in an individual case, and much negotiation is required to ensure that each service can apply the majority of their budget to their main task. In the case of medicine this is the intervention against disease, but a broad view is likely to prove more beneficial than a narrow one.

The second issue concerning the assignment of responsibility is of a more profound nature. It concerns the justification for any medical intervention intended to help people who have a disease. Recently, this issue has become confused. It has been said that disease must be treated because it will save society money. By spending several thousand pounds to cure a disease, the argument goes, the individual, freed from disease, will be able to contribute financially to society for many years, which will amply repay the investments made. Of course, the argument is flawed: it is not certain that the person who had the disease will find or maintain a job and contribute to society. There is no guarantee that the same individual will stay free of disease and that the State will not have to spend more money on his/her health. It is not certain how long a person who has been cured of a disease will live and receive retirement benefits: and so forth.

However, even if the economic argument were not flawed, it should never become the main reason for providing health care. Care for the sick members of a society is an ethical imperative, even if significant amounts of money are spent and not recouped. This consideration is important because it moves the burden of deciding whether a particular person merits care from the health system to the political arena. The task of the health care specialist is to provide the best possible treatment or support for those members of society who are not well: the political structure of the country has to decide on the total amount of money that will be spent on health.

With these considerations in mind it is possible to propose that needs for health care be defined as,

the agglomerate of those demands of people having a health problem, their families and their communities to which the health care system can respond by an effective intervention. In this context, effective interventions are those that have a predictable and significant positive effect on the problem and are acceptable to the individuals who have the problem and to those who care for them.

This definition would allow a pragmatic assessment of needs for care and is cast in the spirit of seeking an alliance between patients, their families, their communities and the health care system. Its acceptance would avoid the pitfall of deciding that illness without an organic substrate is not a legitimate reason for seeking and obtaining help. Similarly, it would avoid equating epidemiological estimates of the prevalence of mental disorders with needs, regardless of the capacity of the health sector to respond to it. It underlines the need to assess interventions scientifically and ensures that only those interventions that are effective are used. It also implies that it is the health sector's responsibility to decide which of the interventions should be applied on ethical and scientific grounds, while the decision not to provide the resources necessary to provide the best treatment remains in the political domain.

Reproduced with permission.

Jacques Louis David (1748–1825): *Les Sabines* (*The Sabine Women*) (1799). (Courtesy of the Louvre, Paris, and Bridgeman Art Library, London.)

14

Why are mental and neurological disorders not being prevented?

Primary prevention of mental and neurological disorders is possible in many instances: correcting iodine deficiency in young women might, for example, to a large extent prevent the occurrence of cretinism.

Primary prevention of psychiatric disorders is, however, not explicitly described as a goal or duty of psychiatry. To an extent this is because many of the preventive interventions are the task of services other than medical and, if they do fall to health services, they are usually not in the classical domain of psychiatry. While this is so, psychiatry should still not neglect its role in ensuring the application of measures of primary prevention to mental and neurological disorders. Psychiatrists and other mental health workers have to accept their role in the advocacy of preventive intervention, accept that primary prevention should be an important focus of their research and invest much more time and effort into teaching about primary prevention of mental and neurological disorders.

More than a decade ago the Director General of the World Health Organization (WHO) presented to the World Health Assembly a document (WHO, 1988) listing possible lines of primary prevention of mental neurological and psychosocial disorders. The report mentioned secondary prevention (treatment of mental disorders) and tertiary prevention (the reduction of disability due to mental disorder), but did not dwell upon them: it concentrated on primary prevention of mental, neurological and psychosocial disorders. The World Health Assembly is the highest international authority in the field of health. Ministers or official representatives of governments of all the Member States of the World Health Organization attend these meetings to consider policies and programmes at national and international level. The Assembly considered the proposals contained in the document and accepted them enthusiastically. Many delegates spoke. A resolution was unanimously adopted. Member States were requested to implement the recommendations contained in the document of the Director General and the Director General was instructed to inform the Assembly about the work done worldwide, in 3 years' time.

Three years later the Director General presented a follow-up report. While optimistic in tone, the report did not bring forward news of a multitude of preventive interventions in the WHO member states. Some countries reported on the preparation of preventive interventions. Meetings were held at regional and national level to discuss action. A number of publications were produced and distributed. Results of research showing effects of small-scale interventions in a variety of situations were made available to the WHO. On the whole, however, the primary prevention of mental and neurological disorders continued to be a neglected part of mental health and public health programmes worldwide.

National efforts seem to have had a similar fate. Reports listing possible interventions as well as declarative and policy documents that were produced at country level usually had little mobilizing effect. The huge potential of primary prevention of mental and neurological disorders remained unused both in countries that have expressed their determination to carry out preventive activities and in other countries which have not said so.

Table 1. *Examples of interventions that could contribute to the primary prevention of mental and neurological disorders*

1. Systematic provision of advice to pregnant women not to smoke or drink alcohol and other drugs during pregnancy.
2. Advocacy of iodine supplementation at least for women in childbearing age.
3. Early recognition and correction of sensory deficits in children (e.g. of myopia)
4. Prevention of injuries to the central nervous system (e.g. at work or in traffic)
5. Education of people with diabetes about the prevention of peripheral neuropathy
6. Management of crises at the point of primary contact with health services
7. Improvement of day care facilities
8. Review of legislation on matters particularly relevant to mental health (e.g. concerning adoption of children and child labour)

Why should that be so? Recent – as well as previous – reports demonstrated that mental and neurological disorders are a serious public health problem causing suffering, disability and vast losses to the economy of countries everywhere. Treatment of mental and neurological disorders is possible and often effective, but the application of treatments on a broad scale remains in the area of dreams and future bliss for most countries of the world. The application of primary preventive measures could significantly reduce the numbers of people suffering from these disorders even in countries in which resources for health care are scarce (Sartorius, 2001).

Table 1 provides examples of measures of primary prevention that were included in the report of the Director General of the WHO. Other documents and recommendations refer to and describe numerous other interventions and list the multitude of disorders that are amenable to primary prevention.

Since then, some of the highly industrialized countries have developed and implemented a number of measures of primary prevention of mental disorders. Some of them have done so incompletely, leaving subgroups of the population uncovered, but at least a good start has been made. However, despite the successful application of programmes in some sites and countries, measures of primary prevention have low popularity and even lower application levels in most countries of the world. Several reasons might be responsible for this. The most often quoted reason is that, at present, there are very few measures that are specifically effective in the prevention of particular mental or neurological disorders so that it is more difficult to mobilize the resources for preventive action. A measure that can prevent the appearance of a particular condition will always be more easy to implement than a measure that probably deals with a problem – a risk factor – that contributes to the occurrence of several disorders. Some of the specific measures that are currently available, e.g. early preventive interventions in schools, also have the disadvantage that they usually require considerable expertise as well as human and material investment. But there are other, in my opinion more important, reasons for the neglect of primary prevention in the field of mental health.

First, the execution of most primary preventive interventions depends on the action of social sectors other than health. Mental and psychosocial disorders (such as violence) do not have a single cause but result from a combination of effects of a genetic or other vulnerability, environmental risk factors, personal action and the life path (which is often not a matter of choice for the individual): preventive measures might therefore have to be simultaneously applied by different services which is difficult. The Ministry of Education will decide whether, and how many hours of, its primary and secondary school curriculum will be given to health education or to the inculcation of attitudes such as tolerance to those who are different – for reasons of illness or other reasons. The Ministry of Labour will decide on regulations that govern the maintenance or creation of jobs for people who experience an attack of mental illness. The Ministry of Social Welfare might be responsible for issuing regulations about the help that social workers or other social agency workers can give to families of people who have fallen ill. The Ministry of the Interior will decide whether police will have to go through a period of education on dealing with crisis situation. These and other ministries and agencies might, in fact, be issuing some regulations that will result in the prevention of mental disorders or diminish the risk of becoming afflicted by a mental illness: they, however, neither realize that they have done so nor report on the effects of their action on mental morbidity. What makes things worse is that the various ministries rarely worry about side effects of their action. Thus, for example, it will happen that the Ministries of Education and of Health educate and praise living in families while Ministry of Finance makes the taxes that young people would pay when they are married higher than if they stay single.

Second, even when primary prevention activities are the responsibility of the Ministry of Health it will not be the mental health department that will be in charge of carrying them out. Improved perinatal care will diminish the incidence of brain damage at birth; but perinatal care is the responsibility of the Mother and Child Health Department. Iodinization of salt may lie in the sphere of action of the agency dealing with food and drug control. The control of sensory deficits in children will be the responsibility of the School Health Department. Training of primary care staff in all matters – including crisis management for example, will be the responsibility of the Primary Health Care Department.

Third, psychiatrists and other mental health workers are neither trained for, nor particularly interested in, spending their time in advocating measures that others have to undertake and over which they will have no control. Psychiatrists who have the knowledge about mental diseases and about risks that might cause them, are more likely to seek support for the development of mental health services than for preventive activities. The fact that even those who are most concerned with psychiatric disorders do not make prevention their priority does anything but convince health authorities about the usefulness of preventive action. The fact that prevention will be often taken up by other professionals in the field – psychologists, for example, does not help either. While good at their work, these other mental health workers suffer from the disadvantage of not having much credibility in the medical circles and in the government offices dealing with public health.

Fourth, the preventive interventions are not glamorous. Writing letters and proposals to the ministerial authority that controls the quality and production of food and urging them, yet again, to add iodine to salt is hardly comparable to the amazing world of neuro-imaging, heart replacement or the unravelling of the mysteries of the human genome. What is more, there is little immediate reward for engaging in preventive work. The results of these interventions are sometimes to be expected in 10, 20 or 30 years' time. The motivation to continue preventive work is therefore usually secondary, e.g. to continue receiving a (usually low) salary which, in turn, may help to survive and buy objects or time giving greater pleasure. Compared to the attraction to other types of health work, prevention is not well placed. Emergency medicine, a discipline marked by the emotional engagement in saving human lives and by reward of every success – or a highly paid private practice, have a better chance of attracting the best and most charismatic medical graduates, which in turn decreases the interest of medical students in the subject of prevention and the willingness of the authorities to support preventive work.

Fifth, preventive interventions usually have a low relative success rate. A preventive intervention may, for example, yield a positive result – for example change the behaviour – of 5 or 10% of the target individuals. Compared to the effects of treatment interventions – for example, the administration of an antibiotic in an acute infectious ailment – this is not a very impressive result, and the preventive intervention may be decried as useless and abandoned. Yet, if a preventive intervention had been successful in making 10% of all smokers stop smoking, the gain of the intervention is that hundreds of thousands or millions of people have broken the habit. This is not only important because it saved many lives: the ex-smokers may make the non-smoking minority of people in a country gain strength and perhaps become a majority, which would help to exert pressure on the public opinion and increase the government's investment into smoking cessation. The success of primary prevention of mental and psychosocial disorders thus requires a more sophisticated assessment of success than simple treatment interventions. This difference between the criteria of assessment of success of preventive and treatment interventions is neither sufficiently recognized by health authorities nor used in the selection for health care interventions.

Finally, some behaviours that can lead to, or contribute to, the occurrence of mental (or physical) disorder contribute vast sums to the national budget. Taxes on smoking, the employment of many people in alcohol industry, profits from selling fast and dangerous vehicles (that may contribute to the incidence of head injury) and many other gains for society may vanish if primary prevention of smoking, drinking and high risk taking behaviour were to be successful. Even if it is true that, in the long run, society loses more than it gains by permitting these behaviours to continue, the immediate gains make governments and industries be half hearted in their preventive efforts.

So, what should psychiatrists or other mental health professionals do about primary prevention of mental and neurological disorders? Sit back and lament? Four sources of action seem to be sensible: first, they should advocate (in their roles as experts and advisors to the government, and as citizens) that measures of primary prevention be applied; second, they should continue and promote research on causes of mental and neurological disorders; third, they should ensure that undergraduate and postgraduate education in psychiatry includes a cogent description of possibilities (and limits) of primary prevention in psychiatry; and fourth, they should seek alliance and provide support to those engaged in activities leading to the primary prevention of mental illness.

REFERENCES

Sartorius, N. (2001). Primary prevention of mental disorders. pp. 487–494. In Thornicroft, G. and Szmukler, G. (eds.) *Textbook of Community Psychiatry.* Oxford: Oxford University Press.

World Health Organization (1988). *Prevention of Mental, Neurological and Psychosocial Disorders.* Document WHO/MNH/EVA188.1. Geneva: WHO.

Hieronymus Bosch (*c*.1450–1516): Table top of the Seven Deadly Sins and the Four Last Things (detail). (Courtesy of the Museo del Prado, Madrid, and Bridgeman Art Library, London.)

15

The seven vices of psychiatry

Psychiatry is, in general, not a highly respected discipline and mental health programmes continue to be given low priority, despite the vast scale of mental health
problems and the existence of effective interventions to control them. To an extent,
this can be explained by the stigma attached to mental illness, by the simultaneous
dramatic presence of other problems and by the fact that effective therapeutic intervention became available only recently. To a significant degree, however, psychiatrists
have to blame themselves for this situation. Unless they change their ways, mental
health programmes will continue their arduous and slow development for a long time
to come.

In most parts of the world psychiatry is not recognized as a medical discipline equal to others. Its practitioners are often considered to be charlatans unable to provide real help and likely to do evil things. People suffering from mental illness are not seen as people requiring help, but as weaklings, evil doers or simulants. Their human rights are often not respected, and the care they receive is usually sub-optimal.

There are many reasons for this lamentable situation. They include the stigma attached to mental illness, ignorance of the general public and decision makers about the nature of mental illness and ways of dealing with it, obsolete traditions and laws. But psychiatry also bears a part of the blame. Its sins can be conveniently enumerated under the heading that the Catholic Church listed as deadly sins, preventing souls from entering heaven and reaching bliss – Avarice, Pride, Envy, Anger, Gluttony, Lechery and Sloth[1]

Avarice

Psychiatry cannot be miserly with its money because it does not have it. Most of its resources worldwide lie bonded to the mental hospital buildings and the land on which they were erected. It is not miserly with its complaints about its low priority in public health and about the lack of understanding of its needs by the general public. It is, however, miserly with the knowledge that it has, and that others could use, often better than psychiatrists. It is still difficult to find psychiatrists willing to give much of their time to the training of general practitioners and other health workers.

The need to instruct the general practitioners is particularly great in countries in which the training of the medical student included no training in psychiatry or in which the undergraduate curriculum included only a week-long stay in a mental hospital. The prevalence of mental disorders in those countries is the same as elsewhere. The proportion of people who come to general practitioners or primary care units primarily because of psychological problems is high. Psychiatrists

[1]   In a recent article Fabrega (Febrega 2000) also listed the seven sins of international psychiatry. These, however, refer to very different issues from those addressed in this chapter.

or mental health professionals in those countries often avoid engagement in the training of other health professionals. The frequently cited reason for not doing so is that they are overburdened by their clinical tasks with psychiatric patients. The argument that they can at best treat only a small proportion of those mentally ill in the country themselves and that they must therefore teach and delegate sounds good to the public health person but has little weight with most clinicians.

The psychiatrists are also not seriously engaged in the battle to change the undergraduate instruction which is often wrong in content and structure. Most of the time in the undergraduate curriculum is spent on teaching about the most severe – but also most rare – mental disorders. The teaching is oriented to the provision of knowledge about the form of mental disorders rather than about their management. The facts are provided in a manner that is off-putting: the language of instruction is obtuse, jargon prevails and simple things are said in a complex way. There is no relation between the frequency of a disorder in general practice and the amount of time spent on instruction about it. Most textbooks of psychiatry for the undergraduate take up very little space on practically useful things. There is little advice on how to educate patients to live with their illness and none on how to teach families to help their sick members. Medical students notice this and complete their study of psychiatry convinced of its inability to provide specific means to help in specific situations.

The situation is even worse when it comes to the inculcation of attitudes. Although it is necessary to use a good part of instruction in psychiatry – and of teaching on other subjects – to dispel prejudice and stigma related to mental illness very little time or effort is given to this educational objective. The site of teaching is often on wards of mental hospitals reserved for the care of the chronically mentally ill or disabled. The patients who are brought for demonstration are often those with the most bizarre symptoms. The demonstration of interviewing techniques with less seriously disturbed people is neglected.

Nor is there much teaching about skills necessary for the management of mental illness. Teachers of psychiatry in most countries of the world do not generally believe that medical practitioners will be able, or willing, to use treatment skills even if they were successful in imparting them. The instruction usually stops short of providing advice on action other than referral to a specialist when the practitioner is suspecting mental illness. When teaching about long-term maintenance treatment, the psychiatrists will often spend little time on instruction about ways to motivate patients to participate in their treatment in an active manner or on ways of ensuring cooperation with family members providing care to a mentally ill person at home.

Psychiatry is also miserly in providing its knowledge to colleagues in other medical disciplines. New psychotropic medicaments are used by many specialists without much consultation with psychiatrists, and psychopharmacotherapy of people suffering from mental disorder comorbid with physical illness is given little time in undergraduate education. Evidence about the impact of psychological factors on the immune system is still considered as being relevant only to psychiatry rather than used as a bridge to general medicine. While other medical disciplines gain respectability and place in medical education by flooding all areas of discourse with new facts and theories – even when these are not sufficiently documented – psychiatry provides hints that its practitioners have hidden knowledge and that the discipline as such is so complex that its practices and actions cannot be made transparent.

Psychiatry will have to change its ways, examine its knowledge and translate it into languages understandable to others in the field of medicine and elsewhere. It must no longer be miserly – its knowledge can and should be useful to the people medicine is supposed to serve and to the progress of science in general.

Pride

I often wondered why pride was selected as a deadly sin. Why should one not be proud of achievements, of things done, acquired or given by nature? What is wrong with the painter's admiration of a picture or with the sculptor's pleasure of seeing the torso just produced? Or, why should a government not announce proudly that it has built a marvellous safe road to the south? Why should surgery not be proud of its capacity to replace the heart, liver or kidney?

Pride is blinding. It makes us less aware of our shortcomings, of things still to do, of imperfections of what was achieved. Being aware of the progress we made motivates: being proud of it can make us complacent. Precise description of psychological abnormalities and the formulation of specific criteria for the diagnosis and classification on a number of occasions and by many authors in the past century made the practitioners of the discipline proud of their achievement and obscured the fact that these descriptions are no more than working hypotheses that may be rejected once sufficient knowledge for their testing became available. The illusion of achievement, and the pride about the development of a comprehensive system of operational criteria for the placement of diagnoses into categories of the major classification, is a case in point. Once the categories of the classifications were written, they were accepted as the truth about mental disorders. The fact that there is often much uncertainty about the precise limits of mental disorders was no longer important. The categories produced by a measure of consensus among the makers of the classifications suddenly became true diseases that should be used in conducting etiological and therapeutic research. Proud of their classification, psychiatrists reject to accept facts that put it in doubt. The fact that a drug is not effective in all persons given a particular diagnostic label makes them reject the drug rather than begin doubting classification. Governments have followed the advice of the profession and defined its rules for the acceptance of a particular medicament by the effectiveness of the substance in the alleviation of severity of a syndrome. They disallow the marketing of a drug that is effective in some persons with a given syndrome and not in others.

That pride can be blinding is true; but this effect would not be sufficient to make it a deadly sin. Pride can easily give birth to arrogance, a manner based on exaggerated pride accompanied by a lack of respect for others, no matter who they might be or what they might have done. Intellectual arrogance has been psychiatry's sin on many occasions. Whenever psychiatry made a step forward and allowed pride over the achievement to fuel its arrogance, psychiatry lost. The members of the profession became complacent and found it easy to disregard advice of others. The physical separation of psychiatry with its point of gravity in mental hospitals, far from the centres of towns and the buildings of the medical schools and other medical disciplines, contributed to maintaining arrogance by diminishing the likelihood that serious criticism by other members of the medical profession will render the psychiatrists better aware of the imperfection of their discoveries or achievements.

Envy

Other subjects have more hours in the medical curriculum than psychiatry. The Departments of cardiac surgery are receiving too much money. The distribution of governments' fellowships between disciplines is unjust, others are receiving much more than psychiatry. Others are allowed to prescribe expensive medications but not psychiatrists. There are many instances in which psychiatry has been given less attention and support than the public health importance of mental disorders would warrant, and psychiatrists could complain about it. But, they do more, and truly excel, to the envy of other disciplines' achievements or resources.

The reasons for the perceived injustice and the justification for complaints are rarely examined. In most parts of the world psychiatry has, for many years, been a discipline that was perceived as a discipline without public health attributes. The concentration on schizophrenia, bipolar illness and a small number of other conditions did nothing to convince others of the frequency of mental disorders nor of the relevance of teaching methods of treatment of such disorders to the medical student. Since the central focus of psychiatry was on these disorders, there was little that psychiatry could propose as preventive interventions.

Nor did the frequent complaints of psychiatrists about the disadvantages they had to endure and their envious regard of other disciplines do much to endear them to their colleagues or the decision makers. Instead of studying what made other disciplines progress – for example, the emphasis on the potential that a discipline has, or a clear presentation of easily understandable and credible numbers showing the seriousness of the problem – psychiatrists continued to complain and speak of being unjustly treated and neglected.

The unfavourable comparison of psychiatry with other disciplines harms psychiatry because it is not perceived by anyone except psychiatrists as an injustice but as a reflection of merit in public health terms. 'Look how serious problems we face and how much we can do' is a formula that has brought support to many and works better than the envious statement 'All of you have so much more and this injustice continues'.

Psychiatry should applaud successes of others but also make it clear that it is a discipline based on tremendous advances of its basic sciences. It should also clearly demonstrate that it has developed many practical preventive and curative interventions that are effective, efficient and acceptable to the patient and to the general population. Envy is a deadly sin because it blocks recognition of one's own value and possibilities for action and advancement – by individuals singly and by the profession as a whole.

Anger

Ora tument ira – anger swells the mouth, makes it impossible to those in anger to speak right. It also makes it difficult to think right, to be effective, to discriminate in action. Even Gods when angry, lose judgement, destroy the good together with the bad, punish many without a cause or reason. In myths they sometimes regret what they have done and express regret: but rarely do they repair the damage they have done.

For humans, the most serious form of anger is war, sustained anger inflicting harm, pain and loss to those seen as enemies – all this with little regard to the damage done to oneself. For a long time, and without valid reasons, war has been a way of life for psychiatry. Schools of psychiatry fought one another. Partisans of biological approaches to the understanding of mental functioning have derided those embracing a psychodynamic orientation in psychiatry – who in turn keep attacking – wherever possible – all the defenders of 'mindless' psychiatry. Academic psychiatrists dismiss hospital psychiatry as being intellectually second class and mental hospital staff have little understanding and even fewer good words for the leaders of community or academic psychiatry. Social psychiatry has not only often overemphasized the influence of social factors, but has also attacked other psychiatric orientations, reminding the observer of the religious wars and the behaviour of religious sects all supposedly in the search of enlightenment and all violently critical of all the ways of finding it, except for their own. No other branch of medicine had developed such different orientations nor as much animosity between the defenders of different theoretical and practical orientations. Like Gods in anger, the sects of psychiatry seemed to be ready to reject all the knowledge or insights that sects other than their own held: the good and the bad in others have been equally viciously attacked. Even those psychiatrists who declared themselves eclectic – saying that they were accepting the best from all the orientations of psychiatry – have been unwilling to make peace with any of the warring groups.

A vital step in the development of psychiatry is its unification. It is very unlikely that governments and the rest of medicine will want to listen to members of a profession speaking with a hundred often contradictory voices. While it might be, epistemologically speaking, enriching to search the truth using different paths it is dangerous and detrimental to do so in the manner in which psychiatry has been doing it over the past one hundred years. The crucial task before psychiatry today is to develop a consensus about ways of diagnosing and treating mental illness using the best of available knowledge and experience. The guidelines so developed will not be valid forever: progress of knowledge will make it necessary to revise them perhaps soon: but this revision again should be done in agreement and by the profession as a whole. War and anger within psychiatry is wasteful and diminishes the probability that we shall make progress in knowledge and in its useful application.

Gluttony

The hospices of the recent medieval past provided shelter to the poor, the sick, the old, the mad, the helpless and those in hiding. With time, these asylums lost some of their inhabitants who migrated into old-age homes, hospitals providing treatment, the criminal underground. Those who were disabled because of mental illness or impairment often had nowhere to go. Their numbers grew as urbanization reduced the opportunities for their careers as well-tolerated simpletons in a village, shepherds, helpers in households sufficiently large to feed one more without noticing. Urban development brought with it the growth of the numbers of asylums predominantly reserved for those with disorderly behaviour, those very poor and those sufficiently disabled to be difficult to employ in any job.

In time, asylums grew into mental hospitals housing those ill and those fully or partially recovered but who had nowhere else to go. The numbers of the chronically disabled who had nowhere to go grew faster than the numbers of those with an illness and lead to an expansion of the size of hospitals that sometimes reached the size of towns. The Pilgrim State hospital at a time had some 13 000 inmates and about as many staff; and the Manila or Rio de Janeiro mental hospitals had more than 8 000 inmates each. The numbers of destitutes and paupers who were brought to hospitals also grew, particularly in European countries. The directors of the asylums and the doctors who dealt with mental illness were not particularly concerned by the reasons that made people come to the hospital. Often, their admission was the only way to prevent the dying from hunger, exposure or abuse. The degree of mental abnormality was not the main nor the only criterion for admission to mental hospitals: it still is not in many developing countries[2].

A possible reason for this behaviour of psychiatrists is the history described above and the expectations born out of habit that the mental hospitals will deal with social problems. To an extent, however, it is also likely that the psychiatrists are unwilling to take the drastic

---

[2] Not so long ago, the internment in mental hospitals was used as punishment or as a secure way of removing those disagreeing with the official government policies from the street and from having access to other people, to media and to their workmates. Whether this form of abuse of psychiatry still occurs is sometimes difficult to say. The visit of an important guest from abroad – a head of state, for example, is not so infrequently taken as a sufficient reason to proceed to a preventive 'hospitalization' of some of those known to be difficult, who perhaps had been in hospital on a previous occasion – lest the visiting Head of State would be booed instead of greeted enthusiastically by children enjoying the day off from school in order to be enthusiastic about the visitor. Other forms of abuse, for reasons that are not political, probably also occur: the past several decades have, however, made these events rarer and more difficult to discover.

step of reducing the size of the facility in which they work because in all health systems the reduction of numbers of beds means also a reduction of power and resources. The fact that the knowledge that psychiatry has at its disposal cannot help the poor to become richer is secondary in this equation. There is no doubt that the poor particularly when disabled are often better off in a decently run mental hospital than in the street; there is no doubt either about the fact that the budget for the hospital will be larger the more beds there are and the more patients or inmates there are in those beds.

Psychiatry, however, loses in this game. The gluttonous wish to have more beds, more resources, more staff, more influence – results, in this instance, in making psychiatry different and distant from the rest of medicine. The hospitals cannot resolve social problems; overcrowding and poor care that usually follows reduce the respect that the general population and the rest of medicine have for psychiatry.

Another expression of exaggerated appetite were the numerous claims of psychiatry in fields in which the knowledge of psychiatry has little to offer. Psychiatrists were asked to draw psychological profiles of statesmen whom they have never seen and accepted to do so, although there is nothing in their trade that would qualify them for this task. That they are asked to do so is not their fault: that they accept that task is. Psychiatrists make pronouncements – invited by others or spontaneously – about the psychological meaning of rituals in a cultural setting that they have neither studied nor are qualified to study. Psychiatrists write about 'political psychiatry' about the personality of nations, reasons for war and about too many other things. Much of what they say seems reasonable and much is in harmony with a psychiatric theory that they believe in. The gluttony for authority in all walks of life however does not befit a discipline nor does it help it to focus its forces on the areas which it should cover and in which it should excel[3].

---

[3] This is not to say that mental health programmes must be restricted to the recognition, prevention and treatment of mental disorders. Mental health programmes should have a broad focus, deal with interventions to prevent or manage mental illness as well as with action necessary to deal with psychosocial aspects of health and development in general. The mental health programmes, however, should rely on the knowledge and support of representatives of many social sectors and disciplines: psychiatry is only one of these.

Psychiatry must shed the burden of activities for which it has neither the competence nor the resources. It must emerge leaner and better defined from this process and the sooner it does so the better.

Lechery

Psychiatry's quest for causes of mental disorder was, for a long time, marked by the hope and insistence that a single set of causative mechanisms will explain mental functioning and its abnormalities. For a while, sexual experiences and their aberrations were seen as the pivot of psychological abnormality and the most important factor in human psychological development. Before that, degeneration and vice were seen as the central cause of mental illness and of criminal inclination. Conditioning and related processes were, for some time, seen as the mechanism that holds the answer to all questions about causes. More recently, disturbances of receptors in the central nervous system seem to have gained the priority in explanatory discourses. Each of these attempts at understanding the complex nature of the human mind and of its operation had merit. The mechanisms proposed to explain the brain function had the beauty of an ingenious construction and the value of containing a morsel of truth. There was nothing wrong in proposing them or exploring whether they will hold up under the tests of evidence. What was bad was that they were each time seen as the answer, not one of the answers, nor as part of an answer but as the whole truth, sufficient in itself.

Sexual activity was not the vice of lechery: it was over-indulgence in it that was sinful. Psychiatry also sinned when it was over-indulgent in its explanatory theories. It sinned because it closed other avenues of search whenever it selected causal theory and restricted all attention to a single (promising perhaps) source of explanation. In the East of Europe, during the existence of the Soviet system, psychiatric books had to be prefaced by a clear explanation of the ways in which the material presented in the book supported and strengthened Pavlov's views. In a 'biologically oriented' journal it is difficult to publish a paper if it does not contain numerical data.

Psychoanalysis was hailed as the method that allows the resolution of mental problems and the rebuilding of personalities in more productive and mature ways. For a long time the allegiance to the psychoanalytic method blocked progress in the search for other methods. It was – and in certain countries it still is – almost sacrilegious to oppose psychoanalytic thinking and apply treatment that does not follow the path that psychoanalysis would justify. Attempts to do so were not infrequently interpreted as signs of a morbid opposition to the master and his teaching and had unpleasant consequences for one's career.

Perhaps more than any other discipline psychiatry suffered from over-indulgence in each of its theories and lost time over-exploring one line of enquiry at the expense of neglecting others perhaps just as promising. A more ecumenical attitude would have been better. Maybe the time for it has come so that psychiatry will soon be able to tolerate and even rejoice in the difference of the approaches and directions of study of the members of the profession.

Sloth

Sloth is seen as the worst vice, a sin more pernicious than all the others in Christian lore. Sloth is the enemy of ambition, of effort and of self-reliance. It is the vice that affects all of an individual or group's functions. It is hidden in excuses and apologies, often presented as prudent expectation of the signal to become active again, a signal that will never come or if it does will be neglected.

Progress in the field of psychiatry depends – perhaps more than in any other field – on the amount of investment of time and energy by mental health professionals. Conditions in many mental hospitals remained unchanged or worsened over decades because it was necessary that psychiatrists invest much of their time to convince those responsible to improve them. Reforms of mental health programmes have failed because nobody had the motivation, endurance and patience necessary to change attitudes and educate staff, families, the media and the general public about the new programmes and their role in them. On many occasions, decision makers in the field of health did not provide psychiatric patients with community services because the leaders of the psychiatric profession failed to persuade them that this is so. Even in very poor countries, whenever psychiatrists tried hard and long the conditions of service, training and research improved despite financial scarcity, stigmatization of the profession and the simultaneous presence of other problems. No other recipe seems to work. When staff and leaders are affected by sloth, even major increases of budget for mental health services will have only a short-lasting effect.

It is, however, not easy to find energy for work in the field of psychiatry. Many factors seem to unite in the process of extinguishing ambition, making people disappointed with life and their career and leading them to burn-out syndromes. The profession is stigmatized and until recently had no methods that could dramatically demonstrate its healing potentials or its efficiency in the prevention of disorder.

An attempt to introduce change in the institution or to develop a community programme often required a heroic battle with powerful staff clans fighting against any changes that might reduce their real or perceived benefits. The disestablishment of a hospital could sometimes cause high rates of unemployment in the area in which the hospital was located. Since reforms in the field of psychiatry often require social interventions, local as well as remote political interests can be awakened and mobilized turning the changes of health services into a political confrontation. The introduction of a school mental health programme usually means prolonged negotiations with the school authorities, a long process of training of trainers and teachers and a relentless support to the programme. It is because of these facts that the most dangerous vice of psychiatry and of all the members of mental health professions is the reluctance or refusal to invest energy and time into mental health programmes. Without a commitment and a lot of hard work by all of the mental health professionals psychiatry is unlikely to improve in the near or distant future.

Conclusion and coda

Psychiatry has made significant steps forward but will not fulfil its social role unless it is successful in combating its major real or potential vices. It has to package the knowledge that it has accumulated in a manner that will make it suitable for use by other participants in care – from journalists to nurses and family carers because it cannot expect to deal alone with the problems of mental disorders regardless of how many psychiatrists are trained and available. It has to be aware of its achievements but shed arrogance and show respect for the many from whom it can learn and with whom it has to work. It must build for itself rather than regret that it is less advantaged than others. It must unite, speak with one voice, arrive at a consensus of opinion about crucial issues of psychiatric theory and practice, and be willing to re-examine its consensus whenever new developments of science and additional experience seem to require this. It must become leaner, better defined, shed the responsibility for social problems, reject the unjustified ambitions to be in all fields of human endeavour as their arbiter and leader. It must allow innovation and promote it, avoiding a lock-up in any particular theoretical or dogmatic paradigm. Finally, it must invest much energy and continue doing so if it is to fulfil its social, scientific and humanitarian roles. It cannot afford to rest and be complacent: there are too many tasks before it, tasks that have to performed to advance psychiatry, medicine and human development in general.

REFERENCE

Fabrega, J.J. (2000). Culture, spirituality and psychiatry. *Current Opinion in Psychiatry*, **13**, 525–543.

16

Brueghel's Everyman: a cover page for a book on research in psychiatry

Hieronymus Cock (*c.*1510–70): an engraving (*c.*1558) after *Everyman* by Pieter Brueghel, the Elder (*c.*1515–69). (Private collection, courtesy of Bridgeman Art Library, London.)

Research in the field of psychiatry faces numerous difficulties. Some stem from the uncertainty about the nosological status of diagnoses in psychiatry which, by and large, describe syndromes rather than diseases. The tradition of psychiatry growing in separation from the rest of medicine hampers research on mental disorders. The gaps between the epidemiological, social, biological and other research undertakings also slow down progress and make it more difficult to gain a comprehensive understanding of mental functioning in health and disease. Recent socio-economic changes, e.g. the growing gap in resources available for research in the G7 countries and those available in the developing world and in Eastern Europe, also adversely affect psychiatric research. An effort to unify research efforts or at least assure communication among groups now working in isolation will be useful.

The inscription on Bruegel's drawing called Everyman is *Niemat en kent he selve* – no one knows himself, and the drawing shows a variety of people – each labelled *elck* (meaning 'everyone') searching something in a mass of objects. The objects include scientific instruments, parts of a chessboard, empty and full bags, some labelled and some not. The scene is presided by a painting on the wall showing a person – yet another everyone – contemplating a mask or a head: this person also stands before a messy array of objects. Some of the people in the picture ventured further afield armed with lanterns to search elsewhere.

The verses at the bottom of the engraving say that everyone searches and tries to enrich himself without ever recognizing one's motivation. The caption in Latin at the bottom of the engraving speaks to the same point. It reads (in A. Klein's translation) 'There is no one who does not seek his own advantage everywhere, no one who does not seek himself in all that he does, no one who does not yearn everywhere for private gain – this one pulls, that one pulls – all have the same love of possessing'.

In a pessimistic moment one might suggest this engraving for the cover page of a book describing psychiatric research worldwide. The many that are engaged in it seem to do so without much connection with the others in the same picture. Some have tools – lanterns – others not. Many of those who have the privilege of spending their time searching – with an uncertain hope that they shall find anything – look quite old. The area of investigation is vast and things lie in disorder – it is unclear what might be the object of the searches.

Biological and other sciences have produced a lot of new facts in recent years but no unifying theory that would help to put them in meaningful relationships. The fact that there is very little evidence about the nosological status of psychiatric disorders does not help at all. A condition can be considered to have the status of a disease when its causes and pathogenesis are known, its clinical picture well described, its natural history known and its reaction to treatment and other interventions predictable. None of the mental and behavioural disorders satisfies these requirements. Yet, psychiatric disorders have been described and classified, then reclassified again and again. Cloninger's apt analogy of current efforts in this field – likening classifiers to people moving around chairs on the upper deck of a ship that has a hole in its side and is sinking – describes the situation very well. There is no certainty that the grouping of syndromes in the current classifications reflects the nature of psychiatric illnesses. Yet, research in psychiatry takes the biological and psychological states of individuals showing the same syndrome as their target hoping to discover the causes of the disease. The study of all forms of peripheral neuropathy or of all types of blindness will not tell us much about diabetes. Peripheral neuropathy, irritability, retinopathy, obesity and other symptoms of diabetes are not taken as the subject of research – all of them and others are related by the underlying disturbances of metabolism characteristic of diabetes which can be the subject of etiological and other research.

Psychiatric research has, for a long time, proceeded on the premise that those who show similar symptoms are a homogeneous group and that they suffer from the same underlying physiological disorder that will be discovered if the search lasts long enough. But, without a well-founded theory of psychiatric illness, it is not possible to say whether the findings of psychiatric investigations are irrelevant to the etiology and course of the disease or represent its determinants. Searching for the cause or causes of schizophrenia without knowing whether schizophrenia is a disease or a syndrome commonly present in a number of diseases is a high-risk enterprise. Research conducted under those circumstances produces results that are difficult to interpret. Changes in the metabolism of dopamine might be merely associated with schizophrenia or be produced by the same cause as the syndrome or represent a part of a crucial pathogenetic mechanism for its occurrence.

The difficulties that rise from the uncertainty about the nature of psychiatric diseases and their classification are compounded by the growing gaps between scientists and clinicians and between scientists of different research orientation. The foci of research within epidemiological, biological psychiatry or within other sub-disciplines of psychiatry are selected in the light of previous findings and current preoccupations of the members of that sub-discipline, without much regard to the directions of research that are taken by other sub-disciplines of psychiatry. The jargon and the multitude of technical terms that are used within sub-disciplines of psychiatry make it difficult to remain aware of developments in any but one's own area of work. Collaboration and joint conduct of studies involving scientists belonging to different sub-disciplines – even when they work in the same department or institute – is extremely rare: more frequently researchers in the same institution might be together only when they have to fight battles against common external enemies. When this is not the case, they live in parallel worlds, occasionally meeting and building their conviviality on matters outside psychiatry. As the sophistication of research increases and the focus of investigations narrows, it is becoming increasingly difficult to accommodate the findings of sub-disciplinary research about the disease or a syndrome in a single framework.

Practising psychiatrists are ceasing to be active factors in the development of psychiatric knowledge and the clinical observations that were at the basis of much of what is today known about psychiatric disorders are less and less often being seen as being of value. Standardized assessments of psychiatric conditions have major advantages in that they allow the creation of groups that are homogeneous with respect to a particular measurement: their disadvantage is that they lead to a neglect of phenomena that have not been considered important by the authors of the assessment procedures used.

The widespread use of operational criteria for diagnosis – while increasing the comparability of results obtained in different investigations – diminished the interest in the study of symptoms and signs that are not contributory to the decision about the presence or absence of diagnostic criteria[1]. The fact that the criteria and diagnoses contained in the present classifications are, in most instances, no more than a convention among psychiatrists based on their knowledge at a given point in time is often forgotten. The consequent reification of the criteria and diagnostic systems – the belief that they are the natural boun-

---

[1] The correct and systematic use of operational criteria in diagnostic and therapeutic work has value for public health decision making. It is less helpful in completing the picture of psychiatric disorders and in transcultural research where standardized descriptions have to be complemented with a record of clinical conditions that have not been classifiable in current classificatory categories.

daries between diseases – reduces chances for the discovery of new syndromes or of unexpected connection between symptoms, laboratory findings and epidemiological data.

Until very recently, research was funded in different ways in different countries. In some it was necessary to write a detailed application including a review of the literature, a description of goals and hypotheses that will be tested, a detailed account of methods to be used and a review of the possible impact and use of the results of the research. In others, research moneys were distributed evenly to the departments of the Medical School and institutions engaged in health research. Some countries had a combination of the two systems – providing a reasonable amount for research within the departmental budget and then offering an opportunity to those interested to apply for additional funds to foundations or other donors. There were also instances in which all research money was given to a central institution that was carrying out research or sub-contracting other agencies to do part of it. In a large majority of countries no money was specifically available for research and the heads of departments took on the expenses of research with the other expenses of their departments.

Each of these systems had advantages and disadvantages. Receiving money without having to produce applications made some researchers less motivated to develop proposals and research plans. Some of the money so received might not be used at all and some of it was not spent on research – because the clinical load was too great, because the head of the department had other priorities (for example, teaching), or because of a variety of personal reasons. The advantages of the system were also significant. The researchers could carry out research instead of producing grant applications and running after money for their research. Research could focus on topics that were the personal choice of the researcher rather than the priority of the funding agency. Some of the money could be used to cover unexpected expenses or travel undertaken in connection with the research under way.

Distributing funds on the basis of detailed applications also had many advantages. The funding agency knew in which direction the research might go. The quality of the application was a partial guarantee that the investigators knew their field. The funding agency could use the peer review[2] to protect itself from the accusations of nepotism or funding bias. Research could be gently steered in a particular direction that was neglected. The dark side was that the almost exclusive reliance on grants often meant that the search for money took more time than the research. Some of the best scientists had to delegate their work to others so as to be able to devote time to getting money for their studies. The capacity to produce excellent applications was sometimes not commensurate with the capacity to carry out the research. When money became scarce, the directive role of the funding agency sometimes became oppressive, and innovative research did not have many chances to get support.

What happened recently in the Eastern European countries gave a new meaning to the differences in the way research is funded. Researchers in Eastern European countries suddenly lost the certainty that money for research will be forthcoming as it used to be. Regardless of a department's productivity suddenly, there was less money or no support in the country. There was no other formal source of funding for research either. The only sources of funds were elsewhere. This money from elsewhere was available in one of two ways. The first of these was the participation in collaborative studies in which the research protocols were often cast in stone by the time that the Eastern European researchers were invited to join the studies. Some of those were organized and managed by pharmaceutical companies interested in the effects of specific treatment methods. Some were studies that were part of a political agreement on collaboration. Others were studies run by researchers from the USA and the industrialized countries of Western Europe. The studies that involved investigators from Eastern and Central Europe throughout the process of research planning were extremely rare. In some deplorable and profoundly unethical instances investigators from richer countries carried out research in Eastern European countries to avoid stricter ethical rules for research in their own country or to get more work done for less money since the salaries of research workers in Eastern Europe and in developing countries were much lower than in the West of Europe and in the USA (Sartorius, 1988).

---

[2] There is no certainty nor guarantee that such measures will not be perverted, but in some countries the system seems to work.

The other way to go was to attempt to get money from the European Union, from some of the Foundations and from some of the (Western European) national government agencies that funded research outside its country. The writing of an application for such funds meant a redistribution of time that was not always easy to achieve. Writing applications required skills that were neither taught nor widespread. The development of detailed plans for research well in advance was not customary and seemed an unnecessary imposition. Directing research to certain priorities stated by the granting agency was perceived as a limitation of academic freedom. In most instances the applications had to be produced in a foreign language, usually English, which presented an additional major difficulty and was often done so badly that the application failed on those grounds. Over time, the quality, quantity and originality of research in Eastern and Central Europe deteriorated, stimulating brain drain to the West and into professional roles other than research. The consequences of this loss of human potential are difficult to foresee at this point in time, but it is likely that they will affect the discipline of psychiatry in a negative way for a long time to come.

If Brueghel's engraving were to have been accepted as the cover page of the book on research, it would also have conveyed other messages, in addition to that that searching alone and without a clear idea of what is being sought is likely to be fruitless. It might have reminded the reader that selfish motives are probably just as present in the search for truth and scientific revelation as they are in other fields of human endeavor. The poem at the bottom of the engraving, on the other hand, would have told the observer that in doing research we often learn much about ourselves, about our tolerance of the behaviour of others, about our patience and endurance, and about our willingness to share and help those who are less fortunate than we are.

REFERENCE

Sartorius, N. (1988). Cross-cultural and international collaboration in mental health research and action. Experience from the mental health programme of the World Health Organization. *Acta Psychiatrica Scandinavica*, **78**, Suppl. 344, 71–74.

Hiroshige Ando or Utagawa (1797–1858): *Kominato Bay, Awa Province*. (Courtesy of the Leeds Museums and Galleries [City Art Gallery], Leeds, England, and Bridgeman Art Library, London.)

17

And then there were five . . .

Mental health problems have often been borne in silence without much help from anyone. Over time, people have been seeking solace and help from religious institutions, traditional healers, from their families and more recently from organized health care services.

As more information becomes available through research and other reports, it becomes obvious that good mental health care cannot be provided by the doctor alone: it has to be achieved in collaboration between patients and health care workers. More recently, other partners in the provision of care – family organizations and self-help groups, governmental agencies other than those dealing with health and the health industry – are also being invited to participate in the assessment of mental health problems and in searching for ways to resolve them.

According to Brewer's dictionary of phrase and fable, five is a mystical number, being the sum of 2 and 3, the first even and the first odd compound. One, or unity is God alone, two the diversity and three, being the sum of 1 and 2 combines unity and diversity representing all the powers of nature.

I came across that passage while thinking about the best way to introduce discussions about the implementation of broadly based mental health programmes in South Africa. It coincided, curiously, with the main point of my talk: I wanted to underline the need to expand the doctor-and-patient dyad to include other partners. The game of numbers had strange associations – the one, to the paternalistic, god-like position that doctors were known to take in their work and the two to the vast diversity of people with mental illness. The three – bringing together a doctor recognizing the vast diversity of patients – was a necessary ingredient to success. What I hoped to present was the need to add other significant partners – patients' families, the government agencies and the health care industry to the equation, which made it a five, a pentalogue that would replace the current notions of the need for a dialogue (doctor/patient) or at best a trialogue involving the family[1].

This change to a pentalogue in which five partners should collaborate became necessary because of changes that happened in recent years. These were changes in the ethos of medicine, in the populations' expectations of medicine, in the limits of competence (of doctors, patients and families), in the locus of responsibility for health care and in the criteria of success of health care interventions.

The changes in the ethos of medicine were perhaps the most important of these changes. They happened almost imperceptibly over the past three decades, perhaps because of advances of knowledge and technology and the new order of values in post-industrial societies. Medicine had started as a magical enterprise and its practitioners joined it because they felt that this is their vocation. The wish to help

---

[1] When referring to patients and families, I am also referring to the self-help organizations that they have created and to associations of volunteers united by their wish to improve the lot of people with mental illness. Similarly 'health workers' in this essay is shorthand for the non-governmental professional organizations.

people in distress and other obligations contained in the Hippocratic Oath was – or so it seemed – for most physicians more important than financial or other material gain. In more recent history, examples of imaginary and real doctors – from Dr Martin Arrowsmith to Dr Schweitzer – enticed candidates to enter medicine.

Advances of medicine and the vast development of health service systems gradually introduced the new paradigm of the very competent professional – transplanting hearts and livers, saving lives by the application of the best of knowledge and skill. More recently still, medicine has assumed a new avatar. Managed care in the USA and similar developments in other countries are gradually transforming medicine to a trade. That, in itself might be tolerable: what is less tolerable is that medical practitioners are active participants in the process of selling health as if it was a commodity. They are increasingly often being asked to make medical decisions on economical grounds and accept to do so. Thus, for example, instead of prescribing the best treatment (in accordance with the most recent and reliable scientific findings) they prescribe the least expensive drug; instead of being adamant and staunch defenders of the best treatment (letting the government take responsibility for not providing it) they adjust their stance to the available resources (letting the government get away with inappropriate allocations for health care).

Parallel to the transformation of medicine from a vocation to a profession and now to a trade, the priority of medicine's goals also seems to be changing. Doctors were supposed to save lives, cure the disease and diminish the suffering of their patients, in that order. Other goals were secondary. The order seems to be changing: the patients' duty to live and the doctors' obligation to save and maintain life is being replaced by the patients' right to die and the doctors' duty to help their patients do what they want to do with their life. The proposals to legalize euthanasia in some developed countries and the insistence on informed consent of patients for most interventions (including those necessary to save life) are symptoms of that change which will probably, in time, have a profound impact on the social role of the physicians and the structure of medicine.

Other changes are no less significant. Among them is the attitude to pain. In previous times a certain amount of suffering was expected and both patients and doctors accepted its necessity. In most countries of the world it was (and in many it still is) unthinkable that a dentist would offer anaesthesia to a patient when preparing to repair a carious tooth. In recent years the control of pain has risen in importance. It is becoming accepted that stilling pain and improving the patients' quality of life is a special part of medicine that should be taught and promoted. Hospices for the terminally ill and pain clinics are growing in numbers. The movement to create 'hospitals without pain', is gaining adherents – all of this a far cry from the opposition that the medical profession and government authorities offered so vigorously 20 years ago when the World Health Organization proposed its schedules for the control of pain with various medicaments – including opiates – for patients suffering from cancer.

The appearance of powerful new technology for use in diagnosis and treatment has also contributed to the change of the ethos of medicine. In psychiatry the new technologies have widened the gap between the poor and rich, in both the developed and the developing countries. They have raised ethical and political problems that have no parallel in history. The cost of a single unit of the modern imaging apparatus – which can help enormously in making the correct diagnosis – equals the cost of treatment for all people with the epilepsy in a country of the size of Zambia. Should the developing countries forego the acquisition of such apparatus? Should doctors accept that there are two medicines – one for the poor and one for the rich? And leave research to the countries that 'can afford it'? Or should the medical profession make it their priority to develop a consensus about the best treatment for different types of diseases (thus providing the basis for a political struggle to liberate funds that would allow people everywhere to benefit from the best of medicine)? The lack of agreement on these and similar questions diminished the clarity of rules of medical deontology so that the medical profession operates in considerably greater ambiguity than ever before.

The changes of the ethos of medicine have also been influenced by changes in the expectations from medicine – by both the population and the health workers. The heady expectations of a few decades ago –

that medicine will find silver bullets for all diseases and that it is only a matter of time before the eradication of the plagues of mankind occurs, in recent times gave place to more reasonable (and sometimes too pessimistic) estimations of what can be achieved and by when. After the Second World War the eradication of malaria worldwide seemed to be within reach. A couple of decades later a major killer disease – small-pox – was eradicated, we hope forever. Shortly after that, the World Health Organization's Assembly adopted the goal of Health for All by the Year 2000 without much hesitation and proclaimed that this lofty goal will be achieved through the primary health care that the countries of the world promised to introduce without delay, everywhere[2].

As time went by, the burden of chronic non-communicable diseases became heavier and heavier and the communicable diseases staged an unexpected return resistant to treatment and more deadly than ever. The effort to eradicate diseases was gradually replaced by that of teaching people how to live with diseases and infirmities. Statistics showing that the extension of life expectancy reported in many countries did not increase the number of disability-free years were also sobering as was the realization that most of the new discoveries in medicine increased the cost of health care. For the medical profession and in particular for public health officials, these developments were also a demonstration of the necessity to rely on factors other than advances of technology. Public health rediscovered the role of the family, the power of practitioners of traditional medicine[3], the potential of religious beliefs and of philosophical orientations, the need to understand the traditional and culture-specific ways of dealing with misery and distress – and other factors that were more or less neglected in the preceding decades.

In this context, it also became inevitable that those involved in the planning of services and in their provision begin to rely not only on

---

[2] It is of interest to remember here that the objective of the World Health Organization 'shall be the attainment by all peoples of the highest possible level of health' – a definition that permits the interpretation that the 'highest possible' is 'the highest under the circumstances', thus achieved already.

[3] The practitioners of traditional medicine are numerous in both developing and developed countries. In the 1980s the numbers of those practitioners and of doctors were said to be about equal in France and other countries in which they were counted.

results of scientific explorations and the experience of health personnel but also on the experience of patients, their families and others who cared for people with chronic disorders in the community. In an era of increasing globalization of medical knowledge this very local input serves a corrective and sobering role: the challenge that the advocates of its use face is the reluctance of the majority of the medical professionals – including psychiatrists, to use it. In part, this is a remnant of the doctor–patient relationship in which the patient's disease is the object of therapy and the patient is no more than the battlefield on which the doctor and the disease fight. In part also, it is because obtaining information from patients and relatives does take time and effort which many of the overtaxed physicians cannot liberate. In part also, the reluctance of obtaining information from patients on matters other than the disease – for example, about the consequences of their stigmatization by a diagnosis – is due to the fact that such information is disturbing, possibly reminding the psychiatrist of unpleasant and possibly unnecessary side effects of their diagnostic or other interventions.

Patients' and families' expertise of living with a stigmatizing and punishing illness is not the only source that seems to have more information about the illness than the doctors: the media and more recently Internet made it possible for many to know a great deal, in some instances more than the health workers, about the advances of medicine. The result does not seem to be – as it was predicted by the apostles of health education – a better and more trustful relationship between doctors and their patients. Doctors dislike being faced by patients (and families) who know a great deal about their disease. Patients, on the other hand, lose confidence in their doctors who seem to know less than a website and seek ways to bypass the general practitioner and reach the top specialists.

A fifth set of changes that has influenced the willingness to consider the pentalogue in mental health care (and indeed in all health care) was the transfer of the locus of responsibility for health care. Over the centuries, the responsibility of finding solutions for health problems was first with the patients and their family. It was then transferred or shared with a religious or traditional healer. Subsequently, it was loaded onto institutions which began to depend on the support of the community and society as a whole. The health systems considered as particularly advanced in the middle of the twentieth century had placed most of the responsibility for health care onto a central governmental authority. That authority governed preventive and curative efforts of the peripheral health care agents and supported their efforts by resources and in other ways. Over the years the numerous advantages of that system seemed to wane and a reverse process started. Decentralization was supposed to give power and the money to the peripheral units which, in turn, were to create alliances with the communities in which they practised. Decentralization, however, often meant only a transfer of responsibility without a transfer of authority and funding resulting in disappointment and poorer service. In time, the transfer of responsibility continued even further, returning the primary tasks of looking after the patient to the family (or adoptive family) to a group of patients or to the patients themselves. While representing a vast improvement for some patients and no particular extra burden for some families, other families and patients were left with a distinct disadvantage in comparison with the previous centralized arrangement. Governments often viewed the transfer of responsibility as no more than a way of saving their money (at the expense of the moneys that the families now had to find to look after the patients). The support to families, who now had to take on the extra burden and to patients who had to live on their own, was only rarely and reluctantly provided in these reforms. In some instances the process of returning responsibility stopped half-way and an uneasy uncertainty about the next step characterizes the health system.

It has therefore become obvious that there is a need not only for new alliances among the members of the pentalogue but also for a set of rules that will govern the collaboration between the five partners[4].

The first of these rules is the obligation to recognize that each of the

---

[4] The acceptance of these rules by all concerned is the challenge to which all those concerned have to respond if they want to avoid wastage of life, health and property. Among the rules, there are some that have proven their value in talking with kidnappers of planes and with leaders of warring parties while others are used in selling goods: neither is surprising since the members of the pentalogue are at present often at war with each other and are reluctant – often taught by bitter experience – to accept what looks like a gift from the other members of the pentalogue.

parties has its interests and that all of these interests have to be satisfied, at least to a degree. Patients want to get care quickly and want it delivered with respect of their person and their needs. Families want to be able to continue their productive life and function, want to be spared of bad reputation, want their contribution to the patient's life and welfare recognized, at least in moral terms. Governments want to avoid scandals and spend as little money as possible, because they need money for their many other obligations. Health industry wants to make profit, wants protection against accusations of unethical conduct, which could lead to a bad reputation and unjustified persecution. Health professionals want to do health work, want to be sheltered from suspicion, avoid excessive administrative burden and receive a fair compensation for their labour. Each of the members of the pentalogue has been known to exaggerate their own demands and disregard the interests of others, declaring them irrelevant, immoral, excessive, insignificant, harmful to all others and generally dishonest. A fair alliance implies the need to give and take: it is unlikely that the wishes, needs and interests of all concerned will be satisfied, particularly if each of the potential partners wastes time and energy fighting against all others.

Negotiations about legitimate needs and compromise solutions cannot have value nor permanence unless all partners agree to respect all others and proceed with their discussion with that premise. It is not always easy to generate respect for yesterday's or today's enemy: but respect is a prerequisite for any successful intervention in this field. Respect will allow the acceptance of the third rule – that of distribution of tasks in the field in accordance with demonstrated competence. Families and patients can do many things which they are not allowed to do now and have to be trusted in this respect. The health industry is usually better able to ensure the regularity of supplies of medicaments, transportation of patients to health services, management of hotel services in hospitals and other tasks than either the government or the health professionals. Properly educated health professionals can deal with treatment better when they are guided by humane, medical and scientific principles than when they are forced to do their work considering, at each point economic and administrative requirements. Governments have within their power the possibility of mobilizing sectors other than health in the care for people suffering from an illness and those disabled by it.

Another rule that comes from peace negotiators is that complete agreement among all concerned is usually impossible. Compromises and partial solutions are more likely. Total disarmament before negotiations about peace can commence is an impossible requirement: peace can be discussed and agreed upon while battles are still raging. Perhaps it will not be possible to deal with more than one problem at a time. Maybe the problems of housing can be resolved now: expecting that the application of a solution must be part of a global agreement covering the organization of services, disability pensions, protection from discrimination in all fields and the many other legitimate and important goals of a good service is a wasteful and short-sighted strategy.

The search for synergy is another rule that might make the pentalogue useful. There are usually parts of the agenda of each of the five partners that could be tackled without difficulty in collaboration with others. Starting with tasks that benefit from synergy would allow closer contact among the members of the pentalogue. Success in achieving anything might contribute to respect and trust among the partners. It would allow to test methods of working together, to identify individuals who are the best spokespersons for each of the groups concerned and to convince 'hard core' members of each of the groups that there is something to be gained from collaboration.

A rule that will have to govern not only the collaboration between partners but also the life of each of the groups within itself is the acceptance of the indivisibility of the search for rights and the acceptance of duties of all concerned. The acceptance of that principle also means that the duties and their performance must be made public and accessible to control of quality and of degree of fulfilment. This evaluation should go hand in hand with the examination to the level and manner in which the rights of each of the partners have been respected. Neither of these evaluations needs a complex administrative or other infrastructure if the pentalogue has led to the development of mutual respect and trust among the parties.

It is clear that the continuing existence of the pentalogue depends on its success and achievements. These have to be evaluated jointly by all of its members, who must agree that the findings of this process will be used to correct the course taken by them whenever necessary. True success of the pentalogue will have to find its reflection in at least (i) an improvement of the quality of life of all concerned; (ii) a better cost benefit ratio of the measures undertaken; (iii) an improvement of the social and economic productivity of each and all of the partners; and (iv) an enhancement of the social capital of societies bringing them closer to becoming a civic society.

18

Enabling

Goals of rehabilitation of people who have had a mental illness are changing and so are the principles that govern them. Quality of life and the capacity to contribute to social capital of society are, for example, replacing the preoccupation with re-employment. It is likely that, in the future, rehabilitation will no longer be the task of health and social services: it has to become a joint enterprise of these services and people who have mental impairments and their families.

Michelangelo Buonarroti (1475–1564): Hands of God and Adam, detail from *The Creation of Adam* (1511) from the ceiling of the Sistine Chapel. (Courtesy of the Vatican Museums and Galleries, Vatican City, Rome, and Bridgeman Art Library, London.)

Enabling is not the right word to describe the process that should take place after a person has been visited by an illness but it is better, I think, than the word rehabilitation. The dictionary (Thompson, 1995) defines 'rehabilitate' as 'to restore to effectiveness or normal life by training etc, especially after imprisonment and illness'. Many of the people with a mental impairment never had a 'normal life' before their illness. A proportion of people who have had a mental illness will never be able to restore their effectiveness and often fail to live a normal life after illness regardless of the amount of effort to help them. In both of these instances the goal of the services that are to assist the person who has been through an illness or is impaired will be to create a life and to find or develop situations in which the person can be effective despite the impairments. Employing a person after an episode of illness is not necessarily full rehabilitation – and might, in fact, be closer to prevention of disability and handicap than to rehabilitation.

But, the problem is not only with the word. In the world today there are some 500 million people who suffer from mental disorders. At least a quarter of them have the most serious forms of mental and neurological disorders and a significant proportion of those are or will be impaired by illness even if the best of currently available treatment were to be given to them. It is possible to estimate that at least 150 million people are in this group.

The unjust distribution of human and material resources (and the slowness with which this inequity is redressed) makes it clear that the majority of those who need treatment will not receive it in the near future. Primary prevention of many mental and neurological disorders is possible already, but often remains undone.

What makes the situation worse is that there is every likelihood that the prevalence of mental and neurological disorders will grow in the years to come. There are various reasons for this prediction. Some are demographic: successes of public health programmes have diminished the mortality of children and thus lead to an increase of the adolescent, adult and elderly population, all of whom are at risk for mental disorders characteristic for their age. At present, about half the population of most countries in the developing world is under the age of 15. As they enter adult age, the increase of the numbers of people with schizophrenia, affective disorders and other illnesses frequent in adults – even if the incidence of these disorders remains the same – will be nothing short of spectacular, particularly in the poor countries. Other successes of medicine are also potential contributors to the increasing burden of mental and neurological disorders. Successes of neurosurgeons saving lives of individuals with brain damage or tumours, for example, are still often leaving the survivor with permanent impairments of mental and motor functions. Other reasons for the increased prevalence of mental and neurological disorders include iatrogenic damage, the appearance of new diseases, (such as AIDS) that affect the brain and the increasing numbers of people who are exposed to the simultaneous action of the many risk factors that affect people who are poor, over-burdened and physically ill.

Nor is the world becoming a place where people with mental illness or subsequent impairments will find it easy to survive. The increasing complexity of labour makes it necessary to show diplomas and certificates of ample experience, which cannot be gained without being employed first and for a long time. The growth of demands on the individual produces new 'cases' of disabilities. The introduction of obligatory education in some African countries, for example, suddenly created problems because it became clear that children with some mental impairment, who until then lived well adjusted – though sometimes teased – in their village could not follow school programmes and were therefore labelled as mentally retarded. People who because of their disease were absent from their place of work or their habitat for a number of years are becoming more and more often temporally uprooted on return: like Rip van Winkle, they return to a setting that is so profoundly changed that they cannot recognize it any longer. Worse still, the professional or social skills which they had, and which helped them to live as actively contributing members of their community a decade ago, became obsolete over the years.

At the same time, the capacity of the community to provide care and to offer a life of quality to people disabled by mental illness is diminishing. The families are becoming smaller and more reluctant to carry the burden of care for their members. The vast changes in the social position of women who have been looking after a vast majority of people who are not well, are infirm, dependent because of being too young or too old is of particular importance in this respect. Their entry into the labour force employed by others than the family leaves the disabled members of their family without care.

Other functions of the family that were carried out by women are also affected. The transmission of the cultural traditions and value systems to children – that was taking place in the family – is interrupted. In some countries the care of children is entrusted to hired help: the housemaids so employed are increasingly often coming from countries with a different culture, or in the instance of urban families from villages that live a different life. It might have been hoped that schools will take on the role of the family in this respect: the continuous depletion of resources in the educational sector, the low salaries of teachers and the epidemic of emotional burn-out among them have all but killed that hope. Adolescents enter community life without adherence to scales of values of others in the same society: in many instances, the only common system of values that they have internalized is that transmitted by the media, mainly television and more recently the Internet connections. Their readiness to make active contributions to the care of disabled members of the community is often feeble and the expectation that by some miraculous process governments or other powers will help those in need – as seen on TV – further weakens their participation in activities supposed to help those impaired. In addition, disappointment with authorities in this and other respects makes the adolescents even more uncertain about their position in life and the desirable courses of action in their life thus increasing the risk that their mental health will require additional attention and care from the overburdened health, social and educational services.

The recent trend of increasing insistence on the economic productivity of communities and individuals does not help either. People who have had a mental illness often remain without jobs. Even when they find employment, they might, for a while be less productive than their peers who did not have an illness. The treatment of mental illness costs money and so do the support services on which they have to rely after recovery. The fact that people whose productivity at work is lower often continue to contribute in a major way to the social capital of societies by the things that they do for their family and for other members of the community is forgotten or considered to be of little importance. The use of economic productivity as the main criterion of usefulness of an individual (or a community) and the diminishing attention to the need to increase the social capital of societies exert a negative effect on mental health and will unfortunately continue to do so.

It is thus clear that programmes that were developed to rehabilitate the mentally ill have to be rethought and probably recast in a fundamentally different way. This has to be done in concert with all those concerned – thus not only with the health and social services but also involving the people who had mental illness, their families, the health industry and those responsible for overall development programmes. This paradigm shift is necessary and anything that postpones it will diminish our societies' ethical standing and social productivity.

Some of the principles that will have to govern the shift are known and others are emerging. They are relevant to the rehabilitation of people who had mental illness but also to the rehabilitation of psychiatry as a discipline. They are particularly relevant to countries in which the investments into rehabilitation services are beginning to grow; they are, however, also of importance for countries in which such services are already well funded and for those countries in which no funds whatsoever have been foreseen to help the people with mental illness and their families overcome their illness and its consequences.

First, the goal of rehabilitation must become the improvement of quality of life of those with mental illness and of their immediate family. Employment or integration into a community could be important in this respect: but they must be seen as subsidiary (as should various other goals until now defined as being central to rehabilitation) and included as goals if they contribute to the overall quality of life as perceived by the individuals most concerned.

In most countries of the world the concept of employment has no real meaning. In agricultural communities members of the family or a clan are working on their land and have no salaries, no syndicates, no contracts, no insurance in case of accidents or pensions for old age. When they are sick, they are given shelter in the family compound and fed for a long time, provided that they are not too aggressive or otherwise disturbing. The number of criticisms about their behaviour, or about the fact that they are not participating in the work of the family, is often low. In countries marked by a high level of technological development, on the other hand, it is becoming obvious that it is not necessary nor possible to employ everyone. In some instances those seeking jobs are not driven by the need to earn enough to maintain themselves and their family alive: rather, the search for a job is fuelled by the wish to meet people, gain some money in order to buy luxuries, to be more independent. The numbers of those who are opting for part-time, temporary jobs is growing in many countries. Why should we then insist that full-time employment is the goal of rehabilitation and the main proof of its success?

Finding a job and becoming employed is still considered to be the confirmation of the person's worth, even if it produces less money than the unemployment benefits and might mean additional financial losses due to the need to hire a person who will do chores around the house. Social productivity, help to others, upbringing of children, creative or artistic production – for the fun of it and for a small circle's consumption only – and many other activities that have made our society distinguishable from herds of animals are given incomparably less attention and reward than traditionally structured jobs. Two years ago a national women's group in Canada released a manual on unpaid work that calls on the government to recognize that breast-feeding is an important food production industry and that women who breast-feed should be regarded as part of Canada's labour force (Bellavance, 1999). The group also stated that caring for the sick and the elderly at home is unpaid work and made a number of reasonable claims about the compensation and recognition of such work. A few years before that, Statistics Canada Survey estimated the value of unpaid work at some 40% of the gross national product. Since 1996, questions relating to unpaid work are included in the Canadian national statistical surveys. While this is a move in the right direction, most of those who heard about it paid little attention to it or discussed it with derision.

And yet, the acceptance of the principle of recognition of unpaid work as any other employment and at least in terms of paying for it of insurance, recognition for advancement and respect, is of vast importance for rehabilitation of people with mental illness and of many others suffering from similar disadvantages. A change from the current disregard and debasing attitudes for useful activities that are not paid would not only recognize the work that carers do for people who are disabled: it would also make it possible to recognize the contribution that people with impairments are making to the maintenance of the society and to the enhancement of its social capital.

Related to the change of attitudes and consequent legal action concerning work is also the attitude to leisure. Schools, media and the population at large consider leisure and work as two opposite states rather than as two interchangeable modes of spending our time. From childhood on, all have to learn that leisure is pleasure, that it has to be earned; that work is hard and that it should be made easier, shorter, less demanding. There is little organized education on the ways of spending time and on the blending of leisure and work times. There are numerous books on ways to arrange flowers at home, but few that say how this could be done at the workplace. Education on how to work is considered honourable, education about leisure almost sinful. Schools do not help students to make the most of their entire waking time, do not help pupils to learn to like their work better, look forward to it, perceive it as relaxing. There are no prizes for the pupil who plans and spends his or her hours out of school in a personally and socially rewarding manner. So, when a person cannot find a job or stops working – for example because of an illness – he or she suddenly stands before an abyss of non-organized, non-structured time that does not offer any opportunities for self-affirmation nor chances to regain self-respect that is so often lost in the course of a prolonged illness.

A second principle of importance in the process of care after illness is to replace the rehabilitation *of* people with impairments and disabilities by a rehabilitation (or enabling) *by* and *with* the people who are disabled or handicapped by mental illness or its consequences. If quality of life is to become the central criterion of success of the efforts of health and of rehabilitation services, the opinion of those whose life is being changed must become a determinant factor in all aspects of the rehabilitation process – from its planning and implementation to its evaluation – rather than only an interesting observation casually recorded in the minutes of a meeting. Ensuring that the opinion of patients and carers is taken into account in a serious manner is not easy. It requires a change of attitudes and expectations of health staff and of the users of the service. It also requires careful preparation of discussions that will lead to decision making and the painful process of learning the jargons of patients, families, health and social service staff. Each one of these participants in the process of rehabilitation speaks in their own manner, well understood by others in their group and usually not by others. Unless a determined effort is undertaken to ensure that everybody speaks the language of all the other participants in the process, most of the decisions will be based on a consensus by misunderstanding, and their implementation will create misgivings, doubts and prejudice.

Once all speak the same language and at least to an extent trust one another, the process of learning will change direction – from learning the jargon to learning about the true limits of power and possibility of administrators, staff, patients and families. Eventually, this might lead to concerted action to improve the funding or in other ways make the service more useful and more rewarding for all.

At present, unfortunately the process of learning to work together is often avoided. Representatives of patients and family organizations often represent no one else but themselves and possibly a small group of friends, not the whole patient population. Many of the patient and family organizations count their numbers in tens or hundreds while the total number of people concerned is in hundreds of thousands. Officials in the secretariats of patient groups are often well trained and well versed in the language that needs to be employed to be heard by the government. They use it, often with success, even if members of their organization have other wishes less acceptable to the authorities. It is thus respectable to ask for the creation of jobs for people impaired by mental illness. It is much less acceptable to ask for funds that will make it possible to have free tickets for theatres, although these may do much to brighten the drab existence of people with impairments.

A third principle that should underlie the process of enabling is that people with disabilities are different from one another, that their needs are different and that therefore the rehabilitative process must be organized in a manner that will make it possible to deal with different needs and different people.

Reintegration and rehabilitation should therefore not necessarily aim to return people to the community and the job that they had before. It should not aim either at a standard of behaviour that would be expected in the microenvironment from which the patient came. It should not aim to make people who suffer from the same disease follow the same rehabilitation pathway, and it should not expect that the course of rehabilitation will fit into a scheme that those responsible for rehabilitation (or those in government dealing with mental health care) have envisaged. The rehabilitation process must be flexible and allow adjustments to fit the needs of people who are impaired or disabled[1]. It also means that the staff must be tolerant to differences in behaviour even when these require special adjustments in the rules or rearrangements of a person's surroundings. The promotion of tolerance for difference will be useful in other pursuits of civic society: in the effort to enable people and make them enter or re-enter into their life, it is essential.

The fourth principle that should be incorporated in rehabilitation programmes seems self-evident: disabled people and their impairments change over time and therefore programmes that are supposed to help them must contain the capacity to change without fuss and major legal or other interventions in parallel with the changes in the disabled people. The life expectancy is increasing for all people and particularly so for people with disabilities. This creates new types of situations for which there are no ready solutions. The needs of a disabled adolescent will be very different from the needs of the same person in adulthood or old age. The needs of a disabled person who grows old are very different from his or her needs in adult life.

The health and social services are only slowly awakening to these changes. Public health leaders still announce that care for the mentally

---

[1] In accordance with WHO-introduced terms, impairment refers to a damage of body tissue or function; disability to the failure to perform in personal and social roles; and handicap to social disadvantages due to the disability.

ill should be in, and by, the community. Very often, this advice is irrelevant because of social changes that are happening worldwide. In addition to the changes of the structure of the family and the changes of roles in it, there are also changes in the structure of communities that have somehow escaped the attention of the authorities. When the theories of community care were crafted, the term community referred to a group of people living in the same geographical area, knowing each other and likely to be prepared to help one another in daily life. Urban settings – in which by the year 2025 there will be four-fifths of humankind – do not have many such communities. They exist, for a while, in slums aggregating recent immigrants to towns and sometimes in traditional cores of cities: the rest of the population lives in administratively defined areas in which the population, despite their geographic proximity, have little in common with one another. The mutually helpful links of the city dwellers are often outside of the apartment blocks and groups of houses – sometimes in the same town elsewhere, sometimes in their office or factory, sometimes on the Internet. The provision of services cannot be based on communities defined geographically any longer: other ways of defining 'community', e.g. by levels of mutual trust and reciprocal help, have to be tried out. For the rehabilitation of people with mental illness this change of community structure plays a particularly important role and it is urgent to make administrations aware of the fact that previously held notions about long-term care for people with impairments in the community need a radical revision.

The acceptance of these principles and the consequent changes of service structure and roles will gradually bring those involved in rehabilitation very close to others active in the area of socio-economic development in general. The challenge today is to make it clear that this change of roles and positions of people who are to be rehabilitated and those active in the rehabilitation process is necessary and that it will modify – in siting, timing and partnerships – what they do, while increasing their usefulness and importance.

REFERENCES

Thompson, D. (1995). *The Concise Oxford Dictionary of Current English*, 9th edn. Oxford: Clarendon Press.

Bellavance J-D. (1999). Breast-feeding should be included in GNP. *National Post*, 15 June, p. 1.

Waist pendant representing Idia, mother of Oba Esigie, part of ceremonial costume. Ivory, sixteenth century, Benin. (Courtesy of the British Museum, London, and Bridgeman Art Gallery, London.)

19

Psychiatry in developing countries

Developing countries differ enormously in their cultural and religious traditions, in their size and wealth, their geographic position and their history. They also have similarities and one of these is that their mental health programmes have low priority on the countries' developmental agenda. To an extent, this is because the magnitude and severity of mental health problems have been obscured by the support that people suffering from mental illness in these countries received from their families and communities; to an extent, the neglect of mental ill health is caused by the simultaneous presence of many other problems that the people in the non-industrialized countries have to face.

Recent changes in socio-economic structures, dwindling family size, population growth, the resolution of many health problems and the availability of effective treatments brought the magnitude and severity of mental health problems into the foreground. It has become essential, therefore, to think of the right strategy to deal with mental health problems, which could otherwise slow down overall socio-economic development.

Introduction

The decision as to whether a country is to be called a developing country depends on a number of criteria. Some of them seem straightforward: in general, such countries have a low per capita income, their communication systems are deficient (thus preventing the efficient transport of people, goods and information), health indicators testify to an unnecessary loss of life (e.g. as a result of high child mortality) and to high rates of disease, and the level of education of their populations as a whole is low. When all of these and a number of other signs of the same kind are present, it is easy to reach agreement that the country is lagging behind in development or – if most of the indicators show that the country is in a very difficult situation – to decide that it belongs to the category of 'least developed countries'. At present, there are some 40 countries in the latter category. However, their populations are relatively small and together they represent only a modest proportion of the total population of the world or of the developing countries. The remaining countries outside Europe, the United States, Canada, Australia, New Zealand and Japan are less easy to place within a category, and the United Nations recently proposed splitting this group into two categories (rapidly developing countries and developing countries) and placing Eastern European countries into a separate group because they had characteristics that distinguish it from the rest of the European countries.

However, this apparently convenient division of the world into developing and developed countries does not hold up under scrutiny. First, in many of the so-called developed countries, there are parts (or population groups) that, in all respects, resemble the countries of the developing world. Second, in most developing countries, there are now parts (or population groups) that have achieved a high standard of living and can be favourably compared with the average of the developed world. Third, some of the developing countries are lagging behind in some aspects, e.g. health criteria, while, in terms of other criteria, e.g. per capita income, they are close to or better than some of the developed countries. Fourth, countries are continually changing, and what could be called a developed country today might tomorrow, in most respects, become close to a developing country, and vice versa. Fifth, economic development is not necessarily the final goal of human existence, and if the world is categorized according to non-economic criteria, e.g. in terms of tolerance, non-aggression, and human interdependence, it becomes necessary to redistribute countries among the developed and the developing categories.

In view of all this, it would seem wiser to avoid dividing the world into a small number of rigidly limited categories and to consider instead smaller groups of countries (or even groups of one), recognizing that each nation has its own cultural, economic, intellectual and emotional traditions and characteristics that make it to a significant degree unique. It is possible and more desirable to describe countries in terms of a number of relevant criteria, even if this takes a little more space and time or, if grouping is necessary, to do this bearing in mind that there are many differences between the countries in the group and that most countries in the world are mosaics of developed and developing regions, of modern and traditional parts and of noble and ignoble components. Just how much of each of these is present will vary with time and from one country to another.

Medicine and science reflect the above situation. Even in very poor countries, there are institutions engaged in research and service of outstanding quality, e.g. the Institute of Psychiatry in Mexico City; on the other hand, in the developed world, there are areas in which health care is poor, e.g. in slums or remote areas, a situation made worse by the fact that there is enough money available and that a lack of governmental resources cannot be blamed for the scenes which can be observed.

The differences within and between countries are one of the reasons why it is illusory to hope that a comprehensive description of mental health programmes in the developing countries can be produced in a single book chapter. Two reasons that reduce the chances of producing a well-documented description are the scarcity of data resulting from well-conducted studies of the mental health situation in many of the developing countries and the rapidity of sociocultural, economic and other changes that are present in most of them.

The problems

Four groups of problems beset psychiatry in developing countries: (i) the low value given to mental health by individuals and by society, (ii) the high prevalence of mental and neurological problems, (iii) the disregard for psychosocial aspects of various health and development projects and (iv) the chronic lack of resources.

Low value given to mental health

The value which individuals and societies give to mental health and the normal functioning of the mind is of decisive importance for the development of mental health programmes. Where mental health lies low on the scale of values, it is difficult, if not impossible, to initiate or maintain mental health programmes. The low value of mental health finds its reflection in the low priority given to mental health activities within general health programmes, in the difficulty of recruiting the best postgraduate students to psychiatry, in the feeble, if any, participation of the population in mental health activities and campaigns and in the continuing disregard for opportunities to enhance mental health programmes. At the individual level, the low value of mental health finds its expression in people's willingness to put their mental health and sanity at risk by taking drugs, in the neglect of measures that would protect or enhance the mental health of children and in a variety of other ways. In most developing countries, mental health is not seen as being without any value: rather, it is considered as less precious than many other things or acquisitions ranging from material wealth to sexual attractiveness. Countries are not monolithic in this respect; however, although population groups vary in their appreciation of mental health, few of them place mental health and mental life among their top priorities.

There may be many reasons for this, probably including the vagueness of the definition of mental health and mental illness. Although mental health can, at best, be a component of health (the other equally non-independent component being physical health), the term is used to describe the state of feeling well, the absence of mental illness, normal mental functioning, equanimity, coping capacity and spiritual equilibrium. The vagueness of the concept makes it difficult to rally support for it as an objective of health service programmes and makes educational programmes supposed to help in the promotion of mental health nebulous; this in turn leads to mental health slipping even lower on the scale of values. The loose boundaries of the term also allow various disciplines – ranging from theology to marketing science – and various organizations to produce and promote definitions of mental health to suit their own purposes. Groups of population at large accept one or the other of these definitions (or create another one of their own), which diminishes or removes the pressure on health services to do something about mental health.

Another reason for the low position of mental health on the scale of values is the uncertainty about the limits of mental illness. In industrialized countries, the boundaries between mental illness and stimulation, possession states, laziness, personality variants, artistic creativity, ideological originality and numerous other forms of behaviour and states of mind are somewhat clearer because of the efforts of the medical profession and because of the pressure of insurance systems to make a distinction between what is a medical condition, i.e. for which treatment has to be paid for by the insurance and non-medical condition (for which the health insurance does not pay for treatment).

In developing countries, neither of these two types of pressure are at work. Mental health care workers are often not numerous and often tend to adhere to illness categories created on the basis of experience in other countries. If these do not fit, vague, general terms ('psychotic state') are used. Insurance systems cover only a minute proportion of the population and do not have much weight or interest in precise definitions.

While there is now no doubt about the similarity of the incidence rates of severe mental disorders such as schizophrenia in different countries, there are other psychological disorders whose incidence and prevalence seem to be different in different socio-cultural settings. Most of those conditions can be placed into the categories of major classifications of mental disorders, e.g. the International Classification of Diseases, ICD, but there are some that cannot: people who suffer from them, however, seek help from both traditional healers and modern doctors. These differences in frequency and the so-called culture-specific disorders contribute to shaping the image of mental illness in the setting in which they occur and can contribute to the notion that psychiatry is a branch of medicine that has a blurred focus, that the diseases which it is supposed to treat are not real diseases (there are no culture-specific forms of cardiovascular disease and these 'real' non-communicable diseases are thought to respond to the same treatment in the same way, everywhere) and that the practitioners of psychiatry are closer to spiritual advisors (or traditional healers) than to real doctors.

Culture-specific ways of describing problems, and the abundance of influential traditional health practitioners who contribute their own terms and explanations, further blur the boundaries and concepts of mental disorder. This is good and bad: good because, in many instances, such vagueness of borders diminishes the probability of rejection and stigma because of mental illness, but bad because some of those who have a treatable mental illness do not come to seek help from qualified services even there where they are provided at a cost that the patient and the family could well afford.

It could be argued that, in some particularly disadvantaged areas, it might be better for the population to continue to consider some of the diseases from which it suffers as an inevitable part of the human condition rather than as disease states for which they could obtain treatment if only their government were to provide them with a better health service or with more money that would allow them to purchase good health care. The limitations of this kind of reasoning are dangerously close to a thoroughly unethical position in which ignorance is regarded as an ally diminishing the probability of revolt and postponing changes in the prevailing socio-economic order. This is particularly so in situations in which active involvement of the population (regardless of the state of the country's health services) could prevent the occurrence of diseases or diminish the problems of those who have them. Psychiatry is an excellent example of a field of work in which much could be done even under conditions of poverty and poor health services; it is all the more deplorable that this happens so rarely.

Yet another reason for the low priority given to mental health is probably the fact that, for a very long time, there were no effective methods of medical treatment of mental disorders. While the rest of medicine achieved victory after victory and produced or declared revolutionary advances in its practice, psychiatry still used a variety of treatment methods that did not yield convincingly good results. Some of the methods used were logical in the light of the limited knowledge about mental functioning, while others were innovative; still others were closer to folk healing and religious rites than to medicine. The impression that psychiatry does not have a solid scientific basis and that it is inefficient (and that it should therefore not be given any support except insofar as it can serve to control socially unacceptable behaviour due to mental disorder and impairment) have prevailed in many countries; in the developing world, however, that image of psychiatry in the face of continuously higher demands of the efficient medical disciplines and diminishing resources at the disposal of the health care system have pushed psychiatry lower and lower on the list of priorities. Lack of support has made mental health care facilities deteriorate, decreased the quality of psychiatric training and increased the attractiveness of other disciplines seen as being more lucrative and more interesting for students of health professions.

Frequency of mental disorders in developing countries

The notion that mental disorders in developing countries are less frequent than in the industrialized world was popular among psychiatrists and other medical specialists until relatively recently. Various reasons were put forward for this contention, including the apparently more leisurely pace of life thought to characterize developing countries, the absence of those stresses seen in highly organized industrialized countries, stable and strong family relationships, healthy air and nutrition without artificial additives. For certain mental disorders, the difference was explained by physiological differences: Carothers (1947, 1953), for example, thought that depression would not affect Africans Some of these convictions had to do with prejudice and prevailing social order: Prince (1967) examined publications about the frequency of depression in African countries and reported that, before the early

1960s, there were very few articles stating that African patients had depressive disorders as often as people elsewhere: the majority of papers stated the opposite. In later years – after African countries became independent – the findings changed: depressive disorders were reported to be seen as frequently in Africans as in other citizens of the world. Prince and others felt that this could be related to the change in the way in which doctors were viewing patients (and patients were viewing themselves) before and after gaining political independence. The diagnostic labels that were previously used only for diseases of colonial officers or citizens then became available to everyone.

Gradually, the myth of differences in the incidence of mental disorders between developed and developing countries began to lose strength. It became clear and admitted that stresses exist in all cultural settings, villages as well as towns, and that mental disorders are frequent regardless of the level of industrial development (e.g. Leighton et al., 1963: Sethi et al., 1972). The studies coordinated by the World Health Organization (WHO) – the International Pilot Study of Schizophrenia (WHO, 1975b), the Study of Determinants of Severe Mental Disorders (Jablensky et al., 1992), the studies of depression in different countries (Sartorius et al., 1983) – all seemed to indicate that differences in the frequency of mental disorders, whenever they are reported to exist, are probably due to methodological reasons rather than to a real difference in incidence.

While mental disorders do not seem to vary in incidence among countries, it would not be surprising to find that there are differences in the prevalence of mental disorder. This difference could result from lesser survival chances of the mentally ill in many developing countries or from other factors, e.g. the better prognosis of mental illness in the developing than in the developed countries (WHO, 1979) that has been reported on several occasions. Some of the epidemiological studies of severe mental disorders in developing countries have shown a lower prevalence of these disorders (e.g. Cooper & Sartorius, 1996), but it should be noted that the size of the differences between the findings of the studies in developed countries and those in developing countries often seems to be similar to that found between studies done in the same (developed) country. The differences in the clinical syndromes of diseases such as schizophrenia have been described as well as culture-specific disorders but, on the whole, the differences between mental disorders in different cultures seem to be less pronounced than the similarities, particularly in the instance of severe forms of mental illness. Difference in patterns of alcohol and drug abuse (e.g. between Islamic and other countries) that were found can most probably be attributed to reasons other than the level of economic development (e.g. religion).

The poor foundations of the myth of the happy savage – of the lower frequency of mental disorders in developing countries – crumble even more convincingly when the conditions due to early or later brain damage because of poor perinatal care, frequent infections, malnutrition and under-stimulation are also considered in the assessment of the burden that mental and neurological problems might present in developing countries. Mental retardation related to iodine deficiency disorders, for example, still appears frequently in many areas of the developing world. Conditions such as short, acute psychotic states due to high fever and psychological impairment due to cerebral malaria and encephalitis are also more frequent in the developing world, but often go unreported. Mild degrees of cognitive impairment are probably higher in those developing countries in which the control and correction of sensory deficits such as poor vision is sporadic or non-existent. The all too frequent comorbidity of mental and physical diseases unfortunately continues to obscure the real numbers of people with mental illness because of the tendency to report only one (usually physical) illness per contact with a health service.

The separation of psychiatry from neurology that happened in many countries in the past four decades – useful as it may have been in many instances – has also been detrimental to the assessment of the importance of psychiatry (and of neurology) in developing countries and to the determination of the priority that mental health programmes should have. The notion that psychiatry's field of action are the 'functional' psychoses such as schizophrenia, manic depressive illness and various neurotic states, while various types of damage of the central nervous system (regardless of the presence of psychiatric symptoms), mental retardation, learning difficulties and behavioural disorders should be the domain of the neurologists and other specialists (often not existing in the developing countries) has decreased the estimates of the magnitude of mental and neurological problems in the eyes of the health system authorities and diminished the priority that might have been given to these disorders had they been grouped together. A second, more subtle negative consequence of the division of psychiatry from neurology is that psychiatry is portrayed as a discipline dealing with states without pathological substrates, thus being a discipline that should not be given the same respect (or resources) as other medical disciplines.

For many health decision makers in developing countries, the findings that mental health problems are frequent in general health care services were surprising. Study after study found that as many as 10–20% of those contacting primary health care services in developing countries have psychological problems of varying severity. In rural Senegal, for example, 17% of the 545 children and 16% of the 933 adults who were examined had psychiatric problems, although these were not necessarily recognized as such by the general health care service workers. In other African countries, the situation was similar (see, e.g. German, 1987; Ndetei & Muhangi 1979). Other parts of the developing world have reported similar findings. In South India, general practitioners estimated that 10% of their patients came to them primarily because of psychological problems (Gautam et al., 1980) and a multicentric study coordinated by the WHO also confirmed these results (Sartorius & Harding, 1983; Harding et al., 1983a,b), as did a number of other studies (Sartorius et al., 1990). More recent studies have shown that the situation is similar today and that mental health problems represent a major part of the burden of general health services (Üstün & Sartorius, 1995).

There are good reasons to believe that the prevalence of mental disorders will continue to increase. The main reasons for this include demographic changes and longer life expectancy increasing the numbers of people at risk for different forms of mental illness. It might, of course, happen that better conditions of life and better health services will decrease the numbers of preventable neurological and psychiatric problems due to early trauma, malnutrition and other ills besetting developing countries today; however, it is not easy to predict which will be quicker – the decrease in the incidence of mental and neurological disorders due to brain damage or its increase due to better survival chances.

Another reason for the probable increase of prevalence of mental disorders is the improvement of chances of survival of people suffering from chronic diseases likely to be accompanied by mental disorders such as depression. The dictum that each of our successes in terms of better medical care and saving lives has to be paid for by an increase in risks for other diseases and problems (Gruenberg, 1977) was true when first said and might, regrettably, remain true in the future. The longer life expectancy of people who have a mental disorder may have the same effect on increasing the prevalence of the disorders even if incidence stays the same or slightly diminishes.

Whether the rampant pollution that accompanies industrialization in developing countries will have neuropsychiatric consequences that will increase the incidence of mental disorders is also difficult to foresee; what is more likely, however, is that man-made accidents will happen more often in developing countries and will lead to an increase in the numbers of people with mental disorders. By way of illustration of the approximately 3 million people affected by disasters in the 1967–1991 period, more than 95% were living in the developing countries in Asia and Africa (Desjarlais et al., 1995).

Although it is likely that some of the communicable diseases that can be accompanied by mental disorders will diminish with the improvement of health care and of the health education of populations, other diseases with mental health consequences might appear and be difficult to control for years to come. If this happens, developing countries will suffer more than their developed counterparts because they cannot easily deploy additional resources to counter the new perils. A good example is infection with the human immunodeficiency virus (HIV): if the current estimates of the frequency of psychological problems associated with HIV infection and acquired immunodeficiency syndrome (AIDS) are correct, within two decades there will be more people affected by AIDS-related dementia in Africa than there are hospital beds for all inpatient care on the continent. In many developed countries the AIDS epidemic is almost under control, but in developing countries it is still on the rise. In the instance of AIDS, the psychological problems are not only the dementias appearing late in the course of the disease, but also the early reactions to the infection (Maj et al., 1993) and the problems arising in orphaned children and devastated families.

A further contribution to the burden of mental disorders in the developing world are the mental health consequences of violence on a mass scale (e.g. wars, insurgencies, civil strife) and on an individual level (e.g. crimes) the latter particularly in urban settings. Both forms of violence are incomparably more frequent in the developing world and have taken on epidemic proportions in recent years. Although suicidal behaviour is not necessarily a psychiatric problem, it is necessary to note here that suicide is more frequent in some developing countries than in most developed countries. Sri Lanka, for example, had the world's second highest suicide rate in the early 1990s, and suicide among young rural women in China appears to be the highest in the world (Desjarlais et al., 1995).

Disregard for psychosocial aspects of health and other development programmes

A third obstacle to the development of mental health programmes in developing countries is the restrictive definition of psychiatry as a discipline whose competence and task is to deal only or mainly with the most severely mentally ill. Since psychiatrists often accept this definition and they are the people who run mental health programmes, such programmes will also concentrate on the most severely ill and impaired (and on their inpatient care). The education of medical students – future health care decision makers – will foster the same image of psychiatry and make changes towards a more enlightened view of mental health and psychiatry difficult for years to come.

The restriction of mental health programmes to activities related to the most severe forms of mental disorders also decreases the importance and relevance of mental health programmes. If defined in this way, mental health programmes deal with a small proportion of the population, and their significance for the improvement of the health of the population is minor. If, on the other hand, mental health programmes were to be seen as having to deal with human behaviour, it would be logical that they assume a position in the mainstream of public health efforts and receive significantly more support and emphasis.

Psychiatrists are often reluctant to assume responsibility for the development of broadly conceived mental health programmes which encompass the prevention of mental disorders, the promotion of mental health, the delivery of contributions that psychiatry and behavioural sciences can make to the resolution of psychosocial problems and the treatment and rehabilitation of people with mental illness and impairment. Postgraduate psychiatric training does not prepare psychiatrists for such an array of tasks, and they are rarely willing to devote all their time to the development of mental health programmes. They are also reluctant to see other professionals running such programmes: as a consequence, in most developing countries mental health programmes are narrowly conceived, and the people running them are either reluctant to see them expanded to include the areas outlined above or find it difficult to gather sufficient support to put broad mental health programmes into operation.

And yet it is logical that the role of psychiatrists in most developing countries should be different from that of their counterparts in the industrialized world. The numbers of psychiatrists are so small that in their clinics they can see only a minute proportion of the mentally ill in the country. Initiating and building a mental health programme that will involve a wide variety of professional and non-professional helpers might have an immeasurably more useful effect for the same investment of time and energy. It can be argued that this is not what psychiatrists are for, but the counter-argument is that the identity and tasks of any professional depend on the context, on the setting in which they exercise their profession, and that the role of the psychiatrist in a developing country therefore has to be different. Top officials in developing countries do recognize the need to develop programmes that deal with psychosocial aspects of health and development. They might be inclined to support such programmes if qualified individuals were willing to commit their time and effort to the development of such programmes.

The two most important consequences of the broad conception of mental health programmes are that, firstly, these programmes would gain in importance because they would deal with problems of major importance for health – such as the promotion of healthy behaviour – and secondly, that postgraduate training in psychiatry would have to include a section that would be fundamentally different from what is currently included in postgraduate courses in most developing and developed countries. The reorientation of postgraduate education in psychiatry in order to produce sufficient numbers of leaders of national and regional mental health programmes in developing countries does not mean that the need for psychiatrists with a predominant interest in clinical psychiatry would disappear; the investment in training, however, would have to be differently weighted to allow for the development of mental health programmes and for the growth of services for people suffering from mental illness.

The WHO has promoted the notion that mental health programmes have to be comprehensive and broad if they are to be seen as an important part of the public health enterprise (Sartorius 1978; WHO 1981, 1992a). The arguments put forward were that, first, many mental health problems can only be resolved if the health sector as a whole is involved, second, that many of the public health problems could be resolved more easily if technology developed by mental health programmes, e.g. concerning change of attitudes, humanization of medicine were to be used in general health care, and third, that health programmes cannot make a contribution to the overall socio-economic development unless they incorporate a mental health component. Broad mental health programmes in the form recommended by the WHO have come into existence in a number of developing countries, but are not yet the model programme accepted by all.

Scarcity of resources

The fourth major reason for the slow development of mental health programmes in developing countries is their chronic lack of resources. Annual expenditure for health in some of the least developed countries is a few dollars – as much as one thousand times less than in countries in the industrialized world. The scarcity concerns most of the resources that are necessary for health programmes – qualified staff, facilities, medicaments, laboratories, means of transport. Salaries, if paid at all, are so low that staff have to seek other sources of income – work abroad, private practice or other occupations – often of the most surprising nature. The scarcity of resources is often combined with an almost total neglect of peripheral health care workers, resulting in burn-out, which is increasingly seen as the chief reason for the continuous deterioration of health care in developing countries. Inpatient facilities (antiquated mental hospitals) still represent most of the resources that mental health programmes have. These institutions, which are usually in a dire state, provide a vastly insufficient number of beds for the country; in many African countries, the number of psychiatric beds is in the region of 0.5–5 per 100 000 population. In Asia, the numbers of psychiatric beds are somewhat higher, but still low in comparison with richer countries (e.g. Vietnam, 0.78/100 000; China, 0.73/100 000; the Philippines, 1.13/100 000). In the richest of the developing countries, the situation is somewhat better: even there, however, the low position that psychiatry has in the eyes of decision makers results in a disproportionately low amount of resources for mental health care and other mental health activities. The numbers of psychiatrists vary from 1:5 000 000 in Ethiopia (Alem, 1997) to 1:200 000 in Korea (Shinfuku, 1993), but their distribution is uneven and most of them are practising in urban areas. The number of psychiatric nurses is also low, although here the situation is less distant from numbers in developed countries. Psychiatric social workers are rarely available. Psychologists are more numerous and often face the difficulty of finding employment in mental health care services which traditionally have not included posts for psychologists. In Latin America, the numbers of psychologists are particularly high, and many among them will seek to open a private practice or work in sectors that have nothing to do with health.

Funds for the treatment of those with mental illness are scarce and their availability irregular. The resources necessary for the maintenance of inpatient institutions, patients' food, clothing and other necessities are often not available. Distances between health service centres and the population groups are often large in developing countries, and effective transportation is of essential importance; yet vehicles are few and there is no money for fuel and maintenance and no replacement parts. The distribution of funds between mental health care services and other services is not even, and the low priority of mental health programmes is reflected in a variety of ways when it comes to budgetary provisions, new posts, fellowships, library supplies and other material. The unjust distribution of resources does not only affect the care of patients; it also has negative effects on the morale of the staff working in mental health care service. Many leave the service, and those who can be recruited are often not of the best quality.

Possible solutions

The difficulties alluded to above have not prevented the establishment of mental health programmes in the developing world. Often, such programmes were built around an individual excelling in energy and charisma; there are, however, also programmes that have grown in the absence of such individuals.

Although none of the developing countries has established, consistently maintained and evaluated a comprehensive mental health programme, many have adopted progressive programmes and are implementing them. The elements such programmes comprise are described below.

Promotion of the value of mental health

The promotion of mental health is best understood as the process of moving mental health up on the scale of values of individuals and societies (Sartorius, 1992, 1998). Mental health promotion should thus not be equated with the improvement of the mental health status of the population; improvement will be achieved by programmes of prevention and treatment of mental disorder and by various other means, e.g. better nutrition. Placing mental health high on the scale of values is, however, important for the improvement of mental health because it provides the motivation to undertake preventative and curative measures which will result in better mental health and functioning.

Since the promotion of mental health is a process of changing values, it cannot be the exclusive task of mental health care services or indeed of health services in general. Values are shaped during the upbringing of children, at home and in school, through the media, by examples and models and in other ways. Mental health programmes in the developing countries should see the promotion of mental health (understood in this sense) as their highest priority, because success in placing mental health higher on the scale of values is essential for all other activities in the mental health field. Unfortunately, the mental health promotion programmes in the developing world are few and usually weak.

Psychiatrists will usually not be in charge of mental health promotion programmes; it is important, however, that they should participate in them and advocate them, because the success of such programmes will help in the development of programmes of care and rehabilitation of people with mental illness. Sometimes, they can initiate such programmes; in Pakistan, for example, the department of psychiatry of the University of Islamabad has been the driving force behind a programme designed to promote mental health in schools (Mubbashar, 1999). In other settings, mental health promotion activities have been embedded in programmes of general health promotion and community development (Badura & Kickbusch 1991; Trent 1992).

Primary prevention of mental disorders

In developing countries, possibilities for the primary prevention of mental disorders (e.g. due to early damage of the central nervous system) are particularly numerous but are usually neglected (Sartorius & Henderson, 1992) (see Chapter 14).

Treatment of mental disorders

There are a number of examples of countries or areas in which mental health care has been provided through general and primary health care agents (WHO, 1984, 1990). The effects have, on the whole, been rewarding. The results have indicated an increased coverage of care for people with serious mental illness and an increased satisfaction of general health care workers trained to deal with mental illness. In some developing countries, e.g. Thailand and Uganda, the treatment of mental disorders and the promotion of mental health have been included in national health care plans as one of the priorities for action. A large number of manuals enabling general practitioners and primary health care workers to deal with mental disorders have been produced and used in training programmes in many countries. The WHO has even complemented its the tenth revision of ICD (ICD-10) by a classification for use in primary health care (ICD-10 PHC). This document has been produced in order to facilitate reporting about mental illness in primary health care facilities. The PHC version of ICD-10 has only 22 categories see Table 1.

Each is accompanied with specific instructions on how to recognize the conditions to be classified and how to treat people who have them once they are recognized. (WHO, 1996).

In developed countries, the treatment of mental disorders in the general health care system is, to a certain degree, a matter of choice of those concerned – the patients, their families, the general practitioner and the psychiatrist. In developing countries, it is not: if mental health care is not provided through the general and primary health care worker, it will not – for an immense proportion of the population – be provided at all.

The treatment of mental disorders, particularly those that are likely to produce a lasting impairment has to be linked to a process of rehabilitation. In developing countries, a very small proportion of the most severely ill are inpatients in the mental hospitals mainly built in the colonial times. Most of the remaining patients who were not rejected by their families (because the family could not afford to feed them or could not tolerate their socially unacceptable behaviour) used to stay with them and were partly integrated into the life of the family and the community. Families have thus played a central role in the life of patients during and after the disease. Current processes of urbanization and the nuclearization of families diminish the capacity of families to provide long-term care to their sick members; at present, most of the developing countries have not found an answer to the challenge of such care under conditions of the dwindling capacities of families to help.

The life of those suffering from a severe mental illness is difficult in all types of countries. In developing countries, the situation is the same or worse. While the families and communities of people who suffer from

Table 1. *Mental health categories in the primary health care version of ICD-10 (ICD-10 PHC)*

F00	Dementia
F05	Delirium
F10	Alcohol use disorders
F11	Drug use disorders
F17.1	Tobacco use
F20	Chronic psychotic disorders
F23	Acute psychotic disorders
F31	Bipolar disorder
F32	Depression
F40	Phobic disorders
F41.0	Panic disorder
F41.1	Generalized anxiety
F41.2	Mixed anxiety and depression
F43	Adjustment disorder
F44	Dissociative disorder
F45	Unexplained somatic complaints
F48.0	Neurasthenia
F50	Eating disorders
F51	Sleep problems
F52	Sexual disorders
F70	Mental retardation
F90	Hyperkinetic disorder
F91	Conduct disorder
F98.0	Enuresis

mental illness show compassion and understanding at the beginning of the illness (unless the behaviour of the mentally ill is very disturbing, bringing shame to the family or community or endangering the life of others), their capacity to care and look after these individuals is usually soon exhausted. Sometimes, those with a severe mental illness are ejected from their setting and become vagrant psychotics; sometimes, they remain hidden in some dark corner of the house for many years; often, they die a premature death because of the increased risks to their health, their diminished capacity to cope and their lesser ability to request or obtain medical help. The introduction of psychiatric services, in collaboration with and through general health services, is therefore a life-saving operation in addition to being a process of bringing people with mental illness relief and support.

REFERENCES

Alem, A. (1997). Mental health in rural Ethiopia. University of Umea, Umea.

Badura, B. & Kickbusch, I. (1991). *Health Promotion Research*. World Health Organization, Copenhagen (regional publications).

Carothers, J.C. (1947). A study of mental derangement in Africans and an attempt to explain its peculiarities, more especially in relation to the African attitude to life. *Journal of Mental Science*, **93**, 548–56.

Carothers, J.C. (1953). The *African Mind in Health and Disease*. Geneva: World Health Organization. (WHO monograph series no. 17).

Cooper, J.E. & Sartorius, N. (eds.) (1996). *Mental Disorders in China*. London: Gaskell.

Desjarlais, P., Eisenberg, L., Good, B. & Kleinman, A. (eds.) (1995). *World Mental Health: Problems and Priorities in Low-income Countries*. Oxford: Oxford University Press.

Gautam, S., Kapur, R.I. & Shamasundar, C. (1980). Psychiatric morbidity and referral in general practice – a survey of general practitioners in Bangalore City. *Indian Journal of Psychiatry*, **22**, 295–297.

German, G.A.G. (1987). The extend of mental health problems in Africa today. An update of epidemiological knowledge. *British Journal of Psychiatry*, **151**, 435–439.

Gruenberg, E.M. (1977). The failures of success. *Milbank Memorial Fund Quarterly*, **55**, 3–24.

Harding, T.W., Climent, C.E., Diop, M. et al. (1983a). The WHO Collaborative Study on Strategies for Extending Mental Health Care. II. The development of new research methods. *American Journal of Psychiatry*, **140**, 1474–1480.

Harding, T.W., D'Arrigo Busnello, E., Climent, C.E. et al. (1983b). The WHO Collaborative Study on Strategies for Extending Mental Health Care. III. Evaluative design and illustrative results. *American Journal of Psychiatry*, **140**, 1481–1485.

Jablensky, A., Sartorius, N., Ernberg, G. et al. (1992). Schizophrenia: manifestations, incidence and course in different cultures. A World Health Organization Ten Countries Study. *Psychological Medicine Monograph* Suppl **20**, 1–97.

Leighton, A.H., Lambo, T.A., Hughes, C.G., Leighton, D.C., Murphy, J.M. &

Cornell, B.M. (1963). *Psychiatric Disorders Among the Yoruba*. New York: Cornell University Press.

Maj, M., Starace, E. & Sartorius, N. (1993). *Mental Disorders in HIV-1 Infection and AIDS*. Seattle: Hogrefe and Huber. (WHO expert series of biological psychiatry, vol. V).

Mubbashar, M.H. (1999). Mental health services in rural Pakistan. In *Common Mental Disorders in Primary Mental Health Care*, ed. M. Tansella & G. Thornicroft. London: Routledge.

Ndetei, D.M. & Muhangi, J. (1979). The prevalence and clinical presentation of psychiatric illness in a rural setting in Kenya. *British Journal of Psychiatry*, **135**, 269–272.

Prince, R. (1967). The changing picture of depressive syndromes in Africa: is it fact or diagnostic fashion? *Canadian Journal of African Studies*, **1**(2), 177–192.

Sartorius, N. (1978). The new mental health programme of WHO. *Interdisciplinary Science Review*, **3**, 202–206.

Sartorius, N. (1992). The promotion of mental health: meaning and tasks. In *Promotion of Mental Health*, vol. 1, ed. D.R. Trent, Aldershot: Avebury. pp. 17–23.

Sartorius, N. (1998) Universal strategies for the prevention of mental illness and the promotion of mental health. In *Preventing Mental Illness*, ed. R. Jenkins & T.B. Üstün, Chichester: Wiley.

Sartorius, N. & Harding, T.W. (1983). The WHO Collaborative Study on Strategies for Extending Mental Health Care. I. The genesis of the study. *American Journal of Psychiatry*, **140**, 1470–1473.

Sartorius, N. & Henderson, A.S. (1992). The neglect of prevention in psychiatry. *Australian and NZ Journal of Psychiatry*, **26**(4), 550–553.

Sartorius, N., Davidian, H., Ernberg, G. et al. (eds.) (1983) *Depressive Disorders in Different Cultures*. Geneva: World Health Organization.

Sartorius, N., Goldberg, D., de Girolamo, G., Costa e Silva, J., Lecrubier, Y. & Wittchen, H.U. (eds.) (1990). *Psychological Disorders in General Medical Settings*. Toronto: Hogrefe and Huber.

Sethi, B.B., Gupta, S.C., & Kumar, P. (1972). A psychiatric survey of 500 rural families. *Indian Journal of Psychiatry*, **94**, 183–196.

Shinfuku, N. (1993). A public health approach to mental health in the Western Pacific Region. *International Journal of Mental Health*, **22**(1), 3–21.

Trent, D. (ed.) (1992). *Promotion of Mental Health*. Aldershot: Avebury.

Üstün, T.B. & Sartorius, N. (eds.) (1995). *Mental Illness in General Health Care. An International Study*. Chichester, UK: Wiley.

WHO (1975a). *Organization of Mental Health Services in Developing Countries*. Geneva: World Health Organization. (Technical report series 564).

WHO (1975b). *Schizophrenia: A Multinational Study.* Geneva: World Health Organization. (Public health papers 63).

WHO (1979). *Schizophrenia: An International Follow-up Study.* Chichester, UK: Wiley.

WHO (1981). *Social Dimensions of Mental Health.* Geneva: World Health Organization.

WHO (1984). *Mental Health Care in Developing Countries: A Critical Appraisal of Research Findings.* Report of a WHO study group. Geneva: World Health Organization. (WHO technical report series 698).

WHO (1990). *The Introduction of a Mental Health Component into Primary Health Care.* Geneva: World Health Organization.

WHO (1992a). *Mental Health Programmes: Concepts and Principles.* Geneva: Division of Mental Health, World Health Organization (Document WHO/MNH/92.11).

WHO (1996). *Diagnostic and Management Guidelines for Mental Disorders in Primary Care* (ICD-10 chapter 5. Primary care version). Seattle: Hogrefe and Humber.

Index

Note to index: page numbers in bold denote tabulated material

administrative domain of mental health
    care 115–17, **119**
advice and consultation 81–7
affordability, criteria for inclusion in
    primary health care 101
affordability trap 160–2
Alma Ata Declaration (primary health
    care) 51, 53–5, 92, 108
anger 193–4
attitudes to mental health care, personal
    domain 111–13, **119**
avarice 188–90

birthrate 28–9
Brundtland, GH, WHO 138

Candau, M, WHO 133
China, Keshan disease (selenium
    deficiency) 57–69
Chisholm, Brock 125
cities 43–56
    Alma Ata Declaration on primary
        health care 53–5, 92, 108
    health care interventions 48–9
    population density 45
    possible areas for action 49–53
    prevalence of mental disorders 46–8
    size 44
community definitions 228–9
compliance, defined 166–7
consultancy 81–7
consumer and health service
    consumption 163–4
contraception 28–9

data presentation 66–9
Declaration of Human Rights, France 14
definitions and usage of terms 157–67
depressive disorders
    developing countries 249
    elderly people 146
    label effect 238
developing countries 231–56
    cities 43–56

definitions 159–60, 232–3
depressive disorders 249
education
    change and immovation 24–6
    and mental impairment 221
    financial support necessary 22–4
    legislation about psychiatric care
        75–6
    legislation on mental health 247
    population growth 26–9
    prevention of mental/neurological
        disorders 179–86, 248–9
    research 61–3
    see also psychiatry in developing
        countries
development, moral, legal and ethical
    definitions 36–8
disease
    communicable, and mental health
        disorders 242
    prevalence and increase 48, 241

education
    change and innovation, developing
        countries 24–6
    and mental impairment, developing
        countries 221
elderly people 141–55
    definitions 143–4
    predictions on health care 144–54
        effective treatment 148–50
        epidemiology 146–8
        financial barriers 153–4
        leisure years gain 150–1
        political power 145–6
        population 144–6
        quality of life 153
        services 152–3
        tolerance levels 151–2
employment 223–6
enabling 219–29
envy 192–3
epidemiology of mental disorders 60
    data 66

epidemiology of mental disorders (*cont.*)
elderly people 146–8
WHO epidemiologist 130
epilepsy, Mozart effect 57–69
ethical issues 34–8

family, and care 221–4
France, Declaration of Human Rights 14
French Revolution 13–20
funding, for research 205–8

gluttony 194–7

health service research 29–32
history of mental health provision
Declaration of Human Rights 13–20
World Health Organization (WHO)
123–39
hospitals, institutional detainment 68,
195
human behaviour, and mental health
243–4

ICD-10 (PHC) 250, **251**
WHO 250
immigration 92
institutional detainment 68, 195
Internet 214

Keshan disease (selenium deficiency)
57–69

labels, use/definitions 157–67
Lambo, TA, WHO 133–4, 137
lechery 197–8
legal issues 36–8
legislation about psychiatric care,
paradox 74–6
leisure years 225
gain by elderly people 150–1
liberty, and mental health programmes
19–20

Mahler, H, WHO 133, 137
medicine
changing goals 211
ethos 210–13
limits of mental health care in general
medical services 107–21
professional domain in mental health
care 117–18, **119**
referral 104
relationship with psychiatry 76–8
mental health care
see also mental health programmes

development dogmas 21–32
developing countries 22–6
health service research benefits
29–32
population growth 26–9
elderly people 141–55
limits in general medical services
107–21, **119**
administrative domain 115–17
introduction of mental health care
118–20
personal domain 111–13
professional domain 117–18, 111–13
social domain 114–15
technological domain 113–14
need for collaboration 209–18
prevalence and increase of disorders 48,
241
rehabilitation 219–29
see also primary health care
mental health programmes
context 13–87
criteria for inclusion in primary health
care 95–101
paradoxes 71–9, 196
legislation about psychiatric care
74–6
relationship between psychiatry and
medicine 76–8
socio-economic development 72–4
and psychiatry 171–255
universal accessibility of care 99–100
mental institutions 68, 195
moral issues 36–8
Mozart effect 57–69
music, and brain function 57–69

Nakijama, H, WHO 137, 138
needs, (individuals, families and
communities) 40–2

overlaps, disease, illness and sickness
definitions 38–40, 174–5

pain 211–12
pentalogue 210–15
rules 215–18
personal domain, attitudes to mental
health care 111–13, **119**
pollution effects 241–2
popular involvement in mental health
care issues 100–1
population, increase in elderly people
144–6
population growth 26–9

prevention of mental/neurological
  disorders 179–86
  developing countries 248–9
pride 190–2
primary health care issues 91–105
  Alma Ata Declaration (WHO) 51, 53–5,
    92, 108
  applications relevant to mental health
    care 102–5
  criteria for inclusion of mental health
    programmes 95–101
    affordability 101
    population involvement 100–1
    public health importance 95–7
    treatment/prevention 97–8
    universal accessibility of care 99–100
  definitions 92–5
  treatment/prevention, *see also*
    prevention of mental/neurological
    disorders
  see also mental health care
Primary Health Care strategy 53–5
professional domain in mental health
  care 117–18, **119**
promotion of mental health values,
  developing countries 247–8
psychiatric care needs assessment 171–7
  disease or illness 38–40, 174–5, 242
  effective interventions 175–7, **181**
  planning – key elements 173–4
  services, developing countries vs.
    developed countries 99
  seven 'vices' 187–200
psychiatry in developing countries
  231–56
  problems
    disregard for psychosocial aspects
      243–5
    frequency of mental disorders 237–43
    low value given to mental health
      234–7
    scarcity of resources 245–7
    separation of neurology 240
  possible solutions 247–52
    primary prevention of mental
      disorders 179–86, 248–9
    promotion of mental health values
      247–8
    treatment of mental disorders
      249–52
    research 61–3
psychosocial issues 96–7
public health, inclusion of mental illness
  in primary health care issues 95–7
publications, imbalance 61

rehabilitation, principles 219–29
research 201–8
  criteria for diagnoses 204
  developing countries 61–3
  funding 205–8
  health services 29–32
  Mozart effect 57–69
  pharmaceutical 62–3
  searching for etiology 202–4
  technological sophistication 62
research dogma, doubts 29–32
rules, pentalogue 215–18

Sauvy, A, on Third World definition
  159–60
schizophrenia
  in cities 47
  definitions 165–6
sloth 198–9
smoking, incubation hypothesis 69
social acceptability of interventions,
  primary health care issues 98–9
social capital, and mental health
  programmes 16–19
social domain of mental health care
  114–15, **119**
socio-economic development, and mental
  health programmes 72–4
stigma, use/definitions 165–7

technological domain
  and ethos 212
  in mental health care 113–14, **119**,
    212–13
  in research 62
terminology, use/definitions 157–67
Third World
  definition 159–60
  see also developing countries

urbanization 43–56

Venezuela, mental health programmes 73
violence 96–7

Western world, definition 158–9
work
  employment 223–6
  and leisure 225
World Health Organization (WHO)
  Alma Ata Declaration 51, 53–5, 92, 108
  broad mental health programmes 245
  Constitution 124
  history of mental health provision
    123–39

World Health Organization (WHO) (*cont.*)
  ICD-10 (PHC) 250, **251**
  infrastructure 125
  mental unit, Expert Committees and
    Scientific Groups 127, **128–9**
  objective 213
  origins of mental health programme
    123–39
    directors 132–8
    overall strategy 136–7
    psychosocial programmes 135–7
    policy of non-interference with
      national systems 132
    *Prevention of Mental, Neurological and
      Psychosocial Disorders* 180
    psychiatric epidemiologist 130